HOLT CALIFORNIA

CALIFORNIA

Earth Science

D1576236

HOLT, RINEHART AND WINSTON

A Harcourt Education Company

Orlando • Austin • New York • San Diego • London

Acknowledgments

Contributing Authors

Katy Z. Allen
Science Writer
Wayland, Massachusetts

Marilyn K. Bachman
Science Teacher
Montecito Union School
Santa Barbara, California

Linda Ruth Berg, Ph.D.
Adjunct Professor of Natural Sciences
St. Petersburg College
St. Petersburg, Florida

Kathleen Meehan Berry
Science Chairman
Canon–McMillan School District
Canonsburg, Pennsylvania

Robert H. Fronk, Ph.D.
Professor
Science and Mathematics
   Education Department
Florida Institute of Technology
Melbourne, Florida

Deborah R. Harden, Ph.D.
Professor
Department of Geology
San Jose State University
San Jose, California

Kathleen Kaska
Life and Earth Science Teacher
Oak Harbor Middle School
Oak Harbor, Washington

J. Richard Kyle, Ph.D.
C. E. Yager Professor of Geology
Department of Geological Sciences
Jackson School of Geosciences
The University of Texas at Austin
Austin, Texas

William G. Lamb, Ph.D.
Winningstad Chair in the Physical Sciences
Oregon Episcopal School
Portland, Oregon

Joel S. Leventhal, Ph.D.
Emeritus Scientist, Geochemistry
U.S. Geological Survey
Denver, Colorado

Peter E. Malin, Ph.D.
Professor of Geology
Division of Earth and Ocean Sciences
Duke University
Durham, North Carolina

Terrie Nolinske, Ph.D.
Vice President of Education
Museum of Science and Industry
Tampa, Florida

Anthony Palaez
Coordinator of Youth and Family Program
Museum of Science and Industry
Tampa, Florida

Robert J. Sager, M.S., J.D., L.G.
Coordinator and Professor of Earth Science
Pierce College
Lakewood, Washington

Lee Summerlin, Ph.D.
Professor of Chemistry (retired)
University of Alabama
Birmingham, Alabama

Consultants

Karen Clay
Inclusion Consultant
Boston, Massachusetts

Belinda Dunnick Karge, Ph.D.
Chair, Department of Special Education
California State University, Fullerton
Fullerton, California

Robin Scarcella
California Inclusion Consultant
Irvine, California

Safety Reviewers

Jim Adams
Science Education Technician (retired)
Las Positas College
Livermore, California

Jack Gerlovich, Ph.D.
Associate Professor
School of Education
Drake University
Des Moines, Iowa

Acknowledgments
continued on p. 698

ISBN 0-03-042658-8

7 8 9 10 11 0914 14 13 12 11 10
4500264477

Contents in Brief

Contents

Contents   **v**

UNIT 2 Earth's Resources

CHAPTER 4

CHAPTER 5

UNIT 3 Plate Tectonics and Earth's Structure

CHAPTER 6

UNIT 4 Shaping Earth's Surface

CHAPTER 9

    Weird Science Strange Soil
    Scientific Discoveries Gobi Dust Delivered to California
    People in Science J. David Bamberger (Habitat Restoration)

Contents   **xi**

UNIT 5 Earth's Oceans and Atmosphere

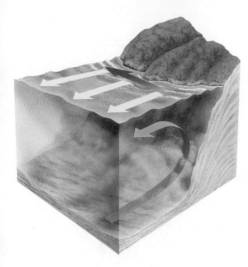 

CHAPTER 15

Contents   **XV**

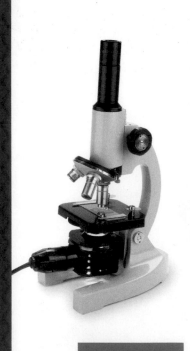

Chapter Previews

Improving Comprehension

Jump-start your learning!
Each chapter starts with a **Chapter Preview** that does two things. The Chapter Preview describes how to make a **Graphic Organizer** to improve your comprehension. And it helps you "unpack" the **California Science Standards,** which will help you better understand what the standards say and mean.

Unpacking the California Standards

Standard 🐻

Organize Activities

Study and Organization Skills

Reading Strategies

There are ways to make reading easier.
Reading Strategies at the beginning of each section will help you remember and organize information as you read the chapter.

Math Practice

Quick Labs

The more labs, the better!

Take a minute to browse the variety of exciting labs in this textbook. All **labs** are designed to help you experience science firsthand. But please don't forget to be safe. Read the Safety First! section before starting any of the labs.

Labs and Activities

Chapter Labs

Explore Activities

Start your engines with an activity!

Get motivated to learn by doing an activity at the beginning of each chapter. The **Explore Activity** helps you gain scientific understanding of the chapter material through hands-on experience.

Internet Activities

Get caught in the Web!

Go to **go.hrw.com** for **Internet Activities** related to each chapter. To find the Internet Activity for a particular chapter, just type in the keyword.

School-to-Home Activities

Science is not just for the classroom!

Bring science into your home by doing **School-to-Home Activities** with a family member or another adult in your household.

Science Skills Activities

Learn and practice the skills of a scientist!

The **Science Skills Activity** in each chapter helps you build investigation and experimentation skills. These skills are essential to learning science.

Science in Action

Science moves beyond the classroom!

Read **Science in Action** articles to learn more about science in the real world. These articles will give you an idea of how interesting, strange, helpful, and action-packed science is. And if your thirst is still not quenched, go to **go.hrw.com** for details about each article.

How to Use Your Textbook

Your textbook may seem confusing at first. But with a little introduction, you'll realize that your science textbook can be a big help. In the next few pages, you'll learn how this textbook can help you become a successful science student. You will also learn how interesting and exciting science can be.

Jump-Start Your Learning

The Chapter Preview helps you brush up on your learning skills and helps you focus on what is important.

> Each chapter starts with instructions on how to make a **Graphic Organizer,** a tool for organizing the information that you read. A sample Graphic Organizer gives you a sneak preview of the major concepts in the chapter.

> California has important **Science Standards** that guide your learning. Use this page to get to know the standards better. The chart contains **Academic Vocabulary** found in the standards. Also, **What It Means** describes each standard in basic terms.

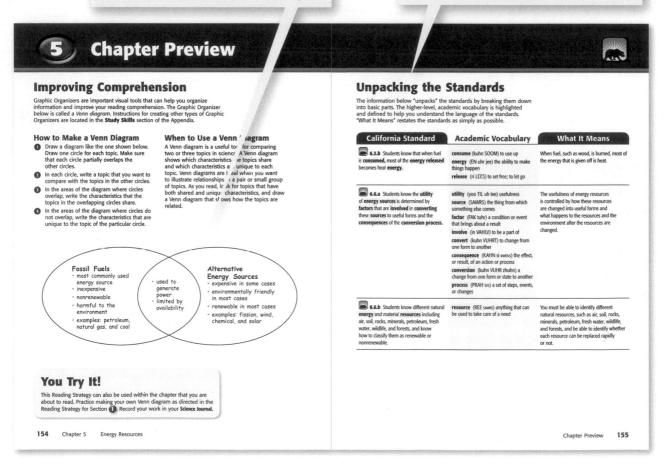

5 Chapter Preview

Improving Comprehension

Graphic Organizers are important visual tools that can help you organize information and improve your reading comprehension. The Graphic Organizer below is called a *Venn diagram.* Instructions for creating other types of Graphic Organizers are located in the **Study Skills** section of the Appendix.

How to Make a Venn Diagram

1. Draw a diagram like the one shown below. Draw one circle for each topic. Make sure that each circle partially overlaps the other circles.
2. In each circle, write a topic that you want to compare with the topics in the other circles.
3. In the areas of the diagram where circles overlap, write the characteristics that the topics in the overlapping circles share.
4. In the areas of the diagram where circles do not overlap, write the characteristics that are unique to the topic of the particular circle.

When to Use a Venn Diagram

A Venn diagram is a useful tool for comparing two or three topics in science. A Venn diagram shows which characteristics the topics share and which characteristics are unique to each topic. Venn diagrams are ideal when you want to illustrate relationships in a pair or small group of topics. As you read, look for topics that have both shared and unique characteristics, and draw a Venn diagram that shows how the topics are related.

Fossil Fuels
- most commonly used energy source
- inexpensive
- nonrenewable
- harmful to the environment
- examples: petroleum, natural gas, and coal

- used to generate power
- limited by availability

Alternative Energy Sources
- expensive in some cases
- environmentally friendly in most cases
- renewable in most cases
- examples: fission, wind, chemical, and solar

You Try It!

This Reading Strategy can also be used within the chapter that you are about to read. Practice making your own Venn diagram as directed in the Reading Strategy for Section 1. Record your work in your **Science Journal.**

Unpacking the Standards

The information below "unpacks" the standards by breaking them down into basic parts. The higher-level, academic vocabulary is highlighted and defined to help you understand the language of the standards. "What It Means" restates the standards as simply as possible.

California Standard	Academic Vocabulary	What It Means
6.3.b Students know that when fuel is **consumed**, most of the **energy released** becomes heat **energy.**	**consume** (kuhn SOOM) to use up **energy** (EN uhr jee) the ability to make things happen **release** (ri LEES) to set free; to let go	When fuel, such as wood, is burned, most of the energy that is given off is heat.
6.6.a Students know the **utility** of **energy sources** is determined by **factors** that are **involved** in **converting** these **sources** to useful forms and the **consequences** of the **conversion process.**	**utility** (yoo TIL uh tee) usefulness **source** (SAWRS) the thing from which something else comes **factor** (FAK tuhr) a condition or event that brings about a result **involve** (in VAHLV) to be a part of **convert** (kuhn VUHRT) to change from one form to another **consequence** (KAHN si kwens) the effect, or result, of an action or process **conversion** (kuhn VUHR zhuhn) a change from one form or state to another **process** (PRAH ses) a set of steps, events, or changes	The usefulness of energy resources is controlled by how these resources are changed into useful forms and what happens to the resources and the environment after the resources are changed.
6.6.b Students know different natural **energy** and material **resources** including air, soil, rocks, minerals, petroleum, fresh water, wildlife, and forests, and know how to classify them as renewable or nonrenewable.	**resource** (REE sawrs) anything that can be used to take care of a need	You must be able to identify different natural resources, such as air, soil, rocks, minerals, petroleum, fresh water, wildlife, and forests, and be able to identify whether each resource can be replaced rapidly or not.

Step into Science

The beginning of each chapter is designed to get you involved with science. You will immediately see that science is cool!

Check out the **Big Idea** to see the focus of the chapter. The entire chapter supports this Big Idea.

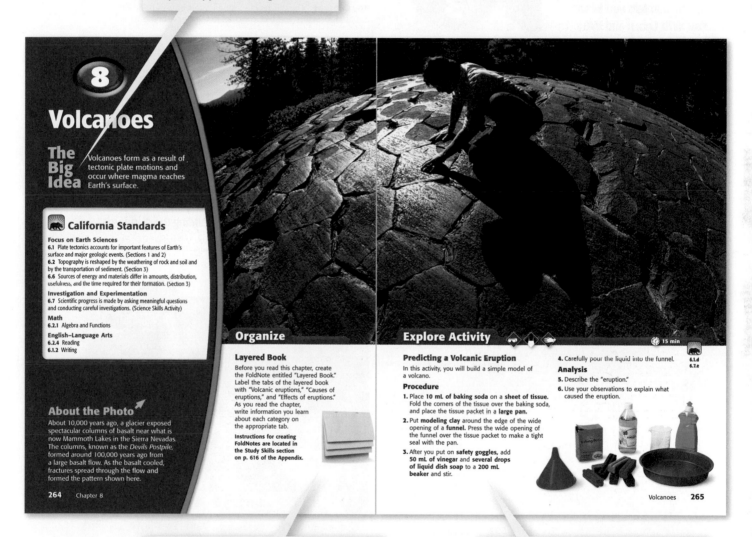

8

Volcanoes

The Big Idea
Volcanoes form as a result of tectonic plate motions and occur where magma reaches Earth's surface.

California Standards

Focus on Earth Sciences
6.1 Plate tectonics accounts for important features of Earth's surface and major geologic events. (Sections 1 and 2)
6.2 Topography is reshaped by the weathering of rock and soil and by the transportation of sediment. (Section 3)
6.6 Sources of energy and materials differ in amounts, distribution, usefulness, and the time required for their formation. (Section 3)

Investigation and Experimentation
6.7 Scientific progress is made by asking meaningful questions and conducting careful investigations. (Science Skills Activity)

Math
6.2.1 Algebra and Functions

English–Language Arts
6.2.4 Reading
6.1.2 Writing

About the Photo
About 10,000 years ago, a glacier exposed spectacular columns of basalt near what is now Mammoth Lakes in the Sierra Nevadas. The columns, known as the *Devils Postpile*, formed around 100,000 years ago from a large basalt flow. As the basalt cooled, fractures spread through the flow and formed the pattern shown here.

264 Chapter 8

Organize

Layered Book
Before you read this chapter, create the FoldNote entitled "Layered Book." Label the tabs of the layered book with "Volcanic eruptions," "Causes of eruptions," and "Effects of eruptions." As you read the chapter, write information you learn about each category on the appropriate tab.

Instructions for creating FoldNotes are located in the Study Skills section on p. 616 of the Appendix.

Explore Activity   15 min

Predicting a Volcanic Eruption
In this activity, you will build a simple model of a volcano.

Procedure
1. Place **10 mL of baking soda** on a **sheet of tissue.** Fold the corners of the tissue over the baking soda, and place the tissue packet in a **large pan.**
2. Put **modeling clay** around the edge of the wide opening of a **funnel.** Press the wide opening of the funnel over the tissue packet to make a tight seal with the pan.
3. After you put on **safety goggles,** add **50 mL of vinegar** and **several drops of liquid dish soap** to a **200 mL beaker** and stir.
4. Carefully pour the liquid into the funnel.   6.1.d 6.7.e

Analysis
5. Describe the "eruption."
6. Use your observations to explain what caused the eruption.

Volcanoes   **265**

You can't be organized enough when learning science. The **FoldNote** provided here gives you note-taking options. These FoldNotes are fun to make and help you understand and remember what you have learned.

It is never too early for exploration in science. The **Explore Activity** gives you a chance to get some hands-on experience right away. Each activity is a lot of fun and introduces you to one or more California Science Standards from the chapter.

Read for Meaning

You want to get the most out of your reading. One way to do so is to take a minute to learn how the sections are organized.

Be sure to start each section by reading the information in the margin. This information tells you **What You Will Learn** and **Why It Matters.** Believe it or not, knowing these things will improve your learning.

Don't skip the **Reading Strategy.** Each strategy provides tips on how to take better notes and how to read for better understanding.

The **Key Concept** sets the stage for your understanding of the section. Read it carefully, and notice how it relates to the chapter's Big Idea. Together, the Big Idea and the Key Concepts give you an excellent overview of the chapter.

SECTION 3

Marine Ecosystems

Key Concept Organisms in marine ecosystems depend on the abiotic factors and biotic factors in their environment.

What You Will Learn

- Three main abiotic factors shape marine ecosystems.
- Producers form the base of the ocean's food chains.
- There are four major ocean zones.
- Different marine ecosystems support different communities of organisms.

Why It Matters

Studying the characteristics of marine organisms will help you understand how the environment affects organisms in marine ecosystems.

Vocabulary
- phytoplankton
- estuary

READING STRATEGY

Outlining In your **Science Journal**, create an outline of the section. Use the headings from the section in your outline.

What covers almost three-fourths of Earth's surface? What holds the largest animals and some of the smallest organisms on Earth? If your answer to both questions is *oceans*, you are correct! Earth's oceans contain many kinds of ecosystems. Scientists call ecosystems in the ocean *marine ecosystems*.

Depth and Sunlight

Marine ecosystems are shaped by abiotic factors. Two of these factors are water dep[th] that passes through water. T[...] 4,000 m, but sunlight does n[...] fore, producers that perform [...] phytoplankton, can survive [...] are tiny producers that f[...] Algae and phytoplankt[...] for food chains. Tiny pr[...]ucers [...] near the surface of the ocea[...]

Do you understand what you are reading? Don't wait until test time to find out. The **Standards Checks** help you see if you are understanding the standards.

Standards Check Why are phytoplankton important to marine ecosystems? 6.5.a, 6.5.c

phytoplankton
(FIET oh PLANGK tuhn) the microscopic, photosynthetic organisms that float near the surface of marine or fresh water
 Wordwise The prefix *phyto-* means "plant."

Figure 1 M[a]rine ecosystems su[pport] a broad diversity [of] life. Large humpbac[k] [w]hales and tiny phytopla[nk]ton live in the oceans.

Notice how vocabulary is treated in the margins. All vocabulary terms are defined in the margins for quick reference. Also look for **Wordwise** items, which help you understand how prefixes and suffixes are used in scientific words.

Keep an Eye on the Headings

Notice how the headings in the textbook are different sizes and different colors. The headings help you organize your reading and form a simple outline, as shown below.

Blue: section title

Red: major subheads

Light blue: minor subheads

One good way to study is to write down the headings in outline form in your notes. Reviewing this outline will give you a good idea of the main concepts in the chapter and will show you how they are related.

Science Is Doing

You get many opportunities throughout the textbook to actually do science.

Each section has at least one **Quick Lab** to help you get real experience doing science. Also look for **School-to-Home Activities** for cool activities that you can do at home.

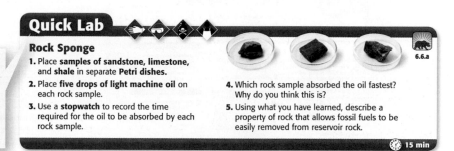

Quick Lab

Rock Sponge

1. Place **samples of sandstone, limestone,** and **shale** in separate **Petri dishes.**
2. Place **five drops of light machine oil** on each rock sample.
3. Use a **stopwatch** to record the time required for the oil to be absorbed by each rock sample.
4. Which rock sample absorbed the oil fastest? Why do you think this is?
5. Using what you have learned, describe a property of rock that allows fossil fuels to be easily removed from reservoir rock.

6.6.a

⏱ 15 min

The **Chapter Lab** at the end of each chapter helps you build your understanding of scientific methods. These labs reinforce the California Science Standards with a hands-on activity.

Using Scientific Methods

Skills Practice Lab

Natural Resources Used at Lunch

Many materials in addition to food are involved in the packaging and delivery of lunches. These materials are made from a variety of natural resources. In this activity, you will determine what types of resources are used in this way at your school.

OBJECTIVES

Categorize common materials left over after lunch.

Compute the amounts in each category, and determine the percentage of each category.

Recommend ways your school can conserve natural resources based on the data you collect and organize in this activity.

MATERIALS

- bags, plastic
- balance, triple beam or electronic
- calculator
- gloves, protective, plastic
- paper towels

SAFETY

Ask a Question

1 What percentage of the materials left over after lunch come from each of the following categories: paper and wood products, plastic, metal, and glass?

Form a Hypothesis

2 Write a hypothesis that is a possible answer to the question above. Explain your reasoning.

Test the Hypothesis

3 Collect all of your lunch waste on the day of the lab activity or the day before the lab activity, depending on whether your class meets before or after lunch. Put all of your lunch waste in a plastic bag, including wrappers, napkins, straws, and disposable trays.

4 Working in groups of three or four students, separate your lunch waste onto paper towels in the following categories: paper and wood, plastic, metal, and glass.

5 Determine the mass of the waste in each category for the entire group. Create a data table similar to the one above, and record the masses.

6 Use the equation below to calculate for each category the average mass of solid waste per student. Use the total mass of waste for each category in your calculation. Record the results in your table.

$$\frac{\text{total mass in category}}{\text{number of students}} = \frac{\text{average mass in}}{\text{category per student}}$$

7 Use the equation below to calculate the percentage of the total waste that is represented by each category. Record the results in your table.

$$\left(\frac{\text{total mass of category}}{\text{total mass for all categories}}\right) \times 100 = \frac{\text{percentage of}}{\text{total waste}}$$

Analyze the Results

8 **Examining Data** Compare your group's percentages for each category with the results from other groups in the class. How and why are the data similar or different?

Data for Leftover Lunch Materials

Category	Total mass for lab group	Average mass per student	Percentage of total waste	Notes
Paper and wood				
Plastic				
Metal				
Glass				
Total			100	

DO NOT WRITE IN BOOK

9 **Classifying** In the "Notes" column of your table, list the natural origin of the materials in each category. List whether each category's materials is made from renewable or nonrenewable resources.

Draw Conclusions

10 **Interpreting Information** What percentage of these lunch leftover materials came from renewable resources? What percentage came from nonrenewable resources?

11 **Making Predictions** Find the mass of leftover materials at your school in each category. Your calculations should be done to find the mass generated each day. You may need to ask your teacher how many students, teachers, and staff members there are at your school.

Big Idea Question

12 **Applying Conclusions** You have been asked to recommend to your school some steps the school can take to conserve material resources. Describe at least two things you would recommend. Base your recommendations on the data you have collected during this activity and on what you know about material resources you have been studying.

144

Chapter Lab 145

Science Skills Activity

| Scientific Methods | Graphs | Data Analysis | Maps |

Investigation and Experimentation
6.7.b Identify changes in natural phenomena over time without manipulating the phenomena (e.g., a tree limb, a grove of trees, a stream, a hillslope).

Identifying Changes over Time

▶ **Tutorial**

The ability to identify changes in a natural system is an important part of Earth science. You can improve your observation skills by practicing the following steps.

Carefully study the original phenomenon.

1 Identify all of the important features of the object or system. To do so, observe details, identify features, and determine the shapes and sizes of different features.

2 Record any important features or details.

Carefully study the phenomenon after the changes have occurred.

1 Locate the features and details that you identified in the original phenomenon.

2 Identify any features or details that differ from their original condition.

3 Analyze differences that you have identified. Look for factors that may have caused or contributed to the changes.

▶ **You Try It!**

Procedure

Mount St. Helens erupted on May 18, 1980. The top photograph at right shows the volcano before the 1980 eruption. The bottom photograph shows Mount St. Helens two years after the eruption. Carefully observe as many details in the two photographs as you can, and answer the questions that follow.

Before

Analysis

1 **Making Observations** How did the volcanic mountain change as a result of the eruption?

2 **Making Observations** How did it affect the wildlife habitats around it?

3 **Applying Concepts** Was the 1980 eruption of Mount St. Helens explosive or nonexplosive? Explain your answer.

4 **Applying Concepts** At which type of plate boundary is Mount St. Helens? Explain your answer.

284 Chapter 8 Volcanoes

Each chapter has one **Science Skills Activity,** which gives you an opportunity to develop your science skills. Scientific methods, doing research, analyzing data, and making graphs are highlighted here. The step-by-step instructions make learning these skills easy.

Review What You Have Learned

You can't review too much when you are learning science. To help you review, a **Section Review** appears at the end of every section and a **Chapter Summary** and **Chapter Review** appear at the end of every chapter. These reviews not only help you study for tests but also help further your understanding of the content.

> Just a few clicks away, each **Super Summary** gives you even more ways to review and study for tests.

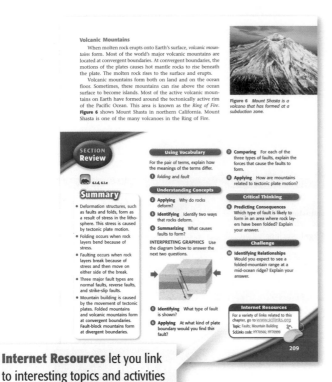

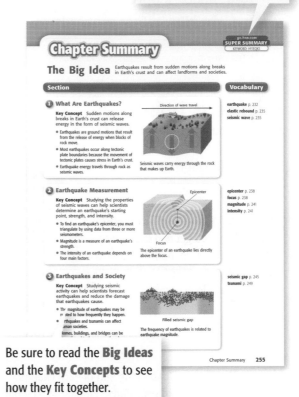

> **Internet Resources** let you link to interesting topics and activities related to the section's content.

> Be sure to read the **Big Ideas** and the **Key Concepts** to see how they fit together.

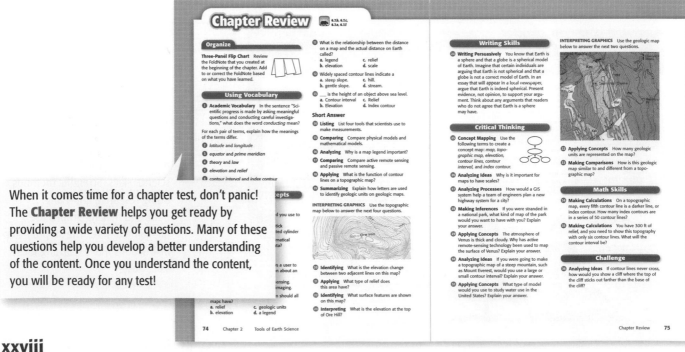

> When it comes time for a chapter test, don't panic! The **Chapter Review** helps you get ready by providing a wide variety of questions. Many of these questions help you develop a better understanding of the content. Once you understand the content, you will be ready for any test!

Review the Standards

Mastering the California Science Standards takes practice and more practice! The **Standards Assessment** helps you review the California Science Standards covered in the chapter. The multiple-choice questions also give you some additional practice with standardized tests.

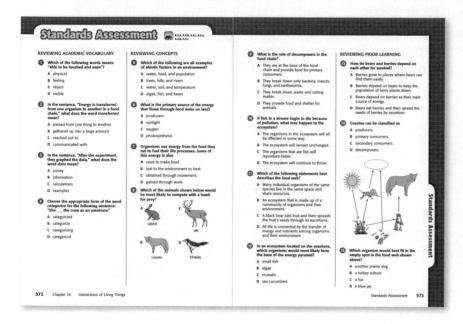

Test-Drive Your Understanding

How well can you use the book now? Use Chapter 1 to answer the questions below and to find out!

1. Which type of Graphic Organizer is used in the Chapter Preview?

2. Which California Science Standards are covered in Chapter 1?

3. What is the Big Idea of this chapter?

4. What will you be doing in the Explore Activity?

5. What is the Key Concept of Section 2?

6. What is the Reading Strategy for Section 1?

7. What new vocabulary terms are introduced in Section 1?

8. How many Standards Checks are in Section 2?

9. What is the name of the Quick Lab in Section 3?

10. On what page does the Chapter Summary appear?

11. How many Standards Assessment questions are there?

12. What is the Super Summary code for Chapter 1?

➚ Be Resourceful—Use the Web!

Internet Resources for Each Section

A box on the Section Review page for each section takes you to resources that you can use for science projects, reports, and research papers. To find information on a topic, go to **scilinks.org** and type in the code provided.

Current Events in Science

Check out the online magazine articles and other materials that go with your textbook at **go.hrw.com.** Click on the textbook icon and the Table of Contents to see all of the resources for each chapter.

Your Online Textbook

If your teacher gives you a special password to log onto the **Holt Online Learning** site, you'll find your complete textbook on the Web. In addition, you'll find some great learning tools and practice quizzes. You'll be able to see how well you know the material from your textbook.

SAFETY FIRST!

Exploring, inventing, and investigating are essential to the study of science. However, these activities can also be dangerous. To make sure that your experiments and explorations are safe, you must be aware of a variety of safety guidelines. You have probably heard of the saying "It is better to be safe than sorry." This is particularly true in a science classroom where experiments and explorations are being performed. Being uninformed and careless can result in serious injuries. Don't take chances with your own safety or with anyone else's.

The following pages describe important guidelines for staying safe in the science classroom. Your teacher may also have safety guidelines and tips that are specific to your classroom and laboratory. Take the time to be safe.

Safety Rules!

Start Out Right

Always get your teacher's permission before attempting any laboratory exploration. Read the procedures carefully, and pay particular attention to safety information and caution statements. If you are unsure about what a safety symbol means, look it up or ask your teacher. You cannot be too careful when it comes to safety. If an accident does occur, inform your teacher immediately no matter how minor the event seems.

Safety Symbols

All of the experiments and investigations in this book and their related worksheets include important safety symbols to alert you to particular safety concerns. Become familiar with these symbols so that when you see them, you will know what they mean and what to do. It is important that you read this entire safety section to learn about specific dangers in the laboratory.

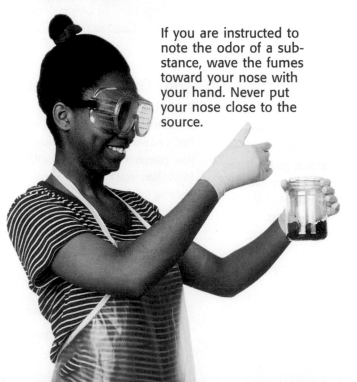

If you are instructed to note the odor of a substance, wave the fumes toward your nose with your hand. Never put your nose close to the source.

Eye protection

Clothing protection

Hand safety

Heating safety

Electric safety

Chemical safety

Animal safety

Sharp object

Plant safety

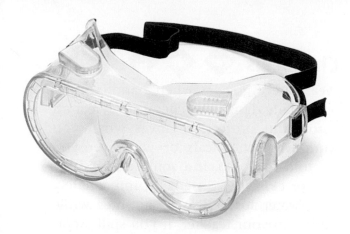

Eye Safety

Wear safety goggles when working around chemicals, acids, bases, or any type of flame or heating device. Wear safety goggles anytime there is the slightest chance that your eyes could be harmed. If anything gets into your eyes, notify your teacher immediately and flush your eyes with running water for at least 15 minutes. Treat any unknown chemical as if it were a dangerous chemical. Never look directly into the sun. Doing so could cause permanent blindness.

Avoid wearing contact lenses in a laboratory situation. Even if you are wearing safety goggles, chemicals can get between the contact lenses and your eyes. If your doctor requires that you wear contact lenses instead of glasses, wear eye-cup safety goggles in the lab.

Safety Equipment

Know the locations of the nearest fire alarms and any other safety equipment, such as fire blankets and eyewash fountains, as identified by your teacher. And know the procedures for using the equipment.

Neatness

Keep your work area free of all unnecessary books and papers. Tie back long hair, and secure loose sleeves or other loose articles of clothing, such as ties and bows. Remove dangling jewelry. Don't wear open-toed shoes or sandals in the laboratory. Never eat, drink, or apply cosmetics in a laboratory setting. Food, drink, and cosmetics can easily become contaminated with dangerous materials.

Certain hair products (such as aerosol hair spray) are flammable and should not be worn while working near an open flame. Avoid wearing hair spray or hair gel on lab days.

Sharp/Pointed Objects

Use knives and other sharp instruments with extreme care. Never cut objects while holding them in your hands. Place objects on a suitable work surface for cutting.

Be extra careful when using any glassware. When adding a heavy object to a graduated cylinder, tilt the cylinder so that the object slides slowly to the bottom.

Heat

Wear safety goggles when using a heating device or a flame. Whenever possible, use an electric hot plate as a heat source instead of using an open flame. When heating materials in a test tube, angle the test tube away from yourself and others. To avoid burns, wear heat-resistant gloves whenever instructed to do so.

Electricity

Be careful with electrical cords. When using a microscope with a lamp, do not place the cord where it could trip someone. Do not let cords hang over a table edge in a way that could cause equipment to fall if the cord is accidentally pulled. Do not use equipment with damaged cords. Do not use electrical equipment near water or when your clothing or hands are wet. Make sure that electrical equipment is in the "off" position before plugging it in. Turn off and unplug electrical equipment when you have finished using it.

Chemicals

Wear safety goggles when handling any potentially dangerous chemicals. Wear an apron and protective gloves when you work with chemicals or whenever you are told to do so. If a spill gets on your skin or clothing, rinse it off immediately with water for at least 5 minutes while calling to your teacher. If you spill a corrosive chemical onto your clothing, rinse it off immediately by using a faucet or the safety shower and remove the affected clothing while calling to your teacher.

Never mix chemicals unless your teacher tells you to do so. Never taste, touch, or smell chemicals unless you are specifically directed to do so. Before working with a flammable liquid or gas, check for the presence of any source of flame, spark, or heat.

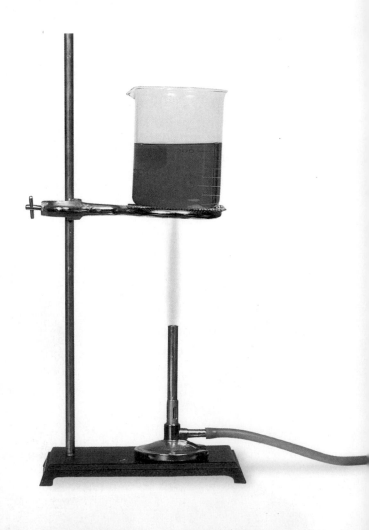

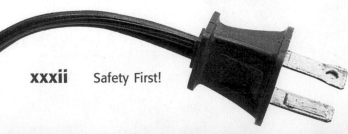

Animal Safety

Always obtain your teacher's permission before bringing any animal into the school building. Handle animals only as your teacher directs. Treat animals carefully and respectfully. Wash your hands thoroughly after handling any animal.

Plant Safety

Do not eat any part of a plant or plant seed used in the laboratory. Wash your hands thoroughly after handling any part of a plant. When in nature, do not pick any wild plants unless your teacher instructs you to do so.

Glassware

Examine all glassware before use. Be sure that glassware is clean and free of chips and cracks. Report damaged glassware to your teacher. Glass containers used for heating should be made of heat-resistant glass.

UNIT 1

TIMELINE

Introduction to Earth Science

In this unit, you will start your own investigation of the planet Earth and of the regions of space beyond it. But first you should prepare yourself by learning about the tools and methods used by Earth scientists. As you can imagine, it is not easy to study something as large as Earth or as far away as Venus. Yet Earth scientists study these planets and more. The timeline shown here identifies a few of the events that have helped shape our understanding of Earth.

1669

Nicolaus Steno accurately describes the process by which living organisms become fossils.

1904

Roald Amundsen determines the position of the magnetic north pole.

1922

Roy Chapman Andrews discovers fossilized dinosaur eggs in the Gobi Desert. They are the first such eggs to be found.

Fossilized dinosaur eggs in the Gobi Desert

1962

By reaching an altitude of over 95 km, the *X-15* becomes the first fixed-wing plane to reach space.

1758

Halley's comet makes a reappearance, which confirms Edmond Halley's 1705 prediction. The comet reappeared 16 years after Halley's death.

1799

The Rosetta stone is discovered in Egypt. It enables scholars to decipher Egyptian hieroglyphics.

1896

The first modern Olympic Games are held in Athens, Greece.

1943

The volcano Paricutín grows more than 200 m tall during its first two weeks of eruption.

Paricutín Volcano

1960

The first weather satellite, *TIROS I,* is launched by the United States.

1970

The first Earth Day is celebrated in the United States on April 22.

1990

The Hubble Space Telescope is launched into orbit. Three years later, faulty optics are repaired during a space walk.

1994

China begins construction of Three Gorges Dam, the world's largest dam. Designed to control the Yangtze River, the dam will supply an estimated 84 billion kilowatt-hours of hydroelectric power per year.

2002

A new order of insects— *Mantophasmatodea*—is found both preserved in 45 million-year-old amber and living in southern Africa.

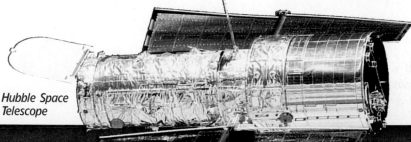

Hubble Space Telescope

Improving Comprehension

Graphic Organizers are important visual tools that can help you organize information and improve your reading comprehension. The Graphic Organizer below is called a *concept map.* Instructions for creating other types of Graphic Organizers are located in the **Study Skills** section of the Appendix.

How to Make a Concept Map

1 Identify main ideas from the text, and write the ideas as short phrases or single words.

2 Select a main concept. Place this concept at the top or center of a piece of paper.

3 Place other ideas under or around the main concept based on their relationship to the main concept. Draw a circle around each idea.

4 Draw lines between the concepts, and add linking words to connect the ideas.

When to Use a Concept Map

Concept maps are useful when you are trying to identify how several ideas are connected to a main concept. Concept maps may be based on vocabulary terms or on main topics from the text. The concept map below shows how the important concepts of this chapter are related. As you read about science, look for terms that can be organized in a concept map.

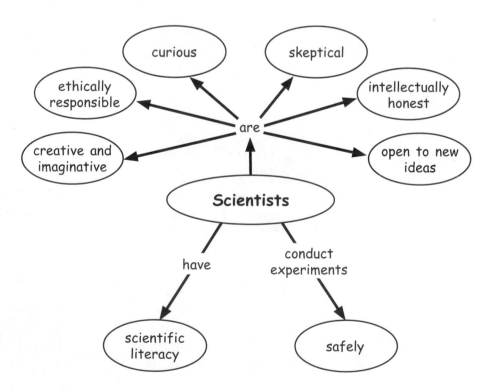

You Try It!

This Reading Strategy can also be used within the chapter that you are about to read. Practice making your own concept map as directed in the Reading Strategy for Section **3**. Record your work in your **Science Journal.**

Unpacking the Standards

The information below "unpacks" the standards by breaking them down into basic parts. The higher-level, academic vocabulary is highlighted and defined to help you understand the language of the standards. "What It Means" restates the standards as simply as possible.

California Standard	Academic Vocabulary	What It Means
6.7.a Develop a hypothesis.		Write a possible explanation for or answer to a scientific research question that can be tested.
6.7.d Communicate the steps and results from an **investigation** in written reports and oral presentations.	**communicate** (kuh MYOO ni KAYT) to make known; to tell **investigation** (in VES tuh GAY shuhn) a detailed search for answers	Clearly explain the steps and the results of an experiment by using written reports and oral presentations.
6.7.e Recognize whether **evidence** is **consistent** with a proposed explanation.	**evidence** (EV uh duhns) information showing whether an idea or belief is true or valid **consistent** (kuhn SIS tuhnt) in agreement	Figure out if observations and information agree or disagree with your previous ideas or explanations.
6.7.g Interpret events by **sequence** and time from natural **phenomena** (e.g., the relative ages of rocks and intrusions.	**interpret** (in TUHR pruht) to tell or explain the meaning of **sequence** (SEE kwuhns) the order in which things come or events happen **phenomenon** (fuh NAHM uh NUHN) any facts or events that can be sensed or described scientifically (plural *phenomena*)	Explain the order of events and time by using natural processes and events. For example, you must be able to tell the ages of rocks and intrusions by the order in which these features formed.
6.7.h Identify changes in natural **phenomena** over time without **manipulating** the **phenomena** (e.g., a tree limb, a grove of trees, a stream, a hillslope).	**identify** (ie DEN tuh FIE) to point out or pick out **manipulate** (muh NIP yoo LAYT) to affect or control	Point out the changes in natural processes or events over time without directly causing changes in the processes or events. For example, you must be able to see how a single tree, a group of trees, a stream, or the slope of a hill changes over time.

1

The Nature of Earth Science

The Big Idea

Scientists use careful observations and clear reasoning to understand processes and patterns in nature.

 California Standards

Investigation and Experimentation
6.7 Scientific progress is made by asking meaningful questions and conducting careful investigations. (Section 2; Science Skills Activity)

Math
6.1.4 Number Sense

English–Language Arts
6.2.4 Reading
6.1.1, 6.1.3, 6.2.1 Writing

About the Photo

Ricardo Alonso, a geologist in Argentina, is measuring the footprints left by a dinosaur millions of years ago. Taking measurements is just one way that scientists collect data to answer questions and test hypotheses.

Organize

Table Fold

Before you read this chapter, create the FoldNote entitled "Table Fold." Label the columns of the table with the titles of the sections in the chapter. Label the rows with "What I know" and "What I have learned." Fill in the first row with what you already know about each section's topic. As you read the chapter, write what you learn in the second row.

Instructions for creating FoldNotes are located in the Study Skills section on p. 618 of the Appendix.

Explore Activity

⏱ **20 min**

Planning the Impossible?

In this activity, you will do some creative thinking to solve what might seem like an impossible problem.

Procedure

1. Examine an **index card.** Your mission is to fit yourself through the card. You can tear, cut, or fold the card. You cannot use tape, glue, or anything else to hold the card together.

2. With a partner, brainstorm ways to complete your mission. Then, record your plan.

3. Test your plan. Did it work? If necessary, get **another index card** and try again. Record your new plan and the results.

4. Share your plans and results with your classmates.

Analysis

5. Why was it helpful to develop a plan in advance?

6. How did testing your plan help you complete your mission?

7. How did sharing your ideas with your classmates help you complete your mission? What did your classmates do differently?

6.7.a

7

Thinking like a Scientist

Key Concept   Scientific progress is made by asking meaningful questions and conducting careful investigations.

▶ You are preparing a gelatin dessert. You mix the gelatin with pineapple. You then put the mixture in the refrigerator to set overnight. In the morning, you find just a pan of liquid with pineapple in it! What happened?

To answer this riddle, you need to think like a scientist. Ask yourself the following questions: Did I mix the gelatin enough? Was the water too hot or too cold? Or did the pineapple ruin my dessert? After some research, you find out that pineapple has an enzyme that prevents gelatin from setting!

Scientific Habits of Mind

Although scientists work in many fields, they share certain habits of mind. Scientists are curious, skeptical, openness to new ideas, creative, and ethical. And they learn from their mistakes. The inventor Thomas Edison once said that he never failed; he just found 10,000 ways that did not work.

Curiosity

Scientists are curious about the world around them. **Figure 1** shows a scientist named Jane Goodall. Goodall was very curious about where chimpanzees lived, what they ate, and how they interacted. Curiosity led Goodall to study chimpanzees for more than 30 years. Goodall's questions, research, and writings changed what scientists know about chimpanzees and other primates.

Figure 1   *Jane Goodall has studied chimpanzees for more than 30 years. Her curiosity helped her make many discoveries about chimpanzees.*

Skepticism

Skepticism is the practice of questioning accepted ideas or claims. Skepticism helps scientists question the assumptions that influence how we see the world. Skepticism helped one scientist discover a major threat to the environment. Rachel Carson, shown in **Figure 2,** was a biologist in the 1950s. At the time, scientists were developing many new kinds of pesticides to kill insects. The companies that made the chemicals said that the chemicals would not harm animals other than insects. Carson did not believe these claims. She questioned whether chemicals that killed insects would also harm other living things.

After much research, Carson wrote a book, *Silent Spring.* The book started debates about the use of pesticides in the United States. Some chemical companies threatened to sue Carson and tried to discredit her. But she stood by her findings, and her work led to controls on pesticide use. In particular, *Silent Spring* led to the banning of a chemical called *DDT.* DDT had threatened bald eagle populations in the United States. By being skeptical and asking questions, Carson encouraged others to think about the world around them.

Openness to New Ideas

Keeping an open mind means considering new ideas. However, this process may be harder than it sounds. Often, people make assumptions about the world based on what they are used to. Scientists in particular should be open to new ideas, even if these ideas differ from their own beliefs. Sometimes, considering an opposing idea can lead to a breakthrough that is the basis of a new discovery.

Figure 2 *Rachel Carson was skeptical of the claims made by pesticide manufacturers. Her research helped bald eagles recover from the effects of pesticides in the environment.*

Quick Lab

Using Curiosity to Make Predictions

How many drops of water do you think you can fit on the head of a penny? Being curious helps you ask questions and motivates you to find answers.

6.7.a
6.7.e

▶ Try It!

1. Predict the number of drops of water that you can place on the head of a penny. Record your prediction.

2. Place a **penny** head side up flat on a **table.**

3. Fill an **eyedropper** with **water.**

4. Count the number of drops of water that you can place on the penny. Stop counting when the water runs down the side of the penny.

▶ Think About It!

5. How many drops of water were you able to place on the penny? Was your prediction correct? Explain your answer.

 10 min

Figure 3 *Creativity helped Andy Michael write "Earthquake Quartet #1." He says that writing the music changed how he thinks about earthquakes.*

Imagination and Creativity

As well as being curious, skeptical, and open minded, scientists need to be creative and imaginative. Being creative helps scientists think about the world in new or different ways. **Figure 3** shows a scientist who used his imagination to connect earthquakes with music! Andy Michael is a seismologist, a scientist who studies earthquakes. Michael also plays the trombone, and he wrote a piece of music called "Earthquake Quartet #1." When the piece is played, the trombone sounds like the stress that builds up inside Earth before an earthquake. Michael also adds earthquake sounds to the music. He says that writing earthquake music helped him think about earthquakes in a different way. He realized that seismologists often do not notice tension building up in Earth's crust because, like the rhythm in a song, the tension is always present.

Intellectual Honesty

Scientists also must demonstrate honesty. Imagine what would happen if you lied about the results of your experiments and other scientists thought that your results were true. Something like this happened in 1989. Two groups of scientists were researching cold fusion. The goal of *cold fusion* is to join the nuclei of two atoms at low temperatures. If cold fusion were achieved, it would create cheap, limitless energy for the world. One group feared that the other group would publish its results first and become famous. So, members of the first group wrote an article claiming that they had achieved cold fusion even though they had not.

The scientific community was excited at first. But no one could repeat the group's results. In short, the scientists were discredited. To ensure honesty, scientists have their work reviewed by other scientists before it is published. This process, which is called *peer review,* is very important in science. Whether scientists are working in a research lab, for a business, or for the government, they must be honest.

Ethical Responsibility

Scientists must never subject anyone's property or any living thing to unnecessary harm. Ethics help guide scientists as they do research. Scientists must use compassion when they care for animals used in research. If scientists use people in research, the scientists must first explain the risks that people may face. When people are informed of risks and choose to participate, this process is known as *informed consent.* Many groups monitor ethics in science. The American Association for the Advancement of Science (AAAS), develops ethics guidelines for scientific research.

What Does a Scientist Look Like?

What do you think of when someone says the word *scientist?* Do you picture a man who has crazy white hair and who wears glasses? Is he also wearing a white lab coat? There are many different scientists. They come from various countries and backgrounds, as shown in **Figure 4.**

Standards Check Who can be a scientist?

Figure 4 **The Faces of Science**

Ⓐ Mae Jemison was a NASA mission specialist. Now, she is adapting space technology to improve the lives of people in West Africa.

Ⓑ David Ho is a researcher who developed new treatments for the virus that causes AIDS.

Ⓒ Stephen Hawking is a theoretical physicist who has taught us about black holes in space.

Figure 5 *You should carefully analyze marketing claims. Advertisers may distort science to convince you to buy their products.*

Scientific Literacy

The goal of science education is to improve scientific literacy. **Scientific literacy** is the understanding of the methods of scientific inquiry, the scope of scientific knowledge, and the role of science in society.

Logic and Analysis

Although you may not become a scientist, learning science and becoming scientifically literate give you skills to use in your daily life. Science teaches you how to ask questions and how to find answers. Science helps you make careful observations. Science teaches you to think logically about information and teaches you how to decide if information is true. Studying science will help you become a better-informed consumer. For example, look at the acne products shown in **Figure 5.** How many of the claims made on the packages can be proven scientifically?

Critical Thinking and Science

Scientists have good critical-thinking skills. When you think critically about something, you think clearly, logically, practically, and realistically. You also gather information, ask questions, make inferences, and try to be objective.

The key to critical thinking is studying the information that you find and asking yourself if the information makes sense. Ask yourself if the person who presents the information is trying to persuade you. Find out how the information was gathered. Ask yourself if the research was done scientifically. Also, find other sources. Find out if they back up the claims being made. Finally, analyze how your opinions might influence how you interpret information. Critical thinking is very important when you are gathering information from the Internet. Many Web sites attempt to influence how you feel about a certain topic or product.

Critiquing the News

With a family member, read a news article, or watch a news broadcast about a current issue in science. In your **Science Journal**, write your first reactions. Include your thoughts, feelings, and questions. Then, answer the following questions:

- Did the report present different sides of the issue?
- Did the report use images or words that made you feel a certain way?
- Did the report provide any facts that helped you form an opinion? Were sources provided for the facts?
- Did the report lack information that might be important?
- When you think more about the issue, does your opinion change?

Science in Our World

Every day, ordinary people make important contributions to the advancement of science. People can help scientists in many ways. For example, people have discovered comets and helped plant trees. And because science affects everyone, people and communities speak out on scientific issues that concern them. These issues may be the research funded by governments, the ethical questions raised by scientific research, or global environmental conditions.

Scientists as Citizens

Scientists have a public place in society, and they use their knowledge and skills to help improve our world. Mario Molina, shown in **Figure 6,** has worked hard to protect Earth's ozone layer. When he was a graduate student in the 1970s, Molina studied chemical compounds called *CFCs,* or chlorofluorocarbons. These chemicals were widely used in aerosol sprays and as refrigerants. Molina discovered that these chemicals could damage the ozone layer of Earth's atmosphere. The ozone layer protects living things on Earth from the sun's harmful ultraviolet (UV) radiation.

Molina warned scientists and others about his discovery, but it took a long time for some people to believe him. He worked for many years to teach people about the link between CFCs and ozone destruction. Finally, in the 1990s, the use of CFCs was banned in most of the world. Today, Molina continues to research ways to help lower the effects of harmful pollutants in the atmosphere.

Standards Check How did Mario Molina contribute to the understanding of the ozone hole?

scientific literacy (SIE uhn TIF ik LIT uhr uh see) the understanding of the methods of scientific inquiry, the scope of scientific knowledge, and the role of science in society

Figure 6 *Mario Molina was awarded the Nobel Prize for his efforts to find the link between CFCs and ozone destruction. In the computer-modeled image of Earth to the left, the Antarctic ozone hole is shown in purple.*

Figure 7 *These students are learning to think like scientists by studying the geology of Mt. Diablo in a special science program.*

From the Classroom to the World

In science, the world is your classroom. If you are interested in science, there are many ways to become involved. There are no limits to what you can do.

Special Science Programs

Students, such as the students in **Figure 7,** can build scientific literacy and learn the skills used by scientists by taking part in special science programs. These skills are questioning, observing, problem solving, and critical thinking. In science programs, students can take part in exciting, hands-on activities, such as exploring tide pools and whale watching. Students can also navigate the ocean by using an ROV, or remotely operated vehicle. Students not only can learn to "fly" an ROV but also can design and build their own ROV! These activities are just a few examples of fun activities in which students can participate at special science programs in California.

Classroom Collaboration

Your class can also take part in science projects that connect classrooms around the world. One such project is the JASON Project. Each year, scientists working on the project lead students, teachers, and other scientists on a virtual two-week research trip. Students talk online with researchers, take part in digital labs, and keep notes in online journals. If your class cannot take part in online projects, you can do a science project at your school. You can volunteer or be an intern in the education department of a local museum. At the museum, you can build skills that may get you a job as a scientist someday!

Summary

- Scientists are curious, creative, skeptical, and open to new ideas.
- It is important for scientists to be honest and ethical in their treatment of humans and other living things.
- People from diverse backgrounds have made many contributions to the advancement of science.
- Increasing scientific literacy and developing critical-thinking skills are goals of science education.
- Scientists always evaluate the credibility of information that they receive.
- Scientists can have public roles in society. In addition to explaining scientific concepts to the media, scientists work to improve the quality of people's lives.
- There are many opportunities to participate in science programs in your community.

Using Vocabulary

1 Write an original definition for *skepticism* and *scientific literacy*.

Understanding Concepts

2 **Listing**   Identify six scientific habits of mind.

3 **Justifying**   Defend the idea that curiosity, skepticism, and openness to new ideas are important in science.

4 **Demonstrating**   Why is it important for scientists to follow a code of ethics when conducting research?

5 **Describing**   Who can be a scientist?

6 **Describing**   Describe the meaning of informed consent.

7 **Applying**   Why is it important to become scientifically literate?

Critical Thinking

8 **Applying Concepts**   Describe a volunteer science opportunity that interests you.

9 **Evaluating Sources**   Explain why scientists must always evaluate sources of information. Why is it important to be particularly skeptical of information found on the Internet?

INTERPRETING GRAPHICS   Use the image below to answer the next two questions.

10 **Evaluating Data**   Which of the statements on the label might make a scientist skeptical?

11 **Analyzing Methods**   How might a scientist determine whether the statements on the label are true?

Challenge

12 **Predicting Consequences**   Scientists on a research team have developed a new drug that they claim can cure cancer. They want to sell the drug, but they have not followed the peer-review process. What are some possible negative consequences of putting the drug on the market? Develop a peer-review process that could be used in researching the drug and that would prevent the negative consequences that you identified.

Internet Resources

For a variety of links related to this chapter, go to www.scilinks.org

Topic: Scientists in California

SciLinks code: HY7C11

Scientific Methods in Earth Science

Key Concept Scientists conduct careful investigations by following standard methods that allow them to collect data and communicate results.

▶ Imagine that you are standing in a thick forest on the bank of a river. Suddenly, you hear a booming noise, and you feel the ground begin to shake. You notice a creature's head looming over the treetops. The creature's head is so high that its neck must be 20 m long! Then, the whole animal comes into view. You now understand why the ground is shaking. The giant animal is *Seismosaurus hallorum* (SIEZ moh SAWR uhs hah LOHR uhm), the "earth shaker," shown in **Figure 1.**

Learning About the Natural World

The description of the *Seismosaurus hallorum* is not based on imagination alone. Scientists have been studying dinosaurs since the 1800s. Scientists gather bits and pieces of information about dinosaurs and their environment. Then, scientists re-create what dinosaurs might have been like hundreds of millions of years ago. But how do scientists put all of the pieces together? How do they know if they have discovered a new kind of dinosaur? Asking such questions is the beginning of a process that scientists use to learn more about the natural world.

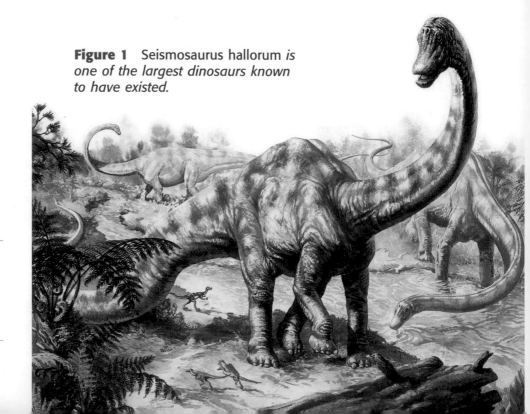

Figure 1 Seismosaurus hallorum *is one of the largest dinosaurs known to have existed.*

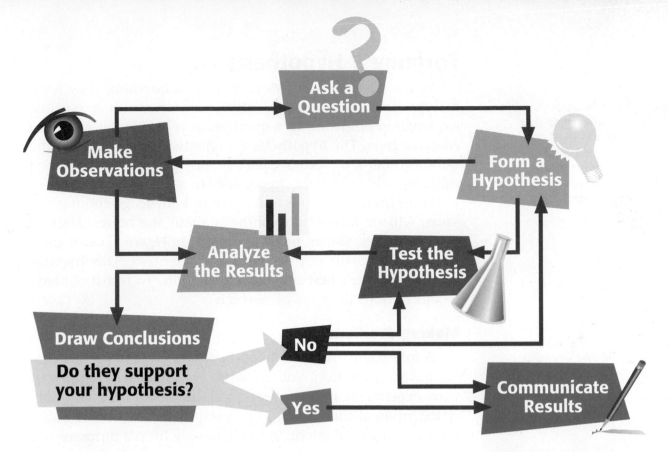

Figure 2 *Steps of scientific methods are illustrated in this flowchart. Notice that there are several ways to follow the paths.*

What Are Scientific Methods?

When scientists observe the natural world, they often think of a question or problem. But scientists don't just guess the answer. Instead, they follow a series of steps called scientific methods. **Scientific methods** are a series of steps that scientists use to answer questions and solve problems. The most basic steps are shown in **Figure 2.**

Although scientific methods have several steps, there is not a set procedure. Scientists may use all of the steps or just some of the steps. They may even repeat some of the steps. Or they may do the steps in a different order. The goal of scientific methods is to come up with reliable answers and solutions. These answers and solutions must be able to stand up to inspection by other scientists.

scientific methods (SIE uhn TIF ik METH uhds) a series of steps followed to solve problems

Asking a Question

Asking a question helps focus the purpose of an investigation. David D. Gillette is a scientist who studies fossils. He examined some bones found by hikers in New Mexico in 1979. He could tell that the bones came from a dinosaur. But he didn't know what kind of dinosaur. So, he may have asked himself, "What kind of dinosaur did these bones come from?" Gillette knew that he would have to use scientific methods to answer this question.

Forming a Hypothesis

hypothesis (hie PAHTH uh sis) a testable idea or explanation that leads to scientific investigation
<u>**Wordwise**</u> The prefix *hypo-* means "under." The root *thesis* means "proposition." Other examples are *hypodermic* and *hypoallergenic.*

When scientists want to investigate a question, they form a hypothesis. A <u>**hypothesis**</u> (plural, *hypotheses*) is a possible explanation or answer to a question. It is sometimes called an *educated guess*. The hypothesis is a scientist's best answer to the question. But a hypothesis can't be just any answer. Someone must be able to test the hypothesis to see if it is true.

From his observations and previous knowledge about dinosaurs, Gillette formed a hypothesis about the bones. He said that the bones, shown being excavated in **Figure 3,** came from a kind of dinosaur not yet known to scientists. This hypothesis was Gillette's best testable explanation. To test it, Gillette would have to do a lot of research.

Making Predictions

Before scientists test a hypothesis, they make predictions. To make a prediction, you say what you think will happen in your experiment or investigation. Predictions are commonly stated in an if-then form. For example, Gillette could make the following prediction: "*If* the bones are from a dinosaur not yet known to scientists, *then* at least some of the bones will not match any dinosaur bones that have been studied before." Sometimes, scientists make many predictions about one experiment. After predictions are made, scientists can do experiments to see which predictions, if any, support the hypothesis.

Figure 3 *Gillette and his team had to dig the bones out of the rock carefully before studying them.*

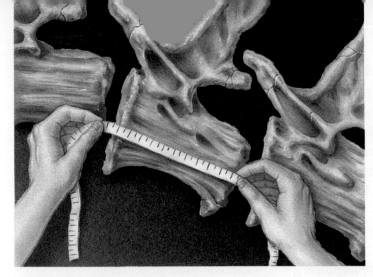

Figure 4 *To test his hypothesis, Gillette took hundreds of measurements of the bones.*

Testing the Hypothesis

To learn if an idea can be supported scientifically, scientists must test the hypothesis. They do so by gathering data. **Data** are any pieces of information gathered through observations or experimentation. The data can help scientists tell if the hypothesis is correct. To test his hypothesis, Gillette took measurements of the bones, as **Figure 4** shows. He compared his measurements with the measurements of bones from known dinosaurs. He also visited museums and talked with other scientists.

Standards Check Why do scientists need to test their hypotheses?

6.7.e

data (DAYT uh) any pieces of information acquired through observation or experimentation

controlled experiment (kuhn TROHLD ek SPER uh muhnt) an experiment that tests only one factor at a time by using a comparison of a control group with an experimental group

Testing with Experiments

To test a hypothesis, a scientist may conduct a controlled experiment. A **controlled experiment** tests only one factor, or *variable*, at a time. All other variables remain constant. By changing only one variable, scientists can see the results of just that one change.

During experiments, scientists must keep accurate records of everything that they do and observe. Accurate record keeping is important for maintaining a scientist's credibility with other scientists and society.

Testing without Experiments

Not all investigations are made by doing controlled experiments. Sometimes, it is not possible to use a controlled experiment to test something. Also, some scientists depend on observations more than they depend on experiments to test their hypotheses. By observing nature, scientists can often collect large amounts of data about their hypotheses. When large amounts of data support a hypothesis, the hypothesis is probably correct.

Analyzing the Results

After they finish their tests, scientists must analyze the results. Analyzing the results helps scientists form explanations based on the evidence that they have collected. To arrange their data, scientists often make tables and graphs. **Table 1** shows how Gillette organized his data. When Gillette analyzed his results, he found that the bones of the unknown dinosaur did not match the bones of any known dinosaur.

Table 1	Comparison of Hip Region Bones		
	Diplodocus	*Apatosaurus*	Unknown dinosaur
Top view			
Side view			

2 m

Drawing Conclusions

After analyzing the results of their tests, scientists must decide if the results support the hypothesis. Discovering that a hypothesis is not true can be as valuable as finding out that it is true. If the hypothesis is not supported, scientists may repeat the investigation to check for mistakes. Or they may look at the original question in a new way, ask new questions, and form new hypotheses. New questions and hypotheses can lead to new investigations and discoveries.

From all of his work, Gillette concluded that the bones found in New Mexico, shown in the model in **Figure 5,** were from an unknown dinosaur. He concluded that the dinosaur was about 35 m (110 ft) long and had a mass of 30 to 70 metric tons. The dinosaur certainly fit the name that Gillette gave it— *Seismosaurus hallorum,* or the "earth shaker."

Careers in Earth Science
Would you like to be an Earth scientist? Write an essay on your investigation of an interesting career. Go to **go.hrw.com,** and type in the keyword HY7WESW.

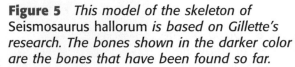

Figure 5 *This model of the skeleton of* Seismosaurus hallorum *is based on Gillette's research. The bones shown in the darker color are the bones that have been found so far.*

Communicating Results

After finishing an investigation, scientists communicate their results. By doing so, they share what they have learned. Scientists communicate by writing reports and by giving talks. They can also put their results on the Internet.

Science depends on sharing information. Sharing allows other scientists to repeat experiments to see if they get the same results. Openness and replication of experiments maintain a scientist's believability with other scientists and society.

Sharing information also helps scientists compare hypotheses and form consistent explanations. When sharing information, scientists sometimes learn that similar investigations gave different results. When different results are found, scientists do more studies to find out if the differences are significant.

 Standards Check What are two reasons that scientists share the results of their investigations? 🐻 **6.7.d**

Is the Case Closed?

Often, the results of an investigation are reviewed year after year as new evidence is found. Sometimes, the new evidence supports the original hypothesis even more. Other times, the hypothesis is questioned. For example, scientists are debating whether *Seismosaurus* is a new genus. Some scientists argue that Gillette's dinosaur belongs to the genus *Diplodocus,* an already known genus. The best way to solve this argument would be to discover at least one more skeleton of the dinosaur. If such a discovery does not support the hypothesis, a new hypothesis may be formed. Either way, Gillete continues the investigation, as shown in **Figure 6.**

Your Investigation

After you complete the Quick Lab on the previous page, write a report on your results in your **Science Journal.** Then, present the findings of your investigation to a member of your family. Encourage your family member to ask questions about your results. After answering any questions, did you decide to change your conclusions? Do you need to do further research?

ACTIVITY

Figure 6 *David Gillette continues to study the bones of* Seismosaurus hallorum *for new views into the past.*

Summary

- Scientific methods are the ways in which scientists follow steps to answer questions and solve problems.
- The steps used in scientific methods are to ask a question, form a hypothesis, test the hypothesis, analyze the results, draw conclusions, and communicate results.
- A controlled experiment tests only one factor at a time so that scientists can determine the effects of changes to just that one factor.
- Accurate record keeping, openness, and replication of results are essential to maintaining a scientist's credibility.
- When similar investigations give different results, the scientific challenge is to verify by further study whether the differences are significant.

Understanding Concepts

1 **Describing** How do scientists communicate the results of an investigation?

2 **Identifying** Identify the steps used in scientific methods, and explain how scientific methods are used to answer questions.

3 **Evaluating** Why are accurate record keeping, openness, and replication of results important?

4 **Applying** What is an observation? Write down one observation about the room that you are in at this moment.

5 **Analyzing** Why do scientists change only one variable in a controlled experiment?

6 **Summarizing** Why do scientists share and compare data?

7 **Justifying** Explain why a hypothesis has to be more than a scientist's best answer to a question.

Critical Thinking

8 **Analyzing Processes** Suppose that two scientists perform the same experiment and find different results. What should the scientists do next?

9 **Predicting Consequences** Explain what might happen if a scientist does not clearly communicate the steps of his or her investigation.

10 **Forming Hypotheses** You find a yellow rock and wonder if it is gold. How could you apply scientific methods to this problem?

INTERPRETING GRAPHICS Use the diagram below to answer the next two questions.

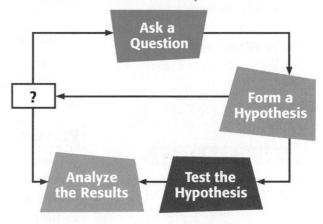

11 **Analyzing Processes** Which steps of scientific methods are missing from the diagram?

12 **Evaluating Data** A scientist has just tested her hypothesis. What is the next step?

Challenge

13 **Forming Hypotheses** New evidence challenges Gillette's hypothesis that the bones came from a dinosaur not yet known to scientists. Form a hypothesis about whether the bones are from a known dinosaur or an unknown dinosaur. Then, explain the process that you would follow to test your hypothesis. Would you need to do additional field investigations?

Internet Resources

For a variety of links related to this chapter, go to www.scilinks.org

Topic: Scientific Methods
SciLinks code: HY71359

Safety in Science

Key Concept Scientific investigations must always be conducted safely.

What You Will Learn

• Following safety rules will help prevent accidents and injury.

• The elements of safety include following safety rules, following directions, being neat, using proper safety equipment, and cleaning up properly.

• If an accident occurs, you should remain calm and should inform your teacher.

Why It Matters

Serious injuries can occur if safety rules are not followed.

Vocabulary

• first aid

READING STRATEGY

Graphic Organizer In your **Science Journal,** create a Concept Map by using the terms *safety in science, precautions, safety symbols, be neat, follow directions, safety equipment, clean up, make work easier, avoid accidents,* and *better results.*

▶ It's a sunny summer day. You and your best friend are going to ride your bikes to the park. You jump on your bike and start pedaling. But then your friend calls to you, "Wait! You forgot your helmet!" Always wearing a helmet when biking is an important safety rule. As **Figure 1** shows, using hand signals is another important rule. Just as you must follow rules to be safe when you are riding a bike, you must follow rules to be safe when you are learning science.

The Importance of Safety Rules

Bicycle safety rules, like all safety rules, have two purposes. Safety rules help prevent accidents and help prevent injury if an accident does happen.

Preventing Accidents

To be safe while doing science activities, you have to learn some safety rules. Perhaps the most important safety rule is to follow directions. The directions of a science activity are made to help you avoid accidents. Following directions also will make your work easier and will help you get better results.

Preventing Injury

If an accident takes place, you or someone nearby could get hurt. Following safety rules after an accident can help avoid or reduce injuries. For example, you should always wear gloves when you clean up a spilled chemical. Wearing gloves will prevent the chemical from touching your skin and causing injury.

Figure 1 *Everyday safety is as important as safety in a science lab.*

Figure 2 Safety Symbols

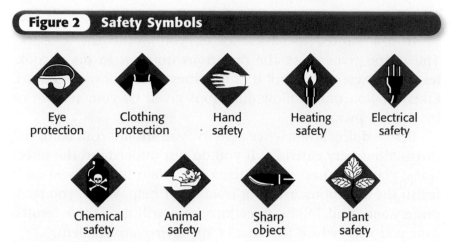

Eye protection   Clothing protection   Hand safety   Heating safety   Electrical safety

Chemical safety   Animal safety   Sharp object   Plant safety

For more safety tips, read the Safety First! section at the front of your book.

Elements of Safety

To have a safe workplace, you must know what precautions should be taken to prevent accidents. Safety has many parts. To be safe, you need to recognize safety symbols, follow directions, be neat, use safety equipment, and clean up after experiments.

Safety Symbols

A red light on a traffic signal has a specific meaning. A red light means that traffic must stop until the light turns green. Signs and symbols that have specific meanings are also used in science. Some of these symbols are safety symbols. They tell you what to do to prevent injury or accidents. For example, the hand safety symbol means that you should wear gloves to protect your hands from dangerous substances or sharp objects. Other safety symbols used in this book are shown in **Figure 2.**

Learn these safety symbols, and learn what they warn you about. For example, the animal safety symbol tells you to take special care of animals used in scientific research. Like the students in **Figure 3,** you must never squeeze or frighten animals. You must follow your teacher's directions on how to pick up animals and throw out animal waste. You should handle only the animals that your teacher gives you. And you should always wash your hands with soap and water after you have touched an animal.

Figure 3 *Treat living things with respect. When doing an experiment that uses animals or insects, do not do anything that could hurt them.*

Reading and Following Directions

If you wanted to bake cookies, you would use a recipe. The recipe gives all of the directions on how to make cookies. When scientists work in a lab, they also follow directions. Likewise, you must follow directions given by your teacher or by the lab procedure.

Before doing any science activity, you should read all of the instructions very carefully. If you do not understand the directions, you should ask your teacher to explain them. If you can't finish the directions, ask your teacher for help. When you read, understand, and follow directions, you will get better results. And you will reduce the chance of having an accident.

Standards Check How can following directions reduce the chance of having an accident?

Neatness

Before starting any experiment, you should clear your work area of books, backpacks, and other unneeded things. These objects can get in the way and can cause an accident. Long hair and loose clothing can get in the way, too, and should be tied back. Also, as **Figure 4** shows, you should prepare neatly your data tables and gather needed equipment before the activity.

During an experiment, arrange your equipment and materials so that they are easy to find and pick up. When instructed to do so, you should label your materials clearly. Some lab materials look alike and can be mixed up. As you collect data, record your findings carefully in your data table or notebook. Neatly recorded data are easier to read and analyze.

Figure 4 *Use a straight edge when making data tables.*

Figure 5 *Because they are working with hot objects, these students are wearing heat-resistant gloves. They are also wearing aprons and goggles to protect themselves from splashes and spills. **What safety symbols would be used for this lab?***

Using Proper Safety Equipment

Safety equipment that you may use in a science lab are goggles, gloves, and aprons. Some of the safety symbols tell you what safety equipment you need. For example, when you see the symbol for eye protection, you must put on safety goggles. Your goggles should fit comfortably but snugly. Your teacher can help you adjust them for a proper fit.

The chemicals that you use may not always be dangerous. But you should wear aprons, goggles, and protective gloves whenever you use chemicals. You should wear protective gloves when handling animals, too. But if you are handling warm objects, you must wear different gloves. You must wear heat-resistant gloves, such as the orange gloves in **Figure 5.**

Proper Cleanup Procedures

At the end of a science activity, you must clean up your work area. Spills and accidents are less likely to happen when everything is put away. You should put caps back on bottles and should return everything to its proper place. You should wash your glassware and should check for chips and cracks. If you find any damaged glassware, you must give it to your teacher. If you have any extra or waste chemicals, you should follow your teacher's directions for disposal. Once your work area is clear, you should wipe it with wet paper towels. Finally, you must wash your hands thoroughly with soap and water.

Figure 6 What to Do After an Accident

Step 1 Remain calm, and assess what happened.

Step 2 Secure the area. Make sure that no one is in danger.

Step 3 Inform your teacher, or call for help.

Step 4 Assist your teacher with cleanup or first aid.

Proper Accident Procedures

Sometimes, accidents happen in a lab even if all safety rules are followed. If an accident happens, you should remain calm. Panicking may make the situation worse. You may be scared, but staying in control will help keep you and others safe.

Steps to Follow After an Accident

The steps that you can follow if an accident occurs are shown in **Figure 6.** You should follow all of the steps in order quickly and carefully. Following the steps will help you and your classmates avoid or reduce injury.

If an accident happens, you must tell your teacher. Tell your teacher even if the accident is minor. You must tell your teacher even if you fear getting in trouble. You will be in more trouble if you don't report an accident. When you report an accident, you should describe exactly what happened. Your teacher will need to know the details, such as what chemicals were spilled or where glassware was broken.

Quick Lab

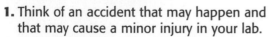

Accident Procedure

1. Think of an accident that may happen and that may cause a minor injury in your lab.

2. Write a procedure that you would follow if this accident happened to you.

3. List the proper safety equipment that you could have used to prevent the injury.

4. Describe other ways in which this accident could have been prevented.

6.7.b

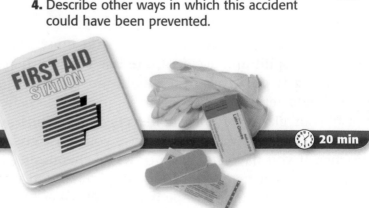

🕐 20 min

Caring for Injuries

If an accident results in an injury, your teacher may have to perform first aid. **First aid** is emergency medical care for someone who has been hurt. First aid is only temporary care. But it can keep a victim stable until complete medical care can be given.

You should not perform first aid unless you have been trained. However, your teacher may need your help. You should know where your classroom's first-aid kit is located. After an accident happens, your teacher may ask you to get your classroom's first-aid kit. You should also be familiar with the contents of the kit and their uses. A first-aid kit commonly contains bandages, antiseptic pads, and protective gloves.

first aid (FUHRST AYD) emergency medical care for someone who has been hurt or who is sick

SECTION Review

Summary

- Following safety rules helps prevent accidents and helps prevent injury when accidents happen.

- Five elements of safety are recognizing safety symbols, following directions, being neat, using safety equipment, and using proper cleanup procedures.

- Animals used in scientific research require special care.

- When an accident happens, assess what happened, secure the area, report the accident, and help care for injuries or help clean up.

- First aid is emergency medical care for someone who has been hurt.

Using Vocabulary

1 Write an original definition for *first aid.*

Understanding Concepts

2 **Listing** List four items that you are likely to find in a first-aid kit.

3 **Analyzing** Why is following all safety rules important?

4 **Summarizing** List and describe five elements of safety.

5 **Listing** List the four steps to follow after an accident.

6 **Summarizing** Why should you always follow directions?

INTERPRETING GRAPHICS Use the diagram below to answer the next question.

7 **Identifying** Identify the meaning of each safety symbol above, and describe an investigation in which you would expect to see each symbol.

Critical Thinking

8 **Making Inferences** Imagine that you are recording the changes that a tadpole goes through when it changes into a frog. Describe how you would care for and handle the tadpole during your experiment.

9 **Applying Concepts** Your lab partner drops a glass bottle of an unknown chemical. The bottle shatters on the floor. What is the first thing you should do?

Challenge

10 **Applying Concepts** Your teacher asks you to teach the safety rules of the science lab to a new student. Prepare a lesson plan that describes all of the safety rules and a procedure to follow if an accident occurs.

Internet Resources

For a variety of links related to this chapter, go to www.scilinks.org
Topic: Safety
SciLinks code: HY71339

Skills Practice Lab

Using Forensics to Catch a Thief

Help! Art thieves have stolen Jasper Rothkenberg's most famous artwork! The criminals stole the painting in broad daylight, and all they left behind were footprints. Can you help solve this mystery and catch the art thieves? To nab the robbers, you need to use forensic print analysis, which is a forensic science that examines shoe prints. In this activity, you will learn how forensic investigators collect information from shoe prints.

OBJECTIVES

Draw conclusions based on observations.

Describe the information that can be obtained from a shoe print.

MATERIALS

- magnifying glass or hand lens
- ruler, metric
- shoe box that contains a shoe print
- shoe print on paper, evidence (Exhibit A)
- shoe prints on paper, from suspects (Exhibit B)

Ask a Question

1 What information can I obtain from a shoe print, and how can this information be used in forensic science?

Form a Hypothesis

2 Write a hypothesis that is a possible answer to the question above. Explain your reasoning.

Test the Hypothesis

3 Look at your shoes. If someone could see only your shoe prints, what would he or she say about you?

Investigation and Experimentation
6.7.a Develop a hypothesis.
6.7.e Recognize whether evidence is consistent with a proposed explanation.

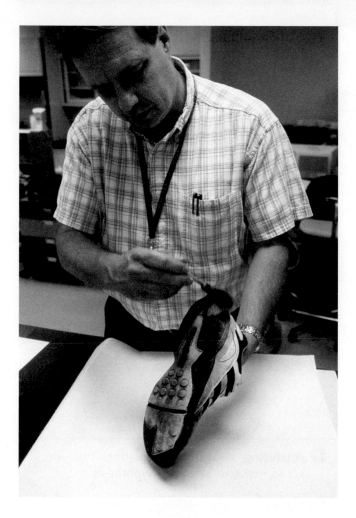

8 Draw a very careful sketch of the print. Make sure that you record every detail that you observe. When you are finished, write a detailed description of the shoe print.

9 Look at some of the other shoe prints in the room. Were any of them made by the same person? How do you know?

10 Now, see if you can practice your skills in matching shoe prints. Look at the shoe print left at the crime scene (Exhibit A). Compare it to the shoe prints of the suspects (Exhibit B).

11 Try to find and then circle five marks, cuts, or flaws that the shoe print of one of the suspects has in common with the shoe print left at the crime scene. In a court case, 12 matches are needed for shoe-print evidence to be accepted.

12 Decide which suspect left the shoe print at the crime scene.

Analyze the Results

13 Explaining Events Describe how flaws on the bottom of a shoe can lead to the identification of suspects.

14 Analyzing Data What other information about the suspect can the shoe print give you?

Draw Conclusions

15 Evaluating Methods Detectives cannot keep a shoe print forever. What are some ways of cataloging shoe-print evidence?

16 Evaluating Data Is a shoe print enough evidence to convict the art thieves? What other kinds of evidence would you look for?

Big Idea Question

17 Applying Conclusions Why is it important for detectives to follow scientific methods?

4 Your group will obtain a shoe box containing a shoe print from your teacher. Examine the shoe print closely, but do NOT touch the shoe print.

5 Discuss what you can learn about the person who made the shoe print. Record your ideas.

6 Examine the shoe print very closely by using a hand lens or magnifying glass. Record your observations.

7 Measure the shoe print by using a metric ruler. What shoe size do you think the shoe is? Do you think that the shoe print was left by a man or by a woman? Record your observations.

Science Skills Activity

Investigation and Experimentation
6.7.a Develop a hypothesis.

Develop a Hypothesis

▶ Tutorial

Scientific investigations commonly begin with observations. You may notice patterns in nature and may think that these patterns need to be explained. Your observations may lead to a question. For example, you may wonder how, why, or when something happens. To answer your question, you can start by forming a hypothesis.

❶ In scientific methods, a hypothesis is a possible answer to a question. Start to form a hypothesis by stating the probable answer to your question based on your observations.

❷ A useful hypothesis must be testable. To determine if your hypothesis is testable, identify experiments that you can perform or observations that you can make to find out whether the hypothesis is true or false.

The scenario below shows how you can develop a hypothesis based on observations.

You observe that your two potted plants have wilted since you last saw them yesterday. You ask the following question: Will these plants grow sturdy if I water them?

❶ You develop the following hypothesis: "The plant that I water will grow sturdy and strong, but the plant that I do not water will continue to wilt."

❷ You test your hypothesis by studying both plants before you water either one to determine the characteristics of each plant. Then, you water one of the plants, but not the other. The next day, you record your observations.

▶ You Try It!

Procedure

Look at the two images of constellations to the right. These two images show the position of the constellations in the sky seen from Denver, Colorado, at 10:00 P.M. on two different nights.

❶ **Comparing** Write a list of the observations that you can make about the two images of constellations.

❷ **Applying** Ask a question about the differences in the locations of the constellations.

❸ **Applying** Form a hypothesis that is a possible answer to your question.

❹ **Analyzing** Describe observations that you could make to test your hypothesis.

Analysis

❺ **Evaluating Hypotheses** Look at a classmate's hypothesis. Is it a possible answer to his or her question, and is it testable?

❻ **Evaluating Conclusions** Imagine that you tested your hypothesis and found that it was false. Was your hypothesis useful? Explain your answer.

February 15 10:00

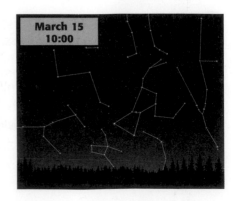

March 15 10:00

Chapter Summary

The Big Idea Scientists use careful observations and clear reasoning to understand processes and patterns in nature.

Section	Vocabulary

① Thinking like a Scientist

Key Concept Scientific progress is made by asking meaningful questions and conducting careful investigations.

- The habits of mind that scientists share include curiosity, skepticism, openness to new ideas, creativity, and ethical responsibility.
- Studying science can help you become a better-informed consumer.
- Most scientists follow a code of ethics so that no living thing is subjected to unnecessary harm.

Scientific habits of mind helped Jane Goodall study chimpanzees.

skepticism p. 9
scientific literacy p. 12

② Scientific Methods in Earth Science

Key Concept Scientists conduct careful investigations by following standard methods that allow them to collect data and communicate results.

- Scientific methods are a series of steps followed to solve problems.
- A scientist must be open to new ideas and must present investigations that can be replicated.
- Scientific investigations often lead to new questions and further investigation.

Scientific methods help scientists study all topics, including dinosaurs.

scientific methods p. 17
hypothesis p. 18
data p. 19
controlled experiment p. 19

③ Safety in Science

Key Concept Scientific investigations must always be conducted safely.

- Following safety rules will help prevent accidents and injury.
- The elements of safety include following safety rules, following directions, being neat, using proper safety equipment, and cleaning up properly.
- If an accident occurs, you should remain calm and should inform your teacher.

Safety equipment and procedures keep you safe when you perform an experiment.

first aid p. 29

Chapter Review

Organize

Folded Table Review the FoldNote that you created at the beginning of the chapter. Add to or correct the Fold-Note based on what you have learned.

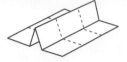

Using Vocabulary

1 Academic Vocabulary In the sentence "The scientist will conduct an experiment all summer," what does the word *conduct* mean?

For each pair of terms, explain how the meanings of the terms differ.

2 *scientific methods* and *scientific literacy*

3 *data* and *hypothesis*

Understanding Concepts

Multiple Choice

4 You are doing a lab in which you use hydrochloric acid. What kind of safety equipment should you wear?
a. goggles
b. goggles and an apron
c. goggles, an apron, and protective gloves
d. goggles, an apron, and heat-resistant gloves

5 Scientists take careful notes during experiments and publish their results in a report. What is one reason for keeping and publishing detailed notes about experiments?
a. The notes help other scientists who want to replicate the experiment.
b. The notes allow scientists to publish longer reports.
c. The notes keep the experiments from having to be repeated.
d. The notes prove the scientists' hypotheses.

Short Answer

6 Identifying Identify the scientific habit of mind that guides scientists to use compassion with animals used in research?

7 Analyzing How could a hypothesis that is shown to be false lead to new scientific investigations?

8 Evaluating Why don't you need to complete the steps of scientific methods in a specific order?

9 Applying Which safety symbols would you expect to see for an experiment that requires handling a frog?

10 Justifying Explain why scientists must communicate their results accurately.

11 Describing Describe the special care that must be taken when animals are used in scientific research.

12 Evaluating Explain how peer review might affect a scientist's view on his or her investigation.

13 Analyzing Why does a scientist need to include the steps of the investigation in his or her report? Why can't the scientist provide only the results?

Writing Skills

14 Outlining Topics Create an outline of the possible steps a scientist will follow to solve a problem.

15 Creative Writing Write a short story about a scientist who had a breakthrough thought while taking part in an artistic activity. The thought helped the scientist answer a scientific question that he or she had been investigating. Explain how the artistic activity helped the scientist think of the investigation in a new way so that he or she could better solve the problem being investigated.

Critical Thinking

16 **Concept Mapping** Use the following terms to create a concept map: *science, scientific methods, hypothesis, problems, experiments, questions,* and *observations.*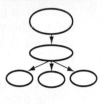

17 **Analyzing Ideas** Richard Feynman, a physicist, once said, "Science is the belief in the ignorance of experts." How would you interpret Feynman's statement in terms of the way in which scientific knowledge grows?

18 **Evaluating Conclusions** How could a scientist respond to another scientist who questioned the first scientist's conclusion?

19 **Identifying Relationships** Science helps us save lives, use resources wisely, and have healthy surroundings. How can healthy surroundings help save lives?

20 **Making Inferences** You build a model boat and predict that it will float. However, your tests show that the boat sinks. What conclusion would you draw? Suggest some logical next steps.

INTERPRETING GRAPHICS Use the illustration below to answer the next two questions.

21 **Applying Concepts** Which safety symbols relate to this diagram?

22 **Evaluating Data** List all of the safety issues that you see in this diagram.

INTERPRETING GRAPHICS Use the graph below to answer the next three questions.

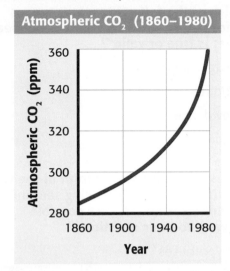

Atmospheric CO_2 (1860–1980)

23 **Evaluating Data** Since 1860, has the level of CO_2 in the atmosphere increased or decreased?

24 **Making Inferences** The line on the graph is curved. What does this curve indicate?

25 **Making Comparisons** Was the rate of change in the level of CO_2 between 1940 and 1960 higher or lower than it was between 1880 and 1900? How can you tell?

Math Skills

26 **Making Calculations** Let's say that Gillette originally estimated *Seismosaurus hallorum* to be about 45 m long and that a reinvestigation of the bones proposes that the dinosaur is only 36 m long. What percentage of the original estimated length is the new estimated length?

Challenge

27 **Analyzing Ideas** Imagine that you are conducting an experiment. You are testing the effects of the height of a ramp on the speed at which a toy car goes down the ramp. What is the variable in this experiment? What factors must be controlled? Write a testable hypothesis for this investigation.

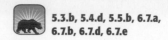
REVIEWING ACADEMIC VOCABULARY

1 Which of the following words means "information showing whether an idea or belief is true or valid"?

A suggestion

B notice

C evidence

D knowledge

2 Choose the appropriate form of the word *hypothesis* for the following sentence: "Scientists form _____ as possible answers to their questions."

A hypotheses

B hypothesis

C hypothesises

D hypothesize

3 Which of the following words is the closest in meaning to the word *select*?

A choose

B repair

C special

D purchase

4 In the sentence "Scientists make sure evidence is consistent with a hypothesis before drawing a conclusion," what does the word *consistent* mean?

A older than

B lacking something

C in agreement

D holding up

REVIEWING CONCEPTS

5 In 1989, a group of scientists claimed to have achieved cold fusion. What evidence showed that they were not telling the truth?

A They admitted that they had created the data.

B Another group achieved cold fusion.

C Other scientists reviewed their data.

D No one could repeat the group's results.

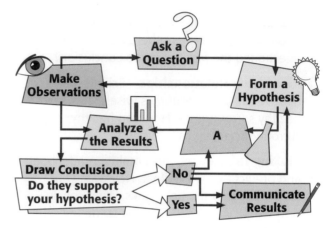

6 Which step belongs at point A in the flowchart of scientific methods above?

A Question the Methods

B Repeat the Hypothesis

C Test the Hypothesis

D Guess an Answer

7 Which of the following statements describes the hypothesis that Rachel Carson developed in the 1950s?

A Chemical manufacturers are developing new ways to kill insects.

B Pesticide use should be limited, and DDT use should be banned.

C A pesticide will not harm organisms other than the insects that it kills.

D Chemicals that harm insects will also harm other living things.

8 Experimentation is an important step in many scientific investigations. What is a controlled experiment?

A an experiment that tests only one factor, called the *variable,* at a time

B an experiment that begins with making predictions about the results

C an experiment performed using the scientific methods as a guide

D an experiment during which a scientist has kept an accurate record

9 Science activities sometimes involve chemicals. Why is it important to wear protective gloves when working with chemicals?

A Some chemicals may burn or irritate your skin.

B All chemicals are dangerous and can easily injure you.

C Experiments are sloppy, and you will probably spill.

D The gloves protect your hands if the chemicals are hot.

10 You are preparing for an experiment in which you will boil water. Which of the safety symbols below would you most likely see in the directions for this experiment?

A

C

B

D

11 Water can exist in three states. Water is a liquid at room temperature. When water freezes, it is called *ice.* What do we call water when it becomes a gas?

A oxygen

B hydrogen

C water vapor

D condensation

12 A weather map shows storms and high pressure in western Canada. The same map shows clear skies and low pressure in central Canada. What is the best weather forecast based on these factors?

A The clear skies and low pressure will move into western Canada.

B The high and low pressure areas will meet to form a closure.

C The high and low pressure areas will meet to form a tornado.

D The storms and high pressure will move into central Canada.

13 Which of the following planets has the shortest year?

A Saturn

B Mars

C Jupiter

D Uranus

Standards Assessment

Science in Action

Weird Science

Raining Fish and Frogs

What forms of precipitation have you seen fall from the sky: rain, snow, hail, sleet, or fish? Fish and frogs might not be a form of precipitation, but as early as the second century, they have been reported to fall from the sky during rainstorms. Scientists think that tornadoes or waterspouts that pull water into clouds can also pull up unsuspecting fish, frogs, or tadpoles that are near the surface of the water. After being pulled up into the clouds and carried a few miles, these reluctant travelers then rain down from the sky.

Language Arts ACTiViTY

Imagine that you are a reporter for your local newspaper. While driving to work on a rainy day in spring, you witness a downpour of frogs and fish. You pull off to the side of the road and interview other witnesses. In your **Science Journal,** write an article that describes this event for the local newspaper.

Science, Technology, and Society

Is There Another Planet?

Can you name all the planets in our solar system? There is Saturn, Neptune, 2003UB313 . . . Wait a minute—2003UB313 is the name of a planet? Scientists at the California Institute of Technology have found a new, large object in our solar system by using the Samuel Oschin Telescope. The telescope operates as a robot and collects data overnight. In the morning, scientists review the data. One morning, scientists found a nice surprise. Way past Pluto, on the outer edge of the solar system, a new object was discovered. Eventually, this object will receive a more fitting name. Until then, 2003UB313 is Cal Tech's lucky number.

Social Studies ACTiViTY

Scientists studied objects in space long before powerful telescopes were invented. Research the history of astronomy. Then, in your **Science Journal,** write a one-page summary of your findings.

Wes Skiles

Diver and Cave Explorer Wes Skiles started diving in his home state of Florida, where he fell in love with the state's hidden underwater caves. These caves were formed by a system of underground rivers that slowly carved their way through the limestone rock. The caves are part of the Floridan Aquifer, one of the largest aquifers in the United States. Skiles travels through these caves like an underwater astronaut. In a diving suit outfitted with space-age gear, he glides through dark worlds that are as silent as outer space.

Skiles is a diver, a cave explorer, and the executive producer of a film and photography company. Skiles and the other members of his production team have traveled all over the world to take photos and make movies of underwater caves and other natural water systems. The movies are usually documentaries about cave exploration or environmental stresses on water systems. The award-winning movies have been shown in theaters and on TV. By watching these movies, you can learn about the beauty and the life of underwater caves and the importance of preserving these ecosystems.

Math ACTiViTY

The Devil's Eye cave system is located northwest of Gainesville, Florida. The system has 30,000 ft of mapped underwater passageways. How many meters of mapped passageways does the cave system have? (Hint: 1 ft = 0.30 m)

Internet Resources

- To learn more about careers in science, visit www.scilinks.org and enter the SciLinks code HY70225.

- To learn more about these Science in Action topics, visit go.hrw.com and type in the keyword HY7WESF.

- Check out articles related to this chapter by visiting go.hrw.com. Just type in the keyword HY7WESC.

Improving Comprehension

Graphic Organizers are important visual tools that can help you organize information and improve your reading comprehension. The Graphic Organizer below is called a *comparison table.* Instructions for creating other types of Graphic Organizers are located in the **Study Skills** section of the Appendix.

How to Make a Comparison Table

1 Draw a table like the one shown below. Draw as many columns and rows as you want to draw.

2 In the top row, write the topics that you want to compare.

3 In the left column, write the general characteristics that you want to compare. As you read the chapter, fill in the characteristics for each topic in the appropriate boxes.

When to Use a Comparison Table

A comparison table is useful when you want to compare the characteristics of two or more topics in science. Organizing information in a table helps you compare several topics at one time. In a table, all topics are described in terms of the same list of characteristics, which helps you make a thorough comparison. As you read, look for topics whose characteristics you may want to compare in a table.

	Tools of measurement	Models	Maps
What they are used for	• to find length, area, mass, volume, or temperature	• to represent things too small or too large to see • to explain the past, present, and future	• to represent features of a physical body, such as Earth
Examples	• balance • meterstick • spring scale • thermometer • stopwatch • graduated cylinder	• physical models • mathematical models • scientific theories and laws	• globe • any representation of a physical body or area

You Try It!

This Reading Strategy can also be used within the chapter that you are about to read. Practice making your own comparison table as directed in the Reading Strategy for Section 1. Record your work in your **Science Journal.**

Unpacking the Standards

The information below "unpacks" the standards by breaking them down into basic parts. The higher-level, academic vocabulary is highlighted and defined to help you understand the language of the standards. "What It Means" restates the standards as simply as possible.

California Standard	Academic Vocabulary	What It Means
6.7.b Select and use **appropriate** tools and **technology** (including calculators, **computers** balances, spring scales, microscopes, and binoculars) to perform tests, collect **data,** and **display data.**	**select** (suh LEKT) to choose; to pick out **appropriate** (uh PROH pree it) correct for the use; proper **technology** (tek NAHL uh jee) tools, including electronic products **computer** (kuhm PYOOT uhr) an electronic device that stores, retrieves, and calculates data **data** (DAYT uh) facts or figures; information **display** (di SPLAY) to show	Choose the correct tools and technology (including calculators, computers, balances, spring scales, microscopes, and binoculars) to perform an experiment. Use these tools and technology to collect facts and figures, and show your research findings.
6.7.c Construct appropriate graphs from **data** and develop **qualitative** statements about the relationships between **variables.**	**construct** (kuhn STRUHKT) to build; to make from parts **qualitative** (KWAWL i TAYT iv) descriptive information that is not expressed as a number and is based on comparisons **variable** (VER ee uh buhl) a factor that changes in an experiment in order to test a hypothesis	Make the correct type of graph to show your facts and figures. Then, write a statement that explains how one variable changes relative to the other variable.
6.7.e Recognize whether **evidence** is **consistent** with a proposed explanation.	**evidence** (EV uh duhns) information showing whether an idea or belief is true or valid **consistent** (kuhn SIS tuhnt) in agreement	Figure out if observations and information agree or disagree with your previous ideas or explanations.
6.7.f Read a topographic map and a geologic map for **evidence** provided on the maps and **construct** and **interpret** a simple scale map.	**interpret** (in TUHR pruht) to tell or explain the meaning of	Read maps that tell you what the shape of the land is and where rock units and structures are located. Make and read a simple map that is drawn to the correct proportions.

2

Tools of Earth Science

The Big Idea

Scientists use a variety of tools, including maps, to perform tests, collect data, and display data.

 California Standards

Investigation and Experimentation
6.7 Scientific progress is made by asking meaningful questions and conducting careful investigations. (Sections 1, 2, 3, and 4, Science Skills Activity)

Math
6.1.3 Number Sense
6.2.3 Algebra and Functions

English–Language Arts
6.1.1 Reading
6.1.1 Writing

About the Photo

This image of Southern California and northern Baja California, Mexico, was taken in October 2003 by NASA's *Aqua* satellite. No less than 10 large brush fires can be seen burning in Southern California. Santa Ana winds—hot, dry winds that blow westward from California's inland deserts—are blowing the smoke from these fires over the Pacific Ocean. The city of San Diego is completely covered in a cloud of smoke from three of these fires.

Organize

Three-Panel Flip Chart

Before you read this chapter, create the FoldNote entitled "Three-Panel Flip Chart." Label the flaps of the three-panel flip chart with "World maps," "Topographic maps," and "Geologic maps." As you read the chapter, write information about each topic under the appropriate flap.

Instructions for creating FoldNotes are located in the Study Skills section on p. 617 of the Appendix.

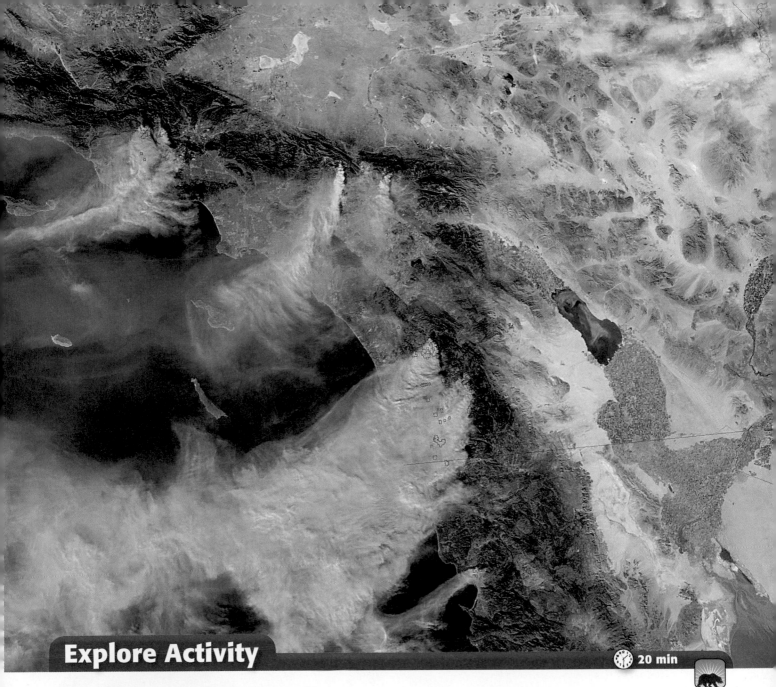

Explore Activity

20 min

6.7.f

Making and Reading Maps

In this activity, you will learn how to read a map and you will make a map.

Procedure

1. Use a **computer drawing program** or **colored pencils** and **paper** to draw a map that shows how to get from your classroom to another place in your school, such as the cafeteria. Make sure that you include enough information for someone unfamiliar with your school to find his or her way.

2. Use a **tape measure** to find the distance between your classroom and the place that you want your map reader to go. Use that distance to create a scale for your map (for example, 1 m on the ground = 1 cm on the map).

3. After you finish drawing your map, switch maps with a partner. Examine your classmate's map, and try to figure out where the map is leading you.

Analysis

4. Does your map reasonably model your school? Explain your answer.

5. Was any information on your map not clear enough? What information could you include to make your map better?

6. Compare your map with your partner's map. How are your maps alike? How are they different?

Tools of Earth Science   **43**

Tools and Measurement

Key Concept Scientists must select the appropriate tools to make measurements and collect data, to perform tests, and to analyze data.

▶ Would you use a hammer to tighten a bolt on a bicycle? You probably wouldn't. To carry out tasks, you need to choose the correct tools. Scientists use many tools. A *tool* is anything that helps you do a task.

Tools for Science

If you observe a jar of pond water, you may see a few insects swimming around. But a microscope can help you see many organisms that you couldn't see before. And a graduated cylinder can help you measure the volume of water in the jar. Different tools help scientists gather different kinds of data.

Tools for Seeing

Microscopes and magnifying lenses are tools that help you see things that are too small to see with only your eyes. Telescopes and binoculars help you make careful observations of things that are too far away to see with only your eyes. The reflecting telescope in **Figure 1** is made up of three major parts—a curved mirror, a flat mirror, and an eyepiece. Light enters the telescope and is reflected from a curved mirror to a flat mirror. The flat mirror focuses the image and reflects the light to the eyepiece.

Figure 1 *By using telescopes, scientists can make detailed studies of distant objects in space, such as the moon.*

Figure 2 Measurement Tools

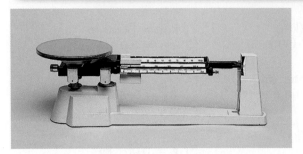

You can use a **balance** to measure mass.

You can use a **meterstick** to measure length.

You can use a **stopwatch** to measure time.

You can use a **thermometer** to measure temperature.

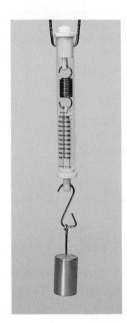

You can use a **spring scale** to measure force.

You can use a **graduated cylinder** to measure volume.

Tools for Measuring

One way to collect data during an experiment is to take measurements. To have the best measurements possible, you need to use the proper tools. Stopwatches, metersticks, and balances are some of the tools that you can use to make measurements. Thermometers, spring scales, and graduated cylinders are also helpful tools. **Figure 2** explains what properties these tools can be used to measure.

Tools for Analyzing

After you take measurements, you need to analyze the data. Perhaps you need to find the average of your data. Calculators are tools that help you do calculations quickly. Or you could show your data in a graph or a figure. A computer that has the correct software can help you make neat figures. In fact, computers have become invaluable tools for collecting, storing, and analyzing data. Of course, even a pencil and graph paper are tools that you can use to graph your data.

Quick Lab

See for Yourself 6.7.b

1. Use a **metric ruler** to measure the length and width of one of your fingernails. Draw and describe the details of your fingernail.

2. Look at the same fingernail through a **magnifying lens.** Now, draw the details of your fingernail as seen with magnification.

3. How does using a magnifying lens change what details you can see?

 15 min

Table 1	Common SI units and Conversion		
Length		**meter (m)** kilometer (km) centimeter (cm)	1 km = 1,000 m 1 cm = 0.01 m
Area		**square meter (m²)** square centimeter (cm²)	1cm² = 0.0001 m²
Mass		**kilogram (kg)** gram (g) milligram (mg)	1 g = 0.001 kg 1 mg = 0.000001 kg
Volume		**cubic meter (m³)** cubic centimeter (cm³) liter (L) milliliter (mL)	1 cm³ = 0.000001 m³ 1 L = 1 dm³ = 0.001 m³ 1 mL = 0.001 L =1 cm³
Temperature*		**kelvin (K)** **celcius (°C)**	0°C = 273 K 100°C = 373 K

*The Celcius (°C) scale is a commonly used non-SI temperature scale.

Measurement

Hundreds of years ago, different countries used different systems of measurement. At one time in England, the standard for an inch was three grains of barley placed end to end. Other modern standardized units were originally based on parts of the body, such as the foot. Such systems were not very reliable. Their units were based on objects that varied in size.

In time, people realized that they needed a simple and reliable measurement system. In the late 1700s, the French Academy of Sciences set out to make that system. Over the next 200 years, the metric system was developed. This system is now called the *International System of Units,* or the *SI.*

The International System of Units

Today, most scientists and almost all countries use the International System of Units. One advantage of using SI measurements is that they allow all scientists to share and compare their observations and results. Another advantage is that all units are based on the number 10. This feature makes changing from one unit to another easy.

Table 1 shows SI units for length, area, mass, volume, and temperature. Become familiar with these units. You will use SI units in the science lab when you collect and analyze data.

Units of Measurement

Measure the width of your desk, but do not use a ruler. Pick an object to use as your unit of measurement. It could be a pencil, your hand, or anything else. Find how many units wide your desk is. Compare your measurement with those of your classmates. Explain why using standard units of measurement is important. Record your work in your **Science Journal.**

Length

How long is your arm? The student in **Figure 3** could describe the length of her arm by using the **meter** (m), the main SI unit of length. Remember that SI units are based on the number 10. If you divide 1 m into 100 parts, each part equals 1 cm. In other words, 1 cm is one-hundredth of a meter. To describe the length of microscopic objects, use micrometers (μm) or nanometers (nm). To describe the length of larger objects, use kilometers (km).

Standards Check What tool would you select to measure the length of an object? 🐻 **6.7.b**

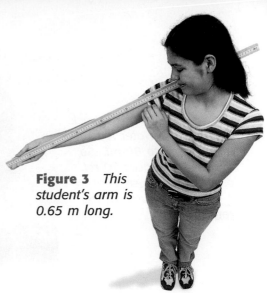

Figure 3 *This student's arm is 0.65 m long.*

Area

How much carpet would it take to cover the floor of your classroom? To answer this question, you must find the area of the floor. **Area** is a measure of how much surface an object has. Area is based on two measurements. For example, to calculate the area of a square or rectangle, you need to measure the length and width. Then, use the following equation for the area of a square or a rectangle:

$$area = length \times width$$

The units for area are square units, such as square meters (m^2), square centimeters (cm^2), and square kilometers (km^2).

meter (MEET uhr) the basic unit of length in the SI (symbol, m)

area (ER ee uh) a measure of the size of a surface or a region

mass (MAS) a measure of the amount of matter in an object

Mass

How many sacks of grain can a mule carry? The answer depends on the strength of the mule and the mass of the sacks of grain. **Mass** is the amount of matter that makes up an object. Scientists often use a balance to measure mass, as shown in **Figure 4.** The kilogram (kg) is the main unit for mass. The kilogram is used to describe the mass of things such as sacks of grain. Many everyday objects are not so large, however. The mass of smaller objects, such as an apple, can be described by using grams (g) or milligrams (mg). One thousand grams equals 1 kg. The mass of large objects, such as an elephant, is given in metric tons. A metric ton equals 1,000 kg.

Figure 4 *This student is using a balance to measure the mass of an apple.*

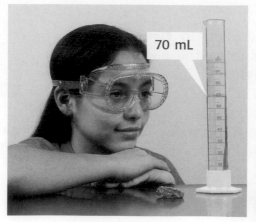

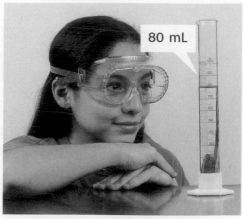

70 mL

80 mL

Figure 5 *Adding the rock changes the water level from 70 mL to 80 mL. So, the rock displaces 10 mL of water. Because 1 mL = 1 cm³, the volume of the rock is 10 cm³.*

Volume

volume (VAHL yoom) a measure of the size of a body or region in three-dimensional space

temperature (TEM puhr uh chuhr) a measure of how hot (or cold) something is; specifically, a measure of the average kinetic energy of the particles in an object

The amount of space that something occupies or the amount of space that something contains is called **volume.** The volume of a large, solid object is given in cubic meters (m^3). The volumes of smaller objects can be given in cubic centimeters (cm^3) or cubic millimeters (mm^3). To find the volume of an irregularly shaped object, measure the volume of liquid that the object displaces. This process is shown in **Figure 5.** To calculate the volume of a box-shaped object, you can multiply the object's length by its width and then by its height.

The volume of a liquid is often given in liters (L). Liters are based on the meter. A cubic meter ($1 \ m^3$) is equal to 1,000 L. So, 1,000 L will fit into a box measuring 1 m on each side. A milliliter (mL) will fit into a box measuring 1 cm on each side. So, 1 mL = 1 cm^3. Graduated cylinders are used to measure liquid volume in milliliters.

Standards Check What tool would you select to measure the volume of a small, irregularly shaped object? 6.7.b

Temperature

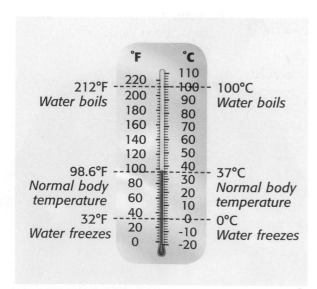

°F	°C	
212°F *Water boils*	220 200 180 160 140 120	110 100 90 80 70 60 50 — 100°C *Water boils*
98.6°F *Normal body temperature*	100 80 60 40	40 37°C 30 *Normal body* 20 *temperature* 10
32°F *Water freezes*	20 0	0 0°C -10 *Water freezes* -20

To find out how hot or cold something is, scientists measure temperature. **Temperature** is a measure of the average kinetic energy of the particles that make up an object. You may use degrees Fahrenheit (°F) to describe temperature. Scientists often use degrees Celsius (°C). However, the kelvin (K) is the SI base unit for temperature. The thermometer in **Figure 6** shows how two of these units are related.

Figure 6 *This thermometer shows the relationship between degrees Fahrenheit and degrees Celsius.*

Writing Numbers in Scientific Notation

Scientific measurement often involves numbers that are very large or very small. For example, light moves through space at a speed of about 300,000,000 m/s. That's a lot of zeros! To make very large numbers and very small numbers more manageable, scientists use a shorthand called *scientific notation*. Scientific notation is a way to express a quantity as a number multiplied by 10 to the appropriate positive or negative power, as shown in **Table 2.** For example, the measurement 300,000,000 m/s can be written as 3.0×10^8 m/s in scientific notation.

Table 2	Powers of 10
Power of 10	**Decimal equivalent**
10^3	1,000
10^2	100
10^{-1}	1.0
10^{-2}	0.1
10^{-3}	0.01

SECTION Review

6.7.b

Summary

- Scientists use tools to make observations, take measurements, and analyze data.
- Scientists must select the appropriate tools for their observations and experiments to take appropriate measurements.
- Scientists use the International System of Units (SI) so that they can share and compare their observations and results with other scientists.
- Scientists have determined standard ways to measure length, area, mass, volume, and temperature.
- Scientific notation is a way to express numbers that are very large or very small.

Understanding Concepts

1. **Identifying** Identify the appropriate tools to measure length, area, mass, and volume.

2. **Comparing** Compare three units that are used to measure temperature.

3. **Analyzing** What is the advantage of using scientific notation to express numbers that are very small and very large?

4. **Applying** What tools could you choose if you wanted to see something far away?

Critical Thinking

5. **Making Inferences** Many nations worked together to build the *International Space Station.* Predict what might have happened if they had not used the International System of Units during construction.

6. **Applying Concepts** Describe two ways that you could determine the volume of a pair of dice.

INTERPRETING GRAPHICS Use the diagram below to answer the next two questions.

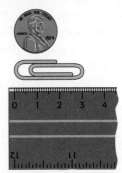

7. **Evaluating Data** What is the approximate diameter of the penny?

8. **Evaluating Data** What is the approximate length of the paper clip?

Math Skills

9. **Making Calculations** What is the area of a room that is 10 m long and 10 m wide?

Internet Resources

For a variety of links related to this chapter, go to www.scilinks.org

Topic: SI Units
SciLinks code: HY71390

Models in Science

Key Concept Models are ways of representing real objects or processes to make the natural world easier to understand.

What You Will Learn

- Physical models and mathematical models are two common types of scientific models.
- Theories and laws are models that describe how the universe works.

Why It Matters

Models allow scientists to study phenomena that may be impossible to investigate in the natural world.

Vocabulary

- model
- law
- theory

READING STRATEGY

Asking Questions Read this section silently. In your **Science Journal,** write down questions that you have about this section. Discuss your questions in a small group.

▶ A crash-test dummy, a mathematical equation, and a road map are all models that represent real things. A **model** is a representation of an object or a process that allows scientists to study something in greater detail. Models allow scientists to change variables without affecting or harming the subject that they are studying. For example, scientists use crash-test dummies to study the effects of car accidents on people.

Types of Models

Models can represent things that are too small to see, such as atoms. Models can also represent things that are too large to see entirely, such as Earth. Models can be used to explain the past and present and to predict the future. Two common kinds of scientific models are physical models and mathematical models.

Standards Check Why are different-sized models used to represent different things? 6.7.b

Physical Models

Physical models are models that you can touch. Physical models often look like the things they represent, but physical models have limitations. For example, because Earth is nearly a sphere, a globe most accurately represents Earth. But to make a map, you make a flat model of Earth's surface. In the process of making a map, you change the distances between points, and the map becomes inaccurate, as shown in **Figure 1.**

Figure 1 *This orange is a physical model of Earth. Notice how the shapes of the continents change when the orange peel is flattened.*

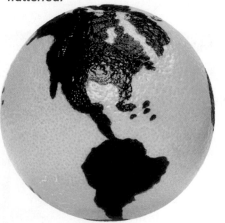

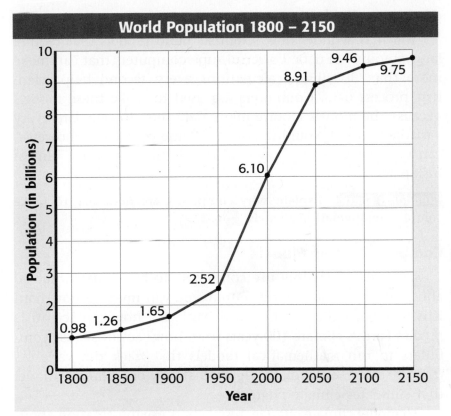

World Population 1800 – 2150

Investigation and Experimentation
6.7.b Select and use appropriate tools and technology (including calculators, computers, balances, spring scales, microscopes, and binoculars) to perform tests, collect data, and display data.
6.7.c Construct appropriate graphs from data and develop qualitative statements about the relationships between variables.
6.7.e Recognize whether evidence is consistent with a proposed explanation.

Figure 2 *This graph was the product of mathematical models that were processed by a computer.*

Mathematical Models

A *mathematical model* is made up of mathematical equations and data. Some mathematical models are simple. These models allow you to calculate things such as how far a car will travel in an hour or how much you would weigh on the moon. Other models are so complex that computers are needed to process them. **Figure 2** shows a graph made by computer models of population growth. Because so many variables affect population changes, scientists use computers to create mathematical models of population growth.

model (MAHD'l) a pattern, plan, representation, or description designed to show the structure or workings of an object, system, or concept

Quick Lab

Reading a Graph

6.7.c

Use the **graph** in **Figure 2** to answer the following questions.
1. The horizontal axis is called the *x*-axis. In this graph, the *x*-axis indicates time. Locate the year 1800 on the *x*-axis.
2. The vertical axis is called the *y*-axis. In this graph, the *y*-axis indicates world population. Find the world population in 1800.

3. Was the population in 1800 higher or lower than in 1900? Was the population in 1900 higher or lower than in 2000?
4. In general, is population increasing or decreasing?
5. Based on the trend you see in the graph, was the world population in 1000 more likely higher or lower than it was in 1800? Is world population likely to be higher in 2200 than in 2000? Explain your answers.

 10 min

Computer Models

You may wonder how scientists build models that require large amounts of data. Powerful supercomputers that can make more than 30 trillion calculations every second help scientists process data. Computers are used to make these models because the models require many data sets. To calculate every variable by itself would take years. Some computers, however, can perform all of the calculations at the same time, almost instantly.

Standards Check Explain why computers are necessary to make complex mathematical models. 🐻 **6.7.b**

Combinations of Models

Scientists commonly use computers to build mathematical and physical models. For example, you can imagine how hard it is to predict the weather next week. So, how can scientists predict Earth's climate 100 years from now? Scientists use computers to run mathematical models that track the variables that affect Earth's climate. **Figure 3** shows one climate model that simulates climate change.

To model climate change, researchers use information about current and past land and ocean-water temperatures around Earth. They also use information about weather patterns, ocean currents, and carbon dioxide levels in the atmosphere. These models do not make exact predictions about future climates, but they estimate what might happen if variables change.

Figure 3 *Supercomputers help scientists create very complex models that predict the results of climate change.*

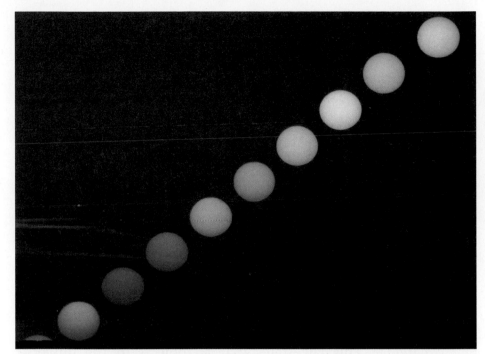

Figure 4 *For thousands of years, people watched the sun appear to move across the sky. From this pattern, they incorrectly developed a theory that Earth was the center of our solar system.*

Patterns in Nature

It is possible for scientists to make models because events in nature often follow predictable patterns. For example, if you drop a ball from a certain height, you can predict how high it will bounce. Another pattern in nature is yearly migration of some animals. Observing patterns in nature is the basis of science. These observations lead to explanations about the way the world works. Although these explanations are supported by observations, they may not be accurate. For example, **Figure 4** shows that the sun appears to move across the sky. For thousands of years, people observed this pattern and incorrectly concluded that Earth was the center of our solar system.

Theories and Laws

Observing patterns in the natural world can lead to the development of scientific theories and laws. The words *law* and *theory* have special meanings to scientists. In science, a **law** is a statement or equation that reliably predicts events under certain conditions. A theory is not a guess, or hypothesis. A **theory** is a scientific explanation that encompasses many scientific observations and may include many hypotheses and laws.

You may think that scientific theories are less important or less useful than scientific laws. But theories are very powerful explanations of the way the world works. Theories do not eventually become laws. Instead, theories are fully formed scientific explanations that are supported by evidence and data from many scientific disciplines.

law (LAW) a descriptive statement or equation that reliably predicts events under certain conditions

theory (THEE uh ree) a system of ideas that explains many related observations and is supported by a large body of evidence acquired through scientific investigation

Theories and Scientific Observations

Like all scientific theories, the theory of an Earth-centered universe was supported by scientific evidence. But even if a theory is supported by most scientific evidence, the theory may not be correct.

Over time, scientists observed movements of planets across Earth's sky that did not fit the theory of an Earth-centered universe. Sometimes, planets appeared to be moving backward across Earth's sky. Four moons were seen traveling around Jupiter. The movement of Jupiter's moons showed that objects can revolve around objects other than Earth. Scientists developed a new theory to incorporate their new observations. They suggested that Earth and the other planets in our solar system travel around the sun, as shown in **Figure 5.**

Laws and Theories

In 1665, Sir Isaac Newton discovered the *law of universal gravitation.* This law states that all objects in the universe, including the sun and planets, attract each other with a force called *gravity.* Scientists used this law to strengthen the theory of a sun-centered solar system. Gravity holds the planets in their orbits as they travel around the sun.

Standards Check What effect can new observations have on a scientific theory? 6.7.e

SCHOOL to HOME

A Community Solar System

The world's largest solar-system model is in Peoria, Illinois. This model shows the distance between the planets and the sun and shows the relative sizes of these bodies. The 11 m–wide dome of a planetarium represents the sun, and the 2.5 cm–wide Pluto is in a furniture store 64 km from the planetarium! With your class, plan a solar-system model in your community.

 ACTIVITY

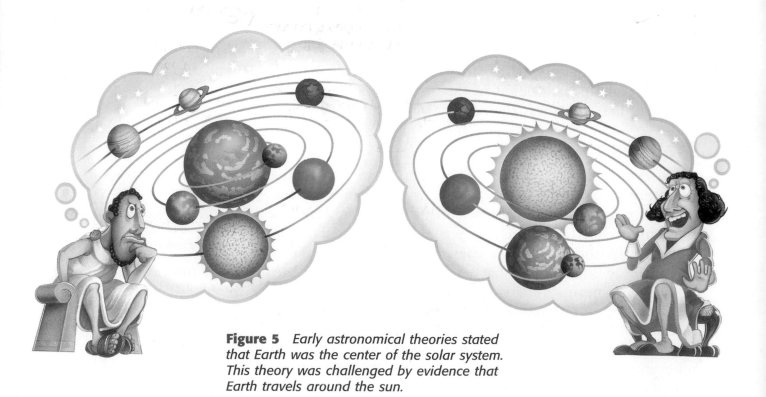

Figure 5 *Early astronomical theories stated that Earth was the center of the solar system. This theory was challenged by evidence that Earth travels around the sun.*

Limitations of Models

Although models are important scientific tools, all models are limited because they are simplified versions of the systems that they try to explain. Simplification makes a model easy to understand and use, but information is left out when a model is made.

All models can change. Models can change if a scientist finds new data or thinks about concepts in a new way. Scientists work to continually improve the models that we use to understand the world. Sometimes, new technology challenges existing models. Or, technology may help create new models that allow us to understand the world differently.

INTERNET ACTIVITY

Maps of the Future

How is technology changing maps? Design a map that might be available in the future, and make a poster of it for your class. Go to **go.hrw.com,** and type in the keyword HY7MAPW.

SECTION Review

 6.7.b, 6.7.c, 6.7.e

Summary

- Scientists must choose the right type of model to study a topic.

- Physical models, mathematical models, and computer models are common types of scientific models.

- Events in nature usually follow patterns. Scientists develop theories and laws by observing these patterns.

- Theories and laws are models that describe how the universe works. Theories and laws can change as new information becomes available.

- All models have limitations, and all models can change based on new data or new technology.

Using Vocabulary

1. Write an original definition for *law* and *theory*.

Understanding Concepts

2. **Summarizing** Explain why scientists use models.

3. **Analyzing** Describe how computers have helped scientists develop more-accurate climate models.

4. **Applying** Explain which type of model you would use to study the flight of birds.

5. **Listing** Give examples of a physical model and a mathematical model.

6. **Identifying** Give one example of how a law or a theory changed when new information became available.

Critical Thinking

7. **Applying Concepts** Do all events in nature follow a pattern? Explain your answer.

8. **Making Comparisons** What is the difference between theories and laws? Are laws more important than theories? Explain.

9. **Applying Concepts** Is a scientific theory inaccurate if it is not supported by a scientific law or laws? Explain your answer.

Math Skills

10. **Making Calculations** If Earth's human population was 1.65 billion in 1900 and 6.10 billion in 2000, predict the human population in 2100 if population continues to increase at the same rate.

Challenge

11. **Making Inferences** Why is a graph a mathematical model?

Internet Resources

For a variety of links related to this chapter, go to www.scilinks.org

Topic: Using Models
SciLinks code: HY71588

Mapping Earth's Surface

Key Concept Maps are tools that are used to display data about a given area of a physical body.

map (MAP) a representation of the features of a physical body such as Earth

▶ The Greeks thought of Earth as a sphere almost 2,000 years before Ferdinand Magellan began his round-the-world voyage in 1519. The observation that a ship sinks below the horizon as it sails into the distance supported the idea of a spherical Earth. If Earth were flat, the ship would not sink below the horizon.

The way in which people have seen the world has been reflected in their maps. A **map** is a representation of the features of a physical body such as Earth. If you were to look at a world map from the second century, you might not recognize the physical features that are represented. However, if you looked at a map of Earth's surface made from a photograph taken from a satellite, you might see physical features of Earth you never knew existed.

Standards Check What is a map? 6.7.f

Finding Directions on Earth

Although Earth's shape is not a true sphere, it is best represented by a sphere. A sphere has no top, bottom, or sides to use as reference points for specifying locations on its surface. However, Earth's axis of rotation can be used to establish reference points. The points at which Earth's axis of rotation intersects Earth's surface are the geographic North and South Poles, which are shown in **Figure 1.** The poles are used as reference points for finding location.

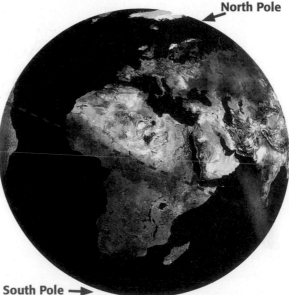

Figure 1 *The geographic North Pole is a good reference point for describing locations in Earth's northern hemisphere.* **What is a good reference point for describing locations in the southern hemisphere?**

Making a Compass

6.7.b

▶ Try It!

1. Do this lab outside. Carefully rub a **steel sewing needle** against a **magnet** in the same direction 40 times.

2. Float a **1 cm × 3 cm piece of tissue paper** in a **bowl of water**.

3. Place the needle in the center of the tissue paper. Observe the direction that the needle points.

▶ Think About It!

4. Compare your needle with a **magnetic compass.** Are both compasses pointing in the same direction?

5. How could you improve your compass?

🕐 **20 min**

Using a Compass

Earth's core generates a magnetic field that causes Earth to act as a giant magnet. Therefore, Earth has two magnetic poles that are located near the geographic poles. A *compass* is a tool that uses Earth's natural magnetism to show direction. A compass needle points to the magnetic north pole. Therefore, a compass will show you which direction is north.

Finding Locations on Earth

All of the houses and buildings in your neighborhood have addresses that give their location. But how would you find the location of something such as a city center or tip of an island? These places can be given an "address" by using *latitude* and *longitude*.

Latitude

The **equator** is a circle halfway between the North and South Poles that divides Earth into the Northern and Southern Hemispheres. Imaginary lines drawn around Earth parallel to the equator are called lines of latitude, or *parallels*. **Latitude** is the distance north or south from the equator. Latitude is expressed in degrees, as shown in **Figure 2.** The equator represents 0° latitude. The North Pole is 90° north latitude, and the South Pole is 90° south latitude. North latitudes are found between the equator and the North Pole. South latitudes are found between the equator and the South Pole.

equator (ee KWAYT uhr) the imaginary circle halfway between the poles that divides the Earth into the Northern and Southern Hemispheres
<u>Wordwise</u> The root *equ-* means "even" or "equal." Other examples are *equal, equidistant,* and *equality.*

latitude (LAT uh TOOD) the distance north or south from the equator; expressed in degrees

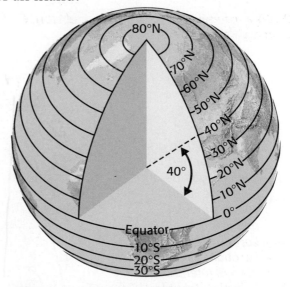

Figure 2 *Degrees latitude are a measure of the angle made by the equator and the location on Earth's surface, as measured from the center of Earth.*

Longitude

Lines of longitude, or *meridians,* are imaginary lines that connect both poles. **Longitude** is the distance east and west from the prime meridian. Like latitude, longitude is expressed in degrees, as shown in **Figure 3.** The **prime meridian** is the line that represents 0° longitude. Unlike lines of latitude, lines of longitude are not parallel. Lines of longitude touch at the poles and are farthest apart at the equator.

Unlike the equator, the prime meridian does not completely circle the globe. The prime meridian runs from the North Pole through Greenwich, England, to the South Pole. The 180° meridian lies on the opposite side of Earth from the prime meridian. Together, the prime meridian and the 180° meridian divide Earth into the Eastern and Western Hemispheres. East lines of longitude are found east of the prime meridian, between 0° and 180° longitude. West lines of longitude are found west of the prime meridian, between 0° and 180° longitude.

Using Latitude and Longitude

Points on Earth's surface can be located by using latitude and longitude. Lines of latitude and lines of longitude cross. They form a grid system on globes and maps. This grid system can be used to find locations north or south of the equator and east or west of the prime meridian.

Figure 4 shows you how latitude and longitude can be used to find the location of your state capital. First, locate the star that represents your state capital on the map. Then, use the lines of latitude and longitude closest to your state capital to estimate its approximate latitude and longitude.

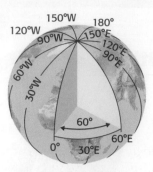

Figure 3 *Degrees longitude are a measure of the angle made by the prime meridian and the location on Earth's surface, as measured from the center of Earth.*

longitude (LAHN juh TOOD) the distance east or west from the prime meridian; expressed in degrees

prime meridian (PRIEM muh RID ee uhn) the meridian, or line of longitude, that is designated as 0° longitude

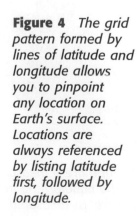

Figure 4 *The grid pattern formed by lines of latitude and longitude allows you to pinpoint any location on Earth's surface. Locations are always referenced by listing latitude first, followed by longitude.*

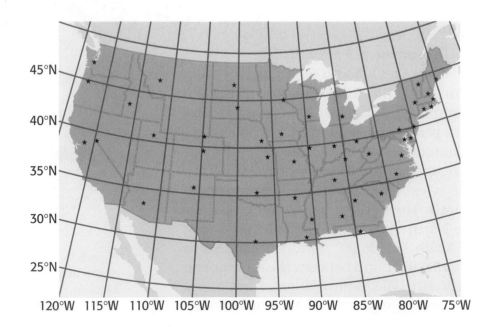

Information Shown on Maps

Maps provide information through the use of symbols. To read a map, you must understand the symbols on the map and be able to find directions and calculate distances. Regardless of the kind of map you are reading, a map typically contains the information shown in **Figure 5.** This information includes a title, an indicator of direction, a scale, a legend, and a date.

Standards Check What information should every map contain?
🐻 **6.7.f**

Figure 5 *This road map of Sacramento, California, contains all of the needed information to use the map.*

The **title** gives you information about the subject of the map.

The **legend** is a list of symbols used in the map that need explanations.

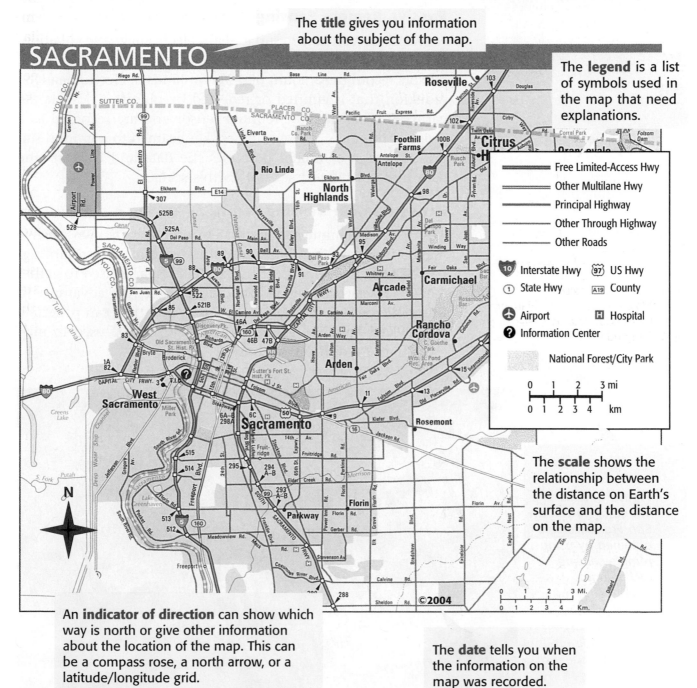

An **indicator of direction** can show which way is north or give other information about the location of the map. This can be a compass rose, a north arrow, or a latitude/longitude grid.

The **scale** shows the relationship between the distance on Earth's surface and the distance on the map.

The **date** tells you when the information on the map was recorded.

Modern Mapmaking

Data used in many of today's maps are provided by the process of *remote sensing*. **Remote sensing** is a way to gather information about an object without directly touching or seeing the object. Today, most maps are made from photographs taken by mapping cameras that are mounted on low-flying aircraft. However, mapmakers are beginning to rely on more sophisticated instruments. These instruments are carried on both aircraft and Earth-orbiting satellites. **Figure 6** shows an image taken by a satellite.

Passive Remote Sensing

All objects on Earth's surface emit electromagnetic radiation, such as heat or X rays. In a passive remote-sensing system, sensors record the amount of different kinds of electromagnetic radiation that is emitted or reflected by objects. The data are gathered by a satellite-mounted sensor and are recorded as a series of numbers. These numbers are beamed to a ground station. There, a computer processes the data and converts the data into a satellite image of Earth's surface.

Active Remote Sensing

An active remote-sensing system produces its own electromagnetic radiation and measures the strength of the return signal. In an active remote-sensing system, radar is used to gather data. Radar gathers data by using microwaves. An advantage to using microwaves for remote sensing is that they can penetrate clouds and water. Therefore, microwaves can be used to map areas that are difficult to study.

Figure 6 *This image of downtown San Francisco was obtained by using remote-sensing technology.*

Figure 7 How GPS Works

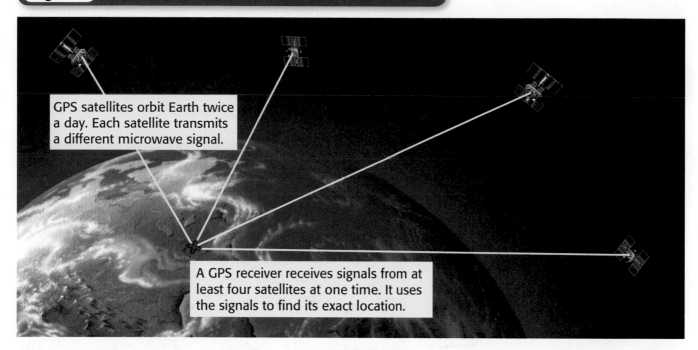

GPS satellites orbit Earth twice a day. Each satellite transmits a different microwave signal.

A GPS receiver receives signals from at least four satellites at one time. It uses the signals to find its exact location.

Global Positioning System

Did you know that satellite technology can actually keep you from getting lost? The *global positioning system* (GPS) can help you find where you are on Earth. GPS is a system of orbiting satellites that send radio signals to receivers on Earth. The receivers calculate the latitude, longitude, and elevation of a given place. **Figure 7** shows how GPS works.

GPS was invented in the 1970s by the U.S. Department of Defense for military use. However, during the last 30 years, GPS has made its way into people's daily lives. Mapmakers use GPS to check the location of boundary lines between countries and states. Airplane and boat pilots use GPS for navigation. Businesses and state agencies use GPS for mapping and environmental planning. Many new cars have GPS units that show information on a screen on the dashboard. Some GPS units are small enough to wear on your wrist, as shown in **Figure 8,** so you can know your location anywhere you go!

Standards Check How can GPS technology be used as a tool to gather data? 6.7.b

Remote Sensing

A GPS satellite is orbiting 20,200 km above the surface of Earth. If a microwave travels at the speed of light (300,000,000 m/s), how long does a microwave take to travel from the satellite to the ground and back to the satellite?

Figure 8 *This tiny GPS unit may come in handy if you are ever lost.*

Geographic Information Systems

Geographic information systems (GISs) are computerized systems that visually present information about an area. A GIS organizes information in overlapping layers. Scientists can compare the layers to answer questions. **Figure 9** shows how GISs helped scientists plan conservation areas for Florida black bears near Ocala National Forest, located northwest of Orlando.

Figure 9 How GIS Works

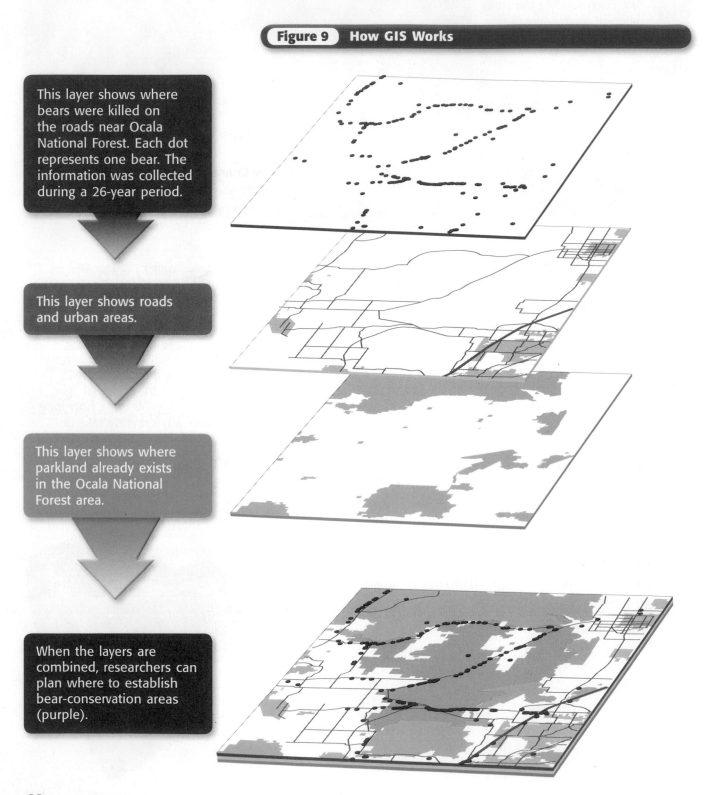

This layer shows where bears were killed on the roads near Ocala National Forest. Each dot represents one bear. The information was collected during a 26-year period.

This layer shows roads and urban areas.

This layer shows where parkland already exists in the Ocala National Forest area.

When the layers are combined, researchers can plan where to establish bear-conservation areas (purple).

Summary

- A map is a representation of the features of a physical body such as Earth.
- A compass is a tool that uses the natural magnetism of Earth to show direction.
- Latitude and longitude can be used to find points on Earth's surface.
- Most maps contain a title, a scale, a legend, an indicator of direction, and a date.
- Modern mapmakers use data gathered by remote-sensing technology to make most maps.
- Remote sensing is a way to collect information about an object without being in physical contact with the object.
- The global positioning system (GPS) calculates the latitude, longitude, and elevation of locations on Earth's surface.
- Geographic information systems (GISs) are computerized systems that allow mapmakers to store and use many types of data.

Using Vocabulary

1 Write an original definition for *map, equator,* and *prime meridian.*

Understanding Concepts

2 **Analyzing** Explain how a compass can be used to find direction on Earth.

3 **Comparing** Compare latitude and longitude.

4 **Listing** List five pieces of information found on maps. Explain how each is important to reading a map.

5 **Comparing** Compare passive remote sensing and active remote sensing.

6 **Summarizing** Describe how GPS can help you find your location on Earth.

INTERPRETING GRAPHICS Use the map legend below to answer the next question.

7 **Analyzing** How many different types of highways are shown on this map?

Critical Thinking

8 **Applying Concepts** While exploring the attic, you find a treasure map. The map shows buried treasure at a point with coordinates 97°N and 188°E. Explain why the treasure cannot be buried at this location.

9 **Making Inferences** Imagine that you were making a map of North America. Would you use a scale of a few kilometers, tens of kilometers, or hundreds of kilometers? Explain your answer.

10 **Analyzing Ideas** Imagine that you are a mapmaker. You have been asked to map an area that is covered with heavy forest. Would you be more likely to map the area using active or passive remote sensing? Explain your answer.

Math Skills

11 **Making Calculations** If a sensor mounted on a satellite scans an area that is 30 m × 30 m, how many square meters is the sensor scanning?

Challenge

12 **Analyzing Ideas** Explain why Earth's magnetic poles have changed throughout history while Earth's geographic poles have remained constant.

Maps in Earth Science

Key Concept Topographic and geologic maps include detailed information about Earth's surface and composition.

What You Will Learn

- Contour lines show elevation and landforms by connecting points of equal elevation.
- Geologic maps show the distribution of geologic features in a given area.

Why It Matters

Topographic maps and geologic maps tell scientists important information about the features of Earth's surface.

Vocabulary

- topographic map
- elevation
- relief
- geologic map

READING STRATEGY

Clarifying Concepts Take turns reading this section out loud with a partner. Stop to discuss ideas that seem confusing.

▶ Imagine that you are going on a camping trip in the wilderness. To be prepared, you want to take a compass and a map. But what kind of map should you take? Because there won't be any roads in the wilderness, you can forget about a road map. Instead, you will need a topographic map.

Topographic Maps

A **topographic map** is a map that shows surface features, or topography (tuh PAHG ruh fee), of an area. Topographic maps show both natural features, such as rivers, lakes, and mountains, and features made by humans. Topographic maps also show elevation. **Elevation** is the height of an object above sea level. The elevation at sea level is 0 m.

Contour Lines

On a topographic map, *contour lines* are used to show elevation. Contour lines are lines that connect points of equal elevation. For example, one contour line would connect points on a map that have an elevation of 100 m. Another line would connect points on a map that have an elevation of 200 m. **Figure 1** illustrates how contour lines show the shape of the landscape.

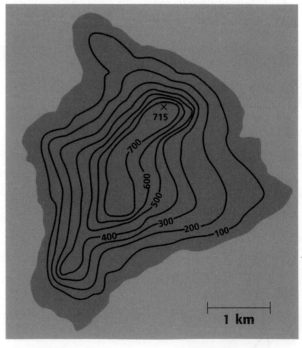

Figure 1 *A drawing gives little information about the elevation of the island (left). In the topographic map (right), contour lines have been drawn to show elevation.*

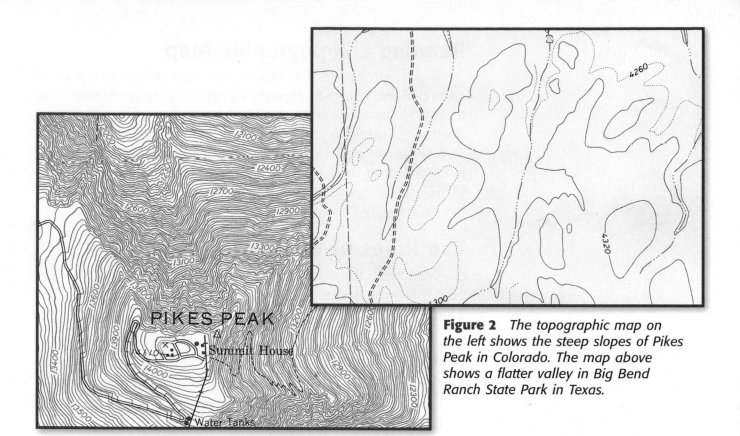

Figure 2 *The topographic map on the left shows the steep slopes of Pikes Peak in Colorado. The map above shows a flatter valley in Big Bend Ranch State Park in Texas.*

Contour Interval

The difference in elevation between one contour line and the next is called the *contour interval*. For example, a map that has a contour interval of 20 m would have contour lines every 20 m of elevation change, such as 0 m, 20 m, 40 m, and 60 m. A mapmaker chooses a contour interval based on the size of the area being mapped and the area's relief.

Relief is the difference in elevation between the highest and lowest points of the area being mapped. For example, the relief of an area that has mountains is high. Therefore, a large contour interval, such as 100 m, would be used. A flat area has low relief. In that case, a small contour interval, such as 10 m, would be used. The spacing of contour lines also indicates slope, as shown in **Figure 2.** Contour lines that are close together show a steep slope. Contour lines that are spaced far apart show a gentle slope.

Standards Check How could you use a topographic map to determine the relief of an area? **6.7.f**

Index Contour

On most topographic maps, an index contour is used to make reading the map easier. An *index contour* is a darker, heavier contour line that is usually every fifth line and that is labeled by elevation. You can see index contours on both of the topographic maps shown in **Figure 2.**

topographic map (TAHP uh GRAF ik MAP) a map that shows the surface features of Earth

elevation (EL uh VAY shuhn) the height of an object above sea level

relief (ri LEEF) the variations in elevation of a land surface

Investigation and Experimentation
6.7.f Read a topographic map and a geologic map for evidence provided on the maps and construct and interpret a simple scale map.

Reading a Topographic Map

Topographic maps, like other maps, use symbols to represent parts of Earth's surface. **Figure 3** shows a topographic map. The legend shows some of the symbols that represent features on the map. Colors are also used to represent features of Earth's surface. In general, buildings, roads, bridges, and railroads are black. Contour lines are brown. Major highways are red. Bodies of water, such as rivers, lakes, and oceans, are blue. Cities and towns are gray or red, and wooded areas are green.

The Rules of Contour Lines

Reading a topographic map takes training and practice. The following rules will help you understand how to read topographic maps:

- Contour lines never cross. All points along a contour line represent one elevation.

- Contour line spacing depends on the slope of the ground. Contour lines that are close together show a steep slope. Contour lines that are far apart show a gentle slope.

- Contour lines that cross a valley or stream are V shaped. The V points toward the area of higher elevation. If a stream flows through the valley, the V points upstream.

- The tops of hills, mountains, and depressions are shown by closed circles. Depressions are marked with short, straight lines inside the circle that point downslope to the depression.

Quick Lab

Modeling Topography

An easy way to model the topography of a landform is to use clay to make a physical model. In this lab, your will mark contour lines on a clay landform.

6.7.f

▶ **Try It!**

1. Shape **modeling clay** into an irregular shape.

2. Hold a **metric ruler** vertically next to the clay landform.

3. Have a partner use a **plastic knife** to mark a line 2 cm from the base of the landform. Make sure to mark the line all the way around the landform.

4. Continue drawing lines at 2 cm intervals until you get to the top of the landform.

▶ **Think About It!**

5. View the landform from the side. Notice the uniformity of the lines you have marked.

6. View the landform from above. Look at the pattern of lines. What do these lines represent? How do these lines relate to a topographic map?

7. Are there any spots on your landform where you would expect rivers to develop?

 15 min

Figure 3 **Topographic Map of El Capitan**

Contour lines that are far apart show a gentle slope.

Contour lines that cross a valley or stream are V shaped. The V points toward the higher elevation.

The tops of hills are shown by closed circles.

Contour lines that are close together show a steep slope.

Vegetated areas are green.

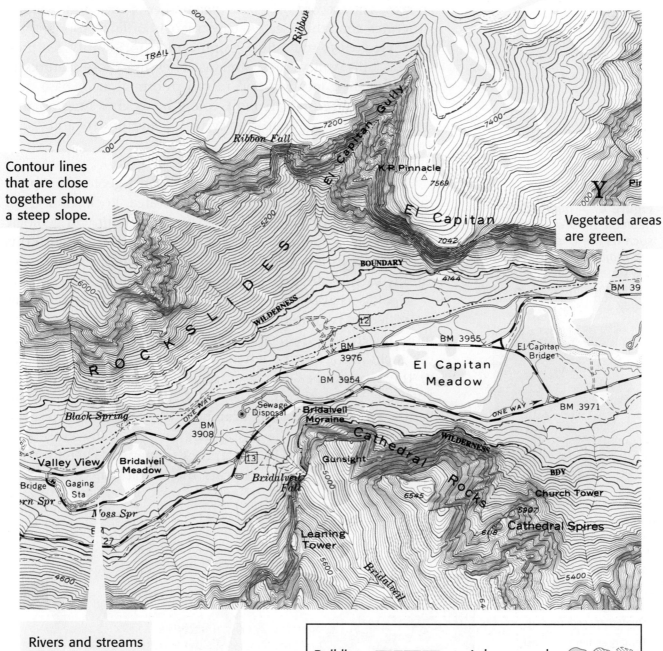

Rivers and streams are blue.

Contour lines are brown.

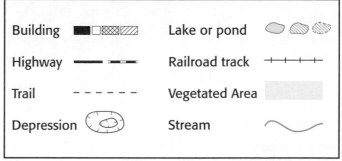

Building	■□▨▨	Lake or pond	⬭⬭⬭
Highway	— ▬ ▬	Railroad track	++++++
Trail	- - - - -	Vegetated Area	▨
Depression	⬭⬭	Stream	～

Geologic Maps

Maps that show the distribution of geologic features in a given area are called **geologic maps. Figure 4** shows a geologic map. Geologic features include different types of rocks and rock structures, such as folded, tilted, or broken rocks.

Geologists make geologic maps by physically walking over an area. They record on a *base map* bodies of rock and geologic structures that they see. A base map is often a topographic map. Geologists use a topographic map to identify features, such as hills, valleys, and streams. They use those features to help find their location and record information. A base map is commonly printed in light colors or as gray lines so that information on the map is easy to see and understand.

Rock Units on Geologic Maps

The most important features shown on a geologic map are rocks that are seen at the surface of an area. Rocks of a given rock type and age range are called a *geologic unit.* On geologic maps, geologic units are identified by color. Geologic units of similar ages are given shades of colors in the same color family, such as different shades of blue.

Geologists also give each geologic unit a set of letters. This set of letters is commonly a capital letter followed by one or more lowercase letters. The capital letter stands for the age of the rock. The lowercase letters represent the name of the unit or the type of rock. For example, the El Capitan Granite in Yosemite Valley, shown in **Figure 4,** dates to the Cretaceous Period. On geologic maps, a capital *K* (the letter for *Cretaceous*) is placed on rock of the El Capitan Granite. A lowercase *ec* is used to designate the El Capitan rock formation. Therefore, the letter pair *Kec* is used to indicate the El Capitan Granite.

geologic map (JEE uh LAHJ ik MAP) a map that records geologic information, such as rock units, strutural features, mineral deposits, and fossil localities

Figure 4 *A generalized geologic map of California, such as the one below, shows the major geologic units in the state. The inset is a close-up geologic map of Yosemite Valley.*

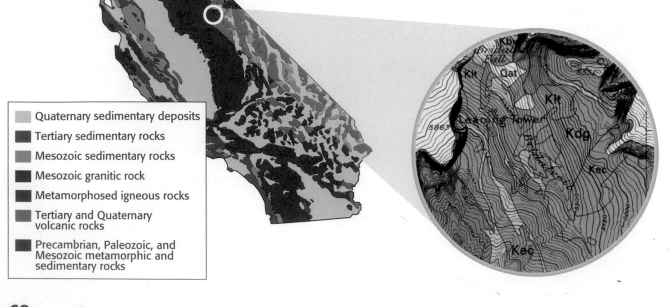

- Quaternary sedimentary deposits
- Tertiary sedimentary rocks
- Mesozoic sedimentary rocks
- Mesozoic granitic rock
- Metamorphosed igneous rocks
- Tertiary and Quaternary volcanic rocks
- Precambrian, Paleozoic, and Mesozoic metamorphic and sedimentary rocks

Other Structures on Geologic Maps

Geologic units are not the only geologic features shown on geologic maps. A contact line shows places where two geologic units meet, called *contacts*. In addition, contact lines can be used to identify where rocks have been deformed. The shapes of contact lines indicate where rock layers have been folded. Other symbols are used to show whether rocks are horizontal or tilted. Geologic maps also show the locations of breaks in rocks called *faults*. These structures and many others are recorded on geologic maps.

Standards Check Describe how you could use a geologic map to find a place where rocks have been deformed. 🐾 6.7.f

---

SECTION Review

 6.7.f

Summary

- Contour lines connect points of equal elevation. They are used to show the shape of landforms.
- The contour interval is determined by the size and relief of an area.
- Geologic maps are designed to show the distribution of geologic features in a given area.
- Geologic units are the most important features shown on a geologic map.
- Geologic maps also show places where geologic units meet, where rocks are folded, and where rocks are broken.

Using Vocabulary

1. Write an original definition for *topographic map, elevation,* and *relief.*

Understanding Concepts

2. **Comparing** Compare an index contour with a contour line.

3. **Analyzing** How does the relief of an area determine the contour interval used on a map?

4. **Listing** What do colors represent on a geologic map?

5. **Applying** Explain how letters are used to describe rock units on geologic maps.

Critical Thinking

6. **Making Inferences** The highest point at the top of a hill is represented by an × and not by a contour line. Why?

7. **Understanding Processes** Why do geologists use topographic maps as base maps?

8. **Applying Concepts** Why is only one contour interval used on a topographic map?

Math Skills

9. **Making Calculations** The contour line at the base of a hill on a map reads 90 m. There are five contour lines between the base of the hill and the top of the hill. If the contour interval is 30 m, what is the elevation of the highest contour line?

Challenge

10. **Applying Concepts** How does the information provided on the legend of a topographic map differ from the information provided on the legend of a geologic map?

Internet Resources

For a variety of links related to this chapter, go to www.scilinks.org
Topic: Topographic Maps
SciLinks code: HY71536

Skills Practice Lab

Topographic Tuber

Imagine that you live on top of a tall mountain and often look down on the lake below. Every summer, an island appears. You call it "Sometimes Island" because it goes away again during heavy fall rains. This summer, you begin to wonder if you could make a topographic map of Sometimes Island. You don't have fancy equipment to make the map, but you have an idea.

Ask a Question

1 How do I make a topographic map?

Form a Hypothesis

2 Write a hypothesis that is a possible answer to the question above. Describe the method you would use to make a topographic map.

Test the Hypothesis

3 Place a mark at the storage container's base. Label this mark "0 cm" with a transparency marker.

4 Measure and mark 1 cm increments up the outside of the container until you reach the top of the container. Label these marks "1 cm," "2 cm," "3 cm," and so on.

5 The scale for your map will be 1 cm = 10 m. Draw a line 2 cm long in the bottom right-hand corner of the lid. Place marks at 0 cm, 1 cm, and 2 cm. Label these marks "0 m," "10 m," and "20 m."

6 Place the potato, flat side down, in the center of the container.

7 Place the lid on the container, and seal it.

Investigation and Experimentation

6.7.b Select and use appropriate tools and technology (including calculators, computers, balances, spring scales, microscopes, and binoculars) to perform tests, collect data, and display data.

6.7.f Read a topographic map and a geologic map for evidence provided on the maps and construct and interpret a simple scale map.

8. Viewing the potato from above, use the transparency marker to accurately trace the outline of the potato where it rests on the bottom of the container. The floor of the container corresponds to the summer water level in the lake.

9. Label this contour "0 m." (For this activity, assume that the water level in the lake during the summer is the same as sea level.)

10. Pour water into the container until it reaches the line labeled "1 cm."

11. Again, place the lid on the container, and seal it. Part of the potato will be sticking out above the water. Viewing the potato from above, trace the part of the potato that touches the top of the water.

12. Label the elevation of the contour line you drew in step 11. According to the scale, the elevation is 10 m.

13. Remove the lid. Carefully pour water into the container until it reaches the line labeled "2 cm."

14. Place the lid on the container, and seal it. Viewing the potato from above, trace the part of the potato that touches the top of the water at this level.

15. Use the scale to calculate the elevation of this line. Label the elevation on your drawing.

16. Repeat steps 13–15, adding 1 cm to the depth of the water each time. Stop when the potato is completely covered.

17. Remove the lid, and set it on a tabletop. Place tracing paper on top of the lid. Trace the contours from the lid onto the paper. Label the elevation of each contour line. Congratulations! You have just made a topographic map!

Analyze the Results

18. **Analyzing Data**   What is the contour interval of this topographic map?

19. **Analyzing Data**   By looking at the contour lines, how can you tell which parts of the potato are steeper?

20. **Analyzing Data**   What is the elevation of the highest point on your map?

Draw Conclusions

21. **Drawing Conclusions**   Would this method of measuring elevation be an effective way to make a topographic map of an actual area on Earth's surface? Explain your answer.

22. **Drawing Conclusions**   By how many meters does the imaginary lake's water level drop in the summer? Explain your answer.

Big Idea Question

23. **Drawing Conclusions** How can a topographic map be a useful tool for a scientist?

Science Skills Activity

Investigation and Experimentation
6.7.f Read a topographic map and a geologic map for evidence provided on the maps and construct and interpret a simple scale map.

Reading a Topographic Map

▶ Tutorial

All Earth scientists must be able to read a topographic map. Reading a topographic map takes training and practice. The following rules will help you understand how to read topographic maps.

① Contour lines never cross. All points along a contour point represent one elevation.

② Contour lines that are close together show a steep slope. Contour lines that are far apart show a gentle slope.

③ Contour lines that cross a valley or stream are V shaped. The V points toward the area of highest elevation. If a stream or river flows through a valley, the V points upstream.

④ The tops of hills, mountains, and depressions are shown by closed circles. Depressions are marked with short, straight lines inside the circle that point downslope to the depression.

▶ You Try It!

Imagine that you were given the topographic map at right and the clues below to reach a hidden treasure. Use the clues to navigate through the map to locate the treasure.

① Begin at the point labeled "BM 3953."

② Proceed west along the secondary highway until the road crosses the small stream.

③ Follow the stream upstream.

④ At 4,660 ft, the stream will fork. Follow the fork that leads up the gentler slope.

⑤ Continue uphill until you reach the pack trail at 7,460 ft.

⑥ Continue southeast along the pack trail until the trail forks.

⑦ Take the fork of the pack trail that goes slightly downhill.

⑧ Follow the pack trail to the 7,569 ft level.

⑨ At what landmark is the treasure located?

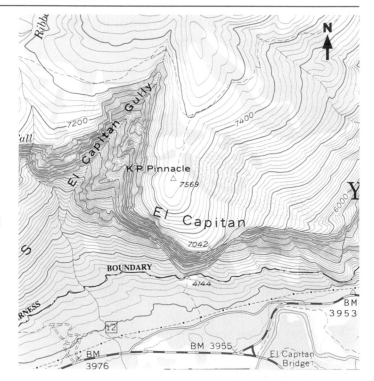

Chapter Summary

The Big Idea
Scientists use a variety of tools, including maps, to perform tests, collect data, and display data.

Section	Vocabulary

1 Tools and Measurement

Key Concept Scientists must select the appropriate tools to make measurements and collect data, to perform tests, and to analyze data.

- Scientists use tools to make observations, take measurements, and analyze data.
- Scientists have determined standard ways to measure length, area, mass, volume, and temperature.

Graduated cylinders and beakers are used when dealing with volume of fluids.

meter p. 47
area p. 47
mass p. 47
volume p. 48
temperature p. 48

2 Models in Science

Key Concept Models are ways of representing real objects or processes to make the natural world easier to understand.

- Physical models and mathematical models are two common types of scientific models.
- Theories and laws are models that describe how the universe works.

This orange is a physical model of Earth.

model p. 50
law p. 53
theory p. 53

3 Mapping Earth's Surface

Key Concept Maps are tools that are used to display data about a given area of a physical body.

- Maps can be used to find locations on Earth and to represent information about features of Earth's surface.
- Most maps are made from data collected by a process called remote sensing.

Models of Earth use longitude as one way to reference location.

map p. 56
equator p. 57
latitude p. 57
longitude p. 58
prime meridian p. 58
remote sensing p. 60

4 Maps in Earth Science

Key Concept Topographic and geologic maps include detailed information about Earth's surface and composition.

- Contour lines show elevation and landforms by connecting points of equal elevation.
- Geologic maps show the distribution of geologic features in a given area.

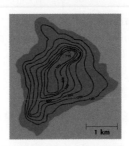

A topographic map uses contour lines to show changes in elevation.

topographic map p. 64
elevation p. 64
relief p. 65
geologic map p. 68

Chapter Review

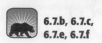

Organize

Three-Panel Flip Chart   Review the FoldNote that you created at the beginning of the chapter. Add to or correct the FoldNote based on what you have learned.

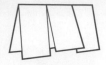

Using Vocabulary

1 **Academic Vocabulary**   In the sentence "Scientific progress is made by asking meaningful questions and conducting careful investigations," what does the word *conducting* mean?

For each pair of terms, explain how the meanings of the terms differ.

2 *latitude* and *longitude*

3 *equator* and *prime meridian*

4 *theory* and *law*

5 *elevation* and *relief*

6 *contour interval* and *index contour*

Understanding Concepts

Multiple Choice

7 Which of the following tools would you use to measure volume?
   a. a spring scale   **c.** a meterstick
   b. a thermometer   **d.** a graduated cylinder

8 Which of the following is a mathematical model that is constructed from data?
   a. a law   **c.** a graph
   b. a map   **d.** a theory

9 A computerized system that allows a user to enter different types of information about an area is called
   a. GIS.   **c.** remote sensing.
   b. GPS.   **d.** satellite imaging.

10 Which of the following information should all maps have?
   a. relief   **c.** geologic units
   b. elevation   **d.** a legend

11 What is the relationship between the distance on a map and the actual distance on Earth called?
   a. legend   **c.** relief
   b. elevation   **d.** scale

12 Widely spaced contour lines indicate a
   a. steep slope.   **c.** hill.
   b. gentle slope.   **d.** stream.

13 ___ is the height of an object above sea level.
   a. Contour interval   **c.** Relief
   b. Elevation   **d.** Index contour

Short Answer

14 **Listing**   List four tools that scientists use to make measurements.

15 **Comparing**   Compare physical models and mathematical models.

16 **Analyzing**   Why is a map legend important?

17 **Comparing**   Compare active remote sensing and passive remote sensing.

18 **Applying**   What is the function of contour lines on a topographic map?

19 **Summarizing**   Explain how letters are used to identify geologic units on geologic maps.

INTERPRETING GRAPHICS   Use the topographic map below to answer the next four questions.

20 **Identifying**   What is the elevation change between two adjacent lines on this map?

21 **Applying**   What type of relief does this area have?

22 **Identifying**   What surface features are shown on this map?

23 **Interpreting**   What is the elevation at the top of Ore Hill?

Writing Skills

24 Writing Persuasively You know that Earth is a sphere and that a globe is a spherical model of Earth. Imagine that certain individuals are arguing that Earth is not spherical and that a globe is not a correct model of Earth. In an essay that will appear in a local newspaper, argue that Earth is indeed spherical. Present evidence, not opinion, to support your argument. Think about any arguments that readers who do not agree that Earth is a sphere may have.

Critical Thinking

25 Concept Mapping Use the following terms to create a concept map: *map, topographic map, elevation, contour lines, contour interval,* and *index contour.*

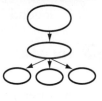

26 Analyzing Ideas Why is it important for maps to have scales?

27 Analyzing Processes How would a GIS system help a team of engineers plan a new highway system for a city?

28 Making Inferences If you were stranded in a national park, what kind of map of the park would you want to have with you? Explain your answer.

29 Applying Concepts The atmosphere of Venus is thick and cloudy. Why has active remote-sensing technology been used to map the surface of Venus? Explain your answer.

30 Analyzing Ideas If you were going to make a topographic map of a steep mountain, such as Mount Everest, would you use a large or small contour interval? Explain your answer.

31 Applying Concepts What type of model would you use to study water use in the United States? Explain your answer.

INTERPRETING GRAPHICS Use the geologic map below to answer the next two questions.

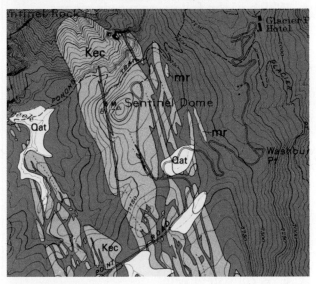

32 Applying Concepts How many geologic units are represented on the map?

33 Making Comparisons How is this geologic map similar to and different from a topographic map?

Math Skills

34 Making Calculations On a topographic map, every fifth contour line is a darker line, or index contour. How many index contours are in a series of 50 contour lines?

35 Making Calculations You have 300 ft of relief, and you need to show this topography with only six contour lines. What will the contour interval be?

Challenge

36 Analyzing Ideas If contour lines never cross, how would you show a cliff where the top of the cliff sticks out farther than the base of the cliff?

Standards Assessment

5.3.a, 5.4.d, 5.6.b, 6.7.b, 6.7.c, 6.7.e, 6.7.f

REVIEWING ACADEMIC VOCABULARY

1 Which of the following words means "correct for the use or proper"?

A available

B capable

C appropriate

D interested

2 Which of the following sets of words best completes the following sentence: "Scientists must be certain that an explanation ___ the evidence available"?

A consists with

B consists of

C is consistent with

D is consistent of

3 In the sentence "Graphs can help scientists learn more about how variables are related," what does the word *variables* mean?

A factors that remain the same

B factors that change

C locations on a map

D qualities of a substance

4 Which of the following words is closest in meaning to the word *data*?

A ideas

B graphs

C theories

D information

REVIEWING CONCEPTS

5 Which of the following tools would you use to measure the mass of a rock?

A thermometer

B spring scale

C graduated cylinder

D balance

6 Which part of a map might be used to show the distance between two points?

A latitude lines

B longitude lines

C scale

D legend

7 For what would a global positioning system be most useful?

A finding out exactly where you are on Earth

B finding your way underground

C predicting the weather

D creating a map of a distant country

8 Which tool might you use to measure the area of a playing field?

A microscope

B balance

C tape measure

D stopwatch

9 Which of the following is an example of a model?

A a hypothesis about weather patterns

B an article about a destructive tornado

C a computer program that predicts tornadoes

D a law that describes how air molecules interact

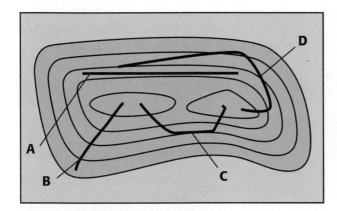

10 Which of the paths marked on the topographic map above would you choose if you wanted to avoid climbing up or down hills?

A path A

B path B

C path C

D path D

11 Which features are most prominently shown on a geologic map?

A landmarks

B mountains and valleys

C water bodies

D geologic units

REVIEWING PRIOR LEARNING

12 If a weather map shows an area of high air pressure in the north and an area of low pressure in the south, what prediction can be made about the weather?

A Clouds from the south will travel north.

B Clouds from the north will travel south.

C Clouds from the north and south will remain where they are.

D Clouds from the south will travel north and south.

13 Which of the following statements is a hypothesis that might be tested by using scientific tools?

A An earthquake occurred on November 15, 1805.

B An earthquake might be predicted by measuring slight tremors in Earth.

C The current system for measuring earthquakes is outdated.

D Earthquake prevention should be a higher priority in many cities.

14 Which of the following is shown on the map of Earth above?

A land covering 3/4 of Earth

B land covering 2/3 of Earth

C water covering 2/3 of Earth

D water covering 1/2 of Earth

Science in Action

Scientific Discoveries

The Lost City of Ubar

According to legend, the city of Ubar was a prosperous ancient city. Ubar was most famous for its frankincense, a tree sap that had many uses. As Ubar was in its decline, however, something strange happened. The city disappeared! According to legend, Ubar was swallowed up by the desert. It wasn't until present-day scientists used information from a shuttle imaging radar system aboard the space shuttle that this lost city was found! Using radar, scientists were able to "see" beneath the huge dunes of the desert, where they finally found the lost city of Ubar.

Science, Technology, and Society

Geocaching in California

Wouldn't it be exciting to go on a hunt for buried treasure? Thousands of people around the world participate in geocaching, which is an adventure game for GPS users. In this adventure game, individuals and groups of people put *caches,* or hidden treasures, in places all over the world. Once the cache is hidden, the coordinates of the cache's location are posted on the Internet. Then, geocaching teams compete to find the cache. Geocaching should be attempted only with parental supervision.

Roads appear as purple lines on this computer-generated remote-sensing image.

Social Studies ACTIVITY

Ubar was once a very wealthy, magnificent city. Its riches were built on the frankincense trade. Research the history of frankincense. In your **Science Journal,** write a paragraph that describes how frankincense was used in ancient times and how it is used today.

Language Arts ACTIVITY

Why was the word *geocaching* chosen for this adventure game? Use the Internet or another source to find the origin and meaning of the word *geocaching.*

Matthew Henson

Arctic Explorer Matthew Henson was born in Maryland in 1866. When Henson was a young boy, his parents, who were freeborn sharecroppers, died. Henson then went to look for work as a cabin boy on a ship. Several years later, Henson had traveled around the world and had become educated in the areas of geography, history, and mathematics. In 1898, Henson met Lieutenant Robert E. Peary of the U.S. Navy. Peary was the leader of Arctic expeditions between 1886 and 1909.

Peary asked Henson to accompany him as a navigator on several trips, including trips to Central America and Greenland. One of Peary's passions was to be the first person to reach the North Pole. Henson's vast knowledge of mathematics and carpentry made Peary's trek to the North Pole possible. In 1909, Henson was the first person to reach the North Pole. Part of Henson's job as navigator was to drive ahead of the party and blaze the first trail. As a result, Henson often arrived ahead of everyone else. On April 6, 1909, he reached the approximate North Pole 45 minutes before Peary. Upon his arrival, Henson exclaimed, "I think I'm the first man to sit on top of the world!"

Math ACTiViTY

On the last leg of their journey, Henson and Peary traveled 664.5 km in 16 days! On average, how far did Henson and Peary travel each day?

Internet Resources

- To learn more about careers in science, visit **www.scilinks.org** and enter the SciLinks code HY70225.
- To learn more about these Science in Action topics, visit **go.hrw.com** and type in the keyword HY7TESF.
- Check out articles related to this chapter by visiting **go.hrw.com**. Just type in the keyword HY7TESC.

Improving Comprehension

Graphic Organizers are important visual tools that can help you organize information and improve your reading comprehension. The Graphic Organizer below is called a *spider map.* Instructions for creating other types of Graphic Organizers are located in the **Study Skills** section of the Appendix.

How to Make a Spider Map

1. Draw a diagram like the one shown below. In the circle, write the main topic.
2. From the circle, draw legs to represent the main ideas or characteristics of the topic. Draw as many legs as you want to draw. Write an idea or characteristic along each leg.
3. From each leg, draw horizontal lines. As you read the chapter, write details about each idea on the idea's horizontal lines. To add more details, make the legs longer and add more horizontal lines.

When to Use a Spider Map

A spider map is an effective tool for classifying the details of a specific topic in science. A spider map divides a topic into ideas and details. As you read about a topic, look for the main ideas or characteristics of the topic. Within each idea, look for details. Use a spider map to organize the ideas and details of each topic.

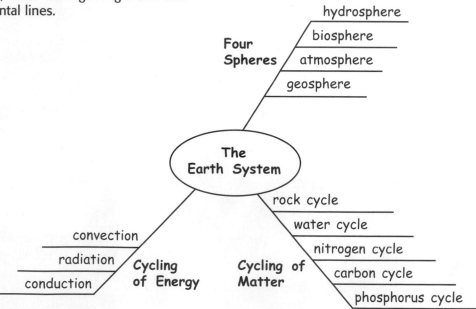

You Try It!

This Reading Strategy can also be used within the chapter that you are about to read. Practice making your own spider map as directed in the Reading Strategies for Section ❶ and Section ❸. Record your work in your **Science Journal.**

Unpacking the Standards

The information below "unpacks" the standards by breaking them down into basic parts. The higher-level, academic vocabulary is highlighted and defined to help you understand the language of the standards. "What It Means" restates the standards as simply as possible.

California Standard	Academic Vocabulary	What It Means
6.1.b Students know Earth is composed of several **layers:** a cold, brittle lithosphere; a hot, convecting mantle; and a dense, metallic core.	**layer** (LAY uhr) a separate or distinct portion of matter that has thickness	Earth is made of several layers: a cold, brittle outer layer called the *lithosphere*; a hot, middle layer called the *mantle*; which circulates heat; and a dense core made of metals such as iron and nickel.
6.3.d Students know heat **energy** is also **transferred** between objects by radiation (radiation can travel through space).	**energy** (EN uhr jee) the ability to make things happen **transfer** (TRANS fuhr) to carry or cause to pass from one thing to another	Heat and energy can move from one place to another by radiation, the process by which the energy moves through matter or empty space.
6.4.a Students know the sun is the **major source** of **energy** for **phenomena** on Earth's surface; it powers winds, ocean currents, and the water **cycle.**	**major** (MAY juhr) of great importance or large scale **source** (SAWRS) the thing from which something else comes **phenomenon** (fuh NAHM uh NUHN) any facts or events that can be sensed or described scientifically (plural *phenomena*) **cycle** (SIE kuhl) a repeating series of changes	The sun is the main source of energy for processes on Earth. Energy from the sun powers winds, ocean currents, and the water cycle.
6.4.b Students know solar **energy** reaches Earth through radiation, mostly in the form of **visible** light.	**visible** (VIZ uh buhl) that can be seen	Energy from the sun reaches Earth through radiation. Most of this energy is light that humans can see.
6.4.c Students know heat from Earth's interior reaches the surface **primarily** through convection.	**primarily** (prie MER uh lee) mainly	Heat from deep inside Earth reaches Earth's surface mainly by the movement of hot material in Earth's mantle.

The following identifies other standards that are covered in this chapter and where you can go to see them unpacked: **6.3.a** (Chapter 13), **6.3.c** (Chapter 13), **6.4.d** (Chapter 12), **6.5.a** (Chapter 16), and **6.5.b** (Chapter 16)

3

Earth's Systems and Cycles

The Big Idea

Many phenomena on Earth's surface are affected by the transfer of energy through Earth's systems.

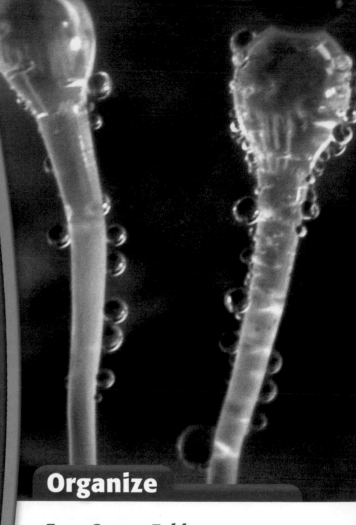

California Standards

Focus on Earth Sciences

6.1 Plate tectonics accounts for important features of Earth's surface and major geologic events. (Section 1)

6.3 Heat moves in a predictable flow from warmer objects to cooler objects until all the objects are at the same temperature. (Sections 1, 2, and 3)

6.4 Many phenomena on Earth's surface are affected by the transfer of energy through radiation and convection currents. (Sections 1, 3, and 4)

6.5 Organisms in ecosystems exchange energy and nutrients among themselves and with the environment. (Section 1 and 4)

Investigation and Experimentation

6.7 Scientific progress is made by asking meaningful questions and conducting careful investigations. (Science Skills Activity)

Math

6.1.4 Number Sense

6.2.1 Algebra and Functions

English-Language Arts

6.2.4 Reading

6.1.3 Writing

About the Photo

From close-up, a shotgun fungus may look like something from another planet. But really it is one of many decomposers that play an important part in the cycling of energy and nutrients through Earth's environment.

Organize

Four-Corner Fold

Before you read this chapter, create the FoldNote entitled "Four-Corner Fold." Label each flap of the four-corner fold with the title of one of the sections in the chapter. As you read the chapter, add details from each section under the appropriate flap.

Instructions for creating FoldNotes are located in the Study Skills section on p. 617 of the Appendix.

Explore Activity

🕐 **20 min**

Heat Transfer by Radiation

In this lab, you will observe temperature variations due to the transfer of heat by radiation.

Procedure

1. Fold a **piece of black construction paper** in half lengthwise to form a sleeve into which a **thermometer** can be fully inserted. Use a **stapler** to secure the bottom and side of the sleeve.

2. Use a **piece of white construction paper** to make a second sleeve.

3. Use **two identical thermometers** to observe and record the room temperature.

4. Insert one thermometer into the black sleeve. Insert the other thermometer into the white sleeve.

5. Place the sleeves, including their thermometers, side-by-side in direct sunlight. Put them where nobody will touch them.   6.3.a
6.4.b

6. After 15 min, observe and record the temperature reading on each thermometer.

Analysis

7. How did the thermometer readings differ after 15 min? Explain why.

8. Explain how this activity can be used to demonstrate the transfer of energy from the sun.

9. Did the black sleeve and white sleeve have to be similar in shape and size? Explain your answer.

The Earth System

Key Concept Earth is a complex system made up of many smaller systems through which matter and energy are continuously cycled.

▶ Next time that you are outside, look up at the sky and down at the ground. What do they have in common? They are always changing. Some changes on Earth happen slowly, and others happen quickly. Some changes are driven by energy from inside Earth. Others are driven by energy from the sun. All of these changes are part of Earth's system.

Earth: An Overview

Earth is the third planet from our sun. Of all of the planets in our solar system, Earth is the only planet known to have abundant liquid water on its surface. As **Figure 1** shows, water covers about 71% of Earth's surface. This water is called the *global ocean*. The global ocean is part of Earth's hydrosphere. The *hydrosphere* is the portion of Earth that is water. The three other major spheres of Earth are the biosphere, atmosphere, and geosphere. The *biosphere* is the part of Earth where life exists. The *atmosphere* is a mixture of gases that surround Earth. The *geosphere* is the mostly solid, rocky part of Earth.

Energy and matter are cycled through and between the spheres. These four spheres make up the Earth system. The cycling of matter and energy in the Earth system makes life on Earth possible.

Figure 1 *The view from space shows that water covers most of Earth's surface.*

Figure 2 The Layers of Earth

Earth's Compositional Layers

Crust The crust is the thin and solid outermost compositional layer of Earth. The crust is 5 to 70 km thick and is made mostly of silicate minerals.

Mantle The mantle is 2,900 km thick. The mantle is slightly denser than the crust.

Core The core has a radius of 3,400 km. This layer, which contains iron and nickel, is about twice as dense as the mantle.

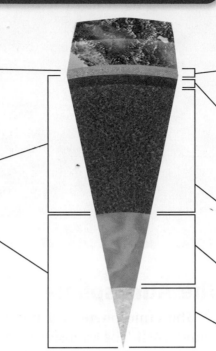

Earth's Physical Layers

Lithosphere The lithosphere is 15 to 300 km thick. This rigid layer of Earth is divided into pieces called *tectonic plates.*

Asthenosphere The asthenosphere is a solid, plastic layer upon which the tectonic plates move.

Mesosphere The mesosphere is the lower, solid layer of the mantle.

Outer Core The outer core is made of liquid iron and nickel.

Inner Core The inner core is also made up of iron and nickel but is under so much pressure that it is solid.

Geosphere

The geosphere is the solid rock of Earth. The geosphere can be divided into layers, as **Figure 2** shows. These layers are based on chemical composition and physical properties.

The Compositional Layers

Earth can be divided into three layers based on chemical composition. The **crust** is the thin, outermost layer of Earth. It is made up largely of silicon, oxygen, and aluminum. The **mantle** is the hot layer of rock between Earth's crust and core. It is made of denser silicate minerals. The mantle has less aluminum and more magnesium than the crust does. The central part of Earth is the **core.** It is made of iron and nickel.

The Physical Layers

Earth can also be divided into five layers based on physical properties. The *lithosphere* is Earth's cold, brittle, outermost layer. It is divided into pieces called *tectonic plates.* These plates move slowly on the *asthenosphere,* which is solid but flows like putty. The *mesosphere*—the solid, lower layer of the mantle—lies below the asthenosphere. The *outer core* is made of liquid iron and nickel. At Earth's center is the *inner core.* The inner core is also made of the metals iron and nickel, but it is solid. Because the core is made of these metals, it is very dense.

Standards Check List and describe the compositional and physical layers of Earth's geosphere. 6.1.b

crust (KRUHST) the thin and solid outermost layer of Earth above the mantle

mantle (MAN tuhl) the layer of rock between Earth's crust and core

core (KAWR) the central part of Earth below the mantle

Wordwise **mesosphere**
The root *mes-* means "middle."

Figure 3 *Clouds, such as these over the Sierra Nevada range are usually found in the lowest atmospheric layer, the troposphere.*

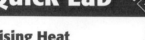

The Atmosphere

The atmosphere is a mixture of invisible gases that surround Earth. The atmosphere extends outward to about 500 km from the surface of Earth. But most of the atmospheric gases lie within 8 to 12 km of Earth's surface. Earth's atmosphere is made up of four layers.

Layers in the Atmosphere

The *troposphere* is the atmospheric layer in which we live. It extends outward to about 12 km from Earth's surface. Weather phenomena, such as the clouds shown in **Figure 3,** usually occur in the troposphere. The *stratosphere* is the layer directly above the troposphere. Temperatures in the stratosphere increase with altitude. Above the stratosphere is the *mesosphere,* which is the coldest layer of the atmosphere. Above the mesosphere is the *thermosphere,* which is the uppermost layer of the atmosphere. Like temperatures in the stratosphere, temperatures in the thermosphere increase with altitude.

Energy Flow in the Atmosphere

The sun radiates the main source of energy that reaches Earth's surface. Solar radiation heats Earth's surface unevenly. This uneven heating causes the air in the atmosphere to move. For example, cold air is denser than warm air. So, cold air in the atmosphere sinks. As the cold air sinks, it forces warm, less-dense air out of the way. This movement of air distributes energy throughout the atmosphere. The transfer of energy, especially heat, due to the movement of matter, such as air, is called **convection.**

Standards Check Explain how energy is distributed in the atmosphere.
6.4.d

The Hydrosphere

Earth's hydrosphere is made up of the water in, on, and surrounding Earth. The hydrosphere includes the water in the oceans, lakes, rivers, glaciers, and polar icecaps. Clouds, rain, and snow are also parts of the hydrosphere. Even water that is in rock deep underground is part of the hydrosphere.

The Global Ocean

As **Figure 4** shows, most of the water on Earth is in the global ocean. The global ocean covers a surface area of about 335 million square kilometers. It holds more than 97% of all of the water on Earth. However, ocean water contains salt. Therefore, the water cannot be used as drinking water.

Energy Flow in the Ocean

The sun's energy heats ocean water unevenly. Thus, the temperature of the water varies. The temperature of ocean water ranges from warm at the equator to near freezing at the poles. The temperature of ocean water also decreases with depth. Differences in temperature cause differences in density. The salt in ocean water also affects the density of ocean water. Differences in the density of ocean water cause the water to move by convection. This movement of matter caused by differences in density is called a **convection current.** Convection currents distribute energy in the ocean.

Standards Check Explain how energy is distributed in the ocean.
🐻 **6.4.d**

convection (kuhn VEK shuhn) the movement of matter due to differences in density; the transfer of energy due to the movement of matter

Wordwise The prefix *con-* means "with" or "together." The root *vect-* means "to carry."

convection current (kuhn VEK shuhn KUHR uhnt) any movement of matter that results from differences in density; may be vertical, circular, or cyclical

Figure 4 *Most of Earth's surface, about 71%, is covered by water.*

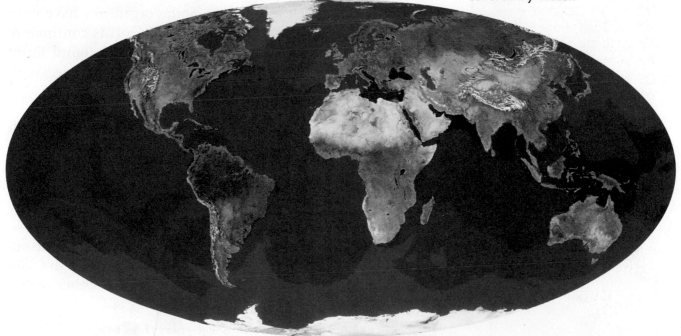

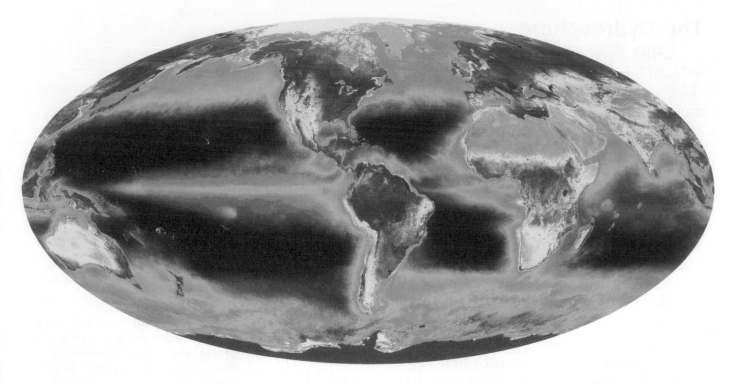

Ocean chlorophyll concentration

Low   High

Amount of land vegetation

Low   High

Figure 5 *The colors in this map show the relative concentrations of plant life across the surface of Earth. The red areas of the map represent lakes, bays, and wetlands where life is especially abundant.*

The Biosphere

The biosphere is made up of living organisms and the areas of Earth where life is found. The biosphere includes Earth's surface, the lower part of the atmosphere, and most of the hydrosphere. As **Figure 5** shows, plants and algae are found in the oceans as well as on land. Some organisms have even been found living deep in Earth's crust. Scientists continue to discover life in new environments. These newly found forms of life expand the known boundaries of the biosphere.

Factors Necessary for Life

The biosphere has certain factors that plants and animals need in order to live. Liquid water and a suitable habitat are very important for the survival of living things. Most plants and animals can also live only in environments that have moderate temperatures. You will not find a lizard living at the North Pole. The temperature is too cold!

A stable source of energy is equally important to organisms. For example, plants and algae get their energy from the sun. They use energy from the sun to produce food. Other organisms get their food by eating plants and algae.

Standards Check How do plants get energy? 6.5.a

Energy and Matter Flow in the Biosphere

Energy enters the biosphere as sunlight. Plants change this energy into chemical energy through the process of photosynthesis. Then, the energy is passed to organisms that eat the plants. Energy and matter is also passed between organisms when they eat one another. The transfer of energy and matter does not stop when a living thing dies. Dead organisms are consumed by decomposers, such as bacteria and fungi. The decomposers break down the remains into simple materials. These materials, such as carbon dioxide, are used by plants to make food during photosynthesis.

Standards Check Explain how energy is transferred in the biosphere.

 6.5.a

SECTION Review

 6.1.b, 6.3.c, 6.4.a, 6.4.b, 6.4.d, 6.5.a, 6.5.b

Summary

- The four divisions of Earth are the hydrosphere, atmosphere, geosphere, and biosphere.
- The geosphere is divided into layers based on composition and physical properties.
- Convection moves energy through the atmosphere and through the hydrosphere.
- Energy in the biosphere is transferred from the sun to plants and then from one organism to another.

Using Vocabulary

1 Write an original definition for *crust, core,* and *mantle.*

Understanding Concepts

2 **Identifying** Identify the layers of Earth by their composition and physical properties.

3 **Describing** Describe how energy is transferred in the ocean and in the atmosphere.

4 **Identifying** Identify the layer of the atmosphere in which we live.

5 **Analyzing** Explain how energy from the sun supports life on Earth.

6 **Listing** List two factors that are needed to support life.

7 **Summarizing** Describe how matter is transferred in the biosphere.

Critical Thinking

8 **Analyzing Processes** What is the major source of energy that powers the convection currents in the atmosphere and oceans?

9 **Analyzing Ideas** How might Earth be different if its surface were heated evenly?

10 **Evaluating Sources** From what source do most organisms on Earth get their energy?

Math Skills

11 **Making Calculations** If Earth's atmosphere is 500 km thick and life is found up to 8 km from Earth's surface, what percentage of the atmosphere contains life?

Challenge

12 **Evaluating Conclusions** The uneven heating of Earth's surface causes convection currents in the ocean and in the atmosphere. Explain why Earth's surface is heated unevenly even though the sun's energy output is mostly constant.

Internet Resources

For a variety of links related to this chapter, go to www.scilinks.org
Topic: Biosphere
SciLinks code: HY70162

Heat and Energy

Key Concept Heat flows in a predictable way from warmer objects to cooler objects until all of the objects are at the same temperature.

▶ Imagine that you are outside on a hot day. You step on a shady porch where a fan is blowing. You feel cool there. Then, your friend comes out onto the porch from an air-conditioned house. She says that she feels hot! Whether you think something is hot or cold depends on your point of reference. If you really want to be clear about how hot or cold something is, you must talk about its temperature.

What Is Temperature?

You might think of temperature as a measure of how hot or cold something is. But using the terms *hot* and *cold* can be unclear. Using the word *temperature* instead of the words *hot* and *cold* is much clearer. Scientifically, **temperature** is a measure of the average kinetic energy of the particles in an object.

Temperature and Kinetic Energy

All matter is made up of constantly moving particles, such as atoms or molecules. The particles are moving even though you cannot see them moving. When particles are in motion, they have *kinetic energy*. The faster that the particles move, the more kinetic energy that they have. The temperature of a substance depends on the kinetic energy of all of the particles that make up the substance. The more kinetic energy that the particles of an object have, the higher that the temperature of the object is. **Figure 1** shows two substances that have different temperatures.

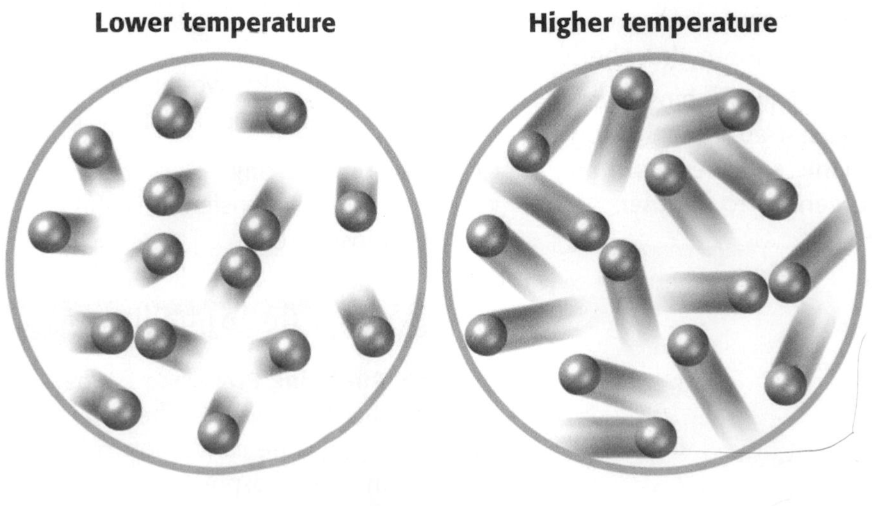

Lower temperature   **Higher temperature**

Figure 1 *The gas particles on the right are moving faster and have a higher average kinetic energy than the particles on the left do. So, the gas on the right is at a higher temperature than the gas on the left is.*

Average Kinetic Energy of Particles

Particles of matter move at random and at different speeds. As a result, the particles have different amounts of kinetic energy. But the *average* kinetic energy of all of the particles in an object can be measured. When you measure an object's temperature, you measure the average kinetic energy of all of the particles in the object.

The temperature of a substance depends on the average kinetic energy of all particles in the substance. The temperature does not depend on the amount of particles. A teapot holds more tea than a teacup does. But if the atoms of tea in both containers have the same average kinetic energy, then the tea in the pot and the tea in the cup are at the same temperature.

Thermal Expansion

When a substance's temperature increases, the substance's particles have more kinetic energy. Thus, the particles move faster and move apart. As the space between the particles increases, the substance expands. The increase in volume resulting from an increase in temperature is called *thermal expansion.*

Thermal expansion is the process that causes hot-air balloons to rise. **Figure 2** shows a hot-air balloon being filled with hot air. Heat is added to the air inside the balloon. The air expands as its particles gain kinetic energy and move faster and farther apart. As the air expands, it becomes less dense than the air outside the balloon. The less-dense air inside the balloon is forced upward by the colder, denser air outside the balloon. As a result, the balloon goes up, up, and away!

Thermal expansion is also the mechanism by which thermometers measure temperature. Thermometers hold a fluid, such as mercury or alcohol. This fluid expands by known amounts for a given change in temperature. A scale on the thermometer shows the temperature based on how much the fluid expands.

This same principle affects air movement in the atmosphere. It also affects water movement in the oceans and rock movement in the geosphere.

6.3.a Students know energy can be carried from one place to another by heat flow or by waves, including water, light and sound waves, or by moving objects.
6.3.c Students know heat flows in solids by conduction (which involves no flow of matter) and in fluids by conduction and by convection (which involves flow of matter).
6.3.d Students know heat energy is also transferred between objects by radiation (radiation can travel through space).

temperature (TEM puhr uh chuhr) a measure of how hot (or cold) something is; specifically, a measure of the average kinetic energy of the particles in an object

Figure 2 *Thermal expansion of heated gases gets these hot-air balloons off the ground.*

What Is Heat?

You might think of the word *heat* when you imagine something that feels hot. But heat also has to do with things that feel cold. In fact, heat is what causes objects to feel hot or cold. Heat also causes objects to get hot or cold under the right conditions. You may often use the word *heat* to mean different things. However, in this chapter, the word *heat* has only one meaning. **Heat** is the energy that is transferred between objects that are at different temperatures.

Transferring Heat

Why do some things feel hot or cold? Heat is passed from one object to another according to the difference in temperature. Energy is always passed from the object that has the higher temperature to the object that has the lower temperature. When you touch something "cold," heat flows from your body to that object. When you touch something "hot," heat flows from the object into your body.

Imagine that you are getting a checkup. The doctor places a metal stethoscope on your back. You jump a little and say, "Whoa! That's cold!" You may feel like the girl in **Figure 3** does. Why did the metal feel cold? It felt cold because your back has a higher temperature than the metal does. Your back is about 30°C. But the metal is about 20°C, or room temperature. When the metal touches your back, heat is passed from your back to the metal. This heat passes very quickly, so the metal feels cold to you. But why does the metal quickly stop feeling cold? No more heat is being transferred to the metal because the temperature of the metal is equal to the temperature of your skin.

Figure 3 *The metal stethoscope feels cold because heat flows from the girl's warm skin to the cold metal!*

Heat and Thermal Energy

When heat is transferred between objects, the thermal energy of each object changes. **Thermal energy** is the total kinetic energy of the particles that make up a substance. Thermal energy depends partly on temperature. Something at a high temperature has more thermal energy than something at a lower temperature does. As **Figure 4** shows, thermal energy also depends on the amount of particles in a substance. The more particles in a substance at a given temperature, the greater the thermal energy of the substance.

Reaching the Same Temperature

When things that have different temperatures come into contact, energy will always be transferred. Energy will pass from the warmer object to the cooler object until both have the same temperature. When objects that are touching each other have the same temperature, there is no net change in the thermal energy of either object. Although one object may have more thermal energy than the other object, both objects will be at the same temperature. The process of transferring heat is shown in **Figure 5.**

Standards Check What will happen if two objects at different temperatures come into contact? 🐻6.3.c

Figure 4 *Both soups are at the same temperature, but the pan holds more soup. So, the soup in the pan has more thermal energy than the soup in the bowl does.*

thermal energy (THUHR muhl EN uhr jee) the kinetic energy of a substance's atoms

---

Figure 5 **Transfer of Heat**

❶ Energy is transferred from the particles in the juice to the particles in the bottle. The bottle's particles transfer energy to the particles in the ice water, which causes the ice to melt.

❷ Heat continues to be transferred to the water after all of the ice has melted.

❸ Eventually, the juice, bottle, and water have the same temperature. The juice and bottle have become colder, and the water has become warmer.

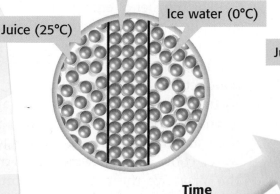

Bottle (25°C)

Juice (25°C)

Ice water (0°C)

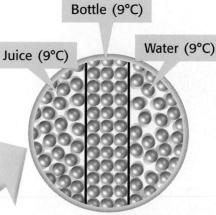

Bottle (9°C)

Juice (9°C)

Water (9°C)

Time

Figure 6 Conduction, Convection, and Radiation

Conduction The end of this spoon will warm up because heat flows from the hot soup to the spoon. Then, the heat flows through the particles that make up the handle.

How Is Heat Transferred?

Heat flows in solids and fluids by conduction and by convection. Heat flows between objects that are not in contact by radiation. These processes are shown in **Figure 6.**

Conduction

conduction (kuhn DUHK shuhn) the transfer of energy as heat through a material

The transfer of heat from one object to another through direct contact is called **conduction.** Heat flows from the particles of the hot soup to the part of the spoon that is in the soup. The particles from that part of the spoon interact with particles in the handle of the spoon. The interaction transfers heat particle by particle all the way up the spoon's handle.

Convection

convection (kuhn VEK shuhn) the movement of matter due to differences in density; the transfer of energy due to the movement of matter

The transfer of energy due to the movement of matter, such as liquid or gas, is called **convection.** When you boil water in a pot, the water moves in a circular pattern. Heat is passed from the hot burner to the pot and from the pot to the water by conduction. As it heats, the water becomes less dense because its higher-energy particles spread apart. The denser, cold water at the top of the pot sinks. As it sinks, the cold water forces the warmer water toward the surface. At the surface, the warm water cools as it passes heat to other water particles and to the air above the pot. At the bottom of the pot, more water is heated by conduction. As the water moves, the energy is spread throughout the water.

Convection Water repeatedly rises and sinks during boiling because of convection.

Radiation The coils of this portable heater warm a room partly by radiating visible light and infrared waves.

Radiation

The transfer of heat or other energy as electromagnetic waves, such as visible light or infrared waves, is called **radiation.** Unlike conduction and convection, radiation can occur between objects that are not in direct contact with each other. Energy can be transferred through empty space by radiation. The sun transfers energy through space by radiation. Most of this energy is emitted as visible light, which you can see. The sun also emits waves of other frequencies, such as infrared waves and ultraviolet waves. But you cannot see these waves.

radiation (RAY dee AY shuhn) the transfer of energy as electromagnetic waves

Standards Check How is radiation different from conduction? **6.3.d**

Quick Lab

Heat Exchange

6.3.a
6.3.c
6.7.c

1. Fill a **film canister** with **hot water.** Insert a **thermometer apparatus** prepared by your teacher. Record the temperature.

2. Fill a **250 mL beaker** two-thirds full with **cool water.** Insert **another thermometer** into the cool water. Record the temperature of the water.

3. Place the canister in the cool water. Every 30 s, record the temperature measured by each thermometer.

4. When the thermometers read nearly the same temperature, stop and graph your data. Plot temperature (*y*-axis) versus time (*x*-axis).

5. Describe what happens to the rate of energy transfer as the two temperatures get closer.

 20 min

States of Matter

The matter that makes up an ice cube has the same chemical composition whether the ice is frozen or has melted. The matter is simply in a different form, or state. The **states of matter** are the physical forms in which a substance can exist. The three states of matter are solid, liquid, and gas. These three states are shown in **Figure 7.**

State and Chemical Properties

Matter is made up of particles that move around at different speeds. A substance's state depends on the speed of its particles, the attraction between them, and the pressure around them. A substance's chemical composition also influences the state of the substance at a given temperature. Different materials are solid at different temperatures. For example, butter is usually solid at room temperature. But milk is liquid at room temperature. Milk is solid at a different temperature than butter is, because milk has a different chemical composition than butter does.

Changes of State

A change of state occurs when a substance changes from one state of matter to another. Changes of state include *condensing* (gas to liquid), *freezing* (liquid to solid), *melting* (solid to liquid), and *evaporating* (liquid to gas). A change of state involves a transfer of heat from one substance to another. Energy is released or added to the substance that changes its state. When it melts or boils, a substance gains energy. When it condenses or freezes, a substance loses energy.

Figure 7 Particles of a Solid, a Liquid, and a Gas

Particles of a solid have a strong attraction between them. The particles are closely locked in position and can only vibrate.

Particles of a liquid are more loosely connected than those of a solid and can collide with and move past one another.

Particles of a gas move fast enough so that they overcome the attractions between them. The particles move independently and collide frequently.

Summary

- Heat moves from warmer objects to cooler objects until all of the objects are at the same temperature.
- Conduction is the transfer of energy as heat through a solid material.
- Convection is the transfer of energy due to the movement of matter.
- Radiation is the transfer of energy as electromagnetic waves. Radiation differs from conduction and convection because radiation can transfer energy through empty space.
- A substance's state of matter depends on the speed of the particles in the substance. Changes of state result from the transfer of energy.

Using Vocabulary

1 Write an original definition for *conduction*, *convection*, and *radiation*.

Understanding Concepts

2 **Comparing** How is temperature related to kinetic energy?

3 **Evaluating** Does temperature depend on the amount of a substance?

4 **Summarizing** Describe the process of thermal expansion.

5 **Analyzing** Explain what happens when two objects at different temperatures are in contact.

6 **Comparing** Describe the differences between conduction, convection, and radiation.

7 **Identifying** How is the state of matter related to the amount of energy in a substance?

Critical Thinking

8 **Making Inferences** Two objects have the same total thermal energy. They are different sizes. Are they at the same temperature? Explain your answer.

9 **Applying Concepts** Why do many metal cooking utensils have wooden handles?

10 **Analyzing Processes** During thermal expansion, what happens to the density of a substance?

11 **Applying Concepts** Energy from the sun comes to Earth by radiation. Why is the energy not transferred by conduction or convection?

INTERPRETING GRAPHICS Use the diagram below to answer the next two questions.

Substance A   **Substance B**

12 **Making Comparisons** Which substance has more kinetic energy? Explain your answer.

13 **Making Comparisons** Which substance is more likely to be a gas? Explain your answer.

Challenge

14 **Evaluating Data** A glass of cold water was placed on a table in a warm room. The particles of cold water had a low average kinetic energy. The average kinetic energy in the cold water increased, while the average kinetic energy of the part of the table under the glass decreased. Explain what happened.

Internet Resources

For a variety of links related to this chapter, go to www.scilinks.org

Topic: What Is Heat?
SciLinks code: HY71661

The Cycling of Energy

Key Concept Various heat-exchange systems work in the Earth system and affect phenomena on Earth's surface.

What You Will Learn

- Heat flow is the transfer of energy from a warmer object to a cooler object.
- Energy from the sun, the major source of energy for phenomena on Earth's surface, is transmitted to Earth by radiation.
- Heat from Earth's interior reaches the surface mostly by convection.

Why It Matters

The movement of energy through Earth's systems is a major factor in most of Earth's processes.

Vocabulary

- heat flow
- electromagnetic spectrum

READING STRATEGY

Graphic Organizer In your **Science Journal,** make a Spider Map that shows the ways in which energy moves through Earth's systems.

6.3.a Students know energy can be carried from one place to another by heat flow or by waves, including water, light and sound waves, or by moving objects.
6.3.c Students know heat flows in solids by conduction (which involves no flow of matter) and in fluids by conduction and by convection (which involves flow of matter).
6.3.d Students know heat energy is also transferred between objects by radiation (radiation can travel through space).
6.4.a Students know the sun is the major source of energy for phenomena on Earth's surface; it powers winds, ocean currents, and the water cycle.
6.4.b Students know solar energy reaches Earth through radiation, mostly in the form of visible light.
6.4.c Students know heat from Earth's interior reaches the surface primarily through convection.
6.4.d Students know convection currents distribute heat in the atmosphere and oceans.

▶ You are on a camping trip with your family. It is a warm, sunny day. But you see clouds forming in the sky. Suddenly, a strong wind starts to blow, and the air feels cooler. Soon, you hear thunder, and a downpour of rain follows. Why did the weather change so quickly? The answer involves the movement of energy through Earth's atmosphere.

The Flow of Energy

Energy can be carried from one place to another by heat flow, by waves, or by moving objects. **Heat flow** is the transfer of energy from a warmer object to a cooler object. Waves—such as water waves, light waves, and sound waves—transfer energy through vibrations. Waves move energy, but they do not move matter from one place to another. Objects carry energy while they are moving. As they move, the objects pass the energy to objects that they touch.

Energy moves through Earth's systems, as **Figure 1** shows. The sun is the major source of energy for the Earth system. Heat from Earth's interior also supplies energy, but the amount of energy is much smaller. Energy from the sun and from Earth's interior moves through the geosphere, hydrosphere, biosphere, and atmosphere. The processes that move the energy are radiation, convection, and conduction.

Standards Check List two sources from which Earth receives its energy. 🐻 **6.4.a**

Figure 1 **Energy Transfer through Earth's Systems**

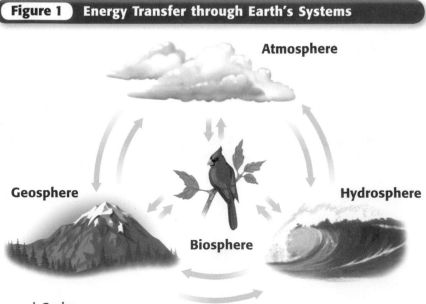

Atmosphere

Geosphere

Hydrosphere

Biosphere

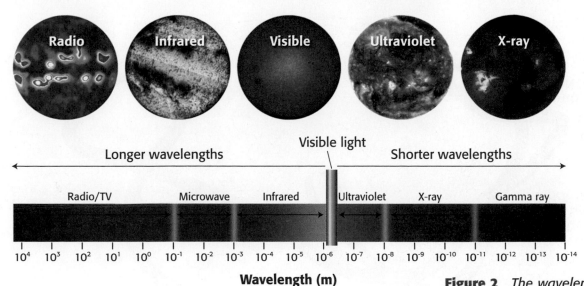

| | | | Visible light | | |
| Longer wavelengths | | | | Shorter wavelengths | |

Radio/TV   Microwave   Infrared   Ultraviolet   X-ray   Gamma ray

10^4 10^3 10^2 10^1 10^0 10^{-1} 10^{-2} 10^{-3} 10^{-4} 10^{-5} 10^{-6} 10^{-7} 10^{-8} 10^{-9} 10^{-10} 10^{-11} 10^{-12} 10^{-13} 10^{-14}

Wavelength (m)

Figure 2 *The wavelengths of the radiation emitted by the sun range throughout the electromagnetic spectrum. Five images of the sun are shown above. Each image shows radiation emitted at different wavelengths.*

Radiation

We live almost 150 million kilometers from the sun. But the sun is the source of 99% of the energy on Earth. Energy from the sun is transmitted through space by radiation.

The Electromagnetic Spectrum

You can see the visible light that the sun radiates. But the sun also radiates other forms of energy that you cannot see. All energy from the sun travels in waves. These waves are called *electromagnetic radiation.* Electromagnetic radiation includes a wide range of wavelengths, which are collectively referred to as the **electromagnetic spectrum.** As **Figure 2** shows, wavelengths range from long, such as the wavelengths of radio waves, to short, such as the wavelengths of gamma rays.

All of the energy that Earth receives from the sun moves through space as electromagnetic radiation. Wavelengths in or close to the visible range make up the largest amount of energy that is given off by the sun. Some of the energy can pass through Earth's atmosphere and reach Earth's surface.

Earth and Energy from the Sun

The Earth receives most of its energy from the sun. This energy drives the water cycle and makes life possible on Earth. The energy that Earth receives from the sun is absorbed by the atmosphere, geosphere, and hydrosphere. Then, the energy is changed into thermal energy. This thermal energy is then transferred through Earth's systems by convection and conduction.

Standards Check Explain how Earth receives energy from the sun.

6.4.b

heat flow (HEET FLOH) another term for *heat transfer,* the transfer of energy from a warmer object to a cooler object

electromagnetic spectrum (ee LEK troh mag NET ik SPEK truhm) all of the frequencies or wavelengths of electromagnetic radiation

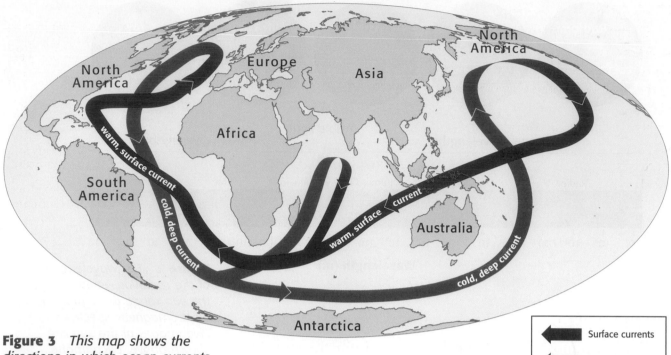

| ← | Surface currents |
| ← | Deep currents |

Figure 3 *This map shows the directions in which ocean currents flow. Surface currents are shown in red. Deep currents are shown in blue. Together, the currents form the ocean conveyor belt.*

Calculating Change

The surface temperature of ocean water near the equator can be as high as 30°C. But the surface temperature of polar ocean water can be as low as −2°C. If the temperature of a sample of ocean water is 30°C, what will the temperature be if it drops by 70%? Record your work in your **Science Journal.**

Convection

Most energy is moved through Earth's systems by convection. Convection occurs in fluids, such as water and air. But some convection occurs in solids that can flow like putty. The uneven heating of matter drives convection. Most matter becomes less dense when heated. Hotter, less dense matter rises through surrounding matter. As the hot matter rises, it cools and becomes denser. As a result, this matter sinks back toward the heat source where it is warmed again. This movement of matter that results from differences in density is called a *convection current.*

Convection in the Ocean

Convection currents occur in the ocean because of differences in the density of ocean water. The uneven heating of ocean water causes these differences. The differences in density are also caused by differences in the salinity of ocean water. Salinity is the amount of salt in water. In the ocean, convection causes deep currents. Deep currents are streamlike movements of water far below the ocean surface. As **Figure 3** shows, deep currents flow from the North Atlantic Ocean to Antarctica. Then, they flow around Antarctica and into the Pacific Ocean. The cold bottom water then flows northward toward Alaska. This journey takes more than a thousand years.

Convection in the Atmosphere

The process of convection in the atmosphere is shown in **Figure 4.** If Earth's surface is warmer than the air, conduction will heat the air touching the ground. As this air becomes warmer, it becomes less dense and rises. The warm air moves upward, away from Earth's surface. As the air rises, it cools. The air becomes denser and begins to sink back toward Earth's surface. As the cooled air sinks, it forces warm air away from Earth's surface. This cycle causes winds and moves energy through the atmosphere.

Convection in the Geosphere

Earth may seem solid and rigid to you. But inside Earth, solid rock is slowly moving. Energy produced deep inside Earth heats rock in the mantle. The heated rock is under high pressure. So, the rock becomes plastic without melting, which causes the rock to flow like putty. As it becomes less dense, the heated rock rises toward Earth's surface. The cooler, denser rock surrounding the heated rock sinks, as **Figure 5** shows. In this way, heat inside Earth moves toward the cooler crust. This movement of rock is a convection current. Convection currents in the mantle cause the movement of tectonic plates.

Standards Check How does convection occur in the geosphere?
6.4.c

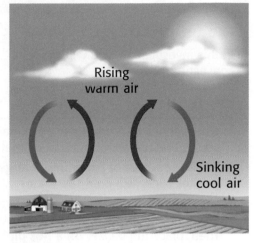

Figure 4 *Convection currents in the atmosphere form when cold air sinks and forces warm air away from Earth's surface.*

Figure 5 *Convection currents in the geosphere carry heat from Earth's interior toward the surface.*

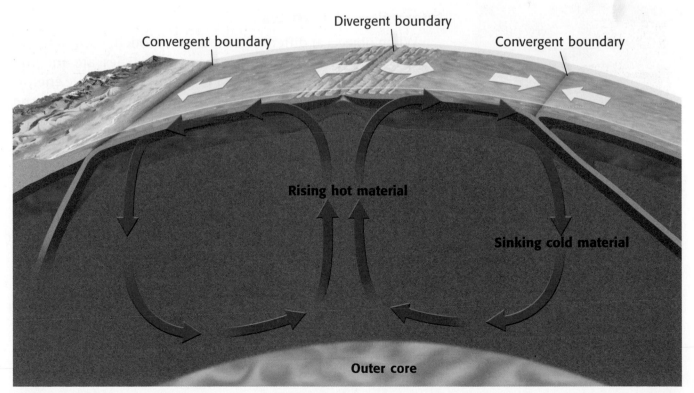

Quick Lab

Modeling Convection

In this investigation, you will model a convection current.

▶ Try It!

1. Tear a **sheet of blue paper** into small pieces that are about 1 cm in diameter.

2. Place the pieces of paper into a **large beaker** filled with **cold tap water.**

3. Let the pieces of paper absorb enough water to sink to the bottom of the beaker. Then, place the beaker on a **hot plate,** and heat the beaker and water.

4. Observe the pieces of paper as the water heats up. Draw a diagram of what you see. Label the heat source. Use arrows to show the movement of the pieces of paper.

▶ Think About It!

6.3.c
6.4.c
6.4.d

5. How does the movement of the pieces of paper relate to convection in the ocean, in the atmosphere, and in the geosphere?

6. Draw another diagram of energy flow in the Earth system. Show convection, conduction, and radiation occurring between and through the geosphere, atmosphere, and global ocean.

🕐 **20 min**

Conduction

Why does a spoon in a bowl of hot soup feel warm? The spoon feels warm because energy from the soup warms the spoon by conduction. This conduction of heat occurs because the spoon's particles interact with the soup's particles.

Interaction of Particles

When objects at different temperatures touch, their particles interact with one another. Because its particles are moving faster, the warmer substance has a higher average kinetic energy. The fast-moving particles transfer energy to the particles in the cooler substance, which has a lower average kinetic energy. The transfer of energy causes the particles in the cooler substance to move faster. So, the cooler substance becomes warmer.

Conduction Between Systems

Energy can be transferred between the geosphere and the atmosphere by conduction, as **Figure 6** shows. When Earth's surface is warmer than the atmosphere, the ground will transfer energy to the atmosphere. When air comes into direct contact with the warm surface of Earth, energy is passed to the atmosphere by conduction. If the atmosphere is warmer than Earth's surface, energy flows from the atmosphere to Earth.

Standards Check How does the geosphere transfer energy to the atmosphere? 🐻 **6.3.c**

Figure 6 *Conduction of heat from the geosphere to the atmosphere occurs only within a few centimeters of Earth's surface, where the air touches the ground. Transfer of heat from the geosphere to the atmosphere occurs only when the atmosphere is cooler than the geosphere, such as at night or on cold days.*

Earth's Energy Budget

Energy on Earth moves through and between four spheres. These four spheres are open systems, which means that they constantly exchange energy with one another. For example, solar radiation heats Earth's surface. And Earth's surface heats air in the lower atmosphere by conduction.

Energy is neither created nor destroyed. It is simply transferred between spheres or converted into another form of energy. You can think of the movement of energy between each of Earth's spheres as part of an energy budget. In a system, additions in energy are balanced by subtractions in energy. For example, energy that is taken away from the atmosphere may be added to the oceans or to the geosphere.

SECTION Review

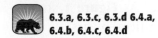

6.3.a, 6.3.c, 6.3.d 6.4.a, 6.4.b, 6.4.c, 6.4.d

Summary

- Energy can be transferred from one place to another by heat flow, by waves, or by objects that are moving.
- Heat flow is the transfer of energy from a warmer object to a cooler object.
- Energy from the sun reaches Earth by radiation.
- Energy is transferred through the oceans, the atmosphere, and the geosphere by convection.
- Energy is transferred between the geosphere and the atmosphere by conduction.

Using Vocabulary

Use a term from the section to complete each sentence below

1. ___ is the transfer of energy from a warmer object to a cooler object.

2. The ___ is all of the frequencies or wavelengths of electromagnetic radiation.

Understanding Concepts

3. **Comparing** How is radiation different from convection and conduction?

4. **Analyzing** How does energy from the sun reach Earth?

5. **Evaluating** Why must substances be touching in order for conduction to occur?

6. **Describing** Explain how energy is transferred in the ocean.

Critical Thinking

7. **Making Comparisons** Why is the sun's energy needed for ocean currents and winds to occur?

8. **Making Inferences** Explain why the transfer of heat through a spoon in a bowl of hot soup is not caused by convection.

9. **Evaluating Conclusions** Explain how all of the water in a tea kettle can be the same temperature even if the kettle is heated only from the bottom.

Challenge

10. **Predicting Consequences** What would Earth be like if heat could not be transferred through Earth's systems? What would Earth be like if energy from the sun could not reach Earth by radiation?

Internet Resources

For a variety of links related to this chapter, go to www.scilinks.org
Topic: The Atmosphere
SciLinks code: HY70112

The Cycling of Matter

Key Concept   Over time, matter—such as rock, water, carbon, and nitrogen—is transferred between organisms and the physical environment.

▶ You probably know people who recycle paper, plastic, and aluminum. But did you know that Earth also recycles? Very little new matter enters the Earth system. So, existing matter must cycle continuously for this planet to support life. Water, carbon, nitrogen, phosphorus, and even rocks move through cycles. If these materials did not cycle, Earth could not support life.

The Changing Earth

As matter cycles through the Earth system, the matter changes. Earth's surface also changes. Some of the processes that cause change may take millions of years. For example, mountains that are thousands of meters high form at rates of only a few centimeters per year. Over time, this slow rate of change adds up to big changes. Many changes have taken place on Earth over a long period of time. As **Figure 1** shows, Earth's history spans 4,600 million (4.6 billion) years!

Some changes happen very quickly. You may see them take place in a single day. For example, the weather may change from one hour to the next. Some cycles include steps that take millions of years and steps that take days or hours. All of the steps of all of these cycles constantly change Earth's surface.

Ma = millions of years ago

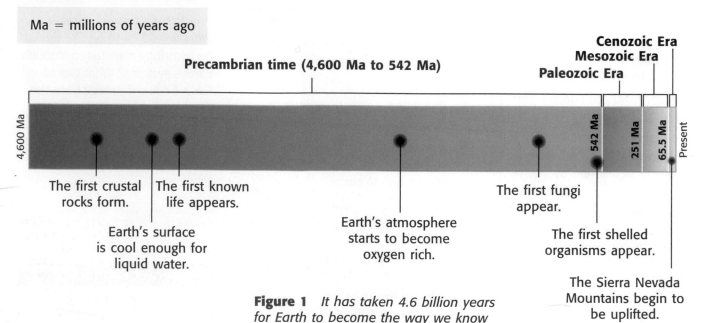

Precambrian time (4,600 Ma to 542 Ma)

Cenozoic Era
Mesozoic Era
Paleozoic Era

4,600 Ma

542 Ma

251 Ma

65.5 Ma

Present

The first crustal rocks form.

The first known life appears.

Earth's surface is cool enough for liquid water.

Earth's atmosphere starts to become oxygen rich.

The first fungi appear.

The first shelled organisms appear.

The Sierra Nevada Mountains begin to be uplifted.

Figure 1   *It has taken 4.6 billion years for Earth to become the way we know it today.* **How many millions of years ago did the first life appear?**

Figure 2   **The Rock Cycle**

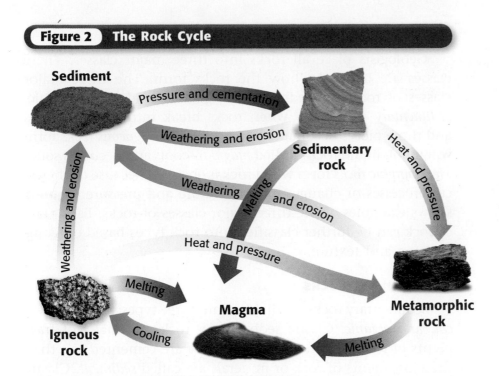

The Rock Cycle

One cycle that takes millions of years is the rock cycle. The **rock cycle** consists of the processes by which rocks change from one form to another. Several geologic processes can change rock from one type to another. These processes include melting, cooling, cementation, heat, pressure, weathering, and erosion. *Weathering* is the process by which rock is broken down by wind, water, and temperature changes. *Erosion* is the process by which wind, water, ice, or gravity transport parts of the weathered rock from one location to another. A diagram of these processes is shown in **Figure 2.**

rock cycle (RAHK SIE kuhl) the series of processes in which rock forms, changes from one type to another, is destroyed, and forms again by geologic processes

Pathways in the Rock Cycle

Rocks may follow a number of pathways in the rock cycle. For example, if it is exposed to weathering and erosion, igneous rock may become sedimentary rock. But under intense pressure and heat, igneous rock may become metamorphic rock. The pathway that a rock follows in the rock cycle is determined by the forces that act on the rock.

Forces That Change Rock

A rock's location determines the forces that will act on the rock. At Earth's surface, rock exposed to agents of weathering and erosion, such as wind and water, may become sedimentary rock. But deep inside Earth, rock exposed to high heat and pressure may become igneous rock or metamorphic rock.

6.4.a Students know the sun is the major source of energy for phenomena on Earth's surface; it powers winds, ocean currents, and the water cycle.
6.5.a Students know energy entering ecosystems as sunlight is transferred by producers into chemical energy through photosynthesis and then from organism to organism through food webs.
6.5.b Students know matter is transferred over time from one organism to others in the food web and between organisms and the physical environment.

Classes of Rocks

Geologists place all rocks into three major classes. These classes are based on how the rocks form. The three major classes of rocks are sedimentary, igneous, and metamorphic. *Sedimentary rocks* form when rocks break into smaller pieces and those pieces become cemented together. *Igneous rocks* form when hot, liquid rock—called *magma*—cools and becomes solid. *Metamorphic rocks* form when rock is changed because of chemical processes or changes in temperature and pressure. **Figure 3** shows examples of the three major classes of rocks. Each class of rock can be further classified into rock types based on composition and texture.

Sedimentary Rocks

Sedimentary rocks are divided into three types: *clastic, chemical,* and *organic*. Clastic sedimentary rocks are made of fragments of rock or minerals. Before they are cemented together, these fragments of rock or minerals are called *sediment*. Clastic sedimentary rocks form when sediments are buried, put under pressure, and cemented by minerals such as calcite and quartz. Chemical sedimentary rocks form when minerals crystallize from a solution, such as ocean water. The minerals are buried, put under pressure, and cemented together. Organic sedimentary rocks form when the shells and skeletons of dead marine animals are buried and cemented by calcite or quartz.

SCHOOL to HOME

Modeling the Rock Cycle

At home, you can use ordinary clay to model the steps of the rock cycle. Flatten two pieces of blue clay and two pieces of red clay. All four pieces should be the same size and as flat as pancakes. Lay the four pieces of clay on top of one another. Be sure to alternate the colors. Gently press the pieces together without changing their shape. Now, you have a model of sedimentary rock. Next, apply pressure to your sedimentary rock by twisting and squeezing the rock. What class of rock did you just model? Which process of the rock cycle did you model to form this class of rock?

ACTIVITY

Figure 3 **Classes of Rocks**

Sedimentary rock

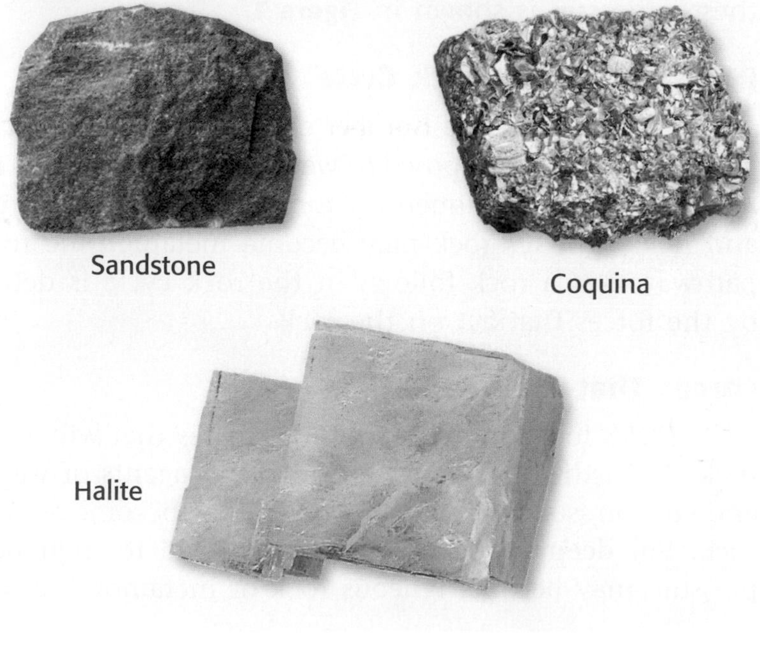

Sandstone

Coquina

Halite

Igneous Rocks

Igneous rocks are divided into groups based on the texture of the rock, or the size of the crystals in the rock. Magma that slowly cools deep inside Earth forms coarse-grained rocks made of large crystals. Lava that erupts at Earth's surface and quickly cools forms fine-grained rocks made of very small crystals.

Igneous rock can also be classified by its chemical composition. The chemical composition of an igneous rock is determined by the type of rock that initially melts to form magma. Magma from melted crustal material tends to form light-colored igneous rocks, such as granite. Magma from Earth's mantle forms dark-colored igneous rocks, such as basalt.

Metamorphic Rocks

Metamorphic rock is rock that forms from other rocks as a result of intense heat, pressure, or chemical processes. Most metamorphic changes happen deep within Earth's crust at depths greater than 2 km. At these depths, pressure can be many times greater than it is at Earth's surface. Temperature is also much higher at these depths than it is at Earth's surface.

There are two types of metamorphic rocks. The minerals of *foliated* metamorphic rock, such as gneiss, are arranged in planes or bands. The minerals of *nonfoliated* metamorphic rock, such as marble, are not arranged in planes or bands.

INTERNET ACTIVITY

Rock Brochure

Watch out, world. Here come some new rock stars! Create a brochure that classifies "rock stars." Go to **go.hrw.com,** and type in the keyword HY7MINW.

Igneous rock

Granite

Basalt

Metamorphic rock

Gneiss

Marble

Quick Lab

Modeling the Water Cycle

6.4.a

1. Start with a **large, sealable, plastic freezer bag.** Be sure that the bag is clean and dry and has no leaks. Place a **small, dark-colored bowl** inside the bag. Position the bag so that the opening is at the top.

2. Fill the bowl halfway with **water.** Place a three drops of **red food coloring** in the water. Seal the bag.

3. Place the bowl and bag under a strong and warm light source, such as a **lamp** or direct sunlight.

4. Leave the bag in the light for one hour. Observe the bag at regular intervals.

5. How does this activity model the sun's role in the water cycle?

⏱ **20 min**

The Water Cycle

The **water cycle** is the continuous movement of water between the atmosphere, the land, and the oceans, as shown in **Figure 4.** The sun is the major source of energy that powers the water cycle. Energy from the sun heats the water on Earth. This heating of water causes water to change states. For example, liquid water changes to water vapor.

Steps of the Water Cycle

Evaporation is the process in which liquid water changes into gaseous water vapor. Water vapor is also released into the air through pores on the leaves of plants. This process is known as *transpiration*. If air that contains water vapor cools, the water vapor turns into liquid water droplets and forms clouds. The change from a gas to a liquid is called *condensation*. When water droplets become large enough, they fall back to Earth as *precipitation,* such as rain.

Pathways of the Water Cycle

Most precipitation falls directly into the ocean and never reaches the land surface. Precipitation that does reach the land surface may fill lakes, streams, and rivers and eventually return to the ocean. Water moving over the land surface is called *runoff.* Gravity may move the water downward through spaces in rock or soil, where the water becomes groundwater.

Standards Check What is the major source of energy for the water cycle? 🐻 **6.4.a**

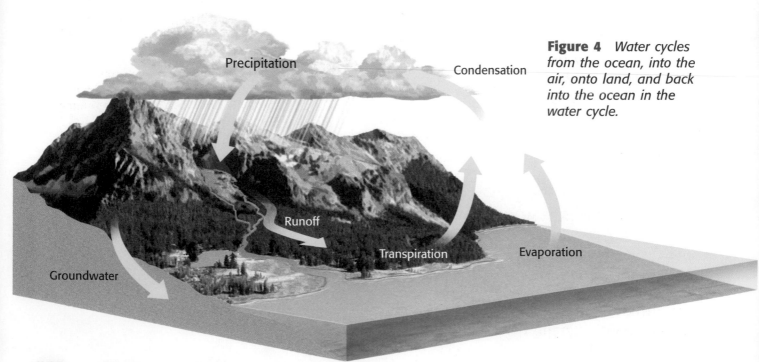

Figure 4 *Water cycles from the ocean, into the air, onto land, and back into the ocean in the water cycle.*

Precipitation

Condensation

Runoff

Transpiration

Evaporation

Groundwater

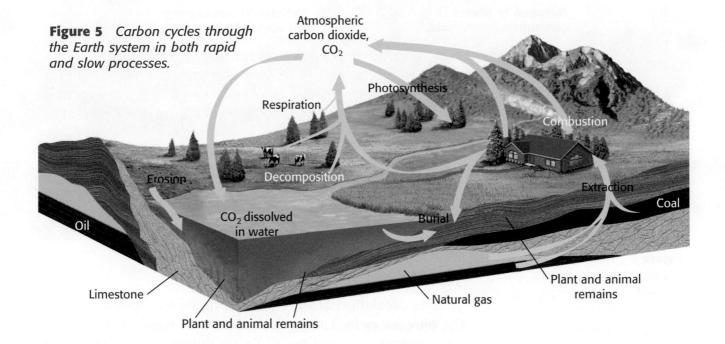

Figure 5 *Carbon cycles through the Earth system in both rapid and slow processes.*

Atmospheric carbon dioxide, CO_2

Respiration

Photosynthesis

Combustion

Erosion

Decomposition

Extraction

Coal

Oil

CO_2 dissolved in water

Burial

Plant and animal remains

Limestone

Plant and animal remains

Natural gas

The Carbon Cycle

Carbon is an important element that cycles through the Earth system. Carbon is part of the proteins, fats, and carbohydrates in living things. But carbon is not only in living things. Carbon is also in the atmosphere, the water, the land, and the remains of living things. The cycling of carbon between Earth's spheres is called the **carbon cycle,** as shown in **Figure 5.**

Short-Term Processes

Parts of the carbon cycle are relatively rapid processes. To build plant material, plants use energy from the sun; from carbon dioxide, CO_2; and from water. When animals eat the plants, the energy in the plants is transferred to the animals. When the animals break down food to release energy, carbon is returned to the air as CO_2. Then, the CO_2 is reused by plants. When a living thing dies, other organisms break down the remains. This process, called *decomposition*, releases the carbon from the dead organism back into the cycle.

Long-Term Processes

Other parts of the carbon cycle are much slower processes. In some cases, dead organisms are buried before they decompose. Their bodies chemically change as they are compacted for millions of years. This process forms rock, such as limestone, or fossil fuels, such as coal, gas, and oil. When humans burn these fuels, carbon returns to the atmosphere as carbon dioxide. This process of burning fuel is called *combustion*.

water cycle (WAWT uhr SIE kuhl) the continuous movement of water between the atmosphere, the land, and the oceans

carbon cycle (KAHR buhn SIE kuhl) the movement of carbon from the nonliving environment into living things and back

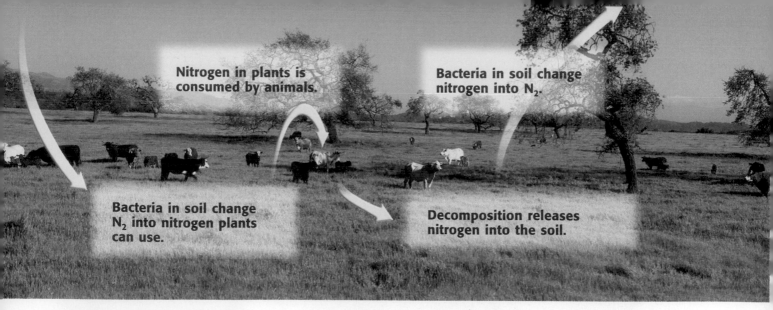

Nitrogen in plants is consumed by animals.

Bacteria in soil change nitrogen into N$_2$.

Bacteria in soil change N$_2$ into nitrogen plants can use.

Decomposition releases nitrogen into the soil.

Figure 6 *The nitrogen cycle includes bacteria, plants, and animals.*

nitrogen cycle (NIE truh juhn SIE kuhl) the process in which nitrogen circulates among the air, soil, water, plants, and animals in an ecosystem

The Nitrogen Cycle

The circulation of nitrogen among Earth's spheres is called the **nitrogen cycle.** This cycle is shown in **Figure 6.** Nitrogen is an important nutrient for all living things. Certain bacteria in soil change atmospheric nitrogen, N$_2$, into forms of nitrogen that plants can use. Other organisms get the nitrogen that they need by eating plants. When organisms die, decomposers release nitrogen from the dead organisms back into the soil. Then, plants use some of this nitrogen. Some bacteria in soil change this nitrogen into atmospheric nitrogen, which returns to the air.

The Phosphorus Cycle

Like carbon and nitrogen, phosphorus is found in living things. Phosphorus is also found in soil, rock, and water. The roots of plants absorb phosphorus from the soil. Then, animals obtain phosphorus when they eat the plants. When the animals die, the phosphorus returns to the soil through decomposition.

Other Cycles in Nature

Other forms of matter on Earth also pass through cycles. Many of the minerals that living things need, such as the mineral calcium, are cycled through the environment. When a living thing dies, every substance in its body is recycled.

Each cycle is connected to other cycles in many ways. Some forms of nitrogen and carbon are carried through the environment by water. Many nutrients pass from soil to plants to animals and back. Living things play an important part in each of the cycles and depend on the cycles for survival.

Standards Check How is matter passed from one living thing to another? **6.5.b**

Summary

- The processes that cycle matter in the Earth system can be relatively rapid or may take millions of years.
- The rock cycle is the series of processes in which rock changes from one form to another by geologic processes.
- The three major classes of rocks are sedimentary, igneous, and metamorphic.
- Water moves continuously from the ocean, to the atmosphere, to land, and back to the ocean through the water cycle.
- In the carbon cycle, carbon is cycled in both rapid processes and slow processes.
- Types of matter that are cycled through the Earth system include carbon, phosphorus, and nitrogen.

Using Vocabulary

1. Write an original definition for *rock cycle, water cycle, carbon cycle,* and *nitrogen cycle.*

Understanding Concepts

2. **Describing** Describe how igneous rock can form into sedimentary rock.

3. **Describing** Describe the sun's role in the water cycle.

4. **Describing** Describe how sedimentary rock can form into metamorphic rock.

5. **Identifying** Identify the steps in the water cycle.

6. **Identifying** Identify the origin from which all living things on Earth get their energy.

7. **Describing** Explain the role that plants play in the carbon cycle.

8. **Summarizing** How is matter transferred from one organism to another?

9. **Summarizing** How is energy from the sun transferred from plants to animals?

Critical Thinking

10. **Analyzing Processes** What is the importance of gravity in the movement of water through the water cycle?

11. **Making Comparisons** Compare the role of decomposers with the role of plants in the carbon cycle.

12. **Analyzing Processes** How is combustion part of the carbon cycle?

13. **Making Comparisons** Compare combustion and decomposition.

INTERPRETING GRAPHICS Use the diagram below to answer the next two questions.

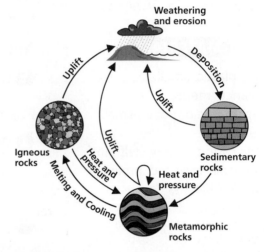

14. **Analyzing Processes** Describe what needs to happen in order for metamorphic rock to change into igneous rock.

15. **Identifying Relationships** What type of rock forms when igneous rock is weathered and eroded?

Challenge

16. **Identifying Relationships** Organisms get their energy from eating other organisms. Where do plants get their energy? What would happen to all of the organisms on Earth if plants did not have this source of energy?

Internet Resources

For a variety of links related to this chapter, go to www.scilinks.org
Topic: Water Cycle; Cycles of Matter
SciLinks code: HY71626; HY70373

Inquiry Lab

OBJECTIVES

Develop a system that prevents energy transfer by conduction, convection, and radiation.

Determine which materials most efficiently prevent energy transfer.

MATERIALS

- bag, plastic, small
- balance, metric
- cup, plastic or paper, small
- ice cube
- milk carton, empty, half-pint
- materials, assorted, provided by your teacher

Stop the Energy Transfer

An ice cube's greatest enemy is the transfer of thermal energy, or heat. Energy can be transferred to an ice cube by conduction (the transfer of energy through direct contact), convection (the transfer of energy by the movement of a liquid or a gas), and radiation (the transfer of energy through matter or space). Your challenge in this activity is to design the best system possible to protect an ice cube from all three types of energy transfer.

Ask a Question

1 What materials most efficiently prevent energy transfer?

Form a Hypothesis

2 Design a system to protect an ice cube against each type of energy transfer. Describe your proposed design.

Test the Hypothesis

3 Use a plastic bag to hold the ice cube and any water if the ice cube melts. You may use any of the materials provided by your teacher to protect the ice cube. However, the whole system must fit inside a milk carton.

4 Find and record the mass of the empty cup. Then, find and record the mass of an empty plastic bag.

6.3.a Students know energy can be carried from one place to another by heat flow or by waves, including water, light and sound waves, or by moving objects.
6.3.c Students know heat flows in solids by conduction (which involves no flow of matter) and in fluids by conduction and by convection (which involves flow of matter).
6.3.d Students know heat energy is also transferred between objects by radiation (radiation can travel through space).

Investigation and Experimentation
6.7.a Develop a hypothesis.
6.7.e Recognize whether evidence is consistent with a proposed explanation.

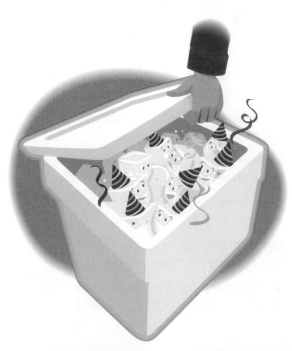

5 Find and record the combined mass of the ice cube and cup.

6 Quickly wrap the protective material around the bag containing the ice cube. Remember that the package must fit in the milk carton.

7 Place your ice cube in the "thermal zone" set up by your teacher. After 10 min, remove the ice cube from the zone.

8 Open the bag. If there is any water in the bag, pour the water into the cup. Find and record the combined mass of the cup and water.

9 Find the mass of the water by subtracting the mass of the empty cup from the mass of the cup and water. Record the mass of the water.

10 Use the same method to determine the mass of the ice cube.

11 Use the following equation to find and record what percentage of the ice cube melted:

$$\% \ melted = \frac{\text{mass of water}}{\text{mass of ice cube}} \times 100$$

Analyze the Results

12 Analyzing Results Compare the results of your design with the results of other designs in your class. How well did your design protect against heat flow?

Draw Conclusions

13 Defending Conclusions Was your design effective at protecting the ice cube from heat flow? How could you improve your design?

Big Idea Question

14 Drawing Conclusions In this lab, the radiation, conduction, and convection of thermal energy was the enemy of your ice cube. In the entire Earth system, do you think the transfer of heat has negative consequences? Describe how the Earth system would be affected if heat could not be transferred.

Science Skills Activity

Investigation and Experimentation

6.7.d Communicate the steps and results from an investigation in written reports and oral presentations.

Communicating Results

 **Tutorial**

Part of the scientific process is communicating the steps and results of an investigation clearly. You can write clear steps and results by following these helpful hints.

Written Report

1 Write each step clearly and fully. Do not skip any steps, and make sure that all of the steps are in order. Sometimes, it helps to perform the process while you are writing the steps.

2 Get a second opinion. Almost everything that you have read—including books, magazines, and even this text book—has been reviewed and rewritten several times. Before you hand in a written report, have someone review it. The person will probably have some suggestions for improving your report.

Scientists also give oral presentations to communicate the steps and results of an investigation. By following these helpful hints, you can improve your oral presentation skills.

Oral Presentation

1 Use visuals. When you use diagrams and charts or demonstrate a process, your audience may better understand what you are trying to communicate. Think about the methods that your teacher uses to present information. What visuals that were used by your teacher helped you learn a process?

2 Practice often. Many people get nervous when speaking in front of a large group. If you practice in front of the mirror or with a friend, you will feel better prepared for the real thing.

▶ You Try It!

You will write a procedure for creating a model of the water cycle. Then, you will demonstrate your model to the class. Follow the steps below to help you prepare for your presentation.

Written Report

1 Write a report that describes how to create a water-cycle model from materials provided by your teacher. Include instructions for testing the model.

2 Exchange your report with a classmate's report. Follow your classmate's report. Do you understand the report? Suggest ways in which your classmate can improve his or her report.

3 Return the report to your classmate. With your classmate, discuss the suggestions on both reports.

4 Edit your report based on the suggestions from your classmate.

Oral Presentation

5 With your classmate, take turns giving oral presentations of the models based on the written reports. Provide each other with feedback about the presentations.

6 Now that you are ready, give the class an oral presentation of your model.

7 How did the model help you communicate the process of the water cycle? How would your presentation be different if you did not use the model?

8 Did your classmate's advice help you with your written report and your presentation to the class? What advice was most helpful?

Chapter Summary

The Big Idea
Many phenomena on Earth's surface are affected by the transfer of energy through Earth's systems.

Section		Vocabulary

① The Earth System

Key Concept Earth is a complex system made up of many smaller systems through which matter and energy are continuously cycled.

- Energy and matter flow through Earth's four spheres: the geosphere, atmosphere, hydrosphere, and biosphere.
- Energy flows through the atmosphere and hydrosphere mostly by convection.

The global ocean covers 71% of Earth's surface.

crust p. 85
mantle p. 85
core p. 85
convection p. 86
convection current p. 87

② Heat and Energy

Key Concept Heat flows in a predictable way from warmer objects to cooler objects until all of the objects are at the same temperature.

- Temperature is a measure of the average kinetic energy of particles in an object.
- Heat is energy that is transferred between objects.
- Heat flows by conduction, convection, and radiation.

Convection currents transfer heat through a fluid.

temperature p. 90
heat p. 92
thermal energy p. 93
conduction p. 94
convection p. 94
radiation p. 95

③ The Cycling of Energy

Key Concept Various heat-exchange systems work in the Earth system and affect phenomena on Earth's surface.

- Heat flow is the transfer of energy from a warmer object to a cooler object.
- Energy from the sun, the major source of energy for phenomena on Earth's surface, is transmitted to Earth by radiation.
- Heat from Earth's interior reaches the surface mostly by convection.

Heat is transferred in the atmosphere by convection.

heat flow p. 98
electromagnetic spectrum p. 99

④ The Cycling of Matter

Key Concept Over time, matter—such as rock, water, carbon, and nitrogen—is transferred between organisms and the physical environment.

- The rock cycle is the series of processes in which rock changes from one form to another.
- In the water cycle, water condenses, precipitates, and evaporates through the various spheres of Earth.
- Nitrogen, carbon, and phosphorus cycle between Earth's spheres.

Sandstone is an example of a sedimentary rock.

rock cycle p. 105
water cycle p. 108
carbon cycle p. 109
nitrogen cycle p. 110

Chapter Review

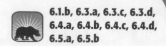

6.1.b, 6.3.a, 6.3.c, 6.3.d,
6.4.a, 6.4.b, 6.4.c, 6.4.d,
6.5.a, 6.5.b

Organize

Four-Corner Fold Review the FoldNote that you created at the beginning of the chapter. Add to or correct the FoldNote based on what you have learned.

Using Vocabulary

1 Academic Vocabulary In the sentence "Energy is transferred through space by radiation," what does the word *transferred* mean?
a. removed   **c.** deleted
b. passed   **d.** emptied

For each pair of terms, explain how the meanings of the terms differ.

2 *atmosphere* and *hydrosphere*

3 *deep current* and *surface current*

4 *crust* and *mantle*

5 *convection* and *conduction*

6 *rock cycle* and *water cycle*

7 *carbon cycle* and *nitrogen cycle*

Understanding Concepts

Multiple Choice

8 The part of Earth where life exists is called the
a. geosphere.   **c.** hydrosphere.
b. atmosphere.   **d.** biosphere.

9 How is most energy transferred through the ocean?
a. by radiation   **c.** by conduction
b. by convection   **d.** by diffusion

10 Which of the following processes is NOT part of the water cycle?
a. condensation   **c.** radiation
b. evaporation   **d.** precipitation

Short Answer

11 Identifying In which of Earth's compositional layers does convection occur?

12 Analyzing How does solar energy reach Earth?

13 Identifying What powers winds, ocean currents, and the water cycle?

14 Evaluating How do differences in temperature cause convection currents?

15 Analyzing Explain why radiation does NOT occur in Earth's mantle.

16 Evaluating Describe the role of particles in the transfer of heat.

INTERPRETING GRAPHICS Use the illustration below to answer the next three questions.

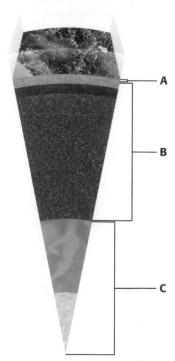

17 Identifying Which letter represents the core of Earth?

18 Applying Which letter represents the compositional layer of Earth where convection occurs?

19 Listing List the compositional layer of Earth that each letter in the diagram represents. Then, list the physical layers that relate to each compositional layer.

Writing Skills

20 Outlining Topics Imagine a sedimentary rock changing into a metamorphic rock, then into an igneous rock, and back into a sedimentary rock. Logically present the steps that the rock goes through as it changes from one kind of rock to another. Clearly explain relationships between each step.

Critical Thinking

21 Concept Mapping Use the following terms to create a concept map: *geosphere, crust, mantle, inner core, outer core, core, lithosphere, asthenosphere, mesosphere, compositional layers,* and *physical layers.*

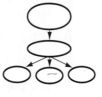

22 Identifying Relationships Explain why organisms are dependent on a continuous supply of energy from the sun.

23 Analyzing Ideas How do differences in density cause currents to flow both in the surface waters of the ocean and in the bottom waters of the ocean?

24 Analyzing Processes How would the carbon cycle and the nitrogen cycle be affected if decomposers were removed from Earth's biosphere?

25 Evaluating Data The movement of liquid metal can generate electric fields and magnetic fields. What characteristic of Earth's interior is probably responsible for Earth's magnetic field?

26 Identifying Relationships Describe two ways in which your daily activities affect the water cycle.

27 Applying Concepts Using what you learned about heat flow and the transfer of energy, describe how the warm ocean currents off the coast of northwestern Europe affect the climate of northwestern Europe.

INTERPRETING GRAPHICS Use the chart below to answer the next three questions.

Percentage of Solar Radiation		
Surface	Reflected (%)	Absorbed (%)
Soils (dark colored)	5–10	90–95
Desert	20–40	60–80
Grass	5–25	75–95
Forest	5–10	90–95
Snow	50–90	10–50
Water (high sun angle)	5–10	90–95
Water (low sun angle)	50–80	20–50

28 Evaluating Data Which surface reflects the highest percentage of solar radiation?

29 Making Comparisons List three surfaces that absorb a high percentage of solar radiation.

30 Evaluating Data At which time of day would you expect the ocean to absorb the most solar radiation: noon or early morning?

Math Skills

31 Making Calculations If the radius of Earth is 6,500 km and the radius of Earth's core is 3,400 km, what percentage of Earth's radius does the core represent?

32 Making Calculations The global ocean covers 335 million square kilometers, which is 71% of Earth's surface. In terms of square kilometers, how much of Earth's surface is covered by land?

Challenge

33 Analyzing Ideas The knobs on a water faucet are labeled "H" for hot and "C" for cold. When you first turn on the hot water, the water that comes out is cool. Is the label on the knob wrong? Explain your answer.

Standards Assessment

4.2.a, 5.2.f, 5.3.b, 5.4.a,
6.1.b, 6.3.a, 6.3.c, 6.3.d,
6.4.a, 6.4.b, 6.4.c, 6.4.d,
6.5.a, 6.5.b

REVIEWING ACADEMIC VOCABULARY

1 In the sentence "The sun provides energy for many phenomena on Earth's surface, including ocean currents," what does the word *phenomena* mean?

A any serious issue caused by natural factors

B any facts or events that can be sensed or described scientifically

C any ocean movement

D cycles

2 Choose the appropriate form of the word *predict* for the following sentence: "Heat moves in a _____ flow from warmer objects to cooler objects until all are the same temperature."

A prediction

B predicted

C predictable

D predictably

3 Which of the following words is the closest in meaning to the word *transfer*?

A move

B stop

C replace

D expand

4 In the sentence "Heat in the atmosphere is distributed by convection currents," what does the word *distributed* mean?

A spread out over a wide area

B focused in a specific area

C reduced to a small amount

D raised to a higher level

REVIEWING CONCEPTS

5 Which of the following describes Earth's lithosphere?

A the solid center of Earth

B the lower layer of Earth's mantle

C the invisible gases around Earth

D the cold, brittle, outermost layer of Earth

6 What happens when a substance's kinetic energy increases?

A The particles expand.

B The particles move more quickly.

C The particles form a solid.

D The particles move more slowly.

7 What is one reason that a room on the upper floor of a house may be warmer than a room on the bottom floor?

A Wind blows hot air to the top of the house.

B The top floor of the house is closer to the sun and is therefore warmer.

C The warm air in the house rises to the top floor.

D The energy of the cooler air on the lower floors pushes the warm air up.

8 Which section of the diagram depicts Earth's mantle?

A section A

B section B

C section C

D section D

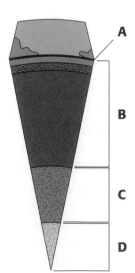

9 By which of the following methods does the sun heat Earth?

A radiation

B convection

C conduction

D evaporation

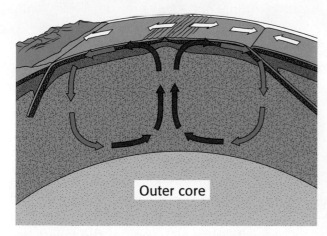

Outer core

10 What process does the diagram above show?

A how radiation is sent from Earth's core

B how Earth's crust cools the geosphere by conduction

C how water currents affect the geosphere

D how energy travels through the geosphere by convection

11 Which of the following is an example of the transfer of matter?

A A deer eats the leaves from a tree.

B The sun's energy heats the atmosphere.

C A bag of popcorn is heated in a microwave.

D A mass of warm air rises into the sky.

REVIEWING PRIOR LEARNING

12 Plants are able to make their own food, which gives them energy. Plants change energy from the sun into chemical energy by the process of _____.

A heat transfer.

B radiation.

C photosynthesis.

D convection.

13 The sun heats Earth's surface unevenly. What is one result of the uneven heating of Earth?

A movements in Earth's crust

B the convection of air currents

C radiation entering the atmosphere

D the shifting of the tides

14 Water can exist in three states: solid, liquid, and gas. What happens to liquid water when it evaporates?

A Its molecules move closer together.

B It falls to the ground.

C It rises into the air.

D It becomes a solid.

15 The energy of the sun makes life on Earth possible. How does energy from the sun end up in people and animals?

A Sunlight shines directly onto people and is converted into energy.

B Sunlight is converted into chemical energy by plants. It is then transferred to people and animals when they eat the plants.

C The sun's energy is absorbed by the water, which people and animals drink.

D The sun's energy travels through the air on convection currents.

Science in Action

Scientific Discoveries

The Deep Freeze

All matter is made up of tiny, constantly vibrating particles. Temperature is a measure of the average kinetic energy of those particles. The colder a substance gets, the slower its particles move. Scientists are interested in how matter behaves when it is cooled to almost absolute zero, the absence of all thermal energy, which is about –273°C. In one method, scientists aim lasers at gas particles, which holds the particles so still that their temperature is less than one-millionth of a degree from absolute zero. It's like turning on several garden hoses and pointing each from a different angle at a soccer ball so that the ball won't move in any direction.

Weird Science

Giant Trees

You already know that trees are an important part of the carbon, nitrogen, and phosphorus cycles. But do you know that California is home to one of the tallest tree species? The average Redwood can range from 60 to 100 m tall. Some Redwoods are even taller than the Statue of Liberty! The tallest Redwood is named *Tall Tree*. It is located at Redwood National Park and is over 122 m tall. Even thinking of looking up at this tree can make your neck hurt! But Redwoods are not simply impressive for their heights. They also live for a long time. Redwoods may live for up to 2,000 years!

Language Arts ACTiViTY

Imagine being 2,000 years old. In your **Science Journal**, write a creative short story in which you are a Redwood. Describe what your life is like.

Math ACTiViTY

Think of the coldest weather that you have ever been in. What was the temperature? Convert this temperature into kelvins. Compare this temperature with absolute zero.

People in Science

Michael Reynolds

Earthship Architect   Would you want to live in a house without a heating system? You could if you lived in an Earthship! Earthships are the brainchild of Michael Reynolds, an architect in Taos, New Mexico. These houses are designed to make the most of our planet's most abundant source of energy, the sun.

Each Earthship takes full advantage of passive solar heating. For example, large windows face south in order to maximize the amount of energy that the house receives from the sun. Each home is partially buried in the ground. The soil helps retain energy that comes in through the windows of the house.

The massive, thick outer walls of Earthships also help absorb the sun's energy. The walls may be made with crushed aluminum cans or stacks of old automobile tires filled with dirt. These materials absorb the sun's energy and naturally heat the house. Because it maintains a temperature of about 15°C (about 60°F), an Earthship can keep its occupants comfortable through all but the coldest winter nights.

Social Studies ACTIVITY

Find out more about Michael Reynolds and other architects who have invented unique ways of building houses that are energy-efficient. Present your findings.

Internet Resources

- To learn more about careers in science, visit **www.scilinks.org** and enter the SciLinks code HY70225.

- To learn more about these Science in Action topics, visit **go.hrw.com** and type in the keyword HY7ESCF.

- Check out articles related to this chapter by visiting **go.hrw.com**. Just type in the keyword HY7ESCC.

Earth's Resources

In this unit, you will learn about the resources that humans use for energy and for material needs. All of the resources that humans use come from Earth or from the sun. You will learn how these resources form, how long they take to form, and how they are used to generate energy and to produce the objects that we use every day. This timeline shows some of the events that have occurred through human history as new resources and new ways to use resources have been discovered.

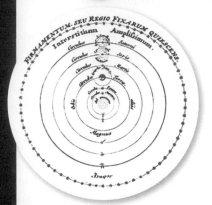

1543

Nicolaus Copernicus argues that the sun rather than Earth is the center of the universe.

1860

Fossil remains of *Archaeopteryx,* a species that may link dinosaurs and birds, are discovered in Germany.

1936

Hoover Dam is completed. This massive hydroelectric dam, standing more than 221 m, required 3.25 million cubic yards of concrete to build.

1975

Tabei Junko of Japan becomes the first woman to successfully climb Mount Everest, 22 years after Edmund Hillary and Tenzing Norgay first conquered the mountain in 1953.

1681

The dodo, a flightless bird, is driven to extinction by the actions of humans.

1739

Georg Brandt identifies a new element and names it *cobalt*.

1848

James Marshall discovers gold at Sutter's Mill in California, which begins the California gold rush. Prospectors during the gold rush of the following year are referred to as "forty-niners."

1947

Willard F. Libby develops a method of dating prehistoric objects by using radioactive carbon.

1955

Using 1 million pounds of pressure per square inch and temperatures of more than 1,700°C, General Electric creates the first artificial diamonds from graphite.

1969

Apollo 11 astronauts Neil Armstrong and Edwin "Buzz" Aldrin bring 22 kg of moon rocks and soil back to Earth.

1989

Russian engineers drill a borehole 12 km into Earth's crust. The borehole is more than 3 times as deep as the deepest mine shaft.

1997

Sojourner, a roving probe on Mars, investigates a Martian boulder nicknamed Yogi.

1999

A Japanese automaker introduces the first hybrid car into the U.S. market.

Improving Comprehension

Graphic Organizers are important visual tools that can help you organize information and improve your reading comprehension. The Graphic Organizer below is called a *comparison table*. Instructions for creating other types of Graphic Organizers are located in the **Study Skills** section of the Appendix.

How to Make a Comparison Table

1 Draw a table like the one shown below. Draw as many columns and rows as you want to draw.

2 In the top row, write the topics that you want to compare.

3 In the left column, write the general characteristics that you want to compare. As you read the chapter, fill in the characteristics for each topic in the appropriate boxes.

When to Use a Comparison Table

A comparison table is useful when you want to compare the characteristics of two or more topics in science. Organizing information in a table helps you compare several topics at one time. In a table, all topics are described in terms of the same list of characteristics, which helps you make a thorough comparison. As you read, look for topics whose characteristics you may want to compare in a table.

	Oxygen	Petroleum	Minerals	Plants	Animals
Where they are found	• the atmosphere	• Earth's crust	• various places in Earth's crust	• many places on Earth	• many places on Earth
Examples of what they are used for	• life processes • rocket fuel	• to make gasoline and other fuels • to manufacture polymers for products such as plastics, clothing, and plumbing supplies	• to make objects used daily, such as parts of bicycles, computers, food containers, and airplanes • industrial processes • environmental processes	• food • clothing • lumber • paper • fuel • other materials, such as rubber	• transporting humans and cargo • farming • food • fertilizer and fuel (in the case of animal wastes)
Renewable?	yes	no	some	yes	yes

You Try It!

This Reading Strategy can also be used within the chapter that you are about to read. Practice making your own comparison table as directed in the Reading Strategy for Section **2**. Record your work in your **Science Journal**.

Unpacking the Standards

The information below "unpacks" the standards by breaking them down into basic parts. The higher-level, academic vocabulary is highlighted and defined to help you understand the language of the standards. "What It Means" restates the standards as simply as possible.

California Standard	Academic Vocabulary	What It Means
6.6.b Students know different natural **energy** and material **resources** including air, soil, rocks, minerals, petroleum, fresh water, wildlife, and forests, and know how to classify them as renewable or nonrenewable.	**energy** (EN uhr jee) the ability to make things happen **resource** (REE SAWRS) anything that can be used to take care of a need	You must be able to identify different natural resources, such as air, soil, rocks, minerals, petroleum, fresh water, wildlife, and forests, and be able to identify whether each resource can be replaced rapidly or not.
6.6.c Students know the natural origin of the materials used to make common objects.		You must be able to identify the natural resources that are used to make common objects.

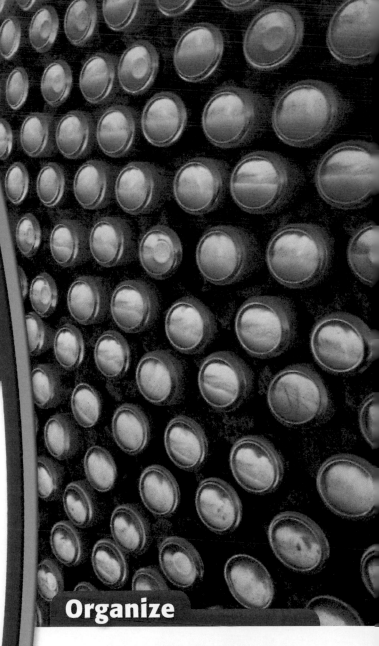

4

Material Resources

The Big Idea

Material resources differ in amounts, distribution, usefulness, and the time required for their formation.

 California Standards

Focus on Earth Sciences
6.6 Sources of energy and materials differ in amounts, distribution, usefulness, and the time required for their formation. (Sections 1, 2, and 3)

Investigation and Experimentation
6.7 Scientific progress is made by asking meaningful questions and conducting careful investigations. (Science Skills Activity)

Math
6.1.1 Statistics, Data Analysis, and Probability
6.1.4, 6.2.1 Number Sense

English–Language Arts
6.1.1, 6.2.4 Reading
6.1.3, 6.2.3 Writing

About the Photo

Would you believe that this house is made from empty soda cans and old tires? Well, it is! *The Castle,* named by its designer, architect Mike Reynolds, is located in Taos, New Mexico. It not only uses recycled materials but also saves Earth's energy resources. All of the energy used to run this house comes directly from the sun, and the water used for household activities is rainwater.

Organize

Two-Panel Flip Chart

Before you read this chapter, create the FoldNote entitled "Two-Panel Flip Chart." Label one flap "Renewable" and the other "Nonrenewable." As you read the chapter, write information about each type of resource, including examples of each type, under the appropriate flap.

Instructions for creating FoldNotes are located in the Study Skills section on p. 618 of the Appendix.

Explore Activity

What Is Your Classroom Made Of?

Complete the following activity to see if you can determine the natural origin of materials used to make common objects in your classroom.

Procedure

1. On a **sheet of paper,** make three columns. Label one column "Object," the second column "Parts of the object," and the third column "Natural origin."

2. Look around your classroom. Choose a few objects to put on your list under "Object."

3. With a partner, discuss each item that you have chosen. List the parts of each object in the second column on your paper. For example, for the object "window," parts of the window could be "glass" and "frame."

Analysis

6.6.c

4. With your partner, discuss the natural origin of the parts of each object and add the natural origins to the third column of your table. For example, for "glass," the natural origin could be "sand."

5. If you can, describe the manufacturing process for some of the objects on your list.

6. What do you think are the costs that are included in the purchase price of some of the objects on your list?

Natural Resources

Key Concept   Different energy and material resources can be classified as renewable or nonrenewable.

▶ What do the water you drink, the paper you write on, the gasoline used in the cars you ride in, and the air you breathe have in common? All of these items are Earth's resources or are made from Earth's resources.

Earth's Resources

Earth provides everything needed for life except energy from the sun. Earth's atmosphere provides the air you breathe, maintains air temperatures, and produces rain. The oceans and other waters of Earth give you food and water. Earth's soil gives nutrients, such as iron, to the plants you eat. These resources from Earth are called natural resources.

A **natural resource** is any natural material that is used by humans. Examples of natural resources are air, soil, fresh water, petroleum, rocks, minerals, forests, and wildlife. Most resources are used in products that make people's lives easier and more comfortable, as shown in **Figure 1.** The energy we get from many of these resources, such as gasoline and wind, ultimately comes from the sun's energy.

Figure 1   **Natural Resources**

This pile of lumber is made of wood, which comes from trees.

The gasoline in this can and the can itself are both made from oil pumped from Earth's crust.

Electrical energy generated by these wind turbines ultimately comes from the sun's energy.

Figure 2 *Trees and fresh water are just a few of the renewable resources available on Earth.*

Renewable Resources

Some natural resources can be replaced in a relatively short time. A **renewable resource** is a natural resource that can be replaced at the same rate at which the resource is used. **Figure 2** shows two renewable resources. However, renewable resources can be used up too quickly. For example, trees are renewable. But some forests are being cut down faster than new forests can grow to replace them.

Nonrenewable Resources

A **nonrenewable resource** is a resource that forms at a much slower rate than the rate at which it is used. These resources may take thousands or millions of years to form. For example, coal takes millions of years to form. Once coal is used up, it is no longer available. Petroleum and natural gas are other examples of nonrenewable resources. When these resources become scarce, humans will have to find other resources to use instead.

Standards Check What is the difference between a renewable resource and a nonrenewable resource? **6.6.b**

natural resource (NACH uhr uhl REE SAWRS) any natural material that is used by humans, such as water, petroleum, minerals, forests, and animals

renewable resource (ri NOO uh buhl REE SAWRS) a natural resource that can be replaced at the same rate at which the resource is consumed

nonrenewable resource (NAHN ri NOO uh buhl REE SAWRS) a resource that forms at a rate that is much slower than the rate at which the resource is consumed

6.6.b Students know different natural energy and material resources, including air, soil, rocks, minerals, petroleum, fresh water, wildlife, and forests, and know how to classify them as renewable or nonrenewable.

Quick Lab

Renewable or Not?

1. Gather two **paper cups,** and fill one 3/4 full with **water.**

2. Put three holes in the bottom of the second cup with a **sharpened pencil.** Make a pencil mark on the inside of the second cup about 2 cm from the bottom.

3. Hold the second cup over a **basin** or **sink.** Pour water into the second cup, and try to keep the water level even with the mark.

4. How does the rate at which you pour water into the cup relate to the water level in the cup?

5. Which part of this model represents the use of a resource? Which part represents the formation of a resource?

6. What makes a resource renewable? What makes a resource nonrenewable?

6.6.b

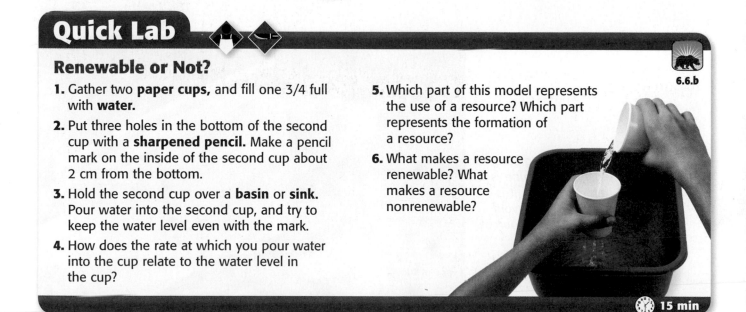

🕐 **15 min**

recycling (ree SIE kling) the process of recovering valuable or useful materials from waste or scrap
Wordwise The prefix *re-* means "again." The root *cycl-* means "circle" or "wheel."

Conserving Natural Resources

Whether the natural resources you use are renewable or nonrenewable, you should be careful how you use them. To conserve natural resources, you should try to use them only when necessary. For example, leaving the water running while brushing your teeth wastes clean water. Running the water only to rinse your toothbrush saves water that you or others may need in the future.

Conserving resources also means taking care of the resources even when you are not using them. For example, it is important to keep lakes, rivers, and other water resources free of pollution. Polluted lakes and rivers can affect the water you drink. Also, polluted water resources can harm the plants and animals, including humans, that depend on them to survive.

Energy Conservation: Reducing the Use

The energy we use to heat our homes, drive our cars, and run our computers comes from natural resources. The ways in which we choose to use energy every day affect the availability of the natural resources. Most of the natural resources that provide us with energy are nonrenewable resources. So, if we don't limit our use of energy now, the resources may not be available in the future.

As with all natural resources, conserving energy is important. You can conserve energy by being careful to use only the resources that you need. For example, turn lights off when you are not using them. And make sure the washing machine is full before you start it, as shown in **Figure 3.** You can also ride a bike, walk, or take a bus because these methods use fewer resources than a car does.

Figure 3 *Making sure the washing machine is full before running it is one way you can avoid wasting natural resources.*

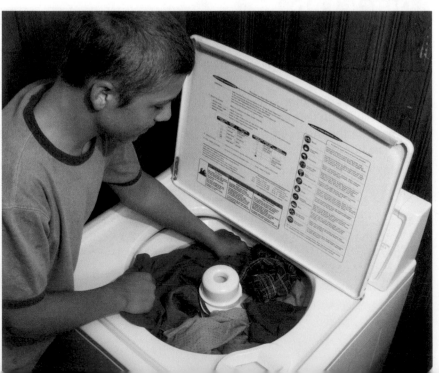

Reusing and Recycling Resources

Another way to conserve natural resources is to recycle, as shown in **Figure 4**. **Recycling** is the process of recovering materials from waste or scrap. Recycling reduces the amount of natural resources that must be obtained from Earth. For example, recycling paper reduces the number of trees that must be cut down to make new paper. Recycling also conserves energy. Energy is needed to recycle materials. But less energy is needed to recycle an aluminum can than is needed to make a new one!

Newspaper, glass, aluminum cans, some plastic packaging, and cardboard boxes can be recycled. Most plastic containers have a number on them. This number informs you what kind of plastic makes up the container. Plastic products with the numbers 1 and 2 can be recycled in most places. Check with a nearby recycling center to see what kinds of materials the center recycles.

Figure 4 *You can recycle many household items to help conserve natural resources.* **Which recyclable resources are shown in this photograph?**

Standards Check How can energy and material resources be conserved through recycling? 6.6.b

---

SECTION
Review

6.6.b

Summary

- We use natural resources such as fresh water, petroleum, and trees to make our lives easier and more comfortable.

- Renewable resources can be replaced in a relatively short time, but nonrenewable resources may take thousands or even millions of years to form.

- Natural resources can be conserved by using only what is needed, by taking care of resources, and by reusing and recycling.

Using Vocabulary

1 Write an original definition for *natural resource, recycling, renewable resource,* and *nonrenewable resource.*

Understanding Concepts

2 Summarizing How do humans use most natural resources?

3 Comparing Compare the rates at which renewable and nonrenewable resources form.

Critical Thinking

4 Applying Concepts Describe three ways you could conserve natural resources.

5 Making Inferences How can people's actions affect renewable and nonrenewable resources?

Math Skills

6 Making Calculations A faucet drips for 8.6 h, and 3.3 L of water drips out every hour. What is the total number of liters of water that drip out?

Challenge

7 Predicting Consequences An island mostly covered with trees was home to a small group of humans. The trees were a renewable resource. How might a change in the human population affect whether the trees remain a renewable resource?

Internet Resources

For a variety of links related to this chapter, go to www.scilinks.org
Topic: Renewable Resources; Nonrenewable Resources
SciLinks code: HY71291; HY71044

Rock and Mineral Resources

Key Concept Minerals and ores are important sources of materials that are used to make common objects.

What You Will Learn

- Minerals are naturally formed, crystalline solids that form in a variety of environments.
- Ore is mined to remove rocks and minerals from Earth so that the rocks and minerals can be used to make a variety of objects.

Why It Matters

Many of the objects you use every day are made from minerals.

Vocabulary

- mineral
- ore

READING STRATEGY

Graphic Organizer In your **Science Journal,** make a Comparison Table that compares metals and nonmetals. In your table, include properties of, examples of, and products made from metals and nonmetals.

▶ You use things made from minerals every day. For example, the fluoride in your toothpaste comes from the mineral fluorite. But what are minerals? Are minerals the same as rocks?

Minerals and Rocks

A **mineral** is a naturally formed, usually inorganic solid that has a crystalline structure. Minerals form in a variety of environments in Earth's crust, as shown in **Figure 1.** Different minerals form in these environments depending on the physical conditions and the chemicals present. Most minerals form very slowly. Some minerals take millions of years to form.

Rock is the natural material that makes up most of the solid part of Earth's surface. A rock may be a collection of one or more minerals. A rock can also include solid, nonmineral material such as coal or volcanic glass.

Standards Check List five ways that minerals form. 6.6.b

Figure 1 **How Minerals Form**

Evaporation of Salt Water When a body of salt water dries up, minerals such as gypsum and halite are left behind.

Metamorphism Changes in pressure, temperature, or chemical makeup that happen during *metamorphism* cause different minerals to form. These minerals include garnet, graphite, magnetite, and talc.

6.6.b Students know different natural energy and material resources, including air, soil, rocks, minerals, petroleum, fresh water, wildlife, and forests, and know how to classify them as renewable or nonrenewable.
6.6.c Students know the natural origin of the materials used to make common objects.

Characteristics of Minerals

So, what makes a mineral a mineral? Geologists use five main characteristics to identify a mineral.

- Geologists define minerals as being naturally formed. If a diamond is made in a laboratory, it is called a *synthetic diamond* to distinguish it from a naturally formed mineral.

- Minerals are also solids. So, the ice in a glacier is a mineral, but liquid water is not a mineral.

- Minerals usually form by inorganic processes. In other words, they are usually not formed by or from living things. Coal is not a mineral because it forms from the remains of plants.

- Minerals are crystals. Crystals are solids whose particles, such as atoms or ions, are arranged in repeating and regular geometric patterns. Volcanic glass is not a mineral because the atoms in glass are not arranged in any pattern. In other words, volcanic glass is not crystalline.

- Minerals have consistent chemical compositions. For example, every sample of the mineral fluorite is made of calcium and fluorine atoms. The chemical composition of minerals is what makes some of them valuable resources.

mineral (MIN uhr uhl) a natural, usually inorganic solid that has a characteristic chemical composition and an orderly internal structure

Deposition When surface water and groundwater carry dissolved materials into lakes and seas, minerals such as calcite and dolomite crystallize and sink to the sea or lake floor.

Reactions Between Hot Water and Rocks When groundwater is heated by magma, the water reacts with minerals to form a hot liquid solution. Dissolved metals and other elements crystallize out of the hot fluid to form new minerals. Gold, copper, sulfur, pyrite, and galena form this way.

Cooling of Plutons As magma rises upward through the crust, the magma sometimes stops moving before it reaches the surface. As the magma cools slowly, mineral crystals form. Eventually, the entire magma body solidifies to form a *pluton*. Mica, feldspar, and quartz are some of the minerals that form this way.

ore (AWR) a natural material whose concentration of economically valuable minerals is high enough for the material to be mined profitably

Mining

Many kinds of rocks and minerals are mined from the ground so they can be made into objects we need. Geologists use the term **ore** to describe a deposit that is large enough and has enough of the desired material to be mined for profit. Rocks and minerals are removed from the ground by one of two methods—surface mining or subsurface mining. The method miners choose depends on how close to the surface the ore is located.

Standards Check Why do we mine rocks and minerals? 6.6.c

Surface Mining

If ore is found at or near the surface of Earth, surface mining is used to remove the ore. Types of surface mines include open-pit mines, quarries, and strip mines.

Open-pit mining is used to remove large, near-surface deposits of valuable minerals such as gold and copper. As shown in **Figure 2,** ore is mined from the top down in an open-pit mine. Explosives are often used to break up the overlying rock and the ore. The ore is then loaded into haul trucks and transported from the mine for processing. Quarries are open pits that are used to mine building stone, crushed rock, sand, and gravel. Coal that is near the surface is removed by surface coal mining. Surface coal mining is sometimes known as *strip mining* because the coal is removed in strips that may be 50 m wide and as long as 1 km.

Figure 2 *In open-pit mines, the ore is mined downward in layers. The stair-step excavation of the walls keeps the sides of the mine from collapsing. Giant haul trucks (inset) are used to transport ore from the mine.*

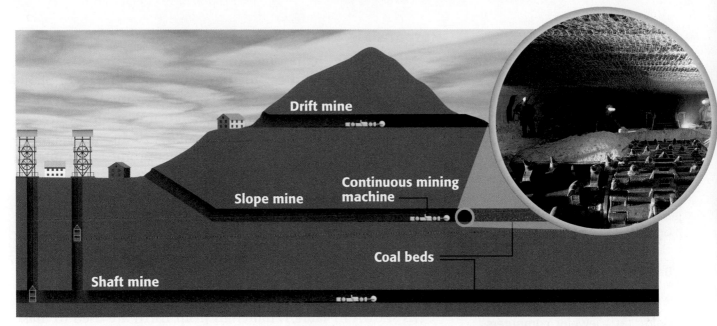

Subsurface Mining

Subsurface mines are used when ore is too deep within Earth to be surface mined. As shown in **Figure 3,** subsurface mining requires that tunnels be dug into the ground horizontally or at an angle. If a mineral deposit extends deep within Earth, however, a vertical shaft is sunk. This shaft may connect tunnels that intersect the ore at different levels. Iron, coal, and salt can be mined in subsurface mines.

Figure 3 *In subsurface mining, machines such as continuous mining machines (inset) are used to extract ore and load it onto conveyors or shuttle cars.*

Quick Lab

Chocolate Ore

Materials from Earth are mined only if there are ore deposits concentrated enough to make the mining profitable. This activity demonstrates how miners find the concentration of an ore.

6.6.c

▶ Try It!

1. Gather a **chocolate chip cookie** and some "mining tools" such as **paper clips** and **toothpicks.**

2. Determine the mass of your whole cookie on a **laboratory balance.** Record the mass.

3. Use your mining tools to mine the chocolate out of your cookie by separating the cookie from the chocolate chips.

4. Collect all of the chocolate chips from your cookie, and determine the total mass of the chocolate by using the balance.

▶ Think About It!

5. Calculate the percentage of chocolate ore in your cookie by dividing the mass of the chocolate by the mass of the whole cookie and multiplying the result by 100.

6. Compare your percentage of chocolate ore with the results of your classmates. Are some cookies richer in chocolate ore than others are?

7. What determines whether a deposit of a natural material is an ore? Did your cookie contain enough chocolate to be considered chocolate ore? Explain your answer.

 30 min

Table 1	Common Uses of Minerals and Rocks
Material	**Uses**
Copper	electrical wire, plumbing, coins
Diamond	jewelry, cutting tools, drill bits
Galena	lead in batteries, ammunition
Bauxite	aluminum cans, foil, appliances, utensils
Gold	jewelry, computers, spacecraft, dentistry
Gypsum	wallboards, plaster, cement
Halite	salt for nutrition, highway de-icer, water softener
Quartz	glass, silicon for computer chips
Silver	photography, electronic products, jewelry
Sphalerite	zinc for jet aircraft, spacecraft, paints

Responsible Mining

Mining gives us resources we need, but it may also create problems. Mining can destroy or disturb the habitats of plants and animals. Also, waste products from a mine may get into water sources and pollute surface water and groundwater.

The harmful effects of mining can be reduced by returning the land to its original state when mining is completed. The process by which land used for mining is returned to its original state or better is called *reclamation*. Reclamation of land used for mining has been required by law since the mid-1970s. Another way to reduce the harmful effects of mining is to reduce our need for the resources being mined.

Making Common Objects

As shown in **Table 1,** materials from Earth are used to make many common objects. Some minerals, such as diamonds, can be used as they are. But most materials, such as bauxite, must be processed. Bauxite is used to produce the metal aluminum.

Metals

Some minerals or products obtained from minerals are metals. Metals have shiny surfaces, are opaque to light, and are good conductors of heat and electricity. Some metals and mixtures of metals are strong and do not rust. Other metals can be pounded or pressed into different shapes or stretched thinly without breaking. These properties make metals useful in aircraft, automobiles, computers, and spacecraft. **Figure 4** shows some parts of a bicycle that are made from metals.

Figure 4 **Some Materials Used in the Parts of a Bicycle**

Handlebars
titanium from ilmenite

Frame
aluminum from bauxite

Spokes
iron from magnetite

Pedals
beryllium from beryl

Nonmetals

Other minerals and materials are nonmetals. Nonmetals have shiny or dull surfaces, may be translucent to light, and are good insulators of heat and electricity. Nonmetallic minerals are some of the most widely used minerals. For example, calcite is a major component of cement. Cement is used in roads, buildings, bridges, and other structures. Sand is a source of silica, which has uses that range from making glass to producing computer chips. The mineral gypsum is shown in **Figure 5.** Gypsum is used to make fertilizer, plaster board for construction, and plaster of Paris.

Standards Check List two nonmetallic minerals and a common object that can be made from each of the minerals. 6.6.c

Figure 5 *This gypsum rose is one form of the mineral gypsum.*

SECTION Review

6.6.b, 6.6.c

Summary

- A mineral is a naturally formed, inorganic solid that has a definite crystalline structure and a consistent chemical composition.

- Environments in which minerals form may be located at or near Earth's surface or deep below the surface.

- Two types of mining are surface mining and subsurface mining.

- Two ways to reduce the harmful effects of mining are through the reclamation of mined land and the recycling of mineral products.

- Both metals and nonmetals are used to make common objects.

Using Vocabulary

1. Write an original definition for *mineral* and *ore.*

Understanding Concepts

2. **Identifying** What are five things that must be true in order for a substance to be considered a mineral?

3. **Describing** Are minerals renewable resources or nonrenewable resources?

4. **Comparing** What are the two main types of mining, and how do they differ?

5. **Listing** List three metals, and name a common object made from each metal.

Critical Thinking

6. **Making Inferences** Name two minerals that might be found at the site of an ancient ocean.

7. **Analyzing Ideas** How does reclamation protect the environment around a mine?

8. **Applying Concepts** How does the recycling of mineral products reduce the costs of manufacturing objects from minerals?

Math Skills

9. **Making Calculations** A copper mine has removed 120,000 metric tons of earth from the mine in a week. If the copper ore at the mine contains 0.7% copper, how much copper was mined during this time?

Challenge

10. **Making Inferences** A variety of economic and technological factors determine whether a rock or mineral deposit is considered an ore. Name two factors that could influence whether a deposit is considered an ore. Explain your answers.

Internet Resources

For a variety of links related to this chapter, go to www.scilinks.org
Topic: Mining Minerals
SciLinks code: HY70968

Using Material Resources

Key Concept A variety of natural resources are used to make common objects.

▶ Where do you get things you need, such as food and clothing? You may say they come from a store. But where does the store get the things it sells? All of the objects that you need to live come from Earth itself.

Resources from Earth

Earth's resources can be divided into energy resources and material resources. Energy resources are natural resources that humans use to generate energy. **Material resources** are natural resources that humans use to make objects or that are consumed as food and drink. These resources come from Earth's atmosphere, crust, and oceans and from the organisms that live on Earth.

Resources from the Atmosphere

Perhaps the most valuable resource in the atmosphere is the oxygen required for plant and animal life. Oxygen is also used to burn rocket fuel, as shown in **Figure 1.** Other valuable chemicals are found in Earth's air. Nitrogen from the atmosphere is used as a fertilizer for agricultural plant growth. Argon is an atmospheric gas that is used inside light bulbs. Argon keeps the glowing filament in the light bulb from burning up.

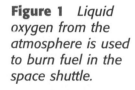

6.6.b Students know different natural energy and material resources, including air, soil, rocks, minerals, petroleum, fresh water, wildlife, and forests, and know how to classify them as renewable or nonrenewable.
6.6.c Students know the natural origin of the materials used to make common objects.

Figure 1 *Liquid oxygen from the atmosphere is used to burn fuel in the space shuttle.*

Figure 2 **A Mineral Resource: Salt from Solar Evaporation**

❶ Ocean water contains dissolved salt. Most of this salt is sodium chloride. Sodium chloride is also called halite *and* table salt.

❷ Ocean water is held in ponds. The water evaporates and leaves behind the salt.

❸ Salt is used to flavor and preserve food, to manufacture other chemicals, and to clear ice from roads.

Rock and Mineral Resources

Minerals ranging from common sand to rare elements such as gold and platinum are used to make objects that we use daily. Earth materials are used for construction and other industrial purposes. Iron is used to make steel that serves as the framework for large buildings. Aluminum provides food and beverage packaging but is used in larger quantities to build airplanes. Copper wiring allows electricity to be distributed efficiently. Gold is used in small quantities in computers and other electronic products. Platinum serves an essential environmental role in catalytic converters that reduce car exhaust emissions. Salt can be harvested from sea water, as shown in **Figure 2.** In addition to its use on food, salt serves as a source of chlorine for water treatment and for other industrial processes.

Petroleum

A liquid mixture of complex hydrocarbons that is found in Earth's crust is called **petroleum.** You may think of petroleum as a resource that is used to provide gasoline and other fuels. But petroleum is also the raw material for other products. Some compounds in petroleum are the source of products such as waxes, tar, and asphalt. Petroleum is also the raw material for the manufacture of various types of polymers.

Polymers—sometimes called *plastics*—are made from chemicals that are separated out of petroleum. Polymers are used to make materials such as clothing and pipes for plumbing. **Figure 3** shows some of the many products that are made of polymers from petroleum.

Standards Check How is petroleum used as a material resource?
🐻 6.6.c

material resource (muh TIR ee uhl REE SAWRS) a natural resource that humans use to make objects or to consume as food and drink

petroleum (puh TROH lee uhm) a liquid mixture of complex hydrocarbon compounds; used widely as a fuel source
Wordwise The root *petr-* means "rock." Another example is *petrify.*

Figure 3 *This bicyclist is using a helmet, a watch, a bicycle, gloves, and clothing that are made partly or entirely from petroleum.*

Figure 4 **Meeting Human Needs with Natural Resources**

Some objects, such as sweaters, can be made from a single natural resource. A sweater can be made from wool or cotton or synthetic fiber.

Synthetic fiber comes from petroleum.

Cotton comes from plants.

Wool comes from sheep.

Other objects, such as houses, are made from a combination of different natural resources.

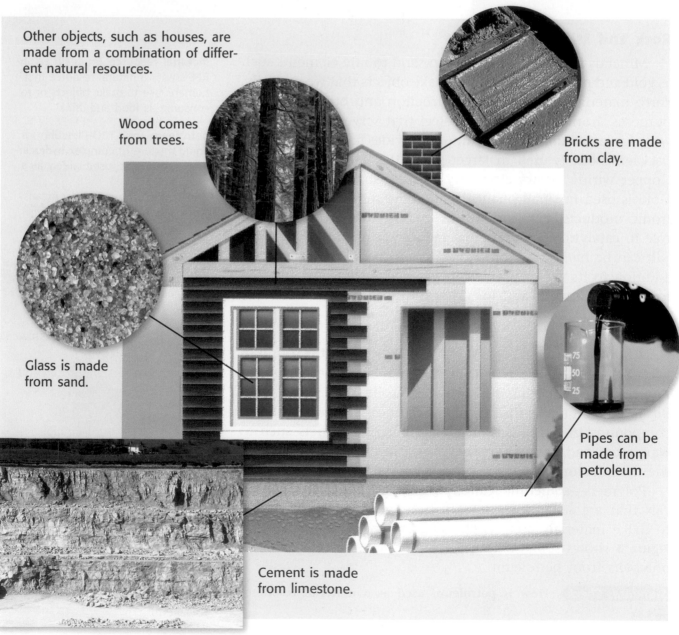

Wood comes from trees.

Bricks are made from clay.

Glass is made from sand.

Pipes can be made from petroleum.

Cement is made from limestone.

Resources from Living Things

Many material resources that we use are provided by living things, such as trees in the forest. Resources from living things can be combined with resources from Earth to make products we need. Some of these products are shown in **Figure 4.**

Plant Resources

Plants store energy as sugars and starches in seeds, nuts, fruits, and roots. Humans harvest and eat plants to get this stored energy. Modern agriculture produces many kinds of plants that provide us with food and drink. Humans also grow food for domesticated animals.

Some plants, such as cotton, produce fibers that can be woven into cloth or braided into ropes or baskets. Trees supply fruit and nut crops, as well as wood for lumber, paper, and fuel. The sap of some trees may be used to make products ranging from rubber, shown in **Figure 5,** to maple syrup. Edible oils are produced from many plants.

Standards Check Name some common objects that are made from plant resources. 6.6.c

Animal Resources

In some parts of the world, animals provide transportation for humans and cargo. Animals help farmers till soil for planting crops. Animals also provide meat, leather, and dairy and egg products. Fibers for clothing are supplied by animals such as sheep, goats, and llamas. And animal wastes are a source of crop fertilizers and cooking fuel for some societies.

INTERNET ACTIVITY

My New Material
Can you think of a new and useful material? Create a new substance, and describe its properties. Go to **go.hrw.com,** and type in the keyword HY7MATW.

Quick Lab

Products from Plants   6.6.c

1. Mix **1 cup sawdust, 1/2 cup flour, 1 TBSP liquid starch,** and **1 cup water** in a **small bowl.** The dough should be fairly stiff, but if it is too dry, add more water.

2. Make an object with your dough, and set it aside to dry for 2 or 3 days. After it is dry, use **sandpaper** to smooth the surface.

3. What is the natural origin of the materials you used to make your object? Are these resources renewable or nonrenewable?

4. What other objects can you name that are made from the materials used here?

⏱ **20 min/day for 2 days**

Figure 5 *Rubber trees are tapped to collect the sap from which rubber is made. Rubber can be used to make tires, although some tires now contain synthetic rubber made from petroleum.*

Figure 6 The Production of Paper

Trees to Wood Trees are cut to obtain one of the raw materials needed.

Wood to Chips Wood is cut into small chips.

Chips to Pulp Wood chips are made smaller and mixed with water and other ingredients to form pulp.

Pulp to Paper Pulp is spread out, pressed, and dried to form paper, which is collected on rolls.

Paper Products Paper is made into many kinds of products.

Recycling

The Costs of Material Resources

The cost of using natural resources is related to the cost of extracting them from rock, water, or the atmosphere. Other costs include those for waste management, processing, packaging, transport, and marketing. Plant and animal resources may have additional costs related to planting, feeding, fertilization, irrigation, and pest control. And the effect of resource use on the environment is a different kind of cost.

Economic Costs

The basic requirement for commercial products is that the total cost of making a product must be less than the price that a buyer is willing to pay for it.

Steps in the manufacture of paper are shown in **Figure 6.** Paper is made mainly from wood pulp. High-purity clays and other ingredients are sometimes added. At each step in the paper making process, there are costs for human labor and safety, for the materials used, and for the energy needed. All of these costs will be added together to determine how much the manufacturer will charge for the finished paper. If a material resource becomes too expensive to obtain, then a cheaper resource must be used instead.

Environmental Costs

The cost of acquiring objects is sometimes more than what is reflected in the price of the object at the store. The price of paper at the store includes the economic costs of making the paper. But does the price take into account the environmental cost of the paper production? Harvesting trees for paper may destroy old-growth forests or at least disrupt local habitats. The manufacturing process may pollute a nearby river or the atmosphere.

If a paper manufacturer installs pollution-control devices in the paper factory, that cost will be added to the monetary cost of making the paper. The price of the paper in the store will increase to reflect the increased cost of manufacturing. Some communities pass laws that require environmental protection procedures. These laws might require reduced emission of pollutants, reclamation of mined land, or the replanting of harvested trees.

Standards Check What are some of the environmental costs of using material resources? 6.6.c

Using Resources Wisely

Reusing and recycling, as shown in **Figure 7,** help reduce the demand for some new resources. But the use of many material resources will continue to increase as the world's population increases. The economic cost of resources is sometimes reduced by improved manufacturing efficiency and by the use of new technologies. The environmental cost of using resources can also be reduced. Resources can be obtained more carefully. Land and habitats that have been damaged by mining and by the harvesting of resources can be restored. In some cases, lowering the environmental costs of using resources costs money. Communities must decide how to balance these factors as they use resources.

Figure 7 *These cubes are made of used metal products that have been compacted and are being sent to a recycling plant.*

SECTION
Review

 6.6.b, 6.6.c

Summary

- Resources from Earth include gases from the atmosphere and rocks, minerals, and petroleum from Earth's crust.

- Living things provide humans with materials, such as food, clothing, and shelter.

- Using natural resources involves both economic and environmental costs.

- Reducing the environmental cost of using resources sometimes involves increasing the economic cost.

Using Vocabulary

1 Write an original definition for *material resource* and *petroleum.*

Understanding Concepts

2 **Listing** What are three resources that can be obtained from the atmosphere? How are these resources used?

3 **Describing** Explain how petroleum is used to make common objects.

4 **Identifying** Give three examples of common objects that are made from plant resources.

Critical Thinking

5 **Analyzing Relationships** Why does protecting the environment sometimes result in an increased price in the store for a product?

6 **Expressing Opinions** Explain why you think it is or is not important to consider environmental costs when determining the price of manufactured materials.

7 **Applying Concepts** List five material resources. List whether they are renewable or nonrenewable. Explain your answers.

Math Skills

8 **Making Calculations** In 1990, world rice production was 350 million tons. In 1999, it had risen to 400 million tons. What was the percentage increase in world rice production between 1990 and 1999?

Challenge

9 **Analyzing Processes** Which energy and material resources are used to make new paper? Which energy and material resources are used to make paper from recycled fiber? Do you think it makes sense to recycle paper? Explain your answer.

Internet Resources

For a variety of links related to this chapter, go to www.scilinks.org

Topic: Natural Resources; Recycling
SciLinks code: HY71015; HY71277

Skills Practice Lab

Categorize common materials left over after lunch.

Compute the amounts in each category, and determine the percentage of the total represented by each category.

Recommend ways your school can conserve natural resources based on the data you collect and organize in this activity.

MATERIALS

- bags, plastic
- balance, triple beam or electronic
- calculator
- gloves, protective, plastic
- paper towels

SAFETY

6.6.b Students know different natural energy and material resources, including air, soil, rocks, minerals, petroleum, fresh water, wildlife, and forests, and know how to classify them as renewable or nonrenewable.
6.6.c Students know the natural origin of the materials used to make common objects.

Investigation and Experimentation
6.7.b Select and use appropriate tools and technology (including calculators, computers, balances, spring scales, microscopes, and binoculars) to perform tests, collect data, and display data.

Natural Resources Used at Lunch

Many materials in addition to food are involved in the packaging and delivery of lunches. These materials are made from a variety of natural resources. In this activity, you will determine what types of resources are used in this way at your school.

Ask a Question

1 What percentage of the materials left over after lunch come from each of the following categories: paper and wood products, plastic, metal, and glass?

Form a Hypothesis

2 Write a hypothesis that is a possible answer to the question above. Explain your reasoning.

Test the Hypothesis

3 Collect all of your lunch waste on the day of the lab activity or the day before the lab activity, depending on whether your class meets before or after lunch. Put all of your lunch waste in a plastic bag, including wrappers, napkins, straws, and disposable trays.

Data for Leftover Lunch Materials

Category	Total mass for lab group	Average mass per student	Percentage of total waste	Notes
Paper and wood				
Plastic				
Metal				
Glass				
Total			100	

DO NOT WRITE IN BOOK

4 Working in groups of three or four students, separate your lunch waste onto paper towels in the following categories: paper and wood, plastic, metal, and glass.

5 Determine the mass of the waste in each category for the entire group. Create a data table similar to the one above, and record the masses.

6 Use the equation below to calculate for each category the average mass of solid waste per student. Use the total mass of waste for each category in your calculation. Record the results in your table.

$$\frac{total\ mass\ in\ category}{number\ of\ students} = \begin{array}{l} average\ mass\ in \\ category\ per\ student \end{array}$$

7 Use the equation below to calculate the percentage of the total waste that is represented by each category. Record the results in your table.

$$\left(\frac{total\ mass\ of\ category}{\begin{array}{c} total\ mass\ for \\ all\ categories \end{array}} \right) \times 100 = \begin{array}{l} percentage\ of \\ total\ waste \end{array}$$

Analyze the Results

8 **Examining Data** Compare your group's percentages for each category with the results from other groups in the class. How and why are the data similar or different?

9 **Classifying** In the "Notes" column of your table, list the natural origin of the materials in each category. List whether each category of materials is made from renewable or nonrenewable resources.

Draw Conclusions

10 **Interpreting Information** What percentage of these lunch leftover materials came from renewable resources? What percentage came from nonrenewable resources?

11 **Making Predictions** Find the mass of leftover materials at your school in each category. Your calculations should be done to find the mass generated each day. You may need to ask your teacher how many students, teachers, and staff members there are at your school.

Big Idea Question

12 **Applying Conclusions** You have been asked to recommend to your school some steps the school can take to conserve material resources. Describe at least two things you would recommend. Base your recommendations on the data you have collected during this activity and on what you know about the material resources you have been studying.

Science Skills Activity

Investigation and Experimentation
6.7.f Read a topographic map and a geologic map for evidence provided on the maps and construct and interpret a simple scale map.

Reading a Geologic Map

▶ Tutorial

All Earth scientists use geologic maps. Geologic maps show the types of rocks found at the surface in a given area. They also show the locations of geologic structures such as faults and folds. The following list will help you read geologic maps.

① Geologic maps are made on a base map that shows things such as topography, roads, and rivers. These features are usually shown in light colors or as gray lines.

② Rock of the same age and type is called a *rock unit*. On geologic maps, each rock unit is represented by a different color. Different units that are similar in age are often represented by different shades of the same color.

③ Each rock unit is identified on a geologic map by a set of letters:
- Capital letters indicate the age of the rock (for example, Q = Quaternary and T = Tertiary).
- Lowercase letters indicate the type of rock (for example, al = alluvium, v = volcanic, and i = intrusive).

④ Other geologic features are indicated on the map by special symbols:
- Faults are shown as thick black lines.
- Contacts between rock units are shown as thin black lines.

▶ You Try It!

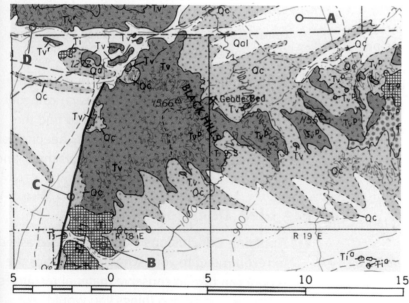

Sedimentary Rocks

| Qal | Alluvium (loose sediment) |

| Qc | Pleistocene nonmarine |

Igneous Rocks

Tertiary intrusive rocks: Ti^r–rhyollite; Ti^a–andesite Ti^b–basalt

Tertiary volcanic: Tv^r–rhyolite; Tv^a–andesite; Tv^b–basalt; Tv^p–pyroclastic rocks

① How many rock units are shown in this map? How many geologic time periods are represented?

② Determine the age and the type of rock at point A and the age and the type of rock at point B.

③ What feature is represented by line C? What feature is represented by line D?

④ Find the Geode Bed on the map. If you wanted to find other areas rich in geodes, what type and age of rock would you look for?

Chapter Summary

The Big Idea
Material resources differ in amounts, distribution, usefulness, and the time required for their formation.

Section

Vocabulary

❶ Natural Resources

Key Concept Different energy and material resources can be classified as renewable or nonrenewable.

- Earth's resources can be classified as renewable or nonrenewable.
- Resources can be conserved by reducing the amount of resources we use and by reusing or recycling them.

Petroleum is a nonrenewable energy and material resource.

natural resource p. 128
renewable resource p. 129
nonrenewable resource p. 129
recycling p. 131

❷ Rock and Mineral Resources

Key Concept Minerals and ores are important sources of materials that are used to make common objects.

- Minerals are naturally formed, crystalline solids that form in a variety of environments.
- Ore is mined to remove rocks and minerals from Earth so that the rocks and minerals can be used to make a variety of objects.

Open-pit mines are one way that ore is removed from Earth.

mineral p. 132
ore p. 134

❸ Using Material Resources

Key Concept A variety of natural resources are used to make common objects.

- Natural resources come from the atmosphere, from Earth's crust, from Earth's oceans, and from living things.
- Both environmental and economic factors must be considered when determining the cost of using natural resources.

Rubber is one of the common objects made from plant material.

material resource p. 138
petroleum p. 139

Chapter Review

6.6.b, 6.6.c

Two-Panel Flip Chart Review the FoldNote that you created at the beginning of the chapter. Add to or correct the FoldNote based on what you have learned.

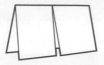

Using Vocabulary

1 **Academic Vocabulary** In the sentence "A mining company will consider the distribution of coal when deciding how to mine the coal," what does the word *distribution* mean?

2 Write an original definition for *natural resource* and *material resource.*

For each pair of terms, explain how the meanings of the terms differ.

3 *mineral* and *ore*

4 *renewable resource* and *nonrenewable resource*

Understanding Concepts

Multiple Choice

5 Which of the following resources is a renewable resource?
  a. coal
  b. trees
  c. petroleum
  d. iron ore

6 Which of the following resources is a nonrenewable resource?
  a. copper ore
  b. trees
  c. fresh water
  d. wildlife

7 The process by which land used for mining is returned to its original state is called
  a. recycling.
  b. regeneration.
  c. reclamation.
  d. renovation.

8 Natural resources can be conserved by
  a. using only what is needed.
  b. protecting the quality of resources such as air and water.
  c. reusing and recycling.
  d. All of the above

9 Which of the following can be made from metals?
  a. plaster board
  b. bicycle frames
  c. glass
  d. All of the above

10 Which of the following can be made from trees?
  a. rubber
  b. paper
  c. lumber
  d. All of the above

Short Answer

11 **Listing** Describe three ways that humans use natural resources.

12 **Summarizing** Explain the five characteristics of a mineral.

13 **Describing** Describe two environments in which minerals form. List a mineral that is formed in each environment.

14 **Listing** List two common objects for which the natural origin is a metal and two common objects for which the natural origin is a nonmetal.

15 **Listing** List two common objects for which the natural origin is a plant resource and two common objects for which the natural origin is an animal resource.

16 **Comparing** Compare surface and subsurface mining.

17 **Identifying** Identify two common objects that are made from petroleum.

Writing Skills

18 **Outlining Topics** Outline the process of making paper from trees.

Critical Thinking

19 Concept Mapping Use the following terms to create a concept map: *natural resources, renewable resources, nonrenewable resources, material resources, petroleum, iron, trees,* and *energy resources.*

20 Evaluating Assumptions Why do we need to conserve renewable resources even though they can be replaced?

21 Applying Concepts Describe the different ways that you can conserve natural resources at home.

22 Applying Concepts Could a resource that was once renewable become nonrenewable? Explain your answer.

INTERPRETING GRAPHICS Use the graph below to answer the next three questions.

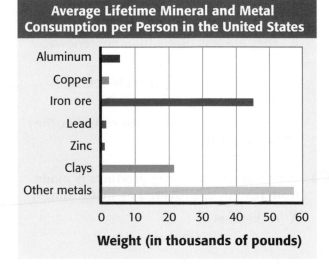

Average Lifetime Mineral and Metal Consumption per Person in the United States

Weight (in thousands of pounds)

23 Evaluating Data Which resource is used the most? Which resource is used the least?

24 Applying Concepts Are the resources shown in the graph energy resources or material resources? Explain your answer.

25 Making Inferences Explain how the practice of recycling could affect the information on the graph for aluminum and copper.

26 Making Comparisons Explain the difference between metals and nonmetals. Give examples of each.

27 Applying Concepts Give examples of environmental concerns that would be taken into account by a mining company as it creates a reclamation plan for an open-pit mine.

28 Identifying Relationships Explain why the environmental costs of producing paper may or may not be reflected in the price of the paper in the store.

29 Predicting Consequences Imagine that a nonrenewable material resource used to make computers begins to run out. Devise two different plans to address the shortage. Explain how each plan would work and how each plan might affect the price of computers.

Math Skills

INTERPRETING GRAPHICS Use the table below to answer the next three questions.

Mass of Paper Products		
Product	**Tons produced**	**Percentage recycled**
Newspapers	13,620	56.4
Books	1,140	14.0
Magazines	2,260	20.8
Office papers	7,040	50.4

30 Making Calculations How many tons of all types of paper products were generated?

31 Making Calculations How many tons of newspapers were recycled?

32 Making Calculations How many total tons of paper products in all categories were recycled?

Challenge

33 Analyzing Relationships Petroleum is used to generate energy and to make common objects such as plastics. Describe how the uses of petroleum might change as petroleum becomes more scarce.

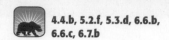

REVIEWING ACADEMIC VOCABULARY

1 Which of the following words best completes the following sentence: "Scientists must _____ the correct tools for their experiments"?

A selection

B selective

C selected

D select

2 Which of the following words means "the application of science for practical purposes"?

A science

B technology

C information

D experimentation

3 Which of the following words is closest in meaning to the word *idea*?

A hypothesis

B evidence

C concept

D prediction

4 In the sentence "Scientists conduct experiments to test new hypotheses," what does the word *conduct* mean?

A to carry out or do

B to transmit or send

C manner of action

D standard of behavior

5 Which of the following words is closest in meaning to the word *required*?

A desired

B needed

C intended

D available

REVIEWING CONCEPTS

6 Which of the following resources is nonrenewable?

A wind

B trees

C natural gas

D sunlight

7 Which of the following observations is evidence that a material is not a mineral?

A The material occurs naturally.

B The material has a crystalline structure.

C The material is inorganic.

D The material has a varied chemical composition.

8 Which of the following is true of renewable resources?

A They must be converted into nonrenewable resources.

B They are less useful than nonrenewable resources.

C Many of them can become scarce if used too quickly.

D No matter how much we conserve, they will one day be gone.

9 Which of the following products is made from resources provided by living things?

A rocket fuel

B rope

C copper wiring

D plastic

10 How does reclamation reduce the harmful effects of mining?

A by reducing the use of minerals

B by returning mines to their natural state

C by mining minerals more efficiently

D by avoiding mining in protected areas

11 Which of the following is a common way that minerals are formed?

A They are left behind when salt water evaporates.

B They are formed from plant material that collects in swamps.

C They are created by mineral manufacturers.

D They are formed when the sun's rays interact with soil.

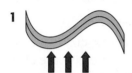

1

Water is heated by magma.

2

Hot water and metallic elements form a solution.

3

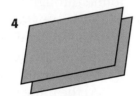

4

New minerals are formed.

12 The diagram above shows one way in which new minerals are formed. Which step is most likely missing from this process?

A The elements crystallize.

B The elements dissolve.

C The elements mix with organic compounds.

D The elements combine with other elements.

13 Which of the following costs might not be included in the price of a plastic product?

A the cost of the raw material—petroleum

B the cost of manufacturing the product

C the environmental cost of drilling for petroleum

D the cost of advertising the product

REVIEWING PRIOR LEARNING

14 What is the product of photosynthesis represented by the arrows in the diagram above?

A carbon dioxide

B carbon monoxide

C oxygen

D nitrogen

15 Which of the following statements is true of fresh water used in California?

A It is derived primarily from desalinated ocean water.

B It is a renewable resource that can be used freely.

C It will one day be gone in spite of conservation.

D It is a limited resource that should be conserved.

16 Which of the following is a physical property of minerals measured by the Mohs scale?

A hardness

B color

C ability to conduct electricity

D crystalline structure

Standards Assessment

Science in Action

Science, Technology, and Society

Gold—the State Mineral of California

Long ago, molten rock began cooling under Earth's surface. As this magma cooled, gold separated from it and solidified into grains, fingers, and leaves of gold. Some was concentrated in veins within the mineral quartz. About 200 million years later, gold was discovered in California. People from all over the world began rushing to California in 1849 to find gold and make their fortunes.

Gold is rare and beautiful and is soft enough to be formed into jewelry. It doesn't tarnish or rust, even in salt water. So, gold coins can be found even in old shipwrecks! Gold also transmits electricity. And because it doesn't corrode, gold is used for important electronic components in manufactured items such as computers, air-bag sensors, and microwave ovens.

Language Arts ACTiViTY

Research the myth of King Midas, and find out what happened that made him horrified at the sight of gold. In your **Science Journal**, write an essay about why it's important to be careful what you wish for.

Weird Science

Wieliczka Salt Mine

Imagine an underground city that is made entirely of salt. Within the city are churches, chapels, rooms of many kinds, and salt lakes. Sculptures of biblical scenes, saints, and famous historical figures carved from salt are found throughout the city. Even chandeliers of salt hang from the ceilings. Such a city is located in the Wieliczka (vie LEECH kah) Salt Mine, which is 16 km southeast of Krakow, Poland.

As the mine grew over the past 700 years, it turned into an elaborate underground city. Miners constructed chapels to patron saints so miners could pray for a safe day in the mine. Miners also developed superstitions about the mine. So, images that were meant to bring good luck were carved in salt. In 1978, the mine was added to UNESCO's list of endangered world heritage sites. Many of the sculptures in the mine have begun to dissolve because of the humidity in the air. Efforts to save the treasures in the mine from further damage were begun in 1996.

Social Studies ACTiViTY

Research some aspect of the role of salt in human history. For example, subjects might include the Saharan and Tibetan salt trade or the use of salt as a form of money in ancient Poland or Rome. Report your findings in a one-page essay. Record your work in your **Science Journal**.

Jamie Hill

The Emerald Man Jamie Hill was raised in the Brushy Mountains of North Carolina. While growing up, Hill gained firsthand knowledge of the geology of North Carolina and the fabulous green crystals that could be found in the mountains. These green crystals were emeralds. Emerald is the green variety of the silicate mineral beryl and is a valuable gemstone. Emerald crystals form in igneous rocks called *pegmatites* that form in pockets, or openings, in rock.

Since 1985, Hill has been searching for pockets containing emeralds in rock near the small town of Hiddenite, North Carolina. He has been amazingly successful. Hill has discovered some spectacular emerald crystals. The largest of these crystals weighs 858 carats and is on display at the North Carolina Museum of Natural Science. Estimates of the total value of the emeralds that Hill has discovered so far are well in the millions of dollars. Hill's discoveries have made him a celebrity, and he has appeared both on national TV and in magazines.

Math ACTiViTY

An emerald discovered by Jamie Hill in 1999 was cut into a 7.85-carat stone that sold for $64,000 per carat. What was the total value of the cut stone? Record your work in your **Science Journal.**

Internet Resources

- To learn more about careers in science, visit **www.scilinks.org** and enter the SciLinks code HY70225.
- To learn more about these Science in Action topics, visit **go.hrw.com** and type in the keyword HY7MARF.
- Check out articles related to this chapter by visiting **go.hrw.com.** Just type in the keyword HY7MARC.

Improving Comprehension

Graphic Organizers are important visual tools that can help you organize information and improve your reading comprehension. The Graphic Organizer below is called a *Venn diagram*. Instructions for creating other types of Graphic Organizers are located in the **Study Skills** section of the Appendix.

How to Make a Venn Diagram

1 Draw a diagram like the one shown below. Draw one circle for each topic. Make sure that each circle partially overlaps the other circles.

2 In each circle, write a topic that you want to compare with the topics in the other circles.

3 In the areas of the diagram where circles overlap, write the characteristics that the topics in the overlapping circles share.

4 In the areas of the diagram where circles do not overlap, write the characteristics that are unique to the topic of the particular circle.

When to Use a Venn Diagram

A Venn diagram is a useful tool for comparing two or three topics in science. A Venn diagram shows which characteristics the topics share and which characteristics are unique to each topic. Venn diagrams are ideal when you want to illustrate relationships in a pair or small group of topics. As you read, look for topics that have both shared and unique characteristics, and draw a Venn diagram that shows how the topics are related.

Fossil Fuels
- most commonly used energy source
- inexpensive
- nonrenewable
- harmful to the environment
- examples: petroleum, natural gas, and coal

- used to generate power
- limited by availability

Alternative Energy Sources
- expensive in some cases
- environmentally friendly in most cases
- renewable in most cases
- examples: fission, wind, chemical, and solar

You Try It!

This Reading Strategy can also be used within the chapter that you are about to read. Practice making your own Venn diagram as directed in the Reading Strategy for Section **1**. Record your work in your **Science Journal.**

Unpacking the Standards

The information below "unpacks" the standards by breaking them down into basic parts. The higher-level, academic vocabulary is highlighted and defined to help you understand the language of the standards. "What It Means" restates the standards as simply as possible.

California Standard	Academic Vocabulary	What It Means
6.3.b Students know that when fuel is **consumed,** most of the **energy released** becomes heat **energy.**	**consume** (kuhn SOOM) to use up **energy** (EN uhr jee) the ability to make things happen **release** (ri LEES) to set free; to let go	When fuel, such as wood, is burned, most of the energy that is given off is heat.
6.6.a Students know the **utility** of **energy sources** is determined by **factors** that are **involved** in **converting** these **sources** to useful forms and the **consequences** of the **conversion process.**	**utility** (yoo TIL uh tee) usefulness **source** (SAWRS) the thing from which something else comes **factor** (FAK tuhr) a condition or event that brings about a result **involve** (in VAHLV) to be a part of **convert** (kuhn VUHRT) to change from one form to another **consequence** (KAHN si KWENS) the effect, or result, of an action or process **conversion** (kuhn VUHR zhuhn) a change from one form or state to another **process** (PRAH SES) a set of steps, events, or changes	The usefulness of energy resources is controlled by how these resources are changed into useful forms and what happens to the resources and the environment after the resources are changed.
6.6.b Students know different natural **energy** and material **resources** including air, soil, rocks, minerals, petroleum, fresh water, wildlife, and forests, and know how to classify them as renewable or nonrenewable.	**resource** (REE SAWRS) anything that can be used to take care of a need	You must be able to identify different natural resources, such as air, soil, rocks, minerals, petroleum, fresh water, wildlife, and forests, and be able to identify whether each resource can be replaced rapidly or not.

5

Energy Resources

The Big Idea

Sources of energy differ in quantity, distribution, usefulness, and the time required for formation.

 California Standards

Focus on Earth Sciences

6.3 Heat moves in a predictable flow from warmer objects to cooler objects until all the objects are at the same temperature. (Sections 1 and 2)

6.6 Sources of energy and materials differ in amounts, distribution, usefulness, and the time required for their formation. (Sections 1 and 2)

Investigation and Experimentation

6.7 Scientific progress is made by asking meaningful questions and conducting careful investigations. (Science Skills Activity)

Math

6.2.0 Number Sense

English–Language Arts

6.2.4 Reading

6.1.0 Writing

About the Photo

There are more than 5,000 wind turbines at the Altamont Pass Wind Resource Area, located between Tracy and Livermore, California. The spinning turbines run electric generators that convert the mechanical energy of the wind into electrical energy. The turbines at Altamont generate enough electric power for about 180,000 homes.

Organize

Double Door

Before you read this chapter, create the FoldNote entitled "Double Door." Write "Fossil fuels" on one flap of the double door and "Alternative energy" on the other flap. As you read the chapter, compare the two topics, and write characteristics of each topic on the inside of the appropriate flap.

Instructions for creating FoldNotes are located in the Study Skills section on p. 615 of the Appendix.

Explore Activity

🕐 **20 min**

Spinning in the Wind

In this activity, you will observe how a mechanical device can harness the energy of moving air.

Procedure

1. Slip a piece of **wagon-wheel pasta** onto a **toothpick** axle. Make sure that the wheel spins freely.

2. Remove the wheel, and press a rim of **modeling clay** onto the wheel. Insert broken pieces of pasta around the clay rim to act as blades.

3. Test your wind turbine by blowing gently on the pasta blades. Make sure that no one is in front of you when you blow on the turbine.

4. Change your turbine design to make the wheel spin more efficiently.

5. Continue improving your turbine's design until your turbine spins as efficiently as it can.

6.6.a

Analysis

6. What caused the wind turbine to spin?

7. How did you improve the efficiency of your turbine?

8. How might a wind turbine be used to generate electrical energy?

157

SECTION 1

Fossil Fuels

Key Concept Most of the energy used by humans comes from fossil fuels, which are made up of ancient plant and animal matter that stored energy from the sun.

What You Will Learn

- Fossil fuels are important energy resources.
- Fossil fuels form slowly over very long periods of time.
- Fossil fuels are found and obtained in different ways.
- Fossil fuels are nonrenewable and create pollution when burned.

Why It Matters

Fossil fuels, such as oil and coal, provide energy that you use every day.

Vocabulary

- energy resource
- fossil fuel
- petroleum
- natural gas
- coal
- acid precipitation

READING STRATEGY

Graphic Organizer In your **Science Journal,** create a Venn Diagram that compares petroleum, natural gas, and coal.

How does a sunny day 200 million years ago relate to your life today? If you traveled to school today or used a product made of plastic, you likely used some of the energy from sunlight that warmed Earth several hundred million years ago.

The fuels that are used to run cars, planes, and factories and to generate electrical energy are energy resources. **Energy resources** are natural resources that humans use to generate energy. Most of the energy that we use comes from a group of natural resources called fossil fuels. A **fossil fuel** is a nonrenewable energy resource that forms from the remains of plants and animals that lived long ago. Petroleum, coal, and natural gas are examples of fossil fuels.

Fossil Fuels as Energy Resources

When fossil fuels are burned, they release energy. Most of the energy released is heat. Power plants and machines use that heat to produce electrical energy. Electrical energy is used to power lights, such as the lights shown in **Figure 1,** and is used in many other ways. But the use of a fossil fuel is limited by the way in which the fuel is obtained and by the availability of the fuel. It is also limited by the process in which the fuel is converted into energy and by the results of that process. Fossil fuels can be obtained and used relatively inexpensively. Thus, they are the most commonly used energy resource. However, fossil fuels are nonrenewable. Replacing fossil fuels that have been burned takes millions of years. Therefore, like other resources, fossil fuels must be conserved.

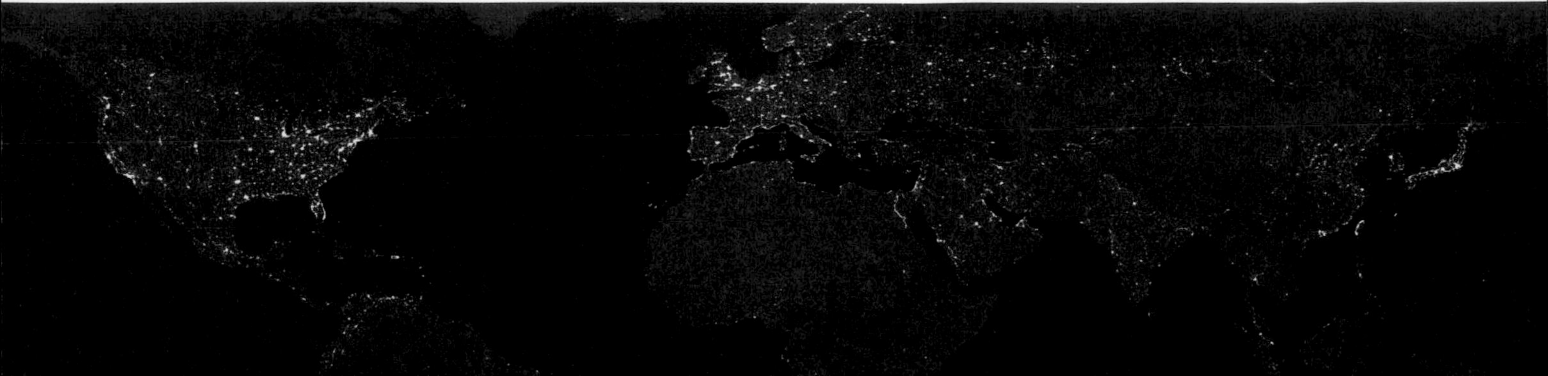

Figure 1 *Light produced from electrical energy can be seen in this composite satellite image.*

Figure 2 *This refinery uses a process called* distillation *to separate petroleum into various types of petroleum products.*

Types of Fossil Fuels

All living things contain the element carbon. Because fossil fuels form from the remains of plants and animals, all fossil fuels contain carbon, too. Most of the carbon in fossil fuels exists as hydrocarbons, which are hydrogen-carbon compounds. Fossil fuels may exist as liquids, gases, or solids.

Liquid Fossil Fuels: Petroleum

A liquid mixture of complex hydrocarbon compounds is called **petroleum.** Petroleum is commonly known as *crude oil.* Petroleum is separated into several kinds of products in refineries, such as the one shown in **Figure 2.** Examples of products separated from petroleum are gasoline, jet fuel, kerosene, diesel fuel, and fuel oil. Petroleum is also used to make plastics.

More than 40% of the world's energy comes from petroleum products. Petroleum products are the main fuel for airplanes, trains, boats, ships, and automobiles. Crude oil is so valuable that it is often called *black gold.*

Standards Check Which kind of resource is petroleum: renewable or nonrenewable? 🐻 **6.6.b**

Gaseous Fossil Fuels: Natural Gas

A gaseous mixture of hydrocarbons is called **natural gas.** Most natural gas is used for heating, but some is used for generating electrical energy. Your kitchen stove may be powered by natural gas. Some motor vehicles use natural gas as fuel. An advantage of using natural gas is that burning natural gas causes less air pollution than burning petroleum does. But natural gas is very flammable. Sometimes, gas leaks lead to fires or deadly explosions.

Methane, CH_4, is the main component of natural gas. But other components, such as butane and propane, can be separated from natural gas, too. Butane and propane are used as fuel for camp stoves and outdoor grills.

energy resource (EN uhr jee REE SAWRS) a natural resource that humans use to generate energy

fossil fuel (FAHS uhl FYOO uhl) a nonrenewable energy resource formed from the remains of organisms that lived long ago; examples include oil, coal, and natural gas

petroleum (puh TROH lee uhm) a liquid mixture of complex hydrocarbon compounds; used widely as a fuel source
 Wordwise The root *petr-* means "rock." Another example is *petrify.*

natural gas (NACH uhr uhl GAS) a mixture of gaseous hydrocarbons located under the surface of Earth, often near petroleum deposits; used as a fuel

6.3.b Students know that when fuel is consumed, most of the energy released becomes heat energy.
6.6.a Students know the utility of energy sources is determined by factors that are involved in converting these sources to useful forms and the consequences of the conversion process.
6.6.b Students know different natural energy and material resources, including air, soil, rocks, minerals, petroleum, fresh water, wildlife, and forests, and know how to classify them as renewable or nonrenewable.

Figure 3 *The photo at right shows a turbine at the old Folsom coal-fired power plant near Sacramento. The map above shows the locations of coal-fired power plants throughout California.*

coal (KOHL) a fossil fuel that forms underground from partially decomposed plant material

Solid Fossil Fuels: Coal

The solid fossil fuel that humans use most is coal. **Coal** is a fossil fuel that forms underground from partially decomposed plant material. Coal was once the major source of energy in the United States. When fossil fuels, including coal, are burned, most of the energy released is heat. As a result, people burned coal in stoves to heat their homes. They also used coal in transportation. Many trains in the 1800s and early 1900s were powered by coal-burning steam locomotives.

As cleaner energy resources became available, people reduced their use of coal. They began to use coal less because burning coal produces large amounts of air pollution. Now, people use forms of transportation that use petroleum products instead of coal as fuel. In the United States, coal is now rarely used as fuel for heating. However, many power plants burn coal for heat to turn turbines that generate electrical energy. These power plants use pollution controls such as scrubbers and filters to prevent air pollution from the burning of coal. The power plant in **Figure 3** burned coal to produce electricity.

Standards Check Why is coal a useful fuel for heating? 6.3.b

Quick Lab

Rock Sponge

1. Place **samples of sandstone, limestone, and shale** in separate **Petri dishes.**

2. Place **five drops of light machine oil** on each rock sample.

3. Use a **stopwatch** to record the time required for the oil to be absorbed by each rock sample.

6.6.a

4. Which rock sample absorbed the oil fastest? Why do you think this is?

5. Using what you have learned, describe a property of rock that allows fossil fuels to be easily removed from reservoir rock.

 15 min

How Do Fossil Fuels Form?

All fossil fuels form from the buried remains of ancient organisms. But fossil fuels differ in the ways in which they form and in the kinds of organisms from which they form.

Formation of Petroleum and Natural Gas

Petroleum and natural gas form mainly from the remains of microscopic sea organisms. When these organisms die, their remains settle on the ocean floor. There, the remains are buried in sediment. Over time, the sediment is compacted and slowly becomes rock. Through physical and chemical changes over millions of years, the remains of the organisms become petroleum and natural gas. Gradually, more rocks form above the rocks that contain the fossil fuels. Under the pressure of overlying rocks and sediments, the fossil fuels can move through permeable rocks. *Permeable rocks* are rocks through which fluids, such as petroleum and gas, can move. As **Figure 4** shows, these permeable rocks become reservoirs that hold petroleum and natural gas.

The formation of petroleum and natural gas is an ongoing process. Part of the remains of today's sea life will become petroleum and natural gas millions of years from now.

Renewable Energy Resources

The world's need for energy is increasing daily. Write a persuasive essay about the use of renewable energy resources. Go to **go.hrw.com,** and type in the keyword HY7ENRW.

Figure 4 *Petroleum and gas move through permeable rock. Eventually, these fuels collect in reservoirs. Rocks that are folded upward are excellent fossil-fuel traps.*

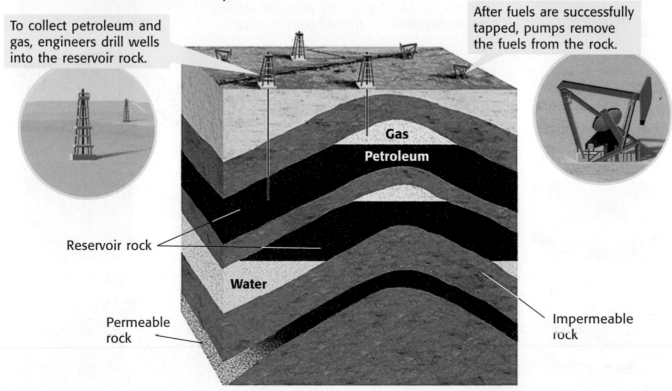

To collect petroleum and gas, engineers drill wells into the reservoir rock.

After fuels are successfully tapped, pumps remove the fuels from the rock.

Gas

Petroleum

Reservoir rock

Water

Permeable rock

Impermeable rock

Formation of Coal

Coal forms underground over millions of years when pressure and heat cause changes in the remains of swamp plants. When these plants die, they sink to the bottom of the swamp. If they do not decay completely, coal formation may begin. The stages of the formation of coal are shown in **Figure 5.**

The first step in the formation of coal is the change of plant remains into peat. Peat is brown, crumbly matter made mostly of plant material and water. Peat is not coal. In some parts of the world, peat is dried and burned for heat or as fuel. If the peat is buried by sediment, pressure and heat increase and the peat is converted into coal. The pressure and heat force water and gases out of the coal. As a result, the coal becomes harder, and its carbon content increases. The amount of heat and pressure determines the type of coal that forms. Lignite forms first, followed by bituminous coal and, finally, anthracite. The formation of coal can stop at any stage of the process.

Today, all three types of coal are mined throughout the world. The greater the carbon content of the coal, the more cleanly the coal burns. But when burned, all types of coal release heat and pollute the air.

Figure 5 | Formation of Coal

Stage 1: Formation of Peat
Sunken swamp plants that have not decayed completely can change into peat. About 60% of an average sample of dried peat is carbon.

Stage 2: Formation of Lignite
If sediment buries the peat, pressure and temperature increase. The peat slowly changes into a type of coal called *lignite.* Lignite is harder than peat, and about 70% of an average sample of lignite is carbon.

Stage 3: Formation of Bituminous Coal
If more sediment is added, pressure and temperature force more water and gases out of the lignite. Lignite slowly changes into bituminous coal. About 80% of an average sample of bituminous coal is carbon.

Stage 4: Formation of Anthracite
If more sediment accumulates, temperature and pressure continue to increase. Bituminous coal slowly changes into anthracite. Anthracite is the hardest type of coal. About 90% of an average sample of anthracite is carbon.

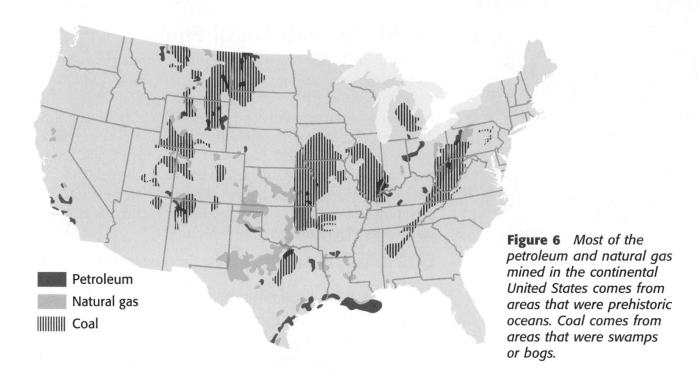

Petroleum
Natural gas
||||||| Coal

Figure 6 *Most of the petroleum and natural gas mined in the continental United States comes from areas that were prehistoric oceans. Coal comes from areas that were swamps or bogs.*

Where Fossil Fuels Are Found

Fossil fuels are found in many parts of the world. Some fossil fuels are found on land. Other fossil fuels are found beneath the ocean in Earth's crust. As **Figure 6** shows, the United States has large reserves of petroleum, natural gas, and coal. Despite its large reserves of petroleum, the United States imports petroleum. More than one-half of the petroleum used by the United States is imported from the Middle East, South America, Africa, Canada, and Mexico.

How Fossil Fuels Are Obtained

Humans use several methods to remove fossil fuels from Earth's crust. The method that is used to remove a fuel depends on the type of fuel and the location of the fuel. People remove petroleum and natural gas from the ground by drilling wells into rock that contains these resources. Oil wells exist on land and in the ocean. For offshore drilling, engineers mount drills on platforms that are secured to the ocean floor or that float at the ocean's surface. **Figure 7** shows an offshore oil rig.

People obtain coal either by mining deep beneath Earth's surface or by surface mining. Surface mining, or strip mining, is the removal of soil and surface rock to reveal underlying coal deposits.

Standards Check How are natural gas and petroleum removed from the ground? 🐻 **6.6.a**

Figure 7 *Large oil rigs, some of which are more than 300 m tall, operate offshore in many places, such as the Gulf of Mexico and the North Sea.*

1994

1935

Figure 8 *Notice how this statue looked before the effects of acid precipitation.*

acid precipitation (AS id pree SIP uh TAY shuhn) rain, sleet, or snow that contains a high concentration of acids

Problems with Fossil Fuels

Fossil fuels provide the energy that humans need. But the methods of obtaining and using these fuels can affect the environment negatively. For example, when coal is burned without pollution controls, sulfur dioxide is released. Sulfur dioxide combines with moisture in the air to produce sulfuric acid. Sulfuric acid is one of the acids in acid precipitation. **Acid precipitation** is rain, sleet, or snow that has a high concentration of acids, often because of air pollutants. Acid precipitation negatively affects wildlife, plants, buildings, and statues, as **Figure 8** shows.

Standards Check How can burning fossil fuels affect rain? 6.6.a

Problems with Coal Mining

The mining of coal can also create environmental problems. Surface mining removes soil. Most plants need soil for growth, and some animals need soil for shelter. If land is not properly restored after surface mining, wildlife habitats can be destroyed. Coal mining can lower water tables and can pollute water supplies with heavy metals. The potential for underground mines to collapse endangers the lives of miners.

Petroleum Problems

Producing, transporting, and using petroleum can cause environmental problems and can endanger wildlife. In June 2000, the carrier *Treasure* sank off the coast of South Africa and spilled more than 400 tons of oil. The toxic oil coated thousands of blackfooted penguins, as **Figure 9** shows. The oil hindered the penguins from swimming and catching fish for food.

Smog

Burning petroleum products causes an environmental problem called smog. *Smog* is photochemical haze that forms when sunlight acts on industrial pollutants or gasoline engine exhaust. Smog is particularly serious in cities such as Los Angeles. In Los Angeles, millions of automobiles burn gasoline. The mountains that surround Los Angeles prevent the wind from blowing pollutants away. This combination of factors causes smog build up.

Figure 9 *The oil spilled from the carrier* Treasure *endangered the lives of many animals, including blackfooted penguins.*

Summary

- Energy resources are natural resources that humans use to produce energy.

- Fossil fuels are nonrenewable resources that form slowly over long periods of time from the remains of dead organisms. Petroleum, natural gas, and coal are fossil fuels.

- When fossil fuels are burned, they release energy. Most of that energy is heat energy.

- How humans use fossil fuels depends on the availability of the fuel, the ways in which the fuels are converted into energy, and the effects of converting the fuels into energy.

- Fossil fuels are found all over the world. The United States imports more than half of the petroleum that it uses from the Middle East, South America, Africa, Mexico, and Canada.

- Fossil fuels are obtained by drilling oil wells, mining below Earth's surface, and strip mining.

- Acid precipitation, smog, water pollution, and the destruction of wildlife habitats are some of the environmental problems created by the use of fossil fuels.

Using Vocabulary

1 Use *petroleum, fossil fuel,* and *acid precipitation* in separate sentences.

Understanding Concepts

2 **Applying** Describe how fossil fuels are converted into usable energy.

3 **Identifying** Identify a solid fossil fuel, a liquid fossil fuel, and a gaseous fossil fuel.

4 **Summarizing** Briefly describe how petroleum and natural gas form.

5 **Identifying** Explain why fossil fuels are nonrenewable resources.

6 **Listing** List two advantages of using fossil fuels.

Critical Thinking

7 **Making Comparisons** What is the difference between the organic material from which coal forms and the organic material from which petroleum and natural gas form?

8 **Making Inferences** Why can carpooling and using mass-transit systems minimize some problems associated with the use of fossil fuels?

Math Skills

INTERPRETING GRAPHICS The pie graph below shows what percentage of the oil produced in the world each region produces. Use the pie graph below to answer the next two questions.

Oil Production by Region

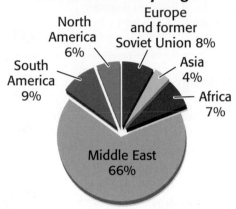

North America 6%

Europe and former Soviet Union 8%

South America 9%

Asia 4%

Africa 7%

Middle East 66%

9 **Analyzing Data** Which region produces the most oil?

10 **Making Calculations** What percentage of oil produced in the world is produced in regions other than North and South America?

Challenge

11 **Applying Concepts** If an oil spill occurred off the coast of California and ocean currents travel at 10 km/h, how long would the oil take to reach a shoreline that is 500 km away?

Internet Resources

For a variety of links related to this chapter, go to www.scilinks.org

Topic: Fossil Fuels

SciLinks code: HY70614

Alternative Energy

Key Concept Each alternative energy resource has both benefits and drawbacks.

What You Will Learn

● Many types of alternative energy resources are used to generate power.

● Alternative energy resources produce less pollution than fossil fuels do.

● The use of alternative energy resources has both advantages and disadvantages.

Why It Matters

Alternative energy becomes more important as fossil fuels are depleted and as environmental concerns become greater.

Vocabulary

• nuclear energy
• wind power
• chemical energy
• solar energy
• hydroelectric energy
• biomass
• gasohol
• geothermal energy

READING STRATEGY

Outlining In your **Science Journal,** create an outline of the section. Use the headings from the section in your outline.

6.3.b Students know that when fuel is consumed, most of the energy released becomes heat energy.
6.6.a Students know the utility of energy sources is determined by factors that are involved in converting these sources to useful forms and the consequences of the conversion process.
6.6.b Students know different natural energy and material resources, including air, soil, rocks, minerals, petroleum, fresh water, wildlife, and forests, and know how to classify them as renewable or nonrenewable.

▶ What would your life be like if you couldn't turn on lights, microwave your dinner, take a hot shower, or take the bus to school? Most of your energy needs are met by the use of fossil fuels. However, a variety of technologies have been invented to convert energy from alternative sources. Some alternative energy sources are easily converted into usable forms of energy. Others are unreliable, expensive, or difficult to convert. The energy sources that are easiest and most cost effective to convert are most valuable. In addition, each source of energy has both advantages and disadvantages.

Nuclear Energy

The energy released when the nuclei of atoms are split or combined is called **nuclear energy.** Nuclear energy can be obtained by two main processes: fission and fusion.

Splitting the Atom: Fission

Fission is a process in which the nuclei of radioactive atoms are split into two or more smaller nuclei, as **Figure 1** shows. When fission takes place, a large amount of energy is released. This energy can be used to generate electrical energy. All nuclear power made by humans is generated by fission.

Figure 1 *During nuclear fission, a neutron collides with the nucleus of a uranium-235 atom. The nucleus splits into two smaller nuclei, called* fission products, *and two or more neutrons.*

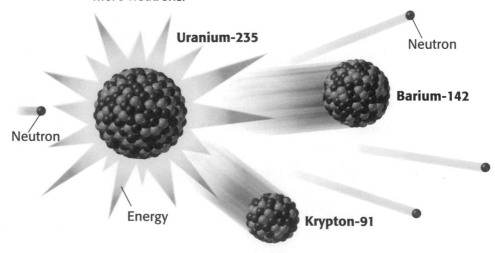

Uranium-235

Neutron

Neutron

Barium-142

Energy

Krypton-91

Advantages and Disadvantages of Fission

Nuclear fission produces a large amount of energy. This source of energy does not cause the problems that fossil fuels do. Because no fuel is burned, nuclear power does not cause air pollution. In addition, mining the fuel for nuclear power does not result in massive strip mines or cause the loss of wildlife habitat.

Nuclear power also has drawbacks. For example, nuclear power plants produce dangerous radioactive wastes. These wastes must be stored for a very long period of time where the radiation that they emit cannot harm anyone. Another problem is the potential for releasing harmful radiation into the environment accidentally. In addition, nuclear plants must release extra heat from the fission reaction. The heat may disrupt the local ecosystem. Thus, cooling towers, such as the ones shown in **Figure 2,** must be used to cool water before the water is released into local rivers or the ocean.

Standards Check What are the advantages of producing energy through fission? 6.6.a

Figure 2 *The San Onofre Nuclear Generating Station in north San Diego County in California provides electrical energy for the surrounding area.*

Combining Atoms: Fusion

Another method of obtaining energy from nuclei is fusion, shown in **Figure 3.** *Fusion* is the joining of two or more nuclei to form a larger nucleus. This process happens naturally in the sun and releases a large amount of energy.

Advantages and Disadvantages of Fusion

Fusion has two main advantages. First, fusion produces few dangerous wastes. Second, the fuels for fusion cannot be exhausted, so fusion is a renewable source of energy. The main disadvantage of fusion is that the reaction can take place only at very high temperatures. So, it is difficult to control the reaction and to keep the reaction going. Currently, the technology to make fusion a source of energy is not available.

nuclear energy (NOO klee uhr EN uhr jee) the energy released by a fission or fusion reaction

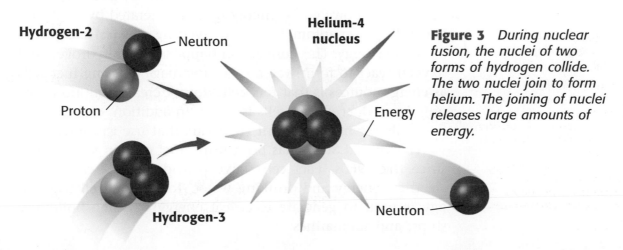

Figure 3 *During nuclear fusion, the nuclei of two forms of hydrogen collide. The two nuclei join to form helium. The joining of nuclei releases large amounts of energy.*

Figure 4 *These wind turbines are at a wind farm in Altamont Pass near Livermore, California. Notice the white pick-up truck, which shows how large the turbines are.* **What can you conclude about the space needed for wind power?**

Wind Energy

Wind is caused indirectly by solar energy because the atmosphere is heated more at middle latitudes than at other latitudes. Because moving air has kinetic energy, energy can be harnessed from wind. **Wind power** is the use of a windmill to drive an electric generator. Clusters of wind turbines, such as the ones shown in **Figure 4,** can generate a large amount of electrical energy. Wind energy is renewable and does not cause any pollution. But, in many areas, the wind isn't strong enough or frequent enough to generate energy on a large scale.

Standards Check Why is wind a useful energy source in some locations, but not in others? 6.6.a

Chemical Energy from Fuel Cells

When you think of fuel for a car, you most likely think of gasoline. However, not all vehicles are fueled by gasoline. Some vehicles are powered by energy that is generated by fuel cells. Fuel cells power automobiles by converting **chemical energy** into electrical energy. This conversion happens when hydrogen and oxygen react to form water. One advantage of using fuel cells as energy sources is that fuel cells do not create pollution. The only byproduct of fuel cells is water. In addition, cars that use fuel cells are more efficient than cars that use gasoline.

The United States has been using fuel cells in space travel since the 1960s. Fuel cells have provided space crews with electrical energy and drinking water. Today, fuel-cell technology is used to generate electrical energy in some buildings, ships, and submarines.

wind power (WIND POW uhr) the use of a windmill to drive an electric generator

chemical energy (KEM i kuhl EN uhr jee) the energy released when a chemical compound reacts to produce new compounds

Solar Energy

Almost all forms of energy, such as wind energy and the energy of fossil fuels, come from the sun. The energy received by Earth from the sun in the form of radiation is **solar energy.** Earth receives more than enough solar energy to meet all of our energy needs. Because Earth continuously receives solar energy, this energy is a renewable resource.

Standards Check Why is solar energy a renewable resource?
 6.6.b

Uses of Solar Energy

Sunlight can be changed into electrical energy through the use of solar cells or photovoltaic cells. You may have used a calculator powered by solar cells. Solar energy can also be used directly to heat buildings and to generate electrical energy. However, the technology that is used to generate electrical energy from solar energy is very expensive.

Advantages and Disadvantages of Solar Energy

One of the best things about solar energy is that it doesn't produce pollution. Because it comes from the sun, solar energy is renewable. But some climates don't have enough sunny days to benefit from solar energy. And despite the fact that solar energy is free, solar cells and solar collectors are more expensive to make than other energy systems.

solar energy (SOH luhr EN uhr jee) the energy received by Earth from the sun in the form of radiation

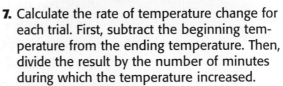

Alternative Energy in Your Community

Find out which alternative energy sources are used in your community. You may be able to find out by calling your local power company. Some alternative energy sources are wind power, solar power, nuclear power, and fuel cells. Present your findings to your family or class.

ACTIVITY

Quick Lab

Solar Collector

6.6.a

1. Line the inside of a **small, shallow pan** with **black plastic.**

2. Use **tape** to attach a **thermometer** to the inside of the pan.

3. Fill the pan with enough **room-temperature water** to cover the bulb of the thermometer.

4. Use a **large rubber band** or **string** to fasten **clear plastic wrap** over the pan. Be sure that you can read the thermometer.

5. Place the pan in a sunny area. Use a **stopwatch** to record the temperature every 5 min until the temperature stops rising. Discard the water.

6. Repeat steps 1–5, but do not line the pan with black plastic.

7. Calculate the rate of temperature change for each trial. First, subtract the beginning temperature from the ending temperature. Then, divide the result by the number of minutes during which the temperature increased.

8. Which trial had a greater rate of temperature change? Why?

9. How can water and solar energy be used to generate electrical energy?

 40 min

Figure 5 *Large amounts of water allow this California dam to generate electrical energy.*

Hydroelectric Energy

Humans have used the energy of falling water for thousands of years. Water wheels have been around since ancient times. Today, the energy of falling water is used to turn turbines that generate electrical energy. Electrical energy produced by moving water is called **hydroelectric energy.**

Advantages of Hydroelectric Energy

After a dam and a hydroelectric power plant are built, generating hydroelectric energy is inexpensive. In addition, hydroelectric energy causes no air pollution and little other pollution. Hydroelectric energy is renewable because it is driven by the water cycle, which is driven by solar energy.

Disadvantages of Hydroelectric Energy

Like wind energy, hydroelectric energy is not available everywhere. It can be produced only where large volumes of moving water can be harnessed. Huge dams, such as the one in **Figure 5,** must be built on major rivers to capture enough water to generate large amounts of electrical energy.

Building a large dam necessary for a hydroelectric power plant has many costs other than the financial costs. The habitats of wildlife living in the river are disrupted. Fish cannot migrate. Water trapped upstream of a dam may flood farmland and wildlife habitats. Downstream, the amount of sediment that reaches beaches and other sites is reduced. In addition, a dam can decrease water quality and can cause erosion. A dam also may cause flooding disasters if the dam is damaged or collapses.

Standards Check What are six potential costs of building a dam for a hydroelectric power plant? 6.6.a

hydroelectric energy
(HIE DROH ee LEK trik EN uhr jee)
electrical energy produced by the flow of water
Wordwise The root *hydr-* means "water." Other examples are *hydrate*, *hydraulics,* and *hydrogen.*

Energy from Living Things

Plants absorb energy from the sun and store this energy for later use. Leaves, wood, and other parts of plants contain stored energy. Even the dung of plant-grazing animals has a lot of stored energy. These sources of energy are called biomass. **Biomass** is organic matter that can be a source of energy.

Biomass is most commonly used in its solid form. **Figure 6** shows a woman who is preparing cow dung that will be dried and used for fuel. Biomass can also be changed into liquid fuel. Plants that contain sugar or starch can be made into alcohol. The alcohol can be used as a fuel. Alcohol can also be mixed with gasoline to make a fuel called **gasohol.**

biomass (BIE oh MAS) plant material, manure, or any other organic matter that is used as an energy source

gasohol (GAS uh HAWL) a mixture of gasoline and alcohol that is used as a fuel

Burning Biomass

The most common way to release biomass energy is to burn biomass. When biomass is burned, energy is released as heat. This heat can be used to cook food, to heat a house, or to drive an engine. Scientists estimate that 14% of the energy used in the world comes from the burning of wood and animal dung.

Advantages and Disadvantages of Biomass

Biomass is inexpensive and can be replaced quickly. Therefore, it can be considered a renewable resource. However, biomass is renewable only when the rate at which the fuel is used does not exceed the rate at which the fuel is replaced. If biomass is used too quickly, habitats may be destroyed and species may become extinct. In that case, the biomass may be considered a nonrenewable resource. Some types of biomass production can require land that could be used for growing food. If that land is not protected, it may become unusable in the future.

Kilometers per Acre

Imagine that you own a car that runs on alcohol made from corn that you grow. You drive your car about 24,000 km per year, and you get 900 L of alcohol from each acre of corn that you process. If your car has a gas mileage of 11 km/L, how many acres of corn must you process to fuel your car for a year? Record your work in your **Science Journal.**

Figure 6 *In many parts of the world where firewood is scarce, people burn animal dung for energy.*

Energy from Within Earth

When *magma*, or melted rock, contacts solid rock, the solid rock heats up. If the solid rock contains groundwater, the water is heated, too. The energy in the hot water can be used to generate electrical energy. The energy produced by the heat within Earth is called **geothermal energy.**

geothermal energy
(JEE oh THUHR muhl EN uhr jee) the energy produced by heat within Earth

Geothermal Energy

Geothermal power plants pump steam and hot water from rock beneath Earth's surface, as shown in **Figure 7.** The hot water and steam turn turbines that generate electricity. Geothermal energy can also be used to heat buildings. In this process, hot water and steam are used to heat a fluid. Then, the fluid is pumped through a building. Energy from the fluid escapes into the building and heats the building.

Advantages and Disadvantages of Geothermal Energy

Geothermal energy is renewable. It comes from water heated by magma in Earth's interior. Because Earth's core will be very hot for billions of years, geothermal energy will be available for a long time. It adds few pollutants to the air or the land. However, this energy can be used only where magma is near Earth's surface.

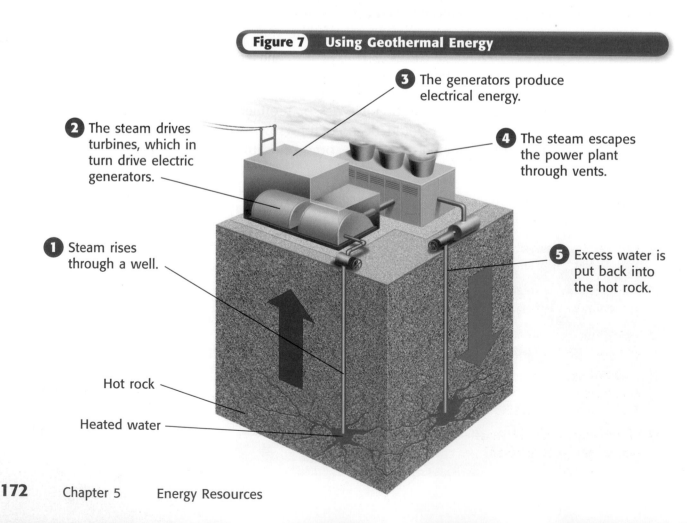

Figure 7 Using Geothermal Energy

3 The generators produce electrical energy.

2 The steam drives turbines, which in turn drive electric generators.

4 The steam escapes the power plant through vents.

1 Steam rises through a well.

5 Excess water is put back into the hot rock.

Hot rock

Heated water

Summary

- The usefulness of a resource depends on how easy converting the resource into energy is, how expensive the resource is, and how much of the resource is available.

- Fission and fusion are processes that release nuclear energy. The byproducts of fission are heat and radioactive waste.

- Wind power, solar energy, hydroelectric energy, biomass, and geothermal energy are renewable resources that emit very little pollution.

- Not all alternative energy resources can be generated in all areas. Some alternative energy resources are very expensive.

- Every energy resource has advantages and disadvantages.

Using Vocabulary

1 Write an original definition for *nuclear energy, solar energy, wind power, hydroelectric energy,* and *biomass.*

Understanding Concepts

2 **Describing** Describe two ways that solar energy can be converted into a useful form of energy.

3 **Identifying** Identify where the production of hydroelectric energy is practical.

4 **Listing** List the forms of renewable energy that are currently in use.

5 **Summarizing** Explain the process in which geothermal energy is produced.

6 **Evaluating** Evaluate the advantages and disadvantages of nuclear energy.

7 **Concluding** Decide which alternative energy resources would be best for where you live. Explain why you chose these energy resources.

8 **Classifying** When biomass is burned, what type of energy is released?

Critical Thinking

9 **Analyzing Methods** If you were going to build a nuclear power plant, why wouldn't you build it in the middle of a desert?

10 **Predicting Consequences** If an alternative energy resource could successfully replace crude oil, how might the use of that resource affect the environment?

Math Skills

INTERPRETING GRAPHICS Use the graph below to answer the next two questions.

How Energy Is Used in the United States

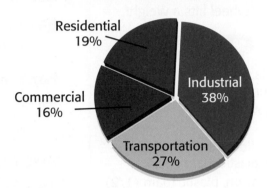

Residential 19%
Industrial 38%
Commercial 16%
Transportation 27%

11 **Analyzing Data** What percentage of energy used in the United States is used for commercial and industrial purposes?

12 **Analyzing Data** What percentage of energy used in the United States is not used for residential purposes?

Challenge

13 **Applying Concepts** Imagine that you live on the moon. Why wouldn't some of the sources of energy used on Earth work on the moon? Explain your reasons.

Internet Resources

For a variety of links related to this chapter, go to www.scilinks.org

Topic: Energy Resources
SciLinks code: HY70515

173

Using Scientific Methods

Model-Making Lab

Making a Water Wheel

Lift Enterprises is planning to build a water wheel that will lift objects in the same way that a crane does. The president of the company has asked you to modify the basic water wheel design so that the water wheel will lift objects more quickly.

Ask a Question

1 What factors influence the rate at which a water wheel lifts a weight?

Form a Hypothesis

2 Formulate a testable hypothesis that is a possible answer to the question in step 1.

Test the Hypothesis

3 Build a water wheel model. Using the permanent marker, draw a line around five of the egg cups of the egg carton. Cut off these cups along the lines that you have drawn.

4 Push the wooden skewer through the center of the flat side of the plastic foam circle so that half of the skewer appears on either side of the plastic foam circle.

5 Open the five paper clips, and bend each paper clip into the shape of a U. Using one U-shaped paper clip for each egg cup, push one end of the paper clip through the egg cup and the plastic foam circle. Push the other end into the plastic foam circle above the egg cup so that each egg cup is attached to the plastic foam circle. The open side of each egg cup should face up.

OBJECTIVES

Create a model of a water wheel.

Determine factors that influence the rate at which a water wheel lifts a weight.

MATERIALS

- bottle, soda, 2 L, filled with water
- clay, modeling
- coin
- dried flower holder, 2 in. × 4 in. plastic foam circle
- egg carton, plastic foam (1/2)
- marker, permanent, black
- paper clips (5)
- scissors
- skewer, wooden (1)
- storage box, plastic
- tape, transparent
- thread, 30 cm long
- watch or clock that indicates seconds

SAFETY

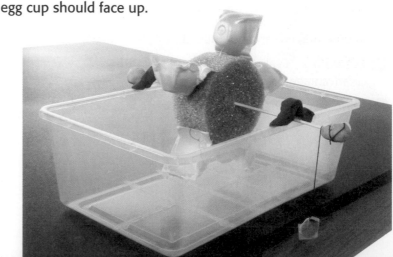

6.6.a Students know the utility of energy sources is determined by factors that are involved in converting these sources to useful forms and the consequences of the conversion process.

Investigation and Experimentation
6.7.a Develop a hypothesis.

174 Chapter 5 Energy Resources

6 Balance the wheel and skewer on the plastic storage box so that the skewer extends evenly over both sides of the box. The wheel should spin freely.

7 Mold a clay arch onto each side of the plastic box so that the skewer is free to turn under each arch.

8 Attach a small ball of clay to each end of the skewer. The balls should be the same size.

9 Wrap the thread twice around one of the clay balls. Tape the thread to the clay ball. (As the water wheel turns, the thread should wrap around the clay. The other ball of clay balances the weight and helps keep the water wheel turning smoothly.)

10 Wrap the free end of the thread one complete time around the coin. Tape the thread on both sides of the coin. The result is the basic design of Lift Enterprises' water wheel.

11 Slowly pour water from the 2 L soda bottle onto the egg cups so that the water wheel spins. Use a clock to measure how quickly the coin rises. Record your observations.

12 Lower the coin to the starting position. Modify your apparatus to make the coin rise faster. Describe the changes that you made to your apparatus. Repeat step 11. Did the coin rise faster or slower this time?

13 Repeat step 12 twice. Each time, modify your apparatus so that it raises the coin even faster.

Analyze the Results

14 Analyzing Results Which of your modifications made the coin rise faster?

15 Analyzing Results What modifications made by your classmates made the coin rise faster?

Draw Conclusions

16 Drawing Conclusions What factors influence how quickly you can lift the coin? Explain your answer.

17 Applying Conclusions What recommendations for improving the water wheel would you make to the president of Lift Enterprises?

Big Idea Question

18 Applying Conclusions What factors influence how useful flowing water is as an energy source?

Science Skills Activity

Investigation and Experimentation
6.7.c Construct appropriate graphs from data and develop qualitative statements about the relationships between variables.

Constructing Graphs from Data

▶ Tutorial

1 Follow these steps to build your graph.

- Draw the axes for your graph on a sheet of graph paper.
- Write the title of your graph on the top of the graph.
- Write the title of the *x*-axis in terms that describe the type of data and the units of the data. Usually, the independent variable is placed on the *x*-axis.
- Determine a scale for the *x*-axis that includes the range of your data. Write the numbers of the scale next to the tick marks of the *x*-axis.
- Write the title of the *y*-axis in terms that describe the type of data and the units of the data. Usually, the dependent variable is placed on the *y*-axis.
- Determine a scale for the *y*-axis that includes the range of your data. Write the numbers of the scale next to the tick marks of the *y*-axis.

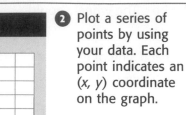

2 Plot a series of points by using your data. Each point indicates an (*x*, *y*) coordinate on the graph.

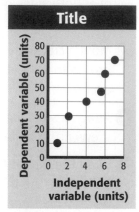

3 On the graph, draw a straight line that best fits the points that you have plotted.

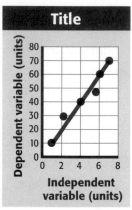

▶ You Try It!

Use the data in the table to construct a graph. Then, use the graph to answer the questions below. (Note: *kWh* means "kilowatt-hour," which is a measure of energy use.)

1 Identifying Relationships Write a statement that describes the relationship between the outdoor temperature and the amount of energy used by a refrigerator in a kitchen.

2 Making Inferences Explain why you think this relationship exists. Which variable is the "cause," and which variable is the "effect?"

3 Predicting Consequences Using these data, what can you predict about the costs of running a refrigerator during different seasons?

Outdoor Temperature and Energy Used by a Refrigerator in a Kitchen	
Outdoor Temperature (°C)	Energy Use (kWh/day)
7	1.7
13	1.9
17	2.2
21	2.5
28	2.9
31	3.1

Chapter Summary

The Big Idea

Sources of energy differ in quantity, distribution, usefulness, and the time required for formation.

Section

Vocabulary

1 Fossil Fuels

Key Concept Most of the energy used by humans comes from fossil fuels, which are made up of ancient plant and animal matter that stored energy from the sun.

- Fossil fuels are important energy resources.
- Fossil fuels form slowly over very long periods of time.
- Fossil fuels are found and obtained in different ways.
- Fossil fuels are nonrenewable and create pollution when burned.

Wells reach reservoirs of natural gas and petroleum deep in the ground.

energy resource p. 158
fossil fuel p. 158
petroleum p. 159
natural gas p. 159
coal p. 160
acid precipitation p. 164

2 Alternative Energy

Key Concept Each alternative energy resource has both benefits and drawbacks.

- Many types of alternative energy resources are used to generate power.
- Alternative energy resources produce less pollution than fossil fuels do.
- The use of alternative energy resources has both advantages and disadvantages.

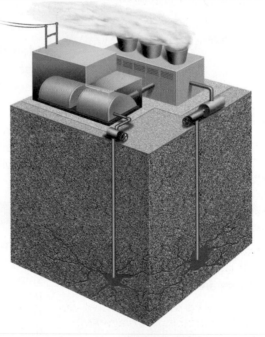

Geothermal power plants use heat from Earth's interior to generate electricity.

nuclear energy p. 166
wind power p. 168
chemical energy p. 168
solar energy p. 169
hydroelectric energy p. 170
biomass p. 171
gasohol p. 171
geothermal energy p. 172

Chapter Review

 6.3.b, 6.6.a, 6.6.b

Organize

Double Door Review the Fold-Note that you created at the beginning of the chapter. Add to or correct the FoldNote based on what you have learned.

Using Vocabulary

1 **Academic Vocabulary** Which of the following words means "to change from one form to another"?
a. interpret
b. convert
c. consume
d. transfer

Correct each statement by replacing the underlined term.

2 A liquid mixture of complex hydrocarbon compounds is called <u>natural gas</u>.

3 The alternative energy resource that uses moving water to produce electricity is called <u>solar energy</u>.

For each pair of terms, explain how the meanings of the terms differ.

4 *solar energy* and *wind power*

5 *biomass* and *coal*

Understanding Concepts

Multiple Choice

6 Which of the following sources of energy is NOT renewable?
a. geothermal energy
b. petroleum
c. nuclear energy
d. biomass

7 Both lignite and anthracite are forms of
a. petroleum.
b. natural gas.
c. coal.
d. gasohol.

8 The use of which of the following forms of energy contributes to smog?
a. hydroelectric energy
b. solar energy
c. wind energy
d. energy from fossil fuels

9 To produce energy, nuclear power plants use a process called
a. fission.
b. fusion.
c. fractionation.
d. None of the above

10 Geothermal energy is heat energy from
a. the sun.
b. biomass.
c. the ocean.
d. Earth.

Short Answer

11 **Listing** Why are fossil fuels and biomass useful as sources of energy?

12 **Evaluating** Are fossil fuels nonrenewable resources? Explain your answer.

13 **Describing** Explain how fossil fuels are located and obtained.

14 **Applying** What factors determine whether a source of energy is useful?

15 **Identifying** Identify the advantages and disadvantages of using fossil fuels as energy resources. Then, list the benefits and drawbacks of four alternative energy resources.

16 **Describing** How could building a hydroelectric dam affect the surrounding environment and wildlife?

Writing Skills

17 **Communicating Key Concepts** Write an essay that would clearly explain the relationship between the use of fossil fuels and pollution to a third-grade student. Your essay should have a thesis, should include evidence that supports your ideas, and should have a conclusion.

Critical Thinking

18 Concept Mapping Use the following terms to create a concept map: *fossil fuels, wind energy, energy resources, biomass, renewable resources, solar energy, nonrenewable resources, natural gas, coal,* and *petroleum.*

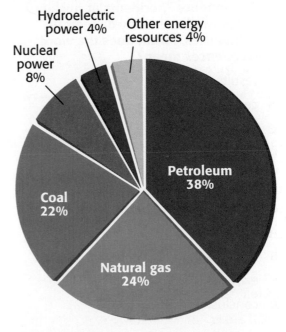

19 Evaluating Assumptions If sunlight is free, why is generating electrical energy from solar cells expensive?

20 Evaluating Assumptions Why do renewable resources need to be conserved?

21 Identifying Relationships Why does the location where coal usually forms differ from the locations where petroleum and natural gas form?

INTERPRETING GRAPHICS Use the graph below to answer the next two questions.

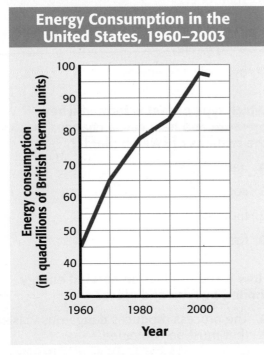

Energy Consumption in the United States, 1960–2003

22 Identifying Relationships In what year was the most energy consumed?

23 Identifying Relationships How do you think energy consumption will be affected if the U.S. population increases by 5% in the next five years?

Math Skills

24 Making Conversions An oil tanker hit a coral reef and spilled 800,000 mL of oil into the ocean. If the oil spread evenly over 100 km², how many liters of oil does each square kilometer contain?

INTERPRETING GRAPHICS Use the graph below to answer the next two questions.

Energy Used in the World by Source

Hydroelectric power 4%

Other energy resources 4%

Nuclear power 8%

Petroleum 38%

Coal 22%

Natural gas 24%

25 Analyzing Data What percentage of the energy used in the world comes from natural gas?

26 Analyzing Data What percentage of the energy used in the world comes from solid and liquid fossil fuels?

27 Analyzing Data What percentage of the energy used in the world does not come from a fossil fuel?

Challenge

28 Identifying Relationships Explain why the energy obtained from many of our resources ultimately comes from the sun.

6.3.b, 6.4.a, 6.6.a, 6.6.b, 6.6.c, 6.7.f

REVIEWING ACADEMIC VOCABULARY

1 In the sentence "Energy is released when fuel is consumed," what does the word *consumed* mean?

A absorbed

B used up

C engaged fully

D spent wastefully

2 In the sentence "Accidents at nuclear facilities can have many dangerous consequences," what does the word *consequences* mean?

A results

B causes

C origins

D accidents

3 Which of the following words is the closest in meaning to the word *utility*?

A excitement

B usefulness

C expense

D conclusion

4 Choose the appropriate form of the word *convert* for the following sentence: "The usefulness of a fuel type depends partly on the _____ process."

A converting

B converted

C conversion

D converter

5 Which of the following words is the closest in meaning to the word *factor*?

A something that prevents a result

B something that predicts a result

C something that is unrelated to a result

D something that brings about a result

REVIEWING CONCEPTS

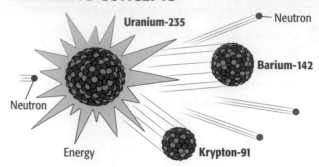

6 What type of energy is produced from the reaction shown in the diagram above?

A hydroelectric energy

B nuclear energy

C solar energy

D chemical energy

7 Which of the following is a nonrenewable energy source?

A solar energy

B coal energy

C wind energy

D hydroelectric energy

8 Which type of fuel is formed when pressure and heat cause changes in the remains of swamp plants?

A natural gas

B coal

C biomass

D fission

9 How is the production of wind energy limited by time and place?

A The process produces dangerous wastes that must be contained.

B Water must be nearby to convert turbine movement to hydroelectricity.

C Wind farms may destroy the habitats of native wildlife on a large scale.

D Winds must be strong and frequent in the area.

10 Which of the following is a main disadvantage of atomic fusion?

   A It is nonrenewable.

   B It produces dangerous radiation.

   C It results in loss of wildlife habitats.

   D It is difficult to control and keep going.

11 What is the most common way to release biomass energy?

   A burn it

   B recycle it

   C convert it into petroleum

   D compress and heat it

12 What is the source of fossil fuels?

   A plants and animals that died long ago

   B the combination of hydrogen and oxygen into water

   C the flow of water

   D the collision of atoms

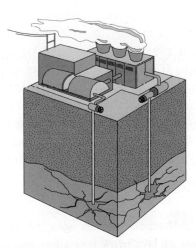

13 The figure above shows the conversion of one type of energy to another type of energy. Which conversion does it show?

   A gasoline to kinetic energy

   B geothermal energy to electrical energy

   C wind to electrical energy

   D fission to electrical energy

REVIEWING PRIOR LEARNING

14 What is the source for almost all energy on Earth?

   A coal

   B water

   C the sun

   D nuclear fission

15 Which natural material is used to make glass?

   A petroleum

   B sand

   C trees

   D salt from the ocean

16 Which type of map records geologic information, such as rock units, structural features, and mineral deposits?

   A a geologic map

   B a topographic map

   C a resource map

   D a contour map

17 Which of the following determines whether a natural resource is a renewable resource or a nonrenewable resource?

   A whether the resource is a material resource or an energy resource

   B whether the resource is expensive to obtain and use

   C whether the use of the resource harms the environment

   D whether the resource can be replaced at the same rate at which it is consumed

Standards Assessment

Science in Action

Place to Visit

Calistoga's Old Faithful Geyser

The Old Faithful Geyser in Calistoga, California, is one of only three Old Faithful geysers in the world. These geysers have predictable eruptions on a regular basis. Old Faithful in Calistoga shoots a stream of boiling water into the air every 45 minutes. The water reaches a height of 20 m to more than 33 m. Geysers do not erupt only from boiling water, however. Some geysers erupt because of gas pressure in the ground. When water boils or when gas pressure is high, a stream of water may escape from the ground in the form of a geyser.

Language Arts ACTiViTY

Find out about geothermal power plants. Would geothermal energy be a good source of energy where you live? Why or why not? Write an essay about how geothermal power plants generate electricity. Record your work in your **Science Journal**.

Science, Technology, and Society

Hybrid Cars

One solution to the pollution problem caused by the burning of fossil fuels for transportation purposes is to develop cars that depend less on fossil fuels. One such car is called a *hybrid*. Instead of using only gasoline for energy, a hybrid car uses gasoline and electricity. Because of its special batteries, the hybrid needs less gasoline to run than a car powered only by gasoline does. Some hybrids have a gas mileage of 60 mi/gal! Currently, several models are available. You may see even more hybrid cars on the roads in the near future.

Math ACTiViTY

Charlie's pickup truck has a gas mileage of 17 mi/gal. Charlie drives his truck an average of 12,000 mi per year. Then, he sells the truck and buys a new hybrid car that has a gas mileage of 45 mi/gal. If gasoline costs $3.25 per gallon, how much money will Charlie save in a year by driving the hybrid car instead of the truck? Record you work in your **Science Journal**.

Fred Begay

Nuclear Physicist Generating energy by combining atoms is called *fusion*. This process is being developed by nuclear physicists, such as Fred Begay at the Department of Energy's Los Alamos National Laboratory. Begay hopes to someday make fusion an alternative source of energy. Because fusion is the process that generates energy in the sun, Begay uses NASA satellites to study the sun. Begay explains that it is necessary to develop skills in abstract reasoning to study fusion. As a Navajo, Begay developed these skills while growing up at his Navajo home in Towaoc, Colorado, where his family taught him about nature. Today, Begay uses his skills not only to help develop a new energy resource but also to mentor Native American and minority students. In 1999, Begay won the Distinguished Scientist Award from the Society for Advancement of Chicanos and Native Americans in Science.

Social Studies ACTIVITY

Research the lifestyle of Native Americans before 1900. Then, create a poster that compares resources that Native Americans used before 1900 with resources that many people use today.

Internet Resources

- To learn more about careers in science, visit **www.scilinks.org** and enter the SciLinks code HY70225.
- To learn more about these Science in Action topics, visit **go.hrw.com** and type in the keyword HY7ENRF.
- Check out articles related to this chapter by visiting **go.hrw.com**. Just type in the keyword HY7ENRC.

Plate Tectonics and Earth's Structure

In this unit, you will learn what a dynamic planet Earth is. Earth's landmasses are changing position continuously as they move across Earth's surface as part of tectonic plates. As plates move, mountain ranges form, earthquakes happen, and volcanoes form. This timeline shows some of the events that have occurred as scientists have tried to understand our dynamic Earth.

1864

Jules Verne's *A Journey to the Center of the Earth* is published. In this fictional story, the heroes enter and exit Earth through volcanoes.

1912

Alfred Wegener proposes his theory of continental drift.

1979

Volcanoes are discovered on Io, one of Jupiter's moons.

1980

Mount St. Helens erupts after an earthquake triggers a landslide on the volcano's north face.

Io, one of Jupiter's moons

1883

When Krakatau erupts, more than 36,000 people are killed.

1896

Henry Ford builds his first car.

The Quadricycle, Henry Ford's first car

1906

San Francisco burns in the aftermath of an earthquake.

1935

Charles Richter devises a system of measuring the magnitude of earthquakes.

1951

Color television programming is introduced in the United States.

1962

A worldwide network of seismographs is established.

1982

Compact discs (CDs) and compact-disc players are made available to the public.

1994

An eight-legged robot named Dante II descends into the crater of an active volcano in Alaska.

Dante II

1997

The population of the Caribbean island of Montserrat dwindles to less than half its original size as frequent eruptions of the Soufriere Hills volcano force evacuations.

2003

An earthquake of magnitude 4.6 strikes Alabama. It is one of the largest earthquakes ever recorded for this area.

Improving Comprehension

Graphic Organizers are important visual tools that can help you organize information and improve your reading comprehension. The Graphic Organizer below is called a *process chart*. Instructions for creating other types of Graphic Organizers are located in the **Study Skills** section of the Appendix.

How to Make a Process Chart

1 Draw a box. In the box, write the first step of a process, chain of events, or cycle.

2 Under the box, draw another box, and draw an arrow to connect the two boxes. In the second box, write the next step of the process or the next event in the timeline.

3 Continue adding boxes until each step of the process, chain of events, or cycle is written in a box. For cycles only, draw an arrow to connect the last box and the first box.

When to Use a Process Chart

Science is full of processes. A process chart shows the steps that a process takes to get from one point to another point. Timelines, chains of events, and cycles are examples of the kinds of information that can be organized well in a process chart. As you read, look for information that is described in steps or in a sequence, and draw a process chart that shows the progression of the steps or sequence.

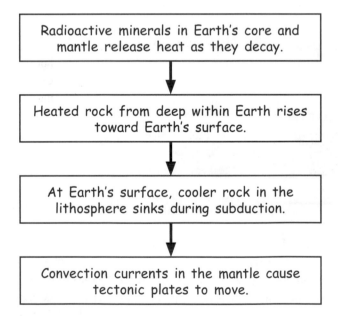

Radioactive minerals in Earth's core and mantle release heat as they decay.

↓

Heated rock from deep within Earth rises toward Earth's surface.

↓

At Earth's surface, cooler rock in the lithosphere sinks during subduction.

↓

Convection currents in the mantle cause tectonic plates to move.

You Try It!

This Reading Strategy can also be used within the chapter that you are about to read. Practice making your own process chart as directed in the Reading Strategies for Section **1** and Section **4**. Record your work in your **Science Journal.**

Unpacking the Standards

The information below "unpacks" the standards by breaking them down into basic parts. The higher-level, academic vocabulary is highlighted and defined to help you understand the language of the standards. "What It Means" restates the standards as simply as possible.

California Standard	Academic Vocabulary	What It Means
6.1.a Students know **evidence** of plate tectonics is **derived** from the fit of the continents; the **location** of earthquakes, volcanoes, and midocean ridges; and the **distribution** of fossils, rock types, and ancient climatic zones.	**evidence** (EV uh duhns) information showing whether an idea or belief is true or valid **derive** (di RIEV) to figure out by reasoning **location** (loh KAY shuhn) a place or position **distribution** (DIS tri BYOO shuhn) the relative arrangement of objects or organisms in time or space	Support for the idea that Earth's surface is made of slabs of rock that move around comes from how continents fit together, where earthquakes happen, where volcanoes and mid-ocean ridges are located, where rocks and fossils are found, and where climate was different in the geologic past.
6.1.b Students know Earth is composed of several **layers:** a cold, brittle lithosphere; a hot, convecting mantle; and a dense, metallic core.	**layer** (LAY uhr) a separate or distinct portion of matter that has thickness	Earth is made of several layers: a cold, brittle outer layer called the *lithosphere*; a hot, middle layer called the *mantle*, which circulates heat; and a dense core made of metals such as iron and nickel.
6.1.c Students know lithospheric plates the size of continents and oceans move at rates of centimeters per year in **response** to movements in the mantle.	**response** (ri SPAHNS) an action brought on by another action; a reaction	Earth's crust and upper mantle are broken into large plates that are the size of oceans and continents. These plates move at rates of centimeters per year as the hot, convecting mantle moves.
6.1.f Students know how to explain **major features** of California geology (including mountains, faults, volcanoes) in terms of plate tectonics.	**major** (MAY juhr) of great importance or large scale **feature** (FEE chuhr) the shape or form of a thing; characteristic	You must know how to explain how the movement of tectonic plates affected the formation of rocks and landforms (such as mountains, faults, and volcanoes) in California.
6.4.c Students know heat from Earth's interior reaches the surface **primarily** through convection.	**primarily** (prie MER uh lee) mainly	Heat from deep inside Earth reaches Earth's surface mainly by the movement of hot material in Earth's mantle.

The following identifies other standards that are covered in this chapter and where you can go to see them unpacked: **6.1.d** (Chapter 7), and **6.1.e** (Chapter 7)

6

Plate Tectonics

The Big Idea

Plate tectonics accounts for important features of Earth's surface and major geologic events.

California Standards

Focus on Earth Sciences
6.1 Plate tectonics accounts for important features of Earth's surface and major geologic events. (Sections 1, 2, 3, and 4)
6.4 Many phenomena on Earth's surface are affected by the transfer of energy through radiation and convection currents. (Section 2)

Investigation and Experimentation
6.7 Scientific progress is made by asking meaningful questions and conducting careful investigations. (Science Skills Activity)

Math
6.2.3 Algebra and Functions

English–Language Arts
6.1.1, 6.2.4 Reading
6.1.3 Writing

About the Photo

The San Andreas fault stretches across the California landscape like a giant wound. The fault, which is 2,600 km long, breaks Earth's crust from Northern California to Mexico. Because the North American plate and the Pacific plate slip past one another along the fault, many earthquakes happen there.

Organize

Key-Term Fold

Before you read the chapter, create the FoldNote entitled "Key-Term Fold." Write a key term from the chapter on each tab of the key-term fold. As you read the chapter, write the definition of each key term under the tab.

Instructions for creating FoldNotes are located in the Study Skills section on p. 617 of the Appendix.

Explore Activity

🕐 10 min

Continental Collisions

Continents wander around the globe. As they move, they may collide with one another. In this activity, you will model the collision of two continents.

Procedure

1. Obtain **two 1 cm–thick stacks of paper.**

2. Place the two stacks of paper on a **flat surface,** such as a desk.

3. Very slowly, push the stacks of paper together so that they collide. Continue to push the stacks until the paper in one of the stacks folds over.

Analysis

6.1.e

4. What happens to the stacks of paper when they collide?

5. Are all of the pieces of paper pushed upward? If not, what happens to the pieces that are not pushed upward?

6. What type of landform will most likely result from this continental collision?

Earth's Structure

Key Concept Earth is composed of several layers. The continents are part of the uppermost layer, and they move slowly around Earth's surface.

What You Will Learn

- Earth's interior can be divided into layers based on chemical composition and physical properties.
- Scientists use seismic waves to study Earth's interior.
- Continents are drifting apart from each other now and have done so in the past.

Why It Matters

The way Earth's layers interact causes major geologic events, such as earthquakes and volcanoes, to happen.

Vocabulary

- core
- mantle
- crust
- lithosphere
- asthenosphere
- continental drift
- sea-floor spreading

READING STRATEGY

Graphic Organizer In your **Science Journal,** create a Process Chart that describes the break-up of Pangaea.

▶ If you tried to dig to the center of Earth, what do you think you would find? Would Earth be solid or hollow? Would it be made of the same material throughout?

The Layers of Earth

Actually, Earth is made of several layers. The types of materials that make up each layer vary from layer to layer. The materials in each layer have characteristic properties. Scientists think about Earth's layers in two ways—in terms of their chemical composition and in terms of their physical properties.

The Compositional Layers of Earth

Figure 1 shows how Earth is divided into three layers based on chemical composition. In Earth's center is the dense, metallic **core,** which is made up mainly of the metal iron. The dense, thick middle layer is the **mantle.** The mantle is made up largely of silicon, oxygen, and magnesium. The surface layer, or **crust,** is composed mostly of silicon, oxygen, and aluminum.

Standards Check Describe Earth's compositional layers. 🐻 6.1.b

Figure 1 **Earth's Compositional Layers**

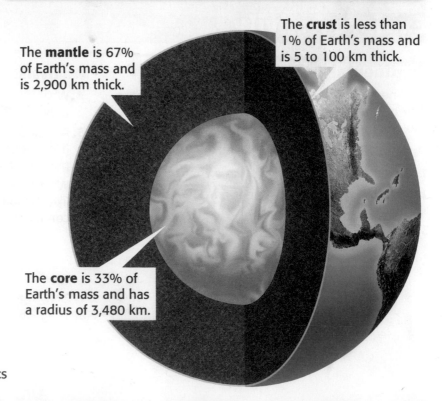

The **mantle** is 67% of Earth's mass and is 2,900 km thick.

The **crust** is less than 1% of Earth's mass and is 5 to 100 km thick.

The **core** is 33% of Earth's mass and has a radius of 3,480 km.

6.1.a Students know evidence of plate tectonics is derived from the fit of the continents; the location of earthquakes, volcanoes, and midocean ridges; and the distribution of fossils, rock types, and ancient climatic zones.
6.1.b Students know Earth is composed of several layers: a cold, brittle lithosphere; a hot, convecting mantle; and a dense, metallic core.

Figure 2 The Physical Structure of Earth

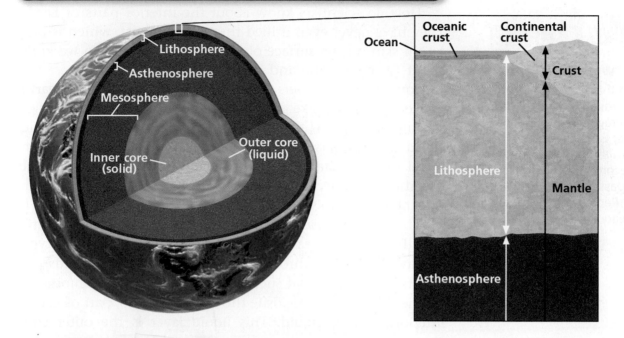

Continental and Oceanic Crust

There are two types of crust: continental and oceanic. Continental crust is thicker than oceanic crust. Both types are made mainly of the elements oxygen, silicon, and aluminum. But oceanic crust has almost twice as much iron, calcium, and magnesium as continental crust does. These three elements form minerals that are denser than the minerals in continental crust. These dense minerals make the thin, oceanic crust heavier than the thicker continental crust. But compared with Earth's other layers, both types of crust are rocky, thin, and fractured.

The Physical Structure of Earth

Figure 2 shows how Earth is divided into five layers based on physical properties. Earth's outer layer is the **lithosphere,** which is a cool, rigid layer that includes the crust and the upper part of the mantle. The lithosphere is divided into pieces called *tectonic plates.* Below the lithosphere is the **asthenosphere,** which is a layer of the mantle that is made of very slow-flowing solid rock. This property of flow allows tectonic plates to move on top of the asthenosphere. Below the asthenosphere is the *mesosphere,* which is the lower part of the mantle. The mesosphere flows even more slowly than the asthenosphere.

Earth's core has two layers. The *outer core* is a layer of liquid iron and nickel. At Earth's center is the solid *inner core.* This layer is made mostly of iron and nickel. The inner core's temperature is estimated to be between 4,000°C and 5,000°C. The inner core is very hot, but it is solid because it is under enormous pressure.

core (KAWR) the central part of Earth below the mantle

crust (KRUHST) the thin and solid outermost layer of Earth above the mantle

mantle (MAN tuhl) the layer of rock between Earth's crust and core

lithosphere (LITH oh SFIR) the solid, outer layer of Earth that consists of the crust and the rigid upper part of the mantle
Wordwise The root *lith-* means "stone."

asthenosphere (as THEN uh SFIR) the soft layer of the mantle on which the tectonic plates move

Seismic Wave Travel Time

Suppose that a seismic wave travels through Earth's mantle at an average velocity of 8 km/s. If Earth's mantle is 2,900 km thick, exactly how many seconds will the wave take to pass through Earth's mantle? Record your work in your **Science Journal.**

Mapping Earth's Interior

How do scientists know about the interior parts of Earth? They have never even drilled through the crust, which is only a thin skin on the surface of the planet. So, how do we know about Earth's mantle and core?

Some of the answers to these questions come from earthquakes. An earthquake produces vibrations called *seismic waves.* Seismic waves travel through Earth at various speeds. Machines called *seismometers* measure the time seismic waves take to travel various distances from an earthquake's center. Scientists use these distances and times to calculate the density and thickness of Earth's layers.

The speed of seismic waves is affected by the type of material that the waves are traveling through. For example, some types of waves can travel through rock but not through liquids. Scientists have found that such waves do not reach seismometers on the side of Earth opposite the earthquake. So, part of Earth's interior must be liquid. This liquid layer is the outer core. **Figure 3** shows how seismic waves travel through Earth.

Standards Check How are seismic waves used to map Earth's interior?
6.1.b

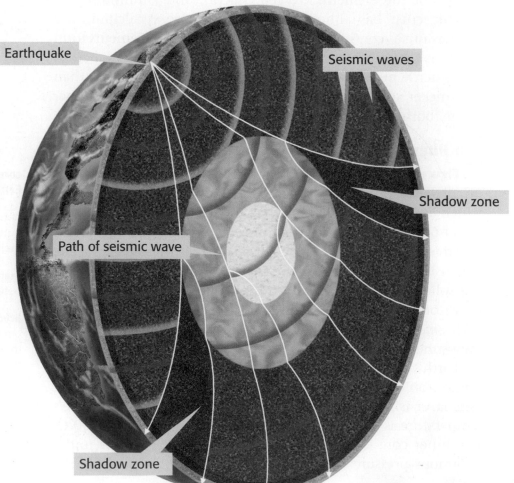

Figure 3 *By measuring changes in the speed of seismic waves that travel through Earth's interior, scientists have learned that Earth is made up of several layers. Shadow zones are places where no seismic waves are detected. Each earthquake has its own shadow zone.*

Earthquake

Seismic waves

Shadow zone

Path of seismic wave

Shadow zone

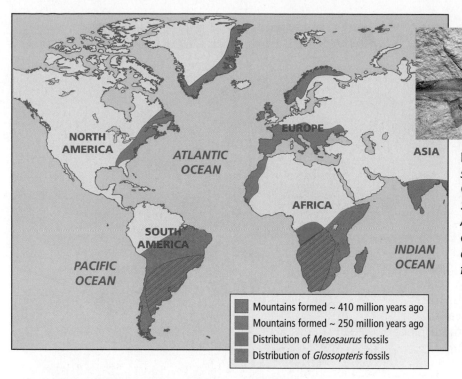

Figure 4 *Fossils of organisms such as* Mesosaurus *and* Glossopteris *were found in both South America and western Africa. The map shows mountain chains of similar ages that exist on separate continents that are far from each other.*

Map labels:
NORTH AMERICA, ATLANTIC OCEAN, EUROPE, ASIA, AFRICA, SOUTH AMERICA, PACIFIC OCEAN, INDIAN OCEAN

Legend:
- Mountains formed ~ 410 million years ago
- Mountains formed ~ 250 million years ago
- Distribution of *Mesosaurus* fossils
- Distribution of *Glossopteris* fossils

Continental Drift

Have you ever looked at a map of the world and noticed how the coastlines of continents on opposite sides of the oceans appear to fit together like the pieces of a puzzle? Is it just coincidence that the coastlines appear to fit together well?

Restless Continents

Alfred Wegener (VAY guh nuhr), a scientist, studied these puzzle pieces. In the early 1900s, he wrote about his hypothesis of *continental drift*. **Continental drift** is the idea that a single large landmass broke up into smaller landmasses to form the continents, which then drifted to their present locations. This idea explains how the continents seem to fit together.

Evidence for Continental Drift

Continental drift also explained why fossils of the same plant and animal species are found on continents that are far from each other. Many of these ancient species could not have crossed an ocean. **Figure 4** shows that continental drift explains such a pattern of fossil locations. The locations of mountain ranges and of similar types of rock also show this pattern. Scientists have used rock and fossil evidence to reconstruct past patterns of climate regions. The distribution of these ancient climatic zones supports the idea of continental drift, too.

Standards Check List three lines of evidence for continental drift.
6.1.a

continental drift (KAHN tuh NENT uhl DRIFT) the hypothesis that states that the continents once formed a single landmass, broke up, and drifted to their present locations

Figure 5 The Drifting Continents

245 Million Years Ago
Pangaea existed when some of the earliest dinosaurs were roaming Earth. The continent was surrounded by a sea called *Panthalassa,* which means "all sea."

135 Million Years Ago
Gradually, Pangaea broke into two big pieces. The northern piece is called *Laurasia.* The southern piece is called *Gondwana.*

65 Million Years Ago
By the time the dinosaurs became extinct, Laurasia and Gondwana had split into smaller pieces.

The Breakup of Pangaea

Wegener made many observations before proposing that a single large continent gave rise to today's continents. He called this single large continent *Pangaea* (pan JEE uh), which is Greek for "all Earth."

By using many geological observations, scientists have determined that Pangaea existed about 245 million years ago. Pangaea split into two continents—Laurasia and Gondwana—about 135 million years ago. As shown in **Figure 5,** these two continents split again and formed the continents of today. The continents slowly moved to their present positions. As the continents drifted, they collided with each other, which caused landforms such as mountain ranges, volcanoes, ocean trenches, and mid-ocean ridges to form.

Standards Check Briefly describe the movement of the continents over the past 245 million years. 6.1.a

Sea-Floor Spreading

When Wegener put forth his hypothesis of continental drift, many scientists would not accept his hypothesis. The calculated strength of rock made such movement of Earth's crust seem impossible. During Wegener's life, no one was able to prove his hypothesis. Not until many years after Wegener's death did scientists find evidence of forces that moved continents.

Mid-Ocean Ridges—a Magnetic Mystery

A chain of submerged mountains runs through the center of the Atlantic Ocean. This mountain chain is part of a worldwide system of mid-ocean ridges. Mid-ocean ridges are underwater mountain chains that run through Earth's ocean floor.

In the 1960s, scientists who were studying the ocean floor discovered a strange property of mid-ocean ridges. As part of their research, these scientists dragged a magnetic recorder through the water above a mid-ocean ridge. They discovered patterns of magnetism in the sea-floor rocks! The pattern they observed on one side of the ridge was a mirror image of the pattern on the other side of the ridge, as shown in **Figure 6.** Why were the rocks magnetized? What could have caused this pattern in the rocks? The scientists determined that the magnetism of the rocks aligned with Earth's magnetic field as it was when the rocks formed.

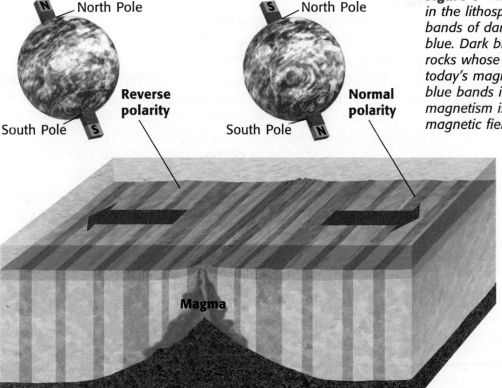

North Pole

Reverse polarity

South Pole

North Pole

Normal polarity

South Pole

Magma

Figure 6 *Magnetic reversals in the lithosphere are shown as bands of dark blue and light blue. Dark blue bands indicate rocks whose magnetism matches today's magnetic field. Light blue bands indicate rocks whose magnetism is opposite to today's magnetic field.*

Figure 7 Sea-Floor Spreading

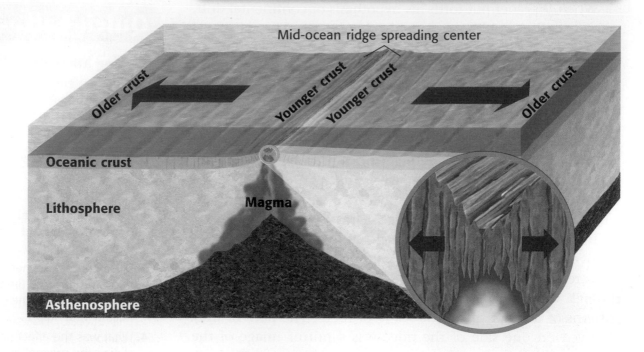

Magnetic Reversals—Mystery Solved

Throughout Earth's history, the north and south magnetic poles have changed places many times. The process by which Earth's magnetic poles change places is called *magnetic reversal.* So, how does this process explain the magnetic patterns on the sea floor?

As rock forms from magma, or molten rock, minerals that contain iron form. Some of these minerals are magnetic and act like compasses. They form so that their magnetic fields align with the magnetic field of Earth. When the molten rock cools, these tiny compasses are locked in position in the rock. After Earth's magnetic field reverses, new magnetic minerals that align in the opposite direction form.

Sea-Floor Spreading

At a mid-ocean ridge, magma rises through fractures in the sea floor. As the magma cools, it forms new rock. As this new rock forms, the older rock gets pulled away from the mid-ocean ridge. The process by which new sea floor forms as old sea floor is pulled away is called **sea-floor spreading,** and is shown in **Figure 7.**

As it spreads away from a mid-ocean ridge, the sea floor carries with it a record of magnetic reversals. This record of magnetic reversals provides evidence that the continents are moving. Sea-floor spreading is now known to be a mechanism by which continents move.

sea-floor spreading (SEE FLAWR SPRED ing) the process by which new oceanic lithosphere (sea floor) forms as magma rises to Earth's surface and solidifies at a mid-ocean ridge

Summary

- Earth is made up of three layers—the crust, the mantle, and the core—based on chemical composition. Of these three layers, the core is made up of the densest materials. The crust and mantle are made up of materials that are less dense than the core.

- Earth is made up of five layers—the lithosphere, the asthenosphere, the mesosphere, the outer core, and the inner core—based on physical properties.

- Knowledge about the layers of Earth comes from the study of seismic waves caused by earthquakes.

- Wegener hypothesized that continents drift apart from one another now and that they have drifted in the past.

- Magnetic reversals that occur over time are recorded in the magnetic pattern of the oceanic crust, which provides evidence of sea-floor spreading and continental drift.

- Sea-floor spreading is the process by which new sea floor forms at mid-ocean ridges.

Using Vocabulary

For each pair of terms, explain how the meanings of the terms differ.

1 *crust* and *mantle*

2 *lithosphere* and *asthenosphere*

Understanding Concepts

3 Listing List the layers of Earth by their chemical composition and by their physical properties.

4 Applying Explain how earthquakes allow scientists to study Earth's interior.

5 Inferring Describe evidence that supports the existence of Pangaea.

6 Summarizing Explain how continental drift explains today's position of the continents.

7 Analyzing Explain the process by which new sea floor forms at mid-ocean ridges.

8 Summarizing Briefly explain how magnetic reversals provide evidence for sea-floor spreading.

INTERPRETING GRAPHICS Use the diagram below to answer the next two questions.

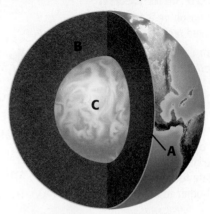

9 Identifying Which layer, A, B, or C, is the densest of Earth's compositional layers?

10 Identifying Which layer, A, B, or C, accounts for 67% of Earth's mass?

Critical Thinking

11 Making Comparisons Explain how the crust differs from the lithosphere.

12 Analyzing Ideas How do the physical properties of the asthenosphere support the ideas of continental drift and sea-floor spreading?

13 Applying Concepts Explain how sea-floor spreading provides a mechanism by which continents move.

Challenge

14 Applying Concepts If rocks found in North America and rocks found in Europe are the same, what does this indicate about the North American and European continents?

Internet Resources

For a variety of links related to this chapter, go to www.scilinks.org

Topic: Composition of the Earth; Structure of the Earth

SciLinks code: HY70329; HY71468

The Theory of Plate Tectonics

Key Concept Tectonic plates the size of continents and oceans move at rates of a few centimeters per year in response to movements in the mantle.

What You Will Learn

- Earth's lithosphere is broken into pieces called *tectonic plates*.
- Heat from Earth's interior causes convection in the mantle.
- Tectonic plates move at an average rate of a few centimeters per year.

Why It Matters

The theory of plate tectonics is a cornerstone of Earth science. Understanding plate tectonics will help you understand other topics of Earth science.

Vocabulary

- plate tectonics
- tectonic plate

READING STRATEGY

Clarifying Concepts Take turns reading this section out loud with a partner. Stop to discuss ideas that seem confusing.

▶ How much force does it take to move a continent? Where could all of the energy for such force possibly come from? As scientists' understanding of mid-ocean ridges and magnetic reversals grew, scientists formed a theory to explain how continents move. **Plate tectonics** is the theory that Earth's lithosphere is divided into tectonic plates that move around on top of the asthenosphere. In this section, you will learn what causes tectonic plates to move.

Tectonic Plates

Pieces of the lithosphere that move around on top of the asthenosphere are called **tectonic plates.** Earth's major tectonic plates are shown on the map in **Figure 1.** Note that tectonic plates differ in size. Some tectonic plates contain both continental and oceanic crust. Also note that some tectonic plates contain mostly oceanic crust, whereas others contain mostly continental crust.

Figure 1 Earth's Major Tectonic Plates

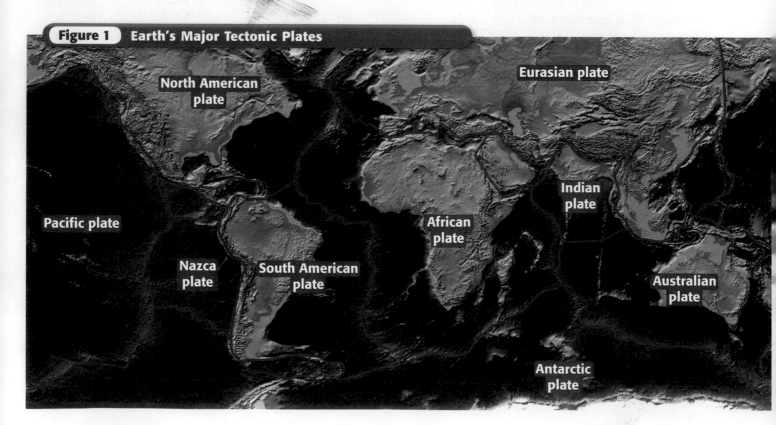

North American plate

Eurasian plate

Pacific plate

Indian plate

African plate

Nazca plate

South American plate

Australian plate

Antarctic plate

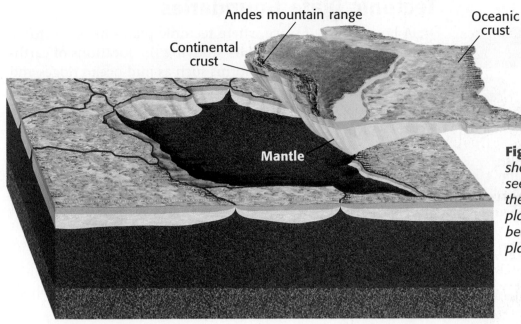

Continental crust

Andes mountain range

Oceanic crust

Mantle

Figure 2 *This image shows what you might see if you could lift the South American plate out of its position between other tectonic plates.*

A Tectonic Plate Close-Up

Earth's lithosphere is like a giant jigsaw puzzle, and tectonic plates are like the pieces of the jigsaw puzzle. What would a tectonic plate look like if you could lift it out of this rocky jigsaw puzzle? **Figure 2** shows what the South American plate might look like. Notice that this tectonic plate consists of not only the upper part of the mantle but also both oceanic crust and continental crust. The thickest part of the South American plate is the part underneath the thick continental crust of the Andes Mountains. The thinnest part of this plate is located at the mid-ocean ridge in the Atlantic Ocean.

Like Ice Cubes in a Bowl of Punch

Think about ice cubes floating in a bowl of punch. If there are enough cubes, they will cover the surface of the punch and bump into one another. Parts of the ice cubes are below the surface of the punch and displace the punch. Large pieces of ice displace more punch than small pieces of ice do. Tectonic plates "float" on the asthenosphere in a similar way. The plates cover the surface of the asthenosphere, and they touch one another and move around. The lithosphere displaces the asthenosphere. Thick tectonic plates, such as those made of continental lithosphere, displace more asthenosphere than do thin plates, such as those made of oceanic lithosphere.

Standards Check Why do tectonic plates made of continental lithosphere displace more asthenosphere than tectonic plates made of oceanic lithosphere do? **6.1.c**

plate tectonics (PLAYT tek TAHN iks) the theory that explains how large pieces of Earth's outermost layer, called *tectonic plates,* move and change shape

tectonic plate (tek TAHN ik PLAYT) a block of lithosphere that consists of the crust and the rigid, outermost part of the mantle

6.1.b Students know Earth is composed of several layers: a cold, brittle lithosphere; a hot, convecting mantle; and a dense, metallic core.
6.1.c Students know lithospheric plates the size of continents and oceans move at rates of centimeters per year in response to movements in the mantle.
6.1.e Students know major geologic events, such as earthquakes, volcanic eruptions, and mountain building, result from plate motions.
6.4.c Students know heat from Earth's interior reaches the surface primarily through convection.

Tectonic Plate Boundaries

A boundary is a place where tectonic plates meet. Tectonic plate boundaries are located by studying the locations of earthquakes, volcanoes, and landforms such as mid-ocean ridges and ocean trenches. Plate boundaries are divided into three types based on how the tectonic plates move relative to one another. **Figure 3** shows examples of tectonic plate boundaries.

Convergent Boundaries

The boundary at which two tectonic plates collide is a *convergent boundary.* At a convergent boundary, three types of collisons may happen. The three types of collisions and their results are outlined in the following list:

- Two plates made of continental lithosphere may collide. This collision may form a high mountain range, which develops over a period of millions of years.

- A plate of oceanic lithosphere may collide with a plate of continental lithosphere. The denser oceanic crust sinks, or subducts, beneath the less-dense continental crust. This process is called *subduction.* Subduction may cause a chain of volcanoes to form parallel to the plate boundary.

- If two plates of oceanic lithosphere collide, the denser of the two plates will subduct. A series of volcanic islands, called an *island arc,* may form parallel to the plate boundary.

Figure 3 Tectonic Plate Boundaries

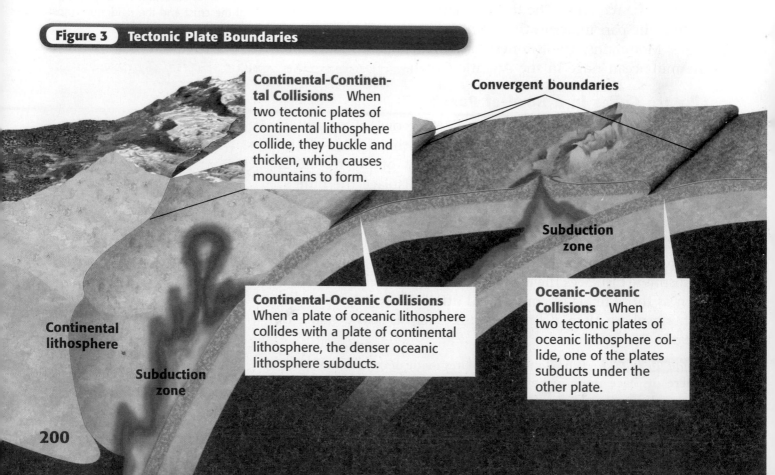

Continental-Continental Collisions When two tectonic plates of continental lithosphere collide, they buckle and thicken, which causes mountains to form.

Convergent boundaries

Subduction zone

Continental lithosphere

Subduction zone

Continental-Oceanic Collisions When a plate of oceanic lithosphere collides with a plate of continental lithosphere, the denser oceanic lithosphere subducts.

Oceanic-Oceanic Collisions When two tectonic plates of oceanic lithosphere collide, one of the plates subducts under the other plate.

200

Divergent Boundaries

The boundary at which two tectonic plates separate is a *divergent boundary*. Some divergent boundaries appear on land, such as in Iceland and eastern Africa. However, most divergent boundaries happen on the sea floor. These boundaries are characterized by mid-ocean ridges. As the plates pull away from each other, fractures form in the oceanic lithosphere. Magma rises through these fractures to the ocean floor. There, the magma solidifies to form new lithosphere.

Transform Boundaries

The boundary at which two tectonic plates slide past one another horizontally is a *transform boundary*. Most transform boundaries occur in the sea floor at mid-ocean ridges. At these locations, transform boundaries run perpendicular to the ridge where plates are pulling apart. The transform boundaries cause offsets between shorter segments of the ridge. These offsets give mid-ocean ridges the zigzag patterns that are seen on maps of the sea floor.

A well-known example of a transform boundary that occurs both on the sea floor and on land is the San Andreas fault system in California. The fault system is located where the Pacific and North American plates are sliding past each other.

Standards Check Compare the three types of plate boundaries.
6.1.e

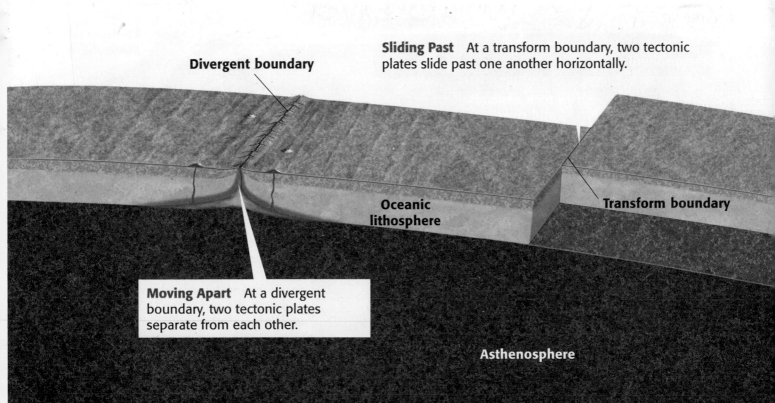

Divergent boundary

Sliding Past At a transform boundary, two tectonic plates slide past one another horizontally.

Oceanic lithosphere

Transform boundary

Moving Apart At a divergent boundary, two tectonic plates separate from each other.

Asthenosphere

Causes of Tectonic Plate Motion

What causes the motion of tectonic plates? Tectonic plate motion is the result of density differences that are caused by the flow of heat within Earth. Earth's core and mantle are very hot because they contain minerals that have radioactive atoms. These atoms release heat as they decay. Heat always flows from a warmer area to a colder area. Thus, heat from Earth's center flows toward the surface. However, rock is a poor conductor of heat. Therefore, most of the transfer of heat happens through convection.

When rock is heated, it expands, becomes less dense, and rises toward the surface of Earth. At the surface, cold, dense rock of the lithosphere tends to sink during subduction. This process causes *convection currents* in the mantle. **Figure 4** shows three mechanisms of convection that drive tectonic plate motion.

Standards Check How does mantle convection cause plate motion?
6.1.c, 6.4.c

Figure 4 **Three Possible Driving Forces of Plate Tectonics**

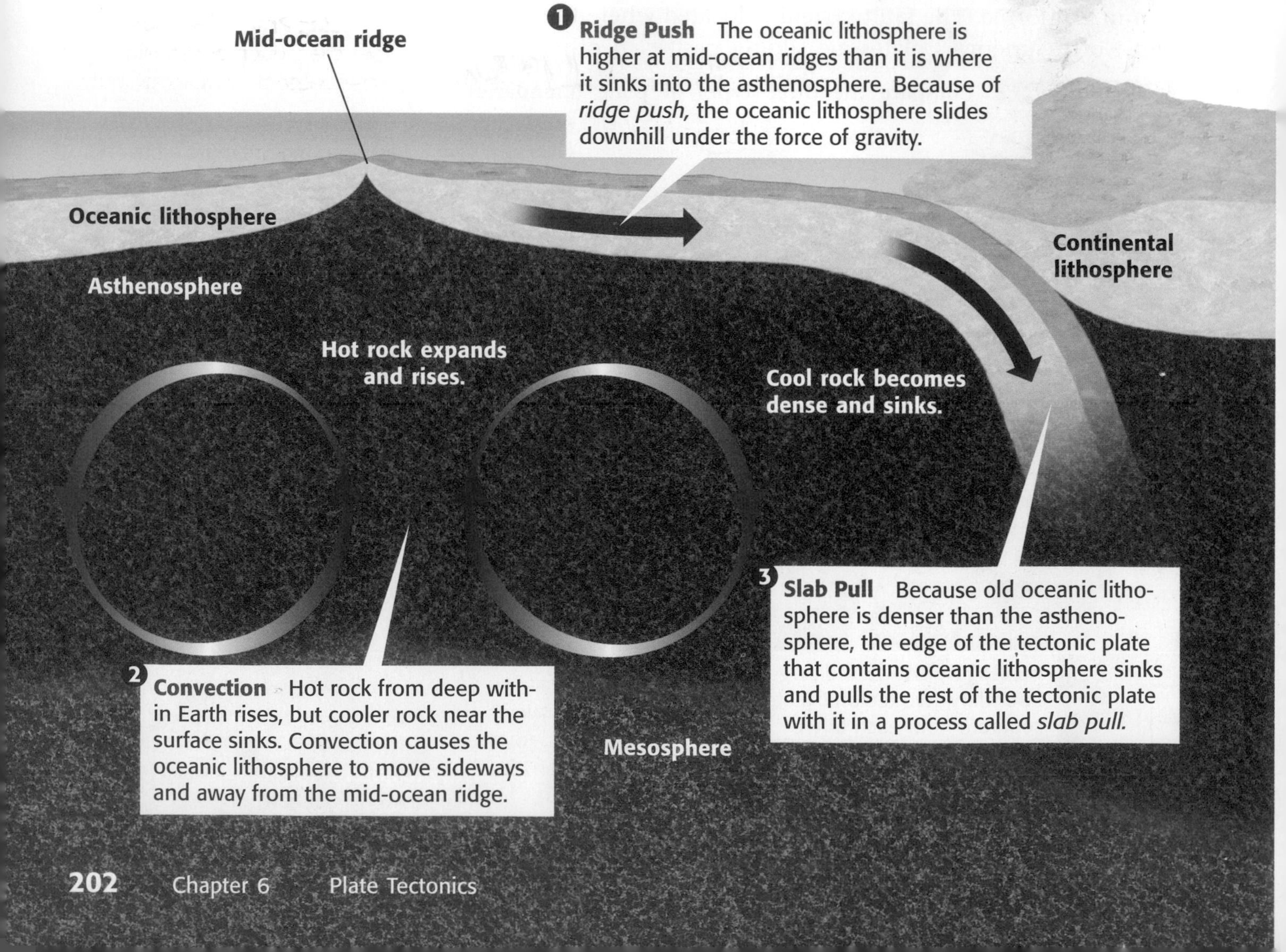

Mid-ocean ridge

❶ **Ridge Push** The oceanic lithosphere is higher at mid-ocean ridges than it is where it sinks into the asthenosphere. Because of *ridge push,* the oceanic lithosphere slides downhill under the force of gravity.

Oceanic lithosphere

Asthenosphere

Continental lithosphere

Hot rock expands and rises.

Cool rock becomes dense and sinks.

❷ **Convection** Hot rock from deep within Earth rises, but cooler rock near the surface sinks. Convection causes the oceanic lithosphere to move sideways and away from the mid-ocean ridge.

❸ **Slab Pull** Because old oceanic lithosphere is denser than the asthenosphere, the edge of the tectonic plate that contains oceanic lithosphere sinks and pulls the rest of the tectonic plate with it in a process called *slab pull.*

Mesosphere

Tracking Tectonic Plate Motion

Tectonic plate movement is so gradual that it is measured in centimeters per year. The average rate of movement for different plates ranges between 2.5 cm/year and 15 cm/year. To measure the rate of tectonic plate movement on continents, scientists use GPS. Radio signals are continuously beamed from satellites to GPS ground stations, which record the exact distance between the satellites and the ground station. Over time, these distances change slightly. Scientists use these distances to measure rates of plate motion. However, scientists use sea-floor spreading to measure the rate of movement of oceanic plates.

Standards Check How fast do tectonic plates move? 6.1.c

INTERNET ACTIVITY

Alien Planet Adventure
Create a planet that might be described in a science fiction book. Describe the interactions of the planet's core, mantle, and crust. Go to **go.hrw.com,** and type in the keyword HY7TECW.

SECTION Review

 6.1.b, 6.1.c, 6.1.e, 4.4.c

Summary

- Plate tectonics is the theory that explains how pieces of Earth's lithosphere move and change shape.
- Tectonic plates are large pieces of the lithosphere that move around on top of the asthenosphere.
- Boundaries between tectonic plates are classified as convergent, divergent, or transform.
- Convection is the main driving force of plate tectonics.
- Tectonic plates move a few centimeters per year. Scientists measure this rate by using GPS or by using sea-floor spreading.

Using Vocabulary

1. Write an original definition for *plate tectonics* and *tectonic plate.*

Understanding Concepts

2. **Applying** What is the theory of plate tectonics?

3. **Applying** Describe a tectonic plate.

4. **Summarizing** Describe the three types of plate boundaries.

5. **Applying** Explain how heat in Earth's interior is transferred by convection.

6. **Summarizing** What three mechanisms may drive tectonic plate movement?

7. **Identifying** Approximately how fast do tectonic plates move?

Critical Thinking

8. **Identifying Relationships** When convection takes place in the mantle, why does cool rock material sink and warm rock material rise?

9. **Analyzing Processes** Why does oceanic lithosphere sink beneath continental lithosphere at convergent boundaries?

10. **Analyzing Processes** How does the motion of tectonic plates relate to continental drift?

11. **Identifying Relationships** How do mountain building and volcanoes relate to plate motion at convergent boundaries?

Math Skills

12. **Making Calculations** If a tectonic plate has moved 125 cm in a 25-year period, what is its average rate of movement in cm/year?

Challenge

13. **Analyzing Processes** How are ridge push and slab pull related to convection in Earth's mantle?

Internet Resources

For a variety of links related to this chapter, go to www.scilinks.org

Topic: Plate Tectonics
SciLinks code: HY71171

Deforming Earth's Crust

Key Concept Tectonic plate motions deform Earth's crust. Deformation causes rock layers to bend and break and causes mountains to form.

What You Will Learn

- Stress is placed on rock as plates move. The stress causes rock to fold and break.
- The formation of mountains results from the motion of tectonic plates.

Why It Matters

Tectonic plate motion shapes and reshapes Earth's surface.

Vocabulary

- folding
- fault

READING STRATEGY

Summarizing Read this section silently. In pairs, take turns summarizing the material. Stop to discuss ideas and words that seem confusing.

▶ Have you ever tried to bend something, only to have it break? Take long, uncooked pieces of spaghetti, and bend them very slowly and only a little. Now, bend them again, but this time, bend them much farther and faster. What happened?

Deformation

How can a material bend at one time and break at another time? The answer is that the stress you put on the material was different each time. *Stress* is the amount of force per unit area on a given material. The same principle applies to the rocks in Earth's crust. Rock reacts differently when different amounts of stress are applied.

The process by which the shape of a rock changes in response to stress is called *deformation*. In the example above, the spaghetti deformed in two different ways—by bending and by breaking. **Figure 1** illustrates this concept. The same process happens in rock layers. Rock layers bend when stress is placed on them. But when enough stress is placed on rocks, the rocks may break.

Standards Check Describe two ways in which rock layers can deform when stress is placed on them. 🐻 **6.1.d**

Figure 1 *When a small amount of stress is placed on uncooked spaghetti, the spaghetti bends. Additional stress causes the spaghetti to break.*

6.1.a Students know evidence of plate tectonics is derived from the fit of the continents; the location of earthquakes, volcanoes, and midocean ridges; and the distribution of fossils, rock types, and ancient climatic zones.

6.1.d Students know that earthquakes are sudden motions along breaks in the crust called faults and that volcanoes and fissures are locations where magma reaches the surface.

6.1.e Students know major geologic events, such as earthquakes, volcanic eruptions, and mountain building, result from plate motions.

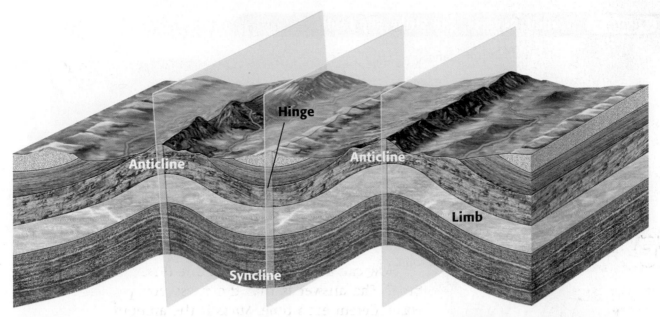

Labels on image: Hinge, Anticline, Anticline, Limb, Syncline

Figure 2 *Anticlines and synclines are two types of folds. The folds to the left and right are anticlines. The fold in the center is a syncline. The blue planes represent surfaces that run through each hinge and divide the folds into two limbs.* **How many limbs does each fold have?**

Folding

The bending of rock layers in response to stress in Earth's crust is called **folding.** Scientists assume that all rock layers started as horizontal layers. So, when scientists see a fold, they know that deformation has taken place. All folds have a hinge and two limbs. Limbs are the sloping sides of a fold. A hinge is the bend where the two limbs meet.

Anticlines and Synclines

Two of the most common types of folds—anticlines and synclines—are shown in **Figure 2.** An *anticline* is a fold in which the oldest rock layers are in the center of the fold. In many anticlines, the rock limbs slope down from the center to form an arch. In the diagram, a syncline is shown between two anticlines. A *syncline* is a fold in which the youngest rock layers are in the center of the fold. In many synclines, the limbs slope up from the center to form a trough. Folds can be large or small. Anticlines can be from tens of meters wide to hundreds of kilometers wide. Small folds are measured in centimeters.

Shapes of Folds

The rock layers in the folds shown in **Figure 2** bend symmetrically. But rock layers can bend into folds that are not symmetrical. Such folds are *asymmetrical* (AY suh ME tri kuhl) *folds.* In an asymmetrical fold, one limb may dip more steeply than the other limb does. An *overturned fold* is a fold in which one limb is tilted beyond 90°. Rock layers may also be bent so much that a fold appears to be lying on its side. Geologists call this type of lying-down fold a *recumbent fold.*

folding (FOHLD ing) the bending of rock layers due to stress

Figure 3 Normal, Reverse, and Strike-Slip Faults

Fault plane

Footwall

Hanging wall

The footwall is the block of rock that lies below the plane of the fault. The hanging wall is the block that lies above the plane of the fault.

Normal Fault *When rocks are pulled apart because of tension, normal faults form.*

Faulting

When rock is placed under so much stress that it can no longer stretch or flow, it may break. The surface along which rocks break and slide past each other is called a **fault.** The blocks of crust on each side of the fault are called *fault blocks.*

When a fault is not vertical, there are two kinds of fault blocks—the *hanging wall* and the *footwall.* The illustration at the far left of **Figure 3** shows the difference between a hanging wall and a footwall. Faults are classified into three categories according to how the fault blocks move relative to each other. The type of fault that forms can be used to determine the type of stress that caused the fault.

fault (FAWLT) a break in a body of rock along which one block slides relative to another

Standards Check How do faults form? 6.1.d

Normal Faults

A *normal fault* is shown in **Figure 3.** Along a normal fault, the hanging wall moves down relative to the footwall. Normal faults usually form where tectonic plate motions cause tension. Tension is stress that pulls rocks apart. Therefore, normal faults are common at mid-ocean ridges. At mid-ocean ridges, plate separation causes oceanic lithosphere to break into fault blocks.

Reverse Faults

A *reverse fault* is shown in **Figure 3.** Along a reverse fault, the hanging wall moves up relative to the footwall. This movement is the reverse of a normal fault. Reverse faults usually form where tectonic plate motions cause compression. Compression is stress that pushes rocks together. Therefore, reverse faults are common in subduction zones. In subduction zones, oceanic lithosphere descends into the asthenosphere.

Reverse Fault *When rocks are pushed together by compression, reverse faults form.*

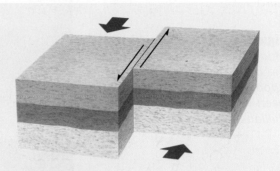

Strike-Slip Fault *When rocks are moved horizontally by opposing forces, strike-slip faults form.*

Strike-Slip Faults

A *strike-slip fault* is shown in **Figure 3.** Along a strike-slip fault, the two fault blocks move past each other horizontally. Imagine that you are standing on one side of a strike-slip fault looking across the fault. If the fault blocks moved, the ground on the other side of the fault would appear to move to your left or right. Strike-slip faults usually form where tectonic plate motions cause shear stress parallel to Earth's surface. Shear stress is stress that pushes different parts of the rock in different directions. Therefore, strike-slip faults are common along transform boundaries.

Standards Check Compare how the three types of faults form. 6.1.d

Recognizing Faults

Some faults are only a few meters long. Other faults are several hundred kilometers long. So, how can you recognize a fault when you see one? Movement along faults causes rock layers to become offset. Therefore, layers of different kinds of rock that sit side-by-side indicate offset along a fault. In addition, features such as grooves, striations, or polished surfaces called *slickensides* indicate where rocks have moved.

Fault offset is particularly obvious along faults that break Earth's surface for many kilometers. A landform on one side of a fault may be offset on the other side of the fault. For example, streams commonly change the direction they flow at a fault. In addition, manmade objects, such as fences and curbs, may be offset. Another feature that indicates fault offset is a scarp. A *scarp* is a row of cliffs formed by faulting. Scarps form when rock on one side of a fault is raised vertically relative to rock on the other side of the fault. Faults scarps may be several centimeters to tens of meters high.

Quick Lab

Modeling Strike-Slip Faults

6.1.d

1. Use **modeling clay** to construct a block that is 15 cm × 15 cm × 10 cm. Use different colors of clay to represent different horizontal layers.

2. Using **scissors**, cut the block down the middle. Place **two 4 in. × 6 in. index cards** inside the cut so that the two blocks slide freely.

3. Using gentle pressure, slide the two blocks horizontally past one another.

4. How does this model illustrate the motion along a strike-slip fault?

15 min

Figure 4 *The Appalachian Mountains were once as tall as the Himalaya Mountains. But the Appalachian Mountains have been worn down by hundreds of millions of years of erosion.*

Plate Tectonics and Mountain Building

As tectonic plates move around Earth's surface, the edges of the plates grind against each other. These interactions cause a great deal of stress in Earth's crust because the plates have a great deal of mass. Over long periods of time, this process may crumple and push up the margins of the plates. When this happens, great mountain-building events may occur.

Standards Check How do mountains form? 🐻 **6.1.a, 6.1.d, 6.1.e**

Folded Mountains

When rock layers are squeezed together and pushed upward, *folded mountains* form. These mountain ranges form at convergent boundaries where continents have collided. When continents collide, compression folds and uplifts the rock. **Figure 4** shows the Appalachian Mountains, an example of folded mountains.

Fault-Block Mountains

When tension in Earth's crust causes the crust to break into a large number of normal faults, *fault-block mountains* form. These mountains form when tension causes large blocks of Earth's crust to drop down relative to other blocks. The Tetons, shown in **Figure 5,** are a range of fault-block mountains.

Figure 5 *The Tetons in Idaho and Wyoming formed as a result of tension that caused Earth's crust to break into a series of normal faults.*

Volcanic Mountains

When molten rock erupts onto Earth's surface, *volcanic mountains* form. Most of the world's major volcanic mountains are located at convergent boundaries. At convergent boundaries, the motions of the plates causes hot mantle rocks to rise beneath the plate. The molten rock rises to the surface and erupts.

Volcanic mountains form both on land and on the ocean floor. Sometimes, these mountains can rise above the ocean surface to become islands. Most of the active volcanic mountains on Earth have formed around the tectonically active rim of the Pacific Ocean. This area is known as the *Ring of Fire*. **Figure 6** shows Mount Shasta in northern California. Mount Shasta is one of the many volcanoes in the Ring of Fire.

Figure 6 *Mount Shasta is a volcano that has formed at a subduction zone.*

SECTION Review

6.1.d, 6.1.e

Summary

- Deformation structures, such as faults and folds, form as a result of stress in the lithosphere. This stress is caused by tectonic plate motion.

- Folding occurs when rock layers bend because of stress.

- Faulting occurs when rock layers break because of stress and then move on either side of the break.

- Three major fault types are normal faults, reverse faults, and strike-slip faults.

- Mountain building is caused by the movement of tectonic plates. Folded mountains and volcanic mountains form at convergent boundaries. Fault-block mountains form at divergent boundaries.

Using Vocabulary

For the pair of terms, explain how the meanings of the terms differ.

1. *folding* and *fault*

Understanding Concepts

2. **Applying** Why do rocks deform?

3. **Identifying** Identify two ways that rocks deform.

4. **Summarizing** What causes faults to form?

INTERPRETING GRAPHICS Use the diagram below to answer the next two questions.

5. **Identifying** What type of fault is shown?

6. **Applying** At what kind of plate boundary would you find this fault?

7. **Comparing** For each of the three types of faults, explain the forces that cause the faults to form.

8. **Applying** How are mountains related to tectonic plate motion?

Critical Thinking

9. **Predicting Consequences** Which type of fault is likely to form in an area where rock layers have been folded? Explain your answer.

Challenge

10. **Identifying Relationships** Would you expect to see a folded-mountain range at a mid-ocean ridge? Explain your answer.

California Geology

Key Concept Major features of California geology can be explained in terms of plate tectonics.

What You Will Learn

- Plate tectonics has been the most important force in shaping California's geologic history.
- The San Andreas fault marks a transform boundary between the North American plate and the Pacific plate.

Why It Matters

California has earthquakes, volcanoes, and mountains as a result of tectonic plate motion.

Vocabulary

- batholith
- accreted terrane

READING STRATEGY

Graphic Organizer In your **Science Journal,** create a Process Chart about how the plate boundary between the North American plate and the Pacific plate in California has developed.

Most people who live in California know that earthquakes are caused by the movement of Earth's plates. However, few Californians realize that plate tectonics is important in many other aspects of California geology. The region that we know as California has been at an active plate boundary for the past 225 million years. As a result, plate tectonics has been the most important force in shaping California's geologic history. The current tectonic setting of California is shown in **Figure 1.**

Building California by Plate Tectonics

Before about 225 million years ago, North America's western edge was much farther east than it is now. The area where Nevada and the eastern deserts of California are today was the west coast of North America. Most of what is now California was either part of a distant oceanic plate or did not exist.

When Pangaea began to break up, the North American plate moved west. The continent's western edge became an active convergent plate boundary. A long period of subduction began. This subduction was the beginning of the most important period of geologic "building" in California, which took place between about 160 million and 100 million years ago.

Standards Check How did the breakup of Pangaea affect the tectonic setting of western North America? 6.1.f

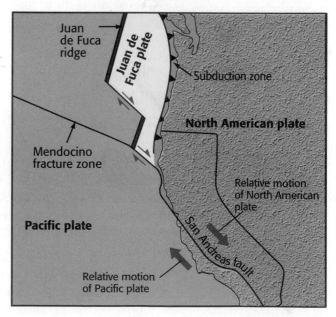

Figure 1 *The map at the right shows the current tectonic setting of California. The San Andreas fault marks a transform boundary between the North American plate and the Pacific plate. Subduction of the Juan de Fuca plate is still occurring in the northernmost part of the state.*

Juan de Fuca ridge

Juan de Fuca plate

Subduction zone

North American plate

Mendocino fracture zone

Relative motion of North American plate

Pacific plate

San Andreas fault

Relative motion of Pacific plate

Figure 2   Changing Tectonic Plate Boundaries

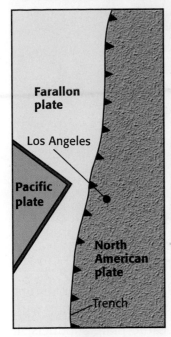
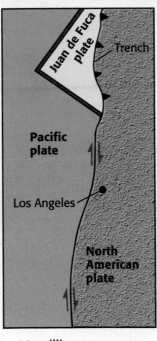
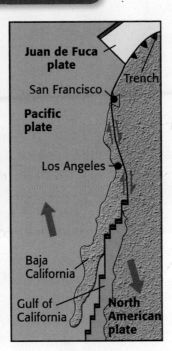

30 million years ago   10 million years ago   Present

Ancient Plate Boundaries

Three major tectonic plates influenced California's geologic history. Those plates were the North American plate, the Farallon plate, and the Pacific plate. As these plates interacted, the modern plate boundary between the North American and Pacific plates developed, as shown in **Figure 2.**

A convergent boundary existed between the North American and Farallon plates. The Farallon plate subducted beneath the North American plate. The subduction zone ran along the entire length of California. It was active for over 100 million years. It ran in a direction similar to today's plate boundary—roughly parallel to the coast.

The Transform Boundary Is Born

The ancient Farallon Plate lay between the North American and Pacific plates. As the Farallon plate subducted, the Pacific plate moved closer and closer to North America. Sometime around 25 million years ago, the Farallon plate was completely subducted at one part of the boundary. The Pacific plate touched North America for the first time. When this happened, the transform boundary was born.

As the Farallon plate continues to subduct, the transform boundary continues to grow longer. Today, it is about 2,600 km long. In fact, the Juan de Fuca plate off northern California is part of what remains of the ancient Farallon plate.

6.1.f Students know how to explain major features of California geology (including mountains, faults, volcanoes) in terms of plate tectonics.

Figure 3 *El Capitan, at left, is located on the north side of Yosemite Valley in the Sierra Nevadas. The granite rocks of the Sierra Nevadas formed over a timespan of more than 100 million years.*

batholith (BATH oh LITH) a large mass of igneous rock in Earth's crust that, if exposed at the surface, covers an area of at least 100 km²

accreted terrane (uh KREET uhd ter RAYN) a piece of lithosphere that becomes part of a larger landmass when tectonic plates collide at a convergent boundary

Subduction and Volcanism

The subduction of the Farallon plate had two major results. It caused rock to melt and caused chunks of rock to collide with the North American continent. As an oceanic plate subducts, it heats up. As a result, it releases water and other fluids into the surrounding rock. This fluid lowers the melting point of the surrounding rock. The rock melts to form magma, or molten rock.

The Sierra Nevada Batholith

The subduction of the Farallon plate caused a great deal of magma to form in the lithosphere. This magma solidified between about 210 million and 100 million years ago to form a mass of granite known as the *Sierra Nevada batholith*. A **batholith** is a large mass of igneous rock that forms deep below the surface. We can think of batholiths as the "roots" of subduction zone volcanoes. A chain of huge volcanoes must have formed above the giant magma chamber. These volcanoes probably stood about twice as tall as today's Sierra Nevadas! The granite batholith is exposed at Earth's surface in the Sierra Nevada mountain range, as **Figure 3** shows.

The Cascadia Subduction Zone

Today, off the northern coast of California, the Juan de Fuca plate is subducting beneath the North American plate. The convergent boundary begins near Cape Mendocino and extends north off the coasts of Oregon, Washington, and British Columbia. This area is known as the *Cascadia subduction zone*. As a result of the subduction zone, a chain of active volcanoes is present in the Cascade Mountains of California, Oregon, and Washington. These volcanoes include Lassen Peak and Mount Shasta in California. These volcanoes are the southernmost volcanoes of the Cascade volcanic chain.

Subduction and Accretion

During subduction, pieces of the plate that subducts may be scraped off and attached to the overriding plate. This process, called *accretion,* forms mountain chains. These mountain chains are parallel to the plate boundary. The rocks in California's Coast Ranges and Transverse Ranges are thought to have formed in this way. The Central Valley, Los Angeles Basin, and Ventura Basin separate some of these mountain ranges.

Accreted Terranes

The chunks of lithosphere that are scraped off of subducting plates and added to the edge of a continent are called **accreted terranes.** Geologists can identify accreted terranes because the rocks that make up a terrane differ from the surrounding rocks. For example, terrane rocks may differ in age from the surrounding rocks. In addition, the terrane is commonly surrounded by faults. Many accreted terranes are made up of marine sedimentary rocks, volcanic rocks erupted on the ocean floor, and unusual rocks from the mantle.

Standards Check How did accretion help shape California's geology? 6.1.f

California Gold

In the foothills along the western side of the Sierra Nevadas are rocks that contain most of California's gold. These rocks are thought to be accreted terranes. This gold-containing rock, which has been very important in California's history, formed near submarine volcanic vents before being accreted. After the terranes were accreted, the gold became concentrated in the quartz veins of the Mother Lode. California gold is shown in **Figure 4.**

Figure 4 *Much of California's gold is found in quartz veins in the Mother Lode country of northern California.*

Quick Lab

Modeling Accretion

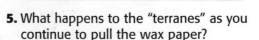

1. Use **one color of modeling clay** to make a continental landmass. Use **several other colors of clay** to make several small "terranes."

2. Place all of the terranes on a **piece of wax paper** at various intervals.

3. Hold the continent just off the edge of a table.

4. Pull the wax paper under the continent so that the terranes move toward the continent.

5. What happens to the "terranes" as you continue to pull the wax paper?

6. How does pulling the wax paper under the continent model subduction at a convergent boundary?

7. How does this lab model the accretion of terranes to a continent during subduction at a convergent boundary?

6.1.f

 20 min

Finding Faults

With an adult, go to the USGS California Educational Resources site on the Internet. Find the fault map titled "Major Faults of California." Use the map to locate the fault nearest your home. Record your findings in your **Science Journal.**

ACTiViTY

The San Andreas Fault System

Today, California is home to the most famous transform plate boundary in the world, the San Andreas fault system. The San Andreas fault, which is the major fault in this system, forms the boundary between the Pacific plate and the North American plate. Most of California is part of the North American plate. But a small part of California, west of the San Andreas fault, lies on the Pacific plate. Along the boundary formed by the San Andreas fault, the Pacific plate is moving to the northwest relative to the North American plate. On land, the San Andreas fault system extends in a northwest direction for about 1,000 km, from the border between California and Mexico to Cape Mendocino in northern California.

Plate Motion on the San Andreas Fault System

Scientists consider the San Andreas fault to be the boundary between the two plates, but not all of the plate motion takes place on the San Andreas fault itself. In the San Francisco Bay area and in southern California, plate motion takes place on other faults of the San Andreas system. These faults lie east and west of the San Andreas fault, as shown in **Figure 5.** In these areas, it is best to think of the boundary between the Pacific plate and the North American plate as a zone rather than as a line. So, we see that even the question, "Where is the exact boundary between the Pacific and North American plates?" has no simple answer.

Standards Check Why is it difficult to distinguish the boundary between the North American plate and the Pacific plate? 6.1.f

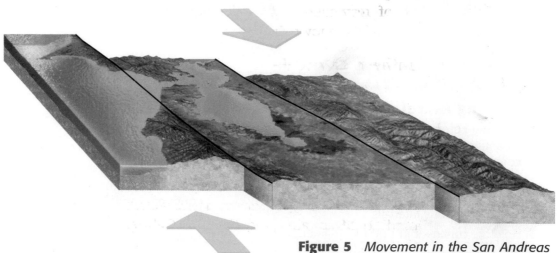

Figure 5 *Movement in the San Andreas fault system takes place along multiple faults. As a result, the boundary between the Pacific plate and the North American plate is not easy to define.*

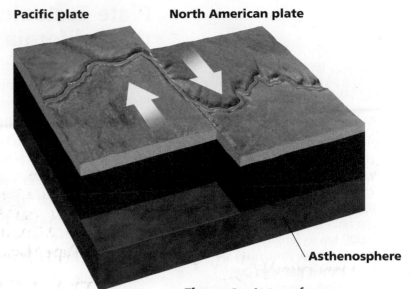

Pacific plate

North American plate

Asthenosphere

Figure 6 *At transform boundaries, plates slide past one another horizontally, causing offset. The course of the stream in the photo is offset because the Pacific plate and the North American plate are moving past one another along the San Andreas fault.*

Offset on the San Andreas Fault System

The Pacific plate and the North American plate have been moving along the San Andreas fault system for about 25 million years. During the last 16 million years, the separation, or offset, along the fault has been about 315 km. Geologists study the history of the plate boundary by matching up unusual rocks that have been separated by the fault. By dating these rocks, geologists know when the rocks formed. The geologists can use that time to determine when those areas were not separated. By measuring offset today, geologists estimate the amount and the rate of movement along the fault. Offset along the San Andreas fault is shown in **Figure 6.**

Compression in Southern California

In southern California, the San Andreas fault takes a huge bend as it passes east of the city of Los Angeles. Because of this bend, the Pacific plate and the North American plate are colliding as they move past each other. As a result, the motion along the boundary is partly convergent.

Because southern California is being compressed, areas near the bend are being uplifted or dropped down along active faults. The San Bernardino Mountains and the San Gabriel Mountains are examples of tectonically created mountain ranges. The Los Angeles Basin is a large depression bordered by active faults that form the borders of the surrounding mountains.

Plate Tectonics and the California Landscape

Movement Along the San Andreas Fault

The San Andreas fault began to form approximately 25 million years ago. During that 25-million-year period the fault has grown to be 2,600 km in length. On average, how much has the fault grown per year over 25 million years?

Much of California's landscape has been formed by plate tectonics. Even though most of the motion along the plate boundary is transform motion, compression along the boundary has recently uplifted California's rugged mountains. The steep, rocky coastlines of central and northern California have also been formed by uplift along the plate boundary.

The major river valleys and mountain ranges and the coastline are oriented in a northwesterly direction. They have this orientation because northwest is parallel to the faults of the plate boundary. But the Transverse Ranges, which stretch 500 km across southern California, do not have this orientation. Motion along faults in the San Andreas fault system has oriented these mountains in an east-west direction. **Figure 7** shows a map of California's major geologic regions and the rocks in them.

Standards Check Explain how the California landscape is influenced by the San Andreas fault system. 🐻 **6.1.f**

Figure 7 *This map shows the major geologic regions of California. Note the different rock types that make up each geologic region.*

Summary

- Plate tectonics has been the most important force in the shaping of California's geology.
- When Pangaea broke apart, the western edge of North America became an active plate boundary.
- Between 225 million and 25 million years ago, subduction took place along all of California.
- During subduction, California grew larger as accreted terranes were added to the North American continent.
- A transform boundary formed about 25 million years ago, when the Pacific plate met the North American plate.
- Along the San Andreas fault, the Pacific plate is moving northwest relative to the North American plate.
- The motions of tectonic plates have caused mountains and valleys to form in California.

Using Vocabulary

1 Use *batholith* and *accreted terrane* in separate sentences.

Understanding Concepts

2 Identifying Explain what the rocks of the Sierra Nevadas tell geologists about the geologic history of California.

3 Analyzing Explain how the formation of Lassen Peak and Mount Shasta are related to subduction.

4 Summarizing Briefly explain how the transform boundary between the Pacific plate and the North American plate formed.

5 Analyzing Explain why there is no clearly defined boundary between the Pacific plate and the North American plate.

6 Analyzing Explain how convergent motion along the San Andreas fault has shaped the southern California landscape.

Critical Thinking

7 Applying Concepts Which type of fault is most common in the San Andreas fault system?

8 Making Inferences Why are California's mountains and valleys generally parallel to the coast?

INTERPRETING GRAPHICS Use the diagram below to answer the next two questions.

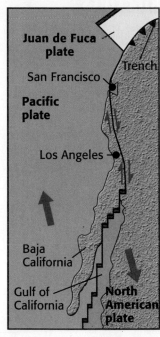

9 Analyzing Data In what direction is the North American plate moving relative to the Pacific plate?

10 Analyzing Data What type of structure has formed where the Juan de Fuca plate is subducting beneath the North American plate?

Challenge

11 Making Inferences Explain how a geologist might determine if rocks are part of an accreted terrane.

Internet Resources
For a variety of links related to this chapter, go to www.scilinks.org
Topic: California Geology
SciLinks code: HY7C04

Model-Making Lab

Sea-Floor Spreading

The places on Earth's surface where plates pull away from one another have many names. They are called *divergent boundaries, mid-ocean ridges,* and *spreading centers.* The term *spreading center* refers to the fact that sea-floor spreading happens at these locations. In this lab, you will model the formation of new sea floor at a divergent boundary. You will also model the formation of magnetic patterns on the sea floor.

Procedure

① Cut two pieces of unlined paper into identical strips that are each 7 cm wide and 30 cm long.

② Cut a slit 8 cm long across the center of the bottom of a shoe-box.

③ Lay the strips of paper together on top of each other end to end so that the ends line up. Push one end of the strips through the slit in the shoe box, so that a few centimeters of both strips stick out of the slit.

④ Place the shoe box open side down on a table, and make sure that the ends of the paper strips are sticking up out of the slit.

⑤ Separate the strips, and hold one strip in each hand. Pull the strips apart. Then, push the strips down against the shoe box.

⑥ Use a marker to mark across the paper strips where they exit the box. One swipe with the marker should mark both strips.

⑦ Pull the strips evenly until about 2 cm of paper have been pulled through the slit.

⑧ Mark the strips with the marker again.

⑨ Repeat steps 7 and 8, but vary the length of paper that you pull from the slit. Continue this process until both strips are completely pulled out of the box.

Analyze the Results

10 Evaluating Models How does this activity model sea-floor spreading?

11 Analyzing Models What do the marker stripes in this model represent?

Draw Conclusions

12 Analyzing Methods If each 2 cm of the paper's length is equivalent to 3 million years, how could you use your model to determine the age of certain points on your model sea floor?

13 Applying Conclusions Imagine that you are given only the paper strips with marks already drawn on them. How would you use the paper strips to reconstruct the way in which the sea-floor formed?

Big Idea Question

14 Drawing Conclusions How does the pattern of magnetic reversals provide evidence that tectonic plates are moving?

Science Skills Activity

Interpreting Time from Natural Phenomena

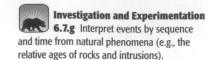

Investigation and Experimentation
6.7.g Interpret events by sequence and time from natural phenomena (e.g., the relative ages of rocks and intrusions).

▶ Tutorial

Earth scientists use a variety of methods to determine the time at which events happened in Earth's history. One way that scientists can determine the age of rocks on the sea floor is by studying the magnetic properties of the rock.

Throughout Earth's history, Earth's magnetic field has reversed from time to time. The orientation of Earth's magnetic field is called *polarity.* Scientists have learned what the pattern of magnetic reversals has been over the last 200 million years by determining the age of the rocks that formed during each reversal. Scientists can use these patterns to determine the age of rocks. This process is most useful for determining the age of sea-floor rocks.

- Geologists use the color black to identify rock that has normal polarity. Rocks that have normal polarity formed when the orientation of Earth's magnetic field was the same as it is now.
- Geologists use the color white to identify rock that has reverse polarity. Rocks that have reverse polarity formed when the orientation of Earth's magnetic field was opposite to the present orientation.
- The length of time between reversals of the magnetic field varied. Each time interval between reversals was unique. The relative length of each interval creates a pattern that does not repeat. This pattern tells scientists the date of the magnetic reversal.

▶ You Try It!

A timescale of magnetic reversals is shown below. Notice that the pattern of black and white intervals corresponds to a timescale of 5 million years. You will use the patterns in that timescale to identify the ages of "sea-floor rocks" in the diagram below.

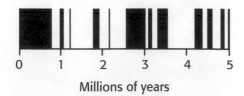

Millions of years

❶ **Identifying** What point most likely represents the location of a mid-ocean ridge? Explain your answer.

❷ **Identifying** Which two points mark rocks that are approximately the same age? Explain your answer.

❸ **Applying** How old is the rock at point C? (Hint: look for a pattern of polarity changes in the timescale that matches the pattern in the sea floor around point C.)

❹ **Applying** Which point—B, C, or D—is located in rock that is about 3 million years old? Explain your answer.

❺ **Applying** Which formed first: rock at point A or rock at point C? Explain your answer.

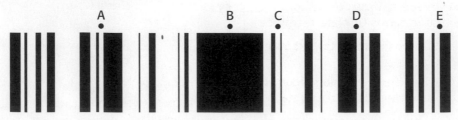

Chapter Summary

The Big Idea
Plate tectonics accounts for important features on Earth's surface and major geologic events.

Section

Vocabulary

① Earth's Structure

Key Concept Earth is composed of several layers. The continents are part of the uppermost layer, and they move slowly around Earth's surface.

- Earth's interior can be divided into layers based on chemical composition and physical properties.
- Scientists use seismic waves to study Earth's interior.
- Continents are drifting apart from each other now and have done so in the past.

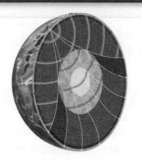

Following an earthquake, seismic waves move through Earth's interior.

core p. 190
mantle p. 190
crust p. 190
lithosphere p. 191
asthenosphere p. 191
continental drift p. 193
sea-floor spreading p. 196

② The Theory of Plate Tectonics

Key Concept Tectonic plates the size of continents and oceans move at rates of a few centimeters per year in response to movements in the mantle.

- Earth's lithosphere is broken into pieces called *tectonic plates*.
- Heat from Earth's interior causes convection in the mantle.
- Tectonic plates move at an average rate of a few centimeters per year.

The South American plate consists of both oceanic and continental lithosphere.

plate tectonics p. 198
tectonic plate p. 198

③ Deforming Earth's Crust

Key Concept Tectonic plate motions deform Earth's crust. Deformation causes rock layers to bend and break and causes mountains to form.

- Stress is placed on rock as plates move. The stress causes rock to fold and break.
- The formation of mountains results from the motion of tectonic plates.

A fault separates a hanging wall fault block from a footwall fault block.

folding p. 205
fault p. 206

④ California Geology

Key Concept Major features of California geology can be explained in terms of plate tectonics.

- Plate tectonics has been the most important force in shaping California's geologic history.
- The San Andreas fault marks a transform boundary between the North American plate and the Pacific plate.

California's gold originally formed in oceanic crust.

batholith p. 212
accreted terrane p. 213

Chapter Summary **221**

Chapter Review

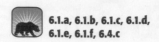

6.1.a, 6.1.b, 6.1.c, 6.1.d, 6.1.e, 6.1.f, 6.4.c

Organize

Key-Term Fold Review the FoldNote that you created at the beginning of the chapter. Add to or correct the FoldNote based on what you have learned.

Using Vocabulary

1 Academic Vocabulary Which of the following words means "a separate or distinct portion of matter that has thickness"?
a. fault
c. layer
b. boundary
d. fold

For each pair of terms, explain how the meanings of the terms differ.

2 *lithosphere* and *asthenosphere*

3 *plate tectonics* and *tectonic plate*

4 *folding* and *fault*

Understanding Concepts

Multiple Choice

5 The strong, lower part of the mantle is a physical layer called the
a. lithosphere.
c. asthenosphere.
b. mesosphere.
d. outer core.

6 Subduction occurs at which of the following tectonic plate boundaries?
a. a divergent plate boundary
b. a transform plate boundary
c. a convergent plate boundary
d. a strike-slip plate boundary

7 The surface along which rocks break and slide past each other is called a(n)
a. anticline.
c. fault.
b. syncline.
d. fault block.

8 Which type of plate boundary is the San Andreas fault?
a. divergent
c. transform
b. convergent
d. strike-slip

INTERPRETING GRAPHICS The illustration below shows the relative velocities (in centimeters per year) and directions in which tectonic plates are separating and colliding. Arrows that point away from one another indicate plate separation. Arrows that point toward one another indicate plate collision. Use the illustration below to answer the next two questions.

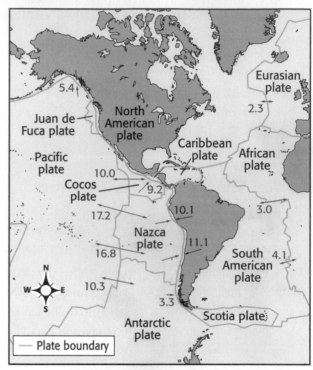

9 Which of the following boundaries is a convergent boundary?
a. the boundary between the Nazca plate and the Pacific plate
b. the boundary between the Nazca plate and the South American plate
c. the boundary between the North American plate and the Eurasian plate
d. the boundary between the African plate and the South American plate

10 Which two tectonic plates are moving away from each other fastest?
a. the African plate and the South American plate
b. the Antarctic plate and the Pacific plate
c. the Nazca plate and the Pacific plate
d. the Cocos plate and the Pacific plate

Short Answer

11 Listing List the layers of Earth by chemical composition and by physical properties.

12 Summarizing Describe the three types of tectonic plate boundaries and the motion that occurs at each type of boundary.

13 Analyzing How is heat from Earth's interior transferred to Earth's surface by convection?

14 Identifying How fast do Earth's tectonic plates move?

15 Summarizing Describe the three major types of faults and the type of stress that forms each fault.

16 Analyzing Explain how compression in southern California has caused basins and mountain ranges to form.

Writing Skills

17 Outlining Topics Outline the steps that occurred in the formation of the San Andreas fault. Begin your outline with the break-up of Pangaea. Present each step in a logical, clear fashion, with the relationship between each step identified.

Critical Thinking

18 Concept Mapping Use the following terms to create a concept map: *sea-floor spreading, convergent boundary, divergent boundary, subduction zone, transform boundary,* and *tectonic plate.*

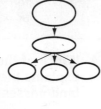

19 Applying Concepts Folded mountains usually form at the edge of a tectonic plate. How can you explain folded mountain ranges located in the middle of a tectonic plate?

20 Making Inferences How can more than one type of motion occur along a plate boundary?

21 Applying Concepts How do convection currents cause tectonic plates to move?

INTERPRETING GRAPHICS Use the diagram below to answer the next four questions.

Composition	Structure
Crust (60 km)	Lithosphere (150 km)
Mantle (2,831 km)	Asthenosphere (260 km)
	Mesosphere (2,481 km)
Core (3,480 km)	Outer core (2,259 km)
	Inner core (1,221 km)

22 Analyzing Data How far beneath Earth's surface would you have to go before you were no longer passing through rock that is composed mostly of silicon, oxygen, and aluminum?

23 Analyzing Data How far beneath Earth's surface would you have to go to find liquid iron and nickel?

24 Analyzing Data At what depth would you find mantle material but still be within the lithosphere?

25 Analyzing Data How far beneath Earth's surface would you have to go to find solid rock that flows slowly?

Math Skills

26 Making Calculations Assume that a very small tectonic plate is located between a mid-ocean ridge and a subduction zone. At the ridge, the plate is growing at a rate of 5 km every 1 million years. At the subduction zone, the plate is subducting at the rate of 10 km every 1 million years. If the plate is 100 km across, in how many million years will the plate disappear?

Challenge

27 Making Inferences How might the shape of California change over the next few million years?

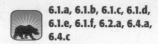
REVIEWING ACADEMIC VOCABULARY

1 Which of the following words means "to move from one place to another"?

A transfer

B replace

C translate

D relate

2 In the sentence "The locations of volcanoes and earthquakes are evidence of plate tectonics," what does *evidence* mean?

A questions that must be answered

B information that cannot be explained

C observations that support a theory

D a theory that is based on reason

3 Which of the following words means "a separate or distinct portion of matter that has thickness"?

A support

B lever

C sediment

D layer

4 In the sentence "Earth has a hot metal core," what does the word *core* mean?

A the innermost part

B a set of subjects

C the most important part

D a basis to build on

5 Choose the appropriate form of the word *primary* for the following sentence: "Heat from Earth's interior reaches the surface _____ through convection."

A primary

B primaries

C primacy

D primarily

REVIEWING CONCEPTS

6 In which of the following settings does a transform boundary occur?

A where two tectonic plates slide past one another horizontally

B where two tectonic plates collide

C where two tectonic plates separate

D where a dense tectonic plate sinks beneath a less-dense tectonic plate

7 Why are most major mountain ranges and river valleys in California oriented in a northwest-southeast direction?

A They are oriented perpendicular to the plate boundary.

B They are oriented parallel to the plate boundary.

C Their orientation has been changed by tension along the San Andreas fault system.

D Their orientation has been changed by compression along the San Andreas fault system.

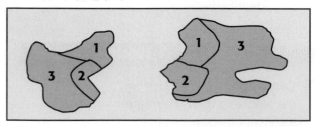

8 Which of the following statements best explains the relative positions of the two landmasses shown above?

A An earthquake split the tectonic plate in two, separating the landmasses.

B Sea-floor spreading pushed the two landmasses apart.

C Subduction occurred, causing the land between the two landmasses to sink.

D Sea-floor spreading pushed the two landmasses toward each other.

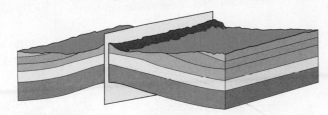

9 Which of the following types of folds is shown in the diagram above if the dark gray layer is the oldest?

    A an asymmetrical fold

    B an overturned fold

    C an anticline

    D a syncline

10 Which of the following ranges of rates describes average yearly tectonic plate movement?

    A 5.0 mm/year to 30.0 mm/year

    B 2.5 cm/year to 15.0 cm/year

    C 1.0 m/year to 5.0 m/year

    D 1 km/year to 2.5 km/year

11 The process by which new oceanic lithosphere forms as magma rises to Earth's surface and solidifies at a mid-ocean is called

    A plate tectonics.

    B sea-floor spreading.

    C magnetic reversal.

    D continental drift.

12 Which of the following is the plastic layer of the mantle on which the tectonic plates move?

    A the mesosphere

    B the lithosphere

    C the asthenosphere

    D the outer core

REVIEWING PRIOR LEARNING

13 What is the dominant process in which water reshapes the landscape?

    A glaciers scouring rock

    B water running downhill

    C waves striking a coastline

    D rivers overflowing their banks

14 Which of the following is most likely to cause rocks to break down?

    A a seasonal lack of rainfall in an area

    B repeated freezing of water and thawing of ice

    C changes in air pressure due to weather

    D changes in soil thickness due to erosion

15 Which of the following phenomena is most likely to be affected by weather patterns?

    A an earthquake

    B a volcano

    C continental drift

    D erosion

16 What source of energy powers the phenomena that occur between Earth's surface and the atmosphere?

    A continental drift

    B heat in Earth's core

    C solar radiation

    D Earth's rotation

Standards Assessment

Science in Action

Science, Technology, and Society

Modeling Earth's Magnetic Field

Flow of heat from Earth's core drives Earth's magnetic field. But how do scientists study heat flow in Earth's core? Two California researchers, Gary Glatzmaier and Paul Roberts, have created a three-dimensional model of the heat flow that drives Earth's magnetic field. Glatzmaier and Roberts' model simulates a magnetic field very similar to the magnetic field of Earth. In fact, their model has been able to simulate reversals of Earth's magnetic field that are similar to magnetic reversals that have taken place over the past several hundred thousand years of Earth history.

Social Studies ACTiViTY

Scientists have hypothesized how Earth might be affected if its magnetic poles reversed. Research some of these hypotheses, and record your findings in your **Science Journal.**

Scientific Discoveries

Megaplumes

Eruptions of boiling water from the sea floor form giant, spiral disks that twist through the oceans. Does this sound like science fiction? Oceanographers have discovered these disks at eight locations at mid-ocean ridges over the past 20 years. These disks, which may be tens of kilometers across, are called *megaplumes*. Megaplumes are like blenders. They mix hot water with cold water in the oceans. Megaplumes can rise hundreds of meters from the ocean floor to the upper layers of the ocean. They carry gases and minerals and provide extra energy and food to organisms in the upper layers of the ocean.

Language Arts ACTiViTY

The prefix *mega-* is used with words such as *plume* to indicate large size. In your **Science Journal,** make a list of 10 words in which the prefix *mega-* is used. Include a definition of each term.

Alfred Wegener

Continental Drift Alfred Wegener's greatest contribution to science was the hypothesis of continental drift. This hypothesis states that continents drift apart from one another and have done so in the past. To support his hypothesis, Wegener used geologic, fossil, and glacial evidence gathered on both sides of the Atlantic Ocean. For example, Wegener recognized similarities between rock layers in North America and Europe and between rock layers in South America and Africa. He believed that these similarities could be explained only if these geologic features, which are now separated by oceans, were once part of the same continent.

Although continental drift explained many of his observations, Wegener could not find scientific evidence to develop a complete explanation of how continents move. Most scientists were skeptical of Wegener's hypothesis and dismissed it as foolishness. It was not until the 1950s and 1960s that the discoveries of magnetic reversals and sea-floor spreading provided a possible mechanism for continental drift.

Math ACTiViTY

The distance between South America and Africa is 7,200 km. As new crust forms at the Mid-Atlantic Ridge, South America and Africa are moving away from each other at a rate of about 3.5 cm/year. How many millions of years ago were South America and Africa joined?

Internet Resources

- To learn more about careers in science, visit **www.scilinks.org** and enter the SciLinks code HY70225.

- To learn more about these Science in Action topics, visit **go.hrw.com** and type in the keyword HY7TECF.

- Check out articles related to this chapter by visiting **go.hrw.com.** Just type in the keyword HY7TECC.

Improving Comprehension

Graphic Organizers are important visual tools that can help you organize information and improve your reading comprehension. The Graphic Organizer below is called a *cause-and-effect map*. Instructions for creating other types of Graphic Organizers are located in the **Study Skills** section of the Appendix.

How to Make a Cause-and-Effect Map

1. Draw a box, and write a cause in the box. You can have as many cause boxes as you want. The diagram shown here is one example of a cause-and-effect map.

2. Draw another box to the right of the cause box to represent an effect. You can have as many effect boxes as you want. Draw arrows from each cause box to the appropriate effect boxes.

3. In the cause boxes, explain the process that makes up the cause. In the effect boxes, write a description of the effect or details about the effect.

When to Use a Cause-and-Effect Map

A cause-and-effect map is a useful tool for illustrating a specific type of scientific process. Use a cause-and-effect map when you want to describe how, when, or why one event causes another event. As you read, look for events that are either causes or results of other events, and draw a cause-and-effect map that shows the relationships between the events.

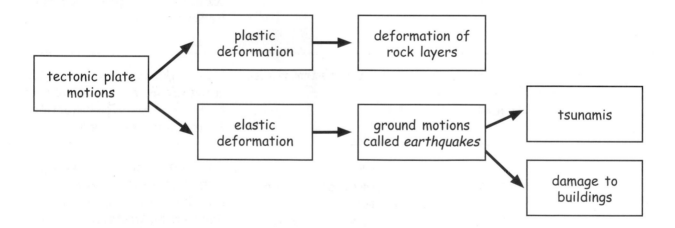

You Try It!

This Reading Strategy can also be used within the chapter that you are about to read. Practice making your own cause-and-effect map as directed in the Reading Strategies for Section ❶ and Section ❸. Record your work in your **Science Journal.**

Unpacking the Standards

The information below "unpacks" the standards by breaking them down into basic parts. The higher-level, academic vocabulary is highlighted and defined to help you understand the language of the standards. "What It Means" restates the standards as simply as possible.

California Standard	Academic Vocabulary	What It Means
6.1.a Students know **evidence** of plate tectonics is **derived** from the fit of the continents; the **location** of earthquakes, volcanoes, and midocean ridges; and the **distribution** of fossils, rock types, and ancient climatic zones.	**evidence** (EV uh duhns) information showing whether an idea or belief is true or valid **derive** (di RIEV) to figure out by reasoning **location** (loh KAY shuhn) a place or position **distribution** (DIS tri BYOO shuhn) the relative arrangement of objects or organisms in time or space	Support for the idea that Earth's surface is made of slabs of rock that move around comes from how continents fit together, where earthquakes happen, where volcanoes and mid-ocean ridges are located, where rocks and fossils are found, and where climate was different in the geologic past.
6.1.d Students know that earthquakes are sudden motions along breaks in the crust called faults and that volcanoes and fissures are **locations** where magma reaches the surface.	**location** (loh KAY shuhn) a place or position	Earthquakes are sudden movements along breaks in Earth's surface called *faults,* and volcanoes are places where molten rock reaches the surface.
6.1.e Students know **major** geologic events, such as earthquakes, volcanic eruptions, and mountain building, result from plate motions.	**major** (MAY juhr) of great importance or large scale	Important global events, such as earthquakes, volcanic eruptions, and mountain building, are caused by the movement of Earth's crust and upper mantle.
6.1.g Students know how to determine the epicenter of an earthquake and know that the effects of an earthquake on any **region vary,** depending on the size of the earthquake, the distance of the **region** from the epicenter, the local geology, and the type of **construction** in the **region.**	**region** (REE juhn) an area **vary** (VER ee) differ; to have more than one possible state **construction** (kuhn STRUHK shuhn) the type of buildings in an area; the way something is built	You must know how to find an earthquake's starting point and must know that how much damage an earthquake causes depends on the size of the earthquake, the distance from the starting point, the type of rock under a place, the materials used in buildings, and the way in which the buildings were made.
6.2.d Students know earthquakes, volcanic eruptions, landslides, and floods change human and wildlife habitats.		Earthquakes, volcanic eruptions, landslides, and floods change the surroundings in which humans and wildlife live.

The following identifies other standards that are covered in this chapter and where you can go to see them unpacked: **6.3.a** (Chapter 10)

Earthquakes

The Big Idea

Earthquakes result from sudden motions along breaks in Earth's crust and can affect landforms and societies.

California Standards

Focus on Earth Sciences

6.1 Plate tectonics accounts for important features of the Earth's surface and major geologic events. (Sections 1, 2, and 3)

6.2 Topography is reshaped by weathering of rock and soil and by the transportation and deposition of sediment. (Sections 2 and 3)

6.3 Heat moves in a predictable flow from warmer objects to cooler objects until all objects are at the same temperature. (Section 1)

Investigation and Experimentation

6.7 Scientific progress is made by asking meaningful questions and conducting careful investigations. (Science Skills Activity)

Math

6.2.3 Algebra and Functions
6.2.4 Mathematical Reasoning

English–Language Arts

6.2.4 Reading
6.1.3 Writing

About the Photo

On October 17, 1989, the Loma Prieta earthquake shook the San Francisco and Monterey Bay area. The magnitude 6.9 earthquake killed 63 people and caused billions of dollars of property damage. The earthquake was caused by the movement of the Pacific plate and the North American plate.

Organize

Pyramid

Before you read this chapter, create the FoldNote entitled "Pyramid." Label the sides of the pyramid with "Where earthquakes happen," "Measuring earthquakes," and "Earthquakes and society." As you read the chapter, add details from each section on the appropriate side of the pyramid.

Instructions for creating FoldNotes are located in the Study Skills section on p. 615 of the Appendix.

Explore Activity

20 min

Investigating Building Materials

In this activity, you will test three materials in a model earthquake setting.

Procedure

1. Gather a **small wooden stick**, a **wire clothes hanger**, and a **plastic clothes hanger**.

2. Draw a straight line on a **sheet of paper**. Use a **protractor** to measure and draw the following angles from center of the line: 20°, 45°, and 90°.

3. Put on your **safety goggles** and a **pair of gloves**. Using the angles that you drew as a guide, try bending each item 20° and then releasing it. What happens? Does it break? If it bends, does it return to its original shape?

4. Using the 45° and 90° angles, repeat step 3.

Analysis

6.1.g
6.7.b

5. How does each of the three materials respond to bending? Compare the responses.

6. Where earthquakes happen, engineers use building materials that are flexible but that do not break or stay bent. Which materials from this experiment would you want building materials to behave like? Explain your answer.

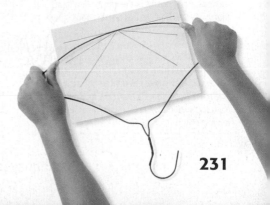

What Are Earthquakes?

Key Concept Sudden motions along breaks in Earth's crust can release energy in the form of seismic waves.

What You Will Learn

- Earthquakes are ground motions that result from the release of energy when blocks of rock move.
- Most earthquakes occur along tectonic plate boundaries because the movement of tectonic plates causes stress in Earth's crust.
- Earthquake energy travels through rock as seismic waves.

Why It Matters

Earthquakes can destroy property and endanger human lives.

Vocabulary

- earthquake   • seismic wave
- elastic rebound

READING STRATEGY

Graphic Organizer   In your **Science Journal,** show the relationship between types of plate motion and major fault types in three Cause-and-Effect Maps.

earthquake (URTH kwayk) a movement or trembling of the ground that is caused by a sudden release of energy when rocks along a fault move

6.1.a Students know evidence of plate tectonics is derived from the fit of the continents; the location of earthquakes, volcanoes, and midocean ridges; and the distribution of fossils, rock types, and ancient climatic zones.

6.1.d Students know that earthquakes are sudden motions along breaks in the crust called faults and that volcanoes and fissures are locations where magma reaches the surface.

6.1.e Students know major geologic events, such as earthquakes, volcanic eruptions, and mountain building, result from plate motions.

6.3.a Students know energy can be carried from one place to another by heat flow or by waves, including water, light and sound waves, or by moving objects.

▶ Have you ever felt the Earth move under your feet? Many people have. Every day, somewhere in the world, earthquakes happen. **Earthquakes** are movements or shaking of the ground that happen when blocks of rock move suddenly and release energy. The transfer of this energy through rock causes the ground to shake.

Standards Check What is an earthquake? 6.1.a

Where Earthquakes Happen

Most earthquakes take place near the boundaries of tectonic plates. However, earthquakes do happen far from tectonic plate boundaries. Large earthquakes have occurred in the interior of the North American plate. For example, earthquakes happened in New Madrid, Missouri, in 1811–1812, and in Charlestown, South Carolina, in 1886. **Figure 1** shows Earth's major tectonic plates and the locations of recent earthquakes.

Tectonic plates move in different directions and at different speeds. Two plates can push toward or pull away from one another. They can also slip slowly past each other horizontally. These movements break Earth's crust into a series of faults. A *fault* is a break in Earth's crust along which blocks of rock slide relative to one another.

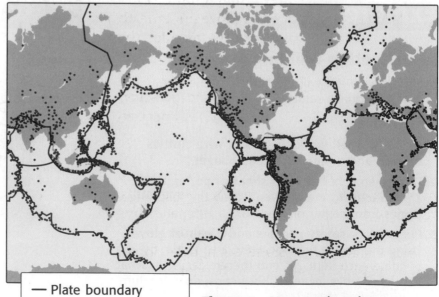

— Plate boundary

• Recorded earthquake

Figure 1   *Most earthquakes occur along tectonic plate boundaries.*

Faults at Tectonic Plate Boundaries

Specific types of plate motion take place at different tectonic boundaries. Each type of motion creates a particular kind of fault. Examine **Figure 2, Figure 3,** and **Figure 4** to learn more about why earthquakes happen at plate boundaries.

Earthquakes at Divergent Boundaries

At divergent tectonic plate boundaries, two tectonic plates pull away from one another. As plates pull away from one another, tension causes the lithosphere to break into a series of fault blocks. Some of these blocks drop down relative to others. The blocks form a series of normal faults. As **Figure 2** shows, earthquakes happen along these normal faults as the blocks move.

A good example of a divergent boundary is a mid-ocean ridge, which is shown in **Figure 2.** At mid-ocean ridges, the oceanic lithosphere is thin and weak. Because oceanic lithosphere is thin, earthquakes that happen along the normal faults are shallow. At divergent boundaries, earthquakes happen at depths of less than 20 km below the ocean floor.

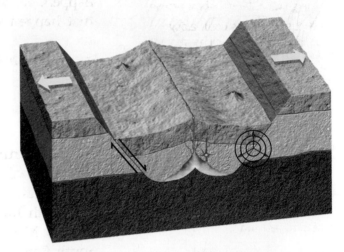

Figure 2 *At divergent boundaries, earthquakes happen along normal faults at depths of less than 20 km.*

Earthquakes at Convergent Boundaries

At convergent tectonic plate boundaries, two tectonic plates collide with one another. When tectonic plates collide, two things may happen. Both plates may crumple up to form mountains. Or one plate can move underneath the other plate and sink into the mantle. The process of one plate moving under another is called *subduction.*

During subduction or mountain building, the rocks that make up the two plates are compressed. Compression causes the lithosphere to break into a series of fault blocks. These blocks are thrust over one another as the plates move. The blocks form a series of reverse faults. As **Figure 3** shows, earthquakes happen along reverse faults. Two types of earthquakes occur at subduction zones. Some earthquakes occur between the downgoing and overlying plates at depths of less than 50 km. Earthquakes also happen inside the downgoing plate to depths of as much as 700 km.

Figure 3 *At convergent boundaries, earthquakes can happen along reverse faults at depths of as much as 700 km.*

Figure 4 *At transform boundaries, earthquakes happen along strike-slip faults at depths of less than 50 km.*

Earthquakes at Transform Boundaries

At transform boundaries, two plates move past one another horizontally. When plates move past one another, the rocks on both sides of the fault are sheared. In other words, they are broken as they grind past one another in opposite directions. The shear stress causes the rock to break into a series of blocks. The blocks form a series of strike-slip faults. As **Figure 4** shows, earthquakes happen along these strike-slip faults as the blocks move.

Most transform boundaries exist between plates made of oceanic lithosphere. However, some transform boundaries occur between plates made of continental lithosphere. Rocks that are deep below Earth's surface tend to react to shear stress by folding rather than by breaking. As a result, earthquakes along strike-slip faults generally occur at shallow depths.

Standards Check Why do earthquakes happen at transform boundaries? 6.1.d

Fault Zones

Places along plate boundaries where large numbers of interconnected faults are located are called *fault zones*. Faults in fault zones have different lengths, occur at different depths, and cut through the lithosphere in different directions. Normal faults, reverse faults, and strike-slip faults can all occur in a single fault zone.

The San Andreas fault zone in California is an example of a fault zone along a transform boundary. The San Andreas fault zone is primarily a strike-slip, or transform, fault system. However, normal and reverse faults do occur at bends in the San Andreas fault. A fault map that shows some of the faults that make up the San Andreas fault zone is shown in **Figure 5.**

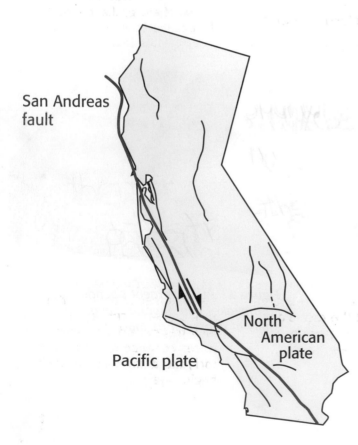

San Andreas fault

Pacific plate

North American plate

Figure 5 *Numerous faults, some of which are shown here, make up the San Andreas fault zone.*

Why Earthquakes Happen

As tectonic plates move, stress on rocks near the edges of the plates increases. In response to this stress, the rock deforms, or changes shape. Rock deforms in mainly two ways. It can deform in a plastic manner, like a piece of clay being molded. Folded rocks, such as the ones shown in **Figure 6,** are a result of *plastic deformation.* Or rock can deform in an elastic manner, like a rubber band being stretched. *Elastic deformation* leads to earthquakes. Think of elastically deformed rock as a stretched rubber band. You can stretch a rubber band only so far before it breaks. When the rubber band breaks, it releases energy as the broken pieces return to their unstretched size and shape. In rock, this elastic movement causes faults to form and releases energy as an earthquake.

Elastic Rebound

The sudden return of elastically deformed rock to its original shape is called **elastic rebound.** Elastic rebound happens when stress on rock along a fault becomes so great that the rock breaks, or fails. This failure causes the rocks on either side of the fault to jerk past one another, as **Figure 7** shows. During this sudden motion, large amounts of energy are released. This energy travels through rock as **seismic waves.** These waves cause the ground to move. The strength of an earthquake is related to the amount of energy that is released during elastic rebound.

Standards Check How does elastic rebound cause earthquakes?
6.1.e

Figure 6 *The forces that formed the San Andreas fault in Southern California also caused the plastic deformation of these rock layers.*

elastic rebound (ee LAS tik REE BOWND) the sudden return of elastically deformed rock to its undeformed shape

seismic wave (SIEZ mik WAYV) a wave of energy that travels through the Earth and away from an earthquake in all directions

---

Figure 7 **Elastic Rebound**

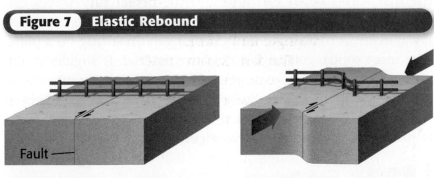

Fault

Tectonic forces push rock on either side of a fault in opposite directions. But the rock is locked in place.

The rock deforms in an elastic manner. When enough energy builds up and the rock along the fault slips, the energy is released as an earthquake.

After the earthquake, surface features may show how the rock on either side of the fault has moved. As tectonic forces continue to act on the rock, the deformation of rock begins again.

Figure 8 Types of Seismic Waves

Direction of wave travel

P waves are body waves that squeeze and stretch rock.

Direction of wave travel

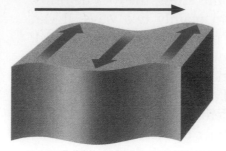

S waves are body waves that shear rock horizontally from side to side.

Direction of wave travel

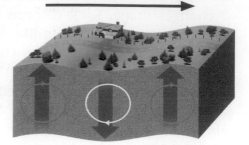

Surface waves can move the ground with a rolling, up-and-down motion.

Earthquake Waves

Earthquakes are the physical result of the movement of energy through Earth as seismic waves. Seismic waves that travel through Earth's interior are called *body waves*. There are two types of body waves: P waves and S waves. Seismic waves that travel along Earth's surface are called *surface waves*. Each type of seismic wave travels through Earth's layers in a different way and at a different speed. Also, the speed of a seismic wave depends on the kind of material the wave travels through.

P Waves

P waves, or pressure waves, are the fastest seismic waves. P waves are also called *primary waves* because they are always the first waves of an earthquake to be detected. P waves can travel through solids, liquids, and gases. To understand how P waves affect rock, imagine a cube of gelatin sitting on a plate. Like most solids, gelatin is an elastic material. It wiggles if you tap it. Tapping the cube of gelatin changes the pressure inside the cube, which momentarily deforms the cube. The gelatin then reacts by springing back to its original shape. This process is how P waves affect rock, as **Figure 8** shows.

S Waves

S waves, or shear waves, are the second-fastest seismic waves. S waves shear rock side to side, as **Figure 8** shows. Unlike P waves, S waves cannot travel through parts of Earth that are completely liquid. Also, S waves are slower than P waves and always arrive later. Thus, another name for S waves is *secondary waves.*

Standards Check How do P waves and S waves differ in the way that they transfer energy? 6.3.a

Quick Lab

Seismic Spring Toys 6.3.a

1. Stretch a **spring toy** lengthwise on a **table.**

2. Hold one end of the spring while a partner holds the other end. Predict how you could move one end of the spring toy to model a P wave. Test your prediction, and describe your results.

3. Repeat step 2 to model an S wave. Describe your results.

4. Did the wave travel faster in step 2 or step 3? Explain your answer.

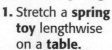 **15 min**

Surface Waves

Surface waves move only along Earth's surface and produce motion only near the top of Earth's crust. Because their energy is focused on Earth's surface, surface waves tend to cause the most damage. In addition, surface waves travel more slowly than body waves do.

There are two types of surface waves. One type of surface wave produces a rolling, up-and-down motion, as **Figure 8** shows. The other type produces a back-and-forth motion like the motion produced by S waves.

Standards Check Explain why surface waves are the most destructive type of seismic wave. 6.3.a

SECTION Review

 6.1.a, 6.1.d, 6.1.e, 6.3.a

Summary

- Earthquakes are motions of the ground that happen as energy travels through rock.

- Earthquakes occur mainly near the edges of tectonic plates.

- Earthquakes are caused by elastic rebound, which is caused by sudden motions along faults. During elastic rebound, rock springs into its original shape and size as stress is released.

- Energy generated by earthquakes travels as body waves through Earth's interior or as surface waves along the surface of Earth.

Using Vocabulary

1. Write an original definition for *earthquake* and *seismic wave.*

Understanding Concepts

2. **Evaluating** How do faults relate to earthquakes?

3. **Classifying** Describe the three types of plate motion and the faults that are characteristic of each motion.

4. **Analyzing** Explain how tectonic plate motion is related to earthquakes.

5. **Explaining** Describe how elastic rebound results in the transfer of energy as seismic waves.

6. **Evaluating** How do the locations of earthquakes support the theory of plate tectonics?

Critical Thinking

7. **Identifying Relationships** Why are surface waves more destructive to buildings than P waves or S waves are?

8. **Applying Concepts** The San Andreas fault system formed as a result of the transform motion of the Pacific and North American plates. What fault type is most common in the San Andreas fault system?

9. **Analyzing Relationships** Where do the majority of earthquakes in the United States occur? Explain.

Challenge

10. **Evaluating Models** Imagine that you are splashing water in a pool. Explain how you could model each type of seismic wave. Then, try to explain why S waves do not travel through liquids.

Internet Resources

For a variety of links related to this chapter, go to www.scilinks.org

Topic: What Is an Earthquake?
SciLinks code: HY71658

Earthquake Measurement

Key Concept Studying the properties of seismic waves can help scientists determine an earthquake's starting point, strength, and intensity.

What You Will Learn

- To find an earthquake's epicenter, you must triangulate by using data from three or more seismometers.
- Magnitude is a measure of an earthquake's strength.
- The intensity of an earthquake depends on four main factors.

Why It Matters

Quickly determining the location and intensity of an earthquake helps reduce the harm that an earthquake can cause.

Vocabulary

- epicenter
- magnitude
- focus
- intensity

READING STRATEGY

Summarizing Read this section silently. In pairs, take turns summarizing the material. Stop to discuss ideas and words that seem confusing.

epicenter (EP i sent uhr) the point on Earth's surface directly above an earthquake's starting point, or focus
Wordwise The prefix _epi-_ means "upon."

focus (FOH kuhs) the location within Earth along a fault at which the first motion of an earthquake occurs

6.1.g Students know how to determine the epicenter of an earthquake and know that the effects of an earthquake on any region vary, depending on the size of the earthquake, the distance of the earthquake from the epicenter, the local geology, and the type of construction in the region.

▶ Imagine walls shaking, windows rattling, glasses and dishes clinking. After only seconds, the vibrating stops and the sounds die away. Within minutes, news reports give information about the strength and the location of the earthquake. How could scientists have learned this information so quickly?

Studying Earthquakes

Scientists use earthquake-sensing instruments called _seismometers,_ or _seismographs,_ to record seismic waves. Seismometers record the vibrations of P waves, S waves, and surface waves as the waves travel through Earth. Seismometers also record the time that seismic waves take to arrive at a seismometer station. Seismometers create a tracing of earthquake motion called a _seismogram._

Determining Location

Scientists use the data from seismograms to find an earthquake's epicenter. An **epicenter** is the point on Earth's surface directly above an earthquake's starting point. A **focus** is the point inside Earth where an earthquake actually begins. **Figure 1** shows the relative locations of an earthquake's epicenter and focus.

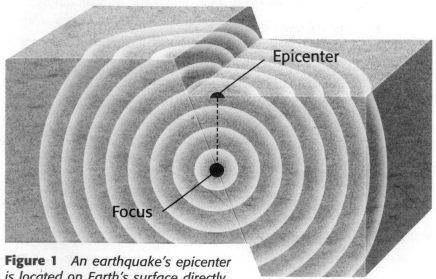

Figure 1 _An earthquake's epicenter is located on Earth's surface directly above the focus._

Figure 2 **Finding an Earthquake's Epicenter**

❶ A circle is drawn around a seismometer station. The radius of the circle equals the distance from the seismometer to the epicenter.

❷ When a second circle is drawn around another seismometer station, the circle overlaps the first circle in two spots. One of these spots is the earthquake's epicenter.

❸ When a circle is drawn around a third seismometer station, all three circles intersect in one spot—the earthquake's epicenter. In this case, the epicenter was in San Francisco.

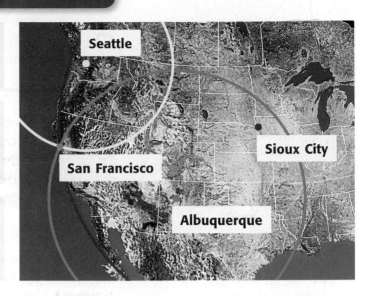

Triangulation

The time between the arrival of the P waves and the arrival of the S waves, called *lag time,* tells scientists how far the waves traveled. The epicenter can then be located by drawing circles around at least three seismometer stations, as **Figure 2** shows. The radius of each circle is equal to the distance from that seismometer to the epicenter. The point at which all of the circles intersect is the epicenter. This process is called *triangulation.* Today, computers perform all of these calculations.

Quick Lab

Locating an Epicenter

In this lab, you will use triangulation to locate the epicenter of an earthquake.

▶ Try It!

1. Locate the following cities on a **map of California:** Stockton, Fresno, and Barstow.

2. Use the data in the table at right and the scale on the map to adjust a **drawing compass.** Adjust the compass so that the distance between the pencil and the metal point equals the distance between Stockton and the epicenter of the earthquake.

3. Place the metal point of the compass directly in the center of Stockton on the map. Turn the compass to draw a circle around Stockton.

Earthquake Data

6.1.g

Seismometer station	Lag time	Distance to epicenter
Stockton	15 s	90 km
Fresno	25 s	195 km
Barstow	70 s	515 km

4. Repeat steps 2 and 3 for Fresno and for Barstow. The three circles intersect in one place.

▶ Think About It!

5. Where was the epicenter of the earthquake?

6. Why did you need data from three seismometers to locate the epicenter?

🕐 **20 min**

find X

Earthquake Start Time

Try this problem to learn how scientists determine when an earthquake began. Imagine that you are racing a friend. You both start at the same time, but you run 10 km/h and your friend runs 5 km/h. If you finish one hour before your friend, how far did you race? Record your work in your **Science Journal.**

Earthquake Magnitude

Seismograms can also provide information about an earthquake's strength. The size of the waves on a seismogram indicates the amount of ground motion. The amount of ground motion can be used to calculate magnitude. **Magnitude** is the measure of an earthquake's strength.

The larger the magnitude of an earthquake is, the stronger the earthquake is. A map of earthquakes that had a magnitude of 4.5 or greater and that happened in California between 1965 and 2005 is shown in **Figure 3.**

Standards Check What is magnitude? 🐾 6.1.g

The Richter Scale

In the past, scientists used the Richter scale to describe magnitude. The Richter scale measures the ground motion from an earthquake and adjusts for distance to find the earthquake's magnitude. On the Richter scale, each increase of one number, such as from 1 to 2, represents a tenfold increase in ground shaking. Richter-scale values generally range from 0 to 9.

The Moment Magnitude Scale

Today, scientists use the moment magnitude scale instead of the Richter scale. The moment magnitude scale is a more accurate measure of the strength of earthquakes. *Moment magnitude (Mw)* represents the size of the area of the fault that moves, the average distance that the fault blocks move, and the rigidity of the rocks in the fault zone. The moment magnitude scale is more closely related to the physical effects that take place at the source of an earthquake than the Richter scale is.

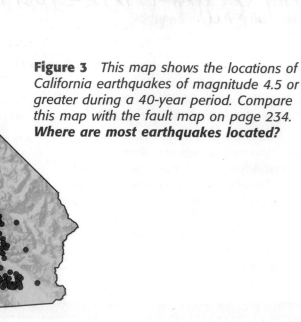

Figure 3 *This map shows the locations of California earthquakes of magnitude 4.5 or greater during a 40-year period. Compare this map with the fault map on page 234.* ***Where are most earthquakes located?***

• Earthquakes

Earthquake Intensity

The effects of an earthquake and how the earthquake is felt by people are known as the earthquake's **intensity.** An earthquake's magnitude is different from its intensity. Magnitude measures how much energy is released by an earthquake. Intensity measures the effects of an earthquake at Earth's surface.

Standards Check What is intensity? 6.1.g

The Modified Mercalli Scale

The Modified Mercalli scale is used to describe an earthquake's intensity. As shown in **Table 1,** the scale ranges from I to XII. Level I earthquakes are barely noticeable, and level XII earthquakes cause total destruction. Intensity values vary from place to place and are usually higher near the epicenter of the earthquake. **Figure 4** shows the damage caused by an earthquake that had a maximum intensity of level IX.

Mapping Earthquake Intensity

Earthquake intensity maps show the level of ground shaking that may be expected to occur in different areas that experience the same earthquake. Data used to make earthquake intensity maps are obtained from information recorded during previous earthquakes. In the San Francisco Bay area, information has been obtained from records of the 1989 Loma Prieta earthquake and even from the 1906 earthquake. These data are used to model differences in the amount of ground shaking that may occur during a future earthquake.

Figure 4 *Intensity values for the 1906 San Francisco earthquake varied from place to place. The maximum intensity level was IX.*

magnitude (MAG nuh TOOD) a measure of the strength of an earthquake

intensity (in TEN suh tee) in Earth science, the amount of damage caused by an earthquake

Table 1	Modified Mercalli Intensity Scale
Intensity	**Description**
I	is not felt except by very few under especially favorable conditions
II	is felt by only few people at rest; delicately suspended items may swing
III	is felt by most people indoors; vibration is similar to the passing of a large truck
IV	is felt by many people; dishes and windows rattle; sensation is similar to a building being struck
V	is felt by nearly everyone; some objects are broken; and unstable objects are overturned
VI	is felt by all people; some heavy objects are moved; causes very slight damage to structures
VII	causes slight to moderate damage to ordinary buildings; some chimneys are broken
VIII	causes considerable damage (including partial collapse) to ordinary buildings
IX	causes considerable damage (including partial collapse) to earthquake-resistant buildings
X	destroys some to most structures, including foundations; rails are bent
XI	causes few structures, if any, to remain standing; bridges are destroyed and rails are bent
XII	causes total destruction; distorts lines of sight; objects are thrown into the air

Figure 5 Liquefaction

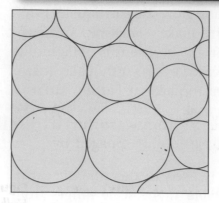

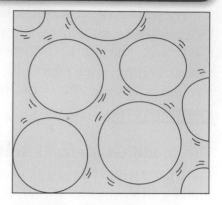

In sandy soils that lie beneath the water table, sand grains are normally in contact with one another.

An earthquake causes sand grains to lose contact with one another and to vibrate more violently.

The Effects of Earthquakes

The effects of an earthquake can vary over a wide area. In addition to the size of the earthquake, three other factors determine the effects of an earthquake on a given area. Those factors are the distance from the epicenter, the local geology, and the type of construction in a region.

Distance from the Epicenter

Have you ever tossed a pebble into a pond? The circles that surround the pebble grow larger, or expand, as they move outward. The same is true of seismic waves as they move away from an epicenter. The total energy in a seismic wave stays relatively constant as the wave travels. So, the amount of energy at any point on the wave decreases as the wave grows increasingly larger. In general, the farther an area is from the epicenter, the less destructive the earthquake will be.

Local Geology

The amount of damage that will be caused by an earthquake depends on the material through which seismic waves travel. In general, solid rock is not likely to increase the intensity or the time that the ground shakes. However, seismic waves are particularly dangerous when they travel through loose soils and sediments that contain large amounts of water. When water-saturated soil or sediment is shaken by seismic waves, the grains that make up the sediment lose contact with one another and are surrounded by water. This process, which is shown in **Figure 5,** is called *liquefaction*. Liquefaction can intensify ground shaking. Liquefaction can also cause the ground to settle. Settling can cause structures to tilt or even collapse.

Earthquake-Resistant Construction

Structures that are made of brick or concrete are not very flexible and are easily damaged by earthquakes, as **Figure 6** shows. Wood and steel are more flexible. Flexible structures are more likely to survive strong ground shaking. In addition, taller buildings are more susceptible to damage than shorter buildings are. Structures that have solid foundations that are firmly anchored in the ground are most likely to be left undamaged by earthquakes.

Standards Check What four factors affect intensity? 6.1.g

Figure 6 *This apartment building in Hollywood, California, was damaged by the Northridge earthquake in January 1994.*

SECTION Review

6.1.g

Summary

- An epicenter is the point on Earth's surface directly above where an earthquake started.

- The distance from a seismometer to an epicenter can be determined by using the lag time between P waves and S waves.

- An earthquake's epicenter can be located by triangulation.

- Magnitude is a measure of an earthquake's strength.

- Intensity is the effects of an earthquake.

- Important factors that determine the effects of an earthquake on a given area are magnitude, distance from the epicenter, local geology, and the type of construction.

Using Vocabulary

1. Use *epicenter* and *focus* in the same sentence.

Understanding Concepts

2. **Summarizing** Briefly explain the steps for locating an earthquake's epicenter.

3. **Comparing** Compare magnitude and intensity.

4. **Summarizing** How is local geology related to earthquake intensity?

5. **Identifying** What four factors affect the intensity of an earthquake?

Critical Thinking

6. **Applying Concepts** Why might an earthquake have more than one intensity value? Explain your answer.

7. **Evaluating Methods** If you were going to construct an earthquake-resistant building, what materials would you use in its construction and why?

INTERPRETING GRAPHICS Use the figure below to answer the next question.

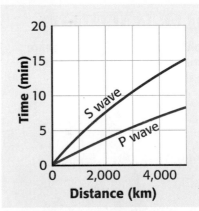

8. **Analyzing Data** If the lag time between the arrival of the P waves and the S waves is 5 min, what is the distance to the epicenter?

Earthquakes and Society

Key Concept Studying seismic activity can help scientists forecast earthquakes and reduce the damage that earthquakes cause.

What You Will Learn

- The magnitude of earthquakes may be related to how frequently earthquakes happen.
- Earthquakes and tsunamis can affect human societies.
- Homes, buildings, and bridges can be strengthened to decrease earthquake damage.

Why It Matters

Adequately preparing for earthquakes will reduce the harm that earthquakes cause.

Vocabulary

- seismic gap
- tsunami

READING STRATEGY

Graphic Organizer In your **Science Journal,** create a Cause-and-Effect Map about tsunamis.

▶ Scientists are not able to predict the exact time and place that an earthquake will happen. They can, at best, make forecasts based on the frequency with which earthquakes take place. Therefore, scientists are always looking for better ways to forecast when and where earthquakes will happen. In the meantime, it is important for people in earthquake zones to be prepared before an earthquake happens.

Earthquake Hazard

Earthquake hazard is a measurement of how likely an area is to have damaging earthquakes in the future. An area's earthquake-hazard level is determined by past seismic activity. **Figure 1** shows earthquake-hazard levels in the continental United States. The more frequently earthquakes happen, the higher the earthquake-hazard level is. California, for example, has a very high earthquake-hazard level because a lot of earthquakes happen there.

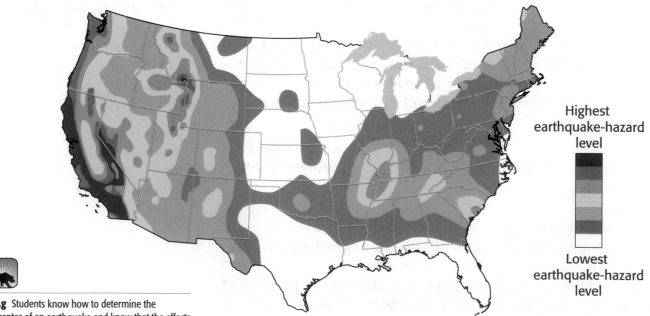

Highest earthquake-hazard level

Lowest earthquake-hazard level

Figure 1 *Earthquake-hazard levels vary throughout the United States because different regions have different levels of seismic activity.*

6.1.g Students know how to determine the epicenter of an earthquake and know that the effects of an earthquake on any region vary, depending on the size of the earthquake, the distance of the region from the epicenter, the local geology, and the type of construction in the region.

6.2.d Students know earthquakes, volcanic eruptions, landslides, and floods change human and wildlife habitats.

Table 1	Worldwide Earthquake Frequency (Based on Observations Since 1900)	
Descriptor	Magnitude	Average number annually
Great	8.0 and higher	1
Major	7.0–7.9	17
Strong	6.0–6.9	134
Moderate	5.0–5.9	1,319
Light	4.0–4.9	about 13,000
Minor	3.0–3.9	about 130,000
Very minor	2.0–2.9	about 1,300,000

Earthquake Forecasting

Forecasting when and where earthquakes will happen or how strong they will be is difficult. However, by studying earthquakes, scientists have discovered some patterns. These patterns allow the scientists to make general predictions.

Strength and Frequency

As you can see in **Table 1,** strong earthquakes are much rarer than weaker earthquakes. The relationship between earthquake strength and frequency is based on the amount of energy that is released during earthquakes. Millions of smaller earthquakes may be required to release the same amount of energy as one large earthquake does. When a large earthquake happens, a huge amount of energy is released. However, many small earthquakes combined release only a small fraction of that energy. Therefore, even though many small earthquakes happen, it is still possible for a large earthquake to happen.

Standards Check What is the relationship between the strength of earthquakes and the frequency with which they happen? 6.1.g

The Gap Hypothesis

One method of forecasting an earthquake's strength, location, and frequency is based on the gap hypothesis. The *gap hypothesis* states that sections of active faults that have had relatively few recent earthquakes are likely to be the sites of strong earthquakes sometime in the future. The areas along an active fault where relatively few earthquakes have happened are called **seismic gaps.** Scientists look for seismic gaps to find places where stress has had a long time to build. When a fault breaks at a seismic gap, this stress is suddenly released. This sudden release causes a large-magnitude earthquake.

INTERNET ACTIVITY

Earthquake Stories
You can create a story with pictures and captions that describes what experiencing an earthquake is like.
Go to **go.hrw.com,** and type in the keyword HY7EQKW.

seismic gap (SIEZ mik GAP) an area along a fault where relatively few earthquakes have occurred recently but where strong earthquakes have occurred in the past

Figure 2   A Seismic Gap on the San Andreas Fault

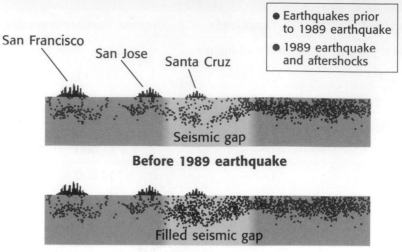

- Earthquakes prior to 1989 earthquake
- 1989 earthquake and aftershocks

San Francisco   San Jose   Santa Cruz

Seismic gap

Before 1989 earthquake

Filled seismic gap

After 1989 earthquake

Quick Lab

Earthquakes and Buildings

6.1.g

1. Use **scissors** to cut **10 drinking straws** so that they fit in the width of a **shoebox.** Place the straws in the shoebox.

2. Cut a **piece of cardboard** from the shoebox lid, and place it on top of the straws. The cardboard should move freely in the shoebox.

3. Build a model structure from **toothpicks** and **marshmallows.**

4. Place your model on top of the cardboard, and move the shoebox back and forth to simulate an earthquake.

5. Was your model damaged? If so, redesign it and test it again.

 30 min

Using the Gap Hypothesis

Because many variables affect when and where an earthquake may happen, not all scientists think that the gap hypothesis is an accurate method of forecasting earthquakes. But some scientists think that the gap hypothesis helped forecast the approximate location and strength of the 1989 Loma Prieta earthquake. The seismic gap that they identified is illustrated in **Figure 2.** In 1988, these scientists predicted that there was a 30% chance that an earthquake with a magnitude of at least 6.5 would fill this seismic gap within the next 30 years. In 1989, the Loma Prieta earthquake of magnitude 6.9 happened in the gap. The scientists' prediction was very close even though forecasting earthquakes is very complicated.

Reducing Earthquake Damage

Much of the loss of human life during earthquakes is caused by buildings that collapse. So, older structures in seismically active areas are being made more resistant to earthquakes. The process of making older structures more resistant to earthquakes is called *retrofitting.* A common way to retrofit a building is to securely fasten the building to its foundation. Another way is to use steel to strengthen brick structures.

A lot has been learned from building failure during earthquakes. Armed with this knowledge, architects and engineers use the newest technologies to design and construct buildings and bridges to better withstand earthquakes. **Figure 3** shows some examples of these technologies.

Standards Check   How does building construction relate to the damage that earthquakes can cause? 6.1.g

Figure 3 Earthquake-Resistant Building Technology

A **mass damper** is a weight placed in the roof of a building. Motion sensors detect building movement during an earthquake and send messages to a computer. The computer then signals controls in the roof to shift the mass damper to counteract the building's movement.

Steel **cross braces** are placed between floors. These braces counteract pressure that pushes and pulls at the side of a building during an earthquake.

The **active tendon system** works much like the mass damper system in the roof. Sensors notify a computer that the building is moving. Then, the computer activates devices to shift a large weight to counteract the movement.

Base isolators act as shock absorbers during an earthquake. They are made of layers of rubber and steel wrapped around a lead core. Base isolators absorb seismic waves and prevent the waves from traveling through the building.

Flexible pipes help prevent waterlines and gas lines from breaking. Engineers design the pipes with flexible joints so that the pipes are able to twist and bend without breaking during an earthquake.

Figure 4 *These students are participating in an earthquake drill.*

Are You Prepared for an Earthquake?

Earthquakes can collapse structures, start fires, and trigger landslides. But you can protect yourself and your property from earthquake damage. Plan ahead so that you will know what to do before, during, and after an earthquake.

Before the Shaking Starts

The first thing you should do is safeguard your home against earthquakes. You can do this by putting heavy objects on low shelves so that they do not fall during an earthquake. You can also talk to a parent about having your home strengthened. Next, you should find places that are safe within each room of your home and outside of your home. Then, make a plan to meet with others (your family, neighbors, or friends) in a safe place after the earthquake. This plan ensures that you will all know who is safe. Waterlines, power lines, gas lines, and roadways may be damaged during an earthquake. So, you should store water, nonperishable food, a fire extinguisher, a flashlight with batteries, a portable radio, medicines, and a first-aid kit in a place that you can access after the earthquake.

Standards Check How do earthquakes change human habitats? **6.2.d**

SCHOOL to HOME

Disaster Planning

With a parent or guardian, create a plan that will protect your family in the event of an earthquake. The plan should include steps to take before, during, and after the disaster. Post your plan in your home so that your family can see it.

ACTIVITY

When the Shaking Starts

If you are indoors, stay indoors until the shaking stops. Crouch or lie face down under a table or desk in the center of a room, as **Figure 4** shows. If you are outside, stay outside. Lie face down away from buildings, power lines, and trees, and cover your head with your hands. If you are in a car on an open road, you should stop the car and remain inside.

After the Shaking Stops

Being in an earthquake is a startling and often frightening experience. After the earthquake, you should remain calm and get your bearings as quickly as possible. Then, identify immediate dangers, such as downed power lines, broken glass, and fire hazards. Always stay out of damaged buildings, and return home only when you are told that it is safe to do so by someone in authority. Be aware that there may be aftershocks, which may cause more damage.

Tsunamis

When earthquakes happen on the ocean floor, they can generate tsunamis. A **tsunami** is an extremely long wave that can travel across the ocean at speeds of up to 800 km/h. Tsunamis most often form when an earthquake causes a vertical movement of the sea floor, which displaces an enormous volume of water. This process is shown in **Figure 5.** Undersea volcanic eruptions, landslides, and even meteorite impacts can also cause tsunamis.

In the open ocean, tsunami waves can seem very small. As tsunami waves enter shallow water along a coastline, the energy of the waves is compressed. As a result, the waves rapidly get taller. By the time tsunami waves reach the shore, waves can be taller than 30 m.

Standards Check How do tsunamis form? 6.2.d

tsunami (tsoo NAH mee) a giant ocean wave that forms after a volcanic eruption, submarine earthquake, or landslide

Figure 5 *An upward shift in the ocean floor causes an earthquake. The energy released by the earthquake pushes a large volume of water upward, which creates a series of tsunami waves.*

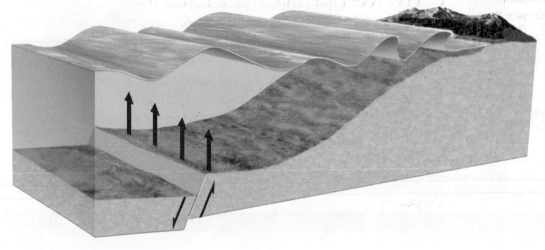

Figure 6 *A tsunami on December 26, 2004, caused widespread destruction in Asia.*

Destructive Tsunamis

Tsunamis can cause large amounts of damage and loss of life by smashing and washing away anything in their paths. During the 20th century, almost 150 tsunamis happened worldwide. **Figure 6** shows the effects of a tsunami that happened in 2004. An undersea earthquake of magnitude 9.3 caused the tsunami. More than 280,000 people died, and 1.25 million people were left homeless. One reason tsunamis cause so many deaths is that the ocean may recede far from the shoreline as the waves approach. When people go to see the exposed ocean floor, they get caught as the waves suddenly rush onto the shore.

Standards Check How do tsunamis change human and wildlife habitats? 6.2.d

Monitoring Tsunamis

Today, tsunamis are monitored by most of the nations that border the Pacific Ocean. Participating nations provide seismic and tide data to the Pacific Tsunami Warning Center (PTWC) in Hawaii. If a large undersea earthquake happens, PTWC will monitor sea level near the epicenter. If a tsunami has been generated, a tsunami watch bulletin is issued for the Pacific Ocean area. If the bulletin is upgraded to a warning, agencies in threatened areas may order residents to evacuate.

Quick Lab

Modeling a Tsunami

In this activity, you will model the events that produce a tsunami.

▶ Try It!

1. Place a **wedge** under a **plastic tub** so that the tub is tilted at a 20° angle.
2. Fill the tub with **water** until 2/3 of the tub is covered in water.
3. Pack a **layer of sand** in the dry end of the container to simulate a shoreline.
4. Punch a hole in a **clear, plastic coffee can lid,** and thread a **piece of string** that is 20 cm long through the hole. Tie the string to the lid.
5. Gently place the coffee lid in the deep end of the tub. Have a partner use several fingers to hold down the lid on the shallow end.

6. Quickly pull up on the string.

▶ Think About It!

7. What does the movement of the lid model?
8. How did the tsunami wave change as it approached the shore?

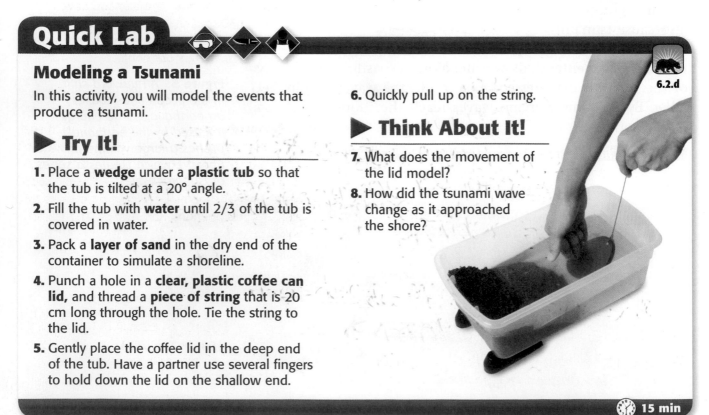

6.2.d

15 min

Summary

- Earthquakes and tsunamis can affect human societies.
- Earthquake hazard is a measure of how likely an area is to have earthquakes in the future.
- Scientists use their knowledge of the relationship between earthquake strength and frequency and of the gap hypothesis to forecast earthquakes.
- Homes, buildings, and bridges can be strengthened to decrease earthquake damage.
- People who live in earthquake zones should safeguard their homes against earthquakes and have an earthquake emergency plan.
- Tsunamis are giant ocean waves that may be caused by earthquakes on the sea floor.

Using Vocabulary

① Write an original definition for *tsunami* and *seismic gap.*

Understanding Concepts

② **Describing**   How is an area's earthquake-hazard level determined?

③ **Summarizing**   Describe the seismic gap hypothesis.

④ **Comparing**   Compare four examples of technologies that are designed to make buildings earthquake resistant.

⑤ **Applying**   Explain how the transfer of energy as seismic waves is related to the frequency and magnitude of earthquakes in a region.

⑥ **Analyzing**   How do earthquakes and tsunamis change human and wildlife habitats?

Critical Thinking

⑦ **Applying Concepts**   Why are large earthquakes less common than small earthquakes?

⑧ **Evaluating Hypotheses**   Scientists predict that there is a 20% chance that an earthquake of magnitude 7.0 or greater will fill a seismic gap during the next 50 years. Is the gap hypothesis incorrect if the earthquake does not happen? Explain your answer.

INTERPRETING GRAPHICS   Use the table below to answer the next two questions.

Earthquake Frequency and Magnitude	
Magnitude	**Annual Frequency**
8.0 and higher	1
7.0 to 7.9	17
6.0 to 6.9	134
5.0 to 5.9	1,319

⑨ **Summarizing Data**   About how many earthquakes of magnitude 6.0 or greater happen each year?

⑩ **Summarizing Data**   How many earthquakes that have magnitudes greater than 7.0 happen in 10 years?

Math Skills

⑪ **Making Calculations**   If a tsunami travels 325 km in 30 min, at what speed is the tsunami moving across the open ocean? Give your answer in kilometers per hour.

Challenge

⑫ **Developing Hypotheses**   People reported seeing animals fleeing for higher ground before the 2004 tsunami reached the shore. After the tsunami, people found that few land animals were killed by the tsunami. Develop a hypothesis that explains this phenomenon, and describe how you would test it.

Inquiry Lab

Earthquake Epicenters

The energy from an earthquake travels as seismic waves in all directions through Earth. P waves travel more quickly than S waves do. That's why P waves are always detected first. The average speed of P waves in Earth's crust is 6.1 km/s. The average speed of S waves in Earth's crust is 4.1 km/s. The difference in arrival time at a seismometer station between P waves and S waves is called *lag time.* In this lab, you will use the lag time to determine the epicenter of an earthquake.

OBJECTIVES

Demonstrate the method scientists use to determine an earthquake's epicenter.

MATERIALS

- calculator (optional)
- compass
- ruler, metric

SAFETY

Procedure

1 The illustration below shows seismometer records made at three seismometer stations following an earthquake. The seismometer traces begin at the left, where the arrival of P waves at each seismometer station is shown at time zero. The second set of waves on each record represents the arrival of S waves.

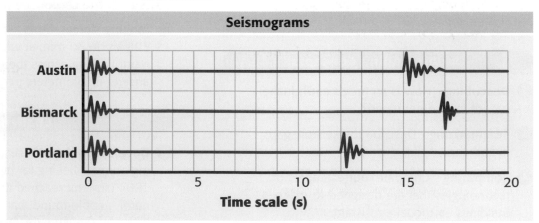

Seismograms

2 Copy the data table below into your notebook.

Epicenter Data Table

City	Lag time (s)	Distance to epicenter (km)
Austin, TX		
Bismarck, ND		
Portland, OR		

6.1.g Students know how to determine the epicenter of an earthquake and know that the effects of an earthquake on any region vary, depending on the size of the earthquake, the distance of the earthquake from the epicenter, the local geology, and the type of construction in the region.

Scale in kilometers

0   600   1200   1800   2400

3 Use the seismograms to find the lag time between the P waves and the S waves for each city. Record these data in your table.

4 The average speed of P waves is 6.1 km/s, and the average speed of S waves is 4.1 km/s. Use the following equation to calculate how long each wave type takes to travel 100 km:

$$100 \text{ km} \div average \text{ } speed \text{ } of \text{ } the \text{ } wave = time$$

5 To find the lag time for earthquake waves at 100 km, subtract the time P waves take to travel 100 km from the time S waves take to travel 100 km. Record the lag time.

6 Use the following formula to find the distance from each city to the epicenter:

$$distance = \frac{measured \text{ } lag \text{ } time \text{ } (s) \times 100 \text{ km}}{lag \text{ } time \text{ } for \text{ } 100 \text{ km} \text{ } (s)}$$

In your data table, record the distance from each city to the epicenter.

7 Trace the map above onto a separate sheet of paper.

8 Use the scale in the map above to adjust your compass so that the radius of a circle with Austin at the center is equal to the distance between Austin and the epicenter of the earthquake.

9 Put the point of your compass at Austin on your copy of the map, and draw a circle.

10 Repeat steps 8 and 9 for Bismarck and Portland. The epicenter of the earthquake is located near the point where the three circles meet.

Analyze the Results

11 **Analyzing Data** How are distance and lag time related to the epicenter of an earthquake?

Draw Conclusions

12 **Drawing Conclusions** Which city is located closest to the epicenter?

Big Idea Question

13 **Drawing Conclusions** Why is determining the epicenter of an earthquake important?

Science Skills Activity

Investigation and Experimentation
6.7.c Construct appropriate graphs from data and develop qualitative statements about the relationships between variables.

Constructing Graphs from Data

▶ Tutorial

Procedure

1. Draw the axes for your graph on a **sheet of graph paper.**

2. Label the *x*-axis in terms that describe the types of data. Determine a scale that includes the range of your data. Write the numbers of the scale on the tick marks of the axis. Title the *x*-axis.

3. Determine a scale for the *y*-axis that includes the range of your data. Write the numbers of the scale on the tick marks of the axis. Label the *y*-axis.

4. Draw bars on your graph. The bar heights should equal the *y*-value for each data set or datapoint on the *x*-axis.

5. Write the title of your graph at the top of your graph.

Analysis

6. Analyze the graph to identify any patterns you see in the data. Patterns in the data usually indicate relationships between variables.

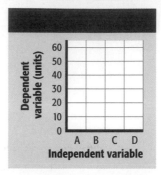

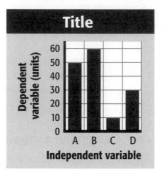

▶ You Try It!

Procedure

Use the data in **Table 1** to construct a bar graph, and then use the graph to make observations about the relationship between the strength of earthquakes and earthquake frequency. Use only the data for great, major, strong, and moderate earthquakes to construct your graph.

Analysis

1. **Identifying Patterns** Write a statement that describes the relationship between earthquake magnitude and earthquake frequency.

2. **Making Comparisons** Examine all of the data in **Table 1.** Compare the average annual number of earthquakes that have a magnitude of 5.0 and greater with the average number of earthquakes that have a magnitude less than 5.0.

3. **Evaluating Results** Why do you think the data for light, minor, and very minor earthquakes were not included in your graph? (Hint: Think about how your graph would look if all of the data in **Table 1** were graphed.)

Table 1	Worldwide Earthquake Frequency	
Descriptor	**Magnitude**	**Average number annually**
Great	8.0 and higher	1
Major	7.0–7.9	17
Strong	6.0–6.9	134
Moderate	5.0–5.9	1,319
Light	4.0–4.9	about 13,000
Minor	3.0–3.9	about 130,000
Very minor	2.0–2.9	about 1,300,000

Chapter Summary

The Big Idea
Earthquakes result from sudden motions along breaks in Earth's crust and can affect landforms and societies.

Section

Vocabulary

1 What Are Earthquakes?

Key Concept Sudden motions along breaks in Earth's crust can release energy in the form of seismic waves.

- Earthquakes are ground motions that result from the release of energy when blocks of rock move.
- Most earthquakes occur along tectonic plate boundaries because the movement of tectonic plates causes stress in Earth's crust.
- Earthquake energy travels through rock as seismic waves.

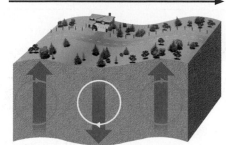

Direction of wave travel

Seismic waves carry energy through the rock that makes up Earth.

earthquake p. 232
elastic rebound p. 235
seismic wave p. 235

2 Earthquake Measurement

Key Concept Studying the properties of seismic waves can help scientists determine an earthquake's starting point, strength, and intensity.

- To find an earthquake's epicenter, you must triangulate by using data from three or more seismometers.
- Magnitude is a measure of an earthquake's strength.
- The intensity of an earthquake depends on four main factors.

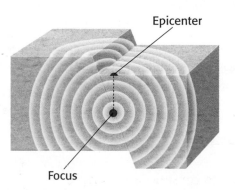

Epicenter

Focus

The epicenter of an earthquake lies directly above the focus.

epicenter p. 238
focus p. 238
magnitude p. 241
intensity p. 241

3 Earthquakes and Society

Key Concept Studying seismic activity can help scientists forecast earthquakes and reduce the damage that earthquakes cause.

- The magnitude of earthquakes may be related to how frequently they happen.
- Earthquakes and tsunamis can affect human societies.
- Homes, buildings, and bridges can be strengthened to decrease earthquake damage.

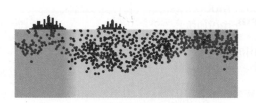

Filled seismic gap

The frequency of earthquakes is related to earthquake magnitude.

seismic gap p. 245
tsunami p. 249

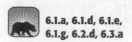
Organize

Pyramid Review the FoldNote that you created at the beginning of the chapter. Add to or correct the FoldNote based on what you have learned.

Using Vocabulary

1 Academic Vocabulary Which of the following words means "a place or position"?
a. distribution
b. distance
c. location
d. source

For each pair of terms, explain how the meanings of the terms differ.

2 *earthquake* and *seismic wave*

3 *epicenter* and *focus*

Understanding Concepts

Multiple Choice

4 Seismic waves are a form of ___ that travels through rock.
a. deformation
b. energy
c. fault
d. earthquake

5 Reverse faults form as a result of
a. divergent plate motion.
b. convergent plate motion.
c. transform plate motion.
d. strike-slip plate motion.

6 Scientists use the Modified Mercalli scale to describe earthquake
a. hazard.   c. magnitude.
b. strength.   d. intensity.

7 A(n) ___ is the shaking of the ground that results from a sudden motion along a break in Earth's crust.
a. fault   c. epicenter
b. earthquake   d. tsunami

Short Answer

8 Describing Explain how tectonic forces created the San Andreas fault zone. What type of fault is typical of this fault zone?

9 Summarizing Describe the method scientists use to locate the epicenter of an earthquake.

10 Comparing How do the Richter scale and the moment magnitude scale differ?

11 Identifying How do earthquake locations support the theory of plate tectonics?

12 Describing How does the Modified Mercalli scale describe earthquake intensity?

13 Describing Explain how undersea earthquakes cause tsunamis.

14 Identifying What four factors affect how much damage is caused by an earthquake?

15 Analyzing How do earthquakes and tsunamis change human and wildlife habitats?

16 Analyzing How does elastic rebound cause the transfer of energy?

INTERPRETING GRAPHICS Use the diagram below to answer the next two questions.

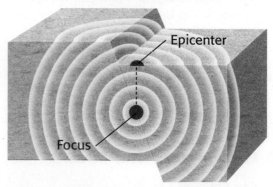

Epicenter

Focus

17 Applying Which type of fault is shown in the illustration?

18 Applying Which type of plate motion produces this type of fault?

Writing Skills

19 Explaining Ideas Write an essay that clearly explains the relationship between earthquakes and plate tectonics to a third-grade student. Your essay should have a thesis statement and include evidence that supports your ideas. Finally, make sure your essay has a conclusion statement.

Critical Thinking

20 Concept Mapping Use the following terms to create a concept map: *focus, epicenter, seismogram, seismic waves, P waves,* and *S waves.*

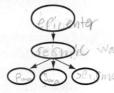

21 Identifying Relationships Would a strong earthquake be more likely to occur along a fault where few earthquakes have happened recently or along a fault where several minor earthquakes have happened recently? Explain your answer.

22 Applying Concepts Japan is located near a point where three tectonic plates converge. What do you think the earthquake-hazard level in Japan is? Explain your answer. *very high*

23 Applying Concepts If you are in a car during an earthquake and are out in the open, are you safest in the car? Can you think of any situation in which you might want to leave a car during an earthquake? Explain your answer. *ground starts to break*

24 Identifying Relationships You use gelatin to simulate rock in an experiment in which you are investigating the way different seismic waves affect rock. In what ways is your gelatin model limited?

25 Identifying Relationships Would an earthquake in the Rocky Mountains in Colorado be likely to form a tsunami? Explain your answer. *No because it is not an ocean.*

26 Analyzing Consequences How can an earthquake that occurs beneath the ocean and far from a populated area cause destruction of property and loss of human life? *It could damage the coastline.*

INTERPRETING GRAPHICS Use the map below to answer the next three questions.

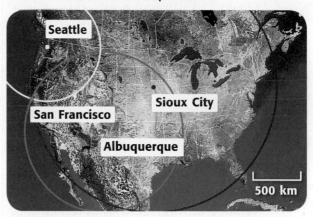

27 Applying Concepts Where was the epicenter of the earthquake? Explain how you determined this.

28 Identifying Relationships If P waves travel at a speed of 6.1 km/s, about how long did the P waves take to reach Albuquerque? (Hint: Use the map's scale.)

29 Identifying Relationships If seismometer data were available from only Seattle and Albuquerque, how many locations could you possibly identify as the epicenter?

Math Skills

30 Making Conversions S waves travel at about 60% of the velocity of P waves. P waves travel at about 6.1 km/s. What is the velocity of S waves?

Challenge

31 Making Inferences Two earthquakes that have similar magnitudes occur in two different parts of the world. One earthquake causes much loss of life and destruction of property, and the other earthquake causes very little property damage and no loss of life. What might explain the difference in the amount of damage caused by the earthquakes?

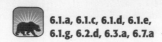

6.1.a, 6.1.c, 6.1.d, 6.1.e,
6.1.g, 6.2.d, 6.3.a, 6.7.a

REVIEWING ACADEMIC VOCABULARY

1 Choose the appropriate form of the word *predict* for the following sentence: "Scientists hope to create tools to make earthquakes more ___."

A prediction

B predictive

C predictable

D predicted

2 Which of the following words means "the relative arrangement of objects or organisms in time or space"?

A organization

B distribution

C evolution

D location

3 Which of the following sets of words best completes the following sentence: "The theory of plate tectonics ___ the fit of continents and other phenomena"?

A derives from

B derives on

C is derived from

D is derived with

4 Choose the appropriate form of the word *locate* for the following sentence: "The ___ of earthquakes and volcanoes gives support to the theory of plate tectonics."

A locate

B localization

C location

D located

REVIEWING CONCEPTS

5 How can scientists tell how far the epicenter of an earthquake is from a seismometer station?

A by calculating the arrival time between P waves and S waves

B by calculating the arrival time between P waves

C by calculating the strength of P waves

D by calculating the difference in the strength of P waves and S waves

6 Earthquakes in California occur mostly along strike-slip faults. Along which type of tectonic plate boundary is California located?

A normal

B transform

C divergent

D convergent

7 Where is the epicenter of an earthquake located?

A directly above the earthquake's focus

B directly below the earthquake's focus

C directly above a seismic gap

D directly below the point of highest intensity

Point A

X   X X X   X   X   X X X X X

8 The diagram above shows an area along a fault. Each *X* shows where an earthquake has occurred. Which term best describes Point A?

A focus

B epicenter

C seismic gap

D tectonic plate boundary

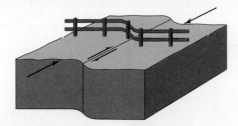

9 **What is happening in the process of elastic rebound shown above?**

A Stress is causing rocks to fold.

B Stress is causing rocks to deform, break, and jerk past one another.

C Stress is causing rocks to move back and forth.

D Stress is causing rocks to shear from side to side.

10 **What do scientists measure when they measure the intensity of an earthquake?**

A the amount of energy released by the earthquake

B the amount of movement that occurs along a fault

C the distance from the earthquake's focus to its epicenter

D the amount of damage done to structures in the area

11 **Which of the following is one way tsunamis affect human and wildlife habitats?**

A Tsunamis cause large areas of coastline to flood.

B Tsunamis cause vertical movement of Earth's crust.

C Tsunamis cause rocks to deform and break.

D Tsunamis cause changes in the average global temperature.

REVIEWING PRIOR LEARNING

12 **A series of earthquakes in a particular area leads scientists to think the area is located above a fault. What is this idea called?**

A observation

B inference

C hypothesis

D experimentation

13 **Which statement best describes what causes movements of tectonic plates?**

A One plate moves under another and slides into the mantle.

B Convective flow in the mantle slowly pushes the plates along.

C Volcanic eruptions create violent forces that push plates along.

D Magma generated in the mantle exerts upward pressure on Earth's surface.

14 **Which of the following statements describes the motion of tectonic plates at a divergent boundary?**

A One tectonic plate separates into two.

B Two tectonic plates collide.

C Two tectonic plates pull away from each other.

D Two tectonic plates move past each other horizontally.

15 **Convective flow in Earth's mantle happens when**

A hot mantle rock rises and cool surface rock sinks.

B hot mantle rock rises and hot surface rock sinks.

C cool mantle rock rises and hot surface rock sinks.

D cool mantle rock rises and cool surface rock sinks.

Science in Action

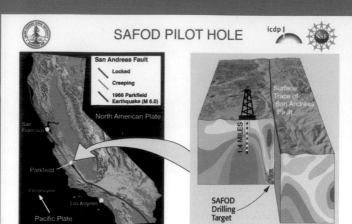

SAFOD PILOT HOLE

Science, Technology, and Society

Waves of the Future

Since 1812, California has been struck by 14 tsunamis that had waves 9 m tall or taller. Six of these tsunamis caused significant damage.

On June 15, 2005, a magnitude 7.2 earthquake occurred 157 km southwest of Crescent City, California. A tsunami warning for the Pacific Coast of North America was in effect for approximately one hour. During that time, residents of Crescent City and other coastal communities evacuated low-lying areas. Though only a 1 cm wave was generated by the earthquake, emergency officials along the Pacific Coast learned about problems with the tsunami warning system.

Scientific Discoveries

SAFOD—An Underground Seismic Observatory

Seismologists are creating an underground observatory in Parkfield, California, to study earthquakes along the San Andreas fault. The observatory will be named the San Andreas Fault Observatory at Depth (SAFOD). A deep hole will be drilled directly into the fault zone near a point where earthquakes of magnitude 6.0 have been recorded. Instruments will be placed at the bottom of the hole, 3 to 4 km beneath Earth's surface. These instruments will take measurements during earthquakes and measure the deformation of rock.

Social Studies ACTiViTY

Research the great San Francisco earthquake of 1906. Find images of the earthquake on the Internet and download them. Create a photo collage of the earthquake that shows San Francisco before and after the earthquake.

Language Arts ACTiViTY

Research the origin and meaning of the word *tsunami*. In your **Science Journal**, write a short essay about your findings.

Hiroo Kanamori

Seismologist Hiroo Kanamori is a seismologist at the California Institute of Technology in Pasadena, California. Dr. Kanamori studies how earthquakes occur and tries to reduce their impact on our society. He also analyzes what the effects of earthquakes on oceans are and how earthquakes create giant ocean waves called *tsunamis*. Tsunamis are very destructive to life and property when they reach land. Kanamori has discovered that even some weak earthquakes can cause powerful tsunamis. He calls these events *tsunami earthquakes,* and he has learned to predict when tsunamis will form. In short, when tectonic plates grind together slowly, special waves called *long-period seismic waves* are generated. When Kanamori sees a long-period wave recorded on a seismogram, he knows a tsunami will form. Because long-period waves travel faster than tsunamis, long-period waves arrive at recording stations earlier. When an earthquake station records an earthquake, information about that earthquake is provided to a tsunami warning center. The center determines if the earthquake may cause a tsunami and, if so, issues a tsunami warning to areas that may be affected.

Math ACTIVITY

An undersea earthquake causes a tsunami to form. The tsunami travels across the open ocean at 800 km/h. How long will the tsunami take to travel from the point where it formed to a coastline 3,600 km away?

Internet Resources

- To learn more about careers in science, visit **www.scilinks.org** and enter the SciLinks code HY70225.

- To learn more about these Science in Action topics, visit **go.hrw.com** and type in the keyword HY7EQKF.

- Check out articles related to this chapter by visiting **go.hrw.com**. Just type in the keyword HY7EQKC.

Improving Comprehension

Graphic Organizers are important visual tools that can help you organize information and improve your reading comprehension. The Graphic Organizer below is called a *concept map.* Instructions for creating other types of Graphic Organizers are located in the **Study Skills** section of the Appendix.

How to Make a Concept Map

1 Identify main ideas from the text, and write the ideas as short phrases or single words.

2 Select a main concept. Place this concept at the top or center of a piece of paper.

3 Place other ideas under or around the main concept based on their relationship to the main concept. Draw a circle around each idea.

4 Draw lines between the concepts, and add linking words to connect the ideas.

When to Use a Concept Map

Concept maps are useful when you are trying to identify how several ideas are connected to a main concept. Concept maps may be based on vocabulary terms or on main topics from the text. The concept map below shows how the important concepts of this chapter are related. As you read about science, look for terms that can be organized in a concept map.

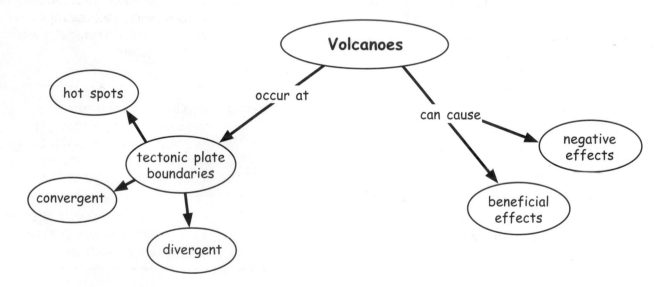

You Try It!

This Reading Strategy can also be used within the chapter that you are about to read. Practice making your own concept map as directed in the Reading Strategies for Section **2** and Section **3**. Record your work in your **Science Journal.**

Unpacking the Standards

The information below "unpacks" the standards by breaking them down into basic parts. The higher-level, academic vocabulary is highlighted and defined to help you understand the language of the standards. "What It Means" restates the standards as simply as possible.

California Standard	Academic Vocabulary	What It Means
6.1.a Students know **evidence** of plate tectonics is **derived** from the fit of the continents; the **location** of earthquakes, volcanoes, and midocean ridges; and the **distribution** of fossils, rock types, and ancient climatic zones.	**evidence** (EV uh duhns) information showing whether an idea or belief is true or valid **derive** (di RIEV) to figure out by reasoning **distribution** (DIS tri BYOO shuhn) information showing whether an idea or belief is true or valid	Support for the idea that Earth's surface is made of slabs of rock that move around comes from how continents fit together, where earthquakes happen, where volcanoes and mid-ocean ridges are located, where rocks and fossils are found, and where climate was different in the geologic past.
6.1.d Students know that earthquakes are sudden motions along breaks in the crust called faults and that volcanoes and fissures are **locations** where magma reaches the surface.	**location** (loh KAY shuhn) a place or position	Earthquakes are sudden movements along breaks in Earth's surface called *faults,* and volcanoes are places where molten rock reaches the surface.
6.1.e Students know **major** geologic events, such as earthquakes, volcanic eruptions, and mountain building, result from plate motions.	**major** (MAY juhr) of great importance or large scale	Important global events, such as earthquakes, volcanic eruptions, and mountain building, are caused by the movement of Earth's crust and upper mantle.
6.2.d Students know earthquakes, volcanic eruptions, landslides, and floods change human and wildlife habitats.		Earthquakes, volcanic eruptions, landslides, and floods change the surroundings in which humans and wildlife live.

The following identifies other standards that are covered in this chapter and where you can go to see them unpacked: **6.6.a** (Chapter 5)

8

Volcanoes

The Big Idea

Volcanoes form as a result of tectonic plate motions and occur where magma reaches Earth's surface.

California Standards

Focus on Earth Sciences

6.1 Plate tectonics accounts for important features of Earth's surface and major geologic events. (Sections 1 and 2)

6.2 Topography is reshaped by the weathering of rock and soil and by the transportation of sediment. (Section 3)

6.6 Sources of energy and materials differ in amounts, distribution, usefulness, and the time required for their formation. (Section 3)

Investigation and Experimentation

6.7 Scientific progress is made by asking meaningful questions and conducting careful investigations. (Science Skills Activity)

Math

6.2.1 Algebra and Functions

English–Language Arts

6.2.4 Reading
6.1.2 Writing

About the Photo

About 10,000 years ago, a glacier exposed spectacular columns of basalt near what is now Mammoth Lakes in the Sierra Nevadas. The columns, known as the *Devils Postpile,* formed around 100,000 years ago from a large basalt flow. As the basalt cooled, fractures spread through the flow and formed the pattern shown here.

Organize

Layered Book

Before you read this chapter, create the FoldNote entitled "Layered Book." Label the tabs of the layered book with "Volcanic eruptions," "Causes of eruptions," and "Effects of eruptions." As you read the chapter, write information you learn about each category on the appropriate tab.

Instructions for creating FoldNotes are located in the Study Skills section on p. 616 of the Appendix.

Explore Activity

15 min

Predicting a Volcanic Eruption

In this activity, you will build a simple model of a volcano.

Procedure

1. Place **10 mL of baking soda** on a **sheet of tissue.** Fold the corners of the tissue over the baking soda, and place the tissue packet in a **large pan.**

2. Put **modeling clay** around the edge of the wide opening of a **funnel.** Press the wide opening of the funnel over the tissue packet to make a tight seal with the pan.

3. After you put on **safety goggles,** add **50 mL of vinegar** and **several drops of liquid dish soap** to a **200 mL beaker** and stir.

4. Carefully pour the liquid into the funnel.

6.1.d
6.7.e

Analysis

5. Describe the "eruption."

6. Use your observations to explain what caused the eruption.

Why Volcanoes Form

Key Concept Volcanoes occur at tectonic plate boundaries and at hot spots, where molten rock, or magma, forms and rises to the surface.

volcano (vahl KAY noh) a vent or fissure in Earth's surface through which magma and gases are expelled

magma (MAG muh) liquid rock produced under Earth's surface; igneous rocks form from magma

▶ A **volcano** is a vent or fissure in Earth's surface through which melted rock and gases pass. An estimated 1,500 volcanoes have been active above sea level during the past 10,000 years of Earth's history. Many more have been active beneath the ocean.

Where Volcanoes Form

The locations of volcanoes are clues that help explain how volcanoes form. The map in **Figure 1** shows the locations of some of the world's major active volcanoes. The map also shows the boundaries between tectonic plates. Tectonic plate boundaries are areas where tectonic plates collide, pull away from one another, or move past one another horizontally. A large number of volcanoes lie directly on tectonic plate boundaries. In fact, the plate boundaries that surround the Pacific Ocean have so many volcanoes that the area is called the *Ring of Fire.*

At tectonic plate boundaries, several processes cause rock to melt at lower-crustal or upper-mantle depths. The molten rock is called **magma.** Because magma is less dense than the solid rock surrounding it, magma travels up toward the surface. When it reaches the surface, magma erupts to form a volcano.

Standards Check Where are most volcanoes located? 6.1.a

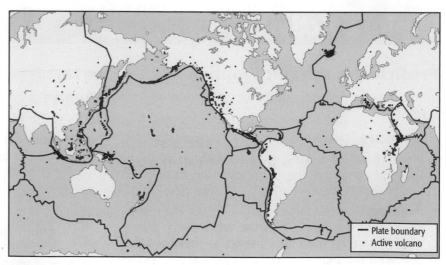

Figure 1 *This map shows the locations of tectonic plate boundaries and many of Earth's active volcanoes.* **How are the locations of volcanoes and plate boundaries related?**

Divergent Boundaries

The boundary between two tectonic plates that are pulling away from one another is called a *divergent boundary*. As tectonic plates pull away from one another, a set of deep vertical fractures called *fissures* form. Molten rock flows through these fissures onto the ocean floor. The molten rock also forms submarine volcanoes. At divergent boundaries, underwater mountain chains known as *mid-ocean ridges* are common. A mid-ocean ridge is shown in **Figure 2.** In fact, most volcanic activity on Earth happens at mid-ocean ridges.

Most divergent boundaries are underwater. However, Iceland is an island that is being pulled apart by a mid-ocean ridge.

Convergent Boundaries

The boundary where two tectonic plates collide is called a *convergent boundary*. As two plates collide, the denser plate slides under the other plate. As the denser plate bends, a deep depression known as a *trench* forms. At a trench, one plate moves downward into the mantle. This process, in which one plate moves beneath another plate, is called *subduction*. It is shown in **Figure 2.** As the plate moves farther downward into Earth's mantle, the rock is subjected to greater heat and pressure. As a result, the plate releases fluids, which causes surrounding rock to melt.

Hot Spots

Volcanically active places that are not located at tectonic plate boundaries are called *hot spots*. Hot spots are thought to lie directly above columns of hot rock that rise through Earth's mantle. These columns are called *mantle plumes*. Mantle plumes are stationary. Therefore, as a tectonic plate moves over a mantle plume, rising magma causes a chain of volcanic islands to form. The Hawaiian Islands, shown in **Figure 2,** have formed as the Pacific plate passes over a mantle plume.

Standards Check How do hot-spot volcanoes differ from other volcanoes? 6.1.e

Figure 2 Locations Where Volcanoes Form

As tectonic plates pull away from one another, magma flows through fractures in the sea floor at mid-ocean ridges.

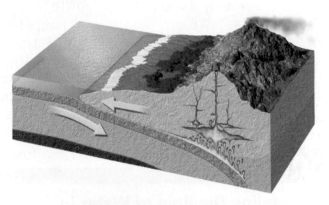

At a convergent boundary, a plate made of dense lithosphere moves beneath another plate.

As a tectonic plate moves over a mantle plume, rising magma may cause a chain of volcanoes to form.

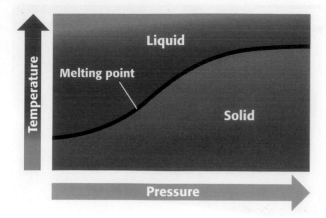

Figure 3 *The curved line indicates the melting point of a rock. As pressure decreases and temperature increases, the rock begins to melt.*

How Magma Forms

Understanding why volcanoes erupt requires an understanding of how magma forms. Magma forms in the deeper parts of Earth's crust and in the uppermost parts of the mantle. In these locations, temperature and pressure are very high. Changes in pressure and temperature cause magma to form. As **Figure 3** shows, rock melts when its temperature increases or when the pressure on the rock decreases. In addition, water can lower the melting temperature of rock and cause the rock to melt.

Increasing Temperature

As a tectonic plate moves downward into the mantle, the plate is exposed to greater temperatures at depth. This increase in temperature may cause the minerals in the rock to melt. But minerals in a rock have different melting temperatures. So, not all of the minerals in the rock melt at the same time. Minerals that have low melting temperatures melt before minerals that have high melting temperatures.

Quick Lab

Modeling the Role of Water in Volcanic Eruptions

Explosive volcanic eruptions can happen when the water content of magma is high. Dissolved water may expand and become a gas if magma rises rapidly and pressure is suddenly released.

A popcorn kernel contains a small amount of water in its core. When heated, this water expands and becomes vaporized water, or gas. The pressure generated inside the core of the kernel increases to the point that the hull of the kernel breaks. The kernel turns inside out, and the gas escapes.

6.1.d

▶ Try It!

1. Select a certain number of **popcorn kernels** to pop.

2. Place the popcorn kernels into an **air popper.** If an air popper is not available, put the popcorn in a **microwavable popcorn popper.**

3. Follow the popping instructions to pop the popcorn.

▶ Think About It!

4. How does water in the core of a popcorn kernel cause popcorn to pop?

5. How does the expansion of water into gas in a popcorn kernel model the expansion of dissolved water in magma?

6. How would a high water content in magma cause an explosive eruption?

 20 min

Decreasing Pressure

Magma can also form when the pressure on a rock decreases. In Earth's mantle, the pressure on rock is so great that the rock cannot expand. Expansion of rock is important in the formation of magma, because magma takes up more space than solid rock does. At divergent boundaries and hot spots, hot mantle rock rises to a shallow depth, where the pressure on the rock decreases. The decrease in pressure allows the hot rock to expand and to melt.

Adding Fluids

Oceanic lithosphere is made up of sediments and volcanic rocks that contain water and other fluids. When oceanic lithosphere moves downward into the mantle at a convergent boundary, the fluids contact the surrounding rock. When the fluids enter the already hot mantle rock, the melting temperature of the hot rock decreases. As a result, the rock begins to melt.

Standards Check How does adding fluids to hot rock cause magma to form? 🐻 6.1.d

INTERNET ACTIVITY

Living with Volcanoes
Investigate the unique characteristics of communities located near volcanoes. Write a short essay on your findings. Go to **go.hrw.com**, and type in the keyword **HY7VOLW**.

SECTION Review

6.1.a, 6.1.d, 6.1.e

Summary

- A volcano is a vent or fissure in Earth's surface through which magma and gases pass.
- Most volcanoes are located at tectonic plate boundaries.
- Volcanic activity occurs at divergent plate boundaries, convergent plate boundaries, and hot spots.
- Magma forms when the temperature of a rock increases, when the pressure on a rock decreases, or when water lowers the melting temperature of a rock.

Using Vocabulary

1 Write an original definition for *volcano* and *magma*.

Understanding Concepts

2 **Applying** How does tectonic plate motion relate to the formation of volcanoes?

3 **Comparing** Compare volcano formation at different plate boundaries.

4 **Summarizing** Briefly explain how volcanoes that are located at hot spots form.

5 **Analyzing** What role do pressure and temperature play in magma formation?

Critical Thinking

6 **Analyzing Ideas** How does the addition of fluid relate to the formation of magma?

Math Skills

7 **Making Calculations** Suppose that 1,500 volcanoes on Earth's surface are active. If 80% of these volcanoes are located at convergent tectonic plate boundaries, how many active volcanoes are located at convergent boundaries?

Challenge

8 **Analyzing Ideas** Explain why the expansion of rock is important in the formation of magma.

Internet Resources

For a variety of links related to this chapter, go to www.scilinks.org
Topic: What Causes Volcanoes?
SciLinks code: HY71654

Types of Volcanoes

Key Concept Tectonic plate motions can result in volcanic activity at plate boundaries.

▶ The process of magma formation is different at each type of plate boundary, where the tectonic setting is unique. Therefore, the composition of magma differs in each of these settings. As a result, tectonic settings determine the types of volcanoes that form and the types of eruptions that take place.

Volcanoes at Divergent Boundaries

At divergent boundaries, plates move away from each other. As the two plates pull away from one another, the lithosphere becomes thinner. A set of deep cracks form in an area called a *rift zone*. Hot mantle rock rises to fill these cracks. As the rock rises, a decrease in pressure causes hot mantle rock to melt and form magma. When the magma reaches Earth's surface, the magma is called **lava.**

Lava at Divergent Boundaries

Lava that flows at divergent boundaries forms from melted mantle rock. As a result, this lava is rich in the elements iron and magnesium and relatively poor in silica. Because of its composition, lava from mantle rock cools to form dark-colored rock. The term **mafic** describes magma, lava, and rocks—such as dark-colored basalt, shown in **Figure 1**—that are rich in iron and magnesium. Because it is low in silica, mafic lava is runny and not sticky. Thus, this type of lava generally produces nonexplosive eruptions. Teide volcano, shown in **Figure 1,** is made largely of basalt.

Standards Check Describe the lava that forms at divergent plate boundaries. 🐻 **6.1.e**

Figure 1 *Teide, located in the Canary Islands, is the third-largest volcano on Earth.*

6.1.d Students know that earthquakes are sudden motions along breaks in the crust called faults and that volcanoes and fissures are locations where magma reaches the surface.

6.1.e Students know major geologic events, such as earthquakes, volcanic eruptions, and mountain building, result from plate motions.

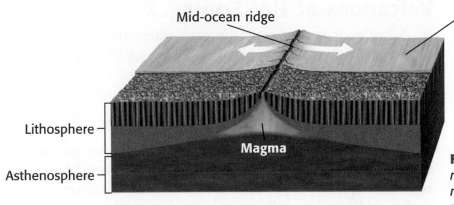

Mid-ocean ridge

Sediments deposited on sea floor

Lithosphere

Magma

Asthenosphere

Figure 2 *At mid-ocean ridges, magma moves upward from the mantle. The magma cools to form new lithosphere on the ocean floor.*

Mid-Ocean Ridges

Mid-ocean ridges are underwater volcanic mountain chains that form where two tectonic plates are moving apart. As the plates move apart, magma from the mantle rises to fill cracks that form in the crust. Some of the magma erupts as basaltic lava on the ocean floor. The magma and lava cool and become part of the oceanic lithosphere, as shown in **Figure 2.** As the plates continue to move, older oceanic lithosphere moves away from the mid-ocean ridge. New cracks form, and new lithosphere forms in the rift zone. The process in which new sea floor forms as older sea floor is pulled apart is called *sea-floor spreading.*

Standards Check Explain how new oceanic lithosphere forms at divergent boundaries. 📖 6.1.e

Fissure Eruptions

The mid-ocean ridge called the *Mid-Atlantic Ridge* is unusually active. This activity has built part of the ridge into a large island known as Iceland. Long linear cracks called *fissures* have formed where the Atlantic and Eurasian plates are moving apart. Basaltic magma rises to Earth's surface through these fissures and erupts nonexplosively. Icelandic volcanoes, such as Krafla, are often associated with large, connected fissure systems. Lava erupts frequently through these fissures. As a result of these eruptions, such as the one shown in **Figure 3,** Iceland is continually getting bigger.

lava (LAH vuh) magma that flows onto Earth's surface; the rock that forms when lava cools and solidifies

mafic (MAF ik) describes magma or igneous rock that is rich in magnesium and iron and that is generally dark in color

How Hot Is Hot?

Inside Earth, magma can reach temperatures as high as 1,400°C! You may be used to Fahrenheit temperatures, so use the following formula to convert 1,400°C to degrees Fahrenheit:

°F = (°C × 9 ÷ 5) + 32

What is the temperature in degrees Fahrenheit? Record your work in your **Science Journal.**

Figure 3 *Krafla volcano in Iceland is a fissure volcano. Frequent fissure eruptions have happened at Krafla.*

271

Volcanoes at Hot Spots

A hot spot is a volcanically active area that is located far from a tectonic plate boundary. A hot spot forms in a tectonic plate over a mantle plume. Mantle plumes are columns of hot, solid rock that rise through the mantle by convection. They are thought to originate at the boundary between the mantle and the outer core.

When the top of a mantle plume reaches the base of the lithosphere, the mantle rock spreads out and "pools" under the lithosphere. Because pressure on the rock in the plume is low at this shallow depth, the rock melts. Large volumes of magma are released onto the ocean floor. Continuous eruptions may produce a volcanic cone. As the plate continues to move over the mantle plume, a chain of volcanoes may form.

Standards Check Explain how mantle plumes generate volcanic activity at hot spots. 6.1.d

Lava at Hot Spots

Because lava at hot spots comes from the mantle, the lava is mafic and fluid. As a result, most eruptions at hot spots are non-explosive. The type of rock that forms from this lava depends on the temperature, gas content, flow rate, and slope of the lava flow. Four types of mafic lava are shown in **Figure 4.**

SCHOOL to HOME

Hot-Spot Volcanoes

With an adult, research a hot-spot volcano, such as Mauna Loa in Hawaii. Create a poster that presents your findings. Include information about how often the volcano has erupted in the past and when the last eruption took place. To enhance your presentation, you may want to include images from the Internet that show recent volcanic eruptions.

ACTIVITY

Figure 4   Four Types of Lava

Aa is lava that forms a thick, brittle crust. The crust is torn into jagged pieces as molten lava continues to flow underneath.

Pahoehoe is lava that forms a thin crust. The crust wrinkles as it is moved by molten lava that continues to flow underneath.

Pillow lava forms when lava erupts underwater. This lava forms rounded lumps that are the shape of pillows.

Blocky lava is cool, stiff lava that does not travel far from the eruption site. Blocky lava usually oozes from a volcano and forms jumbled heaps of sharp-edged chunks.

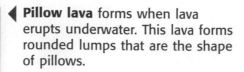

Figure 5 *From sea floor to summit, the Hawaiian shield volcano Mauna Kea is around 10 km tall.*

Shield Volcanoes

Shield volcanoes usually form at hot spots. Shield volcanoes form from layers of lava left by many nonexplosive eruptions. The lava is very runny, so it spreads out over a wide area. Over time, the layers of lava create a volcanic mountain that has gently sloping sides. The sides of shield volcanoes are not very steep, but the volcanoes can be very large. The base of a large shield volcano can be more than 100 km in diameter. Mauna Kea, the Hawaiian shield volcano shown in **Figure 5,** is the tallest mountain on Earth. Measured from its base on the sea floor, Mauna Kea is taller than Mount Everest.

Parts of a Volcano

Most volcanoes share a specific set of features, such as the features shown in **Figure 6.** The magma that feeds the eruptions pools deep underground in a structure called a *magma chamber.* Before erupting as lava from a volcano, magma rises from the magma chamber to Earth's surface through cracks in the crust. This movement of magma through rock causes small earthquakes that can be used to predict an eruption.

At Earth's surface, lava is released through openings called *vents.* Lava may erupt from a central summit crater of a shield volcano. Lava may also erupt from fissures along the sides of a shield volcano. After erupting from a vent, the fluid lavas move downslope in lava flows, long rivers of molten rock. Often, the flow will cool and solidify on top while the interior continues to travel through long, pipelike structures known as *lava tubes.*

Standards Check Describe how earthquakes are related to volcanic eruptions. 🐻 **6.1.e**

Figure 6 *When magma from a magma chamber erupts as lava from a vent, the lava may harden to form a volcanic mountain.*

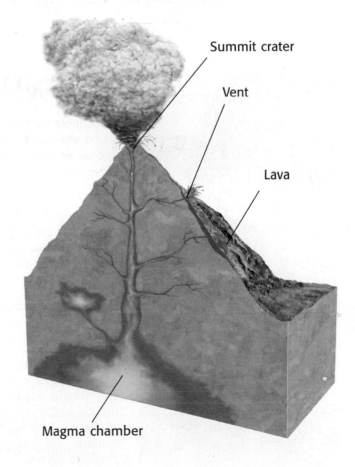

Summit crater

Vent

Lava

Magma chamber

Volcanoes at Convergent Boundaries

At a convergent boundary, a plate that contains oceanic lithosphere may descend into the mantle beneath another plate. The descending lithosphere contains water. As the lithosphere descends into the mantle, temperature and pressure increase. As a result, the subducting lithosphere releases water into the surrounding mantle and the overlying crust. The water lowers the melting temperature of the rock, and the rock melts. The magma that forms rises through the crust and erupts. These eruptions form a chain of volcanoes parallel to the plate boundary.

Lava at Convergent Boundaries

Magmas at convergent boundaries are melted mantle rock and melted crustal rock. So, fluid mafic lava and lava rich in silica and feldspar minerals form at these boundaries. Lavas rich in silica and feldspar cool to form light-colored rocks. The term **felsic** is used to describe magma, lava, and rocks that are rich in silica and feldspars. Silica-rich magma tends to trap water and gas bubbles, which causes enormous gas pressure to develop within the magma. As the gas-filled magma rises to Earth's surface, pressure is rapidly released. This change results in a powerful explosive eruption.

felsic (FEL sik) describes magma or igneous rock that is rich in feldspars and silica and that is generally light in color

Standards Check What is the relationship between high silica content in magma and an explosive eruption? 6.1.d

---

Figure 7 Types of Pyroclastic Material

Volcanic bombs are large blobs of magma that harden in the air.

Lapilli are pebblelike bits of magma that harden before they hit the ground.

Volcanic ash forms when the gases in stiff magma expand rapidly and the walls of the gas bubbles explode into tiny, glasslike slivers.

Volcanic blocks are large, angular pieces of solid rock that erupt from a volcano.

Figure 8 *Pyroclastic flows associated with the 1991 eruption of Mount Pinatubo in the Philippines had temperatures that reached 750°C.*

Types of Pyroclastic Material

Pyroclastic material is particles of lava that form when magma explodes from a volcano and solidifies in the air. Pyroclastic material also forms when powerful eruptions shatter existing rock. **Figure 7** shows four types of pyroclastic material.

<u>Wordwise</u> **pyroclastic**
The prefix *pyr-* means "fire."
The root *cla-* means "to break."
Another example is *pyromaniac.*

Pyroclastic Flows

Pyroclastic flows, such as the one shown in **Figure 8,** are produced when a volcano ejects enormous amounts of hot ash, dust, and toxic gases. This glowing cloud of pyroclastic material can race down the slope of a volcano at speeds of more than 200 km/h. This speed is faster than the speed of most hurricane-force winds! The temperature at the center of a pyroclastic flow can exceed 700°C. At this high temperature, a pyroclastic flow burns everything in its path. These extremes make pyroclastic flows the most dangerous of all volcanic phenomena.

Quick Lab

Modeling an Explosive Eruption

1. Inflate a **large balloon,** and place it in a **cardboard box.**

2. Spread a **sheet** on the floor. Place the box in the middle of the sheet. Mound a thin layer of **sand** over the balloon to make a volcano that is taller than the edges of the box.

3. Lightly mist the volcano with **water.** Sprinkle **tempera paint** on the volcano until the volcano is completely covered.

4. Place **small objects** such as **raisins** randomly on the volcano. Draw a sketch of the volcano.

5. Put on your **safety goggles.** Pop the balloon with a **pin.**

6. Use a **metric ruler** to calculate the average distance that 10 grains of sand and 10 raisins traveled.

7. How did the relative weight of each type of material affect the average distance that the material traveled?

8. Draw a sketch of the exploded volcano.

6.1.d

 20 min

Figure 9 *Parícutin, a cinder cone volcano in Mexico, appeared in a farmer's cornfield in 1943. The volcano erupted for nine years. When Parícutin stopped erupting, its height was 400 m.*

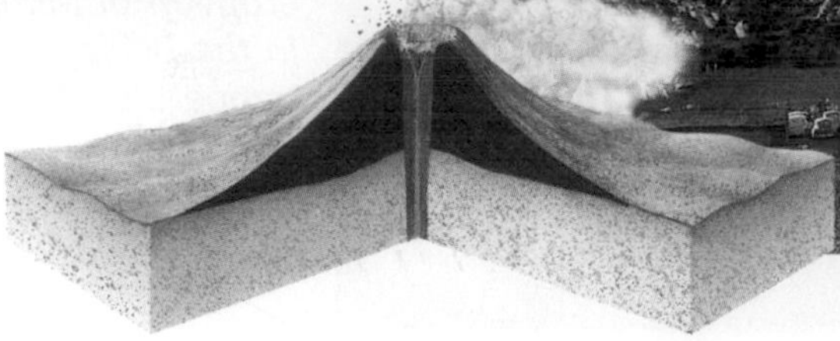

Cinder Cone Volcanoes

Cinder cone volcanoes are the smallest type of volcano. They generally reach heights of no more than 300 m. They are also the most common type of volcano. Cinder cone volcanoes are made of pyroclastic material and most often form from moderately explosive eruptions. As **Figure 9** shows, cinder cone volcanoes have steep sides. They also have a wide summit crater. Unlike other types of volcanoes, cinder cone volcanoes usually erupt only once in their lifetime.

Composite Volcanoes

Composite volcanoes, also called *stratovolcanoes,* are the most recognizable of all volcanoes. Composite volcanoes form from both explosive eruptions of pyroclastic material and quieter flows of lava. The combination of both types of eruptions forms alternating layers of pyroclastic material and lava. Composite volcanoes—such as Mount Fuji, shown in **Figure 10**—have a broad base and have sides that get steeper toward the summit crater. Composite volcanoes may generate many eruptions. However, these eruptions may occur at intervals of hundreds of years or more.

Standards Check How do cinder cone volcanoes differ from composite volcanoes? 6.I.d

Figure 10 *Mount Fuji, located in Japan, is a famous composite volcano. Its lower slopes are broad and gentle, but its upper slopes steepen toward the summit crater.*

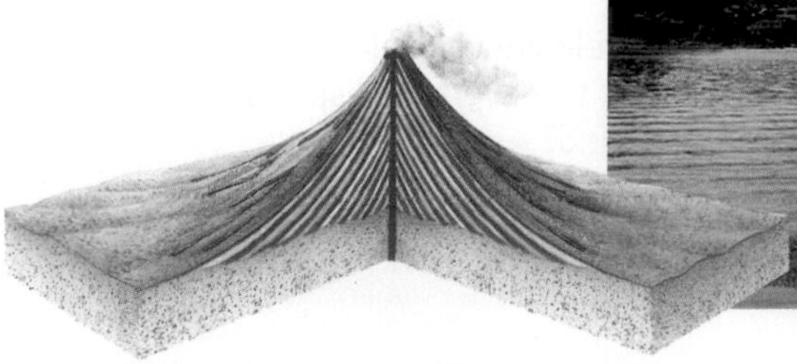

Summary

- Mafic lava erupts quietly through cracks, or fissures, in the lithosphere at divergent boundaries.
- At hot spots, continuous eruptions of mafic magma form chains of volcanoes above mantle plumes.
- Shield volcanoes form from the mafic lava erupted at hot spots.
- At convergent boundaries, eruptions of silica-rich magma are often explosive.
- Composite volcanoes form from the felsic lava erupted at convergent boundaries.

Using Vocabulary

1 Use all of the following terms in the same sentence: *lava, mafic,* and *felsic.*

Understanding Concepts

2 **Listing** List the characteristics of mafic magma.

3 **Summarizing** Summarize the process by which new sea floor forms at mid-ocean ridges.

4 **Identifying** Identify four types of lava that form at hot spots and the characteristics of each type of lava.

5 **Analyzing** Explain why silica-rich magma and magma that contains gas erupt explosively.

6 **Identifying** Identify four types of pyroclastic material and the characteristics of each type of material.

7 **Comparing** Compare shield volcanoes and composite volcanoes.

Critical Thinking

8 **Analyzing Processes** How does magma form at divergent tectonic plate boundaries?

9 **Applying Concepts** Explain why shield volcanoes do not have steep sides but are still very tall.

10 **Applying Concepts** How does the type of lava that forms in a tectonic setting determine the type of eruption that takes place and the type of volcanic mountain that forms in that setting?

INTERPRETING GRAPHICS Use the illustration below to answer the next four questions.

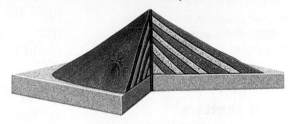

11 **Identifying Relationships** What type of volcano is shown in the illustration?

12 **Identifying Relationships** In which tectonic setting would this type of volcano most likely form?

13 **Applying Concepts** The illustration shows a volcano that is made up of two types of volcanic material. What are these two types of material?

14 **Applying Concepts** What does the material that makes up this volcano tell you about how this volcano erupts?

Math Skills

15 **Making Calculations** If a volcano has a fissure system that is 100 km long and 10 km wide, what is the total area of the fissure system in square kilometers?

Challenge

16 **Identifying Relationships** If you were studying an extinct volcano, how would you determine the type of tectonic setting in which the volcano formed? Explain your reasoning.

Internet Resources

For a variety of links related to this chapter, go to www.scilinks.org
Topic: Volcanic Eruptions
SciLinks code: HY71616

Effects of Volcanic Eruptions

Key Concept The effects of volcanic eruptions can change human and wildlife habitats.

What You Will Learn

- Volcanic eruptions can cause the loss of human life and the devastation of wildlife habitats.
- Volcanic eruptions can cause the average global temperature of Earth to decrease.
- Volcanic eruptions provide benefits to humans and to the environment.

Why It Matters

Volcanic eruptions can be both destructive and beneficial to humans.

Vocabulary

- lahar

READING STRATEGY

Graphic Organizer In your **Science Journal,** create a Concept Map about effects of volcanoes.

lahar (LAH HAHR) a mudflow that forms when volcanic ash and debris mix with water during a volcanic eruption

▶ In 1816, Chauncey Jerome, a resident of Connecticut, wrote that the clothes his wife had laid out to dry had frozen overnight. This event would not have been unusual except that the date was June 10! At that time, residents of New England did not know that the explosion of a volcanic island on the other side of the world had caused changes in the global climate.

Negative Effects of Volcanic Eruptions

Tambora volcano, shown in **Figure 1,** is located on the island of Sumbawa in Indonesia. The volcano erupted explosively in April 1815. Many of the negative images that people have of volcanoes are associated with this powerful eruption. An estimated 92,000 people lost their lives as a result of this event. About 10,000 people who lived in the area of the volcano were killed by pyroclastic flows and falling volcanic debris.

But the effects of the eruption of Mount Tambora were not only local. High in the atmosphere, ash and gases spread around Earth. As a result, the average global temperature decreased by as much as 3°C for one to two years. The lower temperature caused crop failures and starvation, particularly in New England and Europe. These effects led to the deaths of about 82,000 people.

Figure 1 *The 1815 eruption of Mount Tambora caused much loss of life and changed the global climate for one to two years. This is an image of the volcano today as seen from the space shuttle.*

6.2.d Students know earthquakes, volcanic eruptions, landslides, and floods change human and wildlife habitats.
6.6.a Students know the utility of energy resources is determined by factors that are involved in converting these sources to useful forms and the consequences of the conversion process.

Figure 2 *Ash from the eruption of Mount Pinatubo blocked out sunlight in the Philippines for several days. The eruption also affected the global climate.*

Local Effects of Volcanic Eruptions

Volcanic eruptions can cause the loss of human life and can devastate wildlife habitats. The blast from an explosive eruption can knock down trees, destroy buildings, and kill humans and other animals. During an eruption, pyroclastic flows can race down the slope of a volcano and burn everything in their path. The hot volcanic materials can melt the snowcap on a mountain, which can cause devastating floods. Volcanic ash can mix with water to produce **lahars,** fast-moving mudflows that bury everything in their way. The weight of falling ash can collapse structures, bury crops, and damage engines. Volcanic ash can also cause respiratory problems in humans. The result of a volcanic eruption is shown in **Figure 2.**

Global Effects of Volcanic Eruptions

Large volcanic eruptions can affect Earth's climate for several years. During large eruptions, tremendous amounts of volcanic ash and sulfur-rich gases are released and may be pushed into the stratosphere. As the ash and gases spread around the planet, they may absorb and scatter enough sunlight to cause the average global temperature of Earth to decrease. For example, following the 1991 eruption of Mount Pinatubo in the Philippines, the amount of sunlight that reached Earth's surface was estimated to have decreased between 2% and 4%. This decrease caused the average global temperature of Earth to decrease several tenths of a degree Celsius for several years.

Standards Check Explain how large volcanic eruptions can change Earth's average global temperature. 6.2.d

Quick Lab

Modeling Ash and Gases in Earth's Atmosphere   6.2.d

1. Secure a **lamp** that uses a **60 W light bulb** to a table.
2. Use a **light meter** to measure the light bulb's luminosity at a point 30 cm below the bulb.
3. Pour **flour** on a **blank transparency** until an area the size of the opening of the hood of the lamp is covered by the flour.
4. Hold the transparency floured-side up and 30 cm below the light bulb. Use the light meter to measure the luminosity of the light that passes through the transparency.
5. What is the difference in luminosity between the two readings?
6. How does the floured transparency model the effect that volcanic ash and sulfur gases in the atmosphere have on incoming sunlight?

 15 min

Figure 3 *These coffee plants are growing in volcanic soil on a coffee plantation in Ecuador.*

Benefits of Volcanic Eruptions

Volcanic eruptions present various dangers to humans and to wildlife habitats. But volcanoes also provide benefits to humans and to the environment. These benefits include fertile soils, a renewable energy source, and construction materials.

Volcanic Soils

Volcanic soils are some of the most fertile soils on Earth. Volcanic rocks are made of minerals that contain a wide variety of elements that are important to plant growth. When volcanic rocks break down to form soils, these soils contain nutrients that plants can use. Volcanic soils are heavily farmed in many parts of the world, such as at the plantation shown in **Figure 3.**

Geothermal Energy

Magma heats the rocks that surround it. These rocks often hold water that also becomes heated. This heated water, called *geothermal water,* may reach temperatures of hundreds of degrees Celsius. As a result, the water contains large amounts of heat energy. This energy can be tapped by drilling wells to reach the hot water or by pumping water through the heated rocks. The water can be used to drive turbines that generate electricity, to heat homes, to grow crops, and to keep roads free of ice.

The world's largest producer of geothermal energy is currently the Geysers geothermal power plant, near Santa Rosa, California. The city of San Francisco gets some of its electricity from the Geysers plant. The world's greatest consumers of geothermal energy are the residents of Reykjavik, Iceland. In Reykjavik, 85% of the homes are heated by geothermal power. **Figure 4** shows another way in which geothermal energy may be used.

Standards Check List four uses of geothermal energy. 6.6.a

Figure 4 *These Japanese macaques, commonly called* snow monkeys, *are staying warm in the waters of a hot spring during the Japanese winter.*

Other Benefits of Volcanic Eruptions

Volcanic rocks are often used in construction. In about 300 BCE, the Romans began to mix volcanic ash from Mount Vesuvius with wet lime to make concrete. This material was used to build the Colosseum in Rome, shown in **Figure 5.** As recently as the 20th century, volcanic ash was used to make concrete for dams in the United States. Today, basalt and pumice are often used in the construction of roads and bridges and in the production of concrete.

Volcanic rocks have many other uses. Volcanic ash absorbs moisture, so it is used in cat litter. Because pumice is abrasive, it is used in facial scrubs, soaps, cleaners, and polishes. Pumice is also added to soil to allow air and water to circulate more easily through the soil. And because metals in pumice are not water soluble, pumice is used alone or with silica sand to filter drinking water.

Figure 5 *The Colosseum in Rome was built in 80 CE. The fact that the Colosseum still stands today is due in large part to the strength of the materials, including concrete, of which it was built.*

SECTION Review

6.2.d, 6.6.a

Summary

- Volcanic eruptions can have local effects on humans and on wildlife habitats.

- When ash and gases from a large volcanic eruption spread around the planet, they may absorb and scatter enough sunlight to cause a temporary decrease in the average global temperature.

- Benefits that volcanoes provide to humans and to the environment include fertile soil, a renewable energy source, and construction materials.

Using Vocabulary

1 Use the term *lahar* in a sentence.

Understanding Concepts

2 **Summarizing** Describe four local effects of volcanic eruptions.

3 **Analyzing** Explain how large volcanic eruptions can cause global climate change.

4 **Listing** List three benefits that volcanoes provide to humans and to the environment.

5 **Applying** Explain why volcanic soils are some of the most fertile soils on Earth.

Critical Thinking

6 **Identifying Relationships** Describe some qualities of pumice that make pumice a useful ingredient in various products.

7 **Making Comparisons** Compare the short-term effects of a large eruption with the long-term effects of a large eruption.

8 **Identifying Relationships** Explain why a divergent boundary, such as the one in Iceland, would be a good source of geothermal energy.

Challenge

9 **Applying Concepts** Explain how a large volcanic eruption can devastate wildlife habitats.

Internet Resources

For a variety of links related to this chapter, go to www.scilinks.org
Topic: Volcanic Effects
SciLinks code: HY71615

281

Skills Practice Lab

Locating Earth's Volcanoes

OBJECTIVES

Plot the locations of volcanoes by using latitude and longitude.

Describe the locations of volcanic eruptions and the composition of the magma that causes each type of eruption.

MATERIALS

• paper, graph (1 sheet)
• pencils (or markers), red, yellow, and orange
• ruler, metric

Volcanic eruptions range from mild to violent. When volcanoes erupt, they leave behind materials that scientists can use to study Earth's crust. A mild, or nonexplosive, eruption produces thin, runny lava that is low in silica and that flows down the side of the volcano. Explosive eruptions, on the other hand, do not produce much lava. Instead, the explosions hurl ash and debris into the air. The pyroclastic materials left behind are light in color and high in silica. These materials help geologists determine the composition of the crust beneath the volcanoes.

Procedure

1 Copy the map below onto graph paper. Take care to properly line up the grid.

2 Use the latitude and longitude grids on the map to locate each volcano listed on the next page. On your copy of the map, mark the location of each volcano by drawing a circle with a diameter of about 2 mm at that location.

3 Review the eruption type for each volcano. For each explosive eruption, color the circle red. For each nonexplosive eruption, color the circle yellow. For volcanoes that have erupted in both ways, color the circle orange.

6.1.a Students know evidence of plate tectonics is derived from the fit of the continents; the location of earthquakes, volcanoes, and midocean ridges; and the distribution of fossils, rock types, and ancient climatic zones.
6.1.d Students know that earthquakes are sudden motions along breaks in the crust called faults and that volcanoes and fissures are locations where magma reaches the surface.
6.1.e Students know how major geologic events, such as earthquakes, volcanic eruptions, and mountain building, result from plate motions.

Investigation and Experimentation
6.7.f Read a topographic map and a geologic map for evidence provided on the maps and construct and interpret a simple scale map.

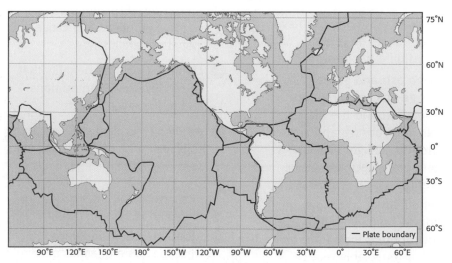

Volcanoes and Eruption Types		
Volcano	**Location**	**Eruption type**
Bezymianny	55.98°N, 160.58°W	explosive and nonexplosive
Cerro Negro	12.5°N, 86.7°W	explosive and nonexplosive
Etna	37.73°N, 15.00°W	explosive and nonexplosive
Fernandina	0.37°S, 91.55°W	nonexplosive
Kilimanjaro	3.07°S, 37.35°E	explosive and nonexplosive
Krafla	65.73°N, 16.78°W	nonexplosive
Lascar	23.32°S, 67.44°W	explosive and nonexplosive
Long Valley	37.6°N, 118.8°W	explosive and nonexplosive
Mauna Loa	19.5°N, 155.6°W	nonexplosive
Mayon	13.3°N, 123.7°E	explosive and nonexplosive
Merapi	7.5°S, 110.4°E	explosive and nonexplosive
Nevado del Ruiz	4.9°N, 75.3°W	explosive and nonexplosive
Piton de la Fournaise	21.23°S, 55.71°E	explosive and nonexplosive
Popocatépetl	19.02°N, 98.62°W	explosive and nonexplosive
Redoubt	60.5°N, 152.7°W	explosive and nonexplosive
Shasta	41.4°N, 122.2°W	explosive and nonexplosive
Soufriere Hills	16.7°N, 62.2°W	explosive and nonexplosive
St. Helens	46.2°N, 122.2°W	explosive and nonexplosive
Stromboli	38.8°N, 15.2°E	explosive and nonexplosive
Taupo	38.8°S, 176.0°E	explosive
Teide (Piton del Teide)	28.3°N, 16.6°W	explosive and nonexplosive
Tristan da Cunha	37.09°S, 12.28°W	explosive and nonexplosive
Unzen	37.09°S, 12.28°W	explosive and nonexplosive
Yellowstone	44.43°N, 110.67°W	explosive

Analyze the Results

4 Examining Data According to your map, where are volcanoes that always have non-explosive eruptions located?

5 Examining Data Where are volcanoes that always erupt explosively located?

6 Examining Data Where are volcanoes that erupt in both ways located?

7 Recognizing Patterns Around what ocean are most of Earth's convergent boundaries located? Explain you answer.

8 Recognizing Patterns What is the composition of continental crust? How do you know?

Draw Conclusions

9 Drawing Conclusions What is the source of materials for volcanoes that erupt in both ways? How do you know?

10 Drawing Conclusions Do the locations of volcanoes that erupt in both ways make sense based on your answer to question 9? Explain your answer.

Big Idea Question

11 Drawing Conclusions How do the locations of volcanoes with respect to tectonic plate boundaries relate to the type of magma that forms and to the type of eruption that will most likely take place?

Science Skills Activity

| Scientific Methods | Graphs | Data Analysis | Maps |

Investigation and Experimentation

6.7.h Identify changes in natural phenomena over time without manipulating the phenomena (e.g., a tree limb, a grove of trees, a stream, a hillslope).

Identifying Changes over Time

▶ Tutorial

The ability to identify changes in a natural system is an important part of Earth science. You can improve your observation skills by practicing the following steps.

Carefully study the original phenomenon.

1 Identify all of the important features of the object or system. To do so, observe details, identify features, and determine the shapes and sizes of different features.

2 Record any important features or details.

Carefully study the phenomenon after the changes have occurred.

3 Locate the features and details that you identified in the original phenomenon.

4 Identify any features or details that differ from their original condition.

5 Analyze the differences that you have identified. Look for factors that may have caused or contributed to the changes.

▶ You Try It!

Procedure

Mount St. Helens erupted on May 18, 1980. The top photograph at right shows the volcano before the 1980 eruption. The bottom photograph shows Mount St. Helens two years after the eruption. Carefully observe as many details in the two photographs as you can, and answer the questions that follow.

Analysis

1 **Making Observations** How did the shape of the volcanic mountain change as a result of the eruption?

2 **Making Observations** How did the eruption affect the wildlife habitats around the volcano?

3 **Applying Concepts** Was the 1980 eruption of Mount St. Helens explosive or nonexplosive? Explain your answer.

4 **Applying Concepts** At which type of tectonic plate boundary is Mount St. Helens located? Explain your answer.

Before

After

Chapter Summary

The Big Idea Volcanoes form as a result of tectonic plate motion and occur where magma reaches Earth's surface.

Section

Vocabulary

1 Why Volcanoes Form

Key Concept Volcanoes occur at tectonic plate boundaries and at hot spots, where molten rock, or magma, forms and rises to the surface.

- Most volcanoes are located at or near tectonic plate boundaries.
- Volcanoes form at divergent boundaries, convergent boundaries, and hot spots.
- The temperature, pressure, and fluid content of rock play roles in the formation of magma.

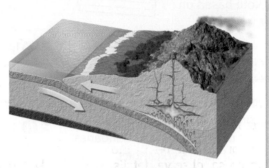

Volcanoes form at convergent boundaries, where one plate subducts beneath another plate.

volcano p. 266
magma p. 266

2 Types of Volcanoes

Key Concept Tectonic plate motions result in volcanic activity at plate boundaries.

- Nonexplosive eruptions of basaltic magma occur at divergent boundaries.
- Shield volcanoes that form from enormous volumes of basaltic magma occur at hot spots.
- Explosive eruptions of silica-rich magma occur at convergent boundaries.

This cutaway diagram shows the interior of a shield volcano.

lava p. 270
mafic p. 270
felsic p. 274

3 Effects of Volcanic Eruptions

Key Concept The effects of volcanic eruptions can change human and wildlife habitats.

- Volcanic eruptions can cause the loss of human life and the devastation of wildlife habitats.
- Volcanic eruptions can cause the average global temperature of Earth to decrease.
- Volcanic eruptions provide benefits to humans and to the environment.

Volcanic eruptions can affect the people who live near the volcano.

lahar p. 279

Organize

Layered Book Review the FoldNote that you created at the beginning of the chapter. Add to or correct the FoldNote based on what you have learned.

Using Vocabulary

① **Academic Vocabulary** Which of the following words best completes the following sentence: The location of tectonic plate boundaries determines the ___ of Earth's volcanoes.
- **a.** eruption
- **b.** production
- **c.** distribution
- **d.** subduction

For each pair of terms, explain how the meanings of the terms differ.

② *magma* and *lava*

③ *mafic* and *felsic*

Understanding Concepts

Multiple Choice

④ The process in which one tectonic plate moves beneath another tectonic plate is called
- **a.** extension.
- **b.** friction.
- **c.** subduction.
- **d.** eruption.

⑤ Magma forms within the mantle most often as a result of
- **a.** high temperature and high pressure.
- **b.** high temperature and low pressure.
- **c.** low temperature and high pressure.
- **d.** low temperature and low pressure.

⑥ Underwater mountain chains that form where two tectonic plates are pulling apart are called
- **a.** hot spots.
- **b.** fissures.
- **c.** rift zones.
- **d.** mid-ocean ridges.

⑦ Lava that flows slowly to form a glassy surface with rounded wrinkles is called
- **a.** aa.
- **b.** pahoehoe.
- **c.** pillow lava.
- **d.** blocky lava.

⑧ Lava escapes from a volcano through a
- **a.** lava tube.
- **b.** vent.
- **c.** magma chamber.
- **d.** mantle plume.

⑨ A type of volcano that typically forms at a hot spot is called a
- **a.** shield volcano.
- **b.** cinder cone.
- **c.** composite volcano.
- **d.** stratovolcano.

⑩ Pebblelike bits of magma that harden before they hit the ground are
- **a.** volcanic ash.
- **b.** lapilli.
- **c.** volcanic blocks.
- **d.** volcanic bombs.

⑪ Explosive volcanic eruptions are most likely to take place
- **a.** at mid-ocean ridges.
- **b.** at hot spots.
- **c.** at convergent boundaries.
- **d.** at fissures.

⑫ A global effect of a large volcanic eruption is
- **a.** the production of pyroclastic flows.
- **b.** the failure of crops.
- **c.** the formation of lahars.
- **d.** the knocking down of trees.

INTERPRETING GRAPHICS Use the illustration below to answer the next question.

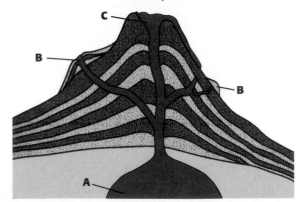

⑬ What is the term for the underground pool of molten rock, labeled "A," that feeds the volcano illustrated above?
- **a.** fissure
- **b.** hot spot
- **c.** vent
- **d.** magma chamber

Short Answer

14 Identifying Identify three ways that magma forms.

15 Comparing Compare shield volcanoes, cinder cones, and composite volcanoes.

16 Analyzing Explain how the presence of water in magma affects a volcanic eruption.

17 Listing List four types of lava and four types of pyroclastic material.

18 Applying Explain how geothermal energy is produced and used.

Writing Skills

19 Creative Writing In this chapter, you have learned that volcanic eruptions result from the movement of tectonic plates. In your own words, explain how magma moves to Earth's surface at divergent boundaries, convergent boundaries, and hot spots. Describe whether eruptions at each location are explosive or nonexplosive. Also, describe the type of rock that is produced by different types of eruptions.

Critical Thinking

20 Concept Mapping Use the following terms to create a concept map: *convergent boundary, divergent boundary, lava, hot spot, mafic, felsic, composite volcano, shield volcano, pyroclastic material,* and *fissure.*

21 Identifying Relationships What is the relationship between a change in the pressure on a rock and the production of magma?

22 Making Comparisons Compare the ways in which magma forms at divergent and convergent boundaries.

23 Applying Concepts Explain how scientists can use rock type to figure out whether an eruption was explosive or nonexplosive.

24 Predicting Consequences Predict some of the possible effects of a decrease in average global temperature following an explosive volcanic eruption.

INTERPRETING GRAPHICS The graph below illustrates the average change in temperature (above or below the average normal temperature) for a community over several years. Use the graph below to answer the next two questions.

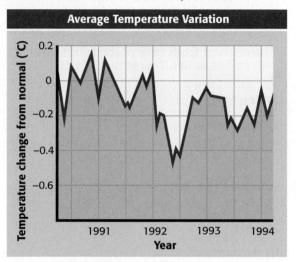

25 Evaluating Data If the variation in temperature over the years was influenced by a major volcanic eruption, when did the eruption most likely take place? Explain your answer.

26 Making Inferences If the temperature were measured only once each year (at the beginning of the year), how would your interpretation be different?

Math Skills

27 Making Calculations A pyroclastic flow travels 5 km in 5 min. What is the rate of speed of the flow in kilometers per hour?

Challenge

28 Applying Concepts Explain how a volcanologist can piece together the history of a volcano by studying the rock that makes up the volcano.

Standards Assessment

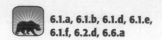

REVIEWING ACADEMIC VOCABULARY

1 In the sentence "Plate tectonics accounts for important features of Earth's surface," what does the word *features* mean?

A to give special importance to

B to have as a characteristic

C prominent parts or characteristics

D the appearance as a whole

2 Which of the following words means "movement from one place to another"?

A location

B transportation

C translation

D subduction

3 Which of the following words is the closest in meaning to the word *concept*?

A idea

B problem

C position

D value

4 Choose the appropriate form of the word *investigate* for the following sentence: "Scientists make careful ___ to determine if their theories are correct."

A investigates

B investigating

C investigations

D investigative

5 In the sentence "Plate tectonics causes many major geologic events," what does the word *major* mean?

A awe-inspiring

B commonplace

C large or important

D great in number

REVIEWING CONCEPTS

6 Under what conditions is rock most likely to melt to form magma?

A high temperature and high pressure

B high temperature and low pressure

C low temperature and high pressure

D low temperature and low pressure

7 What effect might a volcanic eruption have on climate or weather patterns?

A The average global temperature would decrease.

B The average global temperature would increase.

C The average global rainfall would decrease.

D The average global rainfall would increase.

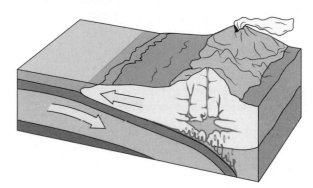

8 As shown in the diagram above, when oceanic lithosphere descends into the mantle,

A it releases water into surrounding rock, which melts.

B it pushes the overlying plate up, forming a chain of volcanoes.

C It cuts off the flow of magma to Earth's surface.

D it creates a mantle plume.

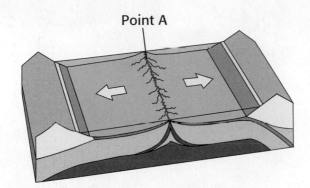

Point A

9 As the plates at a divergent boundary separate, what happens at Point A in the diagram above?

A Molten rock rises to the surface.

B Molten rock sinks into Earth's mantle.

C Solid rock is forced upward so that islands form.

D Oceanic lithosphere subducts.

10 Where are most volcanoes located?

A in trenches

B in subduction zones

C in the middle of tectonic plates

D near the edges of tectonic plates

11 What happens when tectonic plates pass over mantle plumes?

A fissures form

B volcanic hot spots form

C trenches form

D mid-ocean ridges form

12 When tectonic plates separate, magma moves to the surface and new ocean floor forms. What is this process called?

A divergence

B convergence

C subduction

D sea-floor spreading

REVIEWING PRIOR LEARNING

13 Which of the following is a solid fossil fuel?

A petroleum

B natural gas

C uranium

D coal

14 Which of the following layers is the outermost physical layer of Earth?

A core

B mantle

C asthenosphere

D lithosphere

15 A break in a body of rock along which one block slides relative to another is

A an epicenter.

B a fault.

C a focus.

D a fold.

16 The hypothesis that states that the continents once formed a single landmass, broke up, and drifted to their present positions is called

A sea-floor spreading.

B magnetic reversal.

C plate tectonics.

D continental drift.

17 California is a part of which two major tectonic plates?

A Pacific plate and North American plate

B Nazca plate and North American plate

C Pacific plate and Eurasian plate

D Nazca plate and Indian plate

Science
in Action

Science, Technology, and Society

Fighting Lava with Fire Hoses

What would you do if a 20 m wall of lava were moving toward your home? Most people would head for safety. But when an eruption threatened to bury the Icelandic fishing village of Heimaey in 1973, some villagers held their ground and fought back.

Working for 14 hours a day and in conditions so hot that their boots would catch on fire, villagers used fire hoses to spray sea water on the lava flow. For several weeks, the lava moved toward the town. The fight seemed hopeless. But the water eventually cooled the lava fast enough to change the direction of the flow and save the village. It took five months and about 4 billion liters of water to fight the lava flow. When the eruption stopped, villagers found that the island had grown by 20%!

Place to Visit

Devils Postpile National Monument

Where would you go if you wanted to see a wall made of columns of basalt? You would visit Devils Postpile National Monument near Mammoth Lakes in the Sierra Nevadas.

The Devils Postpile formed about 100,000 years ago when a basalt flow filled a valley to a depth of about 120 m. This pool of basalt cooled slowly and uniformly and contracted as it cooled. Contraction caused the basalt to fracture, which caused cracks to spread across the surface of the flow. Eventually, these cracks deepened, and the columns seen today formed. The columns were exposed about 10,000 years ago by the erosive action of a glacier.

Language Arts ACTiViTY

Volcanic terms come from many languages. Use the Internet to research some volcanic terms, and create an illustrated volcanic glossary in your **Science Journal.**

Social Studies ACTiViTY

To try to protect the city of Hilo, Hawaii, from an eruption in 1935, planes dropped bombs on the lava. Do research to find out if this mission was successful. In your **Science Journal,** write a report about other attempts to stop lava flows.

Kristin Martin

Volcanologist   Kristin Martin is a graduate student who is studying volcanology at the University of South Florida (USF) in Tampa. As an undergraduate student majoring in geology at USF, Martin found herself instantly attracted to volcanology. So, after earning her bachelor's degree, she decided to stay at USF to study volcanoes.

Martin has focused her studies on Cerro Negro volcano, which is located in the Central American nation of Nicaragua. She is modeling the way tephra, which is ejected ash and rock fragments, is distributed around Cerro Negro so that she can understand what happens when a volcano erupts. Her research has given her a better understanding of previous eruptions of Cerro Negro volcano. Understanding Cerro Negro volcano is important because the volcano most likely will erupt again.

Martin is fascinated by volcanoes and knows the importance of her work. "Millions of people live in the shadows of active volcanoes all over the world," Martin explains. "Understanding the volcanoes and how and when they may erupt is critical in order to ensure the safety of all the people."

Math ACTiViTY

The 1912 eruption of Mt. Katmai in Alaska could be heard 5,620 km away in Atlanta, Georgia. If the average speed of sound in the atmosphere is 342 m/s, how long after the eruption did the citizens of Atlanta hear the explosion?

Internet Resources

- To learn more about careers in science, visit **www.scilinks.org** and enter the SciLinks code HY70225.

- To learn more about these Science in Action topics, visit **go.hrw.com** and type in the keyword HY7VOLF.

- Check out articles related to this chapter by visiting **go.hrw.com**. Just type in the keyword HY7VOLC.

UNIT 4

TIMELINE

Shaping Earth's Surface

In this unit, you will learn about how the surface of Earth is continuously reshaped. There is a constant struggle between the forces that build up Earth's land features and the forces that break them down. This timeline shows some of the events that have occurred in this struggle as natural changes in Earth's features took place.

320
Million years ago

Vast swamps along the western edge of the Appalachian Mountains are buried by sediment and begin to form the largest coal fields in the world.

6
Million years ago

The Colorado River begins to carve the Grand Canyon, which is roughly 2 km deep today.

10,000
years ago

The Great Lakes form at the end of the last Ice Age.

1930

Carlsbad Caverns National Park is established. It features the nation's deepest limestone cave and one of the largest underground chambers in the world.

Carlsbad Caverns

280
Million years ago

The shallow inland sea that covered much of what is now the upper midwestern United States fills with sediment and disappears.

140
Million years ago

The mouth of the Mississippi River is near present-day Cairo, Illinois.

65
Million years ago

Dinosaurs become extinct.

1775

The Battle of Bunker Hill, a victory for the Colonials, takes place on a drumlin, a tear-shaped mound of sediment that was formed by an ice-age glacier 10,000 years earlier.

1879

Cleopatra's Needle, a granite obelisk, is moved from Egypt to New York City. Within the next 100 years, the weather and pollution severely damage the 3,000-year-old monument.

1987

An iceberg twice the size of Rhode Island breaks off the edge of Antarctica's continental glacier.

1998

Hong Kong opens a new airport on an artificially enlarged island. Almost 350 million cubic meters of rock and soil were deposited in the South China Sea to form the over 3,000-acre island.

2002

A NASA study finds that the arctic ice cap is melting at a rate of 9% per decade. At this rate, the ice cap could melt during this century.

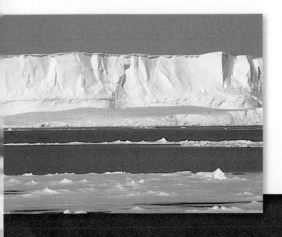

Improving Comprehension

Graphic Organizers are important visual tools that can help you organize information and improve your reading comprehension. The Graphic Organizer below is called a *process chart*. Instructions for creating other types of Graphic Organizers are located in the **Study Skills** section of the Appendix.

How to Make a Process Chart

1 Draw a box. In the box, write the first step of a process, chain of events, or cycle.

2 Under the box, draw another box, and draw an arrow to connect the two boxes. In the second box, write the next step of the process or the next event in the timeline.

3 Continue adding boxes until each step of the process, chain of events, or cycle is written in a box. For cycles only, draw an arrow to connect the last box and the first box.

When to Use a Process Chart

Science is full of processes. A process chart shows the steps that a process takes to get from one point to another point. Timelines, chains of events, and cycles are examples of the kinds of information that can be organized well in a process chart. As you read, look for information that is described in steps or in a sequence, and draw a process chart that shows the progression of the steps or sequence.

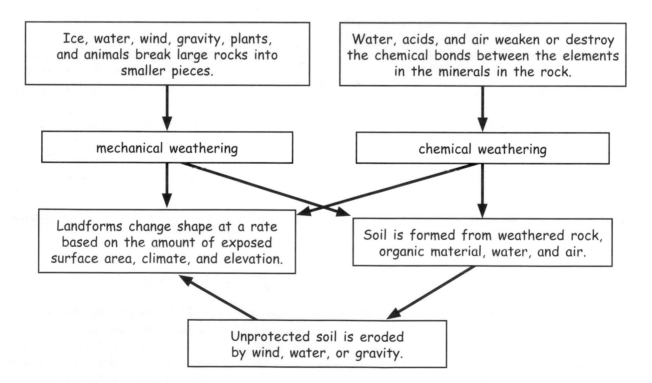

You Try It!

This Reading Strategy can also be used within the chapter that you are about to read. Practice making your own process chart as directed in the Reading Strategies for Section **1** and Section **4**. Record your work in your **Science Journal.**

Unpacking the Standards

The information below "unpacks" the standards by breaking them down into basic parts. The higher-level, academic vocabulary is highlighted and defined to help you understand the language of the standards. "What It Means" restates the standards as simply as possible.

California Standard	Academic Vocabulary	What It Means
6.2.a Students know water running downhill is the **dominant process** in shaping the landscape, including California's landscape.	**dominant** (DAHM uh nuhnt) having the greatest effect **process** (PRAH ses) a set of steps, events, or changes	Water running in rivers and over the land is the most important force in changing the natural shape of Earth's surface.
6.2.b Students know rivers and streams are **dynamic** systems that **erode, transport** sediment, change course, and flood their banks in natural and recurring patterns.	**dynamic** (die NAM ik) active; tending toward change **erode** (ee ROHD) to wear away **transport** (trans PAWRT) to carry from one place to another	Rivers and streams wear away and move rock and soil fragments, change their paths, and overflow their banks in natural patterns that happen over and over and year after year.
6.2.c Students know beaches are **dynamic** systems in which the sand is supplied by rivers and moved along the coast by the action of waves.		Beaches are always changing. Rivers carry sand to beaches and oceans, and ocean waves move the sand along the shoreline.
6.5.e Students know the number and types of organisms an ecosystem can support depends on the **resources available** and on abiotic **factors,** such as quantities of light and water, a **range** of temperatures, and soil composition.	**resource** (REE SAWRS) anything that can be used to take care of a need **available** (uh VAYL uh buhl) that can be used **factor** (FAK tuhr) a condition or event that brings about a result **range** (RAYNJ) a scale or series between limits	The number and kinds of living things that can live in an ecosystem depend on the available resources and on nonliving conditions, such as the amount of light and water, the high and low temperatures, and the makeup of the soil.
6.6.b Students know different natural **energy** and material **resources** including air, soil, rocks, minerals, petroleum, fresh water, wildlife, and forests, and know how to classify them as renewable or nonrenewable.	**energy** (EN uhr jee) the ability to make things happen	You must be able to identify different natural resources, such as air, soil, rocks, minerals, petroleum, fresh water, wildlife, and forests, and be able to identify whether each resource can be replaced rapidly or not.

9

Weathering and Soil Formation

The Big Idea

Weathering is a continuous process that results in the formation of soil and the construction and destruction of landforms.

California Standards

Focus on Earth Sciences

6.2 Topography is reshaped by weathering of rock and soil and by the transportation and deposition of sediment. (Sections 1 and 4)

6.5 Organisms in ecosystems exchange energy and nutrients among themselves and with the environment. (Sections 3 and 4)

6.6 Sources of energy and materials differ in amounts, distribution, usefulness, and the time required for their formation. (Sections 1, 3, and 4)

Investigation and Experimentation

6.7 Scientific progress is made by asking meaningful questions and conducting careful investigations. (Science Skills Activity)

Math
6.2.1 Number Sense

English–Language Arts
6.2.4 Reading
6.1.3 Writing

About the Photo

Do you need a nose job, Mr. President? The process of weathering has caused cracks to form in the carving of President Jefferson that is part of the Mount Rushmore National Memorial in South Dakota. Park rangers use a sealant to protect the memorial from moisture, which can cause further cracking.

Organize

Key-Term Fold

Before you read this chapter, create the FoldNote entitled "Key-Term Fold." Write a key term from the chapter on each tab of the key-term fold. As you read the chapter, write the definition of each key term under the appropriate tab.

Instructions for creating FoldNotes are located in the Study Skills section on p. 617 of the Appendix.

Explore Activity

6.2.a

Break It Down

In this activity, you will test different ways of weathering sticks of chalk.

Procedure

1. Gather **two sticks of chalk,** a **dropper bottle of vinegar,** a **beaker of water,** an **empty beaker** and a **rock.**

2. Using the items that you have gathered, see how many ways you can find to wear away chalk from the sticks or to break the chalk into smaller pieces.

Analysis

3. Discuss with your classmates the methods that they used to weather the chalk.

4. Which methods used by you or your classmates broke the chalk into smaller pieces?

5. Did any of the methods used by you or your classmates seem to make the chalk disappear? What do you think happened to the chalk?

Weathering

Key Concept   Rock is broken down into smaller pieces by mechanical and chemical weathering.

What You Will Learn

- Ice, water, wind, gravity, plants, and animals can cause mechanical weathering by breaking rock into pieces.
- Water, acids, and air can cause chemical weathering of rocks.

Why It Matters

Weathering is the process that allows soil to form and that shapes much of Earth's surface.

Vocabulary

- weathering
- mechanical weathering
- abrasion
- exfoliation
- chemical weathering
- acid precipitation

READING STRATEGY

Graphic Organizer   In your **Science Journal,** create a Process Chart that shows how ice wedging occurs in a cycle to cause mechanical weathering.

weathering (WETH uhr ing) the natural process by which atmospheric and environmental agents, such as wind, rain, and temperature changes, disintegrate and decompose rocks

mechanical weathering (muh KAN i kuhl WETH uhr ing) the process by which rocks break down into smaller pieces by physical means

6.2.a Students know water running downhill is the dominant process in shaping the landscape, including California's landscape.
6.2.b Students know rivers and streams are dynamic systems that erode, transport sediment, change course, and flood their banks in natural and recurring patterns.

▶ If you have ever walked along a trail, you may have noticed small rocks lying around. Where did these small rocks come from? These small rocks came from larger rocks that were broken down. The process by which rock materials are broken down by physical or chemical processes is called **weathering.**

Mechanical Weathering

If you were to crush one rock with another rock, you would be practicing one kind of mechanical weathering. **Mechanical weathering** is the breakdown of rock into smaller pieces by physical means. Agents of mechanical weathering include ice, wind, water, gravity, plants, and even animals.

Ice Wedging

One cause of mechanical weathering is *frost action,* the alternate freezing and thawing of soil and rock. *Ice wedging,* one kind of frost action, is shown in **Figure 1.** Ice wedging starts when water seeps into cracks in rock during warm weather. When temperatures drop, the water freezes and expands. The ice then pushes against the sides of the cracks. This action causes the cracks to widen. As the cycle repeats, the cracks get bigger until the rock finally breaks apart.

Figure 1   *The granite in the photo has been broken down by repeated ice wedging, which is illustrated below.*

Water

Ice

Water

Ice

Figure 2 Three Forms of Abrasion

These river rocks are rounded because they have been tumbled in the riverbed by fast-moving water for many years.

This rock has been shaped by blowing sand. Such rocks are called *ventifacts*.

As rocks grind against each other in a rock slide, the rocks break into smaller and smaller fragments.

Abrasion

As you scrape a piece of chalk against a board, particles of the chalk rub off on the board. The piece of chalk wears down and becomes smaller. The same process, called *abrasion*, happens with rocks. **Abrasion** is the grinding and wearing away of rock surfaces through the mechanical action of other rock or sand particles.

Whenever one rock hits another, abrasion takes place. As **Figure 2** shows, abrasion can happen in many ways. Water can cause abrasion as rocks bump into and scrape each other as they are moved by waves and rivers. Wind causes abrasion by blowing sand and silt against exposed rock. Gravity causes abrasion by causing rocks to grind against one another as they slide downhill.

Standards Check How can sediment transported in a stream cause abrasion? 🐻 **6.2.b**

Exfoliation

As overlying surface material is eroded, some pressure on underlying rocks is removed. This decrease in pressure on the body of rock allows the rock to expand. Sheets of rock may peel away from the main body of rock. **Exfoliation** is the process by which sheets of rock peel away from a large body of rock because pressure is removed.

abrasion (uh BRAY zhuhn) the grinding and wearing away of rock surfaces through the mechanical action of other rock or sand particles

exfoliation (eks FOH lee AY shuhn) the process by which sheets of rock peel away from a large body of rock because pressure is removed

Wordwise The prefix *ex-* means "out." The root *folium* means "leaf." Other examples are *foliage* and *export*.

SCHOOL to HOME

Ice Wedging

To understand ice wedging, try this activity at home with an adult. Fill a small, plastic water bottle with water. Put the cap on tightly. Place the bottle upright in the freezer overnight. In your **Science Journal**, describe what happened to the bottle.

ACTiViTY

Plant Growth

You may not think that plants are strong, but some plants can easily break rocks. Have you ever seen sidewalks and streets that are cracked because of tree roots? The roots of a plant commonly grow into existing cracks in rocks. As the plant grows, the force of its expanding roots becomes so strong that the cracks widen. Roots don't grow fast, but they certainly are powerful! In time, the whole rock can split apart, as **Figure 3** shows.

Figure 3 *Although they grow slowly, tree roots are strong enough to break solid rock.*

Animal Actions

Believe it or not, earthworms cause a lot of weathering. They tunnel through the soil and move soil particles around. This motion breaks some particles into smaller particles. It also exposes fresh surfaces to continued weathering. Some kinds of tropical worms move an estimated 100 metric tons of soil per acre every year! Almost any animal that burrows causes mechanical weathering. Ants, worms, mice, coyotes, and rabbits are just a few of the animals that contribute to weathering. **Figure 4** shows some of these animals in action. The mixing and digging that animals do also contribute to chemical weathering, another kind of weathering.

Standards Check How can animals cause mechanical weathering?
6.2.a

Figure 4 **Weathering Caused by Animals**

Harvester ants cause weathering as they build tunnels and chambers underground.

As earthworms burrow through the ground, they move rock and soil particles and expose new particles to water and air.

When prairie dogs (right) and moles (left) burrow in the ground, they break up soil and loosen rocks to be exposed to further weathering.

Figure 5 Chemical Weathering of Granite

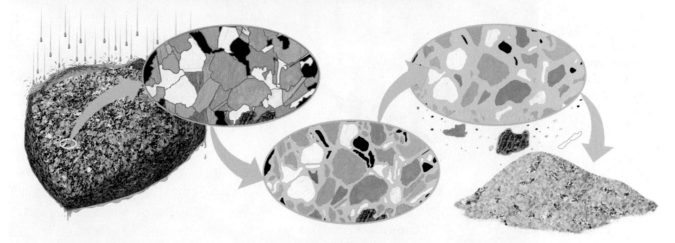

① Rain, dilute acids, and air are made of chemicals that react with the chemicals in granite.

② The bonds between mineral grains weaken as some chemicals in the rock dissolve.

③ When granite is weathered, sediment—particles of sand and clay—forms.

Chemical Weathering

The process by which rocks break down as a result of chemical reactions is called **chemical weathering.** Common agents of chemical weathering are water, acids, and air. These agents chemically break down rocks by reacting with the chemicals that form the rock. These reactions weaken or destroy the bonds between elements in the minerals in the rock.

How Water Chemically Breaks Down Rock

If you drop a sugar cube into a glass of water, the sugar cube will dissolve after a few minutes. In a similar way, water dissolves some of the chemicals that make up rock. Even hard rock, such as granite, can be broken down by water. But this process may take thousands of years or more. **Figure 5** shows how granite is chemically weathered.

Acid Precipitation

Precipitation is naturally acidic. However, rain, sleet, or snow that contains a higher concentration of acid than normal is called **acid precipitation.** Natural sources, such as volcanoes, produce small amounts of sulfuric and nitric acids. Air pollution from the burning of fossil fuels, such as coal and oil, also produces these chemical compounds. These compounds combine with water in the atmosphere to form acids. These acids then fall back to the ground in rain and snow. Because acids are more reactive than regular water is, acid precipitation can cause very rapid weathering of rock.

chemical weathering (KEM i kuhl WETH uhr ing) the process by which rocks break down as a result of chemical reactions

acid precipitation (AS id pree SIP uh TAY shuhn) rain, sleet, or snow that contains a high concentration of acids

Figure 6 *Acid in groundwater has weathered limestone to form Carlsbad Caverns in New Mexico.*

How Acids in Groundwater Weather Rock

In certain places, water flows through rock underground. This water, called *groundwater,* commonly contains dilute acids, such as carbonic or sulfuric acid. When this groundwater comes into contact with limestone, a chemical reaction takes place. This chemical reaction dissolves the rock. Over a long period of time, the dissolving of limestone may form caverns, such as the one shown in **Figure 6.**

How Acids in Living Things Weather Rock

All living things make dilute acids in their bodies. When these living things come into contact with rock, some of the acids are transferred to the rock's surface. The acids react with chemicals in the rock and produce areas of weakness in the rock. The weakened areas are more easily weathered. The rock may also crack in these weakened areas. Even the smallest crack can expose more of the rock to agents of both mechanical weathering and chemical weathering.

Quick Lab

The Reaction of Acids

Ketchup is one example of a food that contains dilute acids. In this lab, you will use ketchup to model how dilute acids react with rock.

1. While wearing **protective gloves,** hold a **penny** that has a dull appearance. Use a **cotton swab** to rub **ketchup** on the penny for several minutes.

2. Rinse the penny.

3. Where did all of the grime on the penny go?

4. How is this process similar to what happens to a rock when the rock is exposed to natural acids?

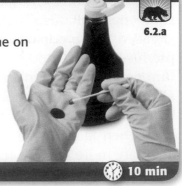

6.2.a

⏱ 10 min

How Air Chemically Weathers Rock

The rocks in **Figure 7** are undergoing chemical weathering. The rocks are orange because oxygen in the air reacts with the iron in the rocks. This process is called *oxidation*.

Oxidation is a chemical reaction in which an element, such as iron, combines with oxygen to form an oxide. This common form of chemical weathering is what causes rust. Cars, bicycles, and other metal objects can experience oxidation if they are exposed to air and rain for a long time. Exposure to rain and other water speeds the process. But the iron would react with oxygen even if no water were present.

Standards Check What is oxidation? 6.2.a

Figure 7 *The color of these rocks in Chaco Canyon, New Mexico, is the result of chemical weathering.*

SECTION Review

6.2.a, 6.2.b

Summary

- Ice wedging is a form of mechanical weathering in which water seeps into cracks in rock and then freezes and expands.

- Wind, water, and gravity cause mechanical weathering by abrasion.

- Animals and plants cause mechanical weathering by mixing the soil and breaking apart rocks.

- Water, acids, and oxygen in the air chemically weather rock by reacting chemically with elements in the rock.

- Oxidation is the process by which oxygen from the air reacts with iron in rocks.

Using Vocabulary

1 Write an original definition for *weathering, mechanical weathering, abrasion, chemical weathering,* and *acid precipitation.*

Understanding Concepts

2 **Listing** List three causes of the chemical weathering of rocks.

3 **Describing** Describe three ways abrasion occurs in nature.

4 **Comparing** Describe the similarity in the ways tree roots and ice mechanically weather rock.

Critical Thinking

5 **Making Inferences** Why does acid precipitation weather rocks faster than normal precipitation does?

6 **Making Comparisons** Compare the weathering processes that affect a rock at Earth's surface and a rock underground.

7 **Predicting Consequences** If moss begins growing on a rock, how might the weathering of this rock change?

Math Skills

8 **Making Calculations** Substances that have a pH of less than 7 are acidic. For every one-point decrease in pH, acidity increases by a multiplication factor of 10. For example, normal precipitation is slightly acidic at a pH of 5.6. Acid precipitation that has a pH of 4.6 is 10 times as acidic as normal precipitation. How many times as acidic as normal precipitation is precipitation that has a pH of 3.6?

Challenge

9 **Evaluating Hypotheses** After observing rocks in the field, a geologist hypothesized that granite weathers more slowly than limestone. Describe how you would test this hypothesis.

Internet Resources

For a variety of links related to this chapter, go to www.scilinks.org

Topic: Weathering
SciLinks code: HY71648

Rates of Weathering

Key Concept The rate at which rock weathers depends on climate, elevation, and the size and makeup of the rock.

What You Will Learn

- Differential weathering is the process by which softer rocks weather more rapidly than harder rocks do.
- Surface area, climate, and elevation are factors that affect the rate at which rock weathers.

Why It Matters

Understanding rates of weathering will help you understand the formation of soil and landforms where you live.

Vocabulary

- differential weathering

READING STRATEGY

Outlining In your **Science Journal,** create an outline of the section. Use the headings from the section in your outline.

▶ Have you ever seen a cartoon in which a character falls off a cliff and lands on a ledge? Natural ledges exist because the rock that makes up the ledges weathered more slowly than the surrounding rock. Weathering generally takes a long time. However, the rate at which a rock weathers depends on climate, elevation, and the chemical makeup of the rock.

Differential Weathering

Hard rocks, such as granite, weather more slowly than softer rocks, such as limestone. **Differential weathering** is the process by which softer, less weather resistant rocks wear away and leave harder, more weather resistant rocks behind. For example, Devils Tower in Wyoming, shown in **Figure 1,** is a result of this process. About 50 million years ago, a mass of molten rock cooled and hardened underground to form igneous rock. The surrounding rock was softer than the igneous rock. As the rocks were weathered for millions of years, the softer rock was completely worn away. The harder, more resistant rock of the tower is all that remains.

Standards Check How does the composition of a rock relate to differential weathering? 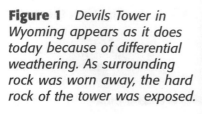 **6.2.c**

Figure 1 *Devils Tower in Wyoming appears as it does today because of differential weathering. As surrounding rock was worn away, the hard rock of the tower was exposed.*

The Surface Area of Rocks

The greater the proportion of a rock that is exposed to weathering, the faster the rock will wear down. However, most weathering takes place only on the outer surface of rock. A large rock has a large surface area that is exposed to weathering. But a large rock also has a large volume. Most of this volume is in the middle of the rock, away from the surface. Therefore, most of the large rock is not exposed to weathering. Because of its volume, the large rock will take a long time to wear down.

If a large rock is broken into smaller pieces, weathering happens much more quickly. The rate of weathering increases because the surface area-to-volume ratio of the small rocks is greater than that of the large rock. So, a greater proportion of a smaller rock is exposed to weathering processes. **Figure 2** shows this concept in detail.

differential weathering
(DIF uhr EN shuhl WETH uhr ing) the process by which softer, less weather resistant rocks wear away at a faster rate than harder, more weather resistant rocks do

6.2.c Students know beaches are dynamic systems in which the sand is supplied by rivers and moved along the coast by the action of waves.

Figure 2 Total Surface Area to Volume

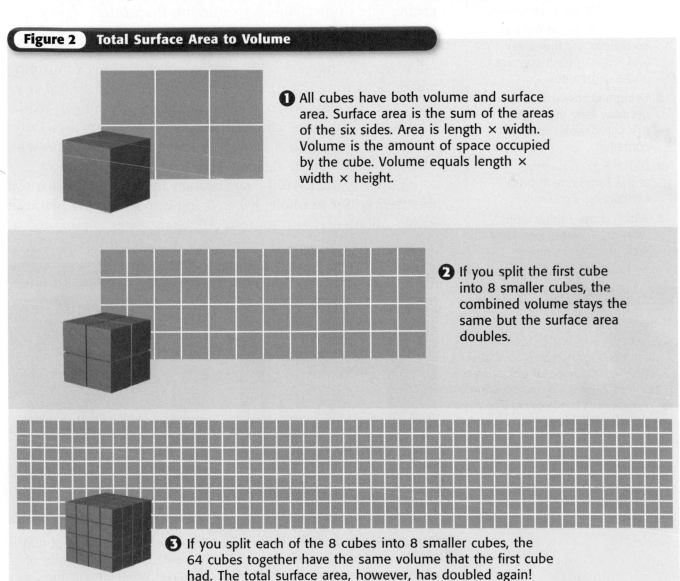

❶ All cubes have both volume and surface area. Surface area is the sum of the areas of the six sides. Area is length × width. Volume is the amount of space occupied by the cube. Volume equals length × width × height.

❷ If you split the first cube into 8 smaller cubes, the combined volume stays the same but the surface area doubles.

❸ If you split each of the 8 cubes into 8 smaller cubes, the 64 cubes together have the same volume that the first cube had. The total surface area, however, has doubled again!

Weathering and Climate

The rate of weathering in an area is greatly affected by the climate of that area. *Climate* is the average weather conditions of an area over a long period of time. For example, the mailboxes shown in **Figure 3** are in areas that have different climates. The mailbox on the left is in an area that has a hot, dry climate. The mailbox on the right is in an area that has a warm, wet climate. As you can see, the mailbox in the area that has a warm, wet climate is rusty.

Temperature

Temperature is a major factor in both chemical and mechanical weathering. Many chemical reactions happen more rapidly at higher temperatures. Cycles of freezing and thawing also increase the chance that ice wedging will take place. Thus, climatic regions that experience many freezes and thaws have a greater rate of mechanical weathering than other regions do.

Moisture

Water can interact with rock as precipitation, as running water, or as water vapor in the air. The rate of chemical reactions may increase when water is present. For example, oxidation, like some other chemical reactions, happens at a faster rate when temperatures are higher and when water is present. The rusty mailbox in **Figure 3** has experienced oxidation.

Water also increases the rate of some methods of mechanical weathering. For example, ice wedging cannot happen without water. Abrasion is also more rapid when water is present.

Quick Lab

How Fast Will It Dissolve?   6.2.c

1. Fill **two small containers** about halfway with **water.**

2. Add **one sugar cube** to one container.

3. Add **one crushed sugar cube** to the other container.

4. Using **one spoon for each container,** stir the water and sugar in each container at the same rate.

5. Using a **stopwatch,** measure how long the sugar takes to dissolve in each container.

6. Did the sugar dissolve at the same rate in both containers? Explain.

7. Which do you think would wear away faster: one large rock or several smaller rocks? Why?

🕐 **20 min**

Figure 3   Water and Rates of Weathering

This mailbox is in an area that has a dry climate, so the rate of chemical weathering is low.

This mailbox is in an area that has a wet climate. The rate of chemical weathering is high.

Other Factors That Affect Weathering

Several other factors affect the rate of weathering. These factors include the following:

- **Elevation** Rocks can be exposed to different weathering environments at different elevations. Rocks at high elevations are exposed to high winds and temperature extremes. They may also be exposed to large amounts of precipitation, which may cause these rocks to weather rapidly. Rocks at sea level can be weathered by the action of ocean waves.

- **Slope** The steep sides of mountains and hills increase the speed of water running downhill. Water that flows rapidly has more energy to break down rock than slow-moving water does. Rainwater that runs down the sides of mountains and hills breaks down and carries away rock.

- **Biological Factors** Organisms in the soil can produce acids that can speed chemical weathering. The activities of burrowing animals and plant roots also speed mechanical weathering.

INTERNET ACTIVITY

Older Than Dirt
What kinds of organisms and processes can change a mountain? Create a poster that shows how a mountain changes over millions of years. Go to **go.hrw.com,** and type in the keyword HY7WSFW.

SECTION Review

 6.2.c

Summary

- Hard rocks weather more slowly than soft rocks.
- The larger the surface area-to-volume ratio of a rock is, the faster the rock will wear down.
- Chemical weathering occurs faster in warm, wet climates than in hot, dry climates.
- Rates of weathering are affected by elevation, by the slope of the ground, and by living things.

Using Vocabulary

1. Write an original definition for *differential weathering*.

Understanding Concepts

2. **Describing** How do the surface area and volume of a rock affect the rate at which the rock weathers?

3. **Summarizing** How does climate affect rates of weathering?

4. **Comparing** How does the weathering of rocks at the peak of a mountain differ from the weathering of rocks at sea level?

5. **Listing** Name two ways in which water may increase the rate of weathering.

6. **Analyzing** How can the process of chemical weathering be influenced by mechanical weathering?

Critical Thinking

7. **Making Inferences** What factors would cause the rate of mechanical weathering to differ for different rocks?

Challenge

8. **Predicting Consequences** You have been asked to choose (1) the kind of rock to use for an outdoor statue and (2) the location for the statue. You want to keep the statue in good condition. What kind of rock do you choose, and what climate do you choose? Explain your choices.

Internet Resources

For a variety of links related to this chapter, go to www.scilinks.org
Topic: Rates of Weathering
SciLinks code: HY71269

From Bedrock to Soil

Key Concept Weathering may lead to the formation of soil, which is an important natural resource.

What You Will Learn

- Soil is a mixture of weathered rock, organic material, water, and air.
- Soil composition, texture, fertility, and pH affect plant growth.
- Climate affects the types of soil that are found in different places.

Why It Matters

Soil is necessary for almost all plant life on land.

Vocabulary

- soil
- bedrock
- parent rock
- humus

READING STRATEGY

Summarizing Read this section silently. In pairs, take turns summarizing the material. Stop to discuss ideas and words that seem confusing.

soil (SOYL) a loose mixture of rock fragments, organic material, water, and air that can support the growth of vegetation

parent rock (PER uhnt RAHK) a rock formation that is the source of soil

bedrock (BED RAHK) the layer of rock beneath soil

6.5.e Students know the number and types of organisms an ecosystem can support depends on the resources available and on abiotic factors, such as quantities of light and water, a range of temperatures, and soil composition.

Most plants need soil to grow. But what exactly is soil? Many people think that soil is just dirt. To a scientist, **soil** is a loose mixture of small mineral fragments, organic material, water, and air that can support the growth of vegetation.

The Source of Soil

Because soils are made from weathered rock fragments, not all soils are the same. The kind of soil that forms depends on the source of the soil. The rock that breaks down into mineral fragments that form a soil is called **parent rock.** Different parent rocks have different chemical compositions. As a result, soils also differ in composition.

Bedrock is the layer of rock beneath soil. In some cases, the bedrock is the parent rock. In these cases, the soil remains above the bedrock that weathered to form the soil. Soil that remains above its parent rock is called *residual soil.* Few soils are residual soils.

Soil can be carried away from its parent rock by wind, water, ice, or gravity. This soil is called *transported soil.* **Figure 1** shows that water is one agent that moves soil from one place to another.

Figure 1 *Rivers, such as the one shown here, may move transported soil long distances from its parent rock.*

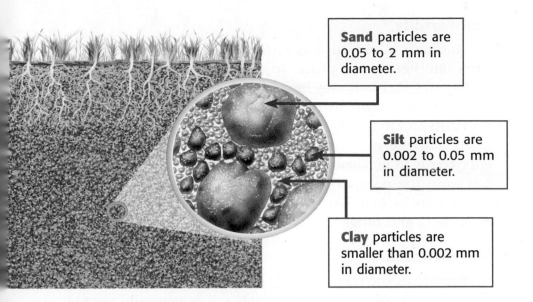

Sand particles are 0.05 to 2 mm in diameter.

Silt particles are 0.002 to 0.05 mm in diameter.

Clay particles are smaller than 0.002 mm in diameter.

Figure 2 *The proportion of different-sized particles in soil determines the texture of the soil. Sand makes up about 40% of the soil illustrated here. Silt and clay each make up about 30% of the soil. All soil particles are less than 2 mm in diameter.*

Soil Properties

Some soils are great for growing plants. Other soils can't support the growth of plants. To better understand soil, you must know about its properties. These properties include soil composition, soil texture, and soil fertility.

Soil Composition

You have learned that soil is made up of mineral fragments, organic material, water, and air. Soil composition describes the kinds and relative amounts of materials that the soil contains. Some soils contain more water or air than other soils do. Moist soil is generally darker than dry soil. Black soil is often rich in organic material. Black soil supports more plant life than a soil that has less organic matter does. The kinds and sizes of mineral particles in soil depend on the parent rock from which the soil formed.

Standards Check How does the amount of organic material in soil affect how well soil will support plant growth? 🐻 6.5.e

Soil Texture

Soil is made of particles of different sizes. These particles can be as large as 2 mm in diameter, as in the case of sand. Other particles can be too small to see without a microscope. *Soil texture* describes the relative amounts of soil particles of different sizes. **Figure 2** shows the soil texture for one kind of soil.

Soil texture affects the consistency of soil. Consistency describes a soil's ability to be broken up for farming. For example, soil that contains a lot of clay can be hard, which makes breaking up the soil difficult. Soil texture also influences *infiltration,* or the ability of water to move into the soil.

Making Soil

You have a 24 kg soil sample. If 60% of the sample is sand, 27% is silt, and 13% is clay, what is the mass of each group of soil particles? Record your work in your **Science Journal.**

Soil Fertility

Nutrients in soil, such as nitrogen, phosphorus, and potassium, are needed for plants to grow. Some soils are rich in nutrients. Other soils may have few nutrients or may be unable to supply the nutrients to plants. The ability of soil to hold nutrients and to supply nutrients to plants is called *soil fertility*. Many nutrients in soil come from the parent rock. Other nutrients come from **humus,** the organic material that forms in soil from the decayed remains of plants and animals. These remains are broken down into nutrients by decomposers, such as bacteria and fungi.

humus (HYOO muhs) dark, organic material formed in soil from the decayed remains of plants and animals

Soil Horizons

Because of the way in which it forms, soil commonly ends up in a series of layers. Humus-rich soil is generally on top. More sediment rests below the humus-rich layer. Bedrock sits below the bottom soil layer. Because the layers are horizontal, soil scientists call these layers *horizons*. **Figure 3** shows what these horizons may look like.

The top layer of soil is commonly called *topsoil*. Topsoil has more humus than lower layers of soil do. The humus is rich in the nutrients that plants need to be healthy.

Figure 3   Soil Horizons

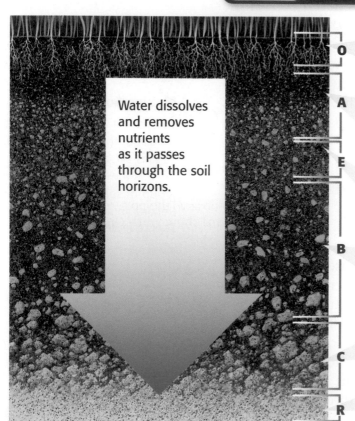

Water dissolves and removes nutrients as it passes through the soil horizons.

O The O horizon is made up of litter from dead plants and animals. It occurs in some areas, such as forests, but not in all soils.

A The A horizon consists of topsoil. Topsoil contains more humus than any other soil horizon does.

E The E horizon is a layer of sediment that is stripped of nutrients as water passes through the sediment.

B The B horizon collects the dissolved substances and nutrients that were removed from the upper horizons.

C The C horizon is made of partially weathered bedrock or of transported sediments.

R The R horizon is made of bedrock that has experienced little or no weathering.

Soil pH

Soils can be acidic, neutral, or basic. The pH scale, which is shown in **Figure 4,** is used to measure how acidic or basic something is. The scale ranges from 0 to 14. The midpoint, which is 7, is neutral. Soil that has a pH below 7 is acidic. Soil that has a pH above 7 is basic.

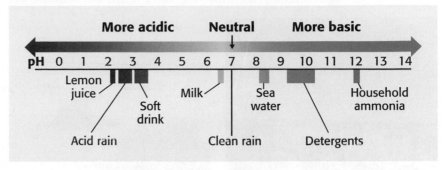

The pH of a soil influences how nutrients dissolve in the soil. Soil pH strongly influences soil fertility. For example, plants are unable to take up certain nutrients from soils that are basic, or that have a high pH. Soils that have a low pH can restrict uptake of other important nutrients by hungry plants. Most plants grow best in soils in the pH range of 5.5 to 7.0. A few plants grow best in soils of higher or lower pH.

Soil pH is determined partly by the soil's parent rock. Soil pH is also affected by the acidity of rainwater, the use of fertilizers, and the extent of chemical weathering.

Figure 4 *This pH scale shows the pH ranges of some common substances.* **Can you find the pH of a beverage that you drink often?**

Standards Check How does soil pH affect plant growth? 🐾 **6.5.e**

Quick Lab

Investigating Plant Growth

The richness of plant growth depends in part on the soil in which the plants are grown. To support vigorous plant growth, soils must have the right characteristics. In this lab, you will investigate how soil texture and composition affect plant growth.

6.5.e

▶ Try It!

1. Prepare **three identical small pots** by filling one with **pea gravel,** one with **sand,** and one with **potting soil.**

2. Following the directions on the **seed package,** plant **four bean seeds** in each pot.

3. Observe the pots every two or three days. Make sure that each pot receives the same amount of sunlight and the same amount of water. Each time you observe the pots, add the same amount of water to each pot. The class can decide together how much water to use based on the size of the pots.

4. Each time you observe the pots, record your observations about what is happening to the seeds.

▶ Think About It!

5. Describe what happened to the seeds in each pot.

6. How was plant growth affected by the different soil compositions used in this lab?

7. What factors other than soil composition may have affected plant growth in this lab?

🕐 **10 min plus follow-up**

Figure 5 Soils in Different Climates

Lush tropical rain forests have surprisingly thin topsoil.

The salty conditions of some desert soils make survival difficult for many plants.

Some arctic soils, such as the soil along Denali Highway in Alaska, cannot support lush vegetation.

Soil and Climate

Soil types vary from place to place, as **Figure 5** shows. The kinds of soils that develop depend on climate. The different characteristics of these soils affect the number and kinds of organisms that can survive in different areas.

Tropical Climates

Tropical rain forests receive a lot of direct sunlight and a large amount of rain. Because of these factors, plants grow year-round. The heat and moisture also cause dead organisms to decay easily. This decay provides rich humus to the soil.

However, soils in tropical rain forests are subjected to heavy rains. The heavy rains in this climate zone *leach,* or remove, nutrients from the topsoil. As a result, many tropical soils are nutrient poor. Another reason that this soil is nutrient poor is that lush vegetation uses up most of the nutrients in the soil.

Desert and Arctic Climates

Desert and arctic climates receive little rainfall. Thus, little leaching of nutrients happens in the soil in these climates. But the lack of rain leads to low rates of chemical weathering and little plant and animal life. As a result, soil forms slowly. Because of the lack of plant and animal life, the soil has little humus. Arctic soil has more humus than desert soil does because the climate slows the breakdown of organic materials.

Sometimes, desert soils can become harsh, even to desert plants! Groundwater in which mineral salts are dissolved seeps into desert soil. When the water evaporates, the salts are left in the soil. These salts can become so concentrated that plants cannot absorb water from the soil.

Temperate Forest and Grassland Climates

Much of the continental United States has a temperate climate. High rates of mechanical weathering cause thick soil layers to form. Temperate areas get a moderate amount of rain. Therefore, rates of chemical weathering are high, but rates of leaching are low.

Temperate soils are some of the most productive soils in the world, as **Figure 6** shows. In fact, the midwestern part of the United States has earned the nickname "breadbasket" for the many crops that the soil in the region supports.

Standards Check Why does soil in temperate climates support a large number of organisms? 6.5.e

Figure 6 *The rich soils in areas that have a temperate climate support a vast farming industry.*

SECTION Review

 6.5.e

Summary

- Soil forms from the weathering of bedrock.

- Soil texture affects how soil can be worked for farming and how well water passes through soil.

- The ability of soil to provide nutrients so that plants can survive and grow is called *soil fertility.*

- The pH of a soil influences which nutrients plants can take up from the soil.

- Different climates have different types of soil, depending on the temperature and rainfall.

- The characteristics of soil affect the number and types of organisms that an area can support.

Using Vocabulary

1. Use *soil, parent rock, bedrock,* and *humus* in separate sentences.

Understanding Concepts

2. **Analyzing** How does flowing water affect the formation of soil?

3. **Summarizing** What components must a soil have in order to support plant life?

4. **Comparing** How does soil texture affect the ability of a soil to support plant life?

5. **Describing** How do soil fertility and pH affect the ability of a soil to support plant life?

6. **Identifying** Which climate has the thickest, most fertile soil?

Critical Thinking

7. **Making Comparisons** Explain why arctic soils and desert soils are similar even though arctic climates are very different from desert climates.

INTERPRETING GRAPHICS The soil profile below shows residual soil. Use the soil profile to answer the next three questions.

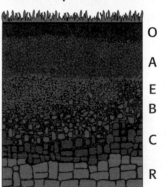

8. **Making Inferences** Which two layers of the soil are least likely to contain humus?

9. **Identifying Relationships** How is the soil composition in the A horizon related to the composition of the R horizon?

10. **Predicting Consequences** Explain whether this soil would support a lot of plant growth.

Soil Conservation

Key Concept Soil is a nonrenewable resource that can be endangered if it is used unwisely.

What You Will Learn

- Soil is important for plants and animals and for the storage of water.
- Farmers use a variety of methods to prevent soil damage and loss.

Why It Matters

Soil must be conserved because soil is a major factor in the growth of plants. Humans and other organisms depend on plants as a source of food.

Vocabulary

- soil conservation
- erosion

READING STRATEGY

Graphic Organizer In your **Science Journal,** create a Process Chart about desertification.

soil conservation
(SOYL KAHN suhr VAY shuhn) a method to maintain the fertility of the soil by protecting the soil from erosion and nutrient loss

erosion (ee ROH zhuhn) the process by which wind, water, ice, or gravity transports soil and sediment from one location to another

▶ Believe it or not, soil can be endangered, just as plants and animals can. Because soil may take hundreds or thousands of years to form, it is not easy to replace. Therefore, soil can be considered a nonrenewable resource. If we do not take care of soils, we can ruin or even lose them. **Soil conservation** is a method to maintain the fertility of the soil by protecting the soil from erosion and nutrient loss.

Standards Check Why is soil a nonrenewable resource? 6.6.b

The Importance of Soil

Soil provides minerals and other nutrients for plants. If the soil loses these nutrients, plants will not be able to grow. In **Figure 1,** the plants on the left are healthy because the soil in which they live is rich in nutrients. The plants on the right are unhealthy because they are not getting enough nutrients. The soil is poor in nutrients and does not provide the plants with the food that they need.

Most land animals get their energy from plants. The animals get their energy either by eating plants or by eating animals that have eaten plants. So, if plants can't get nutrients from the soil, animals can't get nutrients from plants.

Housing

Soil also provides a place for animals to live. Habitat is the term used to describe the region where an animal or plant lives. Earthworms, spiders, ants, moles, and other animals live in soil. If the soil disappears, so does the habitat for these animals.

Figure 1 *Both of these photos show the same crop, but the soil in the photo on the right is poor in nutrients.*

Water Storage

Soil is also very important for water storage. Without soil to hold water, plants would not get the moisture or the nutrients that they need. In addition, soil keeps water from running off, flowing elsewhere, and causing flooding.

Soil Damage and Loss

Soil loss is a major problem around the world. One cause of soil loss is soil damage. Soil can be damaged from overuse by poor farming techniques or by overgrazing. Overused soil can lose its nutrients and become infertile. Plants can't grow in soil that is infertile. Without plants to hold and help cycle water, an area can become a desert. This process is known as *desertification*. Without plants and moisture, the soil can be blown or washed away.

Soil Erosion

When soil is not protected, it can be exposed to erosion. **Erosion** is the process by which wind, water, or gravity transports soil and sediment from one location to another. **Figure 2** shows Providence Canyon in Georgia. The canyon formed when soil eroded because trees were cut down to clear land for farming. Because roots from plants, including trees, anchor the soil, plants keep topsoil from being eroded. Plants also protect the soil by preventing water and wind from flowing freely over the soil and carrying the soil away. By taking care of the vegetation, you also take care of the soil.

Quick Lab

Soil Erosion
1. Place **two large basins** on **books** or **doorstops** so that the basins rest at about a 30° angle.
2. Fill **two square planters,** one with **sod** and one with **potting soil.** The sod and soil should each come to the top of the planters.
3. Put one of the planters at the top of each large basin. Sprinkle about **500 mL of water** on each planter to simulate rain.
4. Which basin shows the most soil erosion? Why?

🕐 **15 min**

Figure 2 *Providence Canyon has suffered soil erosion from the cutting of forests for farmland.*

6.2.a Students know water running downhill is the dominant process in shaping the landscape, including California's landscape.
6.5.e Students know the number and types of organisms an ecosystem can support depends on the resources available and on abiotic factors, such as quantities of light and water, a range of temperatures, and soil composition.
6.6.b Students know different natural energy and material resources, including air, soil, rocks, minerals, petroleum, fresh water, wildlife, and forests, and know how to classify them as renewable or nonrenewable.

Figure 3 **Soil Conservation Techniques**

Contour plowing reduces erosion by slowing the downhill flow of water.

Terracing creates a series of flat fields that prevent the rapid runoff of water.

No-till farming reduces erosion by providing cover that reduces water runoff.

Cover crops, such as soybeans, restore nutrients to soil and reduce soil exposure to wind.

Soil Conservation on Farmland

If farmers plowed rows that ran up and down hills, what might happen during a heavy rain? The rows would act as river valleys and would channel the rainwater down the hill to erode the soil. To prevent this kind of erosion, a farmer could plow across the slope of the hills. This process is called *contour plowing*. In contour plowing, the rows act as a series of dams instead of a series of rivers. **Figure 3** shows contour plowing and three other methods of soil conservation. If the hills are very steep, farmers can use *terracing*. Terracing changes one steep field into a series of small, flat fields. *No-till farming,* the practice of leaving old stalks, provides cover from rain. The cover reduces water runoff and slows soil erosion.

Cover Crops and Crop Rotation

During the early 1900s, the soil in the southern United States had become nutrient poor by the farming of only one crop: cotton. George Washington Carver, the scientist shown in **Figure 4,** urged farmers to plant soybeans and peanuts instead of cotton. Soybeans, peanuts, and some other plants help return important nutrients to the soil. These plants are called *cover crops.* Cover crops are crops that are planted between harvests to replace certain nutrients and to prevent erosion. They prevent erosion by providing cover from wind and rain.

Another way to slow nutrient depletion is through *crop rotation.* If the same crop is grown year after year in the same field, certain nutrients become depleted. To slow this process, a farmer can plant different crops. A different crop will use up fewer nutrients or different nutrients from the soil. Some crops used in crop rotation can even replace soil nutrients.

Standards Check How can crop rotation affect the number of plants that soil can support? 6.5.e

Figure 4 *George Washington Carver taught soil conservation techniques to farmers.*

SECTION Review

 6.2.a, 6.5.e, 6.6.b

Summary

- Soil forms slowly over hundreds or thousands of years. Therefore, soil is considered a nonrenewable resource.

- Soil is important because plants grow in soil, animals live in soil, and water is stored in soil.

- Soil can be eroded by water running downhill or by wind.

- Soil erosion and soil damage can be prevented by no-till farming, contour plowing, terracing, using cover crops, and practicing crop rotation.

Using Vocabulary

1. Write an original definition for *soil conservation* and *erosion.*

Understanding Concepts

2. **Identifying** Is soil a renewable resource or a nonrenewable resource? Explain your answer.

3. **Listing** What are three important benefits that soil provides?

4. **Describing** List and describe five soil conservation methods.

Critical Thinking

5. **Applying Concepts** Why do land animals, including meat eaters, depend on soil?

6. **Making Comparisons** When deciding between contour plowing and terracing, what might a farmer consider?

Math Skills

7. **Making Calculations** A farmer is planting a cover crop. Suppose that the width of each row of cover crop is 80 cm. If the field is 100 m wide, how many rows of cover crop can the farmer plant?

Challenge

8. **Analyzing Processes** A farmer uses three methods of soil conservation on the same field. List three methods that may be used together. Then, describe how each method would benefit the soil in the field.

Internet Resources

For a variety of links related to this chapter, go to www.scilinks.org
Topic: Soil Conservation
SciLinks code: HY71409

Model-Making Lab

Weathering Rocks

Wind, water, and gravity constantly change rocks by causing rock particles to collide. As rocks bump against one another, their shapes change. The kind of mechanical weathering that happens as rocks collide and scrape each other is called *abrasion*. In this activity, you will shake some pieces of limestone to model the effects of abrasion.

Ask a Question

1 How does abrasion break down rocks? How can I use this information to identify rocks that have been abraded in nature?

Form a Hypothesis

2 Formulate a hypothesis that answers the questions above.

Test the Hypothesis

3 Copy the table from the next page onto a piece of poster board. Allow enough space to place rocks in each square.

4 Lay 3 of the limestone pieces on the poster board in the area marked "0 shakes." Be careful not to bump the poster board after you have added the rocks.

5 Place the remaining 21 rocks in the 3 L bottle. Then, fill the bottle halfway with water.

6 Close the lid of the bottle securely. Shake the bottle vigorously 100 times.

7 Remove 3 rocks from the bottle, and place them on the poster board in the box that indicates the number of times that the rocks have been shaken.

8 Repeat steps 6 and 7 six times until all of the rocks have been added to the board.

Analyze the Results

9 Examining Data Describe the surface of the rocks that you placed in the area marked "0 shakes." Are the rocks smooth or rough?

10 Describing Events How did the shape of the rocks change as you performed this activity?

11 Constructing Graphs Using graph paper or a computer, construct a graph that shows how the shape of the rocks changed as a result of the number of times that the rocks were shaken.

12 Recognizing Patterns Write a sentence that describes the relationship between the number of shakes and the shape of the rocks.

Rocks Table	
0 shakes	100 shakes
200 shakes	300 shakes
400 shakes	500 shakes
600 shakes	700 shakes

Draw Conclusions

13 Drawing Conclusions Why did the rocks change?

14 Evaluating Results How did the water change during the activity? Why did it change?

15 Making Predictions What would happen if you used a much harder rock, such as granite, for this experiment?

16 Interpreting Information In what way does the model of abrasion that you created in this lab relate to processes in the natural world?

Big Idea Question

17 Applying Conclusions How can the flow of water in a river cause continuous weathering of rocks?

Science Skills Activity

Investigation and Experimentation
6.7.a Develop a hypothesis.

Developing a Hypothesis

▶ Tutorial

Scientific investigations commonly begin with observations. You may notice something in nature and make some observations about it. Observations can lead to a question. For example, you may wonder how, why, or when something happens. You can start to answer your questions by forming a hypothesis.

1 In scientific methods, a hypothesis is a possible answer to a question. Start to form a hypothesis by stating the probable answer to your question based on your observations.

2 A useful hypothesis must be testable. To determine if your hypothesis is testable, identify experiments that can be performed or observations that can be made to help you find out whether the hypothesis is true or false.

The scenario below shows how you can develop a hypothesis based on observations.

Imagine that you observe two fields next to your bike path. One field contains crops, and one field has been plowed but does not have any crops. You ask the following question: Will soil from these fields end up on the bike path if it rains?

1 You develop the following hypothesis: "Soil from the empty field will wash onto the path when it rains, but soil from the field that has crops will not."

2 You test your hypothesis by studying the soil in both fields before it rains to determine the characteristics of each soil. Then, you ride by the fields after it rains to see if soil from either field is on the bike path.

▶ You Try It!

Procedure

Look at the headstones at right. You have been told that these headstones have been in the same cemetery for the same number of years. Write a list of the observations that you can make about the two headstones.

1 **Comparing**   How do the headstones differ?

2 **Applying**   Form a hypothesis that is a possible answer to the following question: Why do the headstones look different?

3 **Analyzing**   Describe experiments that you could do and observations that you could make to test your hypothesis.

Analysis

4 **Evaluating Hypotheses**   Look at a classmate's hypothesis. Is it a possible answer to his or her question, and is it testable?

5 **Evaluating Conclusions**   Imagine that you tested your hypothesis and found that it was false. Was your hypothesis useful? Explain your answer.

Chapter Summary

The Big Idea Weathering is a continuous process that results in the formation of soil and the construction and destruction of landforms.

Section	Vocabulary

1 Weathering

Key Concept Rock is broken down into smaller pieces by mechanical and chemical weathering.

- Ice, water, wind, gravity, plants, and animals can cause mechanical weathering by breaking rock into pieces.
- Water, acids, and air can cause chemical weathering of rocks.

Water

Ice

Ice wedging is a kind of mechanical weathering.

weathering p. 298
mechanical weathering p. 298
abrasion p. 299
exfoliation p. 299
chemical weathering p. 301
acid precipitation p. 301

2 Rates of Weathering

Key Concept The rate at which rock weathers depends on climate, elevation, and the size and makeup of the rock.

- Differential weathering is the process by which softer rocks weather more rapidly than harder rocks do.
- Surface area, climate, and elevation are factors that affect the rate at which rock weathers.

Greater surface area speeds the rate of weathering.

differential weathering p. 304

3 From Bedrock to Soil

Key Concept Weathering may lead to the formation of soil, which is an important natural resource.

- Soil is a mixture of weathered rock, organic material, water, and air.
- Soil composition, texture, fertility, and pH affect plant growth.
- Climate affects the types of soil that are found in different places.

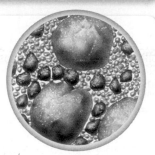

Soils contain particles of different sizes.

soil p. 308
parent rock p. 308
bedrock p. 308
humus p. 310

4 Soil Conservation

Key Concept Soil is a nonrenewable resource that can be endangered if it is used unwisely.

- Soil is important for plants and animals and for the storage of water.
- Farmers use a variety of methods to prevent soil damage and loss.

Terracing can reduce erosion on steep slopes.

soil conservation p. 314
erosion p. 315

Chapter Review

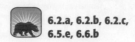 6.2.a, 6.2.b, 6.2.c,
6.5.e, 6.6.b

Organize

Key-Term Fold Review the FoldNote that you created at the beginning of the chapter. Add to or correct the FoldNote based on what you have learned.

Using Vocabulary

1. **Academic Vocabulary** In the sentence "Rivers and streams are dynamic systems that erode, transport sediment, change course, and flood their banks in natural and recurring patterns," what does the word *dynamic* mean?

For each pair of terms, explain how the meanings of the terms differ.

2. *soil conservation* and *erosion*

3. *mechanical weathering* and *chemical weathering*

4. *soil* and *parent rock*

Understanding Concepts

Multiple Choice

5. Which of the following processes is a possible effect of water?
   a. mechanical weathering
   b. chemical weathering
   c. abrasion
   d. All of the above

6. In which climate is the rate of chemical weathering the fastest?
   a. a warm, wet climate
   b. a cold, wet climate
   c. a cold, dry climate
   d. a warm, dry climate

7. If a soil is able to support healthy plant growth, the soil
   a. contains sufficient minerals.
   b. contains humus.
   c. is neither too acidic nor too basic.
   d. All of the above

Short Answer

8. **Listing** Name different ways in which abrasion of rocks can happen.

9. **Concluding** What can happen to soil when soil conservation is not practiced?

10. **Describing** How can crop rotation help maintain the fertility of soil?

11. **Analyzing** Why is soil considered a non-renewable resource?

12. **Summarizing** Why is soil important?

13. **Listing** Which soil conservation techniques can prevent soil erosion?

14. **Describing** Describe how ice wedging weathers rock.

INTERPRETING GRAPHICS The table below shows the volume and surface area of each of three rock samples. Assume that all three samples have the same composition and are located in the same climate. Use the table below to answer the next three questions.

Rock Samples

Sample	Volume (cm³)	Surface area (cm²)
A	80	100
B	240	225
C	800	500

15. **Comparing** Which sample is the largest?

16. **Comparing** Which sample has the highest surface area-to-volume ratio?

17. **Concluding** Which sample would weather at the slowest rate? Why?

Writing Skills

18. **Communicating Concepts** Describe how a mineral grain that is part of a rock at the top of a mountain could end up as part of a sandy beach.

Critical Thinking

19 Concept Mapping Use the following terms to create a concept map: *weathering, chemical weathering, mechanical weathering, abrasion, ice wedging, oxidation,* and *soil.*

20 Making Inferences Mechanical weathering, such as ice wedging, increases surface area by breaking large rocks into smaller rocks. How can mechanical weathering affect the rate of chemical weathering?

21 Analyzing Processes What forms of mechanical and chemical weathering would be most common in a desert? Explain your answer.

22 Applying Concepts If you had to plant a crop on a steep hill, which soil conservation techniques would you use to prevent erosion?

23 Making Comparisons Soil composition, fertility, and pH are important for vigorous plant growth. Explain why each of these soil properties is needed to support plant growth.

INTERPRETING GRAPHICS The table below shows the average rainfall and the average pH of rainfall at three locations. Use the table below to answer the next three questions.

Amount and pH of Rainfall in Three Locations

Location	Average yearly rainfall (cm)	Average pH of rainfall
D	25	3.2
E	193	3.2
F	105	5.9

24 Evaluating Data Which location or locations have the highest average rainfall?

25 Evaluating Data Which location or locations have the most acidic rainfall?

26 Making Inferences At which location would you expect the highest rate of chemical weathering? Explain your answer.

Math Skills

27 Making Calculations What is the total surface area of a cube that measures 4.5 cm on each edge?

28 Making Calculations An area receives 4 cm of rain that has a pH of 3.8 and receives 3 cm of rain that has a pH of 3.2. What is the average pH of these two rainfall events?.

Challenge

INTERPRETING GRAPHICS The graph below shows how water density changes as temperature changes. As most substances get colder, they contract and become denser. But water is unlike most other substances. When water freezes, it expands and becomes less dense. Use the graph below to answer the next three questions.

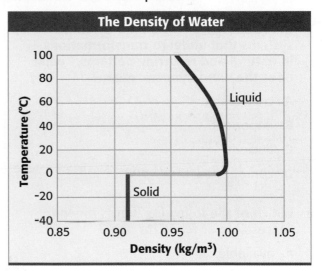

The Density of Water

29 Evaluating Data Which has the greater density: water at 40°C or water at −20°C?

30 Applying Concepts How would the line in the graph look if water behaved like most other liquids?

31 Analyzing Processes Which substance would be a more effective agent of mechanical weathering: water or another liquid? Why?

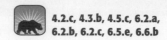

4.2.c, 4.3.b, 4.5.c, 6.2.a,
6.2.b, 6.2.c, 6.5.e, 6.6.b

REVIEWING ACADEMIC VOCABULARY

1 Which of the following words means "having the greatest effect"?

A effective

B dominant

C continual

D major

2 Choose the appropriate form of the word *erode* for the following sentence: "Over long periods of time, wind and water cause ___ to rock formations."

A erode

B erodes

C erosion

D erodible

3 In the sentence "Rivers are dynamic systems that undergo transformations in natural and recurring patterns," what does the word *dynamic* mean?

A changeable

B important

C ancient

D complicated

4 Which of the following words means "accessible or ready for use"?

A available

B appropriate

C ample

D affected

REVIEWING CONCEPTS

5 Which of the following statements describes how a rock changes after it is in a riverbed for a long time?

A The rock rapidly breaks into smaller pieces.

B Chunks of the rock break off, and the rock becomes rougher.

C The edges of the rock are worn away, so its surface becomes smoother.

D The rock absorbs water from the riverbed and becomes softer and smoother.

6 How do acids in groundwater weather rock?

A They wear it away slowly by abrasion.

B They wear it away rapidly by abrasion and gravity.

C Chemicals in the water dissolve the rock.

D Chemicals in the water create deposits on the rock.

Rainfall		
Area	Rainfall Per Year (in.)	Rainfall pH
A	14.2	6.4
B	24.5	2.5
C	25.0	5.7
D	19.8	4.5

7 The table above shows the average rainfall and rainfall acidity in four areas. Which area is likely to undergo the most chemical weathering?

A Area A

B Area B

C Area C

D Area D

8 Why is soil that is rich in humus important to farmers?

A It contains seeds that will grow into plants.

B It contains nutrients that can help plants grow.

C It is finer than other soil, so it allows plants to grow.

D It has a neutral pH, which is important to plant growth.

9 How can contour plowing prevent soil from eroding?

A by turning slopes into a series of smaller, flat fields

B by flattening the contours of a hillside

C by causing rain to run directly down a hillside

D by preventing rain from running directly down a hillside

10 What problems result when soil is overused?

A It becomes dry and washes away.

B It becomes too acidic for plant life.

C It loses its nutrients and becomes infertile.

D It sinks beneath the topsoil and becomes inaccessible.

11 How can plants cause weathering of rocks?

A Plants brush up against rocks and wear them down.

B Plants roots grow into cracks in rocks and break rocks apart.

C Plants absorb nutrients in rocks, so the rocks break apart.

D Plants weigh down on rocks, so the rocks break apart under pressure.

REVIEWING PRIOR LEARNING

12 What is the primary way in which the nutrients inside dead plants are returned to the soil?

A Chemical weathering breaks the plants down into their nutrients.

B Changes in temperature and precipitation cause the plants to die and decompose.

C Decomposers break down the plants and return the nutrients to the soil.

D Erosion from wind and rain causes the plants to break down into their nutrients.

13 Sediment from a riverbed can often be found downstream from the place where it originated. Which of the following statements explains this occurrence?

A The natural flow of water transports silt from one area to another.

B Powerful storms and floods are needed to transport silt to another area.

C Silt in one place is transported by fish and other animals to other areas.

D Silt is frozen in ice and floats downstream when the river thaws.

14 Which of the following changes is most likely to occur in an area where the process of desertification is beginning?

A Plants needing more nutrients will die, while those needing fewer will survive.

B Plants will quickly adapt to the conditions and no longer need as many nutrients.

C Plants will become smaller, but more abundant.

D Plants will gain more nutrients from rainwater.

Standards Assessment

Science in Action

Weird Science

Strange Soil

Mysterious patterns of circles, polygons, and stripes were discovered in the soil in remote areas in Alaska and the Norwegian islands. At first, scientists were puzzled by these strange designs in remote areas. Then, they discovered that these patterns were created by the weathering process in these areas, which includes cycles of freezing and thawing. When the soil freezes, the soil expands. When the soil thaws, the soil contracts. This process moves and sorts the particles of the soil into patterns.

Language Arts ACTiViTy

In your **Science Journal,** write a short story that describes what life would be like if you were a soil circle in one of these areas.

Scientific Discoveries

Gobi Dust Delivered to California

Would you believe that dust from storms in large deserts can be transported over the oceans to different continents? Dust from the Gobi Desert in China has traveled all the way to California! The largest dust storms can pick up millions of tons of dust in Asian deserts. Soil is dry in the spring, and high winds are typical at that time of year. Strong winds that blow east across the Pacific in the spring carry the dust to North America. Scientists in California have measured increased plankton growth in some areas of the Pacific Ocean after dust that contains iron is deposited in the ocean.

Social Studies ACTiViTy

On the Internet or in magazines, find pictures that show dust storms. Use these pictures to make a poster that shows the different cultures affected by dust storms.

J. David Bamberger

Habitat Restoration J. David Bamberger knows how important taking care of the environment is. Therefore, he has turned his ranch into the largest habitat restoration project in Texas. For Bamberger, restoring the habitat started with restoring the soil. One way in which Bamberger restored the soil was to manage the grazing of the grasslands. Because overgrazing causes soil erosion, he wanted to make sure that grazing animals didn't expose the soil. When cattle clear the land of its grasses, the soil is exposed to wind and rain, which can wash the topsoil away.

Bamberger also cleared his land of most of the shrub called *juniper*. Juniper requires so much water per day that it leaves little water in the soil for the grasses and wildflowers. The change in the ranch since Bamberger first bought the ranch in 1959 is most obvious at the fence line of the ranch. Beyond the fence is a small forest of junipers and little other vegetation. On Bamberger's side, the ranch is lush with grasses, wildflowers, trees, and shrubs.

Math ACTIVITY

Bamberger's ranch is 2,300 hectares. There is 0.405 hectare in 1 acre. How many acres is Bamberger's ranch?

Internet Resources

- To learn more about careers in science, visit www.scilinks.org and enter the SciLinks code HY70225.

- To learn more about these Science in Action topics, visit go.hrw.com and type in the keyword HY7WSFF.

- Check out articles related to this chapter by visiting go.hrw.com. Just type in the keyword HY7WSFC.

Improving Comprehension

Graphic Organizers are important visual tools that can help you organize information and improve your reading comprehension. The Graphic Organizer below is called an *idea wheel*. Instructions for creating other types of Graphic Organizers are located in the **Study Skills** section of the Appendix.

How to Make an Idea Wheel

1 Draw a circle. Draw a larger circle around the first circle. Divide the ring between the circles into sections by drawing lines from one circle to the other across the ring. Divide the ring into as many sections as you want.

2 Write a main idea or topic in the smaller circle. Label each section in the ring with a category or characteristic of the main idea.

3 In each section of the ring, include details that are unique to the topic.

When to Use an Idea Wheel

An idea wheel is an effective type of visual organization in which ideas in science can be divided into categories or parts. It is also a useful way to illustrate characteristics of a main idea or topic. As you read, look for topics that are divided into ideas or categories that can be organized around an idea wheel.

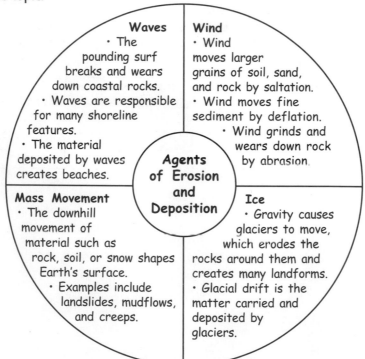

Waves
- The pounding surf breaks and wears down coastal rocks.
- Waves are responsible for many shoreline features.
- The material deposited by waves creates beaches.

Wind
- Wind moves larger grains of soil, sand, and rock by saltation.
- Wind moves fine sediment by deflation.
- Wind grinds and wears down rock by abrasion.

Agents of Erosion and Deposition

Mass Movement
- The downhill movement of material such as rock, soil, or snow shapes Earth's surface.
- Examples include landslides, mudflows, and creeps.

Ice
- Gravity causes glaciers to move, which erodes the rocks around them and creates many landforms.
- Glacial drift is the matter carried and deposited by glaciers.

You Try It!

This Reading Strategy can also be used within the chapter that you are about to read. Practice making your own idea wheel as directed in the Reading Strategies for Section **2** and Section **4**. Record your work in your **Science Journal**.

Unpacking the Standards

The information below "unpacks" the standards by breaking them down into basic parts. The higher-level, academic vocabulary is highlighted and defined to help you understand the language of the standards. "What It Means" restates the standards as simply as possible.

California Standard	Academic Vocabulary	What It Means
6.2.a Students know water running downhill is the **dominant process** in shaping the landscape, including California's landscape.	**dominant** (DAHM uh nuhnt) having the greatest effect **process** (PRAH ses) a set of steps, events, or changes	Water running in rivers and over the land is the most important force in changing the natural shape of Earth's surface.
6.2.c Students know beaches are **dynamic** systems in which the sand is supplied by rivers and moved along the coast by the action of waves.	**dynamic** (die NAM ik) active; tending toward change	Beaches are always changing. Rivers carry sand to beaches and oceans, and ocean waves move the sand along the shoreline.
6.2.d Students know earthquakes, volcanic eruptions, landslides, and floods change human and wildlife habitats.		Earthquakes, volcanic eruptions, landslides, and floods change the surroundings in which humans and wildlife live.
6.3.a Students know **energy** can be carried from one place to another by heat flow or by waves, including water, light and sound waves, or by moving objects.	**energy** (EN uhr jee) the ability to make things happen	Energy is moved from one place to another by heat flow, by waves, or by the movement of objects. Water waves, light waves, and sound waves are kinds of waves.

10

Agents of Erosion and Deposition

The Big Idea

Topography is reshaped by the weathering of rock and soil and by the transportation and deposition of sediment.

California Standards

Focus on Earth Sciences
6.2 Topography is reshaped by the weathering of rock and soil and by the transportation and deposition of sediment. (Sections 1, 2, 3, and 4)
6.3 Heat moves in a predictable flow from warmer objects to cooler objects until all the objects are at the same temperature. (Section 1)

Investigation and Experimentation
6.7 Scientific progress is made by asking meaningful questions and conducting careful investigations. (Science Skills Activity)

Math
6.2.1 Number Sense

English–Language Arts
6.2.4 Reading
6.1.3 Writing

About the Photo

The rugged coastline of Santa Cruz Island, located along the southern California coast, can be seen in this aerial photo. Steep wave cut cliffs, sea caves, beaches, and coves formed as a result of erosion and deposition.

Organize

Layered Book

Before you read this chapter, create the FoldNote entitled "Layered Book." Label the tabs of the layered book with "Shoreline erosion and deposition," "Wind erosion and deposition," and "Erosion and deposition by ice," and "Erosion and deposition by mass movement." As you read the chapter, write information that you learn about each category on the appropriate tab.

Instructions for creating FoldNotes are located in the Study Skills section on p. 616 of the Appendix.

Explore Activity

20 min

6.2.c

Shaping Beaches by Wave Erosion

Above or below ground, water plays an important role in the erosion and deposition of rock and soil. A shoreline is a good example of a place where water shapes Earth's surface by erosion and deposition. Did you know that shorelines are shaped by crashing waves? Build a model shoreline, and see for yourself!

Procedure

1. Make a shoreline by adding **sand** to one end of a **washtub.** Fill the washtub with **water** to a depth of 5 cm. Sketch the shoreline profile (side view), and label it "A."

2. Place a **block** in the water at the end of the washtub opposite the sand.

3. Move the block up and down very slowly to create small waves for 2 min. Sketch the new shoreline profile, and label it "B."

4. Now, move the block up and down more rapidly to create large waves for 2 min. Sketch the new shoreline profile, and label it "C."

Analysis

5. Compare the three shoreline profiles. What happened to the shoreline?

6. How does erosion of the shoreline by small waves differ from erosion by large waves?

Agents of Erosion and Deposition **331**

Shoreline Erosion and Deposition

Key Concept Beaches and shorelines are shaped largely by the action of ocean waves.

What You Will Learn

- Energy from waves crashing against rocks affects shorelines.
- Shoreline features are created by wave erosion.
- Waves deposit sediment at the shore to form beaches.

Why It Matters

Waves erode and deposit materials along beaches and shorelines throughout California and the world.

Vocabulary

- shoreline
- beach
- undertow
- longshore current

READING STRATEGY

Prediction Guide Before reading this section, write each heading from this section in your **Science Journal.** Below each heading, write what you think you will learn.

shoreline (SHAWR LIEN) the boundary between land and a body of water

▶ Two ingredients are needed to make sand: rock and energy. Rock is usually available on the shore. Energy is provided by waves that travel through water. When waves crash into rock over long periods of time, the rock breaks down into smaller pieces that are called *sand*.

The formation and movement of sand by wave erosion and deposition shape the shoreline. A **shoreline** is the place where land and a body of water meet. Waves usually play a major part in building up and breaking down the shoreline.

Wave Energy

As wind moves across the ocean surface, it makes disturbances called *waves*. The size of a wave depends on the strength of the wind and the time that it blows. The stronger the wind is and the longer the wind blows, the bigger the waves are.

Wind that results from summer hurricanes and severe winter storms makes large waves that cause dramatic shoreline erosion. Waves may travel hundreds or even thousands of kilometers from a storm before reaching the shoreline. Some of the largest waves to reach the California coast are produced by storms as far away as Australia. So, the California wave that the surfer in **Figure 1** is riding may have formed on the other side of the Pacific Ocean!

Figure 1 *Waves produced by storms on the other side of the Pacific Ocean propel this surfer toward a California shore.*

6.2.c Students know beaches are dynamic systems in which the sand is supplied by rivers and moved along the coast by the action of waves.
6.3.a Students know energy can be carried from one place to another by heat flow or by waves, including water, light and sound waves, or by moving objects.

Wave Trains

When you drop a pebble into a pond, the pebble makes many ripples, not just one. Waves, like ripples, move in groups, called *wave trains*. **Figure 2** shows a wave train. The waves in a wave train are separated by a period of time called the *wave period*. Wave periods can be observed as the time between breaking waves. Most wave periods are 10 to 20 s long.

As wave trains move away from their source, they travel uninterrupted through deep ocean water. But when a wave in a wave train reaches shallow water, the bottom of the wave drags against the sea floor, which slows the wave down. As a result, the top of the wave moves faster than the bottom of the wave does, and the wave gets taller. Eventually, the wave becomes so tall that it cannot support itself. At that point, it begins to curl and break. Breaking waves are known as *surf*. Now you know why people who ride the waves are called *surfers*.

The Pounding Surf

Look at **Figure 3,** and you will get an idea of how sand is made. A tremendous amount of energy is released when waves break. A crashing wave can break solid rock and can throw broken rocks back against the shore. As water in breaking waves enters cracks in rock, the water helps break off large boulders and wash away fine grains of sand. The loose sand that is picked up by waves wears down and polishes coastal rocks. As a result of these actions, rock is broken down into smaller and smaller pieces that eventually become sand.

Standards Check How do waves break rocks? 🐻 6.3.a

Figure 2 *Because waves travel in wave trains, waves break at regular intervals.*

Figure 3 *The energy of breaking waves is transferred when the waves crash against the shore.*

Wave Erosion

Wave erosion produces a variety of features along a shoreline. *Sea cliffs* form when waves erode and undercut rock to make steep slopes. Waves strike the base of the cliffs. This process wears away the soil and rock and makes the cliffs steeper. The rate at which sea cliffs erode depends on the hardness of the rock and the energy of the waves. Sea cliffs made of hard rock, such as granite, erode very slowly. Sea cliffs made of soft rock, such as shale, erode more rapidly, especially during storms.

Figure 4  **Coastal Landforms Created by Wave Erosion**

Sea stacks are offshore columns of resistant rock that were once connected to the mainland. Sea stacks form when waves erode the mainland and leave behind isolated columns of rock.

Sea arches form when wave action erodes sea caves until arches are cut through the caves.

Sea caves form when waves cut large holes into fractured or weak rock along the base of sea cliffs. Sea caves are common in cliffs that are composed of sedimentary rock.

Shaping a Shoreline

Much of the erosion responsible for landforms that you might see along the shoreline takes place during storms. Large waves caused by storms transfer far more energy than average-sized waves do. This energy is so powerful that it can remove huge chunks of rock. **Figure 4** shows some of the major landscape features that result from wave erosion.

Standards Check Explain why large waves are more able to remove large chunks of rock from a shoreline than average-sized waves are. 🐻 **6.3.a**

Erosion Disasters
Sometimes, Earth changes very quickly. Research some of the dramatic results of those changes. Go to **go.hrw.com,** and type in the keyword HY7ICEW.

Headlands are finger-shaped projections that form when cliffs of hard rock erode more slowly than the surrounding softer rock does. On many shorelines, hard rock forms headlands, and softer rock forms beaches or bays.

Wave-cut terraces form when a sea cliff is worn back from shore, which produces a nearly level platform beneath the water at the base of the cliff.

England

Florida

Hawaii

California

Figure 5 *Beaches are made of various types of materials deposited by waves.* **How are the beach materials in these photos different from each other?**

Wave Deposits

Waves carry a variety of materials, including sand, rock fragments, dead coral, and shells. Often, these materials are deposited on a shoreline, where they form a beach. A **beach** is any area of shoreline that is made up of material deposited by waves. Some beach material is also deposited by rivers and then is moved down the shoreline by waves.

Beach Materials

You may think that all beaches are sandy places at the seashore. However, not all beaches are made of sand. Notice that the beaches shown in **Figure 5** differ in the texture of their materials. The size and shape of beach material depend on how far the material traveled from its source to where it is deposited. They also depend on how the material is eroded by waves. For example, in areas where stormy seas are common, beaches may be made of pebbles and boulders because smaller particles are eroded by waves.

Beach Composition

The color of beach material depends on the material's source. Light-colored sand is the most common beach material. Much of this sand is made of the mineral quartz. Most quartz sand comes from eroded sandstone. Many Florida beaches are made of quartz sand. On many tropical islands, such as the Virgin Islands, beach sand is made of finely ground white coral. But, as **Figure 5** shows, not all beaches are made of light-colored sand. Black sand beaches, such as the ones in Hawaii, are made of eroded lava from Hawaiian volcanoes. This lava is rich in the elements iron and magnesium, which give the sand its dark color.

Standards Check How do source rocks affect beach color? 6.2.c

California Beaches

California has both rocky and sandy shores. Rocky beaches commonly form where mountains or cliffs meet the ocean. Sandy beaches commonly form on the edges of more gently sloping land. Most sandy beaches receive some of their sand from rivers.

The mineral composition of California beaches also varies. The composition and color depend on the source of the sand. For example, the sand at Shelter Cove in Humboldt County is charcoal gray and comes from eroded shale cliffs nearby. The white sand at Carmel is made up of quartz and feldspar. Sands near Santa Cruz contain dark grains of magnetite from igneous rock.

Beach Size

The amount of sand present on a beach can change between seasons. In California, beaches can become narrower in winter as large winter storm waves erode sand away from the beach. Much of the eroded sand is trapped by offshore sandbars and is returned to beaches by small waves during the summer.

Shore Currents

When waves crash on the beach head-on, the water flows back to the ocean underneath new incoming waves. This movement of water carries pieces of sand and rock away from the shore. This kind of water movement is called an **undertow.**

Longshore Currents

When water travels parallel to the shoreline very near shore, the current is called a **longshore current.** Longshore currents are caused by waves hitting the shore at an angle. Waves that break at oblique angles to the shore move sediment along the coast. Waves wash the sand parallel to the direction in which they break. But the return water flow brings sand directly down the slope of the beach. This process results in a zigzag movement of the sand, as shown in **Figure 6.**

Longshore currents transport most of the sediment in beach environments. This process both tears down and builds up the coastline. Unfortunately, longshore currents also carry and spread trash and other ocean pollution along the shore.

Standards Check How do longshore currents move sand? 6.2.c

beach (BEECH) an area of the shoreline that is made up of deposited sediment

undertow (UHN duhr TOH) a subsurface current that is near shore and that pulls objects out to sea

longshore current (LAWNG SHAWR KUHR uhnt) a water current that travels near and parallel to the shoreline

Watching Waves in Action

Ask a parent or guardian to take you to a California beach. While at the beach, notice how the waves come in toward the shore at an angle. Watch how the water moves sand as waves crash into the shore and the water returns toward the ocean. Draw a diagram of the sand's path.

ACTIVITY

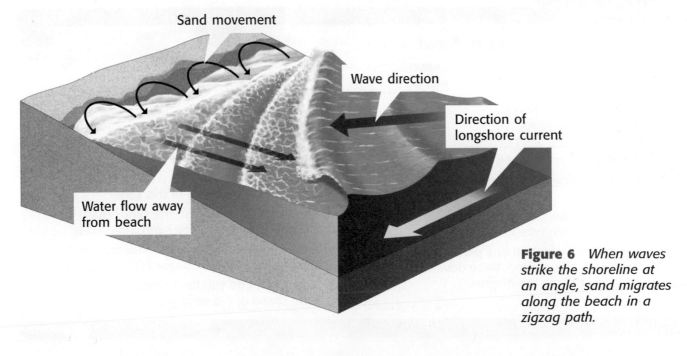

Figure 6 *When waves strike the shoreline at an angle, sand migrates along the beach in a zigzag path.*

Offshore Deposits

Waves that move at an angle to the shoreline push water along the shore and create longshore currents. When waves erode material from the shoreline, longshore currents can transport and deposit this material offshore. This process creates landforms in open water. A *sandbar* is an underwater or exposed ridge of sand, gravel, or shell material. A *barrier spit* is an exposed sandbar that is connected to the shoreline. Cape Cod, Massachusetts, shown in **Figure 7,** is an example of a barrier spit. A *barrier island* is a long, narrow island usually made of sand that forms parallel to the shoreline a short distance offshore.

Figure 7 *A barrier spit, such as Cape Cod, Massachusetts, occurs when an exposed sandbar is connected to the shoreline.*

California Islands

California is unique compared to many states because it has offshore islands. One example of California islands is the Channel Islands. The Channel Islands are located off of the southern California coast. These islands formed millions of years ago. They are thought to have once been part of mainland mountain ranges. Now, they are separated from the mainland by the Santa Monica Channel and the San Pedro Channel. Islands such as the Channel Islands shield the coastline by reducing the impact of storm waves on coastal cliffs.

California's islands can be sanctuaries for birds and marine mammals. Some of the islands are home to rare species because of the islands' isolation from the mainland.

Quick Lab

Observing Differences in Sand

In this activity, you will examine sand collections, observe differences between them, and hypothesize the causes of those differences.

6.2.c

▶ Try It!

1. Gather three or more types of **sand.**
2. Use a **magnifying glass** to examine each type of sand.
3. Describe the grain size, grain shape, and grain color of each type of sand.
4. Drag a **magnet** wrapped in a **plastic bag** through each pile of sand. Write down what, if anything, sticks to the magnet.

▶ Think About It!

5. Do any of the grains of sand look like they came from a rock or mineral you know? What might be the source of this sand?
6. Are there shell fragments in the sand? How did they become part of the sand?
7. Did any sand grains stick to the magnet? What minerals might be magnetic?
8. What processes do you think affected the size and shape of the sand grains?

 20 min

Summary

- A wave is a disturbance in the water that can be caused by wind.
- As waves break against a shoreline, their energy breaks rocks down into sand.
- Six shoreline features that are created by wave erosion are sea cliffs, sea stacks, sea caves, sea arches, headlands, and wave-cut terraces.
- Beaches are made from material deposited by rivers and waves.
- California beaches can be rocky or sandy and can have different mineral compositions.
- Longshore currents cause sand to move in a zigzag pattern along the shore.
- Longshore currents can deposit eroded sediment offshore.

Using Vocabulary

Use a term from the section to complete each sentence below.

1 A(n) ___ is an area made up of material deposited by waves.

2 An area in which land and a body of water meet is a(n) ___.

Understanding Concepts

3 **Summarizing** How do wave deposits affect a shoreline?

4 **Describing** Describe how sand moves along a beach.

5 **Identifying** What are six shoreline features that are created by wave erosion?

6 **Summarizing** How can the energy of water waves affect a shoreline?

Critical Thinking

7 **Applying Concepts** Which wave would have more energy: a small wave or a large wave?

8 **Applying Concepts** Not all beaches are made from light-colored sand. Explain why this statement is true.

9 **Making Inferences** Why are some beaches made of sand and some made of pebbles?

INTERPRETING GRAPHICS Use the photograph below to answer the next three questions.

10 **Evaluating Data** At what kind of angle are the waves approaching the shoreline?

11 **Analyzing Processes** What kind of current does the red arrow represent?

12 **Analyzing Processes** How does this type of current transport sand along a beach?

Math Skills

13 **Making Conversions** Imagine that there is a large boulder on the edge of a shoreline. If the wave period is 15 s long, how many times is the boulder hit by waves in a year?

Challenge

14 **Forming Hypotheses** Seasonal changes in wave action affect beach shorelines. How do you think these seasonal variations would change the way a beach looks?

Wind Erosion and Deposition

Key Concept Wind can cause erosion and can move and deposit sediment.

What You Will Learn

- Wind erosion happens through saltation, deflation, and abrasion.
- Wind can erode and deposit differing amounts and sizes of material, depending on the wind speed.

Why It Matters

Wind erosion and deposition are continually active throughout California and the rest of the world in shaping landscapes.

Vocabulary

- saltation
- deflation
- abrasion
- dune

READING STRATEGY

Graphic Organizer In your **Science Journal,** create an Idea Wheel about the different types of wind erosion.

▶ Have you ever been outside and had a gust of wind blow a stack of papers all over the place? Every time that you caught up with the papers, they moved. If this has happened to you, you have seen how wind erosion works. In the same way that wind moved your papers, wind moves soil, sand, and rock particles. When wind moves soil, sand, and rock particles, it acts as an agent of erosion.

Wind Erosion

Some areas are more vulnerable to wind erosion than other areas are. An area that has little plant cover can be severely affected by wind erosion. These areas lack plant roots, which anchor sand and soil in place. Deserts and coastlines that are made of fine, loose rock material and that have little plant cover are shaped most dramatically by wind.

Saltation

Wind moves material in different ways. Larger grains of soil, sand, and rock are moved by saltation. **Saltation** is the skipping and bouncing movement of sand-sized particles in the direction that wind is blowing. As shown in **Figure 1,** wind causes the particles to bounce. When moving sand grains knock into one another, some grains bounce up in the air, fall forward, and bump other sand grains. These impacts cause other grains to roll and bounce forward.

Figure 1 *Sand grains move by making low, arcing jumps when blown by the wind. Dust is light enough to be carried by the wind.*

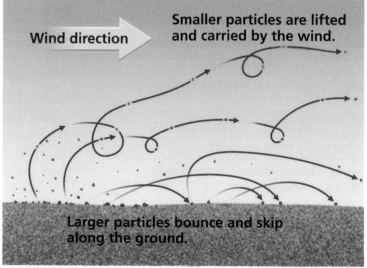

Wind direction

Smaller particles are lifted and carried by the wind.

Larger particles bounce and skip along the ground.

6.2.a Students know water running downhill is the dominant process in shaping the landscape, including California's landscape.

Figure 2 *Desert pavement, such as that found in the Painted Desert in Arizona, forms when wind removes all of the fine materials.*

Deflation

The removal of fine sediment by wind is called **deflation**. This process is shown in **Figure 1.** During deflation, wind removes the top layer of fine sediment or soil. Deflation leaves behind rock fragments that are too heavy to be lifted by the wind. Deflation may cause the formation of *desert pavement,* which is a surface that is made of pebbles and small, broken rocks. An example of desert pavement is shown in **Figure 2.**

If you have ever blown on a layer of dust on a shelf, you may have noticed that a little scooped-out depression formed in the dust. Similarly, in areas that have little plant cover, the wind may scoop out depressions in the landscape. These depressions are called *deflation hollows.*

Abrasion

The grinding and wearing down of rock surfaces by other rock or by sand particles is called **abrasion.** Abrasion happens in areas where there are strong winds, loose sand, and soft rocks. The blowing of millions of sand grains creates a sandblasting effect. This effect helps erode, smooth, and polish rocks.

Standards Check Describe three different ways that wind shapes landscapes. 6.2.a

saltation (sal TAY shuhn) the movement of sand or other sediments by short jumps and bounces that is caused by wind or water

deflation (dee FLAY shuhn) a form of wind erosion in which fine, dry soil particles are blown away

Wordwise The prefix *de-* means "down" or "off." The root *flat-* means "to blow."

abrasion (uh BRAY zhuhn) the grinding and wearing away of rock surfaces through the mechanical action of other rock or sand particles

Quick Lab

Making Desert Pavement

1. Spread a mixture of **dust, sand,** and **gravel** on an **outdoor table.** The mixture represents sediment.

2. Place an **electric fan** at one end of the table.

3. Put on **safety goggles** and a **filter mask.** Aim the fan across the sediment. Set the fan on its lowest speed, and turn the fan on. Record your observations. **Caution:** Make sure the filter mask covers your nose and mouth to prevent sediment inhalation.

4. Set the fan on a medium speed. Record your observations.

5. Finally, set the fan on a high speed so that the fan imitates a desert windstorm. Record your observations.

6. What is the relationship between wind speed and the size of the sediment particles moved?

7. Does the remaining sediment fit the definition of *desert pavement*?

6.2.a
6.7.e

20 min

Figure 3 *These dunes in Death Valley, California, migrate with the wind.*

Wind-Deposited Materials

Wind carries sediment in much the same way that rivers do. And just as rivers deposit their loads, wind drops all of the material that it carries over time. The amount and size of the particles that wind can carry depend on wind speed. The faster wind blows, the more material and the heavier the particles that wind can carry. As wind speed slows, particles are deposited according to weight, from heaviest to lightest. So, heavy particles are deposited first.

Dunes

When wind hits an obstacle, such as a plant or a rock, the wind slows down. As it slows, the wind deposits, or drops, the heaviest material that it is carrying on top of the obstacle. As the material builds up, the obstacle gets larger. This obstacle causes the wind to slow more and deposit more material, which forms a mound. Eventually, the original obstacle is buried. Mounds of wind-deposited sand are called **dunes.** Dunes are common in sandy deserts and along the sandy shores of lakes and oceans. **Figure 3** shows sand dunes in California.

dune (DOON) a mound of wind-deposited sand that moves as a result of the action of wind

California Dunes

California is home to several major dune formations. Dunes are popular for recreational activities like camping. These dune formations are in coastal areas and in desert areas.

A major coastal dune system is the Monterey Bay Dunes, which covers forty square miles. The Algodones Sand Dunes, in southeast California, is the largest desert sand dune system in the state, covering one thousand square miles.

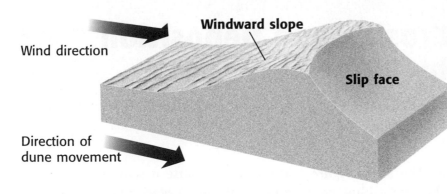

Wind direction

Windward slope

Slip face

Direction of dune movement

Figure 4 *Dunes form from material deposited by wind. The gently sloped side of the dune is called the windward slope. The steeply sloped side of the dune is called the slip face.*

The Movement of Dunes

Generally, dunes move in the same direction the wind is blowing. Wind conditions decide the dune's shape and size. A dune usually has a gently sloped side and a steeply sloped side, as shown in **Figure 4.** Usually, the gently sloped side faces the wind. Wind constantly moves material up this side of the dune. As sand moves over the crest, or peak, of the dune, the sand slides down the slip face and makes a steep slope.

Standards Check How are dunes an example of wind shaping landscapes? 6.2.a

SECTION Review

6.2.a

Summary

- Areas that have little plant cover and desert areas that are covered with fine rock material are more vulnerable to wind erosion than other areas are.

- Saltation is the process in which sand-sized particles move in the direction of the wind.

- Desert pavement, deflation hollows, and dunes are landforms that are created by wind erosion and deposition.

- Dunes move in the direction that the wind blows.

Using Vocabulary

1 Use *saltation, abrasion,* and *deflation* in separate sentences.

Understanding Concepts

2 **Comparing** Compare saltation with deflation.

3 **Describing** Explain the process of abrasion.

4 **Identifying** Identify three landforms that result from wind erosion and deposition.

5 **Summarizing** How do dunes form?

6 **Identifying** In what direction do dunes move?

Critical Thinking

7 **Identifying Relationships** Explain the relationship between plant cover and wind erosion.

8 **Applying Concepts** If you climbed up the steep side of a sand dune, did you most likely travel in the direction that the wind was blowing?

9 **Analyzing Processes** Wind erodes particles in one area and deposits them elsewhere. Which would be deposited farthest from its source: sand or dust?

Challenge

10 **Identifying Relationships** Why might wind erosion be more dominant in shaping the landscape in a dry climate than in a moist climate?

Internet Resources

For a variety of links related to this chapter, go to www.scilinks.org

Topic: Wind Erosion
SciLinks code: HY71669

Erosion and Deposition by Ice

Key Concept   Glaciers shape Earth's surface by moving rock and sediment.

What You Will Learn

- As glaciers move, they form a variety of landforms by removing rock and soil.
- Glaciers deposit rock material when they melt or retreat.

Why It Matters

Glaciers have formed many of the landforms on Earth.

Vocabulary
- glacier
- till
- glacial drift
- stratified drift

READING STRATEGY

Asking Questions   Read this section silently. In your **Science Journal,** write down questions that you have about this section. Discuss your question in a small group.

glacier (GLAY shuhr) a large mass of moving ice

> The ice in **Figure 1** looks blue because it scatters blue light. The bright blue ice is part of a glacier. A **glacier** is an enormous mass of moving ice. There are two kinds of glaciers. Continental glaciers spread across entire continents and produce flattened landscapes. Alpine glaciers form in mountainous areas and produce rugged landscapes.

Glaciers—Rivers of Ice

Glaciers form in areas that are so cold that snow stays on the ground year-round. In polar regions and at high elevations, layers of snow build up year after year. Over time, the weight of the top layers compresses and packs the lower layers. These layers eventually become ice.

How Glaciers Move

Because glaciers are massive, gravity causes glaciers to flow—though slowly—like "rivers of ice." When enough ice builds up on a slope, the ice begins to move downhill. Thick glaciers move faster than thin glaciers do. The steeper the slope is, the faster the glaciers move. Glaciers move by sliding and by flowing.

Standards Check   How are glaciers an example of water shaping a landscape? 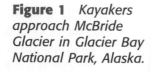 6.2.a

Figure 1   *Kayakers approach McBride Glacier in Glacier Bay National Park, Alaska.*

 6.2.a Students know water running downhill is the dominant process in shaping the landscape, including California's landscape.

Figure 2   **Landscape Features Carved by Alpine Glaciers**

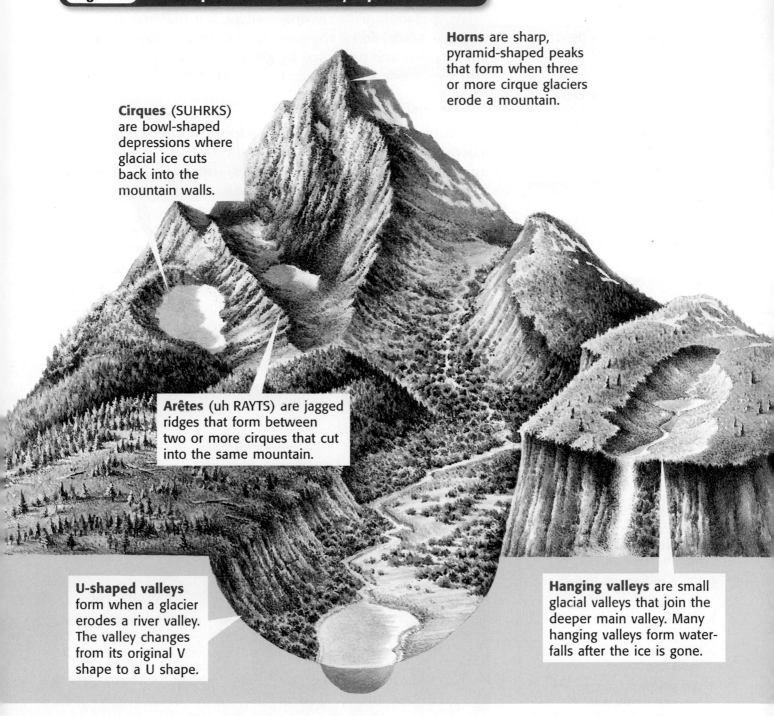

Horns are sharp, pyramid-shaped peaks that form when three or more cirque glaciers erode a mountain.

Cirques (SUHRKS) are bowl-shaped depressions where glacial ice cuts back into the mountain walls.

Arêtes (uh RAYTS) are jagged ridges that form between two or more cirques that cut into the same mountain.

U-shaped valleys form when a glacier erodes a river valley. The valley changes from its original V shape to a U shape.

Hanging valleys are small glacial valleys that join the deeper main valley. Many hanging valleys form waterfalls after the ice is gone.

Landforms Created by Glaciers

Glaciers can produce a variety of landforms as they erode the rocks around them. As a glacier moves, rocks below and beside the glacier are broken and moved. Grooves may form in the rock over which the glacier slides as rocks are dragged beneath the glacier. **Figure 2** shows the kinds of landscape features that are sculpted by alpine glaciers.

glacial drift (GLAY shuhl DRIFT) the rock material carried and deposited by glaciers

till (TIL) unsorted rock material that is deposited directly by a melting glacier

stratified drift (STRAT uh FIED DRIFT) a glacial deposit that has been sorted and layered by the action of streams or meltwater

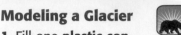
Types of Glacial Deposits

As a glacier melts, it drops all of the material that it is carrying. **Glacial drift** is the general term used to describe all material carried and deposited by glaciers. Glacial drift is divided into two major kinds, *till* and *stratified drift*.

Till Deposits

Unsorted rock material that is deposited directly by the ice when it melts is called **till.** *Unsorted* means that the till is made up of rock material of different sizes—from large boulders to fine sediment. When the glacier melts, the unsorted material is deposited on the surface of the ground.

The most common till deposits are *moraines*. Moraines generally form ridges along the edges of glaciers. Moraines form when glaciers carry material to the front of and along the sides of the ice. As the ice melts, the glacier drops the sediment and rock that it is carrying. This dropped material forms different kinds of moraines. The different kinds of moraines are shown in **Figure 3.**

Figure 3 Types of Moraines

Lateral moraines form along each side of a glacier.

Medial moraines form when valley glaciers that have lateral moraines meet.

Ground moraines form from unsorted materials left beneath a glacier.

Terminal moraines form when sediment is dropped at the front of the glacier.

Stratified Drift

When a glacier melts, streams that carry rock material away from the shrinking glacier form. A glacial deposit that is sorted into layers based on the size of the rock material is called **stratified drift.** Streams carry sorted material and deposit it in front of the glacier in a broad area called an *outwash plain.* Sometimes, a block of ice is left in the outwash plain when a glacier retreats. As the ice melts, sediment builds up around the block of ice, and a depression called a *kettle* forms. Kettles commonly fill with water to form lakes or ponds, such as the lakes shown in **Figure 4.**

Standards Check How is glacial drift related to glaciers reshaping landscapes? 6.2.a

Figure 4 *Kettle lakes form in outwash plains and are common in states such as Minnesota.*

SECTION Review

6.2.a

Summary

- Glaciers are masses of moving ice that shape the landscape by eroding and depositing material.

- Glaciers move by sliding or by flowing.

- Alpine glaciers can carve cirques, arêtes, horns, U-shaped valleys, and hanging valleys.

- Two types of glacial deposits are till and stratified drift.

- Deposition of sediment by glaciers can form several landforms, including kettles.

Using Vocabulary

Use a term from the section to complete each sentence below.

1. A glacial deposit that is sorted into layers based on the size of the rock material is called ___.

2. ___ is all of the material carried and deposited by glaciers.

3. Unsorted rock material that is deposited directly by the ice when the ice melts is ___.

Understanding Concepts

4. **Identifying** Identify two ways in which glaciers move.

5. **Identifying** Identify four types of moraines.

6. **Summarizing** What is a glacier?

7. **Applying** Identify five landscape features that are formed by alpine glaciers.

Critical Thinking

8. **Analyzing Ideas** How can a glacier deposit both sorted and unsorted material?

9. **Applying Concepts** Why are glaciers such effective agents of erosion and deposition?

Challenge

10. **Applying Concepts** How would sea levels be affected if all of Earth's glaciers got bigger and new glaciers formed? How might these new glaciers change global landscapes?

Erosion and Deposition by Mass Movement

Key Concept Gravity causes material to move downslope in a process called *mass movement.*

What You Will Learn

- The angle of repose determines whether mass movement will happen.
- Gravity causes rock falls, landslides, mudflows, and creep.

Why It Matters

Mass movements destroy property and homes. They can destroy wildlife habitats by carrying away plants and animals or by burying a habitat.

Vocabulary

- mass movement
- rock fall
- landslide
- mudflow
- creep

READING STRATEGY

Graphic Organizer In your **Science Journal,** create an Idea Wheel that describes categories of mass movements.

▶ Although you can't see it, the force of gravity is an agent of erosion and deposition. Gravity not only influences water and ice movement but also causes rocks and soil to move downslope. **Mass movement** is the movement of any material, such as rock, soil, or snow, downslope. Mass movement, whether rapid or slow, plays a major role in shaping Earth's surface.

Angle of Repose

In a dry sand pile, sand in the pile moves downhill until the slope of the pile becomes stable, or unchanging. The *angle of repose* is the steepest angle, or slope, at which loose material no longer moves downslope. The angle of repose is demonstrated in **Figure 1.** The angle of repose varies with the type of surface material. Characteristics, such as size, weight, shape, and moisture level, of the material on the surface determine the angle of repose. If the slope of surface material is greater than the angle of repose, mass movement occurs.

mass movement (MAS MOOV muhnt) the movement of a large mass of sediment or a section of land down a slope

rock fall (RAHK FAHL) the rapid mass movement rocks down a steep slope or cliff

landslide (LAND SLIED) the sudden movement of rock and soil down a slope

Figure 1 Angle of Repose

Sand moves downhill because the slope of the sand pile is steeper than the pile's angle of repose.

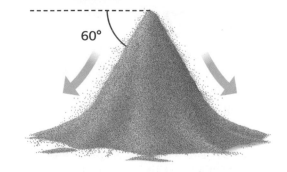

The slope of the sand pile has reached the angle of repose, so the sand pile is stable.

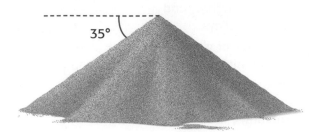

6.2.d Students know earthquakes, volcanic eruptions, landslides, and floods change human and wildlife habitats.

Rapid Mass Movement

The most destructive mass movements happen suddenly and rapidly. Rapid mass movement can be very dangerous and can destroy everything in its path.

Rock Falls

While traveling along a mountain road, you may have noticed signs along the road that warn of falling rocks. A **rock fall** happens when loose rocks fall down a steep slope. Steep slopes sometimes form when a road is built through mountainous areas. Loosened and exposed rocks above the road tend to fall as a result of gravity. The rocks in a rock fall can range in size from small fragments to large boulders.

Landslides

Another kind of rapid mass movement is a landslide. A **landslide** is the sudden and rapid movement of a large amount of material downslope. Landslides can carry away plants and animals or bury their habitats. A *slump,* shown in **Figure 2,** is the most common kind of landslide. Slumping occurs when a block of material moves downslope over a curved surface. Heavy rains, deforestation, construction on unstable slopes, and earthquakes increase the chance that a landslide will happen.

Standards Check How can a landslide affect wildlife habitats? 6.2.d

Figure 2 *This landslide occurred in La Conchita, California, in the spring of 1995.*

Quick Lab

Modeling a Landslide

1. Arrange some **rocks** at one end of a **board.**
2. Carefully and slowly raise the end of the board where the rocks are piled.
3. Hold the board steady at the point where the rocks begin to slide down the board.
4. Have a partner use a **protractor** to measure the angle between the floor and the bottom end of the board. Record this angle.
5. Continue raising the high end of the board until all of the rocks slide.
6. Why do you think the rocks did not slide down the board until a certain angle was reached?
7. What did this measured angle represent?

6.2.d

15 min

Figure 3 *This photo shows one of the many mudflows that have occurred in California during rainy winters.*

Mudflows

A rapid movement of a large mass of mud is a **mudflow.** Mudflows happen when a large amount of water mixes with soil and rock. The water causes the slippery mass of mud to flow rapidly downslope. Mudflows commonly happen in mountainous regions when a long dry season is followed by heavy rains. Deforestation and the removal of ground cover often result in devastating mudflows. As shown in **Figure 3,** a mudflow can carry trees, houses, cars, and other objects that lie in its path.

mudflow (MUHD FLOH) the flow of a mass of mud or rock and soil mixed with a large amount of water

creep (KREEP) the slow downhill movement of weathered rock material

Creep

Even though most slopes appear to be stable, they are actually undergoing slow mass movement. In fact, the ground beneath the tree in **Figure 4** moved so slowly that the tree trunk curved as the tree grew. The extremely slow movement of material downslope is called **creep.** Many factors contribute to creep. Water loosens soil and allows the soil to move freely. In addition, plant roots act as wedges that force rocks and soil particles apart. Burrowing animals, such as gophers and groundhogs, also loosen rock and soil particles. In fact, all rock and soil on slopes travel slowly downhill.

Figure 4 *The shape of this tree trunk indicates that creep has occurred along the slope.*

Mass Movement and Land Use

Mass movement is one factor that must be considered when officials decide how to use land. These officials must determine whether an area is safe for certain uses. If they choose poorly, lives may be lost and property may be damaged when humans get in the way of these powerful natural processes.

Construction in areas that are at risk of natural disasters can be hard to avoid. Land-use decisions should be made after considering many factors, including scientific evidence, to predict mass movement's local impacts. When officials know the likelihood of mass movement, they can take steps to reduce predicted effects.

The effects of major mass movement events are usually unfavorable in the short term. But sometimes, the long-term effects can be beneficial. For example, a landslide may allow fresh minerals to be exposed at the surface. These minerals may then be mined or may break down to form soil.

Standards Check Why must city planners determine the risk of mass movement when deciding how to use land? 🐻 **6.2.d**

Rate of Creep
Creep affects all slopes in varying degrees. Imagine a fence post that is located on the side of a hill. The hill is affected by creep at a rate of 1 cm per year. How many years will the fence post take to move 4 m down the side of the hill? Record your work in your **Science Journal.**

SECTION Review

 6.2.d

Summary

- Gravity causes rocks and soil to move downslope.
- If the slope on which material rests is greater than the angle of repose, mass movement will occur.
- Four types of mass movement are rock falls, landslides, mudflows, and creep.
- Landslides may destroy buildings and change wildlife habitats.

Using Vocabulary

Use a term from the section to complete the sentence below.

1 A(n) ___ occurs when a large amount of water mixes with soil and rock.

Understanding Concepts

2 **Identifying** What is mass movement?

3 **Summarizing** How is the angle of repose related to mass movement?

4 **Applying** How do mass movements affect humans?

Critical Thinking

5 **Identifying Relationships** Which types of mass movement are most dangerous to humans? Explain your answer.

6 **Making Inferences** How does deforestation increase the likelihood of mudflows?

Challenge

7 **Analyzing Ideas** Some long term effects of landslides can be beneficial. What are the benefits of fresh minerals rising to the surface?

8 **Predicting Consequences** Creep is a type of mass movement that occurs slowly. Describe the kinds of effects that you think creep has on trees, buildings, and roads.

Internet Resources

For a variety of links related to this chapter, go to www.scilinks.org

Topic: Mass Movement
SciLinks code: HY70917

Model-Making Lab

OBJECTIVES

Demonstrate the effects of wave action and longshore currents on a beach.

Describe ways to decrease the effects of wave action on beach sand.

MATERIALS

- blocks, plaster (2)
- block, wooden, large
- container, plastic, large
- pebbles
- ruler, metric
- sand (5 to 10 lb)
- water

SAFETY

6.2.c Students know beaches are dynamic systems in which the sand is supplied by rivers and moved along the coast by the action of waves.

Investigation and Experimentation
6.7.a Develop a hypothesis.
6.7.b Select and use appropriate tools and technology (including calculators, computers, balances, spring scales, microscopes, and binoculars) to perform tests, collect data, and display data.

Beach Erosion

Coastal management is a growing concern because beaches are increasingly used for resources and recreation. The supply of sand for many beaches has been cut off by dams built on rivers and streams that once carried sand to the sea. Waves generated by storms also continuously wear away beaches. In some places, breakwaters have been built offshore to protect beaches from washing away. In this lab, you will examine how wave action may change the shape of beaches and how these changes can be reduced.

Ask a Question

1 How does wave action affect the amount of sand on a beach? How can these effects be reduced?

Form a Hypothesis

2 Form a hypothesis that answers your question. Explain your reasoning.

Test the Hypothesis

3 Make a beach in a large, shallow container by placing a mixture of sand and small pebbles at one end of the container. The beach should occupy about one-fourth of the length of the container.

4 In front of the sand, add water to a depth of 2 to 3 cm. Record what happens.

5 Use a large wooden block to generate several waves by moving the block up and down in the water at the end of the container opposite the beach. Continue this wave action until about half of the beach has moved. Describe the beach after this wave action has taken place.

6 Empty the container and repeat steps 3 and 4.

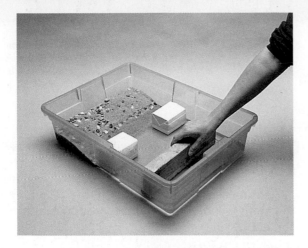

7 Design two breakwaters that change the flow of water along the beach. Draw your designs on a piece of paper. The above photo is a sample of a breakwater arrangement.

8 Have your teacher approve your designs before you build them into your model beach.

9 Use two plaster blocks to model the first breakwater that you designed. Use the wooden block to generate waves as in step 5. Record your observations.

10 Use the wooden block to generate waves that move parallel to the beach. Record your observations.

11 Repeat steps 9 and 10 for your other design. Record your observations.

Analyze the Results

12 Analyzing Results How does wave action build up a beach? How does wave action wear away a beach?

13 Explaining Events Describe what happened to the waves when they encountered the breakwater in step 10.

14 Analyzing Results How do breakwaters modify the effect that longshore currents have on the shape of a beach?

Draw Conclusions

15 Making Predictions Predict what will happen to a beach that is affected by wave action if it has no source of additional sand.

16 Drawing Conclusions What effect would a series of breakwaters have on a beach?

Big Idea Question

17 Evaluating Methods You know that topography is reshaped by the transportation of sediment. How did each of the breakwaters you used affect the transportation of sediment? Which would you recommend for use at a real beach?

Science Skills Activity

Investigation and Experimentation
6.7.b Select and use appropriate tools and technology (including calculators, computers, balances, spring scales, microscopes, and binoculars) to perform tests, collect data, and display data.

Selecting Tools to Collect Data

▶ Tutorial

Scientists need to collect data to perform their work. For scientists to obtain accurate data, they must be able to select appropriate tools for gathering the data. You can select appropriate measuring tools by following these helpful hints.

❶ Identify what characteristic you will be measuring. Are you measuring time, length, volume, temperature, or mass? Different tools are used to measure these characteristics.

❷ Determine the scale of the object you will be measuring. If the object you are measuring is very small or very large, you may want to use different measuring tools.

❸ Decide what units you will use to express your measurement. The scale of the object you are measuring will affect how you express your measurement. For example, a very long length will be better represented by kilometers than by meters.

❹ Choose the best tool for your measurement. Consider the characteristic measured, the object measured, and the scale and units required to select the appropriate measurement tool.

▶ You Try It!

Stopwatch

Balance

Thermometer

Binoculars

Metric ruler

Graduated cylinder

Procedure

Read the following six scenarios. Using the information provided, select from the chart above the appropriate tools to collect the needed data. Each answer should have four parts. For each scenario:

- identify the characteristic to be measured.
- determine the scale of the object to be measured.
- decide what units best express the measurement.
- select the tool or tools you would use to collect the needed data.

❶ You are at a beach and want to collect data about wave period.

❷ You are in the desert and want to collect data about the height of a sand dune.

❸ You are near a kettle lake and want to collect data about the temperature of the water.

❹ You are at a beach and want to know how heavy a handful of sand is.

❺ You are in the mountains and want to collect data about the volume and density of a rock.

❻ You are in a valley and want to see a rock formation on the valley wall.

Chapter Summary

The Big Idea Topography is reshaped by the weathering of rock and soil and by the transportation and deposition of sediment.

Section	Vocabulary

1 Shoreline Erosion and Deposition

Key Concept Beaches and shorelines are shaped largely by the action of ocean waves.

- Energy from waves crashing against rocks affects shorelines.
- Shoreline features are created by wave erosion.
- Waves deposit sediment at the shore to form beaches.

Waves erode and deposit sediment along shorelines.

shoreline p. 332
beach p. 336
undertow p. 337
longshore current p. 337

2 Wind Erosion and Deposition

Key Concept Wind can cause erosion and can move and deposit sediment.

- Wind erosion happens through saltation, deflation, and abrasion.
- Wind can erode and deposit differing amounts and sizes of material, depending on the wind speed.

Wind deposits sediment to form dunes.

saltation p. 340
deflation p. 341
abrasion p. 341
dune p. 342

3 Erosion and Deposition by Ice

Key Concept Glaciers shape Earth's surface by moving rock and sediment.

- As glaciers move, they form a variety of landforms by removing rock and soil
- Glaciers deposit rock material when they melt or retreat.

Alpine glaciers shape the landscape in mountain areas.

glacier p. 344
glacial drift p. 346
till p. 346
stratified drift p. 347

4 Erosion and Deposition by Mass Movement

Key Concept Gravity causes material to move downslope in a process called *mass movement*.

- The angle of repose determines whether mass movement will happen.
- Gravity causes rock falls, landslides, mudflows, and creep.

Landslides are rapid mass movements.

mass movement p. 348
rockfall p. 349
landslide p. 349
mudflow p. 350
creep p. 350

Chapter Review

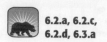 6.2.a, 6.2.c, 6.2.d, 6.3.a

Organize

Layered Book Review the FoldNote that you created at the beginning of the chapter. Add to or correct the FoldNote based on what you have learned.

Using Vocabulary

1. **Academic Vocabulary** In the sentence "Beaches are dynamic systems in which sand is supplied by rivers and moved along the coast by the action of waves," what does the word *dynamic* mean?

For each pair of terms, explain how the meanings of the terms differ.

2. *shoreline* and *longshore current*
3. *beaches* and *dunes*
4. *mudflow* and *creep*

Understanding Concepts

Multiple Choice

5. *Surf* refers to
   a. large storm waves in the open ocean.
   b. giant waves produced by hurricanes.
   c. breaking waves near the shoreline.
   d. small waves on a calm sea.

6. A narrow strip of sand that is formed by wave deposition and is connected to the shore is called a
   a. barrier spit.
   b. sandbar.
   c. wave-cut terrace.
   d. headland.

7. Which of the following terms describes all types of glacial deposits?
   a. glacial drift
   b. dune
   c. till
   d. outwash plain

Short Answer

8. **Identifying** What is the term for a rapid mass movement that flows downhill over a curved surface?

9. **Comparing** Some Earth processes happen quickly, and some Earth processes happen slowly. Which process creates changes in the landscape more slowly, creep or rock fall?

10. **Justifying** Why do waves break when they near the shore?

11. **Analyzing** Why are some areas more affected by wind erosion than other areas are?

12. **Identifying** What kind of mass movement happens continuously?

13. **Identifying** In what direction do sand dunes move?

14. **Describing** Describe the various types of glacial moraines.

15. **Classifying** Wind can shape Earth by erosion and by deposition. Name a landform made by wind erosion and a landform made by wind deposition.

INTERPRETING GRAPHICS Use the diagram below to answer the next three questions.

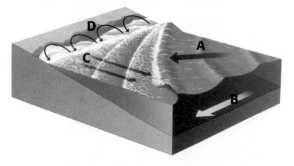

16. **Identifying** What process does this diagram show?

17. **Identifying** What do the lettered arrows **A**, **B**, and **C** represent?

18. **Describing** In what type of pattern does the sand move in **D**?

Writing Skills

19 Communicating Concepts You are interested in purchasing a home that overlooks the ocean. The home that you want to buy sits atop a steep sea cliff. In your own words, describe what factors you would consider when deciding whether you should buy the house. Discuss the most important factors first. Use what you have read about shoreline erosion, mass movement, and land-use decisions.

Critical Thinking

20 Concept Mapping Use the following terms to create a concept map: *wind, saltation, dune, deflation,* and *desert pavement.*

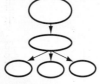

21 Making Inferences How do humans increase the likelihood that wind erosion will occur?

22 Identifying Relationships If the entire ice sheet covering Antarctica melted, what type of landscape would Antarctica likely have?

23 Applying Concepts You are a geologist who is studying rock to determine the direction of flow of an ancient glacier. What clues might help you determine the glacier's direction of flow?

24 Predicting Consequences Describe what kinds of changes could occur in a human habitat if a mudflow occurred in a small mountain town.

25 Predicting Consequences Describe what kinds of changes could occur in a wildlife habitat where creep is happening.

26 Analyzing Processes How do water waves carry and transfer energy from one place to another?

27 Analyzing Relationships Erosion by moving water is a major factor in shaping landscapes. Explain how water waves and glaciers contribute to this component of erosion.

INTERPRETING GRAPHICS The graph below illustrates coastal erosion and deposition at an imaginary beach over a period of eight years. Use the graph to answer the next three questions.

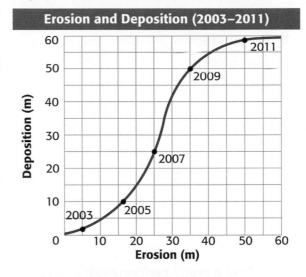

28 Evaluating Data What is happening to the beach over time?

29 Evaluating Data In what year are the amounts of erosion and deposition equal?

30 Forming Hypotheses Based on the erosion and deposition data for 2005, what might have happened to the beach after 2005?

Math Skills

31 Making Calculations If a glacier recedes at the rate of 0.18 km per year, how far will it recede in 3,000 years?

32 Making Calculations If a dune moves 40 m per year, how far does it move in 1 day?

Challenge

33 Making Comparisons The degree of erosion in an area and the types of erosion that affect that area depend on the area's climatic characteristics. Compare how soil in a dry climate and soil in a wet climate would react to high wind speeds. Which soil would be likely to have the most wind erosion?

Standards Assessment

5.3.a, 5.4.b, 5.4.e, 6.2.a,
6.2.c, 6.2.d, 6.3.a, 6.7,
6.7.b

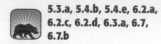

REVIEWING ACADEMIC VOCABULARY

1 Which of the following words means "a detailed search for answers"?

   A conclusion

   B hypothesis

   C investigation

   D report

2 In the sentence "Scientists conduct important experiments to learn more about Earth and its systems," what does the word *conduct* mean?

   A to transmit energy, such as heat

   B to carry out; to do

   C to act in a particular way

   D to lead a group performance

3 Which of the following words is the closest in meaning to the word *display*?

   A show

   B create

   C revise

   D replace

4 In the sentence "Water running downhill is the dominant process in shaping the landscape," what does the word *process* mean?

   A a set of steps, events, or changes

   B a prominent part of an organic structure

   C to subject to analysis or examination

   D to treat or prepare in a series of steps

REVIEWING CONCEPTS

5 How does the energy from a wave in Australia reach the coast of California?

   A Convection currents carry the energy across the ocean.

   B The wave travels in wave trains across the ocean to California.

   C The energy travels in undersea currents to California's coast.

   D The waves disappear for miles and then re-form close to the coast.

6 Which of the following best describes how the sea arch above formed in a coastal area?

   A Salt water dissolves the rock, so a hole is created in the rock formation.

   B A strong storm creates a large hole in the rock formation.

   C The shifting of tectonic plates creates cracks the rock formation.

   D The repeated action of waves slowly wears a hole in the rock formation.

7 Which of the following areas would be most strongly affected by wind erosion?

   A a rain forest

   B a desert

   C a rocky beach

   D a farm

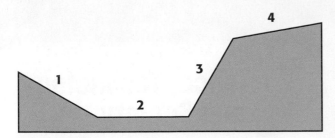

8 Along which section in the diagram above would mass movement be most likely to occur?

A section 1

B section 2

C section 3

D section 4

9 Which of the following statements best explains why sand is different colors at different beaches?

A Varying water temperatures and pressures change the color of sand.

B Sand deposits that formed at different times are different colors.

C Sand is formed from different types of rock, which are different colors.

D Stronger waves bleach sand, so the sand becomes lighter in color.

10 Which of the following phenomena is characterized by the sudden movement of rock and soil down a slope?

A creep

B erosion

C landslide

D volcanic eruption

REVIEWING PRIOR LEARNING

11 Which of the following statements describes the relationship between river water and ocean water?

A Ocean water and river water generally do not interact.

B River water flows into oceans. Water from rivers and oceans evaporates into the atmosphere and falls as precipitation.

C Ocean water flows into rivers and mixes freely with river water.

D Ocean water interacts with river water only when it evaporates and falls into rivers as precipitation.

12 How do oceans affect temperatures on nearby land?

A Oceans always increase temperatures on nearby land.

B Oceans always decrease temperatures on nearby land.

C Oceans moderate temperatures on nearby land.

D Oceans exaggerate temperatures on nearby land.

13 Which of the following statements best describes how air pressure varies with location?

A Air pressure decreases as one moves farther north.

B Air pressure decreases as one moves farther south.

C Air pressure decreases as one moves closer to Earth's surface.

D Air pressure decreases as one moves farther from Earth's surface.

Standards Assessment

Science in Action

Scientific Discoveries

The Lost Squadron

During World War II, an American squadron of eight planes crash-landed on the ice of Greenland. The crew was rescued, but the planes were lost. After the war, several people tried to find the "Lost Squadron." Finally, in 1988, a team of adventurers found the planes by using radar. The planes were buried by 40 years of snowfall and had become part of the Greenland ice sheet! When the planes were found, they were buried under 80 m of glacial ice. Incredibly, the team tunneled down through the ice and recovered a plane. The plane is now named *Glacier Girl*, and it still flies today!

Language Arts ACTiViTY

The crew of the Lost Squadron had to wait 10 days to be rescued by dog sled. If you had been part of the crew, what would you have done to survive? In your **Science Journal**, write a short story that describes your adventure on the ice sheet of Greenland.

Science, Technology, and Society

La Conchita's Recurring Landslides

The coastal community of La Conchita, California, is no stranger to the forces of erosion and deposition. Rapid mass movements, in the form of landslides, have repeatedly affected La Conchita. A major landslide happened in 2005. The 2005 La Conchita landslide damaged 30 homes and killed 10 people. Another major landslide happened in La Conchita in 1995. Geologists think that landslides have been occurring at and near La Conchita for thousands of years.

Math ACTiViTY

Suppose a landslide occurs on a steep slope that is 100 m tall. How long would the sediment at the top of the slope have taken to reach the bottom of the slope if the sediment was traveling at a rate of 12 km/h? Express your answer in seconds. Record your work in your **Science Journal**.

Johan Reinhard

High-Altitude Anthropologist Imagine discovering the mummified body of a girl from 500 years ago! In 1995, while climbing Mount Ampato, one of the tallest mountains in the Andes, Johan Reinhard made an incredible discovery—the well-preserved mummy of a young Inca girl. The recent eruption of a nearby volcano had caused the snow on Mount Ampato to melt which uncovered the mummy. The discovery of the "Inca Ice Maiden" gave scientists a wealth of new information about Incan culture. Today, Reinhard considers the discovery of the Inca Ice Maiden to be his most exciting moment in the field.

Johan Reinhard is an anthropologist. Anthropologists study the physical and cultural characteristics of human populations. Reinhard studied anthropology at the University of Arizona and at the University of Vienna in Austria. Early in his career, Reinhard worked on underwater archeology projects in Austria and Italy and on projects in the mountains of Nepal and Tibet. He made mountains and mountain peoples the focus of his career as an anthropologist. Reinhard spent 10 years in the Himalayas, the highest mountains on Earth. There, he studied the role of sacred mountains in Tibetan religions. Now, Reinhard studies the culture of the ancient Inca in the Andes of South America.

Social Studies AcTiViTY

Find out more about the Inca Ice Maiden or about Ötzi, a mummy that is more than 5,000 years old and that was found in a glacier in Italy. Create a poster that summarizes what scientists have learned from these discoveries.

The Inca Ice Maiden was buried under ice and snow for more than 500 years.

Internet Resources

- To learn more about careers in science, visit **www.scilinks.org** and enter the SciLinks code HY70225.

- To learn more about these Science in Action topics, visit **go.hrw.com** and type in the keyword HY7ICEF.

- Check out articles related to this chapter by visiting **go.hrw.com**. Just type in the keyword HY7ICEC.

Improving Comprehension

Graphic Organizers are important visual tools that can help you organize information and improve your reading comprehension. The Graphic Organizer below is called *combination notes.* Instructions for creating other types of Graphic Organizers are located in the **Study Skills** section of the Appendix.

How to Make Combination Notes

1 Draw a table like the one shown below. Draw the columns to be as long as you want them to be.

2 Write the topic of your notes in the section at the top of the table.

3 In the left column, write important phrases or sentences about the topic. In the right column, draw diagrams or pictures that illustrate the information in the left column.

When to Use Combination Notes

Combination notes let you express scientific information in words and pictures at the same time. Use combination notes to express information that a picture could help explain. The picture could be a diagram, a sketch, or another useful visual representation of the written information in your notes.

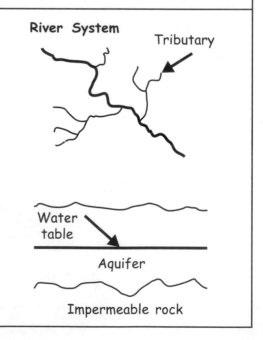

Rivers and Groundwater

Rivers
- A **river system** is a network of streams and rivers that drain an area of its runoff.
- A stream that flows into a lake or into a larger stream is called a **tributary**.

Groundwater
- **Groundwater** is the water in rocks below Earth's surface.
- The rock layer that stores the groundwater and allows it to flow is called an **aquifer**.
- The upper surface of the underground water is called the **water table**.

River System

Tributary

Water table

Aquifer

Impermeable rock

You Try It!

This Reading Strategy can also be used within the chapter that you are about to read. Practice making your own combination notes as directed in the Reading Strategies for Section **1** and Section **2**. Record your work in your **Science Journal.**

Unpacking the Standards

The information below "unpacks" the standards by breaking them down into basic parts. The higher-level, academic vocabulary is highlighted and defined to help you understand the language of the standards. "What It Means" restates the standards as simply as possible.

California Standard	Academic Vocabulary	What It Means
🐻 **6.2.a** Students know water running downhill is the **dominant process** in shaping the landscape, including California's landscape.	**dominant** (DAHM uh nuhnt) having the greatest effect **process** (PRAH ses) a set of steps, events, or changes	Water running in rivers and over the land is the most important force in changing the natural shape of Earth's surface.
🐻 **6.2.b** Students know rivers and streams are **dynamic** systems that **erode, transport** sediment, change course, and flood their banks in natural and recurring patterns.	**dynamic** (die NAM ik) active; tending toward change **erode** (ee ROHD) to wear away **transport** (trans PAWRT) to carry from one place to another	Rivers and streams wear away and move rock and soil fragments, change their paths, and overflow their banks in natural patterns that happen over and over and year after year.
🐻 **6.2.d** Students know earthquakes, volcanic eruptions, landslides, and floods change human and wildlife habitats.		Earthquakes, volcanic eruptions, landslides, and floods change the surroundings in which humans and wildlife live.
🐻 **6.4.a** Students know the sun is the **major source** of **energy** for **phenomena** on Earth's surface; it powers winds, ocean currents, and the water **cycle.**	**major** (MAY juhr) of great importance or large scale **source** (SAWRS) the thing from which something else comes **energy** (EN uhr jee) the ability to make things happen **phenomenon** (fuh NAHM uh NUHN) any facts or events that can be sensed or described scientifically (plural *phenomena*) **cycle** (SIE kuhl) a repeating series of changes	The sun is the main source of energy for processes on Earth. Energy from the sun powers winds, ocean currents, and the water cycle.
🐻 **6.6.b** Students know different natural **energy** and material **resources,** including air, soil, rocks, minerals, petroleum, fresh water, wildlife, and forests, and know how to classify them as renewable or nonrenewable.	**energy** (EN uhr jee) the ability to make things happen **resource** (REE SAWRS) anything that can be used to take care of a need	You must be able to identify different natural resources, such as air, soil, rocks, minerals, petroleum, fresh water, wildlife, and forests, and be able to identify whether each resource can be replaced rapidly or not.

11

Rivers and Groundwater

The Big Idea

Topography is reshaped as water flows downhill in streams and rivers.

California Standards

Focus on Earth Sciences
6.2 Topography is reshaped by the weathering of rock and soil and by the transportation and deposition of sediment. (Sections 1 and 2)
6.4 Many phenomena on Earth's surface are affected by the transfer of energy through radiation and convection currents. (Section 1)
6.6 Sources of energy and materials differ in amounts, distribution, usefulness, and the time required for their formation. (Section 3)

Investigation and Experimentation
6.7 Scientific progress is made by asking meaningful questions and conducting careful investigations. (Science Skills Activity)

Math
6.1.3, 6.1.4 Number Sense
6.2.3 Algebra and Functions

English–Language Arts
6.1.1 Reading
6.1.1, 6.1.2, 6.1.3, 6.2.2, 6.2.5 Writing

About the Photo

Rivers are powerful forces that can cause significant property damage when they flood. When the Cuyama River rose after heavy rainfall, the river split Route 66 between Nipomo and Santa Maria in two.

Organize

Booklet

Before you read this chapter, create the FoldNote entitled "Booklet." On the front cover, title the booklet "Rivers and Groundwater." Label each page of the booklet with the title of one of the sections in the chapter. As you read the chapter, fill in the booklet with details from each section on the appropriate page.

Instructions for creating FoldNotes are located in the Study Skills section on p. 616 of the Appendix.

Explore Activity

⏱ 25 min

The Sun and the Water Cycle

Observe the role of the sun as a source of energy for the water cycle.

Procedure

1. Fill **two sealable plastic bags** with about **100 mL of water.** Seal the bags to prevent the water from leaking.

2. Wrap one of the bags completely in a **sheet of aluminum foil.**

3. Place both sealed bags side by side in direct sunlight. Leave the setup undisturbed.

4. After 15 minutes, remove the aluminum foil cover. Observe the appearance of the contents of the two bags.

5. Record your observations.

Analysis

6.4.a

6. What was the role of the aluminum foil? Could you have used a piece of clear plastic instead? Explain.

7. Compare and contrast the appearance of the contents of the two bags after 15 minutes of exposure to direct sunlight.

8. Explain how this activity can be used to demonstrate the role of the sun as a source of energy for the water cycle.

The Active River

Key Concept Water running downhill is the dominant process in shaping the landscape.

What You Will Learn

- Moving water shapes the surface of Earth by the process of erosion.
- The sun is the major source of energy that drives the water cycle.
- Three factors that affect the rate of stream erosion are gradient, discharge, and load.

Why It Matters

Factors that affect how water moves over the surface of Earth influence the shape of Earth's landscape.

Vocabulary

- erosion
- divide
- water cycle
- channel
- tributary
- load
- watershed

READING STRATEGY

Graphic Organizer In your **Science Journal,** create Combination Notes that express information about the stages of river development both in words and in pictures or diagrams.

▶ Imagine that you fell asleep with your toes dangling in the Colorado River 6 million years ago. Today, you wake up to find that your toes are hanging about 1.6 km (about 1 mi) above the river! The Colorado River carved the Grand Canyon, shown in **Figure 1,** by washing billions of tons of rock and sediment from its riverbed. This process can take millions of years.

Rivers: Agents of Erosion

Six million years ago, the area now known as the Grand Canyon was nearly as flat as a pancake. Tectonic uplift raised the land, and water running downhill became the Colorado River. The Colorado River cut down into the rock and formed the Grand Canyon over millions of years through the process of erosion. **Erosion** is the process by which wind, water, ice, and gravity move soil and sediment from one place to another. Rivers, such as the Colorado River, are agents of erosion that shape Earth's landscape. Because of erosion caused by water, the Grand Canyon is now about 1.6 km deep and 446 km long. In this section, you will learn about stream development and river systems. You will also learn about factors that affect the rate of stream erosion.

Standards Check What is erosion, and how does it shape Earth's landscape? 🐻 **6.2.a, 6.2.b**

Figure 1 *The Grand Canyon is located in northwestern Arizona. The canyon formed over millions of years as running water eroded the rock layers.*

6.2.a Students know water running downhill is the dominant process in shaping the landscape, including California's landscape.
6.2.b Students know rivers and streams are dynamic systems that erode, transport sediment, change course, and flood their banks in natural and recurring patterns.
6.4.a Students know the sun is the major source of energy for phenomena on Earth's surface; it powers winds, ocean currents, and the water cycle.

The Water Cycle

Have you ever wondered where the water in rivers comes from? This water is part of the water cycle. The **water cycle,** shown in **Figure 2,** is the continuous movement of water between the atmosphere, the land, and the oceans. The major source of energy that drives the water cycle is the sun.

Standards Check Describe the water cycle. 🐻6.4.a

erosion (ee ROH zhuhn) the process by which wind, water, ice, or gravity transports soil and sediment from one location to another

water cycle (WAWT uhr SIE kuhl) the continuous movement of water between the atmosphere, the land, and the oceans

Figure 2 The Water Cycle

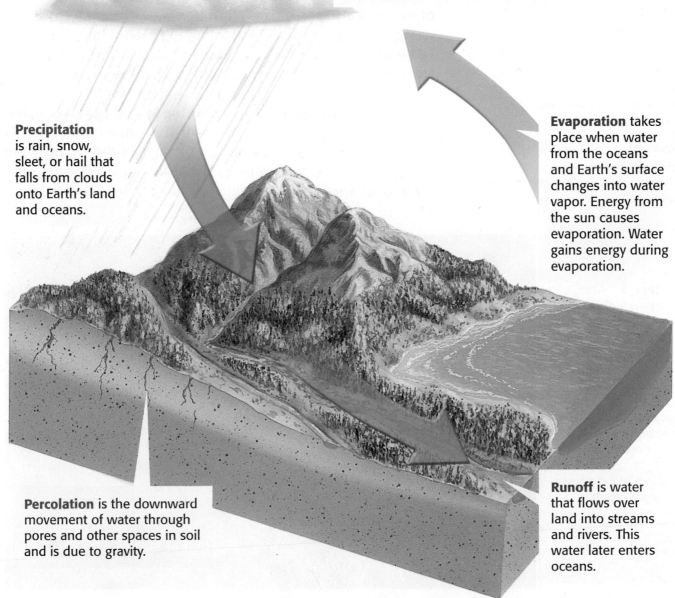

Condensation takes place when water vapor cools and changes into water droplets that form clouds in the atmosphere. Water loses energy during condensation.

Precipitation is rain, snow, sleet, or hail that falls from clouds onto Earth's land and oceans.

Evaporation takes place when water from the oceans and Earth's surface changes into water vapor. Energy from the sun causes evaporation. Water gains energy during evaporation.

Percolation is the downward movement of water through pores and other spaces in soil and is due to gravity.

Runoff is water that flows over land into streams and rivers. This water later enters oceans.

River Systems

The next time you take a shower, notice that individual drops of water join to become small streams. These streams join other small streams and form larger streams. Eventually, all of the water flows down the drain. Every time you shower, you make a model of a river system. A *river system* is a network of streams and rivers that drain an area of its runoff. A stream that flows into a lake or into a larger stream is called a **tributary.**

Standards Check Describe the difference between a tributary and a river system. 🐻 **6.2.b**

Watersheds and Divides

River systems are divided into regions called watersheds. A **watershed** is the area of land that is drained by a river system. Watersheds vary in size. The largest watershed in the United States is the Mississippi River watershed. This watershed has hundreds of tributaries. These tributaries extend from the Rocky Mountains, in the West, to the Appalachian Mountains, in the East. A main stream that drains a large watershed and has many tributaries is called a *river.*

The image in **Figure 3** shows that the Mississippi River watershed covers more than one-third of the United States. Other major watersheds are the Columbia River, the Rio Grande, and the Colorado River watersheds. Watersheds are separated from each other by an area of higher ground called a **divide.**

INTERNET ACTIVITY

Erosion Disasters

What are the differences between youthful, mature, and old rivers? Create a brochure on the recreational activities that you would recommend at each type of river. Go to **go.hrw.com,** and type in the keyword HY7DEPW.

tributary (TRIB yoo TER ee) a stream that flows into a lake or into a larger stream

watershed (WAWT uhr SHED) the area of land that is drained by a river system

divide (duh VIED) the boundary between drainage areas that have streams that flow in opposite directions

channel (CHAN uhl) the path that a stream follows

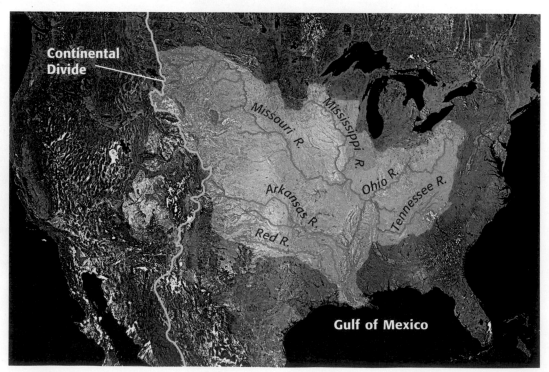

Figure 3 *The Continental Divide runs through the Rocky Mountains. It separates the watersheds that flow into the Atlantic Ocean and the Gulf of Mexico from those that flow into the Pacific Ocean. The Mississippi River watershed is shown in light green.*

Figure 4 **California Rivers That Have Different Gradients**

This stream in John Muir Wilderness has a high gradient. Therefore, the stream flows swiftly downhill over rocks.

Mad River Slough near Eureka, has a low gradient. It flows slowly and has less erosive energy than streams with a high gradient.

Stream Erosion

A stream forms as water erodes soil and rock to make a channel. A **channel** is the path that a stream follows. As the stream continues to erode rock and soil, the channel gets wider and deeper. Over time, tributaries join the main channel. The increased water flow from the tributaries causes the stream to become longer and wider.

Gradient

Figure 4 shows two rivers that have very different gradients. *Gradient* is the measure of the change in elevation over a certain distance. The water in a stream or river that has a high gradient moves very rapidly. This rapid water flow gives the stream or river a lot of energy to erode rock and soil. A river or stream that has a low gradient has less energy for erosion.

Standards Check How does gradient affect the erosion of stream channels? 6.2.b

Discharge

The amount of water that a stream or river carries in a given amount of time is called *discharge*. The discharge of a stream increases when a major storm occurs or when warm weather rapidly melts snow. As the stream's discharge increases, the water's speed and erosive energy increase. The amount of solid material that the stream can carry also increases.

SCHOOL to HOME

Floating down the River

At home with a parent or guardian, study a map of the United States. Find the Mississippi River. Imagine that you are planning a rafting trip down the river. On the map, trace the route of your trip from Lake Itasca, Minnesota, to the mouth of the river in Louisiana. If you were floating down the Mississippi River on a raft, what major tributaries would you pass? What cities would you pass? Mark them on the map. How many kilometers would you travel on this trip?

ACTIVITY

Load

The materials carried by a stream are called the stream's **load.** The three types of load are shown in **Figure 5.** The size of the particles in a stream's load is affected by the stream's speed. Fast-moving streams can carry large particles. Rocks and pebbles bounce and scrape along the bottom and sides of the stream bed. Thus, a stream that has a load of large particles has a high rate of erosion. Streams that move more slowly carry smaller particles and have less erosive energy.

Standards Check How does load affect rates of erosion? 6.2.b

Figure 5   **Three Types of Load**

A stream can bounce large materials, such as pebbles and boulders, along the stream bed. These rocks are called the **bed load.**

A stream can carry sand in suspension. These materials, called the **suspended load,** make the river look muddy.

The **dissolved load** is material carried in solution, which means that the material is dissolved in the water. Sodium and calcium are some of the materials in the dissolved load.

River's Load

As a fast-moving river slows down, some of its load will settle. Use the following procedure to model the ways in which sediments in a river's load may settle.

▶ Try It!

1. Add **water** to a **plastic soda bottle** until the bottle is two-thirds full.

2. Add **30 g (1/4 cup) of soil**, a **large handful of pebbles,** and **40 g (3 Tbsp) of salt** to the bottle.

3. Twist the cap onto the bottle. Shake the bottle vigorously until all of the sediment is mixed in the rapidly moving water.

4. Set the bottle on the table. Draw a diagram of what you observe.

▶ Think About It!

5. Which materials best represent a river's bed load, suspended load, and dissolved load? Label each type of load on your diagram.

6. Which sediment settled first? Which sediment settled last?

7. What can you conclude about the size of the sediment and the rate at which the sediment settles?

6.2.b

🕐 **20 min**

Describing Rivers

William Morris Davis was a geomorphologist who studied how rivers shape the landscape. His studies of rivers in the Appalachian Mountains helped him develop a model to describe the stages of river development. In his model, rivers went through a series of stages. Davis described rivers as evolving from a youthful stage to an old-age stage. He thought that all rivers eroded in the same way and at the same rate.

Today, scientists support a model that differs from Davis's model. Because materials erode at different rates, one river may develop more quickly than another river does. Many factors, such as climate, local geology, gradient, and load, influence the development of a river. Scientists no longer use Davis's model to explain river development. But they still use many of his terms to describe a river. These terms describe a river's general features, not a river's actual age.

Youthful Rivers

A youthful river erodes its channel deeper rather than wider. Its channel is narrow and straight. The river tumbles over rocks in rapids and waterfalls. Youthful rivers have very few tributaries. These rivers flow quickly because they have steep gradients. Many youthful rivers have steep gradients because the areas that these rivers drain have been tectonically uplifted. A youthful river in Wyoming is shown in **Figure 6.**

Figure 6 *This youthful river is located in Yellowstone National Park in Wyoming. Rapids and falls exist where the river flows over hard, resistant rock.*

Standards Check Describe a youthful river. 🐻 **6.2.b**

Figure 7 *A mature river, such as this one in the Amazon basin of Peru, curves back and forth.*

Figure 8 *The rejuvenated river above is located in Canyonlands National Park in Utah.*

Figure 9 *This old river is located in New Zealand.*

Mature Rivers

Unlike a youthful river, a mature river erodes its channel wider rather than deeper. The gradient of a mature river is not as steep as that of a youthful river. Therefore, a mature river has fewer falls and rapids. A mature river is fed by many tributaries. Because of its large watershed, a mature river has more discharge than a youthful river does. A mature river is shown in **Figure 7.** Notice that a mature river tends to curve back and forth. These curves or bends in the river's channel are called *meanders*.

Standards Check Describe the difference between youthful rivers and mature rivers in terms of how these rivers erode their channels. 6.2.b

Rejuvenated Rivers

A rejuvenated (ri JOO vuh NAYT ed) river forms where the land has been raised by tectonic activity. When land rises, the river's gradient becomes steeper and the river flows more quickly. This rapid water flow allows the river to cut more deeply into the valley floor. Steplike formations called *terraces* commonly form on both sides of a stream valley because of rejuvenation, as **Figure 8** shows.

Old Rivers

An old river has a low gradient, so it has little erosive energy. Instead of widening and deepening its banks, the river deposits rock and soil in and along its channel. An old river has wide, flat floodplains, or river valleys, and many bends. An old river also has fewer tributaries than a mature river does. An old river has fewer tributaries because its smaller tributaries have joined together. An old river commonly forms an oxbow lake, such as the one shown in **Figure 9.** An oxbow lake forms when the strip of land that separates parts of a meander is eroded. This process shortens the river's length.

Summary

- Rivers shape Earth's landscape through the process of erosion.
- The sun is the major source of energy that drives the water cycle.
- A river system is made up of a network of streams and rivers.
- A watershed is a region that collects runoff water that then becomes part of a river system that drains into a lake or the ocean.
- Gradient affects the speed at which water flows in a stream. The higher the gradient, the faster the water flows. Water that flows rapidly has a lot of energy for eroding soil and rock.
- When a stream's discharge increases, the stream's erosive energy also increases.
- A stream can carry eroded particles as bed load, suspended load, or dissolved load. A stream that has a load of large particles has a high rate of erosion.
- A river can be described as youthful, mature, old, or rejuvenated based on its characteristics.

Using Vocabulary

1 Use *water cycle*, *tributary*, *channel*, and *load* in separate sentences.

2 Write an original definition for *watershed*, *erosion*, and *divide*.

Understanding Concepts

3 **Evaluating** Explain how gradient affects a stream's erosive energy.

4 **Describing** How did erosion by water running downhill form the Grand Canyon?

5 **Analyzing** Explain how the sun's energy drives the water cycle.

6 **Summarizing** What are three factors that affect the rate of stream erosion?

7 **Comparing** Which type of river is characterized by flat floodplains?

Critical Thinking

8 **Making Inferences** How are river systems part of the water cycle?

9 **Making Comparisons** How do youthful rivers, mature rivers, and old rivers differ?

INTERPRETING GRAPHICS Use the pie graph below to answer the next two questions.

Distribution of Water in the World

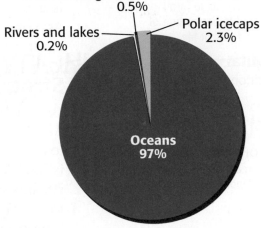

Water underground, in soil, and in air
0.5%

Rivers and lakes
0.2%

Polar icecaps
2.3%

Oceans
97%

10 **Evaluating Data** Where is most of the water in the world located?

11 **Evaluating Data** In what form is the majority of the world's fresh water?

Challenge

12 **Analyzing Processes** Explain how a river system is part of the water cycle. Then, describe how the Earth's water cycle and river systems may be affected if the sun's rays are significantly blocked by pollutants in the atmosphere.

Internet Resources

For a variety of links related to this chapter, go to www.scilinks.org

Topic: Rivers and Streams
SciLinks code: HY71316

Stream and River Deposits

Key Concept Rivers and streams are dynamic systems that erode, transport sediment, change course, and flood their banks in natural and recurring patterns.

What You Will Learn

- Three types of stream deposits are deltas, alluvial fans, and floodplains.
- Rivers and streams flood their banks in natural and recurring patterns, and these floods affect humans and wildlife habitats.

Why It Matters

The cycle of deposition and flooding can bring nutrients to farmland but can also lead to destruction of property and loss of life.

Vocabulary

- deposition
- alluvial fan
- delta
- floodplain

READING STRATEGY

Graphic Organizer In your **Science Journal,** create Combination Notes about the landforms created by stream deposits.

▶ If your job were to carry millions of tons of rock and soil across the United States, how would you do it? You might use a bulldozer or a dump truck, but your job would still take a long time. Did you know that rivers do this job every day?

Rivers and streams carry large amounts of material, such as soil and rock. Acting as liquid conveyor belts, rivers may carry fertile soil to farmland and wetlands. Although erosion is a big problem, rivers also renew soils and form new land. As you will see in this section, rivers make many different landforms on Earth's surface.

Stream Deposits

You have learned how flowing water erodes Earth's surface. After rivers erode rock and soil, they drop, or *deposit*, their load downstream. **Deposition** is the process in which material is laid down or dropped. Rock and soil that are deposited by streams are called *sediment*. Rivers and streams deposit sediment where the speed of the water decreases. **Figure 1** shows how deposition happens as a river meanders.

Figure 1 *Erosion and deposition occur at a bend, or meander, in this Alaskan river.*

Erosion occurs along the outside bank of the bend, where the water flows faster.

Deposition occurs along the inside bank of the bend, where the water flows slower.

6.2.a Students know water running downhill is the dominant process in shaping the landscape, including California's landscape.
6.2.b Students know rivers and streams are dynamic systems that erode, transport sediment, change course, and flood their banks in natural and recurring patterns.
6.2.d Students know earthquakes, volcanic eruptions, landslides, and floods change human and wildlife habitats.

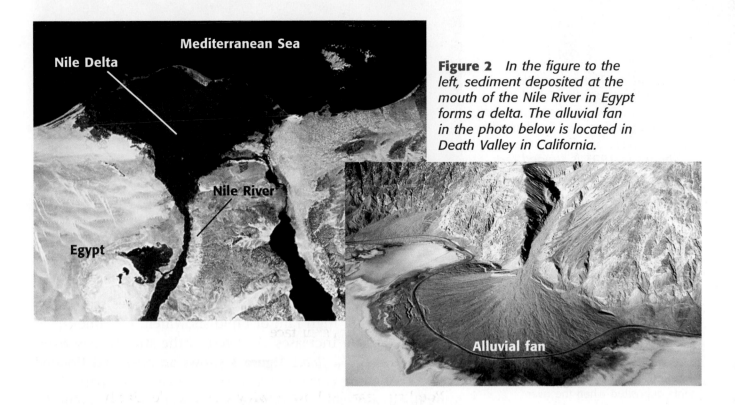

Mediterranean Sea

Nile Delta

Nile River

Egypt

Alluvial fan

Figure 2 *In the figure to the left, sediment deposited at the mouth of the Nile River in Egypt forms a delta. The alluvial fan in the photo below is located in Death Valley in California.*

Deltas

A river's current slows when a river empties into a large body of water, such as a lake or an ocean. As its current slows, a river may deposit its load in a fan-shaped pattern called a **delta.** In **Figure 2,** you can see an astronaut's view of the Nile Delta in Africa. A delta forms on a flat surface and is made mostly of mud. These mud deposits form new land and cause the coastline to grow. The world's deltas are home to a rich diversity of plant and animal life.

In the United States, the Mississippi Delta has formed where the Mississippi River flows into the Gulf of Mexico. Each of the fine mud particles in the delta began its journey far upstream. Parts of Louisiana are made up of particles that came from places as far away as Montana, Minnesota, Ohio, and Illinois!

deposition (DEP uh ZISH uhn) the process in which material is laid down

delta (DEL tuh) a fan-shaped mass of material deposited at the mouth of a stream

alluvial fan (uh LOO vee uhl FAN) a fan-shaped mass of material deposited by a stream when the slope of the land decreases sharply

Alluvial Fans

When a fast-moving mountain stream flows onto a flat plain, the stream slows down quickly. As the stream slows down, it deposits sediment. The sediment forms an alluvial fan, such as the one shown in **Figure 2. Alluvial fans** are fan-shaped deposits of material, that unlike deltas, form on dry land. Alluvial fans can be found in some desert regions of California.

Standards Check How are deltas and alluvial fans examples of ways in which rivers and streams change Earth's landscape? 6.2.a, 6.2.b

Figure 3 *The normal flow of the Mississippi River and the Missouri River is shown in black. The area that was flooded when both rivers overflowed their banks in 1993 is shaded red.*

Mississippi River

Missouri River

Floods

The amount of water in a stream usually varies seasonally. During periods of high rain or rapid snowmelt, the amount of water in a stream increases. As a result, the stream may overflow its banks in a *flood.* **Figure 3** shows an area that flooded in 1993. Flooding can cause a stream to change its path. During a flood, a stream's bank may collapse and may change the water's course. This process commonly forms oxbow lakes.

When a stream floods, a layer of sediment is deposited on the land that is flooded. The area along a river that forms from sediment deposited when a river overflows its banks is called a **floodplain.** Floodplains are rich farming areas because periodic flooding brings new soil to the land.

floodplain (FLUHD PLAYN) an area along a river that forms from sediments deposited when the river overflows its banks

Quick Lab

Make Your Own Lake

In this lab, you will demonstrate how erosion can redirect a stream's course by creating an oxbow lake.

6.2.a
6.2.b

▶ Try It!

1. Cover the bottom of a **plastic tub** with **sand** to a depth of 3 cm.

2. Carve a meandering channel in the sand along the length of the tub. Elevate one end of the tub so that one end of the river channel is higher than the other.

3. Fill completely with **water** a **container that has a closable spout.**

4. Holding the spout over the higher edge of the tub, allow water to flow from the container into the channel.

▶ Think About It!

5. Draw a diagram of what you observe. Label the area where erosion caused the oxbow lake. Draw arrows to show the direction of the stream, including how the direction changed.

6. Explain how this lab shows how water running downhill shapes Earth's landscape.

 20 min

Effects of Floods

Floods are natural events that happen in recurring patterns. These natural events can cause a great deal of damage. Wildlife habitats can be buried or washed away. Human property may be damaged. The flooding of the Mississippi River in 1993 caused damage in nine states. Farms were destroyed, and whole towns were evacuated. Many people have lost their lives to floods. As **Figure 4** shows, flash flooding, which can happen unexpectedly after a severe storm, can take a driver by surprise.

Barriers can help to control floods. One type of barrier is called a *dam*. A dam is a barrier that can redirect and hold a portion of the floodwater in a reservoir. Another type of barrier that can help control flooding is a *levee*. A levee is the buildup of sediment deposited along the channel of a river. This buildup helps keep the river inside its banks. Sandbags can be used to build artificial levees to control water during flooding.

Standards Check List two ways in which floods affect people.
🐻 6.2.d

Figure 4 *Cars driven on flooded roads can easily be carried down to deeper, more dangerous water.*

SECTION
Review

 6.2.a, 6.2.b, 6.2.d

Summary

- Sediment forms several types of deposits, such as deltas, alluvial fans, and floodplains.

- A delta is a fan-shaped deposit of sediment that forms where a river meets a large body of water.

- Alluvial fans can form when a river deposits sediment on land.

- Flooding brings rich soil to farmland and may cause a stream to change course.

- Flooding can also lead to property damage and death.

Using Vocabulary

1. Write an original definition for *deposition* and *floodplain*.

Understanding Concepts

2. **Evaluating** Where do rivers and streams deposit sediments?

3. **Analyzing** Why are floodplains both good and bad areas for people to live?

4. **Evaluating** Describe three landscape features that form as a result of stream deposition.

5. **Identifying** When do floods happen?

Critical Thinking

6. **Applying Concepts** Floods are natural events. Why do humans try to prevent floods?

Math Skills

7. **Using Equations** A river flows at a speed of 8 km/h. If you floated down this river on a raft, how far would you have traveled after 5 h?

Challenge

8. **Predicting Consequences** Dams can cause problems as well as prevent flooding. List reasons why blocking the flow of a river could cause problems. Then, determine strategies to avoid the problems, or provide alternatives to damming.

Internet Resources

For a variety of links related to this chapter, go to www.scilinks.org
Topic: Stream Deposits
SciLinks code: HY71458

SECTION 3

Using Water Wisely

Key Concept Water resources can be endangered by pollution or overuse.

What You Will Learn

- California's water needs are supplied by using groundwater and surface water, by transporting water from one region of California to another, and by importing water from other areas.
- Conserving water and protecting water sources are important in California because the water supply is limited.

Why It Matters

Polluted water can be harmful to you and to the environment.

Vocabulary

- aquifer
- water table
- water pollution
- conservation

READING STRATEGY

Clarifying Concepts Take turns reading this section out loud with a partner. Stop to discuss ideas that seem confusing.

▶ Did you know that almost 65% of your body is made of water? You depend on clean, fresh drinking water to maintain that 65% of you. But the amount of fresh water available on Earth is limited. Only 3% of Earth's water is drinkable. And of the 3% of Earth's water that is drinkable, 75% is frozen in the polar icecaps. Therefore, protecting our water resources is important.

Groundwater

Although you can see some of Earth's water in streams and lakes, you cannot see the large amount of water that flows underground. Rainwater and water from streams seeps through the soil and into underground rock and soil. Then, water collects in spaces between rock particles. The water found inside the rocks below Earth's surface is called *groundwater*. The rock layer that stores groundwater and allows the flow of groundwater is called an **aquifer**. As **Figure 1** shows, the upper surface of underground water is called the **water table**. The water table can rise or fall depending on the amount of water in the aquifer. In wet regions, the water table can be at or just beneath the soil's surface.

Figure 1 *Aquifers contain pores and open spaces to hold water and to allow water to flow.* **After heavy rains, would you expect the water table to rise or drop?**

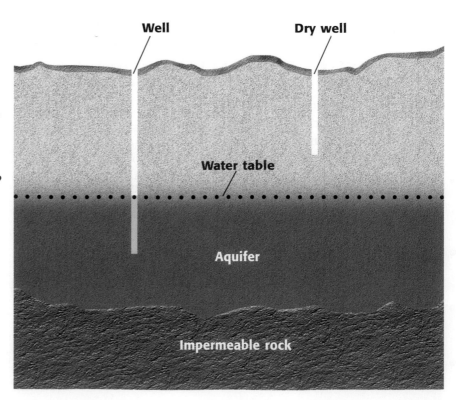

6.6.b Students know different natural energy and material resources, including air, soil, rocks, minerals, petroleum, fresh water, wildlife, and forests, and know how to classify them as renewable or nonrenewable.

378 Chapter 11 Rivers and Groundwater

Water in California

California's aquifers are shown in **Figure 2.** Unfortunately, many of these aquifers are contaminated by pollutants. Also, in some of these aquifers, more water is being pumped out than is being replaced by rain. This process is called an *overdraft*.

Californians get their water not only from the ground but also from surface water, such as rain. Surface water is captured and stored in reservoirs. The water you drink and use to shower in may come from one of these reservoirs.

Where Does It Come From?

The area of California that is north of Sacramento receives about 75% of the annual precipitation in California. But about 75% of the demand for water comes from the area south of Sacramento. Most Californians live in Southern California, and most irrigated farmland is in Central California. Thus, much of the state depends on a system that moves water between places. The California Aqueduct in **Figure 3** carries water from Northern California to Southern California. Still, Northern California's abundant rainfall is not enough to meet the water needs of other parts of the state. Therefore, California receives water from nearby areas, such as Oregon, Colorado, and Mexico.

Standards Check List all sources from which Californians get water.
6.6.b

Where Does It Go?

The agriculture industry in California is the leading producer of crops in the United States. Depending on the year's water balance, this industry can use up to 50% of the state's water supply. The state's water supply also is used for environmental management. Finally, businesses and households use the water supply. This use of water is called *urban use*.

aquifer (AK wuh fuhr) a body of rock or sediment that stores groundwater and allows the flow of groundwater
Wordwise The root *aqui-* means "water." The suffix *-fer* means "to carry."

water table (WAWT uhr TAY buhl) the upper surface of underground water

Figure 2 *The shaded areas of the map below represent aquifers in California. The aquifer represented in dark blue is the Central Valley aquifer system.*

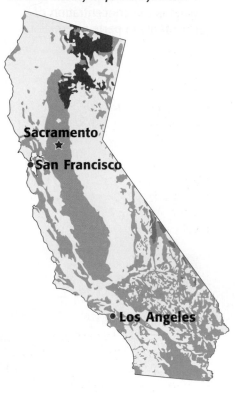

Figure 3 *The California Aqueduct supplies water from Northern California to Los Angeles.*

Water Pollution

Water pollution is waste matter or other material that is introduced into water and that is harmful to organisms. Water pollution is harmful to organisms that live in, drink, or are exposed to the water. Surface water, such as the water in rivers and lakes, and groundwater can be polluted by waste from cities, factories, and farms. Water can become so polluted that it cannot be used anymore. In some cases, it can be deadly.

Sources of Water Pollution

To prevent water pollution, people must understand where pollutants come from. **Figure 4** shows major sources of groundwater pollution. Pollution can come from a single source, such as a factory or a leaking gas station tank. Often, pollution from a single source can be identified and traced to the source. But when pollution comes from various sources, identifying those sources may be hard. For example, a river can be polluted by runoff from any of the land in the river's watershed. If a farm, a road, or any other land surface in a watershed is polluted, runoff from a rainstorm can carry the pollution into a nearby river or lake.

MATH PRACTICE

Parts per Million

The concentration of pollutants in water is commonly expressed in parts per million (ppm). If a 1,000,000 L sample of water contains 5 L of pollutants, the concentration of pollutants is 5ppm. If a 10,000,000 L sample of water contains 40 L of pollutants, what is the concentration of pollutants in parts per million?

Figure 4 **Examples of Groundwater Pollution**

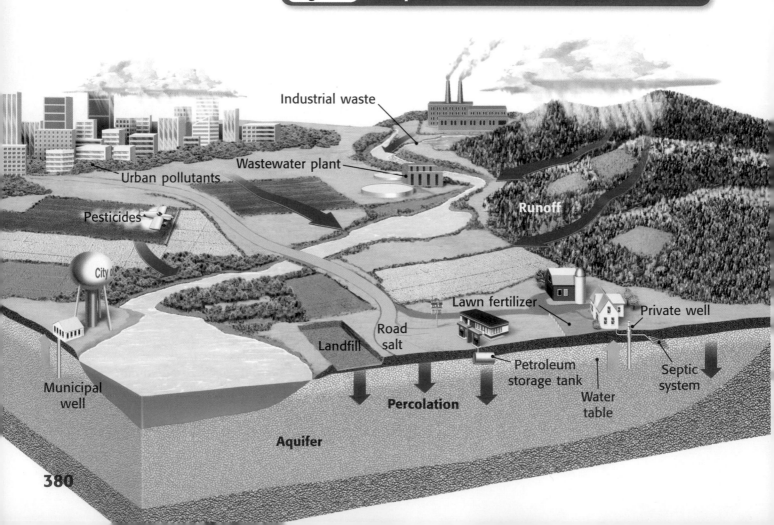

Industrial waste

Wastewater plant

Urban pollutants

Pesticides

Runoff

City of

Lawn fertilizer

Private well

Municipal well

Landfill

Road salt

Petroleum storage tank

Percolation

Water table

Septic system

Aquifer

Figure 5 *The Cuyahoga River in Ohio was so polluted with petroleum and petroleum byproducts that it caught on fire and burned in 1969.*

The Clean Water Act of 1972

In 1969, the Cuyahoga River in Cleveland, Ohio, was so polluted that the river caught on fire and burned for several days, as shown in **Figure 5.** This shocking event helped pass the Clean Water Act of 1972. The stated purpose of the act was to "restore and maintain the chemical, physical, and biological integrity of the nation's waters." The goal of the act was to make all surface water clean enough for fishing and swimming by 1983. This goal was not achieved. However, much progress has been made since the act was passed. The number of lakes and rivers that are fit for swimming and fishing has increased. Many states, including California, have passed stricter water-quality standards of their own.

water pollution (WAWT uhr puh LOO shuhn) waste matter or other material that is introduced into water and that is harmful to organisms that live in, drink, or are exposed to the water

Other Water-Quality Laws

The Clean Water Act of 1972 opened the door for other water-quality laws. For example, the Marine Protection, Research, and Sanctuaries Act of 1972 has strengthened the laws against ocean dumping. The Oil Pollution Act of 1990 requires all oil tankers traveling in U.S. waters to have double hulls by 2015 as an added protection against oil spills. The Safe Drinking Water Act of 1975 introduced programs to protect groundwater and surface water from pollution.

Legislation has improved water quality in the United States. However, the cooperation of individuals, businesses, and the government will be essential to maintain a clean water supply in the future.

Standards Check Summarize how the Clean Water Act of 1972 has helped reduce water pollution. **6.6.b**

Figure 6 *This xeriscaped yard in Arizona features plants that are native to the state.*

Water Conservation

Fresh water is a limited natural resource. To make sure that we have enough clean water to meet our needs, we must conserve it. **Conservation** is the preservation and wise use of natural resources. Water can be conserved in many ways.

Conserving Water in Agriculture and Industry

In agriculture, farmers have learned that most water loss comes from evaporation and runoff. The amount of water loss in agriculture can be reduced by using drip irrigation. Drip irrigation systems deliver small amounts of water directly to plant roots. The plants take up the water before the water can evaporate or run off.

Many industries conserve water by recycling cooling water and wastewater. Instead of discharging used water into a nearby river, businesses often recycle water and use it again.

Conserving Water at Home

While households use less water than the agriculture industry does, conserving water at home is important. A few changes to household water use can add significantly to water conservation. Installing low-flow toilets and shower heads lowers the amount of water used in the bathroom. To conserve water used in landscaping, many people water their lawns at night to reduce the amount of water lost to evaporation. People also save water by landscaping with a technique called *xeriscaping*. Xeriscaping involves designing a landscape with native plants. Native plants don't need to be watered because they receive enough water from the natural environment. **Figure 6** shows one example of xeriscaping.

What You Can Do

Can one person make a difference? When you multiply one by the millions of people who are trying to save water, you can make a big difference. Your behavior alone can help conserve water. For example, you can avoid running the water while brushing your teeth or washing dishes. You can take shorter showers. You can wash the car by using only a bucket and a hose that has a shutoff nozzle. You can run the dishwasher and washing machine only when they are full. As you can see, there are many ways to reduce how much water you use.

conservation (KAHN suhr VAY shuhn) the preservation and wise use of natural resources

Standards Check List four things that you can do to conserve water.
🐻 6.6.b

SECTION Review

 6.6.b

Summary

- An aquifer is a rock and soil layer that stores groundwater and allows the flow of groundwater.

- California receives its water from surface water, from aquifers, and from other areas.

- Water sources can be polluted by cities, factories, and farms.

- Water can be conserved by using only the water that is needed, by recycling water, and by using drip irrigation systems.

Using Vocabulary

Use a term from the section to complete each sentence below.

1 The ___ is the upper surface of underground water.

2 A(n) ___ is a rock and soil layer that stores groundwater.

Understanding Concepts

3 Analyzing Why does Northern California transport water to Southern and Central California?

4 Evaluating How is most of the water used in California?

5 Applying Describe how water is conserved in industry.

Critical Thinking

6 Applying Concepts Name some ways to save water. Do not use examples from this section.

7 Making Inferences Why is it better to water your lawn at night instead of during the day?

8 Evaluating Data Determine how urban growth might affect the water level in an aquifer.

9 Analyzing Processes How is reducing the pollution in streams and groundwater linked to water conservation?

Math Skills

10 Making Calculations Let's say that your family used 360 L of water today and that 25% of this water was used for lawn care. How many liters of water did your family use for lawn care?

Challenge

11 Making Inferences If the Central Valley aquifer system is the largest basin-fill aquifer system in the United States, why does California have an insufficient water supply? Create a water plan that does not require California to rely on out-of-state water.

Internet Resources

For a variety of links related to this chapter, go to www.scilinks.org
Topic: California's Fresh Water
SciLinks code: HY7C05

Model-Making Lab

Carving a Stream

As water moves over land, it erodes the soil and forms a channel. In this lab, you will investigate how gradient and discharge affect how a river erodes its channel and shapes the landscape.

Procedure

1 Your teacher will provide you with a tub that contains moist diatomaceous earth. The earth will be sloped so that one end of the tub contains more earth than the other end does. Place a book under the tub to raise the end of the tub that has the deepest layer of earth.

2 In a pitcher, mix 30 mL of blue food coloring and 4 L of water.

3 Submerge the plastic tubing in the pitcher of blue water until the tubing is full of water and no more bubbles escape.

4 Pinch one end of the tubing closed. Pull the pinched end out of the water while leaving the other end submerged.

5 Hold the pinched end of the tubing over the diatomaceous earth at the elevated end of the tub. Make sure that the pinched end of the tubing is lower than the level of water in the pitcher so that water can be easily siphoned through the tubing. Adjust the tension on the pinched end of the tubing so that water leaks out at about two drips per second. (You may want to use an empty bucket to practice.) Allow the water to drip onto the earth for 5 min.

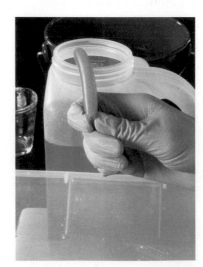

6 Stop the drip, and return the tubing to the pitcher. Draw a diagram of the stream channel. Label the diagram. Note the width of the channel and the accumulation of sediment.

6.2.a Students know water running downhill is the dominant process in shaping the landscape, including California's landscape.
6.2.b Students know rivers and streams are dynamic systems that erode, transport sediment, change course, and flood their banks in natural and recurring patterns.

Investigation and Experimentation
6.7.a Develop a hypothesis.
6.7.d Communicate the steps and results from an investigation in written reports and oral presentations.
6.7.e Recognize whether evidence is consistent with a proposed explanation.

7 Form a hypothesis that explains how the stream channel would differ if a larger volume of water flowed through the channel in the same amount of time.

8 Repeat steps 3–5, but adjust the flow rate of water from the tubing to be about 2 or 3 times the original flow rate. Allow the water to drip for 5 min.

9 Draw and label a diagram of your second stream. Again, note the width of the channel and the accumulation of sediment.

Analyze the Results

10 Making Observations Compare the two streams. How did the increased discharge of water change the stream channel?

11 Making Predictions How would the stream channel change if you increased the gradient?

Draw Conclusions

12 Forming Conclusions Was the hypothesis that you formed in step 7 correct? If not, explain why not. Using your diagrams of both stream channels, explain how water flow can change a stream channel.

Big Idea Question

13 Evaluating Conclusions Using your observations of how running water erodes the landscape, write a report explaining how a real stream would erode the land after a light rain and after a heavy rain. Include an explanation of how gradient might increase erosion. Use your diagrams and report to present your findings to the class.

Science Skills Activity

Investigation and Experimentation
6.7.h Identify changes in natural phenomena over time without manipulating the phenomena (e.g., a tree limb, a grove of trees, a stream, a hillslope).

Identifying Changes over Time

▶ Tutorial

Identifying changes in a natural system is an important part of Earth science. Improve your observation skills by practicing the following steps.

Carefully study the original phenomenon.

- Identify all of the important features of the object or system. To do so, observe details, identify features, and determine the shapes and sizes of different features.
- Record any important features or details.

Carefully study the phenomenon after the changes have occurred.

- Locate the features and details that you identified in the original phenomenon.
- Identify any features or details that differ from their original condition.
- Analyze the changes that you have identified. Look for factors that may have caused the changes.

▶ You Try It!

The following three images are *Landsat* images of the Tri-River area of the midwestern United States. The three images represent the area before, during, and after a flood. Black areas represent water. Green areas represent vegetation and red areas represent soil. Use the images and the key to identify changes that occurred in this area.

1 **Describing** Locate and describe the area of the floodplain. How do you know that the area is a floodplain?

2 **Analyzing** How has the river itself changed? Did any new bodies of water form, or did the course of the river change in any way? Explain your answer.

3 **Evaluating** Much of the lack of vegetation in the November 1993 image is a result of harvesting crops and the loss of tree leaves due to changes in season. However, do you think that the flood might have affected the number of crops for that year's harvest?

August 1991

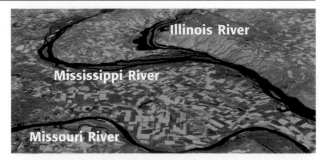

Illinois River
Mississippi River
Missouri River

July 1993

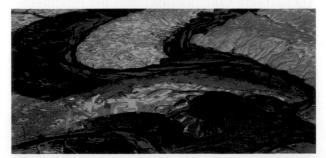

November 1993

Chapter Summary

The Big Idea
Topography is reshaped as water flows downhill in streams and rivers.

Section		Vocabulary

① The Active River

Key Concept Water running downhill is the dominant process in shaping the landscape.

- Moving water shapes the surface of Earth by the process of erosion.
- The sun is the major source of energy that drives the water cycle.
- Three factors that affect the rate of stream erosion are gradient, discharge, and load.

Rivers that have a high gradient have a lot of erosive energy.

erosion p. 366
water cycle p. 367
tributary p. 368
watershed p. 368
divide p. 368
channel p. 369
load p. 370

② Stream and River Deposits

Key Concept Rivers and streams are dynamic systems that erode, transport sediment, change course, and flood their banks in natural and recurring patterns.

- Three types of stream deposits are deltas, alluvial fans, and floodplains.
- Rivers and streams flood their banks in natural and recurring patterns, and these floods affect humans and wildlife habitats.

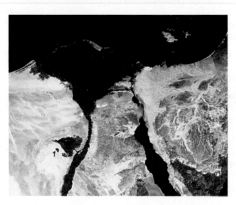

The Nile River delta in Egypt formed as a result of stream deposition.

deposition p. 374
delta p. 375
alluvial fan p. 375
floodplain p. 376

③ Using Water Wisely

Key Concept Water resources can be endangered by pollution or overuse.

- California's water needs are supplied by using groundwater and surface water, by transporting water from one region of California to another, and by importing water from other areas.
- Conserving water and protecting water sources are important in California because the water supply is limited.

Native plants get the water that they need from the natural environment.

aquifer p. 378
water table p. 378
water pollution p. 380

Chapter Review

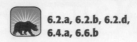

Organize

Booklet Review the FoldNote that you created at the beginning of the chapter. Add to or correct the FoldNote based on what you have learned.

Using Vocabulary

1 **Academic Vocabulary** In the sentence "Water running downhill is the dominant process in shaping the landscape," what does the word *dominant* mean?

Complete each of the following sentences by choosing the correct term from the word bank.

river	tributary
watershed	floodplain

2 A stream that flows into a lake or into a larger stream is a ___.

3 The area along a river that forms from sediment deposited when the river overflows is a ___.

For each pair of terms, explain how the meanings of the terms differ.

4 *divide* and *watershed*

5 *delta* and *alluvial fan*

6 *aquifer* and *water table*

Understanding Concepts

Multiple Choice

7 Which landform is located at the coast?
a. delta
b. floodplain
c. alluvial fan
d. water table

8 Which landscape features are common in youthful river channels?
a. meanders
b. floodplains
c. rapids
d. sandbars

9 Which of the following powers the water cycle?
a. runoff
b. condensation
c. clouds
d. the sun's energy

10 One way to control floods is through
a. soil treatment.
b. alluvial fans.
c. floodplains.
d. artificial levees.

Short Answer

11 **Describing** Describe the stages of the water cycle.

12 **Describing** Describe two techniques for controlling floods.

13 **Analyzing** What factors affect how a river erodes its channel?

14 **Classifying** Identify the four types of rivers based on their characteristics.

15 **Comparing** What is the main difference between an alluvial fan and a delta?

16 **Identifying** Identify three sources from which California receives water.

17 **Identifying** Identify the landscape feature that is an area good for farming.

18 **Listing** List three major ways in which California uses its water.

19 **Listing** Give two examples of how water can become polluted.

20 **Summarizing** Explain how the deposition of sediment by rivers shapes the landscape.

Writing Skills

21 **Writing Persuasively** In an letter to your mayor, suggest ways in which your town can conserve water. Provide detailed examples of water conservation methods. Arrange your examples and reasoning in an effective manner that anticipates and answers the mayor's concerns and counterarguments.

Critical Thinking

22 Concept Mapping Use the following terms to create a concept map: *erosion, channel, watersheds, divide, tributaries, river system, alluvial fan, delta, floodplain,* and *load.*

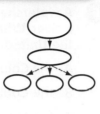

23 Identifying Relationships What is water's role in erosion and deposition?

24 Analyzing Processes What are the features of a river channel that has a steep gradient?

25 Predicting Consequences After heavy rains, would you expect the water table to be higher or lower than normal?

26 Making Inferences The Colorado River is usually grayish brown as it flows through the Grand Canyon. What causes this color?

27 Predicting Consequences What do you think would happen to cities in the southwestern United States if rivers in that area could not be dammed?

INTERPRETING GRAPHICS Use the map below to answer the next three questions.

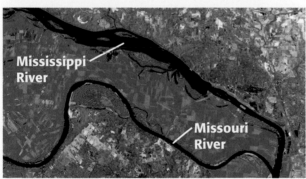

28 Evaluating Data In the map above, which color represents a floodplain? Explain your answer.

29 Predicting Consequences Describe the area of the map where you would most likely find river deposits.

30 Applying Concepts In which area of the map would you build a house? Explain why.

INTERPRETING GRAPHICS Use the graph below to answer the next three questions.

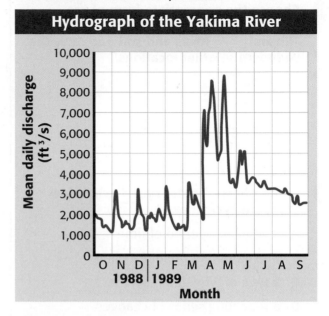

31 Evaluating Data In which months is the river discharge the highest?

32 Applying Concepts Why is the river discharge so high during these months?

Math Skills

33 Making Calculations If the concentration of gasoline in 650,000 L of water is 3 ppm, how many liters of gasoline are in the water?

34 Using Equations A river is 3,705 km long from its headwaters to its delta. The average downstream velocity of the water in the river is 200 cm/s. Use the equation *time = distance ÷ velocity* to determine how many days a sedimentary particle takes to make the trip.

Challenge

35 Analyzing Processes Describe how water running downhill shapes the landscape. Include examples in California. Explain how California's landscape would be different if it were completely flat and lacked gradients.

Standards Assessment

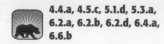

4.4.a, 4.5.c, 5.1.d, 5.3.a,
6.2.a, 6.2.b, 6.2.d, 6.4.a,
6.6.b

REVIEWING ACADEMIC VOCABULARY

1 Choose the appropriate form of the word *erode* for the following sentence: "Rivers _____ rocks and soil and carry the sediment to other locations."

A erode

B erosion

C eroding

D erodes

2 In the phrase "water cycle," what does the word *cycle* mean?

A a very long period of time

B one complete orbit of a planet

C a type of wheeled machine

D a repeating series of changes

3 Which of the following words is the closest in meaning to the word *transport*?

A to deposit

B to carry from one place to another

C to lift

D to flow downhill

4 In the sentence "The sun is a major source of *energy* on Earth," what does the word *energy* mean?

A the action of work

B the life

C the power that makes things happen

D the work that is completed

5 Which of the following words means "a set of steps, events, or changes"?

A process

B practice

C promise

D phenomenon

REVIEWING CONCEPTS

6 A watershed is an area of land drained by a river. What is the largest watershed in the United States?

A the Colorado River watershed

B the Continental Divide watershed

C the Mississippi River watershed

D the Rio Grande watershed

7 A stream's ability to erode is influenced by gradient, discharge, and load. Which of the streams below will most likely have the fastest rate of erosion?

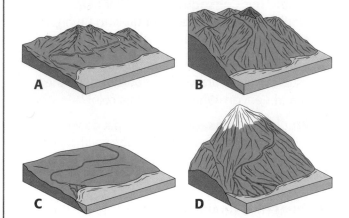

8 Flooding can wash away human and wildlife habitats. But flooding also has benefits. What is one benefit of flooding?

A It creates an artificial levee.

B It erodes the floodplain.

C It allows people to evacuate.

D It deposits rich soil on the land.

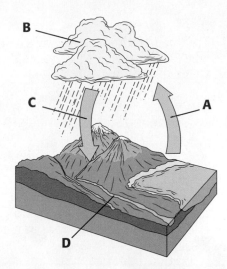

9 At which point in the diagram above is precipitation most likely taking place?

A point A

B point B

C point C

D point D

10 After water falls as precipitation, some of it seeps into the ground and pools in aquifers. What is this process called?

A sedimentation

B condensation

C percolation

D deposition

11 The Colorado River watershed covers parts of Colorado, Utah, Arizona, and California. What are the streams and rivers that flow into the Colorado River called?

A aquifers

B gradients

C tributaries

D deltas

REVIEWING PRIOR LEARNING

12 Where there was once a meadow, there is now a floodplain. What is most likely the reason for this change?

A A delta formed there.

B A river changed its course.

C A stream deepened its channel.

D A new tributary appeared.

13 Water covers three-fourths of Earth's surface. Most of this water is

A groundwater.

B salt water.

C contaminated water.

D fresh water.

14 Water running downhill is a force that reshapes Earth's surface through

A weathering, transport, and deposition.

B evaporation, condensation, and precipitation.

C erosion, pressure, and rock formation.

D channeling, freezing, and boiling.

15 Elements are substances that cannot be broken down any further. How many elements make up water (H_2O)?

A one element

B two elements

C three elements

D four elements

16 The Colorado River deposits layers of sand and soil on its banks. Over many years, what might these layers of sand and soil become?

A conglomerate rock

B igneous rock

C metamorphic rock

D sedimentary rock

Science in Action

Scientific Discoveries

Placer Deposits

Heavy minerals are sometimes deposited at places in a river where the current slows down. This kind of sediment is called a *placer deposit*. Some placer deposits contain gold. During the California gold rush, which began in 1849, many miners panned for gold in the placer deposits of rivers.

Language Arts ACTiViTy

During the California gold rush, many people came from all over the United States to search for gold. Imagine that you are one of those people. Write a short story describing your journey and your excitement while finding gold.

Weird Science

Sunken Forests

Imagine having your own little secret forest. There are plenty of secret forests in Ankarana National Park in Madagascar. Within the limestone mountain of the park, caves have formed from the twisting path of the flowing groundwater. In many places in the caves, the roof has collapsed to form a sinkhole. The light that now shines through the collapsed roof of the cave has allowed miniature sunken forests to grow. Each sunken forest has unique characteristics. Some have crocodiles. Others have blind cavefish. You can even find some species that can't be found anywhere else in the world!

Social Studies ACTiViTy

Do research to find out how the geography of Madagascar contributes to the island's biodiversity. In your **Science Journal**, make a map of the island that highlights some of the island's unique forms of life.

Rita Colwell

A Water Filter for All Have you ever drunk a glass of water through a piece of cloth? Rita Colwell, director of the National Science Foundation, has found that filtering drinking water through a cloth can decrease the number of disease-causing bacteria in the water. This discovery is very important for the people of Bangladesh, where deadly outbreaks of cholera are frequent. People are usually infected by the bacteria that cause cholera by drinking contaminated water. Colwell knew that filtering the water would remove the bacteria and would make the water safe to drink. Unfortunately, filters were too expensive for most of the people to buy. Colwell tried to use a sari to filter the water. A sari is a long piece of colorful cloth that many women in Bangladesh wear as a skirtlike piece of clothing. Using a sari to filter the water did the trick. The number of cholera-causing bacteria in the water decreased. Fewer people contracted cholera, and many lives were saved!

Math ACTIVITY

Using the cloth to filter water reduced the occurrence of cholera by 48%. If 125 out of 100,000 people contracted cholera before the water was filtered, how many people per 100,000 contracted cholera after the water was filtered?

Internet Resources

- To learn more about careers in science, visit **www.scilinks.org** and enter the SciLinks code HY70225.

- To learn more about these Science in Action topics, visit **go.hrw.com** and type in the keyword HY7DEPF.

- Check out articles related to this chapter by visiting **go.hrw.com**. Just type in the keyword HY7DEPC.

Earth's Oceans and Atmosphere

In this unit, you will learn about Earth's oceans and atmosphere, including how they both affect conditions on Earth's land. All together, the oceans cover approximately 70% of Earth's surface. And the atmosphere forms a thin blanket that covers all of Earth's land and water. This timeline shows some of the events that have occurred as scientists have tried to better understand Earth's oceans, atmosphere, weather, and climate.

1281

A sudden typhoon destroys a fleet of Mongolian ships about to reach Japan. This "divine wind," or *kamikaze* in Japanese, saves the country from invasion and conquest.

1920

Serbian scientist Milutin Milankovitch determines that over tens of thousands of years, changes in Earth's motion through space have profound effects on climate.

1982

Weather information becomes available 24 hours a day, 7 days a week, on commercial TV.

1994

The completion of the tunnel under the English Channel makes train and auto travel between Great Britain and France possible.

1718
Gabriel Fahrenheit builds the first mercury thermometer.

1749
Benjamin Franklin explains how updrafts of air are caused by the sun's heating of the local atmosphere.

1778
Carl Scheele concludes that air is mostly made of nitrogen and oxygen.

1872
The *HMS Challenger* begins its four-year voyage. Its discoveries lay the foundation for the science of oceanography.

1943
Jacques Cousteau (shown at right) and Émile Gagnan invent the aqualung, a breathing device that allows divers to freely explore the silent world of the oceans.

1960
Jacques Piccard and Don Walsh dive to a record 10,916 m below sea level in their bathyscaph *Trieste*.

1974
Chlorofluorocarbons (CFCs) are recognized as harmful to the ozone layer.

1998
Ben Lecomte of Austin, Texas, successfully swims across the Atlantic Ocean from Massachusetts to France, a distance of 5,980 km. His record-breaking feat takes 73 days.

1999
The first nonstop balloon trip around the world is successfully completed when Brian Jones and Bertrand Piccard land in Egypt.

2003
A record 393 tornadoes are observed in the United States during one week in May.

The Breitling Orbiter 3 *lands in Egypt on March 21, 1999.*

Improving Comprehension

Graphic Organizers are important visual tools that can help you organize information and improve your reading comprehension. The Graphic Organizer below is called an *idea wheel*. Instructions for creating other types of Graphic Organizers are located in the **Study Skills** section of the Appendix.

How to Make an Idea Wheel

1 Draw a circle. Draw a larger circle around the first circle. Divide the ring between the circles into sections by drawing lines from one circle to the other across the ring. Divide the ring into as many sections as you want.

2 Write a main idea or topic in the smaller circle. Label each section in the ring with a category or characteristic of the main idea.

3 In each section of the ring, include details that are unique to the topic.

When to Use an Idea Wheel

An idea wheel is an effective type of visual organization in which ideas in science can be divided into categories or parts. It is also a useful way to illustrate characteristics of a main idea or topic. As you read, look for topics that are divided into ideas or categories that can be organized around an idea wheel.

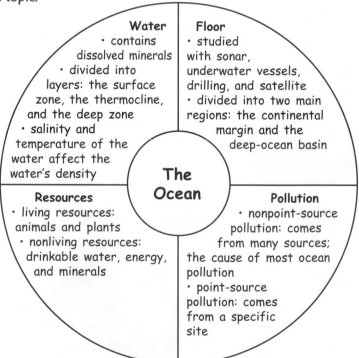

Water
• contains dissolved minerals
• divided into layers: the surface zone, the thermocline, and the deep zone
• salinity and temperature of the water affect the water's density

Floor
• studied with sonar, underwater vessels, drilling, and satellite
• divided into two main regions: the continental margin and the deep-ocean basin

The Ocean

Resources
• living resources: animals and plants
• nonliving resources: drinkable water, energy, and minerals

Pollution
• nonpoint-source pollution: comes from many sources; the cause of most ocean pollution
• point-source pollution: comes from a specific site

You Try It!

This Reading Strategy can also be used within the chapter that you are about to read. Practice making your own idea wheel as directed in the Reading Strategies for Section **2** and Section **4**. Record your work in your **Science Journal.**

Unpacking the Standards

The information below "unpacks" the standards by breaking them down into basic parts. The higher-level, academic vocabulary is highlighted and defined to help you understand the language of the standards. "What It Means" restates the standards as simply as possible.

California Standard	Academic Vocabulary	What It Means
6.1.a Students know **evidence** of plate tectonics is **derived** from the fit of the continents; the **location** of earthquakes, volcanoes, and midocean ridges; and the **distribution** of fossils, rock types, and ancient climatic zones.	**evidence** (EV uh duhns) information showing whether an idea or belief is true or valid **derive** (di RIEV) to figure out by reasoning **location** (loh KAY shuhn) a place or position **distribution** (DIS tri BYOO shuhn) the relative arrangement of objects in time or space	Support for the idea that Earth's surface is made of slabs of rock that move around comes from how continents fit together, where earthquakes happen, where volcanoes and mid-ocean ridges are located, where rocks and fossils are found, and where climate was different in the geologic past.
6.1.d Students know that earthquakes are sudden motions along breaks in the crust called faults and that volcanoes and fissures are **locations** where magma reaches the surface.		Earthquakes are sudden movements along breaks in Earth's surface called *faults,* and volcanoes are places where molten rock reaches the surface.
6.1.e Students know **major** geologic events, such as earthquakes, volcanic eruptions, and mountain building, result from plate motions.	**major** (MAY juhr) of great importance or large scale	Important global events, such as earthquakes, volcanic eruptions, and mountain building, are caused by the movement of Earth's crust and upper mantle.
6.3.c Students know heat flows in solids by conduction (which **involves** no flow of matter) and in fluids by conduction and by convection (which **involves** flow of matter).	**involve** (in VAHLV) to have as a part of	When heat flows in solids, the heat can be transferred without the movement of matter. When heat flows in liquids and gases, the heat can be transferred with or without the movement of matter.
6.4.d Students know convection currents **distribute** heat in the atmosphere and oceans.	**distribute** (di STRIB yoot) to spread out over an area	The movement of air in the atmosphere and of water in the ocean carries heat throughout the atmosphere and oceans.

The following identifies other standards that are covered in this chapter and where you can go to see them unpacked: **6.6.a** (Chapter 5), **6.6.b** (Chapter 4), and **6.6.c** (Chapter 4)

12

Exploring the Oceans

The Big Idea

Oceans cover 71% of Earth's surface and contain natural resources that must be protected.

California Standards

Focus on Earth Sciences

6.1 Plate tectonics accounts for important features of Earth's surface and major geologic events. (Section 2)

6.3 Heat moves in a predictable flow from warmer objects to cooler objects until all the objects are at the same temperature. (Section 1)

6.4 Many phenomena on Earth's surface are affected by the transfer of energy through radiation and convection currents. (Section 1)

6.6 Sources of energy and materials differ in amounts, distribution, usefulness, and the time required for formation. (Sections 3 and 4)

Investigation and Experimentation

6.7 Scientific progress is made by asking meaningful questions and conducting careful investigations. (Science Skills Activity)

Math

6.1.1 Algebra and Functions

6.1.4 Number Sense

English—Language Arts

6.2.4 Reading

6.1.1, 6.1.2, 6.1.3, 6.1.4, 6.2.5 Writing

About the Photo

One way scientists explore oceans is through underwater vessels. This underwater vessel, *Little Hercules,* has no pilot. However, scientists on board the mother ship, *Northern Horizon,* control Little Hercules through a fiber-optic cable that connects the two ships.

Organize

Four-Corner Fold

Before you read this chapter, create the FoldNote entitled "Four-Corner Fold." Label each flap of the four-corner fold with the title of one of the sections in the chapter. As you read the chapter, add details from each section under the appropriate flap.

Instructions for creating FoldNotes are located in the Study Skills section on p. 617 of the Appendix.

Explore Activity

🕐 20 min

Clean up That Spill!

Oil that runs off the land or is spilled from oil tankers pollutes the oceans and harms wildlife. Cleaning up oil in the ocean is very difficult, as you will find out in this activity.

Procedure

1. Pour about **5 mL of vegetable oil** into a **pan of water.**

2. Think of ways in which you can remove the oil from the water without pouring out the water.

3. Using materials that your teacher provides, remove the oil from the pan of water.

Analysis

6.6.a

4. Were you able to remove all of the oil?

5. What was the most effective technique for removing the oil?

6. How is this problem similar to cleaning up an oil spill in the ocean?

Earth's Oceans

Key Concept The characteristics of ocean water, such as temperature and salinity, affect the circulation of the ocean.

▶ Earth is unique in our solar system because 71% of its surface is covered with liquid water. Most of Earth's water is in the *global ocean*. The global ocean is divided by the continents into five main oceans. These five main oceans are shown in **Figure 1.** The global ocean has characteristics that play an important role in regulating Earth's climate.

Divisions of the Global Ocean

The largest ocean is the *Pacific Ocean*. It lies between Asia and the Americas. The volume of the *Atlantic Ocean,* the second-largest ocean, is about half the volume of the Pacific. The *Indian Ocean* is the third-largest ocean. It is located between Africa and Australia. The *Arctic Ocean* is the smallest ocean. This ocean is unique because much of its surface is covered by ice. The *Southern Ocean* extends from the coast of Antarctica to 60° south latitude.

Figure 1 **Parts of the Global Ocean**

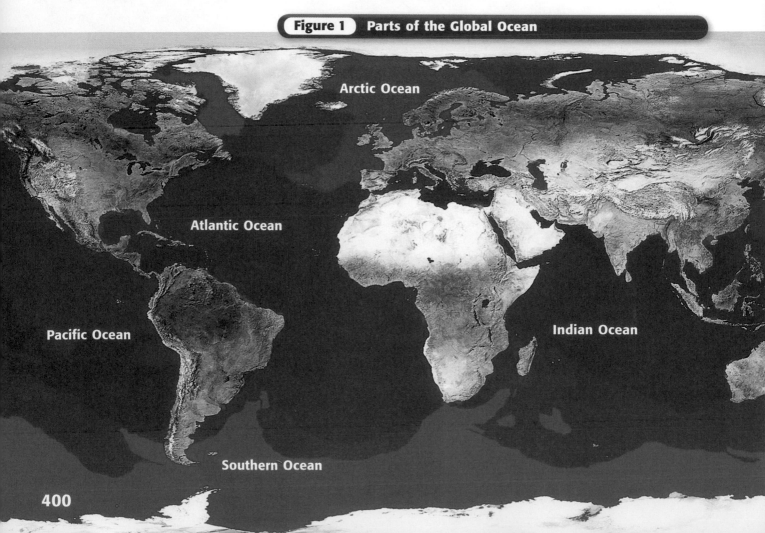

Arctic Ocean

Atlantic Ocean

Pacific Ocean

Indian Ocean

Southern Ocean

Figure 2 *This pie graph shows the relative percentages of dissolved solids (by mass) in ocean water.*

The pie graph shows:
- Sodium 30.6%
- Magnesium 7.7%
- Sulfur 3.7%
- Calcium 1.2%
- Potassium 1.1%
- Other 0.7%
- Chlorine 55.0%

Characteristics of Ocean Water

Ocean water is different from the water that flows from your sink at home. For one thing, you can't drink ocean water. It is too salty and doesn't taste very good. But there are other things that make ocean water special.

Ocean Water Is Salty

Have you ever swallowed water while swimming in the ocean? It tasted really salty, didn't it? Most of the salt in the ocean is the same kind of salt that we sprinkle on our food. This salt is called *sodium chloride*. This compound consists of the elements sodium, Na, and chlorine, Cl. There are many other dissolved solids in ocean water, such as magnesium and calcium. **Figure 2** shows the relative amounts of the dissolved solids in ocean water.

Salts have collected in the ocean for billions of years. As rivers and streams flow toward the ocean, they dissolve minerals from the land. The running water carries these dissolved minerals to the ocean. At the same time, water is *evaporating* from the ocean. As the water evaporates, it leaves the dissolved solids behind. The most abundant dissolved solid in the ocean is sodium chloride.

Salinity

A measure of the amount of dissolved solids in a given amount of liquid is called **salinity**. Salinity is usually measured as grams of dissolved solids per kilogram of water. Every 1 kg (1,000 g) of ocean water has 35 g of dissolved solids in it. Therefore, if you evaporated 1 kg of ocean water, 965 g of fresh water would be removed and 35 g of solids would remain.

salinity (suh LIN uh tee) a measure of the amount of dissolved salts in a given amount of liquid

6.3.c Students know heat flows in solids by conduction (which involves no flow of matter) and in fluids by conduction and by convection (which involves flow of matter).

6.4.d Students know convection currents distribute heat in the atmosphere and oceans.

Figure 3 *Salinity varies in different parts of the ocean because of variations in evaporation, circulation, and fresh water inflow.* ***Does the area of the ocean near the mouth of the Amazon have a high or low salinity? Explain your answer.***

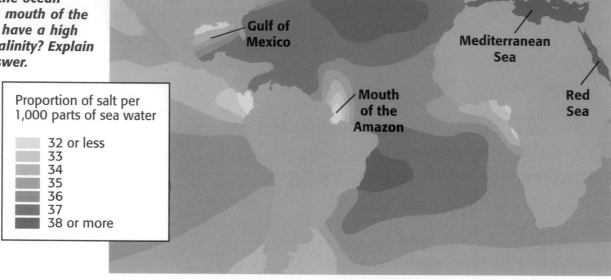

Proportion of salt per 1,000 parts of sea water

- 32 or less
- 33
- 34
- 35
- 36
- 37
- 38 or more

Climate Affects Salinity

Some parts of the ocean are saltier than others, as shown in **Figure 3.** In places that have hotter, drier climates, salinity is usually higher. In these areas, the evaporation rate is high because the temperatures are high. Evaporation removes water but leaves salts and other dissolved solids behind. The salinity of the Red Sea is very high because the hot, dry climate around the Red Sea causes a high rate of evaporation.

Coastal waters commonly have lower salinity than waters farther offshore. Fresh water from streams and rivers on land runs into the ocean in these areas. As the fresh water mixes with the ocean water, the concentration of salts in the ocean water decreases. The mouth of the Amazon is one such location, as shown in **Figure 3.**

Water Movement Affects Salinity

Another factor that affects ocean salinity is water movement. Slower-moving areas of water develop higher salinity. Some parts of the ocean, such as bays, gulfs, and seas, move less than other parts do. Parts of the open ocean that do not have currents running through them can also be slow moving. In **Figure 3,** identify the areas that are most likely to have slower-moving water.

Temperature of Ocean Water

The temperature of ocean water decreases as depth increases. However, this temperature change is not uniform. Water in the ocean can be divided into three layers by temperature. Those three layers are the surface zone, the thermocline, and the deep zone, as shown in **Figure 4.**

Surface Zone

The *surface zone,* or top layer of ocean water, is heated by the sun's energy. Heated ocean water becomes less dense and rises above the denser, cool water. This movement of water caused by differences in density forms convection currents. The convection currents distribute heat in the surface zone down to a depth of about 100 m to 300 m. The convection currents distribute the heat until the temperature is fairly uniform throughout the surface zone.

Standards Check How is heat distributed in the surface zone of the ocean? **6.4.d**

Thermocline

The sun cannot directly heat ocean water below the surface zone. And the heated, less dense water of the surface zone cannot easily mix with the cold, dense water below. Therefore, below the surface zone, the temperature of the water decreases sharply as depth increases. The layer of the ocean in which temperature drops with increased depth faster than it does in other layers is called the **thermocline.** The thermocline's depth varies in different parts of the ocean. However, it may extend between 100 m and 1000 m below the ocean's surface.

How Deep Is It?
One area of the ocean is 4,000 m deep. Its surface zone extends to about 300 m below the surface of the ocean. What percentage of the total depth of the ocean in this particular area is the surface zone? Record your work in your **Science Journal.**

thermocline (THUHR moh KLIEN) a layer in a body of water in which water temperature drops with increased depth faster than it does in other layers

Wordwise The root *therm-* means "heat." The root *clino-* means "slope." Other examples are *incline, decline,* and *thermometer.*

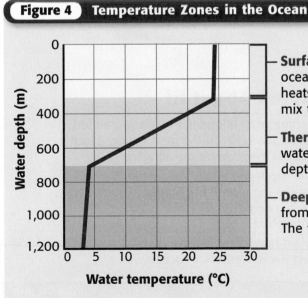

Figure 4 Temperature Zones in the Ocean

Surface zone The *surface zone* is the warm, top layer of ocean water. It can extend to 300 m below sea level. Sunlight heats the top 100 m of the surface zone. Convection currents mix the heated water with cooler water below.

Thermocline The *thermocline* is the second layer of ocean water. In the thermocline, temperature drops with increased depth faster than it does in the other two zones.

Deep zone The *deep zone* is the bottom layer that extends from the base of the thermocline to the bottom of the ocean. The temperature in this zone can range from 1°C to 3°C.

Deep Zone

The layer of the ocean directly below the thermocline is called the *deep zone*. In the deep zone of the ocean, the temperature of the water is usually about 2°C. The colder the water is, the denser it is. The density of cold, deep water controls the slow movement of deep ocean currents. This movement begins when the cold, dense water at the poles sinks and flows beneath warm water.

Surface Temperature Changes

Surface temperatures of different parts of the ocean are different depending on the latitude. Water along the equator is warmer because it receives more direct sunlight than water closer to the poles does. At low latitudes, ocean surface temperatures can be as high as 30°C. But in the polar oceans, temperatures of the ocean surface can be as low as –1.9°C!

The temperature of surface water also changes depending on the time of the year. The ocean surface at higher latitudes receives more direct sunlight during the summer season than during the winter season. Therefore, during summer, the surface water is warmer. For this reason, the Maine beach shown in **Figure 5** is crowded during the summer.

Figure 5 *People in Maine enjoy swimming in the ocean during the summer because the water is warmer during the summer.*

Quick Lab

Density Factors

In this lab you will learn how salinity and temperature affect the density of ocean water.

6.3.c

▶ Try It!

1. Fill a **deep, clear plastic container** half full with **room-temperature water.**

2. In a **1 L beaker**, mix **30 g (1/8 cup) of table salt, three drops of red food coloring,** and 1 L of room-temperature water (about 21°C). Stir the mixture until the salt is dissolved.

3. Slowly add the red saltwater mixture to the water in the clear plastic container. Record your observations. Then, dump out the water and refill the container half full with room-temperature water.

4. In the 1 L beaker, mix a **three drops of blue food coloring** with water that is 8°C.

5. Slowly add the cold, blue water to the clear plastic container. Record your observations.

▶ Think About It!

6. Describe what happened when you added the red salt water to the fresh water. Which is denser: fresh water or salt water?

7. What happened when you added the cold water to the room-temperature water? Which is denser: cold water or room-temperature water?

8. Explain how differences in density may affect the movement of ocean water.

 20 min

Density

Salinity and temperature affect the density of ocean water. The large amount of dissolved solids in ocean water makes ocean water denser than pure fresh water. Ocean water also becomes denser as it becomes colder. Water temperature affects the density of ocean water more than salinity does. Therefore, the densest ocean water is found in the polar regions, where the ocean surface is coldest. Differences in density throughout the global ocean drive the circulation of ocean water, which distributes heat in the ocean.

Standards Check What factors affect the circulation of ocean water?

 6.3.c

SECTION Review

6.3.c, 6.4.d

Summary

- The global ocean is divided by the continents into five main oceans: Pacific Ocean, Atlantic Ocean, Indian Ocean, Southern Ocean, and Arctic Ocean.

- Salts have collected in the ocean for billions of years. Salinity is a measure of the amount of dissolved salts in a given mass of liquid.

- The three temperature zones of ocean water are the surface zone, the thermocline, and the deep zone.

- Temperature and salinity determine the density of ocean water. The density of ocean water drives convection currents.

Using Vocabulary

1. In your own words, write definitions for *salinity* and *thermocline.*

Understanding Concepts

2. **Listing** Name the major divisions of the global ocean.

3. **Analyzing** Why does ocean water taste salty?

4. **Describing** Describe the temperature layers in ocean water.

5. **Comparing** Which is more dense, ocean water or fresh water? Why?

6. **Analyzing** How is heat distributed in the surface zone of the ocean?

7. **Identifying** What causes convection currents?

Critical Thinking

8. **Predicting Consequences** If all ocean water was the same temperature all the way through, how would the movement of ocean water be affected?

INTERPRETING GRAPHICS Use the graph below to answer the next question.

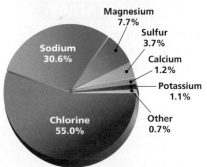

9. **Identifying Relationships** What is the combined percentage of magnesium and sulfur in the dissolved solids in ocean water?

Challenge

10. **Identifying Relationships** How does density of ocean water affect how heat is distributed in the ocean?

Internet Resources

For a variety of links related to this chapter, go to www.scilinks.org

Topic: Exploring Earth's Ocean
SciLinks code: HY70557

SECTION 2

The Ocean Floor

Key Concept Many different technologies have helped scientists study the topography of the ocean basins.

What You Will Learn

- Scientists use sonar, underwater vessels, drilling, and satellites to study the ocean floor.
- Ocean floor features formed because of tectonic plate movement.

Why It Matters

Understanding the topography of the ocean basins helps scientists understand the processes that formed the topography of the continents.

Vocabulary

- abyssal plain
- mid-ocean ridge
- ocean trench

READING STRATEGY

Graphic Organizer In your **Science Journal,** create an Idea Wheel that describes different features of the ocean floor.

What lies at the bottom of the ocean? This question was once unanswerable. By using new technology, scientists have learned a lot about the ocean floor. Scientists have discovered many different landforms on the ocean floor.

Studying the Ocean Floor

How can scientists study the ocean floor when it can be as much as 4,000 m below the ocean surface? Scientists can use underwater vessels to explore the ocean floor. But they can also study the ocean floor from the ocean's surface. They can even study the ocean floor from space!

Seeing by Sonar

Sonar stands for *sound navigation and ranging.* Scientists use sonar to determine the ocean's depth by sending sound pulses from a ship down into the ocean. The sound moves through the water, bounces off the ocean floor, and returns to the ship. The deeper the water is, the longer the round trip takes. Scientists then calculate the depth by multiplying half the travel time by the speed of sound in water (about 1,500 m/s). This process is shown in **Figure 1.**

Figure 1 **Ocean Floor Mapping with Sonar**

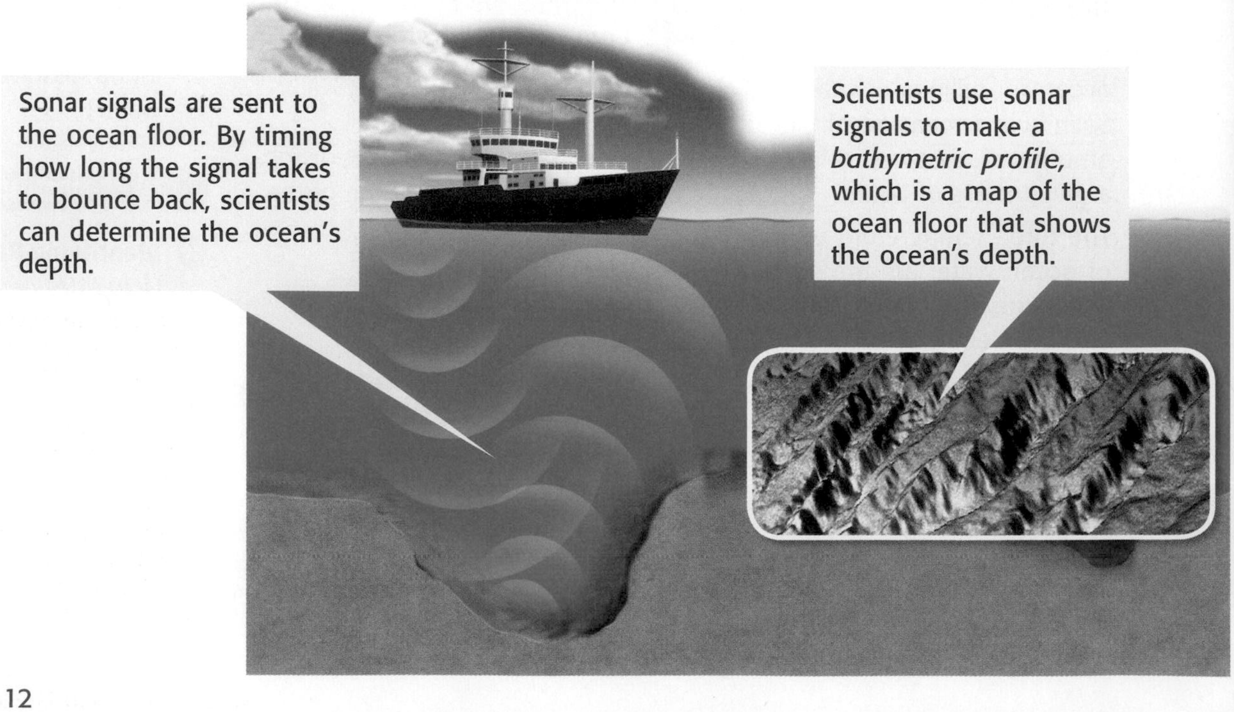
Sonar signals are sent to the ocean floor. By timing how long the signal takes to bounce back, scientists can determine the ocean's depth.
Scientists use sonar signals to make a *bathymetric profile,* which is a map of the ocean floor that shows the ocean's depth.

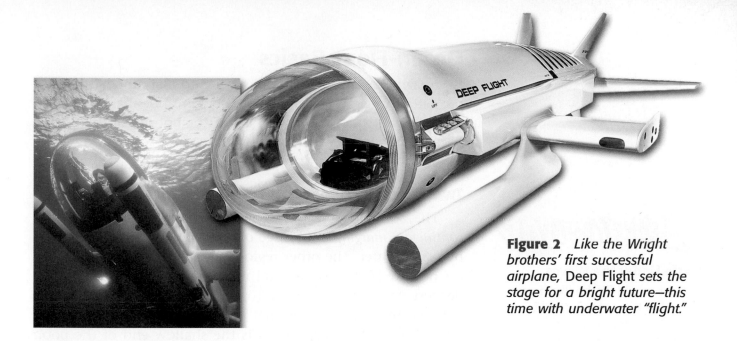

Figure 2 *Like the Wright brothers' first successful airplane,* Deep Flight *sets the stage for a bright future—this time with underwater "flight."*

Underwater Vessels

Just as astronauts explore space by using rockets, scientists explore the oceans by using underwater vessels. One piloted research vessel, *Deep Flight,* is shown in **Figure 2.** Future models of *Deep Flight* will be designed to transport scientists to depths of up to 11,000 m!

Scientists also use remotely operated vehicles, or ROVs, to explore the ocean. One interesting ROV is *JASON II,* which is "flown" from the surface by remote control. *JASON II* can be used to explore the sea floor at depths that are too dangerous for piloted vessels to go.

The Integrated Ocean Drilling Program (IODP)

The Integrated Ocean Drilling Program (IODP) is an international program that studies the sea floor by ocean drilling. Scientists drill cores, or long tubes of rock and sediment, from the sea floor. By studying the layers of rock and sediment from the cores, scientists learn about the history of Earth. For example, through drilling, scientists have found evidence of sea-floor spreading. Sea-floor spreading is a process responsible for the formation of many features on the ocean floor.

Studying via Satellite

Geosat, once a top-secret military satellite, has been used to measure slight changes in the height of the ocean's surface. Different underwater features, such as mountains and trenches, affect the height of the water above them. Scientists measure the different depths of the ocean and use the measurements to make detailed maps of the sea floor. Maps made from satellite data can cover much more territory than maps made by using sonar.

6.1.a Students know evidence of plate tectonics is derived from the fit of the continents; the location of earthquakes, volcanoes, and midocean ridges; and the distribution of fossils, rock types, and ancient climatic zones.

6.1.d Students know that earthquakes are sudden motions along breaks in the crust called faults and that volcanoes and fissures are locations where magma reaches the surface.

6.1.e Students know major geologic events, such as earthquakes, volcanic eruptions, and mountain building, result from plate motions.

Ocean-Floor Basics

Imagine being an explorer assigned to map uncharted areas on Earth. You might think that there are not many areas on Earth left to explore. But what about the bottom of the ocean? Because it is underwater and some areas are so deep, much of the ocean floor is still not completely explored.

Two Major Regions of the Ocean Floor

The ocean floor has two major regions. One region, the *continental margin,* is the edge of the continent that is covered by ocean water. The other region, the *deep-ocean basin,* begins at the end of the continental margin and extends under the deepest parts of the ocean. To get an idea of the difference between the two, imagine that the ocean is a giant swimming pool. The continental margin is the shallow end of the pool. The deep-ocean basin is the deep end of the pool.

Subdivisions of the Ocean Floor

The continental margin is subdivided into the continental shelf, the continental slope, and the continental rise. These divisions are based on depth and changes in slope. The deep-ocean basin consists of the abyssal plain, mid-ocean ridges, rift valleys, and ocean trenches, as shown in **Figure 3.** Mid-ocean ridges and ocean trenches mark the boundaries of Earth's tectonic plates.

INTERNET ACTIVITY

Life Under the Waves

What would life be like if you lived in the ocean? Would you be predator or prey? Describe your life as a sea creature. Go to **go.hrw.com,** and type in the keyword HY7OCEW.

Figure 3 Ocean Floor Features

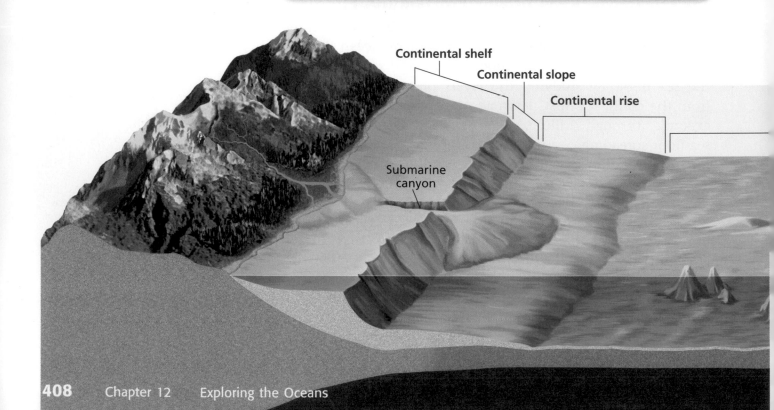

Continental shelf

Continental slope

Continental rise

Submarine canyon

Tectonic Plates and Ocean-Floor Features

If you could go to the bottom of the ocean, you would see the world's longest mountain chain. This mountain chain is about 64,000 km (40,000 mi) long. You would also see canyons deeper than the Grand Canyon. Why does the ocean floor have such impressive features? How did these features form? The answers have to do with plate tectonics.

You may know that the movement of tectonic plates forms features, such as mountains and volcanoes, on land. But these movements also form features on the ocean floor. Convection within Earth causes tectonic plates to move. The plates slide past each other, collide with each other, or move away from each other. As a result, seamounts, mid-ocean ridges, and trenches form. These features can be found on or near the abyssal plain.

Standards Check What process is responsible for the formation of features on the ocean floor? 🐾 **6.1.a, 6.1.d, 6.1.e**

Abyssal Plain

The large, flat, almost level area of the deep-ocean basin is called the **abyssal plain.** Abyssal plains are the flattest regions on Earth. They are covered with layers of fine sediment. Wind and ocean currents carry some of this sediment from the continental margins. Other sediment is made of the remains of marine organisms. Those remains settle to the ocean floor when the organisms die.

abyssal plain (uh BIS uhl PLAYN) a large, flat, almost level area of the deep-ocean basin

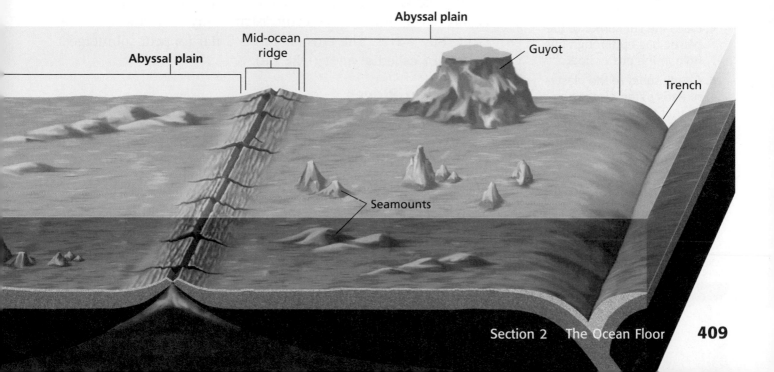

Abyssal plain

Mid-ocean ridge

Abyssal plain

Guyot

Trench

Seamounts

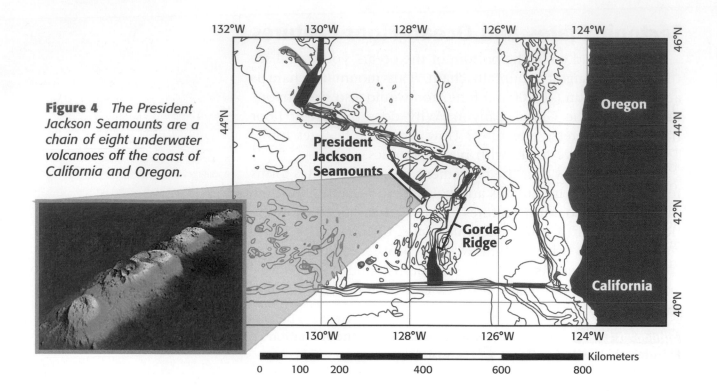

Figure 4 *The President Jackson Seamounts are a chain of eight underwater volcanoes off the coast of California and Oregon.*

Quick Lab

Seamounts   6.1.d

1. Cut a 0.5 cm hole in the center of a **15 cm × 15 cm piece of posterboard.**

2. Fill a **plastic bag** 1/3 full with **plaster of Paris**. Seal the plastic bag.

3. Cut 0.5 cm off of one corner of the plastic bag.

4. Place the cut corner of the plastic bag up through the hole in the poster board.

5. Gently squeeze the plaster of Paris in the plastic bag so that the plaster of Paris comes up through the hole in the poster board.

6. What ocean feature have you modeled?

7. Which area of the ocean floor does your model most likely represent, a hot spot or a tectonic plate boundary?

 15 min

Seamounts

A submerged volcanic mountain on the ocean floor is called a *seamount*. The President Jackson Seamounts are shown in **Figure 4.** Seamounts are at least 1,000 m high. They may form where magma pushes its way between tectonic plates. As the magma cools and builds up, it forms a mountain. Seamounts can also form far away from a tectonic plate boundary. Areas of volcanic activity within the interior of tectonic plates are called *hot spots*. At a hot spot, magma rises up from deep inside Earth and breaks through the overlying plate. The resulting volcano may grow into a seamount.

If a seamount builds up above sea level, it becomes a volcanic island. Over time the volcanic island may sink and become eroded by waves. The erosion forms a flat-topped, submerged seamount called a *guyot* (GEE OH).

Mid-Ocean Ridges

A long, undersea mountain chain that forms along the floor of the ocean is called a **mid-ocean ridge.** For the most part, mid-ocean ridges do not rise above sea level. However, Iceland is one place where a mid-ocean ridge has risen above the ocean's surface. Mid-ocean ridges form where plates move apart from each other. This motion creates a crack in the ocean floor called a *rift*. Magma rises through this rift and cools to form new rock. The ridges are made of this hot, new rock.

Standards Check Explain how the movement of tectonic plates causes the formation of mid-ocean ridges. **6.1.a, 6.1.d, 6.1.e**

Ocean Trenches

Long, narrow depressions located in the deep-ocean basins are called **ocean trenches.** The Mariana Trench, which is in the western Pacific Ocean, is the deepest place in Earth's crust. Trenches form where one tectonic plate moves under another tectonic plate. This process is called *subduction.*

As a plate subducts under another plate, the pressure on the subducting plate rises. Water and other fluids are squeezed out of the rock and sediments. These fluids cause surrounding rock to melt and form magma. The magma rises to the surface to form arcs of volcanoes along the trench. Earthquakes also may occur along subduction zones when one plate subducts under another.

mid-ocean ridge (MID OH shuhn RIJ) a long, undersea mountain chain that forms as magma rises from the asthenosphere when tectonic plates move apart

ocean trench (OH shuhn TRENCH) a long, narrow, and steep depression on the ocean floor that forms when one tectonic plate subducts beneath another plate

SECTION Review

6.1.a, 6.1.d, 6.1.e

Summary

- Scientists study the ocean floor by using sonar, underwater vessels, drilling, and satellites.

- The ocean floor is divided into two regions—the continental margin and the deep-ocean basin.

- The continental margin consists of the continental shelf, the continental slope, and the continental rise.

- The deep-ocean basin consists of the abyssal plain, mid-ocean ridges, trenches, and seamounts.

- Mid-ocean ridges and trenches mark the boundaries of tectonic plates.

Using Vocabulary

Use a term from the section to complete each sentence below.

1 A(n) ___ is an undersea mountain chain that forms along the floor of the ocean.

2 A(n) ___ is a large, flat, almost level area of the deep-ocean basin.

Understanding Concepts

3 Evaluating How does the movement of tectonic plates form ocean trenches?

4 Listing List three technologies for studying the ocean floor, and explain how they are used.

5 Describing Describe how mid-ocean ridges form.

Critical Thinking

6 Analyzing Ideas How are mid-ocean ridges and seamounts related to volcanoes?

7 Making Comparisons How is the formation of mid-ocean ridges and trenches different?

INTERPRETING GRAPHICS Use the diagram below to answer the next question.

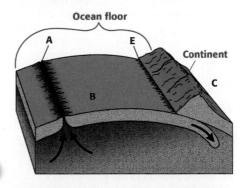

Ocean floor

8 Making Comparisons What letter represents the area where the abyssal plain is located?

Math Skills

9 Using Equations Air pressure at sea level is 1 atmosphere (atm). Underwater, pressure increases by 1 atm every 10 m of depth. What is the pressure at 100 m?

Internet Resources

For a variety of links related to this chapter, go to www.scilinks.org

Topic: Undersea Technology in California

SciLinks code: HY7C13

Resources from the Ocean

Key Concept The ocean is an important source of living and nonliving resources.

What You Will Learn

- The ocean is an important source for food, salt, fresh water, oil, tidal energy, and minerals.
- Oil is the most valuable resource obtained from the ocean.

Why It Matters

Many of the things you eat and the materials you use are made from resources from the ocean.

Vocabulary

- desalination

READING STRATEGY

Outlining In your **Science Journal,** create an outline of the section. Use the headings from the section in your outline.

6.6.a Students know the utility of energy sources is determined by factors that are involved in converting these sources to useful forms and the consequences of the conversion process.
6.6.b Students know different natural energy and material resources, including air, soil, rocks, minerals, petroleum, fresh water, wildlife, and forests, and know how to classify them as renewable or nonrenewable.
6.6.c Students know the natural origin of the materials used to make common objects.

▶ Did you know that without seaweed, your favorite ice cream would be a runny mess? A seaweed called *kelp* is used as a thickener for many food products, including ice cream. Food, raw materials, energy, and drinkable water are all harvested from the ocean. The ocean offers a large number of resources.

Living Resources

People have been harvesting plants and animals from the ocean for thousands of years. Today, harvesting food from the ocean is a multi-billion-dollar industry. As human populations have grown, the demand for these resources has increased. However, the availability of these resources has not.

Fishing the Ocean

Almost 75 million tons of fish are harvested each year. With improved technology, such as the drift nets shown in **Figure 1,** fishers have become better at taking fish from the ocean. Fish are considered a renewable resource. In other words, they can reproduce at the same rate at which they are consumed. However, many people are concerned that we are overfishing our oceans. In addition, animals other than fish, such as dolphins and turtles, can be accidentally caught in fishing nets. The fishing industry is now making efforts to prevent both overfishing and damage to other animals.

Standards Check Why are fish considered a renewable resource?
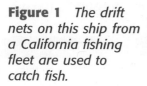 **6.6.b**

Figure 1 *The drift nets on this ship from a California fishing fleet are used to catch fish.*

Farming the Ocean

Overfishing reduces fish populations. Recently, laws regulating fishing have become stricter. Because of this, it is becoming more difficult to supply our demand for fish. Many people have begun to raise ocean fish in fish farms to help meet the demand. **Figure 2** shows one such farm.

Fish are not the only seafood harvested in a farmlike setting. Shrimp, oysters, crabs, and mussels are also raised in enclosed areas near the shore. Even seaweed is harvested. Kelp is a seaweed that is harvested and used as a thickener in jellies and ice cream. Seaweed is also high in protein and is a part of the diets of people around the world.

Standards Check How is seaweed used as a resource? ⬛ **6.6.c**

Nonliving Resources

Humans also harvest many nonliving resources from the ocean. These resources provide raw materials, drinkable water, and energy for our growing population. Some resources are easy to get, whereas others are very difficult to obtain.

Fresh Water and Desalination

Because of the water cycle, fresh water is considered a renewable resource by most countries. However, in parts of the world that have dry climates, fresh water is limited. These countries must desalinate ocean water to obtain fresh water. **Desalination** is the process of removing salt from sea water. Most desalination plants heat ocean water to cause the water to evaporate. Fresh water evaporates and is collected for use. Salt from the water remains behind and is also used as a resource. Unfortunately, desalination can be a very expensive process.

Figure 2 *In Eastport, Maine, this fish farmer shovels salmon chow to Atlantic salmon he is raising in pens at a fish farm.*

desalination (DEE SAL uh NAY shuhn) the process of removing salt from ocean water

Quick Lab

The Desalination Plant

1. Measure **1,000 mL of warm water** in a **beaker.** Pour the water in a **large pot.**
2. Carefully add **35 g of table salt.** Stir the water until all of the salt is dissolved.
3. Place the pot on a **hot plate,** and allow all of the water to boil away.
4. Using a **wooden spoon,** scrape the salt residue from the bottom of the pot.

5. Use a **balance** to measure the mass of the salt that was left in the bottom of the pot. How much salt did you separate from the water?
6. How does this activity model what happens in a desalination plant? What would be done differently in a desalination plant?

⬛ **6.6.c**

🕐 **30 min**

Figure 3 Using Tides to Generate Energy

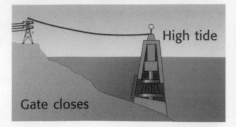

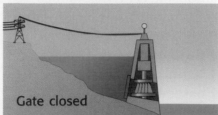

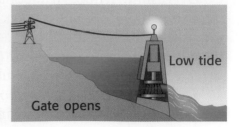

High tide

Gate closes

Gate closed

Low tide

Gate opens

❶ As the tide rises, water enters a bay behind a dam. The gate closes when high tide reaches its peak.

❷ The gate remains closed as the tide falls.

❸ At low tide, the gate opens, and water rushes through the dam. The water moves the turbines, which generate electricity.

Figure 4 *This offshore drilling rig is located near the Channel Islands Park near Santa Barbara.*

Tidal Energy

The ocean can generate energy simply by its constant movement. The gravitational pulls of the sun and the moon cause the ocean to rise and fall as tides. Energy generated from the movement of tides is called *tidal energy.* Humans tap tidal energy by building power plants, as shown in **Figure 3.** Tidal energy is a clean, inexpensive, and renewable resource. Unfortunately, tidal energy is practical only in areas that have a coastline with shallow, narrow channels and a large tidal range.

La Rance is a tidal energy power plant along the coast of France. It is the largest tidal energy power plant in the world. It can generate 240 megawatts of power, and it supplies energy to over 200,000 homes!

Standards Check How can tides be used to generate energy? 6.6.a

Oil and Natural Gas Resources

The most valuable resources in the ocean are oil and natural gas. Oil and natural gas form from the buried remains of living things. The remains take millions of years to change into oil and natural gas. For this reason, oil and natural gas are nonrenewable resources.

Offshore oil and natural gas deposits are found between layers of impermeable rock along continental margins around the world. Engineers must drill a well through the rock to reach these resources. About one-fourth of the world's oil is now obtained from offshore wells. The offshore well shown in **Figure 4** is located off the coast of California.

After oil is obtained from the wells, manufacturers refine the oil to make gasoline. Gasoline is used to power vehicles and generators that make electricity. Oil is also used to make plastic and other synthetic materials.

Sea-Floor Minerals

Many different kinds of minerals can be found on the ocean floor. The minerals are commonly in the form of nodules. *Nodules* are potato-shaped lumps of minerals that crystallize from ocean water. These nodules are made mostly of manganese. Manganese can be used to make certain kinds of steel. Nodules also contain iron, copper, nickel, and cobalt. Other nodules are made of phosphates. Phosphates are commonly used to make fertilizer.

Nodules form from dissolved substances in sea water that stick to solid objects, such as pebbles. As more substances stick to a pebble, a nodule begins to grow. Manganese nodules, shown in **Figure 5,** can be as small as a marble or as large as a soccer ball. However, these nodules are located in the deep parts of the ocean and are costly and difficult to mine.

Figure 5 *Manganese nodules are difficult to mine because they are located on the ocean floor in the deep part of the ocean.*

Standards Check List five minerals that can be found on the sea floor. 6.6.c

---

SECTION Review

 6.6.a, 6.6.b, 6.6.c

Summary

- Humans depend on the ocean for living and nonliving resources.

- Fish and other marine life are caught in the ocean and are being raised in fish farms to help feed growing human populations.

- Nonliving ocean resources include oil and natural gas, fresh water, minerals, and tidal energy.

Using Vocabulary

1. Write an original definition for *desalination.*

Understanding Concepts

2. **Listing** List two renewable resources from the ocean.

3. **Evaluating** What is the natural origin of the material used to make a plastic chair?

4. **Identifying** Name four nonliving resources in the ocean.

5. **Applying** Why are nodules not mined for ores such as manganese and iron?

6. **Listing** List the energy resources that come from the ocean.

7. **Summarizing** Why are people starting to farm the oceans rather than simply fishing or harvesting wild organisms?

Critical Thinking

8. **Analyzing Processes** Why is tidal energy considered renewable?

9. **Analyzing Ideas** Why is tidal energy not a useful energy resource everywhere?

Challenge

10. **Predicting Consequences** Overfishing our oceans could make it more difficult for us to meet our demand for fish. Overfishing can also have other negative consequences. Describe the possible environmental consequences of overfishing.

Ocean Pollution

Key Concept Activities on land and in the ocean contribute to ocean pollution.

▶ It is a hot summer day at the beach. You can hardly wait to swim in the ocean. You run to the surf only to be met by piles of trash washed up on the shore. Where did all that trash come from? People have thrown their trash in the ocean for thousands of years. This trash has harmed the living things in the oceans, as well as the people and animals that depend on them. Fortunately, we are becoming more aware of ocean pollution, and we are learning from our mistakes.

Nonpoint-Source Pollution

There are many sources of ocean pollution. Some of these sources are easily identified, but others are more difficult to pinpoint. **Nonpoint-source pollution** is pollution that comes from many sources rather than from just a single site. Some common sources of nonpoint-source pollutants are shown in **Figure 1.**

Most ocean pollution is nonpoint-source pollution. Human activities on land can pollute rivers, which then flow into the ocean and bring the pollutants they carry with them. Nonpoint-source pollutants are very hard to regulate and control because they enter bodies of water in many different ways. Nonpoint-source pollution can be reduced by using less lawn chemicals and disposing of used motor oil properly.

Figure 1 Examples of Nonpoint-Source Pollution

Oil and gasoline that have leaked from cars onto streets can wash into storm sewers that drain into the ocean.

Boats and other watercraft can leak gasoline and oil directly into bodies of water, including the ocean.

Pesticides and fertilizers from residential lawns, golf courses, and farmland can wash into waterways that flow to the ocean.

Figure 2 *This barge will dump the trash it carries in the ocean. This is an example of point-source pollution.*

Point-Source Pollution

Water pollution caused by a leaking oil tanker, a factory, or a wastewater treatment plant is one type of point-source pollution. **Point-source pollution** is pollution that comes from a specific site. However, even when the source of pollution is known, cleanup of the pollution is difficult.

6.6.a Students know the utility of energy sources is determined by factors that are involved in converting these sources to useful forms and the consequences of the conversion process.

Trash Dumping

People dump trash in many places, including the ocean, as shown in **Figure 2.** In the 1980s, scientists became alarmed by the kinds of trash that were washing up on beaches. Bandages, vials of blood, and syringes (needles) were found among the waste. Some of the blood in the vials even contained the AIDS virus.

The Environmental Protection Agency (EPA) began an investigation and discovered that hospitals in the United States produce an average of 3 million tons of medical waste each year. Because of stricter laws, much of this medical waste is now buried in sanitary landfills. However, dumping trash in the ocean is still a common practice in many countries.

nonpoint-source pollution
(NAHN POYNT SAWRS puh LOO shuhn) pollution that comes from many sources rather than from a single, specific site

point-source pollution
(POYNT SAWRS puh LOO shuhn) pollution that comes from a specific site

Effects of Trash Dumping

Trash thrown into the ocean can affect the organisms that live in the ocean. It also affects those organisms that depend on the ocean for food. Trash such as plastic can be very harmful to ocean organisms. Most plastic materials do not break down for thousands of years. Marine animals can mistake plastic materials for food and choke or become strangled. The sea gull in **Figure 3** is tangled up in a piece of plastic trash.

Figure 3 *Marine animals can be strangled by plastic trash or can choke if they mistake the plastic for food.*

Sludge Dumping

Raw sewage is all of the liquid and solid wastes that are flushed down toilets and poured down drains. After collecting in sewer drains, raw sewage is sent through a treatment plant, where it undergoes a cleaning process that removes solid waste. The solid waste is called *sludge*.

In many areas, people dump sludge into the ocean several kilometers offshore, as shown in **Figure 4.** Sometimes the sludge settles to the ocean floor. However, sometimes currents stir up the sludge and move it closer to shore. This sludge can pollute beaches and can kill marine life. By 1990, the United States alone had discharged 38 trillion liters of treated sludge into the waters along its coasts. Many countries have now banned sludge dumping. Yet it continues to occur in many areas of the world.

Figure 4 *Sludge is the solid part of waste matter and often carries bacteria. Sludge makes beaches dirty and kills marine animals.*

Oil Spills

Oil is in high demand around the world because of its use as an energy source. For this reason, large tankers must transport billions of barrels of oil across the oceans. If not handled properly, these transports can lead to oil spills. **Figure 5** shows some of the major oil spills that have happened off the coasts of North America.

Figure 5   Oil Spills in North America

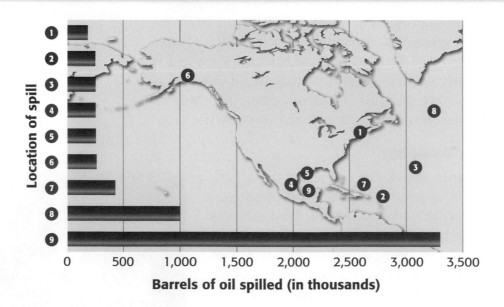

❶ Nantucket, Massachusetts, 1976

❷ Puerto Rico, 1978

❸ Atlantic Ocean, 1988

❹ Tuxpan, Mexico, 1996

❺ Galveston Bay, Texas, 1979

❻ Prince William Sound, Alaska, 1989

❼ Caribbean Sea, 1975

❽ North Atlantic Ocean, 1988

❾ Bay of Campeche, 1979

Effects of Oil Spills

One of the oil spills shown on the map in **Figure 5** happened in Prince William Sound, Alaska, in 1989. A supertanker struck a reef and spilled more than 260,000 barrels of crude oil along the shorelines of Alaska. The amount of spilled oil is roughly equivalent to the water in 125 Olympic-sized swimming pools.

The oil company spent $2.1 billion in trying to clean up the mess. Many Alaskans who made their living from fishing lost their businesses. Alaska's economy will probably continue to suffer for decades. However, there were nonmonetary costs on Alaska's wildlife as well. Although some animals were saved, many plants and animals died as a result of the spill.

Standards Check Describe one nonmonetary cost of oil spills.
🐾 6.6.a

Preventing Oil Spills

In 1990, the Oil Pollution Act was passed. It was a direct response to the oil spill in Prince William Sound. Under the law, all oil tankers operating in United States waters must be protected by double hulls by 2015. If the outer hull of the ship is damaged, an inner hull prevents oil from spilling into the ocean.

Although oil spills can harm plants, animals, and people, these spills are responsible for only about 5% of oil pollution in the oceans, as shown in **Figure 6.** Most of the oil that pollutes the oceans is caused by nonpoint-source pollution on land.

Quick Lab

Oily Feathers

1. Submerge a **feather** in a **cup of water.** 🐾 6.6.a

2. Pull the feather out of the water, and dry it with a **paper towel.**

3. Now, with an **eyedropper,** place a **drop of oil** into the cup of water.

4. Submerge the feather again.

5. Pull the feather out of the water, and try to dry it with the paper towel.

6. How difficult was drying the feather coated with oil compared with drying the feather without oil?

7. Explain how you think oil in the ocean affects wildlife that depend on the ocean.

🕐 **15 min**

Figure 6 *You can see how this oil spill in Galveston, Texas, pollutes the ocean. But as the graph shows, most of the oil that pollutes the oceans comes from everyday human activities.*

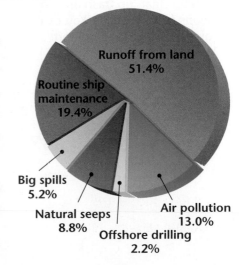

Runoff from land
51.4%

Routine ship
maintenance
19.4%

Big spills
5.2%

Natural seeps
8.8%

Offshore drilling
2.2%

Air pollution
13.0%

Figure 7 *Making an effort to pick up trash on a beach can help make the beach safer for plants, animals, and people.*

Saving Our Ocean Resources

Although humans have done much to harm the ocean's resources, we have also begun to do more to save them. From international treaties to volunteer cleanups, efforts to conserve and protect the ocean's resources are making an impact around the world.

Nations Take Notice

When ocean pollution reached an all-time high, many countries recognized the need to work together to solve the problem. In 1989, a treaty was passed by 64 countries that prohibits the dumping of certain metals, plastics, oil, and radioactive wastes into the ocean. Many other international agreements and laws restricting ocean pollution have been made. However, waste dumping and oil spills still occur. Therefore, waste continues to wash ashore, as shown in **Figure 7.** Enforcing pollution-preventing laws at all times is not always easy.

Citizens Take Charge

Citizens of many countries have demanded that their governments do more to solve the growing problem of ocean pollution. The United States now spends more than $130 million each year to protect the oceans and beaches. Citizens have also begun to take the matter into their own hands. In the early 1980s, citizens began to organize beach cleanups. For example, in **Figure 7,** teens picked up trash on the beaches of Santa Monica. Millions of tons of trash have been gathered from the beaches. And people are being educated about the hazards of ocean dumping.

Coastal Cleanup

You can be a part of a coastal cleanup. Every September, people from all over the world set aside one day to help clean up trash and debris from beaches. You can join this international effort! With a parent or guardian, write a letter to the Ocean Conservancy to see what you can do to help clean up coastal areas.

Laws in the United States

The United States, like many other countries, has taken additional measures to control local pollution. These measures include making laws. In 1972, Congress passed the Clean Water Act. This law put the Environmental Protection Agency in charge of issuing permits for any dumping of trash into the ocean.

Later that year, the U.S. Marine Protection, Research, and Sanctuaries Act was passed. This law prohibits the dumping of any material that would affect human health, the environment, or businesses that depend on the ocean. These laws have helped decrease the pollution entering our oceans.

Oil Spill

A ship spilled 750,000 barrels of oil when it accidentally struck a reef. The oil company was able to recover 65% of the oil that was spilled. How many barrels of oil were not recovered? Record your work in your **Science Journal.**

SECTION Review

 6.6.a

Summary

- The two main types of water pollution are nonpoint-source pollution and point-source pollution.

- Types of nonpoint-source pollution include oil and gasoline from cars, trucks, and watercraft, as well as of pesticides, herbicides, and fertilizers.

- Oil spills harm wildlife and local fishing economies and cost billions of dollars to clean up.

- Efforts to save ocean resources include laws, international treaties, and volunteer cleanups.

Using Vocabulary

1. Write an original definition for *point-source pollution* and *nonpoint-source pollution*.

Understanding Concepts

2. **Applying** Give an example of nonpoint-source pollution.

3. **Listing** List three types of ocean pollution.

4. **Identifying** What is the name for solid raw sewage that is a type of ocean pollution?

5. **Listing** What is a nonmonetary cost of oil pollution?

6. **Identifying** What is the main source of oil pollution?

7. **Summarizing** How does ocean pollution affect people who rely on food from the ocean?

Critical Thinking

8. **Identifying Relationships** Describe measures that governments have taken to control ocean pollution.

9. **Evaluating Data** What were two effects of the oil spill in Alaska in 1989? Describe two ways in which oil spills can be prevented.

10. **Applying Concepts** Give three examples of oil pollution in the ocean that do not come from big oil spills.

11. **Making Comparisons** How can trash dumping and sludge dumping affect food chains in the ocean?

Challenge

12. **Predicting Consequences** Oil spills are one consequence involved with the use of energy resources. What are some other consequences? Explain how these consequences add to the nonmonetary costs of using energy resources.

Internet Resources

For a variety of links related to this chapter, go to www.scilinks.org

Topic: Ocean Pollution
SciLinks code: HY71063

OBJECTIVES

Determine how far a drop of oil can spread over water.

Describe how oil's ability to spread can affect wildlife in the ocean.

MATERIALS

- calculator (optional)
- gloves, protective
- oil, light machine (5 mL)
- pan, large, at least 22 cm in diameter
- pipet
- ruler, metric
- water

SAFETY

Investigating an Oil Spill

Have you ever wondered why it is important to recycle motor oil rather than pour it down the drain or the sewer? Or have you ever wondered why a seemingly small oil spill can cause so much damage? Well, a little oil goes a long way.

Maybe you've heard the phrase "Oil and water don't mix." Oil dropped in water will spread out thinly over the surface of the water. In this activity, you'll learn how far a drop of oil can spread.

Ask a Question

❶ How far will one drop of oil spread in a pan of water?

Form a Hypothesis

❷ Write a hypothesis that could answer the question above.

Test the Hypothesis

❸ Use a pipet to place one drop of oil into the middle of a pan of water. **Caution:** Machine oil is poisonous. Wear goggles and gloves. Keep materials that have had contact with oil out of your mouth and eyes.

6.6.a Students know the utility of energy sources is determined by factors that are involved in converting these sources to useful forms and the consequences of the conversion process.

Investigation and Experimentation
6.7.a Develop a hypothesis.
6.7.e Recognize whether evidence is consistent with a proposed explanation.

4 Observe what happens to the drop of oil for the next few seconds. Record your observations.

5 Using a metric ruler, measure the diameter of the oil slick to the nearest centimeter.

Analyze the Results

6 Analyzing Results What happened to the drop of oil when it came in contact with the water?

7 Analyzing Data Determine the area of the oil slick in square centimeters. Use the formula $A = \pi r^2$ to find the area of a circle. The radius (*r*) is equal to the diameter you measured in step 5 divided by 2. Multiply the radius by itself to get the square of the radius (r^2). Pi (π) is equal to 3.14. Record your answer.

Example

If your diameter is 10 cm,

$r = 5$ cm, $r^2 = 25$ cm^2, $\pi = 3.14$

$A = \pi r^2$

$A = 3.14 \times 25$ cm^2

$A = 78.5$ cm^2

Draw Conclusions

8 Drawing Conclusions Was your hypothesis correct? How does the oil's ability to spread affect its ability to damage wildlife in the ocean?

Big Idea Question

9 Making Predictions "It's only a few drops," you may think as you spill something toxic on the ground. But those drops eventually add up. Just how many drops does it take to make a difference? Describe what you think would happen if someone spilled 4 L of oil into a lake.

Science Skills Activity

Scientific Methods   Graphs   Data Analysis   Maps

Investigation and Experimentation
6.7.g Interpret events by sequence and time from natural phenomena (e.g., the relative ages of rocks and intrusions).

Interpreting Events by Time

► Tutorial

You can interpret events by time in a natural system by learning how to read a line graph. Line graphs can be used to show change over time.

Reading a line graph

1. Data are plotted on a line graph based on changing aspects of the data called *variables.* For example, your height increases as you grow older. Both your height and your age are variables. Height is the *dependent variable* because it depends on your age. Your age is not affected by your height and thus is the *independent variable.*

2. Line graphs will have a horizontal (*x*) axis and a vertical (*y*) axis. The dependent variable is placed on the *y*-axis and the independent variable is placed on the *x*-axis, as shown in the graph to the right.

3. Data are plotted based on the two variables. A line drawn from each data point to the next shows how the dependent variable changes as the independent variable changes.

Look for relationships between variables

4. Look for a trend in the dependent variable. What influence does the independent variable have on the dependent variable?

5. Based on the relationship between the two variables, interpret the changes in the natural system over time. For example, the graph below shows that as age increases, height increases. In other words, you get taller as you get older.

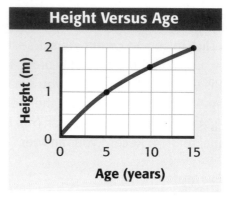

► You Try It!

Procedure

The graph to the right shows the relationship between the age of the sea floor and the depth of the sea floor beneath the ocean's surface. Use the graph to answer the following questions.

Analysis

1. How old is the sea floor at a depth of 4 km?

2. Approximately how deep is the sea floor when it is 55 million years old?

3. What can you infer about the age of very deep sea floor from the data in the graph?

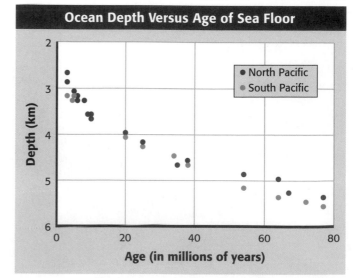

Chapter Summary

go.hrw.com
SUPER SUMMARY
KEYWORD: HY7OCES

The Big Idea
Oceans cover 71% of Earth's surface and contain natural resources that must be protected.

Section		Vocabulary

1 Earth's Oceans

Key Concept The characteristics of ocean water, such as temperature and salinity, affect the circulation of the ocean.

- Ocean water contains dissolved solids that make the water salty.
- The temperature of ocean water varies with depth, latitude, and movement of the water.

The global ocean covers most of Earth's surface.

salinity p. 401
thermocline p. 403

2 The Ocean Floor

Key Concept Many different technologies have helped scientists study the topography of the ocean basins.

- Scientists use sonar, underwater vessels, drilling, and satellites to study the ocean floor.
- Ocean floor features formed because of tectonic plate movement.

Underwater vessels help scientists explore the ocean.

abyssal plain p. 409
mid-ocean ridge p. 410
ocean trench p. 411

3 Resources from the Ocean

Key Concept The ocean is an important source of living and nonliving resources.

- The ocean is an important source for food, salt, fresh water, oil, tidal energy, and minerals.
- Oil is the most valuable resource obtained from the ocean.

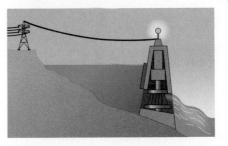

Tides can be used to generate energy.

desalination p. 413

4 Ocean Pollution

Key Concept Activities on land and in the ocean contribute to ocean pollution.

- Most of the pollution in the ocean comes from multiple sources.
- Oil pollution in the ocean harms wildlife and can cost billions of dollars to clean up.
- Laws have been passed to reduce pollution, and organizations are working to clean up the oceans.

Animals can be harmed by ocean pollution.

nonpoint-source pollution p. 416
point-source pollution p. 417

Chapter Review

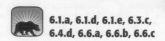
Organize

Four-Corner Fold Review the FoldNote that you created at the beginning of the chapter. Add to or correct the FoldNote based on what you have learned.

Using Vocabulary

1 **Academic Vocabulary** Which of the following words is the closest in meaning to the word *consequence*?
   a. factor
   b. resource
   c. effect
   d. change

For each pair of terms, explain how the meanings of the terms differ.

2 *mid-ocean ridge* and *ocean trench*

3 *seamount* and *abyssal plain*

Understanding Concepts

Multiple Choice

4 Which of the following distributes heat in the ocean?
   a. deep water
   b. salinity
   c. thermocline
   d. convection currents

5 Which of the following is NOT directly formed by the movement of tectonic plates?
   a. mid-ocean ridges
   b. earthquakes
   c. guyots
   d. trenches

6 Which of the following is NOT a possible product of oil?
   a. salt
   b. plastic
   c. energy
   d. synthetic materials

Short Answer

7 **Listing** List all of the possible consequences of oil pollution in the ocean.

8 **Describing** How do oil and natural gas form?

9 **Identifying** Identify five resources obtained from the ocean. Describe them as renewable or nonrenewable.

10 **Comparing** How are temperature, salinity, and density related?

11 **Summarizing** Explain why the surface zone is warmer than the thermocline.

12 **Listing** List the ocean floor features that are formed by the movement of tectonic plates.

13 **Identifying** How does differences in density cause convection currents in ocean water?

14 **Describing** Describe how a mid-ocean ridge forms.

INTERPRETING GRAPHICS Use the diagram below to answer the next two questions.

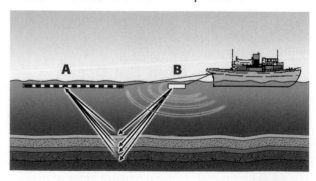

15 **Evaluating** While scientists use the method illustrated above to study the ocean floor, their ship may tow a sound source that emits sound waves. Which letter most likely represents the sound source?

16 **Analyzing** Explain how scientists use the method illustrated above to determine the depth of the sea floor.

Writing Skills

17 Writing from Research Use a variety of sources to research different underwater vessels. Write a brief report on your findings. Create charts, maps, or graphs to illustrate ideas and concepts from your sources.

Critical Thinking

18 Concept Mapping Use the following terms to create a concept map: *abyssal plain, ocean basin, mid-ocean ridge, seamount, ocean trench,* and *global ocean.*

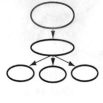

19 Making Inferences What benefit besides being able to obtain fresh water from salt water comes from desalination?

20 Analyzing Methods Some businesses have tried to develop methods of extracting nodules from the ocean. Describe factors that the businesses should consider when determining whether extracting nodules is profitable.

21 Predicting Consequences If the sea level were to fall significantly, what would happen to the continental shelves?

22 Evaluating Assumptions If fish and water are considered renewable resources, why do we need to conserve them?

23 Predicting Consequences Do you think the ocean floor will look the same 1 million years from now? Explain why or why not.

24 Making Inferences Salinity and temperature affect the density of water. Explain how salinity and temperature affect convection currents and the transfer of heat throughout the ocean.

25 Predicting Consequences How might a change in the demand of energy sources affect the amount of pollution in the oceans?

INTERPRETING GRAPHICS Use the graph below to answer the next three questions.

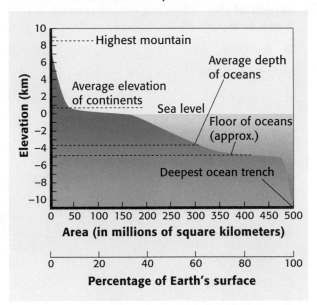

26 Evaluating Data What percentage of Earth's surface is covered by land?

27 Making Comparisons Which is greater: the elevation of the highest mountain above sea level or the depth of the deepest ocean trench below sea level?

28 Identifying Relationships Relative to sea level, how many times greater is the average depth of the ocean than the average elevation of land?

Math Skills

29 Making Calculations The total area of Earth is approximately 511,000,000 km². About 71% of Earth's surface is covered with water. Calculate the area of Earth, in square kilometers, that is covered with water.

Challenge

30 Analyzing Processes In the best conditions, a fish farm can produce more food than an agricultural farm. Explain why this is possible.

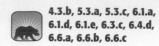
REVIEWING ACADEMIC VOCABULARY

1 Which of the following words means "to have as a part of"?

A exclude

B appropriate

C involve

D viable

2 Choose the appropriate form of the word *convert* for the following sentence: "Photosynthesis is a method of _____ solar energy into chemical energy."

A convert

B converted

C converting

D conversion

3 Which of the following sets of words is the closest in meaning to the word *consequences*?

A the effect of an action or process

B serious problems

C special techniques

D big surprises

4 Which of the following sets of words best completes the following sentence: "Ideas about the habits of deep-sea creatures _____ years of careful study."

A are derived from

B derived by

C are derivative of

D derive in

REVIEWING CONCEPTS

5 Which of the following is true of water in the ocean's thermocline?

A Convection heats all areas of the thermocline equally.

B The sun's rays directly heat the thermocline.

C Temperatures in the thermocline drop as depth increases.

D The thermocline begins at the same depth everywhere.

6 What is the natural origin of the material that is used to make a plastic chair?

A oil

B rubber trees

C seaweed

D chemicals

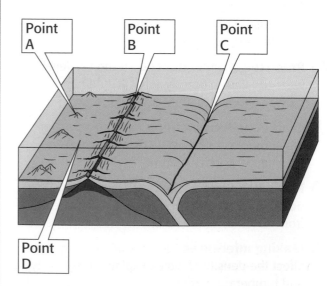

7 At which point in the diagram above is there most likely to be a hot spot?

A Point A

B Point B

C Point C

D Point D

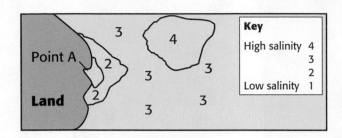

Key

High salinity	4
	3
	2
Low salinity	1

8 **Which of the following features is most likely to be found at Point A in the diagram above?**

A a mountain

B a coral reef

C a fault line

D a river

9 **How do some communities use ocean water to generate energy?**

A by harnessing convection currents

B by damming water at high tide

C by using the water as an electrical conductor

D by tapping the energy in deep-sea water

10 **What factors cause a mid-ocean ridge to form?**

A Tectonic plates pull apart, and magma rises up.

B Magma rises up through a hot spot in the ocean floor.

C One plate is pushed upward when tectonic plates collide.

D Sediment is deposited along the edge of a tectonic plate.

REVIEWING PRIOR LEARNING

11 **Which statement describes the role of ocean water in the water cycle?**

A Ocean water evaporates, condenses, and travels to land as clouds.

B Ocean water flows onto land in the form of rivers.

C Ocean water blows onto land as a result of storms.

D Ocean water evaporates over the ocean and never reaches land.

12 **Which of the following adaptations is most likely to benefit an animal living in the deep zone of the ocean?**

A eyes that can see long distances

B a shell that protects against cold temperatures

C gills that can withstand high salt levels

D skin that can survive quick changes in temperature

13 **An astronaut viewed Earth from space. Which of the following did she observe?**

A The global ocean covers 40 percent of Earth's surface.

B The global ocean and land cover Earth's surface equally.

C The global ocean covers about 71 percent of Earth's surface.

D The global ocean accounts for three-fourths of the water on Earth.

Standards Assessment

Science in Action

Weird Science

Human-Powered Submarine Races

Your friend is furiously pumping the pedals that drive the submarine's propeller as you desperately try to keep the vessel on course. You are piloting a small, human-powered sub and are halfway through the race.

Human-powered submarine racing is a competitive sport for engineering students around the world. These amazing races were started by the Ocean Engineering Department of Florida Atlantic University in Boca Raton. Awards are given to the fastest subs, the subs that have the best design, and the most efficient subs. But all of the participants have fun while gaining experience in designing new and unique technology.

Math ACTiViTY

A human-powered submarine has a mass of about 135 kg. Calculate the weight of this submarine in pounds. (Hint: A 1 kg mass has a weight of about 2.2 lb.)

Science, Technology, and Society

A "Ship" That Flips?

Does your school's laboratory have doors on the floor or tables bolted sideways to the walls? Scripps Institution of Oceanography has a lab like this, and you can find it floating in the ocean. *FLIP*, or *Floating Instrument Platform*, is a 108 m long ocean research vessel that can tilt 90°. *FLIP* is towed to an area that scientists want to study. To flip the vessel, empty chambers within the vessel are filled with water. The *FLIP* begins tilting until almost all of the vessel is underwater. Having most of the vessel below the ocean's surface stabilizes the vessel against wind and waves. Scientists can collect accurate data from the ocean, even during a hurricane!

Social Studies ACTiViTY

Scientists have used ships to help them do research for many years. Find out more about research ships that scientists use. In your **Science Journal,** write a one-page description of one of these research ships.

Jacques Cousteau

Ocean Explorer Jacques Cousteau was born in France in 1910. Cousteau performed his first underwater diving mission at age 10 and became very fascinated with the possibilities of seeing and breathing underwater. As a result, in 1943, Cousteau and Emile Gagnan developed the first aqualung, a self-contained breathing system for underwater exploration. Using the aqualung and other underwater equipment that he developed, Cousteau began making underwater films. In 1950, Cousteau transformed the *Calypso*, a retired minesweeper boat, into an oceanographic vessel and laboratory. For the next 40 years, Cousteau sailed with the *Calypso* around the world to explore and film the world's oceans. Cousteau produced more than 115 films, many of which have won awards.

Jacques Cousteau opened the eyes of countless people to the sea. During his long life, Cousteau explored Earth's oceans and documented the amazing variety of life that they contain. He was an environmentalist, inventor, and teacher who inspired millions with his joy and wonder of the ocean. Cousteau was an outspoken defender of the environment. He campaigned vigorously to protect the oceans and the environment. Cousteau died in 1997 at age 87. Before his death, he dedicated the *Calypso II,* a new research vessel, to the children of the world.

Language Arts ACTIVITY

Ocean pollution and overfishing are subjects of intense debate. Think about these issues, and discuss them with your classmates. Take notes on what you discuss. In your **Science Journal,** write an essay in which you try to convince readers of your point of view.

Cousteau sailed his ship, the *Calypso,* around the world exploring and filming the world's oceans.

Internet Resources

- To learn more about careers in science, visit **www.scilinks.org** and enter the SciLinks code HY70225.

- To learn more about these Science in Action topics, visit **go.hrw.com** and type in the keyword HY7OCEF.

- Check out articles related to this chapter by visiting **go.hrw.com.** Just type in the keyword HY7OCEC.

Improving Comprehension

Graphic Organizers are important visual tools that can help you organize information and improve your reading comprehension. The Graphic Organizer below is called a *cause-and-effect map*. Instructions for creating other types of Graphic Organizers are located in the **Study Skills** section of the Appendix.

How to Make a Cause-and-Effect Map

1 Draw a box, and write a cause in the box. You can have as many cause boxes as you want. The diagram shown here is one example of a cause-and-effect map.

2 Draw another box to the right of the cause box to represent an effect. You can have as many effect boxes as you want. Draw arrows from each cause box to the appropriate effect boxes.

3 In the cause boxes, explain the process that makes up the cause. In the effect boxes, write a description of the effect or details about the effect.

When to Use a Cause-and-Effect Map

A cause-and-effect map is a useful tool for illustrating a specific type of scientific process. Use a cause-and-effect map when you want to describe how, when, or why one event causes another event. As you read, look for events that are either causes or results of other events, and draw a cause-and-effect map that shows the relationships between the events.

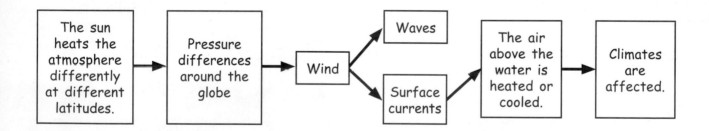

You Try It!

This Reading Strategy can also be used within the chapter that you are about to read. Practice making your own cause-and-effect map as directed in the Reading Strategies for Section **2** and Section **3**. Record your work in your **Science Journal.**

Unpacking the Standards

The information below "unpacks" the standards by breaking them down into basic parts. The higher-level, academic vocabulary is highlighted and defined to help you understand the language of the standards. "What It Means" restates the standards as simply as possible.

California Standard	Academic Vocabulary	What It Means
6.3.a Students know **energy** can be carried from one place to another by heat flow or by waves, including water, light and sound waves, or by moving objects.	**energy** (EN uhr jee) the ability to make things happen	Energy is moved from one place to another by heat flow, by waves, or by the movement of objects. Water waves, light waves, and sound waves are kinds of waves.
6.3.c Students know heat flows in solids by conduction (which **involves** no flow of matter) and in fluids by conduction and by convection (which **involves** flow of matter).	**involve** (in VAHLV) to have as a part of	When heat flows in solids, the heat can be transferred without the movement of matter. When heat flows in liquids and gases, the heat can be transferred with or without the movement of matter.
6.4.a Students know the sun is the **major source** of **energy** for **phenomena** on Earth's surface; it powers winds, ocean currents, and the water **cycle.**	**major** (MAY juhr) of great importance or large scale **source** (SAWRS) the thing from which something else comes **phenomenon** (fuh NAHM uh NUHN) any facts or events that can be sensed or described scientifically (plural *phenomena*) **cycle** (SIE kuhl) a repeating series of changes	The sun is the main source of energy for processes on Earth. Energy from the sun powers winds, ocean currents, and the water cycle.
6.4.d Students know convection currents **distribute** heat in the atmosphere and oceans.	**distribute** (di STRIB yoot) to spread out over an area	The movement of air in the atmosphere and of water in the ocean carries heat throughout the atmosphere and oceans.
6.4.e Students know differences in pressure, heat, air movement, and humidity result in changes of weather.		Changes in the weight of the atmosphere, heat, air movement, and the amount of water in the air cause the conditions of the atmosphere to change.

13

The Movement of Ocean Water

The Big Idea

The movement of ocean water is a major factor in energy transfer on Earth's surface.

California Standards

Focus on Earth Sciences

6.3 Heat moves in a predictable flow from warmer objects to cooler objects until all the objects are at the same temperature. (Sections 1 and 3)

6.4 Many phenomena on Earth's surface are affected by the transfer of energy through radiation and convection currents. (Sections 1 and 2)

Investigation and Experimentation

6.7 Scientific progress is made by asking meaningful questions and conducting careful investigations. (Science Skills Activity)

Math

6.1.4, 6.2.1 Number Sense
6.2.3 Algebra and Functions
6.1.1 Statistics, Data Analysis, and Probability

English–Language Arts

6.1.1 Reading
6.2.1, 6.2.2 Writing

About the Photo

The movement of ocean water is obvious to this surfer in Half Moon Bay, California. Waves form offshore when wind transfers energy to ocean water. As a wave reaches shallow water near the shore, the height of the wave increases. Eventually, the wave curls over, which makes surfing possible.

Organize

Three-Panel Flip Chart

Before you read this chapter, create the FoldNote entitled "Three-Panel Flip Chart." Label the flaps of the three-panel flip chart with "Currents," "Currents and Climate," and "Waves and Tides." As you read the chapter, write information about each topic under the appropriate flap.

Instructions for creating FoldNotes are located in the Study Skills section on p. 617 of the Appendix.

Explore Activity

20 min

6.4.d

The Ups and Downs of Convection

In this activity, you will investigate how warm water and cold water interact.

Procedure

1. Fill a **1,000 mL beaker** 4/5 full with **chilled water.**

2. Attach a 20 cm length of **nylon or cotton string** to an **open film canister** with a lip at the top edge by looping the string beneath the canister's lip. Secure with a knot.

3. Place several **coins** inside the canister. Add two drops of **food coloring** to the canister. Carefully fill the canister with **warm water.**

4. Seal the canister with a lid shaped from a single piece of **aluminum foil.** Crimp the edges of the foil to the canister lip to keep the foil in place.

5. Holding the string, gently lower the canister into the chilled water.

6. Use a **sharpened pencil** to punch several holes in the aluminum foil cover. Observe what happens.

Analysis

7. What happened after the aluminum foil was punctured?

8. What does this result tell you about the movement of warm and cold water in the ocean?

435

Currents

Key Concept The circulation of ocean water distributes water, heat, dissolved gases, and dissolved solids around Earth's surface.

▶ Imagine that you are stranded on a desert island. You put a message asking for help into a bottle and throw the bottle into the ocean. Is there a way to predict where your bottle will end up? Actually, there is a way to predict where the bottle will end up. The oceans contain streamlike movements of water called *ocean currents*. Currents are influenced by a number of factors, including wind, Earth's rotation, and the position of the continents. With knowledge of ocean currents, people are able to predict where objects in the open ocean will be carried.

Surface Currents

Horizontal, streamlike movements of water that occur at or near the surface of the ocean are called **surface currents.** Surface currents can reach depths of several hundred meters. These currents also reach lengths of several thousand kilometers and can travel across oceans. The Gulf Stream, shown in **Figure 1,** is one of the strongest surface currents on Earth. The Gulf Stream transports at least 25 times more water each year than is transported by all of the rivers in the world combined.

Surface currents are controlled by three factors: global winds, the Coriolis effect, and continental deflections. These three factors keep surface currents flowing in distinct patterns around Earth.

Figure 1 *This false-color image taken from an infrared satellite shows the Gulf Stream moving warm water northward along the east coast of the United States.*

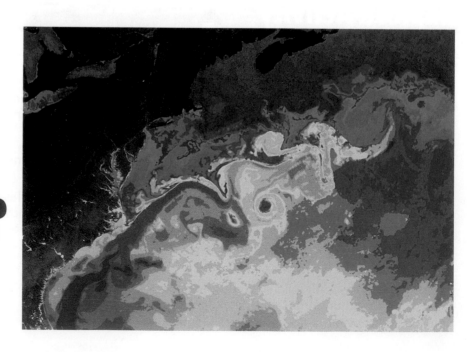

Warm   Cool

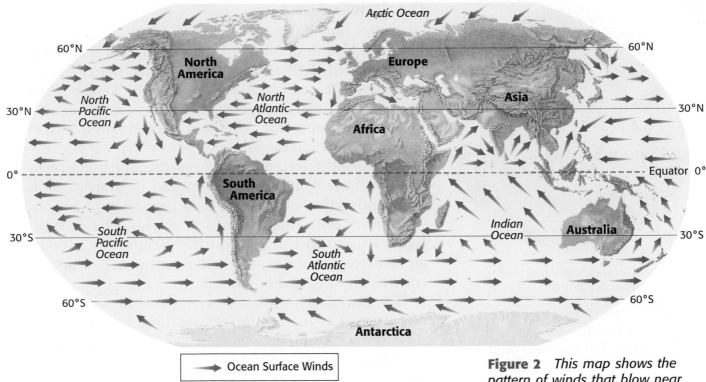

 Ocean Surface Winds

Figure 2 *This map shows the pattern of winds that blow near the surface of Earth's oceans.*

Global Winds

Have you ever blown gently on a cup of hot chocolate? You may have noticed that your breath pushes the hot chocolate across the surface of the liquid in your cup. In much the same way, winds that blow across the surface of Earth's oceans push water across Earth's surface. This process causes surface currents in the ocean.

Different winds cause currents to flow in different directions. The pattern of global winds that blow near the ocean surface is shown in **Figure 2.** Near the equator, the winds blow mostly east to west. Between 30° south latitude and 60° south latitude, winds blow mostly west to east.

How the Sun Powers Ocean Currents

The sun heats air near the equator more than it heats air at other latitudes. Pressure differences form because of these differences in heating. For example, the air that is heated near the equator is warmer and less dense than surrounding air. Warm, less dense air rises and creates an area of low pressure near the equator. Pressure differences in the atmosphere cause the wind to blow. So, the sun causes winds to blow, and winds cause surface currents to form. Therefore, the major source of the energy that powers surface currents is the sun.

Standards Check What is the major source of the energy that powers surface currents in the ocean? 🐻 **6.4.a**

6.3.c Students know heat flows in solids by conduction (which involves no flow of matter) and in fluids by conduction and convection (which involves flow of matter).

6.4.a Students know the sun is the major source of energy for phenomena on Earth's surface; it powers winds, ocean currents, and the water cycle.

6.4.d Students know convection currents distribute heat in the atmosphere and oceans.

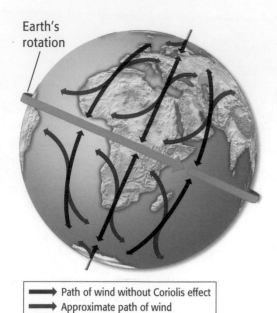

Earth's
rotation

→ Path of wind without Coriolis effect
→ Approximate path of wind

Figure 3 *The Coriolis effect in the Northern Hemisphere causes winds and water traveling north or south to appear to be deflected to the right.*

Coriolis effect (KAWR ee OH lis e FEKT) the curving of the path of a moving object from an otherwise straight path due to Earth's rotation

deep current (DEEP KUHR uhnt) a streamlike movement of ocean water far below the surface

The Coriolis Effect

Earth's rotation causes some wind and ocean currents to be deflected from the paths they would take if Earth did not rotate. This deflection of moving objects from a straight path due to Earth's rotation is called the **Coriolis effect.** Because Earth rotates, points on Earth near the equator travel faster than points closer to the poles. This difference in speed of rotation causes the Coriolis effect. For example, water or wind traveling south from the North Pole actually goes toward the southwest instead of straight south. Wind and water deflect to the right because the water and wind move east slower than Earth rotates beneath them. **Figure 3** shows that in the Northern Hemisphere, currents are deflected to the right. In the Southern Hemisphere, currents are deflected to the left.

The Coriolis effect is most noticeable for objects that travel very fast or that travel over long distances. Over short distances, the difference in Earth's rotational speed from one point to another point is not great enough to cause deflection.

Standards Check How are air and ocean currents deflected by the rotation of Earth? 🐻 **6.4.d**

Continental Deflections

If Earth's surface were covered only with water, surface currents would travel freely across the globe in a very uniform pattern. However, water does not cover the entire surface of Earth. Continents rise above sea level over about one-third of Earth's surface. When surface currents meet continents, the currents are deflected and change direction. Notice in **Figure 4** how the South Equatorial Current turns southward as it meets the coast of South America. The southward-flowing current is called the Brazil Current.

Figure 4 *If South America were not in the way, the South Equatorial Current would probably flow farther west.*

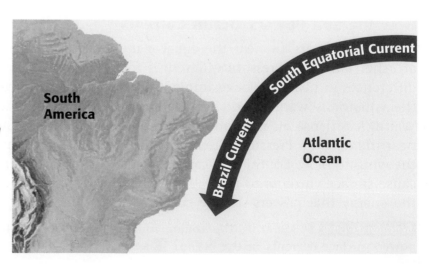

South America

South Equatorial Current

Brazil Current

Atlantic Ocean

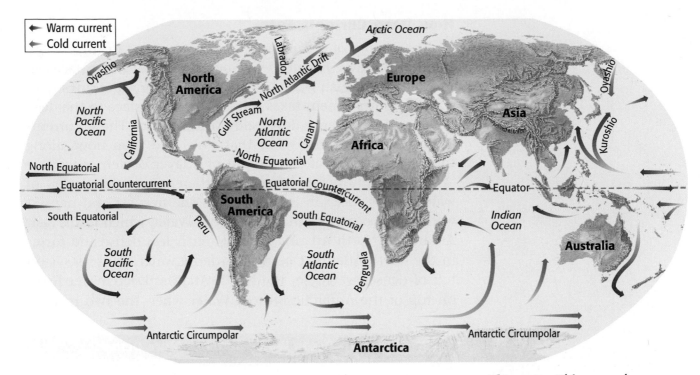

Warm current
Cold current

Arctic Ocean

Labrador

Oyashio

North America

North Atlantic Drift

Gulf Stream

North Pacific Ocean

California

North Atlantic Ocean

Canary

North Equatorial

Europe

Asia

Oyashio

Kuroshio

Africa

North Equatorial

Equatorial Countercurrent

Equatorial Countercurrent

Equator

South America

South Equatorial

South Equatorial

Peru

Benguela

Indian Ocean

Australia

South Pacific Ocean

South Atlantic Ocean

Antarctic Circumpolar

Antarctic Circumpolar

Antarctica

Figure 5 *This map shows Earth's major surface currents.*

How Surface Currents Distribute Heat

The flow of surface currents transfers, or distributes, heat energy from one part of Earth to another. The transfer of energy as a result of the movement of matter is called *convection*. So, surface currents transfer heat energy by convection. As **Figure 5** shows, both warm-water and cold-water currents travel from one ocean to another. Water near the equator absorbs heat energy from the sun. Then, warm-water currents carry the energy from the equator to other parts of the ocean. The heat energy from the warm water is transferred to colder water or to the atmosphere. Cold-water currents absorb heat energy from the atmosphere and from other ocean currents.

Standards Check How do surface currents distribute heat in the oceans? 🐻 **6.3.c, 6.4.d**

Deep Currents

Movements of ocean water far below the surface are called **deep currents.** Unlike surface currents, deep currents are not controlled by wind. Instead, the movement of deep currents is caused by differences in water density. Water that flows deep in the ocean is denser than water at the ocean surface. *Density* is the amount of matter in a given space or volume. The density of ocean water is affected by salinity and temperature. *Salinity* is a measure of the amount of dissolved salts or solids in a liquid. Water with high salinity is denser than water with low salinity. And cold water is denser than warm water.

Wordwise **convection**
The prefix *con-* means "with" or "together." The root *vect-* means "to carry."

Coriolis Effect in Your Sink?

Some people think that the Coriolis effect can be seen in sinks. Does water draining from sinks turn clockwise in the Northern Hemisphere and counter-clockwise in the Southern Hemisphere? Research this question at the library, on the Internet, and in your sink at home with an adult. Write what you learn in your **Science Journal.**

How Deep Currents Form

The density of ocean water can be increased in three ways, as **Figure 6** shows. In these ways, ocean water at the surface can become denser than water below it. The denser water sinks. This downward movement takes water from the surface to the deep ocean. Deep currents flow below the surface. These currents are made up of dense water that sinks and then flows along the ocean floor or along the top of a layer of denser water.

Because the ocean is so deep, there are several layers of water at any location in the ocean. The deepest and densest water in the ocean is Antarctic Bottom Water, which forms near Antarctica. North Atlantic Deep Water is less dense and forms in the North Atlantic Ocean. Less-dense water always stays on top of denser water. So, the North Atlantic Deep Water flows on top of the Antarctic Bottom Water when the two meet.

Figure 6 **How Ocean Water Becomes More Dense**

Decreasing Temperature In Earth's polar regions, cold air chills the water molecules at the ocean's surface. This decrease in temperature causes the molecules to slow down and move closer together. Thus, the water's volume decreases, which makes the water denser.

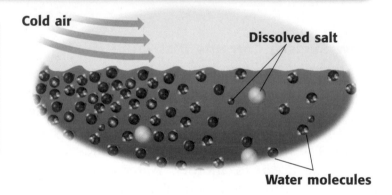

Cold air

Dissolved salt

Water molecules

Increasing Salinity Through Freezing In some places, ocean water freezes at the surface. Ice floats on top of the water because ice is less dense than liquid water. The dissolved solids in the ocean water do not become part of the ice and remain in the water that has not frozen. This process increases the salinity of the water, and the water becomes denser.

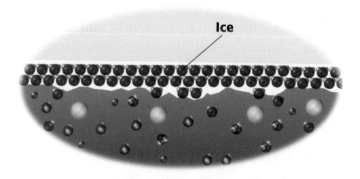

Ice

Increasing Salinity Through Evaporation Salinity also increases through evaporation of surface water. Evaporation is especially common in warm climates. It removes water but leaves solids behind. As a result, salinity increases and the water becomes denser.

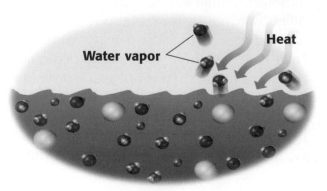

Heat

Water vapor

Quick Lab

Creating Convection Currents

In this investigation, you will use colored ice cubes to model convection currents.

▶ Try It!

1. One day before beginning step 2, make **ice cubes** by using **water** and **food coloring**.
2. Fill a **deep, clear baking dish** with **hot water**.
3. Float one **large, colored ice cube** on the surface of the water at one end of the pan.
4. Trace the path of the colored water as the ice cube melts.

▶ Think About It!

5. In what way was the movement of water that you observed like a convection current?
6. Formulate a hypothesis that describes what you think would happen if the pan was left undisturbed for several hours.
7. If you have time, test your hypothesis by observing the pan after several hours.

🕐 **2 10-min periods on the same day**

Convection Currents

Surface currents and deep currents are linked in the ocean. Together they are called **convection currents** because their movement results partly from differences in water density. Convection currents transfer energy as they flow, as shown in **Figure 7**. Warm water at the ocean surface absorbs energy from the sun. Surface currents carry this energy to colder regions. The warm water loses energy to its surroundings and becomes cooler. As the water cools, it becomes denser and sinks. The cold water travels along the ocean bottom. Then, the deep water rises to the surface as surface water moves away. The cold water warms as it absorbs energy from the sun, and the cycle continues.

convection current (kuhn VEK shuhn KUHR uhnt) any movement of matter that results from differences in density; may be vertical, circular, or cyclical

Standards Check What is a convection current? 🐻 **6.3.c, 6.4.d**

ⓐ Surface currents carry warmer, less-dense water from warm ocean regions to polar regions.

ⓑ Warm water from surface currents cools in polar regions, becomes denser, and sinks to the ocean floor.

ⓒ Deep currents carry colder, denser water along the ocean floor from polar regions to other ocean regions.

ⓓ Water from deep currents rises to replace water that leaves in surface currents.

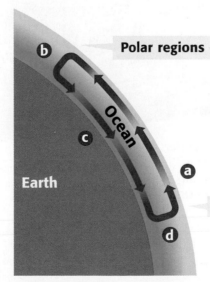

Figure 7 *The warmer, less-dense water in surface currents cools and sinks. This water then becomes the colder, denser water in deep currents.*

Global Circulation

Ocean water circulates through all of Earth's ocean basins. The paths shown in **Figure 8** are like the main highway on which much ocean water flows. If you could follow a water molecule on this path, you would find that the molecule takes more than 1,000 years to come back to its starting point!

Material Transport by Global Circulation

Global ocean circulation moves more than just water—materials in the water are moved as well. Two of the most important materials transported this way are oxygen and nutrients. Oxygen is taken from the surface to the deep ocean by deep currents. Nutrients are brought to the surface as deep water rises to the surface.

Heat Transport by Global Circulation

Global ocean circulation is also very important in the distribution of heat. About half of the heat that is transported around Earth's surface is carried by convection currents in the ocean. Thus, ocean circulation is important in global climate regulation.

Standards Check What are three of the things that are transported by global ocean circulation? 6.4.d

Figure 8 *This map shows the main paths of global ocean circulation. Antarctica is not shown on this map, but the currents at the bottom of the map circulate around Antarctica. These currents are called circumpolar currents.*

SECTION
Review

6.3.c, 6.4.a, 6.4.d

Summary

- Surface currents form as wind transfers energy to ocean water.

- Surface currents are controlled by three factors: global winds, the Coriolis effect, and continental deflections.

- Deep currents form where the density of ocean water increases. Water density depends on temperature and salinity.

- Surface currents and deep currents combine to form convection currents that transfer energy.

- Earth's global circulation moves water through all oceans and distributes materials and heat.

Using Vocabulary

1 Write an original definition for *surface current, deep current,* and *convection current.*

Understanding Concepts

2 Describing Explain ways in which energy from the sun influences surface currents.

3 Listing List three factors that control surface currents, and tell how each factor is important.

4 Describing Describe how temperature and salinity affect the formation of deep currents.

5 Analyzing How do convection currents distribute heat in the oceans?

6 Summarizing Explain how oxygen and nutrients are transported by ocean currents.

Critical Thinking

7 Evaluating Conclusions If there were no land on Earth's surface, what would the pattern of surface currents look like? Explain your answer.

8 Making Comparisons Compare the factors that cause the formation of surface currents and the factors that cause the formation of deep currents.

9 Making Inferences Explain why the Coriolis effect is important in the movement of both wind and ocean currents.

10 Identifying Relationships Explain one way in which ocean currents might change if the polar regions of Earth become warmer.

INTERPRETING GRAPHICS Use the diagram of a convection current in the ocean below to answer the next two questions.

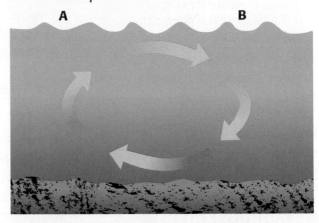

A   B

11 Making Inferences What might be happening at point B to keep this convection current flowing?

12 Analyzing Processes Explain ways in which heat could be transferred by this convection current.

Math Skills

13 Making Calculations The average speed of surface currents is about 20 cm/s. The Gulf Stream flows as fast as 2 m/s. What is the difference in speed between the Gulf Stream and an average surface current?

Challenge

14 Identifying Relationships You have learned how ocean water can become more dense. Describe two ways in which ocean water can become less dense. Explain how the density change would take place in each case.

Internet Resources

For a variety of links related to this chapter, go to www.scilinks.org

Topic: Ocean Currents
SciLinks code: HY71061

<table>
</table>

SECTION 2

Currents and Climate

Key Concept Ocean currents transport energy, affect climate and weather, and distribute nutrients.

What You Will Learn

● Surface currents affect climate by distributing energy around Earth.

● Changes in surface currents, such as El Niño, can cause changes in weather patterns.

Why It Matters

Surface currents affect the climate of many of the most populated areas of the world.

Vocabulary

• El Niño
• La Niña
• upwelling

READING STRATEGY

Graphic Organizer In your **Science Journal,** show the relationship between surface currents and coastal climates in a Cause-and-Effect Map.

6.4.e Students know differences in pressure, heat, air movement, and humidity result in changes of weather.

▶ The Scilly Isles in Great Britain are located as far north as Newfoundland in Canada. But the Scilly Isles have warm weather almost all year long, and Newfoundland has long winters of frost and snow. How can two places at similar latitudes have such different climates? This difference in climate happens because heat is transported by the Gulf Stream.

Surface Currents and Climate

Surface currents greatly affect the climate in many parts of the world. The surface temperature of the water affects the temperature of the air above it. Warm currents heat air and cause warmer air temperatures. Cold currents absorb energy from surrounding air and cause cooler air temperatures. Also, water absorbs and releases heat more slowly than land does. So, sudden changes and extreme temperatures are unusual on land near any large body of water.

Warm-Water Currents and Climate

Surface currents are often warmer than deep currents, but the temperatures of surface currents do vary. Coastal areas that are affected by warm-water currents tend to have warmer climates than inland areas of the same latitude have. **Figure 1** shows the Gulf Stream as it carries heat from the Tropics northward. The heat is absorbed by the atmosphere around Great Britain. As a result, Great Britain has a mild climate for land at such a high latitude. Because of the Gulf Stream, the Scilly Islands have a milder climate than Newfoundland has.

Figure 1 **How Warm-Water Currents Affect Climate**

❶ The Gulf Stream carries warm water from the Tropics to the North Atlantic Ocean.

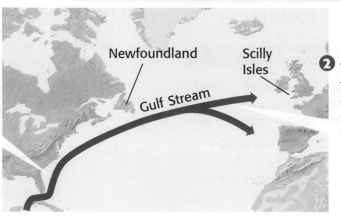

❷ The Gulf Stream flows to the British Isles and creates a relatively mild climate for land at such a high latitude.

Cold-Water Currents and Climate

Coastal areas near cold-water currents feel the effects of the cold water on their climates. **Figure 2** shows how the California Current carries cold water south from the North Pacific Ocean. The California Current moves less water than the Gulf Stream does. But the California Current has a big effect on the climate of the West Coast of the United States. Summer temperatures differ less from winter temperatures along the West Coast than they do inland. Usually, the climate along the West Coast is cooler than the climate of inland areas at the same latitude and elevation.

Standards Check How do ocean currents affect climates? 6.4.e

El Niño and La Niña

Every 2 to 12 years, the South Pacific trade winds move less warm water to the western Pacific than they usually do. Thus, surface-water temperatures along the coast of South America rise. Gradually, this warming spreads westward. This periodic change in the location of warm and cool surface waters in the Pacific Ocean is called **El Niño.** El Niño can last for a year or longer. Sometimes, El Niño is followed by La Niña. **La Niña** is a periodic change in the eastern Pacific Ocean in which the surface-water temperature becomes unusually cool.

El Niño and Weather Patterns

Both El Niño and La Niña change the way the ocean and atmosphere interact. The resulting changes in the circulation of the atmosphere lead to changes in global weather patterns. Changes in the weather during El Niño show how the atmosphere, ocean, and weather patterns are related. Scientists can predict the weather changes on land that might be caused by El Niño by studying the atmosphere and ocean.

INTERNET ACTIVITY

What Is El Niño?
Explore the effects of El Niño and La Niña. Go to **go.hrw.com,** and type in the keyword HY7H20W.

El Niño (el NEEN yoh) a change in the water temperature in the Pacific Ocean that produces a warm current

La Niña (lah NEEN yah) a change in the eastern Pacific Ocean in which the surface water temperature becomes unusually cool

Figure 2 How Cold-Water Currents Affect Climate

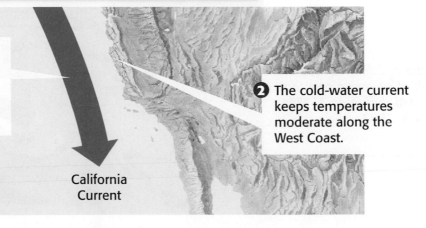

1 Cold water from the northern Pacific Ocean is carried south to Mexico by the California Current.

California Current

2 The cold-water current keeps temperatures moderate along the West Coast.

Quick Lab

Warm Land, Cold Water

6.4.e

1. Mix **ice** and **cool water** in a **22 cm × 22 cm pan.**

2. Fill a **pan of the same size** with **warm sand.**

3. Place the two pans next to each other about 1 cm apart.

4. Put your hand over each pan to see what the temperature is above the sand and above the water.

5. Light a **fireplace match.** Then, quickly blow out the flame, and place the match above the space between the two pans.

6. Observe how the smoke from the match moves.

7. What does the movement of the smoke demonstrate about how cold currents affect nearby land?

 15 min

Studying and Predicting El Niño

Because El Niño occurs every 2 to 12 years, studying and predicting this phenomenon can be difficult. However, it is important for scientists to learn as much as possible about El Niño because of its effects on organisms and land.

One way scientists collect data to predict El Niño is through a network of buoys anchored to the ocean floor along Earth's equator. The buoys record data about water temperature, air temperature, currents, and winds. Buoys sometimes report that the South Pacific trade winds are weaker than usual. Or buoys may report that the surface temperatures of the tropical oceans have risen. If either of these changes happen, scientists can predict that El Niño is likely to occur.

Effects of El Niño

El Niño can alter weather patterns enough to cause disasters in many parts of the world. For example, flash floods and mudslides may happen in areas of the world that usually receive little rain. These areas include Peru and the southern half of the United States. **Figure 3** shows homes that were destroyed by a mudslide that happened during an El Niño event.

While some regions flood, regions that usually get a lot of rain may experience droughts. *Droughts* are unusually long periods during which rainfall is below average. Periods of severe drought can lead to crop failure. During El Niño, severe droughts can occur in Indonesia and Australia.

Standards Check Why is it important to study El Niño events in relation to changes in weather? 6.4.e

Figure 3 *This damage in Southern California was the result of excessive rain that occurred during an El Niño event in 1997.*

Upwelling

At times, local winds blow toward the equator along the northwest coast of South America and the west coast of North America. This wind causes local surface currents to move away from the shore. The warm surface water is then replaced by cold, nutrient-rich water from the deep ocean in a process called **upwelling.** This process is shown in **Figure 4.**

Upwelling is extremely important to ocean life. The nutrients that are brought to the surface of the ocean support the growth of plankton. These tiny plants and animals support other organisms, such as fish and seabirds. On the California coast, upwelling is usually strongest from March to September. Some weather conditions, including El Niño, can interrupt the process of upwelling. When upwelling is reduced, the richness of the ocean life at the surface is also reduced.

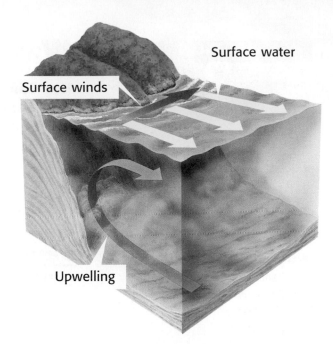

Figure 4 *Upwelling can occur along coastlines when the wind conditions are right.*

SECTION Review

 6.4.e

Summary

- Surface currents cause climates of coastal areas to be more moderate than inland climates at the same latitude and elevation.

- Upwelling is the flow of cold, nutrient-rich water from the deep ocean to the surface.

- During El Niño, warm and cool surface waters change locations. El Niño can cause floods, mudslides, drought, and changes in upwelling.

Using Vocabulary

❶ Use *El Niño, La Niña,* and *upwelling* in separate sentences.

Understanding Concepts

❷ **Describing** How do surface currents affect the climate of land near which they flow?

❸ **Concluding** Why might the climate in Scotland be relatively mild even though the country is located at a high latitude?

❹ **Listing** Name three disasters caused by El Niño.

Critical Thinking

❺ **Applying Concepts** Many marine organisms depend on upwelling to bring nutrients to the surface. How might El Niño affect a commercial fishing fleet?

Math Skills

❻ A fisher usually catches 540 kg of fish off the coast of Peru. During El Niño, the fisher caught 85% less fish. How many kilograms of fish did the fisher catch during El Niño?

Challenge

❼ **Predicting Consequences** Predict what would happen to the weather on the coast of California if the California Current stopped flowing. Explain your answer.

Internet Resources

For a variety of links related to this chapter, go to www.scilinks.org

Topic: El Niño
SciLinks code: HY70468

Waves and Tides

Key Concept Energy is carried through the ocean by tides, which are caused by gravitational attraction between Earth, the moon, and the sun, and by waves.

▶ Have you ever seen a surfer riding waves? Did you ever wonder where the waves come from? A **wave** is any disturbance that transmits energy through matter or empty space. Waves in the ocean carry energy through water.

Standards Check What is a wave, and what do waves in the ocean carry through water? 6.3.a

Waves

Ocean waves are affected by a number of different factors. They can be formed by something as simple as wind or by something as violent as an earthquake. Ocean waves can travel through water slowly or incredibly quickly. The size of an ocean wave depends on the energy the wave carries.

Parts of a Wave

Waves are made up of two main parts—crests and troughs. A *crest* is the highest point of a wave. A *trough* is the lowest point of a wave. Imagine a roller coaster designed with many rises and dips. The top of a rise on a roller-coaster track is similar to the crest of a wave. The bottom of a dip in the track resembles the trough of a wave. The distance between two adjacent wave crests or wave troughs is a *wavelength*. The vertical distance between the crest and trough of a wave is called the *wave height*. **Figure 1** shows the parts of a wave.

wave (WAYV) a periodic disturbance in a solid, liquid, or gas as energy is transmitted through a medium

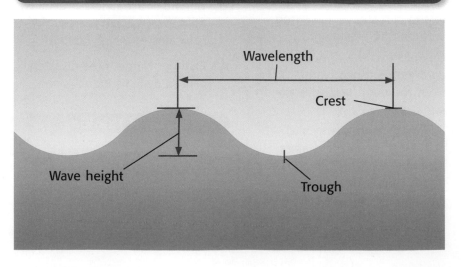

Figure 1 **Parts of a Wave**

Wavelength

Crest

Wave height

Trough

6.3.a Students know energy can be carried from one place to another by heat flow or by waves, including water, light and sound waves, or by moving objects.

Wave Formation

Ocean waves form when energy is transferred from a source to the ocean water. Most ocean waves form as wind blows across the water's surface and transfers energy to the water. The energy is then carried by the wave, usually the entire distance to the ocean shore. Waves can also form from other sources of energy. Underwater earthquakes and landslides, as well as impacts by asteroids or meteorites, can form waves in the ocean.

Standards Check List four sources of energy for ocean waves.
🐻 **6.3.a**

Wave Movement

If you have watched ocean waves, you may have noticed that water appears to move across the ocean's surface. However, this movement is only an illusion. As the energy moves through the water, so do the waves. But the water itself does not travel significantly with the energy. Notice in **Figure 2** that the floating bottle remains in the same spot as the waves travel from left to right. The water only rises and falls in circular movements. This circular movement of water is generally greatest at the ocean surface. Wave energy decreases as the water depth increases. Below a depth of about half a wavelength, water is not affected by the energy of surface waves.

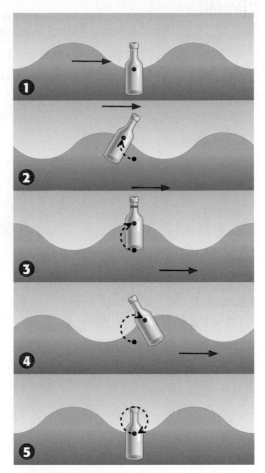

Figure 2 *Like the bottle in this figure, water remains in the same place as waves travel through it.*

Quick Lab

Making Waves

In this lab, you will make waves and observe the motion of the waves and an object on the water.

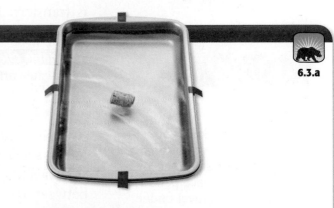

6.3.a

▶ Try It!

1. Fill a **rectangular pan** (40 cm × 30 cm × 10 cm) with **water** to a depth of about 7 cm.

2. Float a **cork** or **piece of foam** near the center of the pan. On each side of the pan, mark the location of the cork with a **small piece of tape**.

3. Hold a **spoon** in the water at one end of the pan. Gently move the spoon into the water to make a wave. Wait 10 s, and repeat.

4. Observe the movement of the waves and the motion of the cork or foam. Sketch how the cork moves relative to the waves.

▶ Think About It!

5. Describe the motion of a wave and the motion of the cork when a wave passes.

6. How does the cork move relative to the tape on the sides of the pan?

7. Explain how energy travels in the waves you were making. How is this energy related to the movement of the cork?

 15 min

Figure 3 Determining Wave Period

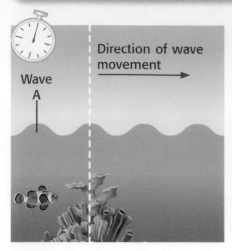

① Notice that the waves are moving from left to right.

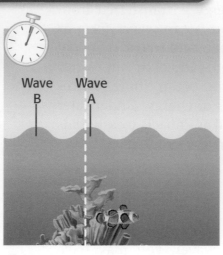

② The clock begins running as Wave A passes the reef's peak.

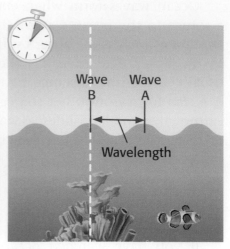

③ The clock stops as Wave B passes the reef's peak. The time shown on the clock (5 s) represents the wave period.

Wave Energy

You have learned that most ocean waves are formed by the wind. Have you ever wondered why these waves are different sizes? When wind begins to blow over water, small waves, or ripples, form. If the wind keeps blowing, the ripples receive more energy and grow into larger waves. The longer the wind blows in the same direction across the water, the more energy is transferred from the wind to the water and the larger the waves become.

Standards Check How does the length of time that wind blows over water affect the amount of energy in a wave? 📖6.3.a

Wave Speed

Waves not only are different sizes but also travel at different speeds. To calculate wave speed, scientists must know the wavelength and the wave period. *Wave period* is the time between the passage of two wave crests (or troughs) at a fixed point, as **Figure 3** shows. Dividing wavelength by wave period gives you wave speed, as shown below.

$$\frac{\text{wavelength (m)}}{\text{wave period (s)}} = \text{wave speed (m/s)}$$

For any given wavelength, an increase in the wave period will decrease the wave speed. For a given wavelength, a decrease in the wave period will increase the wave speed.

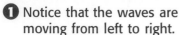

Wave Speed

A surfer wants to know how fast she needs to go to catch a wave. She measures the wavelength and wave period of waves as they travel under her surfboard. One set of waves has waves that have a wavelength of 5 m and a wave period of 3 s. What is the wave speed of these waves?

Waves Reaching the Shore

No matter how waves form, most waves reach the shore. When waves reach the shore, energy from the wave is transferred to the beach environment. The energy of the wave and the angle at which the wave hits the shore determine how much energy is transferred. Some waves, such as tsunamis, transfer large amounts of energy. Tsunamis are huge ocean waves that form as a result of underwater earthquakes or underwater landslides. These events release large amounts of energy. This energy can be carried by tsunamis that may become very big near land. Tsunamis can cause a great deal of damage when they reach the shore and can be dangerous to humans.

Why Waves Break

Have you ever wondered why waves increase in height and crash as they reach the shore? The answer has to do with the depth of the water, as **Figure 4** shows. When waves reach water shallower than one-half their wavelength, they begin to interact with the ocean floor. As waves begin to touch the ocean floor, the waves transfer energy to the ocean floor. As a result, the water particles at the bottom of the wave slow down and the wave height increases. The water at the top of the wave is not slowed as much. So, the top of the wave continues to travel at the original speed. The top of the wave travels faster than the bottom of the wave. Eventually, the high wave crest crashes down onto the ocean floor as a *breaker*.

Standards Check How do waves transfer energy to the ocean floor and to the shore? 🐻 6.3.a

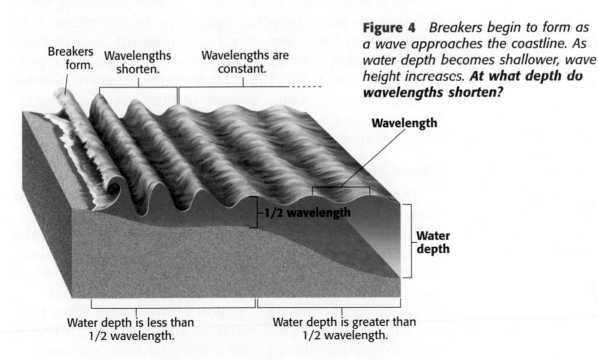

Figure 4 *Breakers begin to form as a wave approaches the coastline. As water depth becomes shallower, wave height increases.* **At what depth do wavelengths shorten?**

Breakers form.
Wavelengths shorten.
Wavelengths are constant.
Wavelength
1/2 wavelength
Water depth

Water depth is less than 1/2 wavelength.
Water depth is greater than 1/2 wavelength.

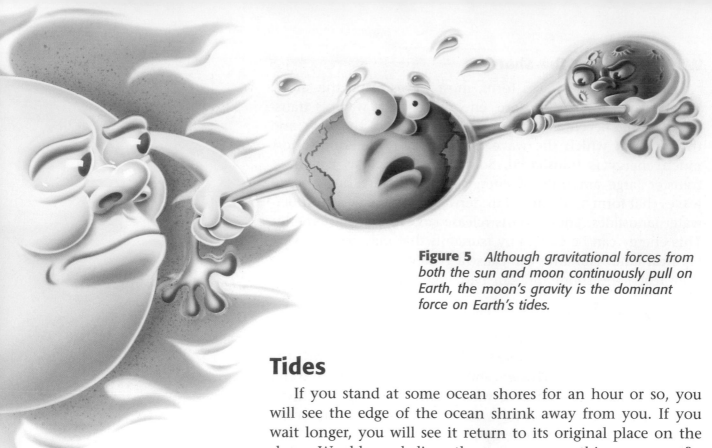

Tides

If you stand at some ocean shores for an hour or so, you will see the edge of the ocean shrink away from you. If you wait longer, you will see it return to its original place on the shore. Would you believe the moon causes this movement?

You have learned how winds and earthquakes can move ocean water. But other forces also move ocean water in regular patterns. **Tides** are daily changes in the level of ocean water. Tides are influenced by the sun and the moon, as **Figure 5** shows, and tides occur in a variety of cycles.

tide (TIED) the periodic rise and fall of the water level in the oceans and other large bodies of water

Why Tides Happen

The gravity of the moon pulls on every particle of Earth. However, the moon's gravitational pull on Earth decreases with distance from the moon. As a result, different parts of Earth are pulled more strongly toward the moon than other parts are. In addition, the pull on liquids is much more noticeable than the pull on solids, because liquids move more easily. Even the liquid in a carton of milk is slightly pulled by the moon's gravity.

Where Tides Happen

The part of the ocean that directly faces the moon is pulled toward the moon with the greatest force. As a result, the water on the side of Earth that faces the moon bulges toward the moon. The solid center of Earth is also pulled toward the moon. However, because it is farther from the moon, the solid Earth is not pulled as strongly as the ocean facing the moon is. The ocean on Earth's far side is pulled with even less force than the solid Earth is. So, the water on the side of Earth that is farthest from the moon bulges away from Earth's center.

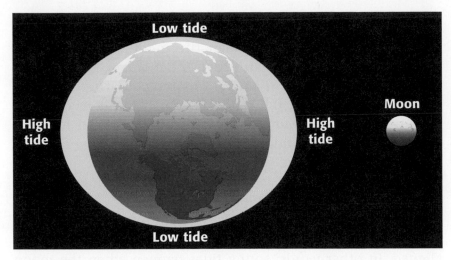

Figure 6 *High tide occurs on the part of Earth that is closest to the moon and on the opposite side of Earth. Low tides occur in the areas between the high tides.*

High Tides and Low Tides

The bulges that form in Earth's oceans as a result of the moon's gravitational pull are called *high tides*. In high-tide areas, shown in **Figure 6,** the water level is higher than the average sea level. In the areas between the high tides, *low tides* form. In low tide areas, the water levels are lower because the water is pulled toward high-tide areas. As the moon moves around Earth, the tidal bulges sweep around the planet in a regular pattern. As a result, many places on Earth experience two high tides and two low tides every day.

Timing the Tides

The moon revolves around Earth much more slowly than Earth rotates. As **Figure 7** shows, a place on Earth that is facing the moon takes 24 h and 50 min to rotate to face the moon again. So, the high tides and low tides at that place happen 50 minutes later each day. If Earth rotated at the same speed that the moon revolved around Earth, the tides would not alternate between high and low.

Tuesday, 11:00 A.M.

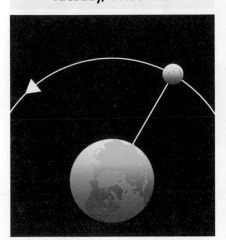

Wednesday, 11:50 A.M.

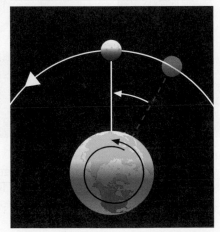

Figure 7 *High and low tides occur about 50 minutes later each day at a given place. This happens because the moon moves only a fraction of its orbit in the time that Earth rotates once.*

Tidal Variations

The sun is much larger than the moon, but the sun is much farther away from Earth than the moon is. So, the sun's pull on tides is weaker than the moon's pull. The combined forces of the sun and the moon on Earth result in different tidal ranges. A *tidal range* is the difference between levels of ocean water at high tide and low tide. Tidal range depends on the positions of the sun, Earth, and the moon.

Spring Tides

Tides that have the largest daily tidal range are **spring tides.** Spring tides happen when the sun, Earth, and the moon are aligned. In other words, spring tides happen when the moon is between the sun and Earth or when the moon and the sun are on opposite sides of Earth. **Figure 8** shows the positions of the sun, Earth, and the moon during spring tides. Spring tides happen during the new-moon and full-moon phases, or every 14 days. During these times, the sun and moon cause one pair of very large tidal bulges.

Neap Tides

Tides that have the smallest daily tidal range are **neap tides.** Neap tides happen when the sun, Earth, and the moon form a 90° angle. **Figure 8** shows the positions of the sun, Earth, and moon during neap tides. Neap tides occur halfway between the occurrence of spring tides, during the first-quarter and third-quarter phases of the moon. During these times, the sun and moon cause two pairs of smaller tidal bulges.

spring tide (SPRING TIED) a tide of increased range that occurs two times a month, at the new and full moons

neap tide (NEEP TIED) a tide of minimum range that occurs during the first and third quarters of the moon

Figure 8   Spring Tides and Neap Tides

Spring Tides   When the sun, Earth, and the moon form a line, the gravitational force of the sun increases the tidal range that results from the gravitational force of the moon.

Neap Tides   When the sun and the moon are at right angles to each other relative to Earth, the gravitational force of the sun decreases the tidal range that results from the gravitational force of the moon.

Summary

- Waves form when the wind's energy is transferred to the surface of the ocean.
- Wave energy travels through water near the water's surface, while the water itself rises and falls in circular movements.
- Waves break when the water depth becomes so shallow that the bottom of the wave transfers energy to the ocean bottom and the shore.
- Tides are caused by the gravitational forces of the moon and the sun on Earth. The moon's gravity is the main force behind the tides.
- The positions of the sun and moon relative to the position of Earth cause tidal ranges.

Using Vocabulary

❶ Write an original definition for *wave*, *tide*, *spring tide*, and *neap tide*.

Understanding Concepts

❷ **Describing** How do ocean waves form?

❸ **Summarizing** Explain how water moves as wave energy travels through it.

❹ **Concluding** What happens as waves from deeper waters enter shallower waters?

❺ **Identifying** What is the main force that causes tides?

❻ **Comparing** Which tides have minimum tidal ranges? Which tides have maximum tidal ranges?

Critical Thinking

❼ **Analyzing Processes** Why do you think earthquakes and underwater landslides cause larger, more-destructive waves than winds do?

❽ **Applying Concepts** Explain how the sun's energy plays a role in the formation of ocean waves.

❾ **Identifying Relationships** If you had a calendar that showed only the phases of the moon, how could you predict when spring tides and neap tides would happen?

❿ **Analyzing Processes** Waves transfer energy to the beach environment when they reach the shore. Describe some of the effects on the natural environment and on human-made structures that are caused by this transfer of energy.

⓫ **Applying Concepts** Many coastal cities build artificial walls or reefs in their harbors to protect the cities from damaging waves, such as tsunamis. How would these structures help protect the cities?

Math Skills

INTERPRETING GRAPHICS The diagram shows an ocean wave with a scale beneath it. Use the diagram below to answer the next two questions.

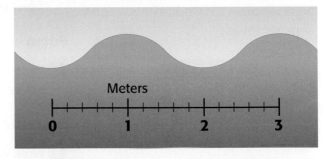

⓬ **Making Calculations** What is the wavelength of the waves shown in the diagram?

⓭ **Using Equations** The wave period for these waves is 3 s. Calculate the wave speed.

Challenge

⓮ **Forming Hypotheses** Develop a hypothesis about how the waves and tides might be different if the amount of energy Earth received from the sun were to increase.

Internet Resources

For a variety of links related to this chapter, go to www.scilinks.org

Topic: Ocean Waves; Tides
SciLinks code: HY71066; HY71525

Model-Making Lab

Modeling the Coriolis Effect

OBJECTIVES

Model the Coriolis effect.

Observe the path of liquid flowing over a spinning sphere.

MATERIALS

- balloons, large, round, light color (2)
- cup, plastic or paper, small
- eye dropper
- food coloring, red or blue
- kite string
- newspapers, scrap
- paper clip
- paper towels

SAFETY

6.4.d Students know convection currents distribute heat in the atmosphere and oceans.

Investigation and Experimentation
6.7.a Develop a hypothesis.

Although you can't feel it move, the ground beneath your feet is moving. And the rotational movement of Earth changes the path of moving objects. Objects north of the equator can curve to the right, and produce a clockwise spin. Objects south of the equator can curve to the left, and produce a counterclockwise spin. This deflection of the path of a moving object is known as the Coriolis effect. It is seen in the curved paths of some wind and ocean currents. In this activity, you will model the Coriolis effect. And you will see how the Coriolis effect affects the movement of water in the ocean.

Ask a Question

1 Does water flow over a spinning sphere differently than it flows over a sphere that is not spinning?

Form a Hypothesis

2 Write a hypothesis that is a possible answer to the question above. Explain your reasoning.

Test the Hypothesis

3 Work with a partner. Inflate and tie a knot in a large, round balloon. Use sheets of scrap newspaper to protect the floor.

4 Tie a 15 cm (about 6 in.) length of kite string to the knot.

5 Position the balloon above the newspaper and hold the knot of the balloon so that the balloon does not move.

6 Put about 5 drops of food coloring in the small cup and then fill the eye dropper with this food coloring.

7 Have your partner use an eye dropper to deliver a large drop of food coloring as close as possible to the knot.

8 Observe the path that the food coloring follows as it moves over the balloon. Record your observations.

9 Set aside the balloon on newspaper. Repeat steps 3 and 4 using the second balloon. Also repeat step 6.

10 Position the balloon above the newspaper and use two hands to twirl the string. The balloon should spin at about 1 revolution per second. The balloon should spin in a counterclockwise direction as you look down toward the knot. You can also bend open the paper clip, tie the end of the string to it, and use it as a crank to spin the balloon.

11 As the balloon is spinning, have your partner use an eye dropper to deliver the food coloring as close a possible to the spinning knot.

12 Keep the balloon spinning, and observe the path that the food coloring follows as it moves over the balloon. Be patient. It make take several seconds for the drop to begin to move. Record your observations.

Analyze the Results

13 Identifying Patterns   If the balloon is a model of Earth, what does the balloon knot represent? Where is the equator located?

14 Analyzing Results   What location(s) on the balloon's surface were spinning fastest? What location(s) on the balloon's surface were spinning slowest?

15 Describing Events   Describe the path of the drop as it moved across the balloon that was not spinning.

16 Describing Events   Think of the spinning balloon as a model of Earth. Describe the path of the drop as it moved over the "Northern Hemisphere". Describe the path of the drop as it moved over the "Southern Hemisphere".

Draw Conclusions

17 Evaluating Results   Compare the paths of the drop on the still sphere, on the "Northern Hemisphere" of the spinning sphere, and on the "Southern Hemisphere" of the spinning sphere. How do your observations compare with your original hypothesis?

18 Evaluating Models   How does your model help explain the Coriolis effect on Earth?

19 Making Predictions   Suppose the balloon was rotated in a clockwise direction. How would that motion affect the path of the drop? Test your hypothesis.

Big Idea Question

20 Drawing Conclusions   How does the Coriolis effect influence the movement of ocean water? Look at a map of surface ocean currents. Explain how the Coriolis effect influences the patterns you see in these currents.

Science Skills Activity

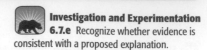

Investigation and Experimentation
6.7.e Recognize whether evidence is consistent with a proposed explanation.

Evaluating Explanations for Evidence

► Tutorial

After scientists make observations and collect data, the scientists develop explanations for the phenomena they observe. Part of the scientific method is to evaluate all evidence to see whether it supports, or is consistent with, proposed explanations. To do this, scientists perform the following steps:

❶ Identify which lines of evidence support the explanation. Most explanations must be supported by at least two different lines of evidence to be considered valid.

❷ Identify any lines of evidence that do not support the proposed explanation. A single line of evidence can disprove an explanation.

❸ Identify any additional lines of evidence that should be considered when evaluating the explanation.

❹ If possible, propose an alternative explanation that could fit the evidence.

❺ Decide whether the original explanation is supported by enough evidence. Determine whether or not the original explanation is disproved by any available evidence. Decide whether an alternative explanation better explains the evidence.

► You Try It!

Imagine that you are reviewing the work of a research team that is studying the differences between the climates of Iceland and Greenland. The team developed the map that you see here. And the team made the following observations:

- Both Iceland and Greenland lie above 60° north latitude.
- Iceland's land surface area is 103,000 km². Greenland's land surface area is 2,166,086 km².
- The average annual temperature for locations in Greenland ranges from −1°C to −30°C. The average annual temperature for locations in Iceland ranges from 6°C to −8°C.
- Iceland is bordered by the North Atlantic Current and the Norway Current. Greenland is bordered by the Labrador Current and the East Greenland Current.

After reviewing the data, the team has proposed the following explanation: The climate of Greenland is cooler than the climate of Iceland because Greenland is very large and because the center of Greenland is far from the warm ocean water.

❶ Which evidence did the scientists collect that supports the proposed explanation?

❷ Do any data suggest that the explanation is untrue? Explain your answer.

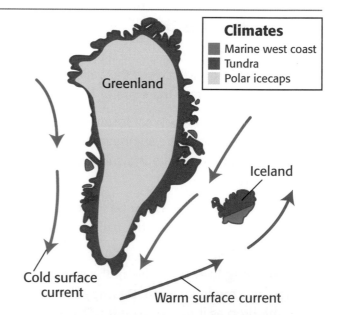

Climates
- ■ Marine west coast
- ■ Tundra
- □ Polar icecaps

Greenland

Iceland

Cold surface current

Warm surface current

❸ What additional evidence would you like to have when deciding whether the team's evidence is consistent with the explanation?

❹ Can you propose another explanation that fits the data? Explain your answer.

❺ Do you think that the evidence is consistent with the team's proposed explanation? Is the explanation correct? Explain your answer.

Chapter Summary

The Big Idea
The movement of ocean water is a major factor in energy transfer on Earth's surface.

Section

Vocabulary

1 Currents

Key Concept The circulation of ocean water distributes water, heat, dissolved gases, and dissolved solids around Earth's surface.

- The sun is the major source of energy that drives wind and ocean currents.
- Surface currents and deep currents form convection currents that move ocean water.

Warm and cold surface currents in the ocean transfer energy around Earth's surface.

surface current p. 436
Coriolis effect p. 438
deep current p. 439
convection current p. 441

2 Currents and Climate

Key Concept Ocean currents transport energy, affect climate and weather, and distribute nutrients.

- Surface currents affect climate by distributing energy around Earth.
- Changes in surface currents, such as El Niño, can cause changes in weather patterns.

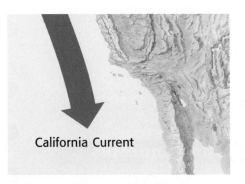

Warm and cold currents affect the climates of nearby landmasses.

El Niño p. 445
La Niña p. 445
upwelling p. 447

3 Waves and Tides

Key Concept Energy is carried through the ocean by tides, which are caused by gravitational attraction between Earth, the moon, and the sun, and by waves.

- Ocean waves transfer energy through water and to the shore when the wave breaks.
- Tides are the periodic rise and fall of the water level in the oceans.

A wave carries energy from one place to another with no net movement of matter.

wave p. 448
tide p. 452
spring tide p. 454
neap tide p. 454

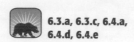
Organize

Three-Panel Flip Chart   Review the FoldNote that you created at the beginning of the chapter. Add to or correct the FoldNote based on what you have learned.

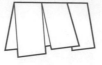

Using Vocabulary

1 **Academic Vocabulary**   In the sentence "The sun is the major source of energy for phenomena such a winds and ocean currents," what does the word *phenomena* mean?
  a. events that are the strongest of their kind
  b. events that can be sensed or described scientifically
  c. events that involve changes in direction
  d. events that have worldwide effects

For each pair of terms, explain how the meanings of the terms differ.

2 *surface current* and *deep current*

3 *El Niño* and *La Niña*

4 *spring tide* and *neap tide*

Understanding Concepts

Multiple Choice

5 Deep water forms in the ocean when
  a. cold air decreases water density.
  b. warm air increases water density.
  c. rain falls into the ocean.
  d. salinity increases.

6 A convection current
  a. can form in air or water.
  b. distributes heat in the oceans.
  c. often forms a circular pattern.
  d. All of the above

7 Tidal range is greatest during
  a. spring tide.
  b. neap tide.
  c. high winds.
  d. the daytime.

8 Energy can be carried from one place to another by
  a. ocean waves.
  b. convection currents.
  c. surface currents.
  d. All of the above

9 Global ocean circulation
  a. does not reach the Indian Ocean.
  b. moves water, materials, and heat.
  c. depends on energy from volcanoes.
  d. All of the above

10 Waves can form in the ocean when
  a. wind blows across the water.
  b. salinity increases.
  c. upwelling increases.
  d. rain or snow fall in the ocean.

Short Answer

11 **Analyzing**   Explain how the sun powers winds and ocean currents.

12 **Describing**   Describe the two parts of a wave. Describe how these two parts relate to wavelength and wave height.

13 **Comparing**   Compare the causes of ocean waves and the causes of tides in the ocean.

14 **Summarizing**   Describe how warm-water currents affect the climate in the British Isles.

15 **Listing**   Describe the factors that form deep currents.

Writing Skills

16 **Communicating Key Concepts**   Write an essay that traces energy from its origin in the sun to the effect of ocean waves on the beach.

Critical Thinking

17 **Concept Mapping**   Use the following terms to create a concept map: *wind, sun, deep currents, water density, ocean currents, energy transfer, surface currents, movement of ocean water,* and *waves.*

18 Identifying Relationships   Why are tides more noticeable in Earth's oceans than on Earth's land?

19 Expressing Opinions   Do you think that studying El Niño and La Niña is important? Explain your answer.

20 Identifying Relationships   Describe how global winds, the Coriolis effect, and continental deflections form a pattern of surface ocean currents on Earth.

21 Analyzing Processes   Compare the way energy moves with the way water moves when a wave travels through ocean water.

22 Analyzing Relationships   What part does upwelling play in the global circulation of ocean water?

23 Analyzing Processes   Describe how heat flow by convection affects Earth's oceans.

INTERPRETING GRAPHICS   The diagram shows some of Earth's major surface currents that flow in the Western Hemisphere. Use the diagram below to answer the next two questions.

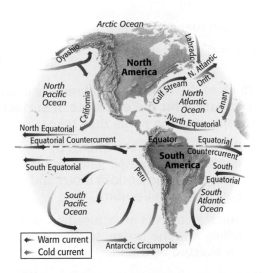

24 Identifying Relationships   How do you think the Labrador Current affects the climate of northeastern Canada?

25 Applying Concepts   Why does the California Current turn the way it does as it approaches the equator?

INTERPRETING GRAPHICS   The graph below shows the average monthly temperature of two locations that are at the same latitude and elevation but are in different parts of the United States. Use the graph to answer the next two questions.

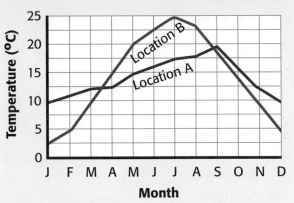

26 Evaluating Data   Which location has the lowest temperatures in the summer?

27 Making Inferences   Which of the two locations is most likely closest to the ocean? Explain your answer.

Math Skills

28 Using Equations   Wave A and wave B each have a period of 8 s. However, the waves have different wavelengths. Wave A has a wavelength of 5 m, and wave B has a wavelength of 7 m. Find the wave speed for each wave, and identify which wave is traveling faster.

Challenge

29 Predicting Consequences   Occasionally, Earth's atmosphere can be filled with debris. For example, dust and ash can come from a volcanic eruption, or in rare cases, from an asteroid impact. Imagine that there was enough debris in the atmosphere to reduce the amount of energy from the sun that reached Earth's atmosphere and oceans. Describe changes in the movement of ocean water that might occur, and give reasons for each change.

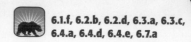

REVIEWING ACADEMIC VOCABULARY

1 Which of the following words is the closest in meaning to the word *predictable*?

A varying in time or place

B unique

C able to be known ahead of time

D wavering in space

2 Which of the following words is the closest in meaning to the word *involves*?

A is a part of

B wants

C gives away

D develops

3 Which of the following words means "a fact or event that can be sensed or described scientifically"?

A time

B date

C appointment

D phenomenon

4 Which of the following words best completes the following sentence: "The air currents _____ heat in the atmosphere"?

A distribute

B detach

C develop

D dissolve

5 Which of the following words means "the thing from which something else comes"?

A preview

B cycle

C source

D event

REVIEWING CONCEPTS

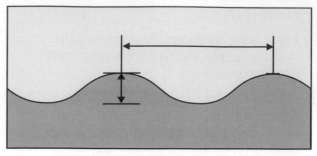

6 Use the diagram above to answer the next question. What does the horizontal arrow at the top of the diagram show?

A wavelength

B crest

C trough

D wave height

7 What is the major source of energy for occurrences on Earth's surface, such as ocean and wind currents?

A the sun

B the moon

C earthquakes

D the Gulf Stream

8 Which of the following statements is an explanation for the existence of surface currents and the paths they take?

A Surface currents are caused by earthquakes, so their paths can be affected by the Coriolis effect and continental deflection.

B Surface currents are caused by rain falling into the ocean, so their paths can be affected by the moon's gravity.

C Surface currents are caused by waves from the Pacific Ocean, so their paths can be affected by the moon's gravity.

D Surface currents are caused by winds, so their paths can be affected by the Coriolis effect and continental deflection.

9 **What is a convection current?**

A Warmer water at the ocean surface flows to cooler regions, cools, and sinks.

B Surface currents blow across the surface of the ocean and warm Earth.

C Warmer water at the bottom of the ocean flows up and cools in a circular pattern.

D Colder water at the top of the ocean flows to warmer regions and causes waves.

10 **What is El Niño?**

A a change in the water temperature in the Atlantic Ocean that produces a warm current

B a change in the Eastern Pacific Ocean in which surface water becomes very hot

C a change in the Eastern Atlantic Ocean in which surface water becomes very cool

D a change in the water temperature in the Pacific Ocean that produces surface water that is warmer than usual

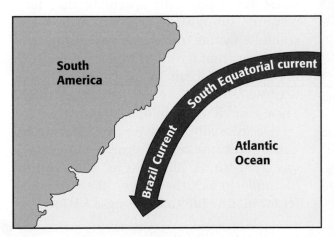

11 **Use the map above to answer the next question. What causes the surface ocean current to change direction?**

A the movement of tectonic plates

B deflection by continents

C a change in the density of the water

D the gravity of the moon

REVIEWING PRIOR LEARNING

12 **If a scientist developed an idea about the movement of ocean water and tested it, what is her original idea called?**

A conclusion

B result

C hypothesis

D test

13 **What do light waves and ocean waves carry from one place to another?**

A pressure

B energy

C electricity

D water

14 **What is the sudden and rapid movement of a large amount of material down a slope called?**

A metamorphism

B creep

C a tsunami

D a landslide

15 **Which of the following may be formed as a river changes course?**

A a plate boundary

B an oxbow lake

C electromagnetic radiation

D a divide

16 **On which of the following tectonic plates does California rest?**

A the North American plate, the Juan de Fuca plate, and the Pacific plate

B the North American plate and the Pacific plate

C the North American plate and the Juan de Fuca plate

D the North American plate

Science in Action

Weird Science

Using Toy Ducks to Track Ocean Currents

Accidents can sometimes lead to scientific discovery. For example, on January 10, 1992, 29,000 plastic tub toys spilled overboard when a container ship traveling northwest of Hawaii ran into a storm. In November 1992, those toys began washing up on Alaskan beaches. When oceanographers heard about this, they placed advertisements in newspapers along the Alaskan coast. The scientists asked people who found the toys to call with their location.

Hundreds of toys were recovered. Using recovery dates and locations and computer models, oceanographers were able to re-create the toys' drift and figure out which currents carried the toys. As for the remaining toys, currents may carry them to a number of different destinations. Some may travel through the Arctic Ocean and eventually reach Europe!

Math ACTiViTy

Between January 10, 1992, and November 16, 1992, some of the toys were carried approximately 3,220 km from the cargo-spill site to the coast of Alaska. Calculate the average distance traveled by these toys per day. (Hint: The year 1992 was a leap year.)

Scientific Discoveries

Red Tides in California

Why is the ocean red along this California coast? It may surprise you to find that the answer is single-celled algae. When certain algae grow rapidly, they clump together on the ocean's surface in what are known as *algal blooms.* These algal blooms have been commonly called *red tides* because the blooms often turn the water red or reddish-brown.

No one is sure about what causes red tides. Some scientists speculate that temperature, sunlight, or layering of the water could be factors in red-tide formation. Others suggest that fertilizers in river water flowing into the ocean might cause red tides. Because fertilizers are nutrients, they might cause a sudden bloom of algal growth.

Occasionally, red tides in California are harmful because certain algae release poisonous compounds. But most red tides are not harmful—in fact, they can be like a huge buffet for marine life that use algae for food!

Social Studies ACTiViTy

Some scientists think that factors related to human activities, such as agricultural runoff into the ocean, are causing more red tides than occurred in the past. Other scientists disagree. Find out more about this issue, and have a class debate about the roles humans play in creating red tides.

Cristina Castro

Marine Biologist Have you ever imagined watching whales for a living? Cristina Castro does. Castro works as a marine biologist with the Pacific Whale Foundation in Ecuador. She is studying the migratory patterns of a whale species known as the *humpback whale*. Each year, humpback whales migrate from feeding areas in the Antarctic to the warm waters off the coast of Ecuador, where the whales breed. Castro's studies take place largely in the Machalilla National Park. The park is a two-mile stretch of beach that is protected by the government of Ecuador.

In her research, Castro focuses on the connection between El Niño events and the number of humpback whales in the waters off the coast of Ecuador. Castro believes that during an El Niño event, the waters off the coast of Ecuador are too hot for the whales. When the whales get hot, they have a difficult time cooling off because they have a thick coat of blubber that provides insulation. So, Castro believes that the whales stay in colder waters during an El Niño event.

Language Arts ACTiViTY

Research the humpback whale's migratory route from Antarctica to Ecuador. In your **Science Journal,** write a short story in which you describe the migration from the point of view of a young whale.

Internet Resources

- To learn more about careers in science, visit **www.scilinks.org** and enter the SciLinks code HY70225.

- To learn more about these Science in Action topics, visit **go.hrw.com** and type in the keyword HY7H2OF.

- Check out articles related to this chapter by visiting **go.hrw.com.** Just type in the keyword HY7H2OC.

Improving Comprehension

Graphic Organizers are important visual tools that can help you organize information and improve your reading comprehension. The Graphic Organizer below is called *combination notes.* Instructions for creating other types of Graphic Organizers are located in the **Study Skills** section of the Appendix.

How to Make Combination Notes

1. Draw a table like the one shown below. Draw the columns to be as long as you want them to be.

2. Write the topic of your notes in the section at the top of the table.

3. In the left column, write important phrases or sentences about the topic. In the right column, draw diagrams or pictures that illustrate the information in the left column.

When to Use Combination Notes

Combination notes let you express scientific information in words and pictures at the same time. Use combination notes to express information that a picture could help explain. The picture could be a diagram, a sketch, or another useful visual representation of the written information in your notes.

The Atmosphere

Air Composition
- The atmosphere is a mixture of gases that surround Earth. This mixture of gases is commonly called *air.*

Air Pollution
- Air pollution is the contamination of the atmosphere by the introduction of pollutants from human and natural sources.
- Air pollution has adverse effects on people and the environment.

You Try It!

This Reading Strategy can also be used within the chapter that you are about to read. Practice making your own combination notes as directed in the Reading Strategies for Section **1** and Section **3**. Record your work in your **Science Journal.**

Unpacking the Standards

The information below "unpacks" the standards by breaking them down into basic parts. The higher-level, academic vocabulary is highlighted and defined to help you understand the language of the standards. "What It Means" restates the standards as simply as possible.

California Standard	Academic Vocabulary	What It Means
6.3.c Students know heat flows in solids by conduction (which **involves** no flow of matter) and in fluids by conduction and by convection (which **involves** flow of matter).	**involve** (in VAHLV) to have as a part of	When heat flows in solids, the heat can be transferred without the movement of matter. When heat flows in liquids and gases, the heat can be transferred with or without the movement of matter.
6.3.d Students know heat **energy** is also **transferred** between objects by radiation (radiation can travel through space).	**energy** (EN uhr jee) the ability to make things happen **transfer** (TRANS fuhr) to carry or cause to pass from one thing to another	Heat and energy can move from one place to another by radiation, the process by which the energy moves through matter or empty space.
6.4.a Students know the sun is the **major source** of **energy** for **phenomena** on Earth's surface; it powers winds, ocean currents, and the water **cycle.**	**major** (MAY juhr) of great importance or large scale **source** (SAWRS) the thing from which something else comes **phenomenon** (fuh NAHM uh NUHN) any facts or events that can be sensed or described scientifically (plural *phenomena*) **cycle** (SIE kuhl) a repeating series of changes	The sun is the main source of energy for processes on Earth. Energy from the sun powers winds, ocean currents, and the water cycle.
6.4.b Students know solar **energy** reaches Earth through radiation, mostly in the form of **visible** light.	**visible** (VIZ uh buhl) that can be seen	Energy from the sun reaches Earth through radiation. Most of this energy is light that humans can see.
6.4.d Students know convection currents **distribute** heat in the atmosphere and oceans.	**distribute** (di STRIB yoot) to spread out over an area	The movement of air in the atmosphere and of water in the ocean carries heat throughout the atmosphere and oceans.
6.4.e Students know differences in pressure, heat, air movement, and humidity result in changes of weather.		Changes in the weight of the atmosphere, heat, air movement, and the amount of water in the air cause the conditions of the atmosphere to change.

The following identifies other standards that are covered in this chapter and where you can go to see them unpacked: **6.3.a** (Chapter 10) and **6.6.a** (Chapter 5)

The Atmosphere

The Big Idea

Earth's atmosphere is a mixture of gases that absorbs solar energy and enables life on Earth.

California Standards

Focus on Earth Sciences
6.3 Heat moves in a predictable flow from warmer objects to cooler objects until all the objects are at the same temperature. (Section 2)
6.4 Many phenomena on Earth's surface are affected by the transfer of energy through radiation and convection currents. (Sections 1, 2, and 3)
6.6 Sources of energy and materials differ in amounts, distribution, usefulness, and the time required for their formation. (Section 4)

Investigation and Experimentation
6.7 Scientific progress is made by asking meaningful questions and conducting careful investigations. (Science Skills Activity)

Math
6.2.1 Number Sense

English–Language Arts
6.2.4 Reading
6.1.3, 6.2.5 Writing

About the Photo

The lighted skyline of San Francisco, California, rises above the clouds in this aerial photograph. The many buildings and clouds are a reminder of society's constant interactions with Earth's atmosphere.

Organize

Booklet

Before you read this chapter, create the FoldNote entitled "Booklet." On the front cover, title the booklet "The Atmosphere." Label the pages of the booklet with the titles of the sections of this chapter. As you read the chapter, write what you learn about each topic on the appropriate page of the booklet.

Instructions for creating FoldNotes are located in the Study Skills section on p. 616 of the Appendix.

Explore Activity

⏱ **25 min**

Sunlight and Temperature Change

In this activity, you will observe a relationship between direct sunlight and temperature change.

Procedure

1. Position **two outdoor thermometers** side by side in **clay** bases, and place them outside.

2. Create **sunshades** to block direct sunlight from falling on each thermometer.

3. Record the temperature displayed on each shaded thermometer.

4. Position a **plastic mirror** so that it reflects sunlight directly onto one of the thermometers. **Caution:** Do not look directly into the sun or its reflection.

5. After 15 min, read the thermometers and record their temperatures.

Analysis

6.4.b
6.7.b

6. Was there any change in observed temperatures? Describe your observations.

7. What is the source of the energy that produced this change? How did the energy reach the thermometers?

8. How might additional mirrors focusing light on the thermometer affect your results?

The Atmosphere   **469**

Characteristics of the Atmosphere

Key Concept Earth's atmosphere absorbs solar energy and transports energy around Earth's surface.

▶ The **atmosphere** is a mixture of gases that surrounds Earth. The atmosphere contains the oxygen you need to live. It also protects you from the sun's damaging rays. Every breath you take, every tree that is planted, and every automobile you ride in affect the atmosphere's composition.

The Composition of the Atmosphere

The mixture of gases that makes up the atmosphere is commonly called *air*. As you can see in **Figure 1,** most of this mixture is nitrogen. About 78% of the atmosphere is nitrogen. Oxygen makes up about 21% of the atmosphere. The other 1% of the atmosphere is made of other gases, such as argon, carbon dioxide, and water vapor. Water vapor is an invisible gas that forms when water reaches a certain temperature. Sometimes, water vapor can make up as much as 4% of the air.

The atmosphere also contains liquids and solids. Liquid water (water droplets) and solid water (snow and ice crystals) are found in clouds. The atmosphere also contains small particles, such as dust, volcanic ash, sea salt, dirt, and smoke. You can turn off the lights at night and shine a flashlight to see some of these tiny particles floating in the air.

Figure 1   **Composition of the Atmosphere**

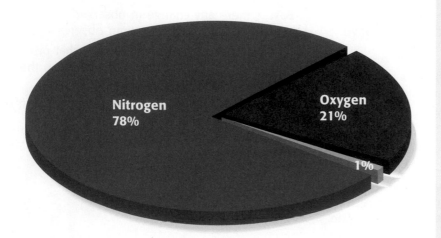

Nitrogen, the most common atmospheric gas, is released when dead plants and dead animals break down and when volcanoes erupt.

Oxygen, the second most common atmospheric gas, is made by living things, such as plants.

Argon, carbon dioxide, water vapor, and other gases make up the remaining 1% of the atmosphere.

Air Pressure and Temperature

What would carrying a column of air that is 500 km high feel like? You carry this load every day! You do not notice the load because your body is used to it. At sea level, a square inch of surface area is under almost 7 kg (15 lb) of air.

Altitude and Air Pressure

Gravity pulls gas molecules in the atmosphere toward Earth's surface. As a result, there are a lot of air molecules near Earth's surface. When a large number of air molecules are contained in a small space, those molecules exert a lot of pressure on one another and on surfaces around them. **Air pressure** is the measure of the force with which air molecules push on a surface. The air pressure at any point in the atmosphere is equal to the weight of the air directly above that point. Air pressure is greatest at Earth's surface because there is a lot of air above Earth's surface. A human pyramid models how air pressure changes in the atmosphere, as shown in **Figure 2.**

Standards Check Why is air pressure highest near Earth's surface?
 6.4.e

Atmospheric Composition and Air Temperature

Air temperature also changes as altitude increases. The temperature differences result from the way that energy is absorbed by gases in the atmosphere. Some parts of the atmosphere are warmer because they contain higher concentrations of gases that absorb energy from the sun or from Earth's surface.

6.4.b Students know solar energy reaches Earth through radiation, mostly in the form of visible light.
6.4.e Students know differences in pressure, heat, air movement, and humidity result in changes of weather.

Quick Lab

Modeling Air Pressure

6.4.e

1. Fill a **plastic cup** to the brim with **water.**
2. Firmly hold an **index card** over the mouth of the cup.
3. Quickly invert the glass over a **sink.**
4. Release the paper square, and observe what happens.
5. How do the effects of air pressure explain your observations?

⏱ **10 min**

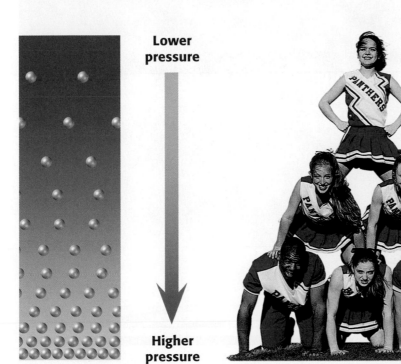

Figure 2 *In the atmosphere, air pressure is greatest at Earth's surface. In a human pyramid, pressure is greatest at the bottom.*

Lower pressure

Higher pressure

Layers of the Atmosphere

Gases in Earth's atmosphere absorb solar energy differently, which causes temperature gradients. The atmosphere is divided into four main layers based on these temperature differences, as shown in **Figure 3.**

The Troposphere: The Layer in Which We Live

The **troposphere** is the layer of the atmosphere that lies next to Earth's surface. This layer contains almost 90% of the atmosphere's total mass. Almost all water vapor, air pollution, and weather are in this layer. Temperature decreases as altitude increases in the troposphere. Differences in air temperature and density cause gases in this layer to mix continuously.

The Stratosphere: Home of the Ozone Layer

The layer above the troposphere is called the **stratosphere.** The air in this layer is thin and has little moisture. In this layer, temperature rises as altitude increases. This rise happens because a layer of gas called *ozone* absorbs radiation from the sun, so the air warms. The *ozone layer* protects life on Earth by absorbing harmful ultraviolet radiation.

troposphere (TROH poh SFIR) the lowest layer of the atmosphere, in which temperature decreases at a constant rate as altitude increases
Wordwise The root *trop-* means "to turn."

stratosphere (STRAT uh SFIR) the layer of the atmosphere that is above the troposphere and in which temperature increases as altitude increases

mesosphere (MES oh SFIR) the layer of the atmosphere between the stratosphere and the thermosphere and in which temperature decreases as altitude increases

thermosphere (THUHR moh SFIR) the uppermost layer of the atmosphere, in which temperature increases as altitude increases

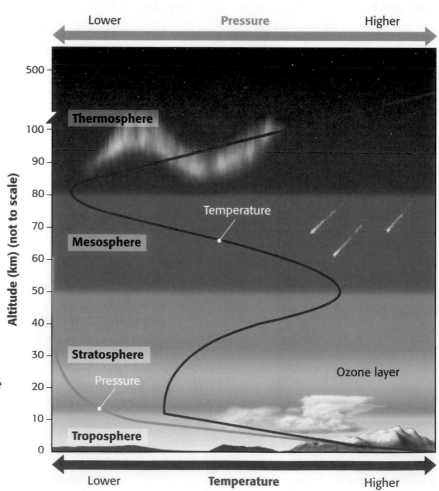

Figure 3 *The layers of the atmosphere are defined by changes in temperature.*

The Mesosphere: The Middle Layer

Above the stratosphere is the mesosphere. The **mesosphere** is the middle layer of the atmosphere. It is also the coldest layer. As in the troposphere, temperature decreases as altitude increases in the mesosphere.

The Thermosphere: The Edge of the Atmosphere

The uppermost atmospheric layer is called the **thermosphere.** In the thermosphere, temperature again increases with altitude. Temperature increases in this layer because atoms of nitrogen and oxygen absorb high-energy solar radiation.

Standards Check Why are temperatures high in the stratosphere and thermosphere? 6.4.b

SECTION Review

6.4.b, 6.4.e

Summary

- Nitrogen and oxygen make up most of Earth's atmosphere.

- Air pressure decreases as altitude increases.

- The composition of atmospheric layers affects their temperature.

- The troposphere is the lowest atmospheric layer. It is the layer in which we live.

- The stratosphere contains the ozone layer, which protects us from harmful ultraviolet radiation.

- The mesosphere is the coldest atmospheric layer.

- The thermosphere is the uppermost layer of the atmosphere.

Understanding Concepts

1. **Applying** Why does the temperature of different layers of the atmosphere vary?

2. **Identifying** What is air pressure?

3. **Summarizing** Why does air pressure decrease as altitude increases?

INTERPRETING GRAPHICS Use the graph below to answer the next two questions.

Composition of the Atmosphere

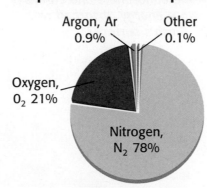

Argon, Ar 0.9%
Other 0.1%
Oxygen, O_2 21%
Nitrogen, N_2 78%

4. **Identifying** What two gases make up most of the atmosphere? What is the combined percentage of the two gases?

5. **Identifying** What percentage of the atmosphere is argon?

Critical Thinking

6. **Applying Concepts** Apply what you know about the relationship between altitude and air pressure to explain why rescue helicopters have a difficult time flying at altitudes above 6,000 m.

7. **Making Comparisons** Compare the four atmospheric layers. How do temperatures and pressures vary between layers?

Math Skills

8. **Making Calculations** The troposphere ends at an altitude of about 12 km. The mesosphere begins at an altitude of about 50 km. What is the approximate thickness of the stratosphere?

473

Atmospheric Heating

Key Concept Heat in Earth's atmosphere is transferred by radiation, conduction, and convection.

▶ You are lying in a park. You feel the warmth of the sun on your face. The sun is nearly 150,000,000 km from Earth! Have you ever wondered how the sun's warmth reaches you?

Radiation: Energy Transfer by Waves

Energy from the sun, or solar energy, takes a little more than eight minutes to travel from the sun to Earth. Solar energy reaches Earth by radiation. **Radiation** is the transfer of energy as waves through space or matter.

The sun radiates a huge amount of energy. Earth receives only about two-billionths of this energy. But this small fraction of energy is enough to drive many processes at Earth's surface. For example, the sun provides the energy that drives winds, the water cycle, ocean currents, and changes in the weather. **Figure 1** shows what happens to solar energy that enters Earth's atmosphere.

Standards Check What is the source of energy that drives most processes at Earth's surface, and how does that energy reach Earth? 🐻 **6.3.a, 6.3.d, 6.4.a, 6.4.b**

Figure 1 *Different amounts of energy from the sun are absorbed, scattered, or reflected by the atmosphere and Earth's surface.* ***Is more energy absorbed or reflected by Earth's surface?***

About **25%** is scattered and reflected by clouds and air.

About **20%** is absorbed by ozone, clouds, and gases in the atmosphere.

About **5%** is reflected by Earth's surface.

About **50%** is absorbed by Earth's surface.

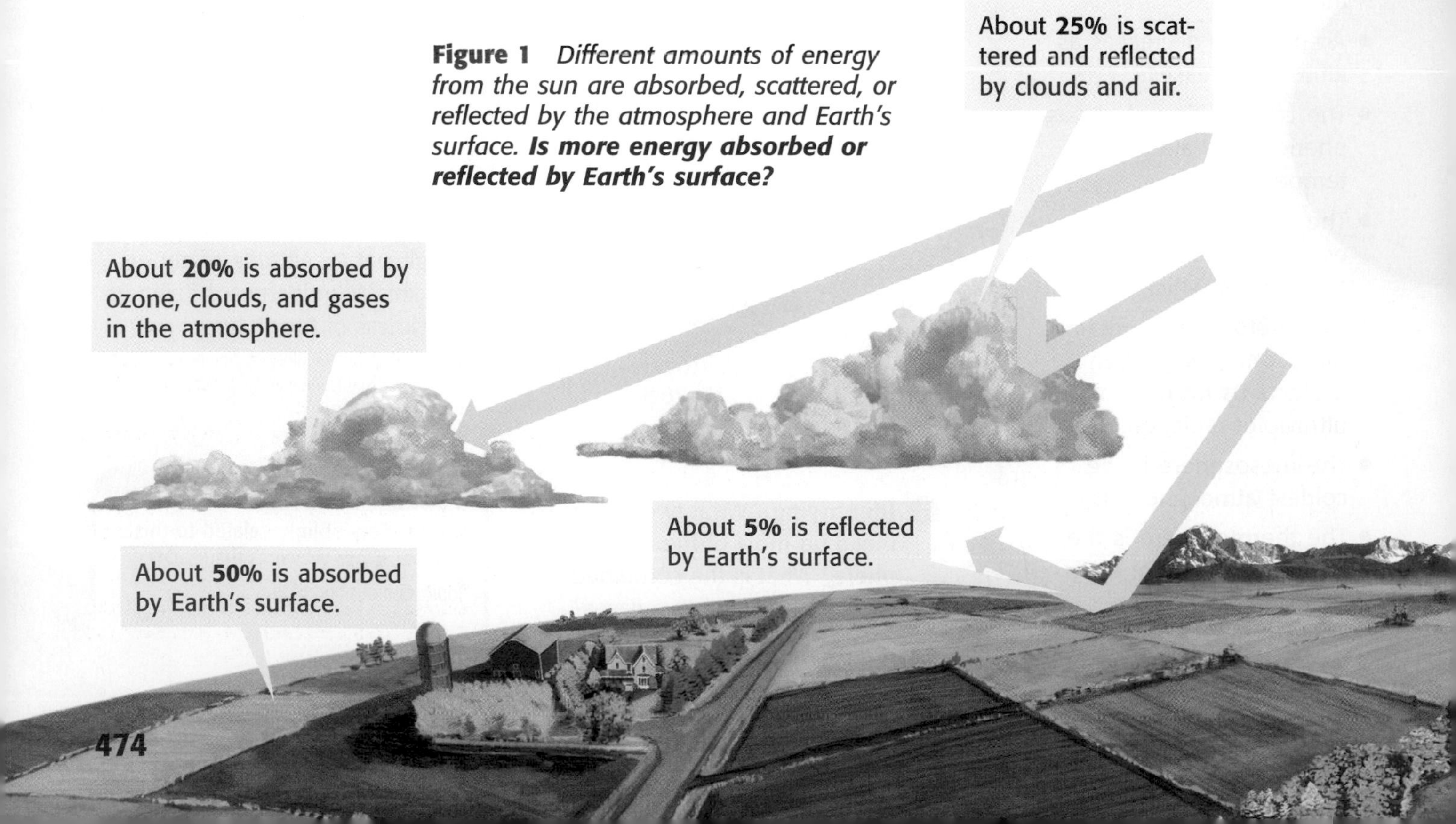

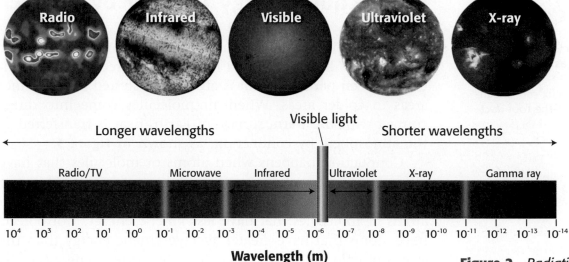

Longer wavelengths | Visible light | Shorter wavelengths

Radio/TV   Microwave   Infrared   Ultraviolet   X-ray   Gamma ray

10^4 10^3 10^2 10^1 10^0 10^{-1} 10^{-2} 10^{-3} 10^{-4} 10^{-5} 10^{-6} 10^{-7} 10^{-8} 10^{-9} 10^{-10} 10^{-11} 10^{-12} 10^{-13} 10^{-14}

Wavelength (m)

Figure 2 *Radiation from the sun includes the entire electromagnetic spectrum. Each image of the sun above the spectrum shows different wavelengths of radiation.*

The Electromagnetic Spectrum

Radiation travels through space in the form of waves at a very high speed—about 300,000 km/s. These waves are called *electromagnetic waves*. Almost all of the energy that reaches Earth from the sun is in the form of electromagnetic waves. The **electromagnetic spectrum,** shown in **Figure 2,** contains all of the kinds of electromagnetic waves.

The kinds of electromagnetic radiation differ in the length of their waves. The distance from any point on a wave to the identical point on the next wave is called the *wavelength*. Visible light consists of waves that have wavelengths that humans can see as different colors. The wavelengths of ultraviolet rays, X rays, and gamma rays are shorter than the wavelengths of visible light. Infared waves and radio waves have wavelengths that are longer than those of visible light.

The Atmosphere and Solar Radiation

Earth's atmosphere affects incoming solar radiation in many ways. The upper atmosphere absorbs almost all radiation that has wavelengths shorter than those of visible light. Nitrogen and oxygen in the thermosphere and mesosphere absorb the X rays, gamma rays, and some ultraviolet rays. In the stratosphere, ultraviolet rays are absorbed by and act upon oxygen molecules to form ozone.

Most incoming infared radiation is absorbed by gases in the troposphere. But some of this longer-wavelength energy reaches Earth's surface. Only a small amount of visible light is absorbed by the atmosphere. As a result, most of the solar rays that reach Earth's surface are visible light.

Standards Check What form of energy is most solar energy that reaches Earth's surface? **6.4.b**

radiation (RAY dee AY shuhn) the transfer of energy as electromagnetic waves

electromagnetic spectrum (ee LEK troh mag NET ik SPEK truhm) all of the frequencies or wavelengths of electromagnetic radiation

6.3.a Students know energy can be carried from one place to another by heat flow or by waves, including water, light and sound waves, or by moving objects.
6.3.c Students know heat flows in solids by conduction (which involves no flow of matter) and in fluids by conduction and by convection (which involves flow of matter).
6.3.d Students know heat energy is also transferred between objects by radiation (radiation can travel through space).
6.4.a Students know the sun is the major source of energy for phenomena on Earth's surface; it powers winds, ocean currents, and the water cycle.
6.4.b Students know solar energy reaches Earth through radiation, mostly in the form of visible light.
6.4.d Students know convection currents distribute heat in the atmosphere and oceans.

Conduction: Energy Transfer by Contact

If you have ever touched something hot, you have experienced the process of conduction. **Conduction** is the transfer of energy, as heat, through a material by direct physical contact between particles. Heat is always transferred from warmer areas to colder areas. When air molecules come into direct contact with the warm surface of Earth, heat is transferred to the atmosphere by conduction, as shown in **Figure 3.**

Conduction happens when atoms or molecules that have different amounts of average kinetic energy collide. Atoms or molecules that have more kinetic energy transfer energy to atoms or molecules that have less kinetic energy. Hot objects have atoms that have greater average kinetic energy than the atoms of cold objects do. Therefore, the kinetic energy of the atoms in the hot object is transferred to the atoms of the cold object. In a solid, the atoms vibrate in place, but energy may still be transferred from atom to atom. This process happens when a pan is placed on a stove and the pan's handle becomes hot. The same mechanism happens in liquids and gases. In liquids and gases, the atoms collide as they slip past one another.

Standards Check How does heat flow by conduction in solids? 6.3.c

Figure 3 *The processes of radiation, conduction, and convection heat Earth and its atmosphere.*

Radiation is the transfer of energy through space as electromagnetic waves.

The movement of air transfers energy by **convection.**

Within a few centimeters of Earth's surface, air is heated by **conduction.**

Modeling Air Movement by Convection

In this lab, you will model how the transfer of energy causes convection currents to form.

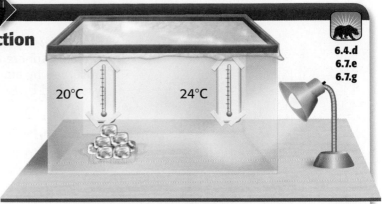

20°C   24°C

6.4.d
6.7.e
6.7.g

▶ Try It!

1. Use **masking tape** to attach **two outdoor thermometers** to the inside of a **15 gal glass aquarium,** one at each end. Make sure the thermometers can be read from outside the aquarium.

2. Stack **24 ice cubes** in one end of the aquarium.

3. Place an **adjustable neck lamp** outside the other end of the aquarium. Point the lamp at the bottom of that end of the aquarium.

4. **Tape** a piece of **plastic cling wrap** over the top of the aquarium, and wait 5 min.

5. Write down the temperature on each thermometer.

6. Light the end of an **incense stick.** Then, quickly blow out the flame.

7. Lift the plastic wrap, and hold the incense stick in the center of the aquarium. Observe the movement of the smoke.

▶ Think About It!

8. How does the temperature at each end of the aquarium affect the movement of the smoke?

9. How does this activity model convection in the atmosphere?

🕐 **20 min**

Convection: Energy Transfer by Motion

If you have ever watched a pot of water boil, you have observed convection. **Convection** is the transfer of heat by the circulation or movement of a liquid or gas. Convection occurs because most fluids, such as liquids and gases, become less dense when they are heated. Because the hot fluid is less dense, it is more buoyant than surrounding cool fluid. Therefore, the hot fluid rises. As hot fluid rises away from a heat source, it may cool, become denser, and sink back to the source to be warmed again. This cycle of warm fluid rising and cool fluid sinking may cause a circular movement called a **convection current.**

Most heat in the atmosphere is transferred by convection, as shown in **Figure 3.** For example, as air is heated by conduction from the ground, the air becomes less dense. The surrounding cool air is denser than the warm air, so the cool air sinks. As the cool air sinks, it pushes the warm air up. The cool air is eventually heated by conduction from the ground, and the process repeats.

convection (kuhn VEK shuhn) the movement of matter due to differences in density; the transfer of energy due to the movement of matter

Wordwise The root *vect-* means "to carry."

convection current (kuhn VEK shuhn KUHR uhnt) any movement of matter that results from differences in density; may be vertical, circular, or cyclical

Standards Check Describe the flow of heat by convection in fluids.

🐻 **6.3.c**

Figure 4 The Greenhouse Effect

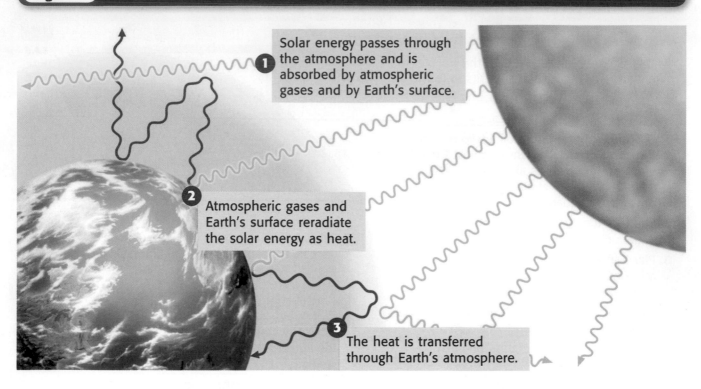

1. Solar energy passes through the atmosphere and is absorbed by atmospheric gases and by Earth's surface.

2. Atmospheric gases and Earth's surface reradiate the solar energy as heat.

3. The heat is transferred through Earth's atmosphere.

The Greenhouse Effect

About 70% of the radiation that enters Earth's atmosphere is absorbed by atmospheric gases and by Earth's surface. This energy is changed into heat that warms the planet. In other words, visible light is absorbed and then is reradiated into the atmosphere as heat.

So, why doesn't this heat escape back into space? Most of it does. But the atmosphere is like a warm blanket that absorbs enough energy to make Earth livable. This process, shown in **Figure 4,** is called the greenhouse effect. The **greenhouse effect** is the process by which gases in the atmosphere, such as water vapor and carbon dioxide, absorb and reradiate heat.

The Radiation Balance: Energy In, Energy Out

For Earth to remain livable, the amount of energy received from the sun and the amount of energy returned to space must be approximately equal. Solar energy that is absorbed by Earth's surface and atmosphere is reradiated into space as heat. Every day, Earth receives more energy from the sun. And every day, Earth releases energy back into space. The balance between incoming energy and outgoing energy is known as the *radiation balance.*

Standards Check How does the sun's radiation make Earth livable?
🐻 **6.3.d**

greenhouse effect (GREEN HOWS e FEKT) the warming of the surface and lower atmosphere of Earth that occurs when water vapor, carbon dioxide, and other gases absorb and reradiate thermal energy

Global Warming

Many scientists are concerned that average global temperatures have increased in the past 100 years. This increase in average global temperatures is called *global warming.* Human activity, such as the burning of fossil fuels, as shown in **Figure 5,** may lead to global warming. Burning fossil fuels releases greenhouse gases, such as carbon dioxide, into the atmosphere. An increase in the amount of greenhouse gases may cause global warming because the gases absorb more heat. If the amount of greenhouse gases in the atmosphere continues to rise, global temperatures may continue to rise. If global warming continues, global climate patterns could be disrupted. However, the causes of global warming are still being debated.

Figure 5 *While in traffic on the Golden Gate Bridge, vehicles burn fossil fuels, which may lead to global warming.*

SECTION Review

 6.3.a, 6.3.c, 6.3.d, 6.4.a, 6.4.b, 6.4.d

Summary

- Energy travels from the sun to Earth by radiation. This energy drives many processes at Earth's surface.
- Energy in Earth's atmosphere is transferred by radiation, conduction, and convection.
- Radiation is the transfer of energy through space or matter by waves.
- Conduction is the transfer of energy by direct contact.
- Convection is energy transfer by the movement of matter.

Using Vocabulary

1. Use *conduction, radiation, convection,* and *global warming* in separate sentences.

Understanding Concepts

2. **Applying** How does the sun affect processes at Earth's surface?

3. **Describing** What is radiation?

4. **Identifying** Identify three ways that energy is transferred in the atmosphere.

5. **Describing** How does radiation differ from conduction and convection?

6. **Summarizing** Describe the electromagnetic spectrum, and explain how this energy reaches Earth.

Critical Thinking

7. **Making Comparisons** How does conduction differ from convection?

8. **Identifying Relationships** How does the process of convection rely on conduction?

9. **Making Comparisons** What is the difference between the greenhouse effect and global warming?

Math Skills

10. **Making Calculations** Find the average of the following temperatures: 22.8°C, 21.7°C, 12.5°C, 18.6°C, 25.7°C, 27.7°C, and 27.8°C.

Challenge

11. **Predicting Consequences** How do you think processes of conduction and convection on Earth would be different if radiation from the sun were not constant or uniform?

Air Movement and Wind

Key Concept Global winds and local winds are produced by the uneven heating of Earth's surface.

▶ As you lie in the park with the sun warming your face, a gentle breeze ruffles your hair. What caused that breeze? The movement of air is caused by differences in air pressure. Differences in air pressure are generally caused by the unequal heating of Earth's surface.

What Causes Wind ?

When the sun warms the surface of Earth, the surface heats the air above it. As a result, the air becomes less dense, which forms an area of low pressure. Areas where cold air sinks toward the surface are areas of high pressure. Colder, denser air from a high-pressure area will flow toward a low-pressure area. As the cold air moves, it pushes the warm, less dense air out of the way. This movement of air is called **wind.** The greater the pressure difference is, the faster the air moves, and the stronger the wind is. As shown in **Figure 1,** these areas of high and low pressure are part of convection cells.

Standards Check What causes wind? 🐻 **6.4.a, 6.4.d**

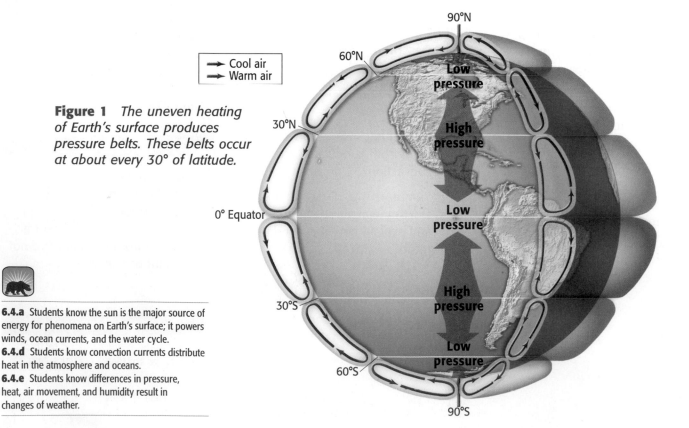

Figure 1 *The uneven heating of Earth's surface produces pressure belts. These belts occur at about every 30° of latitude.*

→ Cool air
→ Warm air

90°N
60°N
Low pressure
30°N
High pressure
0° Equator
Low pressure
High pressure
30°S
Low pressure
60°S
90°S

6.4.a Students know the sun is the major source of energy for phenomena on Earth's surface; it powers winds, ocean currents, and the water cycle.
6.4.d Students know convection currents distribute heat in the atmosphere and oceans.
6.4.e Students know differences in pressure, heat, air movement, and humidity result in changes of weather.

The Coriolis Effect

At the equator, Earth's surface receives a lot of direct sunlight that heats the ground and the air. As a result, air pressure is low at the equator. The poles, however, receive much less direct sunlight. Therefore, the ground and air are not as warm, and air pressure at the poles is high. These pressure differences cause air to circulate from the poles toward the equator. However, winds do not travel directly north or south, because Earth is rotating. The apparent curving of the path of winds and ocean currents due to Earth's rotation is called the **Coriolis effect.** Because of the Coriolis effect in the Northern Hemisphere, winds traveling north curve to the east and winds traveling south curve to the west.

Global Winds

Convection cells, pressure belts, and winds combine with the Coriolis effect to produce air-circulation patterns called *global winds.* **Figure 2** shows the major global wind systems: polar easterlies, westerlies, and trade winds. Winds such as easterlies and westerlies are named for the direction from which they blow. Global winds distribute heat around Earth's surface and affect ocean currents and weather patterns.

Standards Check What causes global wind patterns? 🐻 **6.4.e**

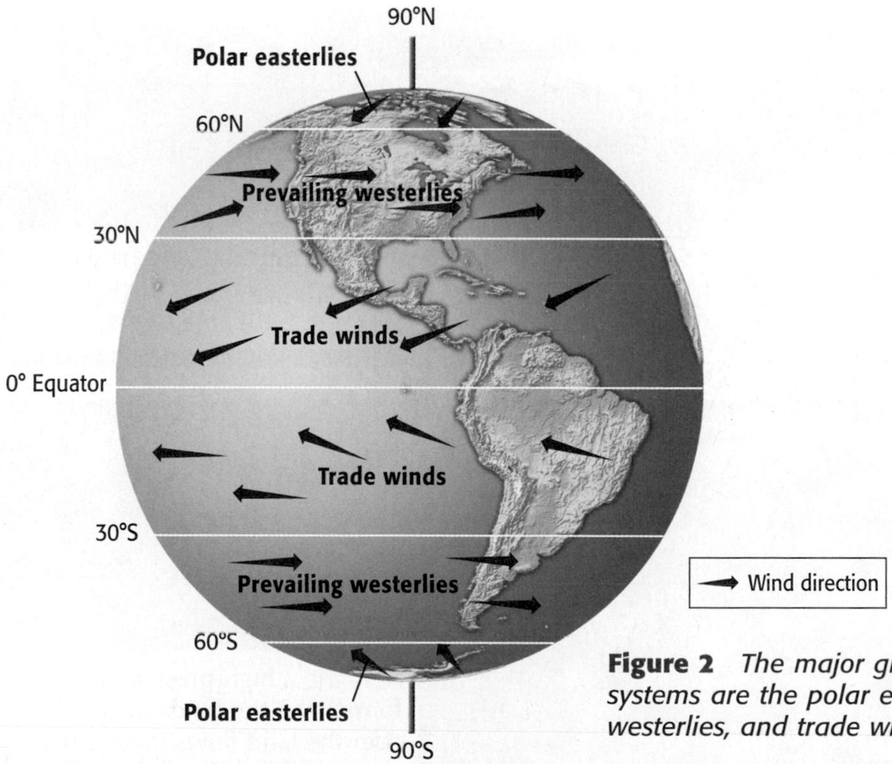

wind (WIND) the movement of air caused by differences in air pressure

Coriolis effect (KAWR ee OH lis e FEKT) the curving of the path of a moving object from an otherwise straight path due to Earth's rotation

90°N

Polar easterlies

60°N

Prevailing westerlies

30°N

Trade winds

0° Equator

Trade winds

30°S

Prevailing westerlies

60°S

Polar easterlies

90°S

 → Wind direction

Figure 2 *The major global wind systems are the polar easterlies, westerlies, and trade winds.*

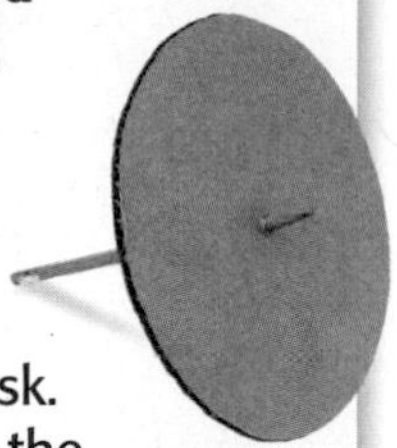

Local Winds

Local winds generally move short distances and can blow from any direction. Like global winds, most local winds result from differences in pressure that are caused by the uneven heating of Earth's surface. However, these pressure differences result from a different process. The pressure differences that cause local winds are caused by the properties of the matter that makes up Earth's surface. For example, some materials, such as rock, heat up more rapidly than other materials. Areas of low pressure form over material that heats up quickly.

Standards Check What causes local winds? 6.4.e

Sea Breezes and Land Breezes

The formation of sea and land breezes is shown in **Figure 3.** During the day, the land heats up faster than the water does. The air above the land becomes warmer than the air above the water. The warm air above the land rises, and the cold ocean air flows in to replace it. At night, the land cools faster than water does. The cold air above the land flows toward the ocean. So, the wind blows toward the ocean at night.

Figure 3 Sea Breezes and Land Breezes

During the day, a high-pressure area forms over the ocean. The cool air over the ocean flows toward the land, producing a sea breeze.

Air over the land heats up very rapidly, and a low-pressure area forms.

Air over the ocean cools slowly, and a low-pressure area forms.

At night, a high-pressure area forms over the land. The cool air over the land flows toward the ocean, producing a land breeze.

Figure 4 **Valley Breezes and Mountain Breezes**

Valley breeze

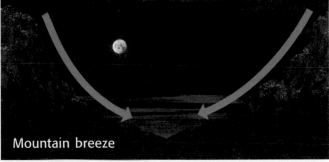

Mountain breeze

Valley Breezes and Mountain Breezes

The formation of valley and mountain breezes is shown in **Figure 4.** During the day, the air along the mountain slopes heats up rapidly. This warm air rises up the mountain slopes, creating a valley breeze. At night, the air along the mountain slopes cools. This cool air moves down the slopes into the valley, producing a mountain breeze.

SECTION Review

6.4.a, 6.4.d, 6.4.e

Summary

- Winds blow from areas of high pressure to areas of low pressure.
- Pressure belts are caused by the uneven heating of Earth's surface by the sun.
- The Coriolis effect causes wind to appear to curve as it moves across Earth's surface.
- Global winds include the polar easterlies, the westerlies, and the trade winds.
- Local winds include sea and land breezes and valley and mountain breezes.

Using Vocabulary

1. Write an original definition for *wind* and *Coriolis effect.*

Understanding Concepts

2. **Applying** Why do pressure belts form in the atmosphere?

3. **Summarizing** What causes winds?

4. **Identifying** What causes the Coriolis effect?

5. **Applying** How does the Coriolis effect affect wind movement?

6. **Comparing** How do the processes that cause global winds and local winds differ?

7. **Summarizing** Describe the difference between sea and land breezes and between valley and mountain breezes.

Critical Thinking

8. **Analyzing Ideas** Would there be winds if Earth's surface were the same temperature everywhere? Explain your answer.

9. **Applying Concepts** Imagine that you are near an ocean in the daytime. How could a local wind help you find the ocean if you don't know the way there?

Challenge

10. **Forming Hypotheses** In the Northern Hemisphere, why do westerlies flow from the west but trade winds flow from the east?

Internet Resources

For a variety of links related to this chapter, go to www.scilinks.org

Topic: Atmospheric Pressure and Winds

SciLinks code: HY70115

The Air We Breathe

Key Concept Air is an important natural resource that is affected by human activities.

▶ In December 1952, one of London's "pea-soup" fogs settled on the city. But this was no ordinary fog—it was thick with coal smoke and air pollution. It burned people's lungs. The sky grew so dark that people could not see far in front of their faces. When the fog lifted four days later, thousands of people were dead!

Air Pollution

London's killer fog shocked the world and caused major changes in England's air-pollution laws. Although this event is an extreme example, air pollution is common in many parts of the world. But what is air pollution? **Air pollution** is the contamination of the atmosphere by the introduction of pollutants from human and natural sources. Air pollutants are classified according to their source as either primary pollutants or secondary pollutants.

Primary Pollutants

Pollutants that are put directly into the air by human or natural activity are *primary pollutants*. Primary pollutants from natural sources include dust, sea salt, volcanic gases and ash, smoke from forest fires, and pollen. Primary pollutants from human sources include carbon monoxide, dust, smoke, and chemicals from paint and other substances. In urban areas, vehicle exhaust is a common source of primary pollutants. Examples of primary pollutants are shown in **Figure 1.**

air pollution (ER puh LOO shuhn) the contamination of the atmosphere by the introduction of pollutants from human and natural sources

Figure 1 **Examples of Primary Pollutants**

Industrial emissions   Vehicle exhaust   Volcanic ash

6.6.a Students know the utility of energy sources is determined by factors that are involved in converting these sources to useful forms and the consequences of the conversion process.

Secondary Pollutants

Pollutants that form when primary pollutants react with other primary pollutants or with naturally occurring substances, such as water vapor, are *secondary pollutants.* Ozone and smog are examples of secondary pollutants. Ozone forms when sunlight reacts with vehicle exhaust and air, as shown in **Figure 2.** You may have heard of "Ozone Action Day" warnings in your community. When such a warning is issued, people are discouraged from outdoor physical activity because ozone can damage their lungs. In the stratosphere, ozone forms a protective layer that absorbs harmful radiation from the sun. Near Earth's surface, however, ozone is a dangerous pollutant that negatively affects the health of organisms.

The Formation of Smog

Smog forms when ozone and vehicle exhaust react with sunlight, as shown in **Figure 2.** Local geography and weather patterns can also contribute to smog formation. Los Angeles, shown in **Figure 3,** is bordered by mountains that restrict the flow of wind and trap pollutants. Although pollution controls have reduced levels of smog in Los Angeles, smog remains a problem for Los Angeles and other large cities.

Standards Check How does the burning of gasoline by cars contribute to air pollution? 6.6.a

❷ Ozone reacts with vehicle exhaust to form smog.

Smog

Ozone

❶ Vehicle exhaust reacts with air and sunlight to form ozone.

Automobile exhaust

Figure 2 *Smog forms when sunlight reacts with ozone and vehicle exhaust.*

Figure 3 *Smog levels in Los Angeles can vary dramatically. During summer, a layer of warm air can trap smog near the ground. However, in the winter, a storm can quickly clear the air.*

Human-Caused Air Pollution

Human-caused air pollution comes from many sources. A major source of air pollution today is transportation. Cars contribute about 10% to 20% of the human-caused air pollution in the United States. However, pollution controls and cleaner gasoline have reduced air pollution from automobiles.

Industrial Air Pollution

Many industrial plants and electric power plants burn fossil fuels, such as coal, to produce energy. Burning some kinds of coal without pollution controls can release large amounts of air pollutants. Some industries also produce chemicals that can pollute the air. Oil refineries, chemical manufacturing plants, and other industries are all potential sources of air pollution.

Standards Check How does burning of fuels to produce energy affect air quality? 6.6.a

Indoor Air Pollution

Sometimes, the air inside a building can be more polluted than the air outside. Some sources of indoor air pollution are shown in **Figure 4.** *Ventilation,* or the mixing of indoor air with outdoor air, can lower indoor air pollution. Another way to lower indoor air pollution is to limit the use of chemical solvents and cleaners.

Figure 4 *Indoor air pollution can come from many sources.*

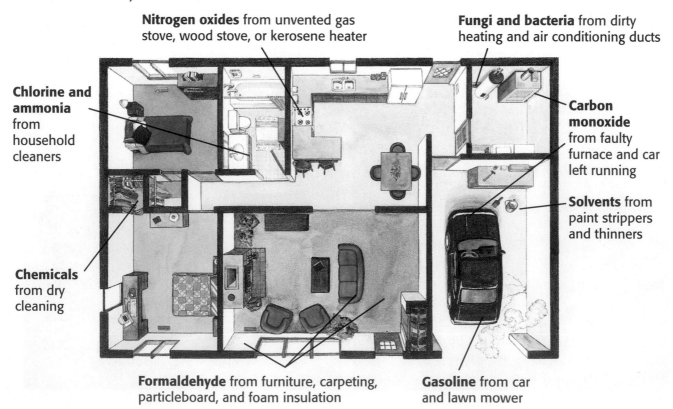

Nitrogen oxides from unvented gas stove, wood stove, or kerosene heater

Fungi and bacteria from dirty heating and air conditioning ducts

Chlorine and ammonia from household cleaners

Carbon monoxide from faulty furnace and car left running

Solvents from paint strippers and thinners

Chemicals from dry cleaning

Formaldehyde from furniture, carpeting, particleboard, and foam insulation

Gasoline from car and lawn mower

Figure 5 *This forest in Poland was damaged by acid precipitation.*

Acid Precipitation

Precipitation such as rain, sleet, or snow that contains acids from air pollution is called **acid precipitation.** When fossil fuels are burned, they can release sulfur dioxide and nitrogen oxide into the atmosphere. When these pollutants combine with water in the atmosphere, they form sulfuric acid and nitric acid. Precipitation is naturally acidic, but sulfuric acid and nitric acid can make precipitation so acidic that it can negatively affect the environment. In most areas of the world, pollution controls have helped lower acid precipitation.

Standards Check What causes acid precipitation? 🐻 6.6.a

Acid Precipitation and Plants

Plant communities have adapted over long periods of time to the natural acidity of the soil in which they grow. Acid precipitation can cause the acidity of soil to increase. This process, called *acidification,* changes the balance of a soil's chemistry in several ways. When the acidity of soil increases, some nutrients are dissolved. Nutrients that plants need for growth may get washed away by rainwater. Increased acidity also causes aluminum and other toxic metals to be released. Some of these toxic metals are absorbed by the roots of plants.

The Effects of Acid Precipitation on Forests

Forest ecology is complex. Scientists are still trying to fully understand the long-term effects of acid precipitation on groups of plants and their habitats. In some areas of the world, however, acid precipitation has damaged large areas of forest. The effects of acid precipitation are most noticeable in Eastern Europe, as shown in **Figure 5.** Forests in the northeastern United States and in eastern Canada have also been affected by acid precipitation.

acid precipitation (AS id pree sip uh TAY shuhn) rain, sleet, or snow that contains a high concentration of acids

Quick Lab

Collecting Air-Pollution Particles

6.6.a
6.7.a

1. Cover **ten 5 in. × 7 in. index cards** with a thin coat of **petroleum jelly.**

2. Hang the cards in various locations inside and outside your school.

3. One day later, use a **magnifying lens** to count the number of particles on the cards.

4. Which location had the fewest particles? Which location had the most particles?

5. Hypothesize why some locations had a higher number of particles than other locations did.

⏱ **10 min/day for 2 days**

Acid Precipitation and Aquatic Ecosystems

Aquatic organisms have adapted to live in water that has a particular range of acidity. If acid precipitation increases the acidity of a lake or stream, aquatic plants, fish, and other aquatic organisms may die. The effects of acid precipitation on lakes and rivers are worst in the spring, when the acidic snow that built up in the winter melts and acidic water flows into lakes and rivers. A rapid change in a body of water's acidity is called *acid shock*. Acid shock can cause large numbers of fish to die. Acid shock can also affect the delicate eggs of fish and amphibians.

To reduce the effects of acid precipitation on aquatic ecosystems, some communities spray powdered lime on acidified lakes in the spring. Lime, a base, neutralizes the acid in the water. Unfortunately, lime cannot be spread to offset all acid damage to lakes.

Standards Check What effects can the burning of fossil fuels have on aquatic ecosystems? 6.6.a

The Ozone Hole

In 1985, scientists reported an alarming discovery about Earth's protective ozone layer. Over Antarctica, the ozone layer was thinning, particularly during the spring. This change was also noted over the Arctic Ocean. Chemicals called *CFCs* were causing ozone to break down into oxygen, which does not block the sun's harmful ultraviolet (UV) rays. The thinning of the ozone layer makes an ozone hole, shown in **Figure 6.** The ozone hole allows more UV radiation to reach Earth's surface. UV radiation is dangerous to organisms because it damages genes and can cause skin cancer.

Cooperation to Reduce the Ozone Hole

In 1987, a group of representatives from several nations met in Canada and agreed to take action to prevent the destruction of the ozone layer. Agreements were made to reduce and eventually ban CFC use, and CFC alternatives were quickly developed. As a result, many people consider ozone protection an environmental success story. The battle to protect the ozone layer is not over, however. CFC molecules can remain active in the stratosphere for 60 to 120 years. So, CFCs released 30 years ago are still destroying ozone today. Thus, the ozone layer will take many years to completely recover.

September 2001

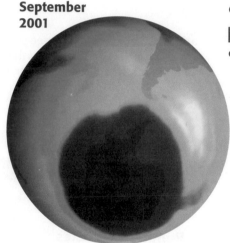

September 2002

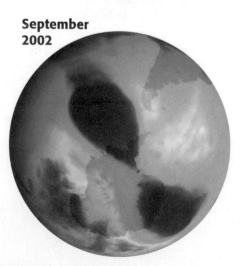

Figure 6 *Polar weather conditions cause the size of the ozone hole (shown in blue) to vary.*

Air Pollution and Human Health

Daily exposure to small amounts of air pollution can cause serious health problems. Children and elderly people are especially vulnerable to the effects of air pollution. So are people who have asthma, allergies, lung problems, and heart problems. **Table 1** shows some of the effects of air pollution on the human body. The short-term effects of air pollution are immediately noticeable. Coughing, headaches, and increases in asthma-related problems are only a few short-term effects. The long-term effects of air pollution, such as lung cancer, are more dangerous. Long-term effects may not be noticed until many years after an individual has been exposed to pollutants.

Table 1	Effects of Air Pollution on Human Health
Short-term effects	headache; nausea; irritation of eyes, nose, and throat; coughing; upper respiratory infections; worsening of asthma and emphysema
Long-term effects	emphysema; lung cancer; permanent lung damage; heart disease

Cleaning Up Air Pollution

Much progress has been made in reducing air pollution. For example, in the United States, the Clean Air Act was passed by Congress in 1970 and was strengthened in 1990. The Clean Air Act is a law that gives the Environmental Protection Agency (EPA) the authority to control the amount of air pollutants that can be released from any source, such as cars and factories. The EPA also checks air quality. If air quality worsens, the EPA can set stricter standards.

Controlling Air Pollution from Industry

The Clean Air Act requires many industries to use pollution-control devices such as scrubbers. A *scrubber* is a device that is used to remove some pollutants before they are released by smokestacks. Scrubbers in coal-burning power plants remove particles such as ash from the smoke. Other industrial plants, such as the power plant shown in **Figure 7,** focus on burning fuel more efficiently so that fewer pollutants are released.

Figure 7 *This power plant in Florida is leading the way in clean-coal technology. The plant turns coal into a gas before it is burned, so fewer pollutants are released.*

The Allowance Trading System

The Allowance Trading System is another initiative to reduce air pollution. In this program, the EPA establishes allowances for the amount of a pollutant that companies can release. A company that releases more than its allowance must pay a fine. A company that releases less than its allowance can sell some of its allowance to a company that releases more. Allowances are also available for the public to buy. So, organizations seeking to reduce air pollution can buy an allowance of 1,000 tons of sulfur dioxide. This purchase reduces the total sulfur dioxide allowances that industries can buy.

Reducing Air Pollution from Vehicles

A large percentage of air pollution in the United States comes from the vehicles we drive. To reduce air pollution from vehicles, the EPA requires car makers to meet a certain standard for vehicle exhaust. Devices such as catalytic converters remove many pollutants from exhaust and help cars meet this standard. Cleaner fuels and more-efficient engines have also helped reduce air pollution from vehicles. Car manufacturers are also making cars that run on fuels other than gasoline. Some of these cars run on hydrogen or natural gas. Hybrid cars, which are becoming more common, use gasoline and electric power to reduce emissions. Other ways to reduce air pollution are to carpool, use public transportation, or bike or walk to your destination, as shown in **Figure 8.**

Figure 8 *In Copenhagen, Denmark, companies lend free bicycles in exchange for publicity. The program helps reduce air pollution and automobile traffic.*

Summary

- Air pollution is the introduction of harmful substances into the air by humans or by natural events.

- Primary pollutants are pollutants that are put directly into the air by human or natural activity.

- Secondary pollutants are pollutants that form when primary pollutants react with other primary pollutants or with naturally occurring substances.

- Transportation, industry, and natural sources are the main sources of air pollution.

- The burning of fossil fuels may lead to air pollution and acid precipitation, which may harm human and wildlife habitats.

- Air pollution can be reduced by legislation, such as the Clean Air Act; by technology, such as scrubbers; and by changes in lifestyle.

Using Vocabulary

Correct each statement by replacing the underlined term.

1 <u>Air pollution</u> is a sudden change in the acidity of a stream or lake.

2 <u>Smog</u> is rain, sleet, or snow that has a high concentration of acid.

Understanding Concepts

3 **Summarizing**   How does smog form?

4 **Comparing**   What is the difference between primary and secondary pollutants?

5 **Identifying**   List five sources of indoor air pollution.

6 **Applying**   How are fossil fuels related to air pollution and acid precipitation?

7 **Listing**   List five short-term effects of air pollution on human health.

Critical Thinking

8 **Analyzing Ideas**   Is all air pollution caused by humans? Explain your answer.

9 **Expressing Opinions**   How do you think that nations should resolve air-pollution problems that cross national boundaries?

10 **Making Inferences**   Why may establishing a direct link between air pollution and health problems be difficult?

INTERPRETING GRAPHICS   The map below shows the pH of precipitation measured at field stations in the northeastern United States. On the pH scale, the lower a number is, the more acidic the solution is. Use the map below to answer the next two questions.

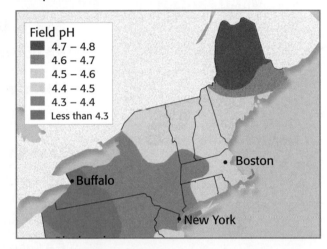

Field pH
- 4.7 – 4.8
- 4.6 – 4.7
- 4.5 – 4.6
- 4.4 – 4.5
- 4.3 – 4.4
- Less than 4.3

Boston
Buffalo
New York

11 **Forming Hypotheses**   Which areas have the most acidic precipitation? Hypothesize why.

12 **Making Inferences**   Boston is a larger city than Buffalo is, but the precipitation measured in Buffalo is more acidic than the precipitation in Boston is. Explain why.

Challenge

13 **Making Inferences**   Do you think that air pollution can extend beyond its source area? How far? How would the pollution move?

Internet Resources

For a variety of links related to this chapter, go to www.scilinks.org

Topic: Air Pollution
SciLinks code: HY70033

Skills Practice Lab

OBJECTIVES

Predict how changes in air pressure affect weather.

Build a barometer to test your hypothesis.

MATERIALS

- balloon
- can, coffee, large, empty, 10 cm in diameter
- card, index
- scissors
- straw, drinking
- tape, masking, or rubber band

SAFETY

6.4.e Students know differences in pressure, heat, air movement, and humidity result in changes of weather.

Investigation and Experimentation
6.7.a Develop a hypothesis.
6.7.e Recognize whether evidence is consistent with a proposed explanation.

Under Pressure!

Imagine that you are planning a picnic with your friends. The temperature this afternoon should be in the low 80s, and the skies should be sunny. These weather conditions sound quite comfortable. But you know that weather can change when air pressure changes. You can use a barometer to keep track of air-pressure changes. In this activity, you will build your own barometer and will discover what this tool can tell you.

Ask a Question

1 How can I use a barometer to detect changes in the weather?

Form a Hypothesis

2 Write a few sentences that answer the question above.

Test the Hypothesis

3 Stretch the balloon a few times. Then, blow up the balloon and let the air out. This step will make your barometer more sensitive to changes in atmospheric pressure.

4 Cut off the open end of the balloon. Next, stretch the balloon over the open end of the coffee can. Then, attach the balloon to the can with masking tape or a rubber band.

5 Cut one end of the straw at an angle to make a pointer.

6 Place the straw on the stretched balloon so that the pointer is directed away from the center of the balloon. Five centimeters of the end of the straw should extend past the edge of the can. Tape the straw to the balloon as shown in the illustration below.

7 Tape the index card to the side of the can as shown in the illustration at right. Congratulations! You have just made a barometer!

8 Now, use your barometer to collect and record information about air pressure. Place the barometer outside for 3 or 4 days. On each day, mark on the index card where the tip of the straw points.

Analyze the Results

9 Explaining Events   What atmospheric factors affect how your barometer works? Explain your answer.

10 Recognizing Patterns   What does it mean when the straw moves up?

11 Recognizing Patterns   What does it mean when the straw moves down?

Draw Conclusions

12 Applying Conclusions   Compare your results with the barometric pressures listed in your local newspaper. What kind of weather is associated with high pressure? What kind of weather is associated with low pressure?

13 Evaluating Results   Does the barometer you built support your hypothesis? Explain your answer.

Big Idea Question

14 Drawing Conclusions   Why is it important to be aware of barometric pressure? How can pressure help scientists to predict weather?

Science Skills Activity

Preparing for an Oral Report

Investigation and Experimentation
6.7.d Communicate the steps and results from an investigation in written reports and oral presentations.

▶ Tutorial

Communicating your results is an important part of any scientific investigation. Sometimes, scientists give oral reports. Preparation is the key to giving a good oral report. The steps outlined below will help you prepare for an oral report.

1. First, research the topic you will be discussing. Ask your teacher what sources you should use for the assignment.

2. To guide your research, make a list of topics you want to discuss in your presentation. You can update this list as you continue to gather information. Remember to take good notes!

3. Think about the order in which you will discuss the information. Create an outline that lists the order of topics.

4. Think about your introduction and conclusion. Your introduction should get your audience's attention. Your conclusion should review the information you have discussed.

5. Practice giving your presentation in front of family members or a mirror.

6. Use your outline as a guide when you give your presentation. Look at your audience, stand straight, stay still, and speak clearly.

▶ You Try It!

Procedure

Some substances that can be air pollutants include dust and smoke particles, pollen, mold spores, and waste gases. If these tiny particles remain suspended in the air for long periods of time, they are called *particulates*.

You will prepare and present an oral report about the particulates you collected when you performed the Quick Lab entitled "Collecting Air-Pollution Particles." Use the library or the Internet to research common particulates, their sources, and factors that affect the amount of particulates in the air. Your presentation should answer the following questions:

1. What are some common particulates? Are these particulates common where you live? Did you collect any of these particulates during your investigation?

2. What are possible sources of common particulates where you live?

3. How does wind affect the amount of particulates in the air?

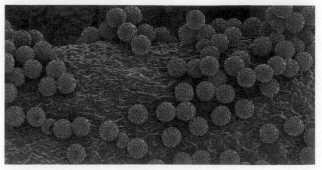

Pollen can be an air pollutant. The two photos above show microscopic views of pollen.

Chapter Summary

The Big Idea
Earth's atmosphere is a mixture of gases that absorbs solar energy and enables life on Earth.

Section

Vocabulary

1 Characteristics of the Atmosphere

Key Concept Earth's atmosphere absorbs solar energy and transports energy around Earth's surface.

- Earth's atmosphere is a mixture of gases that surrounds Earth and absorbs solar radiation.
- Pressure and temperature in the atmosphere change as distance from Earth's surface increases.

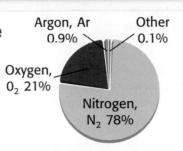

Argon, Ar 0.9% Other 0.1%
Oxygen, O_2 21%
Nitrogen, N_2 78%

Nitrogen is the most common gas in Earth's atmosphere.

atmosphere p. 470
air pressure p. 471
troposphere p. 472
stratosphere p. 472
mesosphere p. 473
thermosphere p. 473

2 Atmospheric Heating

Key Concept Heat in Earth's atmosphere is transferred by radiation, conduction, and convection.

- Solar energy travels through space as radiation and passes through the atmosphere to Earth's surface.
- Energy is carried through the atmosphere by radiation, conduction, and convection.

The atmosphere transfers energy by three processes.

radiation p. 474
electromagnetic spectrum p. 475
conduction p. 476
convection p. 477
convection current p. 477
greenhouse effect p. 478

3 Air Movement and Wind

Key Concept Global winds and local winds are produced by the uneven heating of Earth's surface.

- Uneven heating of Earth's surface by the sun causes differences in air pressure that cause wind.
- Wind patterns can be global or local and are influenced by the rotation of Earth and by geography.

Winds are part of a global air-circulation pattern.

wind p. 480
Coriolis effect p. 481

4 The Air We Breathe

Key Concept Air is an important natural resource that is affected by human activities.

- Air pollution is caused by human activities, such as burning fossil fuels, and by natural events, such as volcanic eruptions.
- Air pollution has short-term and long-term effects on human health.

Smog is a common type of air pollution.

air pollution p. 484
acid precipitation p. 487

Chapter Review

Organize

Booklet Review the FoldNote that you created at the beginning of the chapter. Add to or correct the FoldNote based on what you have learned.

Using Vocabulary

1 Academic Vocabulary Which term—*transfer* or *result*—best completes the following sentence: Convection currents ___ heat in the atmosphere.

For each pair of terms, explain how the meanings of the terms differ.

2 *conduction* and *convection*

3 *radiation* and *electromagnetic spectrum*

4 *wind* and *air pressure*

Understanding Concepts

Multiple Choice

5 What is the most abundant gas in the atmosphere?
a. oxygen
b. hydrogen
c. nitrogen
d. carbon dioxide

6 The ozone layer is located in the
a. stratosphere.
b. troposphere.
c. thermosphere.
d. mesosphere.

7 By which method does most thermal energy in the atmosphere circulate?
a. conduction
b. convection
c. advection
d. radiation

Short Answer

8 Classifying Classify the following pollutants as primary or secondary pollutants: *car exhaust, acid precipitation, smoke from a factory, and fumes from burning plastic.*

9 Analyzing Why does air pressure decrease as altitude increases?

10 Describing Explain why air rises when it is heated.

11 Identifying What is the main cause of temperature changes in the atmosphere?

12 Summarizing What are secondary pollutants, and how do they form? Give an example of a secondary pollutant.

13 Summarizing What is the electromagnetic spectrum? How much of the electromagnetic spectrum is visible light?

14 Describing Describe the relationship between solar energy and global winds.

INTERPRETING GRAPHICS Use the pie graph below to answer the next two questions.

Total World Emissions of CO_2

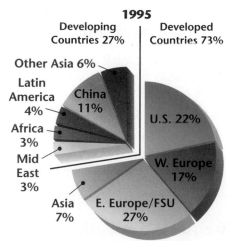

1995
Developing Countries 27%
Developed Countries 73%
Other Asia 6%
Latin America 4%
China 11%
Africa 3%
Mid East 3%
U.S. 22%
Asia 7%
E. Europe/FSU 27%
W. Europe 17%

15 Identifying Which produced more CO_2 emissions in 1995: developing countries or developed countries?

16 Listing Which developed country or group of countries had the highest CO_2 emissions?

Writing Skills

17 Writing Persuasively Write a letter to a family member or friend. Tell him or her about the effects of pollution and explain what he or she can do to reduce pollution.

18 Outlining Topics Outline the steps that you would take to reduce indoor air pollution at your school.

Critical Thinking

19 Concept Mapping Use the following terms to create a concept map: *mesosphere, stratosphere, layers, temperature, troposphere,* and *atmosphere.*

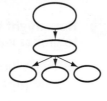

20 Identifying Relationships What is the relationship between the greenhouse effect and global warming?

21 Applying Concepts How do you think the Coriolis effect would change if Earth rotated twice as fast as it does? Explain your answer.

22 Identifying Relationships How are global winds related to convection?

23 Making Comparisons Compare local winds and global winds. Do the two types of winds form in the same way? Explain your answer.

24 Applying Concepts How is radiation fundamentally different from conduction and convection?

25 Making Inferences Is air a renewable or nonrenewable resource? Is stratospheric ozone a renewable or nonrenewable resource? Explain your answers.

26 Analyzing Processes How is heat transferred from the sun to Earth? What carries this energy from the sun to Earth?

27 Applying Concepts Compare the characteristics of visible light to the portions of the electromagnetic spectrum that are not visible. Which characteristics are different?

INTERPRETING GRAPHICS Use the graph below to answer the next three questions.

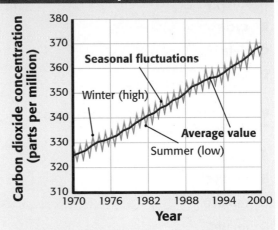

Concentration of Carbon Dioxide in the Atmosphere, 1970–2000

28 Evaluating Data According to the graph, is the carbon dioxide concentration increasing or decreasing with time?

29 Evaluating Data What factors could be contributing to the trend you see in the graph?

30 Making Inferences What can you infer about what will happen to the atmospheric carbon dioxide concentration in future years not shown on this graph? How could this result be avoided?

Math Skills

31 Making Calculations Maximum local wind speeds for each of the last seven days were 12 km/h, 20 km/h, 11 km/h, 6 km/h, 8km/h, 19 km/h, and 17 km/h. What was the average maximum wind speed?

Challenge

32 Predicting Consequences Imagine that there is a planet that has two suns. Assume that the planet and Earth have similar land and water conditions. Describe how two energy sources combined might affect the imaginary planet's winds.

Standards Assessment

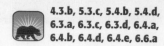

REVIEWING ACADEMIC VOCABULARY

1 Which of the following words means "the power that makes things happen"?

A energy

B cycle

C data

D factor

2 Which of the following words means "to have as a part of"?

A circle

B involve

C replace

D relate

3 In the sentence "Convection currents distribute heat in the atmosphere," what does the word *distribute* mean?

A to require

B to wear away

C to change

D to spread out

4 Which of the following phrases is the closest in meaning to the word *visible*?

A can be heard

B can be measured

C can be seen

D can be selected

REVIEWING CONCEPTS

5 How does Earth's atmosphere affect radiation that travels from the sun?

A Almost all the radiation reaches the surface of Earth.

B Most of the visible light is absorbed by the atmosphere.

C Most visible light reaches the surface of Earth.

D Only infrared radiation reaches the surface undisturbed.

6 How might burning fossil fuels contribute to global warming?

A by polluting water that then becomes acid precipitation in the water cycle

B by breaking down the atmosphere and allowing more radiation in

C by producing carbon dioxide that traps heat in the atmosphere

D by producing pollution that blocks sunlight from reaching Earth

7 Area A, which has high air pressure, is located beside Area B, which has low air pressure. The wind is blowing toward Area B. Which of the following is most likely to occur as the air pressure in Area B increases?

A The wind blowing toward Area B becomes faster.

B The wind blowing toward Area A becomes faster.

C The wind blowing toward Area B becomes slower.

D The wind blowing toward Area A becomes slower.

8 During the day, air over the ocean blows toward the land. Which of the following explains this phenomenon as shown in the figure above?

A Earth's rotation causes air to blow toward land.

B The energy of ocean storms pushes air toward land.

C Air over land heats more quickly, so the air rises and is replaced by air from the ocean.

D Air over land heats more slowly, so the warmer air over the ocean moves in to replace it.

9 Which of the following statements about air pollution is true?

A Cars and trucks produce the majority of air pollution.

B Air pollution does not occur indoors; it occurs only outdoors.

C Air pollution caused by fossil-fuel use can lead to acid precipitation.

D The use of hybrid cars has increased levels of air pollution.

10 Which of the following statements describes how pressure and temperature change as altitude increases?

A Pressure and temperature decrease.

B Pressure and temperature increase.

C Pressure decreases and temperature increases.

D Pressure decreases and temperature fluctuates.

REVIEWING PRIOR LEARNING

11 Which of the following is an example of a secondary pollutant?

A pollen

B smog

C paint chemicals

D vehicle exhaust

12 What effect does the thinning of the ozone layer have on the environment?

A It creates acid precipitation that harms the environment.

B It intensifies the effects of primary and secondary pollutants.

C It creates a greenhouse effect that leads to global warming.

D It increases ultraviolet radiation that can cause skin cancer.

13 Which of the following is most likely to occur when water vapor in a cloud cools?

A It evaporates and rises.

B It moves away to a lower-pressure area.

C It moves away to a higher-pressure area.

D It condenses and falls as precipitation.

A	B	C	D
H H	L L	L H	H L
H LL H	L HH L	L H	L H
HH	L L	L H	

14 In the air-pressure patterns above, H represents high pressure, and L represents low pressure. Which of the air-pressure patterns is most likely to lead to severe weather, such as a hurricane?

A pattern A

B pattern B

C pattern C

D pattern D

Science in Action

Science, Technology, and Society

The HyperSoar Jet

Imagine traveling from Chicago to Tokyo in 72 minutes. If the HyperSoar jet becomes a reality, you may be able to travel to the other side of the world in less time than it takes to watch a movie! To accomplish this amazing feat, the jet would "skip" across the upper stratosphere. To begin skipping, the jet would climb above the stratosphere, turn off its engines, and glide for about 60 km. Then, gravity would pull the jet down to where the air is denser. The denser air would cause the jet to soar upward. In this way, the jet would skip across a layer of dense air until it was ready to land. Each 2-minute skip would cover about 450 km, and the HyperSoar would be able to fly at Mach 10—a speed of 3 km/s!

Social Studies ACTiViTY

Great advances have been made in the technology of flight, and even greater advances are on the horizon. Use the Internet or a library to research the history of flight. Record your findings in your **Science Journal.**

Weird Science

A Very Expensive Time Capsule

Diamonds are beautiful gemstones. And they can be useful in drills and blades, too. But did you know that some diamonds may act like time capsules? Three-billion-year-old diamonds that have this special property have been found in Botswana, Africa. These diamond time capsules contain information about what Earth's atmosphere was like billions of years ago. The diamonds are being studied by a team of scientists from the University of California, San Diego, and from the University of Maryland. The diamonds contain information about forms of sulfur in the atmosphere during the Archean Eon. Geologists and atmospheric chemists hope that the information stored in these diamonds will allow us to better understand how Earth's early atmosphere developed.

Math ACTiViTY

Diamonds take millions of years to form. How long is 1 million years compared to other time intervals? Express 1 million years in decades and centuries.

Ellen Paneok

Bush Pilot For Ellen Paneok, understanding weather patterns is a matter of life and death. As a bush pilot, she flies mail, supplies, and people to remote villages in Alaska that can be reached only by plane. Bad weather is one of the most serious challenges Paneok faces. "It's beautiful up here," she says, "but it can also be harsh." One dangerous situation is landing a plane in mountainous regions. "On top of a mountain you can't tell which way the wind is blowing," Paneok says. In this case, she flies in a rectangular pattern to determine the wind direction. Landing a plane on the frozen Arctic Ocean is also dangerous. In whiteout conditions, the horizon can't be seen because the sky and the ground are the same color. "It's like flying in a milk bottle full of milk," Paneok says. In these conditions, she fills black plastic garbage bags and drops them from the plane to help guide her landing.

Paneok had to overcome many challenges to become a pilot. When she was a child, she lived in seven foster homes before being placed in an all-girls' home at the age of 14. In the girls' home, she read a magazine about careers in aviation and decided then and there that she wanted to become a pilot. At first, she faced a lot of opposition from people who told her that she wouldn't be able to become a pilot. Now, she encourages young people to pursue their goals. "If you decide you want to go for it, go for it. There may be obstacles in your way, but you've just got to find a way to go over them, get around them, or dig under them," she says.

Ellen Paneok is shown at right with two of her Inupiat passengers.

Language Arts ACTiViTY

Beryl Markham lived an exciting life as a bush pilot delivering mail and supplies to remote areas of Africa. Read about her life or the life of Bessie Coleman, one of the most famous African-American women in the history of flying.

Internet Resources

- To learn more about careers in science, visit **www.scilinks.org** and enter the SciLinks code HY70225.

- To learn more about these Science in Action topics, visit go.hrw.com and type in the key-word HY7ATMF.

- Check out articles related to this chapter by visiting go.hrw.com. Just type in the key-word HY7ATMC.

Improving Comprehension

Graphic Organizers are important visual tools that can help you organize information and improve your reading comprehension. The Graphic Organizer below is called a *spider map.* Instructions for creating other types of Graphic Organizers are located in the **Study Skills** section of the Appendix.

How to Make a Spider Map

1 Draw a diagram like the one shown below. In the circle, write the main topic.

2 From the circle, draw legs to represent the main ideas or characteristics of the topic. Draw as many legs as you want to draw. Write an idea or characteristic along each leg.

3 From each leg, draw horizontal lines. As you read the chapter, write details about each idea on the idea's horizontal lines. To add more details, make the legs longer and add more horizontal lines.

When to Use a Spider Map

A spider map is an effective tool for classifying the details of a specific topic in science. A spider map divides a topic into ideas and details. As you read about a topic, look for the main ideas or characteristics of the topic. Within each idea, look for details. Use a spider map to organize the ideas and details of each topic.

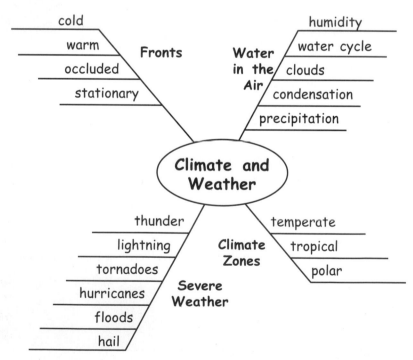

You Try It!

This Reading Strategy can also be used within the chapter that you are about to read. Practice making your own spider map as directed in the Reading Strategies for Section **2** and Section **3**. Record your work in your **Science Journal.**

Unpacking the Standards

The information below "unpacks" the standards by breaking them down into basic parts. The higher-level, academic vocabulary is highlighted and defined to help you understand the language of the standards. "What It Means" restates the standards as simply as possible.

California Standard	Academic Vocabulary	What It Means
6.2.d Students know earthquakes, volcanic eruptions, landslides, and floods change human and wildlife habitats.		Earthquakes, volcanic eruptions, landslides, and floods change the surroundings in which humans and wildlife live
6.4.a Students know the sun is the **major source** of **energy** for **phenomena** on Earth's surface; it powers winds, ocean currents, and the water **cycle.**	**major** (MAY juhr) of great importance or large scale **source** (SAWRS) the thing from which something else comes **energy** (FN uhr jee) the ability to make things happen **phenomenon** (fuh NAHM uh NUHN) any facts or events that can be sensed or described scientifically (plural *phenomena*) **cycle** (SIE kuhl) a repeating series of changes	The sun is the main source of energy for processes on Earth. Energy from the sun powers winds, ocean currents, and the water cycle.
6.4.b Students know solar **energy** reaches Earth through radiation, mostly in the form of **visible** light.	**energy** (EN uhr jee) the ability to make things happen **visible** (VIZ uh buhl) that can be seen	Energy from the sun reaches Earth through radiation. Most of this energy is light that humans can see.
6.4.d Students know convection currents **distribute** heat in the atmosphere and oceans.	**distribute** (di STRIB yoot) to spread out over an area	The movement of air in the atmosphere and of water in the ocean carries heat throughout the atmosphere and oceans.
6.4.e Students know differences in pressure, heat, air movement, and humidity result in changes of weather.		Changes in the weight of the atmosphere, heat, air movement, and the amount of water in the air cause the conditions of the atmosphere to change.

The following identifies other standards that are covered in this chapter and where you can go to see them unpacked: **6.3.c** (Chapter 13), **6.6.a** (Chapter 5)

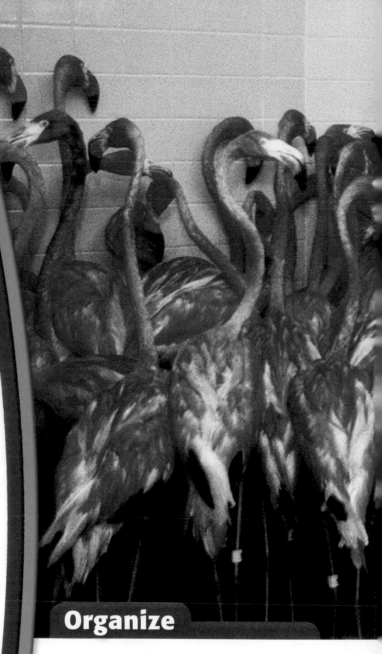

15

Weather and Climate

The Big Idea

Differences in pressure, heat, air movement, and humidity result in changes of weather and thus affect climate.

California Standards

Focus on Earth Sciences

6.2 Topography is reshaped by the weathering of rock and soil and by the transportation and deposition of sediment. (Sections 2 and 4)

6.4 Many phenomena on Earth's surface are affected by the transfer of energy through radiation and convection currents. (Sections 1, 2, 3, and 4)

6.6 Sources of energy and materials differ in amounts, distribution, usefulness, and the time required for their formation. (Section 4)

Investigation and Experimentation

6.7 Scientific progress is made by asking meaningful questions and conducting careful investigations. (Science Skills Activity)

Math

6.1.1 Algebra and Functions

English–Language Arts

6.1.1, 6.2.4 Reading

6.1.1, 6.1.2, 6.1.3, 6.2.1, 6.2.2 Writing

About the Photo

Flamingos in the bathroom? This situation may look like someone's idea of a practical joke, but in fact, it's a practical idea! These flamingos reside at the Miami-Metro Zoo in Florida. They were put in the bathroom for protection against the dangerous winds of Hurricane Floyd in September of 1999.

Organize

Double Door

Before you read this chapter, create the FoldNote entitled "Double Door." Write "Weather" on one flap of the double door and "Climate" on the other flap. As you read the chapter, compare the two topics, and write characteristics of each topic on the inside of the appropriate flap.

Instructions for creating FoldNotes are located in the Study Skills section on p. 615 of the Appendix.

Explore Activity

⏱ **10 min**

The Meeting of Air Masses

In this activity, you will model what happens when two air masses that have different temperature characteristics meet.

Procedure

1. Pour **500 mL of water** into a **beaker**. Pour **500 mL of cooking oil** into a **second beaker.** The water represents a dense, cold air mass. The cooking oil represents a less dense, warm air mass.

2. Predict what would happen to the two liquids if you tried to mix them.

3. Pour the contents of both beakers into a **clear, plastic, rectangular container** at the same time from opposite ends of the container.

4. Observe the interaction of the oil and water.

Analysis

6.4.e

5. What happens when the liquids meet?

6. Does the prediction that you made in step 2 match your results?

7. Using your results, hypothesize what happens when a cold air mass meets a warm air mass.

Water in the Air

Key Concept The sun's energy drives the water cycle and causes differences in humidity that may lead to precipitation.

What You Will Learn

- The amount of water vapor in the air is known as humidity.
- Differences in pressure, temperature, and humidity cause clouds and precipitation.

Why It Matters

Understanding how water moves through the water cycle is the basis for understanding weather.

Vocabulary

- weather
- humidity
- dew point
- relative humidity
- condensation
- precipitation

READING STRATEGY

Summarizing Read this section silently. In pairs, take turns summarizing the material. Stop to discuss ideas and words that seem confusing.

▶ What will the weather be tomorrow? Depending on what you have planned, knowing the answer to this question could be important. A day at the beach in the rain would be no fun!

Weather is the condition of the atmosphere at a certain time and place. The condition of the atmosphere is affected by the amount of water in the air. To understand weather, you need to understand how water moves through the atmosphere.

The Water Cycle

The sun's energy heats Earth's surface and causes water to change states. For example, as the water in the ocean is heated, it may change to water vapor. If the water vapor cools, it may condense to form water droplets that make up clouds. This movement of water between the atmosphere, the land, and the oceans is called the *water cycle*. The water cycle is shown in **Figure 1.**

Standards Check What is the main source of energy for the water cycle? 6.4.a

Figure 1 The Water Cycle

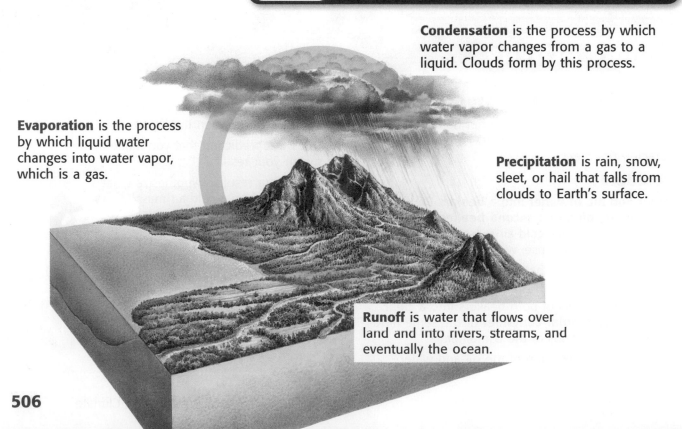

Condensation is the process by which water vapor changes from a gas to a liquid. Clouds form by this process.

Evaporation is the process by which liquid water changes into water vapor, which is a gas.

Precipitation is rain, snow, sleet, or hail that falls from clouds to Earth's surface.

Runoff is water that flows over land and into rivers, streams, and eventually the ocean.

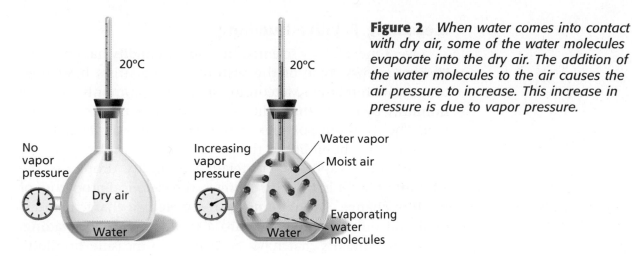

Figure 2 *When water comes into contact with dry air, some of the water molecules evaporate into the dry air. The addition of the water molecules to the air causes the air pressure to increase. This increase in pressure is due to vapor pressure.*

20°C

20°C

No vapor pressure

Increasing vapor pressure

Water vapor

Moist air

Dry air

Evaporating water molecules

Water

Water

Humidity

Water vapor makes up between 1% and 4% of the total composition of Earth's atmosphere by volume. However, this small amount of water vapor greatly affects weather and climate. The amount of water vapor in the air is known as **humidity.**

Humidity depends on the rates of evaporation and condensation. In general, the rate of evaporation increases as air temperature increases. The rate of condensation is determined by vapor pressure. *Vapor pressure* is that part of total atmospheric pressure that is caused by water vapor, as shown in **Figure 2.** As vapor pressure increases, the rate of condensation increases. When the rate of evaporation equals the rate of condensation, the air is saturated with water molecules. The temperature at which this balance happens is called the **dew point.** At temperatures below the dew point, liquid water droplets form on a surface or on tiny particles in the air.

Relative Humidity

A common way for scientists to express the amount of water vapor in the air is by using relative humidity. **Relative humidity** is the ratio of the amount of water vapor in the air to the amount of water vapor needed to reach saturation at a given temperature. In other words, relative humidity is a measure of how close the air is to the dew point. At a certain temperature, air is saturated when it has 24 g of water vapor per 1 m³ of air. But, the air actually has 18 g of water vapor. You can calculate the relative humidity by using the following formula:

$$\frac{actual\ water\ vapor\ content\ (g/m^3)}{saturation\ water\ vapor\ content\ (g/m^3)} \times 100 = relative\ humidity\ (\%)$$

$$\frac{18\ g/m^3}{24\ g/m^3} \times 100 = 75\%$$

weather (WETH uhr) the short-term state of the atmosphere, including temperature, humidity, precipitation, wind, and visibility

humidity (hyoo MID hu tee) the amount of water vapor in the air

dew point (DOO POYNT) at constant pressure and water vapor content, the temperature at which the rate of condensation equals the rate of evaporation

relative humidity (REL uh tiv hyoo MID uh tee) the ratio of the amount of water vapor in the air to the amount of water vapor needed to reach saturation at a given temperature

Relative Humidity

At 25°C, the air is saturated when it contains 24 g/m³ of water vapor. If 1 m³ of air at 25°C contains 11 g of water vapor, calculate the relative humidity. Record your work in your **Science Journal.**

6.4.a Students know the sun is the major source of energy for phenomena on Earth's surface; it powers winds, ocean currents, and the water cycle.
6.4.e Students know differences in pressure, heat, air movement, and humidity result in changes of weather.

Measuring Relative Humidity

Over time, the way scientists measure humidity has changed. **Figure 3** shows some of the instruments scientists have used to measure humidity. Meteorologists today commonly measure humidity by using a humidity sensor that has a thin-film polymer. The thin-film polymer in the sensor absorbs water vapor as the relative humidity in the air rises, and thin-film polymer releases water vapor as the relative humidity drops. As the amount of water in the film changes, the electrical properties of the film change. The amount of stored electric charge is measured and quickly converted into a relative-humidity reading. Other instruments that have been used to measure humidity are hair hygrometers, dew cells, and psychrometers.

Figure 3 Instruments for Measuring Relative Humidity

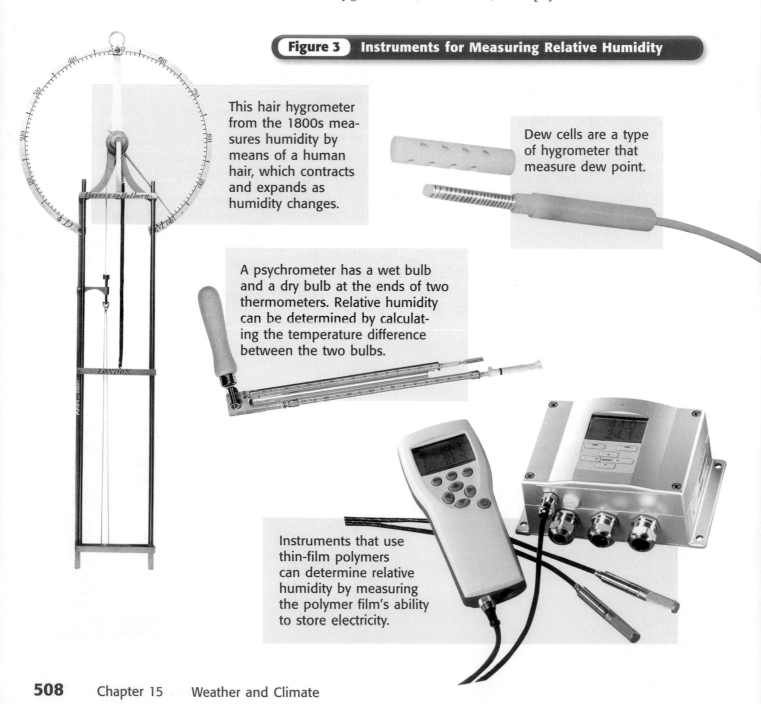

This hair hygrometer from the 1800s measures humidity by means of a human hair, which contracts and expands as humidity changes.

Dew cells are a type of hygrometer that measure dew point.

A psychrometer has a wet bulb and a dry bulb at the ends of two thermometers. Relative humidity can be determined by calculating the temperature difference between the two bulbs.

Instruments that use thin-film polymers can determine relative humidity by measuring the polymer film's ability to store electricity.

Condensation

You have probably seen water droplets form on the outside of a glass of ice water, as shown in **Figure 4.** Where did those water droplets come from? They came from the surrounding air. The droplets formed as a result of condensation. **Condensation** is the process by which a gas, such as water vapor, becomes a liquid. For liquid water droplets to form, the air must be saturated, or have a relative humidity of 100%. Air can become saturated when water vapor enters the air through evaporation. Air can also become saturated when it cools to below its dew point.

Dew Point and Condensation

The dew point is the temperature at which the rate of condensation equals the rate of evaporation. When ice cubes are added to the glass of water, the temperature of the water drops. The cold water absorbs heat from the glass by conduction, and the glass cools, too. By conduction, the glass absorbs heat from the air. As a result, the temperature of the air next to the glass drops to below the dew point. As the condensation rate exceeds the evaporation rate, water droplets form on the glass.

Reaching the Dew Point

When the air is nearly saturated, only a small temperature drop is needed for air to reach its dew point. During the night, grass, leaves, and other things near the ground lose heat. Air may cool to below the dew point when the air touches these cold surfaces. The water droplets that form are called *dew*.

Standards Check How does a drop in temperature cause condensation? 6.4.e

Figure 4 *Water droplets formed when the air around the glass cooled to below the dew point.*

condensation (KAHN duhn SAY shuhn) the change of state from a gas to a liquid

---

Quick Lab

Reaching the Dew Point

1. Pour **room-temperature water** into a **plastic container,** such as a drinking cup, until the water level is near the top of the cup.
2. Observe the outside of the container, and record your observations.
3. Add **one or two ice cubes** to the container of water.
4. Watch the outside of the container for any changes.

5. What happened to the outside of the container?
6. Where did the liquid come from? Explain your answer.
7. Explain how the cooling of the water inside the glass causes the air outside the glass to reach the dew point.

6.4.e

10 min

Clouds and Precipitation

precipitation (pree SIP uh TAY shuhn) any form of water that falls to Earth's surface from the clouds

A cloud is a collection of millions of tiny water droplets or ice crystals. Clouds form as air rises and cools. When the air cools to below the dew point, water droplets or ice crystals form. At temperatures above 0°C, water vapor condenses on small particles in the air and forms tiny water droplets. At temperatures below 0°C, water vapor changes to a solid to form ice crystals.

Types of Clouds

Clouds are classified by their shape and their altitude, as shown in **Figure 5.** The three cloud forms are stratus clouds, cumulus clouds, and cirrus clouds. There are also three altitude groups: low clouds (0 m to 2,000 m), middle clouds (2,000 m to 6,000 m), and high clouds (above 6,000 m).

Standards Check How does air movement cause clouds to form?
6.4.e

High Clouds Because of the cold temperatures at high altitude, high clouds are made up of ice crystals. The prefix *cirro-* is used to describe high clouds.

Middle Clouds Middle clouds can be made up of both water droplets and ice crystals. The prefix *alto-* is used to describe middle clouds.

Low Clouds Low clouds are made up of water droplets. There is no specific prefix to describe low clouds.

Figure 5 Cloud Types Based on Shape and Altitude

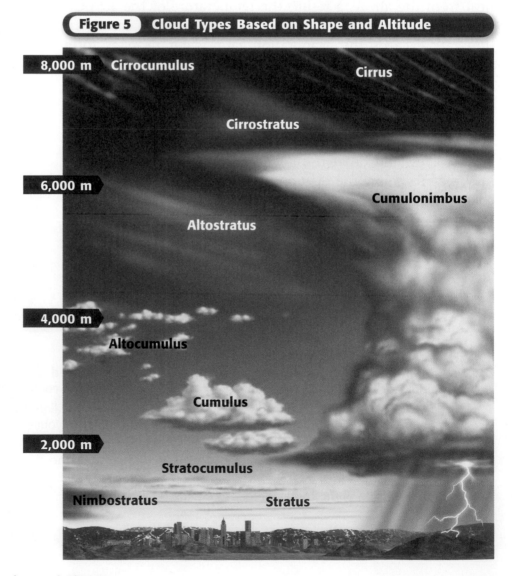

8,000 m — Cirrocumulus — Cirrus

Cirrostratus

6,000 m

Cumulonimbus

Altostratus

4,000 m

Altocumulus

Cumulus

2,000 m

Stratocumulus

Nimbostratus — Stratus

Precipitation

Most cloud droplets have a diameter of about 20 micrometers, which is smaller than the period at the end of this sentence. Droplets of this size fall very slowly through the air. When a droplet reaches a certain size, it falls as precipitation. **Precipitation** is water, in any form, that falls to Earth's surface from the clouds. There are four major forms of precipitation—rain, snow, sleet, and hail. Rain is the most common form of precipitation. Hail, lumps of ice that fall from clouds, is less common. **Figure 6** shows a cross section of a hailstone.

Standards Check What is precipitation, and what causes it? 6.4.e

Figure 6 *The layers in a hailstone show that the hailstone was repeatedly coated in water and then frozen.*

SECTION Review

6.4.a, 6.4.e

Summary

- The sun's energy causes water to change states and to move through the water cycle.
- The amount of water vapor in the air is called *humidity*.
- When the temperature of the air cools to the dew point, the air is saturated and liquid water droplets form.
- Clouds form as air rises and cools, which causes water droplets to form on small particles in the air.
- Precipitation is water, in any form, that falls to Earth's surface from the clouds.

Using Vocabulary

Use a term from the section to complete each sentence below.

1 ___ is the amount of water vapor in the air.

2 ___ is any form of water that falls to Earth's surface from the clouds.

Understanding Concepts

3 Summarizing Explain how relative humidity relates to the amount of water vapor in the air.

4 Describing Describe the four processes in the water cycle.

5 Summarizing What is the dew point?

6 Demonstrating What is the water cycle's energy source?

Critical Thinking

7 Identifying Relationships What happens to the rates of condensation and evaporation as the air temperature drops below the dew point?

INTERPRETING GRAPHICS
Use the illustration below to answer the next two questions.

8 Making Inferences By its shape, name this type of cloud.

9 Evaluating Data Estimate the altitude of this cloud.

Challenge

10 Identifying Relationships One body of air has a relative humidity of 97%. Another has a relative humidity of 44%. At the same temperature, which body of air is closer to its dew point? Explain your answer.

Fronts and Weather

Key Concept Weather results from the movement of air masses that differ in temperature and humidity.

▶ Have you ever wondered how the weather can change so quickly? Changes in weather are caused by the interaction of air masses. An **air mass** is a large body of air that has similar temperature and moisture content throughout.

Fronts

When different air masses meet, the less dense air mass rises over the denser air mass. Warm air is less dense than cold air is. So, when a warm air mass and a cold air mass meet, warm air generally rises. The area in which two or more air masses meet is called a **front. Figure 1** shows the four different kinds of fronts.

Cold Fronts

A cold front forms where cold air moves under warm air. Because the warm air is less dense, the cold air pushes the warm air up. Cold fronts can move quickly and bring heavy rain or snow. Cooler weather follows a cold front. The cooler weather is brought by the cold, dry air mass behind the cold front that pushed up the warm air mass.

Figure 1 The Four Main Types of Fronts

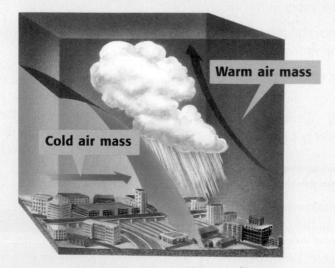

Cold Front

Warm air mass

Cold air mass

Movement of front

Warm Front

Warm air mass

Cold air mass

Movement of front

Warm Fronts

A warm front forms where warm air moves over cold, denser air that is leaving an area. The warm air replaces the cold air as the cold air moves away. Warm fronts generally bring drizzly rain. They also are followed by clear, warm weather.

Occluded Fronts

An occluded front forms when a warm air mass is caught between two colder air masses. One cold air mass moves under and pushes up the warm air mass. The cold air mass then moves forward until it meets the other cold air mass. The advancing cold air masses moves under and pushes up the other cold air mass. Sometimes, though, the two colder air masses mix. An occluded front brings cool temperatures and large amounts of rain and snow.

Standards Check What kind of weather would you expect an occluded front to produce? **6.4.e**

Stationary Fronts

A stationary front forms when a cold air mass and a warm air mass move toward each other. The warm air mass is commonly forced over the cold air mass. However, there is not enough force for either air mass to advance relative to the other. So, the two air masses remain separated. Stationary fronts happen when there is not enough wind to keep the air masses pushing against each other. A stationary front generally causes many days of cloudy, wet weather.

6.2.d Students know earthquakes, volcanic eruptions, landslides, and floods change human and wildlife habitats.
6.4.a Students know the sun is the major source of energy for phenomena on Earth's surface; it powers winds, ocean currents, and the water cycle.
6.4.e Students know differences in pressure, heat, air movement, and humidity result in changes of weather.

air mass (ER MAS) a large body of air throughout which temperature and moisture content are similar

front (FRUNT) the boundary between air masses of different densities and usually different temperatures

Occluded Front

Warm air mass   Warm air mass

Cold air mass   Cold air mass

Stationary Front

Cold air mass   Warm air mass

Movement of front

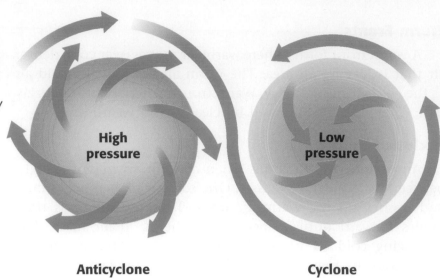

Figure 2 *As the colder, denser air spirals out of the anticyclone, the air may spiral in toward areas of low pressure called* cyclones.

High pressure

Low pressure

Anticyclone

Cyclone

Air Pressure and Weather

You may have heard a weather reporter talking about areas of low pressure and high pressure. These areas of different pressure cause changes in the weather. An area that has lower air pressure than the areas around it do is called a **cyclone.** Cyclones are areas where air rises. As the air in the center of a cyclone rises, the air cools. Clouds form and may cause rainy and stormy weather.

Areas of high air pressure are called *anticyclones.* Anticyclones are areas where air sinks. As the air sinks, it gets warmer and its relative humidity decreases. As a result, the sinking air in an anticyclone brings dry, clear weather. **Figure 2** shows how an anticyclone can form a cyclone.

Standards Check Describe the different kinds of weather that cyclones and anticyclones can form. 🐻**6.4.e**

cyclone (SIE KLOHN) an area in the atmosphere that has lower pressure than the surrounding areas and has winds that spiral toward the center

Wordwise The root *cycl-* means "circle" or "wheel." Other examples are *bicycle, cyclic,* and *cycle.*

Quick Lab

Modeling a Front

1. Use a **bottle opener** to punch one or two holes into the **metal lid** of a **glass jar.**

2. Pour **1 mL of hot water** into the jar. Place the lid on the jar.

3. Place an **ice cube** over the holes in the lid. Make sure the holes are completely covered.

4. Observe the changes that occur within the jar.

5. Draw a diagram of what you observe in the jar.

6. In your diagram, label the location of the warm air mass, the cold air mass, and the front where the two air masses meet. How do you know where the front is located?

🐻 **6.4.e**

🕐 **20 min**

Thunderstorms

A *thunderstorm* is an intense local storm that forms strong winds, heavy rain, lightning, and thunder. Two atmospheric conditions are needed to form thunderstorms: warm and moist air near Earth's surface and an unstable atmosphere. The atmosphere is unstable when cold air is over warm air. When the rising warm air reaches its dew point, the water vapor in the air forms cumulus clouds. If the warm air continues to rise, the cloud may grow into a dark, cumulonimbus cloud. One such cloud is shown in **Figure 3.**

Lightning

Have you ever touched someone after scuffing your feet on the carpet and received a mild shock? If so, you have experienced how lightning forms. While you walk around, friction between the floor and your shoes builds up an electric charge in your body. When you touch someone else, the charge is released. Lightning forms in a similar way. **Lightning** is an electric discharge that happens between a positively charged area and a negatively charged area. This process is shown in **Figure 4.**

Thunder

When lightning strikes, the air along its path is superheated. The superheated air expands rapidly. The rapidly expanding air causes the air to vibrate and release energy as sound waves. The result is **thunder,** which is the sound caused by the fast expansion of air along the lightning strike.

Figure 3 *A typical thunderstorm, such as this one over Los Angeles, California, generates an enormous amount of electrical energy.*

lightning (LIET ning) an electric discharge that takes place between two oppositely charged surfaces, such as between a cloud and the ground, between two clouds, or between two parts of the same cloud

thunder (THUHN duhr) the sound caused by the rapid expansion of air along an electrical strike

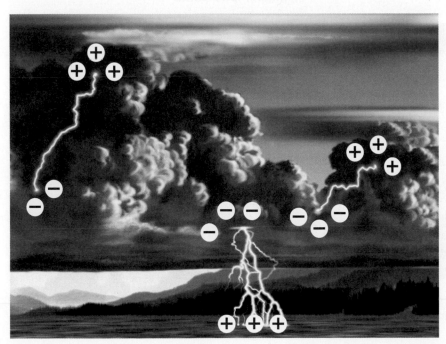

Figure 4 *The upper part of a cloud usually carries a positive electric charge. The lower part of the cloud carries mainly negative charges.*

Tornadoes

tornado (tawr NAY doh) a destructive, rotating column of air that has very high wind speeds and that may be visible as a funnel-shaped cloud

Tornadoes happen in less than 1% of all thunderstorms. A **tornado** is a rapidly, spinning column of air with high wind speeds and low central pressure and that touches the ground. The beginning of a tornado can be seen as a funnel cloud that pokes through the bottom of a cumulonimbus cloud. The funnel cloud becomes a tornado when it touches down on Earth's surface, as shown in **Figure 5.**

Figure 5   **How a Tornado Forms**

❶ Wind moving in two directions causes a layer of air in the middle to begin to spin like a roll of toilet paper.

❷ The spinning column of air is turned to a vertical position by strong updrafts and downdrafts of air located next to each other in the cumulonimbus cloud.

❸ The spinning column of air moves to the bottom of the cumulonimbus cloud and forms a funnel cloud.

❹ A funnel cloud becomes a tornado when it touches the ground.

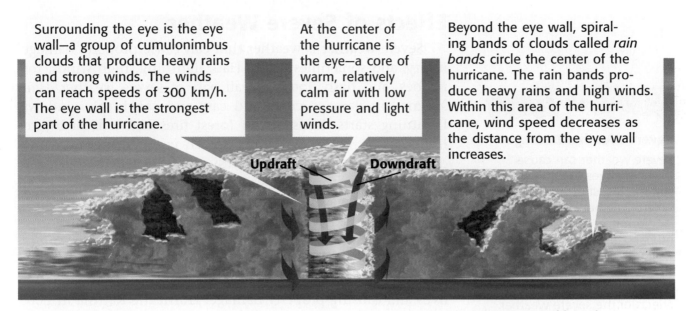

Surrounding the eye is the eye wall—a group of cumulonimbus clouds that produce heavy rains and strong winds. The winds can reach speeds of 300 km/h. The eye wall is the strongest part of the hurricane.

At the center of the hurricane is the eye—a core of warm, relatively calm air with low pressure and light winds.

Beyond the eye wall, spiraling bands of clouds called *rain bands* circle the center of the hurricane. The rain bands produce heavy rains and high winds. Within this area of the hurricane, wind speed decreases as the distance from the eye wall increases.

Updraft   **Downdraft**

Figure 6 *Although hurricanes are very destructive storms, the eye at the center of the tropical storm is relatively calm.*

Hurricanes

A large, rotating tropical weather system that has wind speeds of at least 120 km/h is called a *hurricane*. A hurricane is shown in **Figure 6.** Hurricanes are the most powerful storms on Earth. Hurricanes range in size from 160 km to 1,500 km in diameter. They can travel for thousands of kilometers.

Where Hurricanes Form

Most hurricanes form in the areas between 5° and 20° north latitude and between 5° and 20° south latitude. These storms form over warm, tropical oceans. At higher latitudes, the water is too cold for hurricanes to form.

How Hurricanes Form

A hurricane gets its energy from the evaporation and condensation of water vapor. Once formed, the hurricane is fueled through contact with the warm ocean water. Heat from the sun causes ocean water to evaporate. The evaporation adds moisture to the warm air. As the warm, moist air rises, the water vapor condenses and releases large amounts of energy. A group of thunderstorms forms and moves over tropical ocean waters. The thunderstorms produce a large vortex, or whirl of air.

The hurricane continues to grow as long as it is over warm ocean water. When the hurricane moves over colder waters or over land, the storm loses energy. This loss of energy is the reason that California does not experience hurricanes. Hurricanes approaching California quickly die out over the cold California coastal waters.

Standards Check How does the sun's energy power hurricanes?
6.4.a

Effects of Severe Weather

Severe weather is weather that can cause property damage, injury, and sometimes death. Hail, lightning, high winds, tornadoes, and flash floods are all part of severe weather. Hailstorms can damage crops and cars and can break windows. Lightning starts thousands of forest fires and kills or injures hundreds of people and animals each year. Winds and tornadoes can uproot trees and destroy homes.

Floods caused by heavy rains cause millions of dollars in property damage every year. Flash flooding is also a leading cause of weather-related deaths. Most damage from hurricanes results from flooding caused by heavy rains and storm surges. A *storm surge* is a rise in sea level that forms in the ocean during a storm. The storm surge crashes onto shore, endangering lives and causing property damage. Hurricane Katrina in 2005 caused more damage and deaths to the southeastern coast of the United States from flooding than from high-speed winds.

Standards Check How do floods affect humans? 🐾 **6.2.d**

Severe-Weather Safety

During severe weather, one of the most important things to do is to listen to your local radio or TV stations. Severe-weather announcements will let you know a storm's location. They also tell you if the storm is getting worse. During most kinds of severe weather, it is safest to stay indoors away from windows. However, in some situations, you may need to evacuate. During a flood warning, if you are in a low-lying place, such as the one shown in **Figure 7,** you should move to higher ground. Never enter floodwaters. Even shallow floodwater can be dangerous if it is moving fast.

Figure 7 *In 1998, heavy rains caused flooding in the town of Petaluma, California.*

Summary

- Thunderstorms are weather systems that produce strong winds, heavy rain, lightning, and thunder.

- Lightning is a large electric discharge that occurs between two oppositely charged surfaces. Lightning releases a great deal of energy and can be very dangerous.

- Tornadoes are small, rapidly rotating columns of air that touch the ground and can cause severe damage.

- A hurricane is a large, rotating tropical weather system that has high wind speeds.

- In the event of severe weather, it is important to stay safe. Listen to your local TV or radio stations for updates, and remain indoors and away from windows.

Using Vocabulary

Use a term from the section to complete each sentence below.

1 A ___ is a brief storm that consists of rain, strong winds, lightning, and thunder.

2 ___ is the sound caused by the rapid expansion of air along a lightning strike.

Understanding Concepts

3 Comparing Compare a cold front and a warm front.

4 Analyzing How does energy from the sun lead to the formation of hurricanes?

5 Evaluating What causes lightning?

6 Applying What type of weather would you expect a cold front to produce? a warm front?

7 Applying How do floods affect people?

8 Applying How do heat flow and air movement relate to the formation of thunderstorms?

Critical Thinking

9 Making Comparisons Compare cyclones and anticyclones and the weather patterns that they cause.

10 Identifying Relationships Explain what happens to a hurricane as it moves over land.

11 Identifying Relationships How does severe weather cause floods?

12 Identifying Relationships Flooding can cause property damage and endanger human lives. Describe how flooding might affect wildlife habitats.

INTERPRETING GRAPHICS Use the illustration below to answer the next two questions.

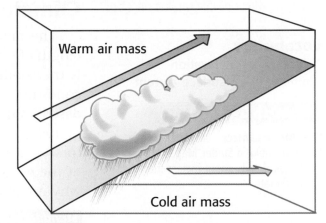

Warm air mass

Cold air mass

13 Analyzing Processes In which direction is the front moving? How can you tell?

14 Evaluating Data What type of front is represented in the illustration?

Challenge

15 Applying Concepts Fronts form when two moving air masses meet. Explain what causes the air masses to move. What would weather be like if air masses did not move? Why don't fronts form between two air masses that have the same temperature?

Internet Resources

For a variety of links related to this chapter, go to www.scilinks.org
Topic: Weather in California
SciLinks code: HY7C08

SECTION 3

What Is Climate?

Key Concept Earth's climate zones are caused by the distribution of heat around Earth's surface by wind and ocean currents.

What You Will Learn

● Climate is the average weather condition in an area over a long period of time.

● Climate is affected by latitude, global winds, topography, proximity to large bodies of water, and ocean currents.

Why It Matters

Climate and seasonal weather patterns determine where people can live on Earth.

Vocabulary

• climate
• latitude
• elevation
• surface current

READING STRATEGY

Graphic Organizer In your **Science Journal,** make a Spider Map that organizes details about factors that affect climate.

▶ Suppose that you receive a call from a friend who is coming to visit you tomorrow. To decide what clothing to bring, he asks about the current weather in your area.

You step outside to see if rain clouds are in the sky and to check the temperature. But what would you do if your friend asked you about the climate in your area? What is the difference between weather and climate?

Climate Versus Weather

The major difference between weather and climate is the length of time over which the conditions are measured. *Weather* is the condition of the atmosphere at a certain time. Weather conditions change from day to day. **Climate,** on the other hand, describes the average weather conditions in an area over a long period of time. Climate is usually described by using two factors—temperature and amount of precipitation. Different parts of the world have different climates, as shown in **Figure 1.** But why are climates so different?

Standards Check Name two factors that are used to describe climate. **6.4.e**

Figure 1 *North America has a variety of climates.* **How does the climate where you live compare to the climate in northern Africa?**

North America

Africa

South America

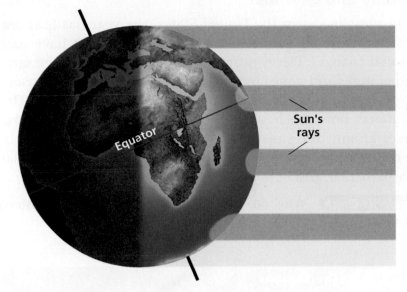

Factors That Affect Climate

For the most part, climate is determined by temperature and precipitation. But what factors affect the temperature and precipitation rates of an area? Those factors include latitude, wind patterns, locations of mountains and large bodies of water, and nearness to ocean currents.

Solar Energy and Latitude

If you look at a globe, you will see horizontal lines that circle the globe. Those lines are called lines of latitude. **Latitude** is the distance north or south from the equator. In general, the temperature of an area depends on its latitude. The higher the latitude is, the colder the climate tends to be. One of the coldest places on Earth, the North Pole, is 90° north of the equator. However, the equator, at latitude 0°, is usually hot.

Latitude affects the temperature of an area because latitude determines the amount of direct solar energy a certain area receives. **Figure 2** shows how the curve of Earth affects the amount of direct solar energy at different latitudes. Notice that the sun's rays travel in a line parallel to one another. The sun's rays hit the equator directly, at almost a 90° angle. At this angle, the solar energy is concentrated on a small area of Earth's surface. That small area receives the maximum amount of solar energy. As a result, that area has high temperatures.

At the poles, the sun's rays strike at a lesser angle than they do at the equator. At this angle, the same amount of solar energy that hits the area at the equator is spread over a larger area at the poles. Because the energy is less concentrated, the poles have lower temperatures than the equator.

climate (KLIE muht) the average weather conditions in an area over a long period of time

latitude (LAT uh TOOD) the distance north or south from the equator; expressed in degrees

6.4.b Students know solar energy reaches Earth through radiation, mostly in the form of visible light.
6.4.d Students know convection currents distribute heat in the atmosphere and oceans.
6.4.e Students know differences in pressure, heat, air movement, and humidity result in changes of weather.

Latitude and Seasons

In most places in the United States, the year has four seasons. But there are places in the world that do not have such seasonal changes. Places near the equator have about the same temperatures and same amount of daylight year-round. Seasons happen because Earth is tilted on its axis at a 23.5° angle. This tilt affects how much solar energy an area receives as Earth moves around the sun. **Figure 3** shows how latitude and the tilt of Earth determine the seasons and the length of the day in a particular area.

Standards Check Why do some places on Earth have seasons?
6.4.b

Figure 3 The Seasons

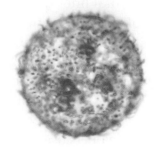

Winter
During winter in the Northern Hemisphere, the Southern Hemisphere has higher temperatures and longer days because it is tilted toward the sun and receives more-direct solar energy. At that time, the Northern Hemisphere has lower temperatures and shorter days because it is tilted away from the sun.

March 21 Spring

June 21 Summer

December 21 Winter

September 22 Fall

Summer
During summer in the Northern Hemisphere, locations in the Northern Hemisphere experience warmer temperatures and longer days because the Northern Hemisphere is tilted toward the sun and receives more-direct solar energy. At the same time, the Southern Hemisphere has colder temperatures and shorter days because it is tilted away from the sun.

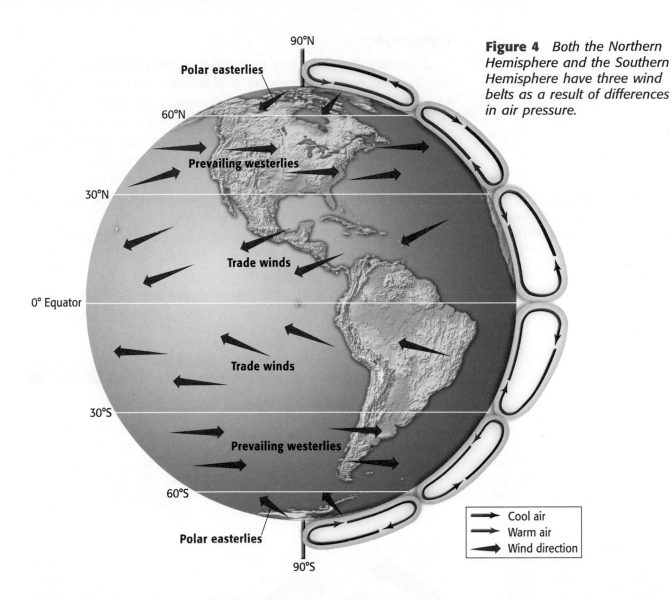

Figure 4 *Both the Northern Hemisphere and the Southern Hemisphere have three wind belts as a result of differences in air pressure.*

90°N

Polar easterlies

60°N

Prevailing westerlies

30°N

Trade winds

0° Equator

Trade winds

30°S

Prevailing westerlies

60°S

Polar easterlies

90°S

→ Cool air
→ Warm air
→ Wind direction

Global Circulation and Winds

Wind moves in predictable patterns across Earth's surface. The patterns of winds are the result of convection currents caused by uneven heating of Earth's surface. This uneven heating forms areas of different air pressure. Wind blows from areas of higher pressure to areas of lower pressure. The major wind belts on Earth's surface are shown in **Figure 4.**

The speed and direction, as well as the temperature and moisture content, of winds affect climate and weather. Winds carry solar energy to and from different locations, so the temperature of both locations changes. Winds also affect the amount of precipitation that a region receives. Winds may carry evaporated water away from the ocean surface. The water vapor is then carried to other places where it may condense and fall as precipitation.

Standards Check How do winds affect the climate of an area?
🐻 6.4.e

Topography

The sizes and shapes of the land-surface features of a region combine to form *topography*. Topography can influence the wind patterns and the transfer of energy in an area. So, topography influences an area's climate by affecting both temperature and precipitation. For example, temperatures in mountainous areas are affected by elevation. **Elevation** is the height of surface landforms above sea level. At high elevations, the temperature of the air is lower. Therefore, as elevation increases, temperature decreases.

Mountains also affect the distribution of precipitation. As air rises to pass over a mountain, the air cools. As a result, clouds form and precipitation may fall. This process causes what is called a *rain-shadow effect*. **Figure 5** shows how a rain shadow affects the climates on two sides of a mountain.

elevation (EL uh VAY shuhn) the height of an object above sea level

surface currents (SUHR fis KUHR uhnt) a horizontal movement of ocean water that is caused by wind and that occurs at or near the ocean's surface

Figure 5 **How Mountains Affect Climate**

The Wet Side
Mountains force air to rise. The air cools as it rises, releasing moisture as snow or rain. The land on the windward side of the mountain is usually green and lush because the air releases its moisture.

The Dry Side
After dry air crosses the mountain, the air begins to sink. As the air sinks, it becomes warmer and absorbs moisture. This process results in dry conditions that may cause desert climates to develop.

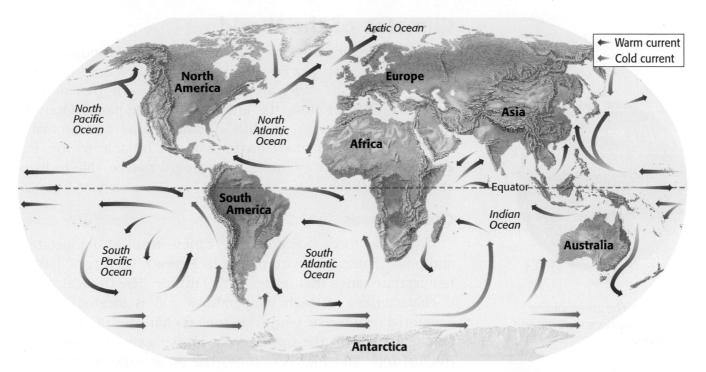

Arctic Ocean

Europe

North America

Asia

North Pacific Ocean

North Atlantic Ocean

Africa

Equator

South America

Indian Ocean

South Pacific Ocean

South Atlantic Ocean

Australia

Antarctica

Figure 6 *The red arrows represent the movement of warm surface currents. The blue arrows represent the movement of cold surface currents.*

Proximity to Large Bodies of Water

Large bodies of water, such as the ocean, can influence an area's climate. Water absorbs and releases heat more slowly than land does. Because of this quality, water helps moderate the temperature of nearby land. Sudden or extreme temperature changes rarely take place on land near large bodies of water.

The state of Michigan, which is surrounded by the Great Lakes, has more-moderate temperatures than other places at the same latitude. California's climate is also influenced by a large body of water—the ocean. The ocean keeps temperatures in California moderate. Other states that are inland but are at the same latitude as California have wide ranges in temperature.

Ocean Currents

The circulation of ocean surface currents has a large effect on an area's climate. **Surface currents** are streamlike movements of water at or near the surface of the ocean, as shown in **Figure 6.** As surface currents move, they carry warm or cool water to different locations. The surface temperature of the water affects the temperature of the air above it. Warm currents heat the surrounding air and cause warmer air temperatures. Cool currents absorb energy from the surrounding air and cause cooler air temperatures. California's climate is affected by a cool ocean current. Cold water from the northern Pacific Ocean is carried south to Mexico by the California current. This current keeps temperatures along the West Coast cooler than inland temperatures all year long.

Quick Lab

A Cool Breeze

6.4.e

1. Hold a **thermometer** next to the top edge of a **cup** of **water** containing **two ice cubes.** Record the temperature next to the cup.

2. Have your lab partner fan the surface of the cup with a **paper fan.** Record the temperature again.

3. Did the temperature change? Why or why not?

4. Explain how this activity models how a large body of water affects climate.

15 min

Climates of the World

Have you seen any polar bears in your neighborhood lately? You probably have not because polar bears live only in very cold arctic regions. Why are the animals in one part of the world so different from the animals in other parts? One of the differences has to do with climate. Plants and animals that are adapted to one climate may not be able to live in another climate. For example, frogs would not be able to live at the North Pole.

Climate Zones

Earth has three major climate zones—tropical, temperate, and polar. These zones are shown in **Figure 7.** Each zone has a temperature range that relates to its latitude. The tropical zone is characterized by high temperatures and is located in the equatorial region. The temperate zone is characterized by lower temperatures than the tropical zone. It is located between the tropical zone and the polar zone. The polar zone, at latitudes of 66.5° and higher, is the coldest climate zone.

In each of these zones, there are several kinds of climates. These different climates result from differences in topography, winds, ocean currents, and geography. **Figure 8** shows the distribution of Earth's climates.

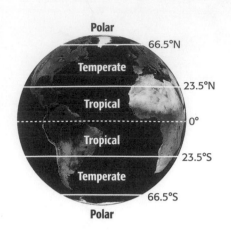

Figure 7 *The three major climate zones are determined by latitude.*

Figure 8 Earth's Climates

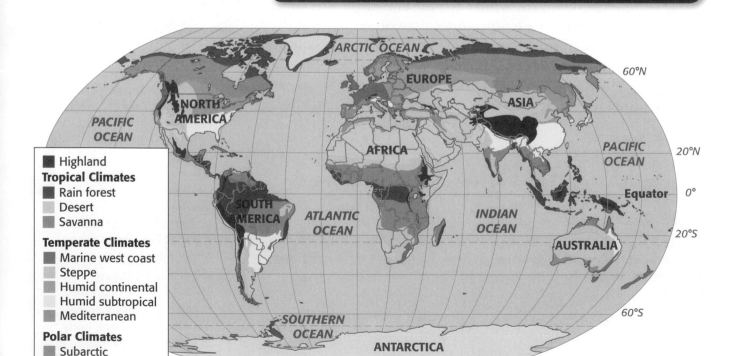

Highland

Tropical Climates
- Rain forest
- Desert
- Savanna

Temperate Climates
- Marine west coast
- Steppe
- Humid continental
- Humid subtropical
- Mediterranean

Polar Climates
- Subarctic
- Tundra
- Polar icecaps

Summary

- Climate is the average weather conditions in an area over a long period of time.
- The curve of Earth's surface affects the amount of direct solar energy that reaches the ground at different latitudes.
- The tilt of Earth on its axis causes the seasons.
- Winds affect the climate of an area by transferring solar energy and by carrying moisture.
- Topography influences an area's climate by affecting both the transfer of energy and the rate of precipitation.
- Large bodies of water and ocean currents influence the climate of an area by affecting the temperature of the air.
- The three main climate zones of the world are the tropical zone, the temperate zone, and the polar zone.

Using Vocabulary

1 Write an original definition for *climate, latitude, elevation,* and *surface current.*

Understanding Concepts

2 Analyzing Explain how topography affects climate.

3 Comparing What is the difference between weather and climate?

4 Identifying Identify five factors that affect climate.

5 Evaluating Explain why there is a difference in climate between areas at 0° latitude and areas at 45° latitude.

6 Identifying What carries solar energy from one place to another in the atmosphere?

Critical Thinking

7 Evaluating Data Describe what you think the climate might be like at the very southern tip of South America.

8 Applying Concepts During what months does Australia have summer? Explain your answer.

9 Predicting Consequences How would global climate be affected if Earth were not tilted on its axis? Explain your answer.

10 Analyzing Ideas Explain why climates cannot be classified only by latitude.

INTERPRETING GRAPHICS Use the diagram below to answer the next three questions.

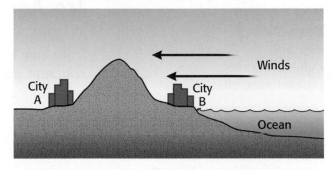

11 Evaluating Data Which city is more likely to have the largest yearly temperature range? Explain your answer.

12 Applying Concepts Which city is more likely to have a dry climate? Explain your answer.

13 Making Comparisons Describe the climates of each city.

Challenge

14 Applying Concepts Describe how latitude, winds, topography, and ocean currents affect the climate of California.

Changes in Climate

Key Concept Climate changes may be caused by natural factors and by human activities and can affect human and wildlife habitats.

What You Will Learn

- Earth's climates have changed throughout geologic history.
- Climate change may be the result of several factors, including natural events and human activity.

Why It Matters

The choices you make may affect the global climate and the environment where you live.

Vocabulary

- ice age
- global warming
- greenhouse effect

READING STRATEGY

Clarifying Concepts Take turns reading this section out loud with a partner. Stop to discuss ideas that seem confusing.

▶ As you have probably noticed, the weather changes from day to day. But have you ever noticed the climate change? You probably haven't, because climates change slowly. What causes climates to change? Studies show that human activity may cause climate change. However, natural factors can also lead to changes in the climate.

Ice Ages

The geologic record shows that Earth's climate has been both much warmer and much colder than it is today. In fact, much of Earth was covered by sheets of ice during certain periods. An **ice age** is a period during which ice forms in high latitudes and moves toward lower latitudes. Scientists have found evidence of many major ice ages during Earth's geologic history. The most recent ice age began about 2 million years ago.

During an ice age, there are periods of cold and periods of warmth. These periods are called *glacial* and *interglacial periods*. During glacial periods, the large sheets of ice advance. As the ice sheets advance, they get bigger and cover a larger area. Because a large amount of ocean water is frozen during glacial periods, the sea level drops. As shown in **Figure 1,** coastlines of the continents once extended farther than they do today.

Figure 1 *During the last glacial period, about 30% of Earth's surface was covered with ice.*

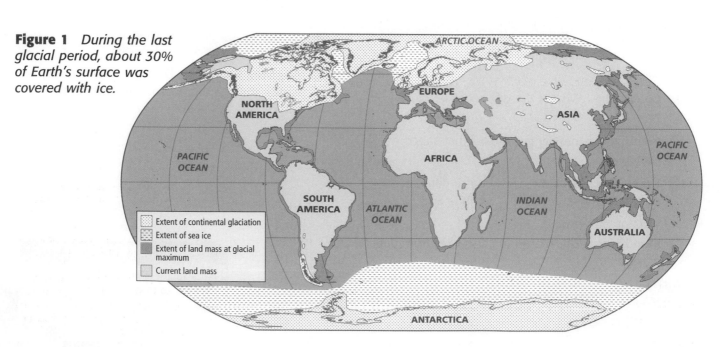

Extent of continental glaciation
Extent of sea ice
Extent of land mass at glacial maximum
Current land mass

Figure 2 The Milankovitch Theory

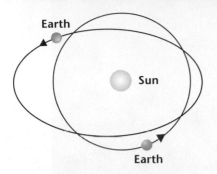

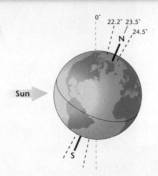

Orbit Earth encounters more variation in the energy that it receives from the sun when Earth's orbit is elongated than it does when Earth's orbit is circular.

Tilt Over a period of about 41,000 years, the tilt of Earth's axis varies between 22.2° and 24.5°. The poles receive more solar energy when the tilt angle is greater.

Wobble The wobble of Earth's axis affects the amount of solar radiation that reaches different parts of Earth's surface at different times of the year.

Causes of Climate Change

Scientists have formed a number of theories to explain ice ages and other forms of climate change. Factors that might cause climate change are changes in Earth's orbit and tilt of its axis, the movement of tectonic plates, the sun's cycle, asteroid impacts, human activity, and volcanic eruptions.

Changes in Earth's Orbit and Tilt

During an ice age, the temperature alternates between cold and warm. The Milankovitch theory explains why an ice age isn't just one long cold spell. Milutin Milankovitch, a scientist from Yugoslavia, proposed that changes in Earth's orbit and in the tilt of Earth's axis cause ice ages. The three main parts of his theory are shown in **Figure 2.** These three factors change the amount or intensity of solar radiation received by Earth. As a result, these factors affect climate.

ice age (IES AYJ) a long period of climatic cooling during which the continents are glaciated repeatedly

Standards Check How do changes in Earth's orbit and tilt influence changes in temperature on Earth? **6.4.a**

Plate Tectonics

Earth's climate is further influenced by plate tectonics and continental drift. A continent's location relative to the equator and poles determines how much solar radiation the continent receives. The continent's location relative to oceans and other continents is also important. The way continents deflect ocean currents and winds has a strong influence on climate. When continents move, the flow of air and moisture around the globe changes. These changes cause changes in climate.

6.2.d Students know earthquakes, volcanic eruptions, landslides, and floods change human and wildlife habitats.

6.4.a Students know the sun is the major source of energy for phenomena on Earth's surface; it powers winds, ocean currents, and the water cycle.

6.4.b Students know solar energy reaches Earth through radiation, mostly in the form of visible light.

6.6.a Students know the utility of energy sources is determined by factors that are involved in converting these sources to useful forms and the consequences of the conversion process.

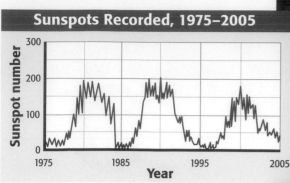

Sunspots Recorded, 1975–2005

Figure 3 *The sun has an 11-year cycle in which it goes from a maximum of activity to a minimum.*

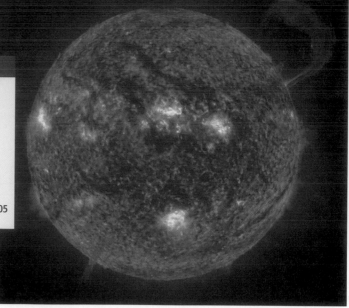

The Sun's Cycle

Some changes in climate can be linked to changes in the sun. You may think that the sun always stays the same. However, the sun is a variable star. In other words, the amount of energy that the sun emits changes over time, as shown in **Figure 3.** The sun follows a regular cycle during which it releases different amounts of energy at different times. Sometimes, the sun produces a low percentage of high-energy radiation. At other times, the sun produces more high-energy radiation.

Because the sun's energy powers most cycles on Earth, these changes affect the amount of energy in Earth's system. These variations in the amount of energy cause slight changes in Earth's climates.

Standards Check How does the sun's cycle affect climate change on Earth? 6.4.a

Asteroid Impacts

Sometimes, asteroids from outer space crash into Earth. An *asteroid* is a small, rocky object that orbits the sun. Scientists think that if an asteroid 1 km wide were to hit Earth, the climate of the whole world could change.

When a large piece of rock slams into Earth, debris from the impact shoots into the atmosphere. *Debris* is dust and smaller rocks. This debris can block some sunlight from reaching Earth's surface. The lack of solar radiation would lower average temperatures, and the decrease in temperature would change the climate. Plants wouldn't get the sunlight they need to grow. Without plants for food, many animals would find it hard to survive. Scientists think that an asteroid that was 10 km in diameter may have struck Earth 65 million years ago. This asteroid impact could have contributed to the extinction of the dinosaurs.

A Century Later

How do changes in climate affect the environment? Predict how the climate of your hometown may change over the next 100 years. Go to **go.hrw.com,** and type in the keyword **HY7CLMW.**

Volcanic Eruptions

Volcanic eruptions can influence climate for a short time. Volcanic eruptions send large amounts of dust, ash, and smoke into the atmosphere. Once in the atmosphere, the dust, smoke, and ash particles act as a shield that blocks some of the sun's rays. When the sun's rays are blocked, solar energy cannot reach Earth's surface. As a result, Earth's surface and atmosphere begin to cool. **Figure 4** shows how dust particles from a volcanic eruption block sunlight.

Standards Check How can volcanic eruptions change the climate?
 6.2.d

Human Activity

Global temperatures have increased about 1°C during the last 100 years. Researchers are not sure if this increase is a natural change or if it is the result of human activities.

A gradual increase in average global temperatures is called **global warming.** Global warming is caused in part by increases in carbon dioxide, CO_2, concentrations. The burning of fuels for transportation and industry releases CO_2 into the atmosphere. Another factor that increases CO_2 concentrations is the burning of forests to clear land for farming. Burning of the trees gives off more CO_2. Because plants use CO_2 to make food, destroying the trees also takes away a natural way of removing CO_2 from the atmosphere.

global warming (GLOH buhl WAWRM ing) a gradual increase in the average global temperature

Figure 4 **Volcanic Dust in the Atmosphere**

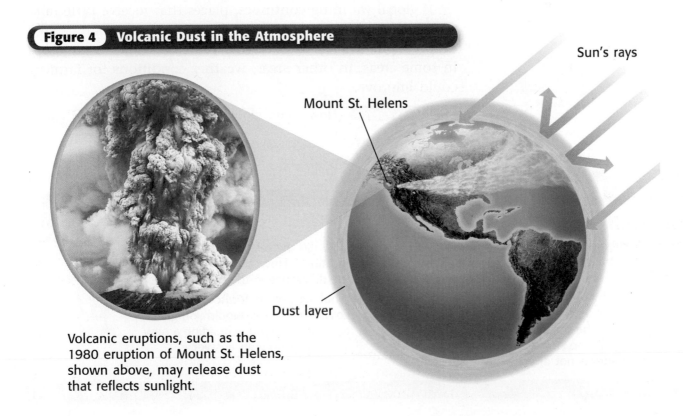

Sun's rays

Mount St. Helens

Dust layer

Volcanic eruptions, such as the 1980 eruption of Mount St. Helens, shown above, may release dust that reflects sunlight.

Global Warming

Global warming is caused by both natural events and by human activities. Earth's natural heating process, in which gases in the atmosphere absorb thermal energy, is called the **greenhouse effect.** To better understand this concept, think about the inside of a car on a hot, sunny day. The inside of the car gets hot because the sun's rays enter the car through the windows. The seats and other surfaces in the car absorb the sun's energy. Then, the surfaces reradiate that energy as heat. However, the car's windows stop most of the heat from escaping. Therefore, the air inside the car gets really hot.

The Greenhouse Effect on Earth

On Earth, instead of glass stopping the heat from escaping, gases, such as CO_2 absorb the heat. As a result, the heat stays in the atmosphere and keeps Earth warm. However, during the last 100 years, global temperatures have increased. Many scientists think that the rise in global temperatures is due to an increase in CO_2 in the atmosphere.

Consequences of Global Warming

Many scientists think that if the global temperature continues to rise, the icecaps will melt. Evidence that this melting has already started is shown in **Figure 5.** When icecaps melt, water stored in the icecaps raises sea level. The rise in sea level could flood low-lying areas, such as coasts.

If global warming continues, places that receive little rain, such as deserts, might receive even less rain because of increased evaporation. Changes in weather patterns could harm crops in some areas. In other areas, weather conditions for farming could improve.

Figure 5 *This ice sheet in Greenland is melting because of an increase in global temperatures.*

Standards Check How could global warming affect coastal cities?
🐻 6.6.a

Quick Lab

Hot Stuff

1. In midafternoon, use a **thermometer** to measure the air temperature over a grassy field or other vegetated area. Make sure to shield the thermometer from sunlight.

2. Measure the air temperature over a parking lot. Take the measurement at the same height above the surface. Make sure the thermometer is not directly in the sunlight.

3. How did the results differ between locations? How would you explain the difference in the results?

4. What suggestion for how to keep cooling costs low would you give to someone who is building a new store? Explain your answer.

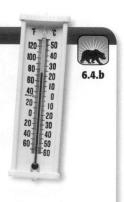

6.4.b

🕐 15 min

What Humans Can Do

Many countries are working together to reduce the potential effects of global warming. Treaties and laws have been passed to reduce pollution. Industrial practices are being monitored and changed. Even community projects to reforest areas have been developed.

Individuals can also help lower the amount of CO_2 in the atmosphere that is caused by pollution. Pollution is caused mostly by the burning of fossil fuels. Fossil fuels are used for running automobiles and generating electricity. Therefore, humans can reduce pollution rates by using less electricity. For example, people can turn off lights that are not in use and turn down the heat in winter.

greenhouse effect (GREEN HOWS e FEKT) when water vapor, carbon dioxide, and other gases absorb and reradiate thermal energy

SECTION Review

 6.2.d, 6.4.a, 6.4.b, 6.6.a

Summary

- Earth's climate has changed repeatedly throughout geologic time.
- The Milankovitch theory states that Earth's climate changes as Earth's orbit and the tilt of Earth's axis change.
- Climate changes may also be affected by continental drift, volcanic eruptions, asteroid impacts, solar activity, and human activity.
- Excess CO_2 is believed to contribute to global warming.

Using Vocabulary

1 Write an original definition for *ice age, global warming,* and *greenhouse effect.*

Understanding Concepts

2 **Analyzing** How does the Milankovitch theory explain climate changes?

3 **Identifying** What factors affect the amount of solar energy that reaches Earth's surface?

4 **Concluding** Explain how global warming could cause flooding.

5 **Listing** List the factors that might cause changes in Earth's climates.

6 **Describing** Explain how the greenhouse effect warms Earth.

Critical Thinking

7 **Analyzing Relationships** How would the warming of Earth affect agriculture in different parts of the world? Explain your answer.

8 **Applying Concepts** Describe how you could decrease the amount of CO_2 released in the atmosphere.

Math Skills

9 **Using Equations** If burning 4 L of gasoline produces 9 kg of CO_2, and a car burns 160 L of gasoline in a month, how much CO_2 did the vehicle release during the month?

Challenge

10 **Predicting Consequences** Can short-term climate changes over a 100-year period be explained by changes in the tilt of Earth's axis? Explain your answer.

Internet Resources

For a variety of links related to this chapter, go to www.scilinks.org

Topic: Changes in Climate
SciLinks code: HY70252

Convection Currents

Why are some days windy and some days not windy? Where does wind come from? Wind is the movement of air that is caused by convection currents. Convection currents are caused by the uneven heating of Earth's surface. Convection currents distribute heat throughout the atmosphere and affect weather all around the world. In this lab, you will create your own convection current.

6.3.c Students know heat flows in solids by conduction (which involves no flow of matter) and in fluids by conduction and by convection (which involves flow of matter).
6.4.d Students know convection currents distribute heat in the atmosphere and oceans.
6.4.e Students know differences in pressure, heat, air movement, and humidity result in changes of weather.

Procedure

1. Cut off the flaps to the opening of your cardboard box.

2. Position the box so that the opening is the side that faces you.

3. Use the utility knife to cut out a flap that can be opened and closed on the side of the box that is next to the opening. The flap should be about half of the area of the side, as shown in the figure above.

4. Open a drawing compass to a radius that is slightly smaller than the base of a chimney lamp. Use the compass to draw two circles on top of the box, at opposite ends of the box.

5. Use a utility knife to cut out the circles you drew on the box.

6. Cover the opening that you created in step 1 with plastic wrap. Use transparent tape to secure and seal the plastic wrap.

7. With tape, secure the chimney lamps over the holes in the top of the box.

8. Using a pair of tongs, place a cup of steaming, hot water into the box through the closable flap. Position the cup under one of the chimney lamps. Close the flap carefully so that no draft is created inside the box.

9. Light an incense stick, and immediately blow it out. Then, hold the smoking end of the incense stick over the mouth of the chimney lamp that does not have the cup of hot water under it.

10. Draw a diagram of what you observe.

Analyze the Results

11. **Analyzing Data** Describe the movement of the smoke.

12. **Analyzing Results** How would you describe the movement of the air above the hot cup of water? Explain why the air moves in this direction.

13. **Explaining Events** What is powering the movement of air in your model?

Draw Conclusions

14. **Interpreting Information** How does your model relate to the movement of air in the atmosphere?

Big Idea Question

15. **Drawing Conclusions** How do convection currents affect weather? What would weather on Earth be like if convection currents did not occur in the atmosphere?

Science Skills Activity

Investigation and Experimentation
6.7.b Select and use appropriate tools and technology (including calculators, computers, balances, spring scales, microscopes, and binoculars) to perform tests, collect data, and display data.

Collecting Weather Data

▶ Tutorial

Scientists use a variety of instruments to collect data. The meteorologists then analyze the relationships between the data and make predictions about the weather.

1 Making a Data Table On a piece of graph paper, make a chart like the one shown to the right. Record today's date above the first two columns labeled "A.M." and "P.M."

2 Measuring Temperature Place a thermometer in the shade where it is not exposed to precipitation. Wait at least 3 minutes. Then, read the temperature. Plot a point for that temperature on your chart.

3 Measuring Atmospheric Pressure Use a barometer to measure the atmospheric pressure to the nearest tenth of a millibar. Plot a point for the atmospheric pressure on your chart.

4 Measuring Weather Conditions Observe the present weather conditions, and record them in your chart. For example, if there is a light rain outside, write *drizzle* in your chart.

▶ You Try It!

Procedure

Identify weather patterns and make weather predictions by following these steps.

1 On a piece of graph paper, create a fresh chart like the one above.

2 Twice daily for a week, at about the same time every day (about 10 hours apart), measure and record the temperature, atmospheric pressure, and weather conditions.

3 Use the data to make two graphs of changing temperature and atmospheric pressure. Do so by connecting the points for temperature with one smooth line and the points for atmospheric pressure with a second smooth line.

Analysis

4 Inferring Relationships In general, what is the relationship between temperature and atmospheric pressure?

5 Drawing Conclusions Did you notice any relationships between the atmospheric pressure and the weather conditions? If so, describe the relationships.

6 Drawing Conclusions How do the relationships between certain weather variables help you predict the weather?

Chapter Summary

The Big Idea
Differences in pressure, heat, air movement, and humidity result in changes of weather and thus affect climate.

Section	Vocabulary

1 Water in the Air

Key Concept The sun's energy drives the water cycle and causes differences in humidity that may lead to precipitation.

- The amount of water vapor in the air is known as humidity.
- Differences in pressure, temperature, and humidity cause clouds and precipitation.

Humidity increases as water vapor enters the air.

weather p. 506
humidity p. 507
dew point p. 507
relative humidity p. 507
condensation p. 509
precipitation p. 511

2 Fronts and Weather

Key Concept Weather results from the movement of air masses that differ in temperature and humidity.

- Differences in pressure, temperature, air movement, and humidity cause changes in weather, including severe weather.
- Severe weather and floods can cause property damage and death.

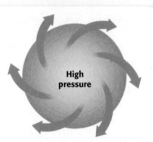

High pressure

An anticyclone is an area of high pressure.

air mass p. 512
front p. 512
cyclone p. 514
lightning p. 515
thunder p. 515
tornado p. 516

3 What Is Climate?

Key Concept Earth's climate zones are caused by the distribution of heat around Earth's surface by wind and ocean currents.

- Climate is the average weather condition in an area over a long period of time.
- Climate is affected by latitude, global winds, topography, proximity to large bodies of water, and ocean currents.

The sun's rays strike Earth at different angles because Earth's surface is curved.

climate p. 520
latitude p. 521
elevation p. 524
surface current p. 525

4 Changes in Climate

Key Concept Climate changes may be caused by natural factors and by human activities and can affect human and wildlife habitats.

- Earth's climates have changed throughout geologic history.
- Climate change may be the result of several factors, including natural events and human activity.

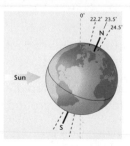

Changes in Earth's tilt over time may cause climate change.

ice age p. 528
global warming p. 531
greenhouse effect p. 532

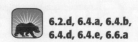 6.2.d, 6.4.a, 6.4.b, 6.4.d, 6.4.e, 6.6.a

Organize

Double Door Review the Fold-Note that you created at the beginning of the chapter. Add to or correct the FoldNote based on what you have learned.

Using Vocabulary

1 Academic Vocabulary Which of the following words is closest in meaning to the word *affected*?
a. worsened **c.** influenced
b. improved **d.** moved

For each pair of terms, explain how the meanings of the terms differ.

2 *relative humidity* and *dew point*

3 *condensation* and *precipitation*

4 *air mass* and *front*

5 *weather* and *climate*

6 *thunder* and *lightning*

Understanding Concepts

Multiple Choice

7 Which of the following is a form of precipitation?
a. fog **c.** snow
b. cloud **d.** dew

8 Fronts that form when a warm air mass is trapped between cold air masses and is forced to rise are
a. snow fronts.
b. warm fronts.
c. occluded fronts.
d. cold fronts.

9 A severe storm that forms when a rapidly rotating funnel cloud touches the ground is a
a. hurricane.
b. tornado.
c. typhoon.
d. thunderstorm.

10 Which of the following would not be a threat to humans or their property?
a. hurricane **c.** thunder
b. tornado **d.** lightning

Short Answer

11 Comparing Explain the relationship between condensation and dew point.

12 Describing Describe the weather conditions along a stationary front.

13 Summarizing Explain how a hurricane develops.

14 Analyzing Describe the water cycle, and explain how it affects weather.

15 Evaluating Explain how wind patterns can influence climate.

16 Concluding How can severe weather affect humans and their property?

17 Identifying Name four factors that cause changes in weather.

INTERPRETING GRAPHICS Use the graph below to answer the next two questions.

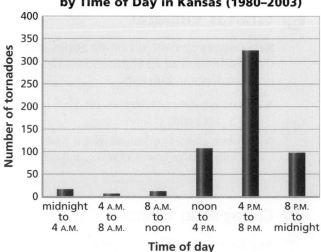

Number of Tornadoes by Time of Day in Kansas (1980–2003)

18 Evaluating During which time of day did the least tornadoes occur?

19 Concluding Would Kansas students be more likely to experience a tornado while they are at school or while they are at home? Explain your answer.

20 Communicating Concepts Write a short essay that explains how pressure, heat, air movement, and humidity result in changes in weather.

Critical Thinking

21 Concept Mapping Use the following terms to create a concept map: *condensation, humidity, water cycle, dew point, precipitation, front, air masses, cyclone, lightning, tornado, thunder,* and *weather.*

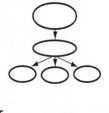

22 Predicting Consequences How might the sun's cycle affect climate changes?

23 Making Inferences If both the air temperature and the amount of water vapor in the air change, is it possible for the relative humidity to stay the same? Explain your answer.

24 Evaluating Conclusions Explain why the climate on the eastern side of the Sierra Nevada differs drastically from the climate on the western side.

25 Identifying Relationships Explain the relationship between the tilt of Earth's axis and seasonal changes at different latitudes.

26 Applying Concepts Explain how convection currents affect wind patterns.

27 Predicting Consequences How would global climate be affected if Earth were not tilted on its axis? Explain your reasoning.

28 Predicting Consequences How would the water cycle be affected if the concentration of CO_2 in the atmosphere increased drastically?

29 Applying Concepts How can human activity affect the global climate?

INTERPRETING GRAPHICS Use the map below to answer the next two questions.

30 Evaluating Data Based on the map, identify two factors that influence the climates of California.

31 Analyzing Processes What major factor influences the amount of annual precipitation in the city of Barstow?

Math Skills

32 Using Equations The temperature is 47°F. Using the equation °C = 5/9 × (°F − 32), find the temperature in degrees Celsius.

Challenge

33 Predicting Consequences Describe how living things might be affected if global temperatures were, on the average, 5°C warmer. Over a long period of time, how might living things adapt to this change in temperature?

Standards Assessment

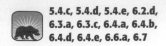

REVIEWING ACADEMIC VOCABULARY

1 In the sentence "Convection is a process that involves the flow of fluids," what does the word *involves* mean?

- **A** takes part in
- **B** is strengthened by
- **C** to have as a part of
- **D** needs

2 Which of the following words means "a repeating series of changes"?

- **A** energy
- **B** cycle
- **C** erosion
- **D** phenomenon

3 In the sentence "Convection currents distribute heat throughout the atmosphere," what does the word *distribute* mean?

- **A** eliminate
- **B** focus all attention on
- **C** to spread over an area
- **D** strengthen

4 Which of the following words is the closest in meaning to the word *investigation*?

- **A** a detailed search for answers
- **B** a series of actions directed toward an aim
- **C** a request for information or for a reply
- **D** an answer to a puzzle or question

REVIEWING CONCEPTS

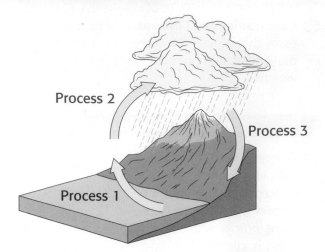

Process 2

Process 3

Process 1

5 Which word best describes Process 2 in the diagram above?

- **A** convection
- **B** condensation
- **C** reclamation
- **D** reformation

6 Carbon dioxide in the atmosphere can lead to global warming. How can carbon dioxide cause this phenomenon?

- **A** It absorbs heat and keeps heat in the atmosphere.
- **B** It creates warm fronts that heat Earth.
- **C** Its natural radiation heats Earth.
- **D** It causes warm ocean currents that heat Earth.

7 How can volcanoes cause climate change?

- **A** by warming Earth with a blanket of dust and ash particles
- **B** by warming Earth with volcanic lava
- **C** by blocking the sun's rays with dust and ash so that Earth cools
- **D** by shifting tectonic plates

8 Why is the climate at the North Pole cooler than the climate near the equator?

   A because the North Pole is farther from the sun

   B because days last much longer at the equator

   C because cold air currents make the North Pole cooler

   D because the sun's rays hit the North Pole at an angle

9 Under which of the following conditions is a hurricane most likely to form?

   A when high and low pressure zones meet over warm land

   B when thunderstorms meet over warm ocean water

   C when thunderstorms meet over cool ocean water

   D when warm and cold fronts meet over warm water

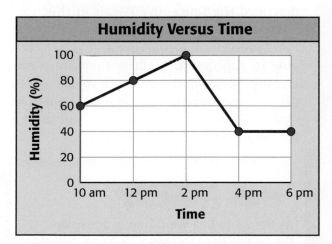

10 Which of the following events most likely occurred at 2:00 pm in the graph above?

   A a cold front

   B a warm front

   C rain showers

   D evaporation

REVIEWING PRIOR LEARNING

11 Which of the following is most likely to occur when warm, humid air comes into contact with a cold air mass?

   A Water on the ground evaporates.

   B Condensation and precipitation occur.

   C A hurricane or tropical storm forms.

   D The cold air mass is pushed upward.

12 Clouds are observed in a high-pressure area over California, and clear skies are observed in a low-pressure area directly to the east. Which of the following is most likely to occur?

   A Wind will blow the clouds in a westerly direction.

   B The warm air will cause the clouds to evaporate.

   C The clouds will move east to the low-pressure area.

   D A thunderstorm will occur between the two areas.

13 Which of the following statements about Earth's atmosphere is true?

   A The atmosphere exerts greater downward than upward pressure.

   B Pressure is highest in upper areas of the atmosphere.

   C Atmospheric pressure increases as altitude decreases.

   D Pressure is equal at all levels of the atmosphere.

14 By what process does the sun heat Earth?

   A conduction

   B evaporation

   C convection

   D radiation

Science in Action

Science Fiction

"All Summer in a Day" by Ray Bradbury

It is raining, just as it has been for seven long years. For the people who live on Venus, constant rain is a fact of life. But today is a special day—a day when the rain stops and the sun shines. This day comes once every seven years. At school, the students have been looking forward to this day for weeks. But Margot longs to see the sun even more than the others do. The reason for her longing makes the other kids jealous, and jealous kids can be cruel. What happens to Margot? Find out by reading Ray Bradbury's "All Summer in a Day" in the *Holt Anthology of Science Fiction.*

Science, Technology, and Society

Santa Ana Winds

". . . those hot dry [winds] that come down through the mountain passes and curl your hair and make your nerves jump and your skin itch." The famous writer Raymond Chandler described the Santa Ana Winds in this way. These dry, warm winds, named after Southern California's Santa Ana Canyon, originate in the desert. Because they are warm and dry, these winds can cause vegetation to dry out and increase the danger of wildfire. Once a fire does start, these winds will fan the flames and spread the fire farther.

Math Activity

As the Santa Ana Winds move downslope, the temperature increases by about 10°C/km of descent. What would be the temperature increase if the winds traveled downslope for 0.75 km?

Language Arts Activity

What would living in a place where it rained all day and every day for seven years be like? In your **Science Journal,** write a short story that describes what your life would be like if you lived in such a place. In your story, describe what you and your friends would do for fun after school.

Cristy Mitchell

Meteorologist Predicting floods, observing a tornado develop inside a storm, watching the growth of a hurricane, and issuing flood warnings are all in a day's work for Cristy Mitchell. As a meteorologist for the National Weather Service, Mitchell spends each working day observing the powerful forces of nature. When asked what makes her job interesting, Mitchell replied, "There's nothing like the adrenalin rush you get when you see a tornado coming!"

Perhaps the most familiar field of meteorology is weather forecasting. However, meteorology is also used in air-pollution control, weather control, agricultural planning, and even criminal and civil investigations. Meteorologists also study trends in Earth's climate.

Meteorologists such as Mitchell use high-tech tools—computers and satellites—to collect data. By analyzing such data, Mitchell is able to forecast the weather.

Social Studies ACTiViTY

An almanac is a type of calendar that contains various information, including weather forecasts and astronomical data, for every day of the year. Many people used almanacs before meteorologists started to forecast the weather on TV. Use an almanac from the library to find out what the weather was on the day that you were born.

Internet Resources

- To learn more about careers in science, visit **www.scilinks.org** and enter the SciLinks code HY70225.

- To learn more about these Science in Action topics, visit **go.hrw.com** and type in the keyword HY7CLMF.

- Check out articles related to this chapter by visiting **go.hrw.com**. Just type in the keyword HY7CLMC.

TIMELINE

Ecology

What did you have for breakfast this morning? Your breakfast was a result of living things working together. For example, milk comes from a cow. The cow eats plants to gain energy. Bacteria help the plants obtain nutrients from the soil. And the soil has nutrients because fungi break down dead trees.

All living things on Earth are interconnected. Our actions have an impact on our environment, and our environment has an impact on us. In this unit, you will study ecology, the interaction of living things. This timeline shows some of the ways that humans have studied and affected Earth.

1661
John Evelyn publishes a book condemning air pollution in London, England.

1771
In his experiments with plants, Joseph Priestley finds that plants use carbon dioxide and release oxygen.

1933
The Civilian Conservation Corps is established. The corps plants trees, fights forest fires, and builds dams to control floods.

1990
To save dolphins from being caught in fishing nets, U.S. tuna processors announce that they will not accept tuna caught in nets that can kill dolphins.

1851

The United States imports sparrows from Germany to defend against crop-damaging caterpillars.

1854

Henry David Thoreau's *Walden* is published. In it, Thoreau asserts that people should live in harmony with nature.

1872

The first U.S. national park, Yellowstone, is established by Congress.

1962

Rachel Carson's book *Silent Spring,* which describes the wasteful use of pesticides and their destruction of the environment, is published.

1970

The Environmental Protection Agency (EPA) is formed to set and enforce pollution-control standards in the United States.

1973

The United States Congress passes the Endangered Species Act.

1993

Americans recycle 59.5 billion aluminum cans (two out of every three cans).

1996

The Glen Canyon Dam is opened, purposefully flooding the Grand Canyon. The flooding helps maintain the ecological balance by restoring beaches and sandbars and rejuvenating marshes.

2002

The U.S. Fish and Wildlife Service installs red neon lights along the Florida coast to replace lights that distract baby sea turtles from finding the ocean when they hatch.

Improving Comprehension

Graphic Organizers are important visual tools that can help you organize information and improve your reading comprehension. The Graphic Organizer below is called a *pyramid chart*. Instructions for creating other types of Graphic Organizers are located in the **Study Skills** section of the Appendix.

How to Make a Pyramid Chart

1 Draw a triangle that is divided into sections like the one shown below. Draw as many sections as you need to draw.

2 Draw a box to the left of the triangle, as shown in the example. Write the topic of your pyramid chart in the box.

3 In each section of your triangle, write information about the topic in the appropriate level of the pyramid.

When to Use a Pyramid Chart

A pyramid chart is used to organize information in a hierarchy of magnitude or detail. As the shape of the pyramid suggests, the pyramid's bottom level contains information that is largest in terms of magnitude and broadest, or least specific, in terms of detail. As you read about science, look for information that you can organize into a hierarchy.

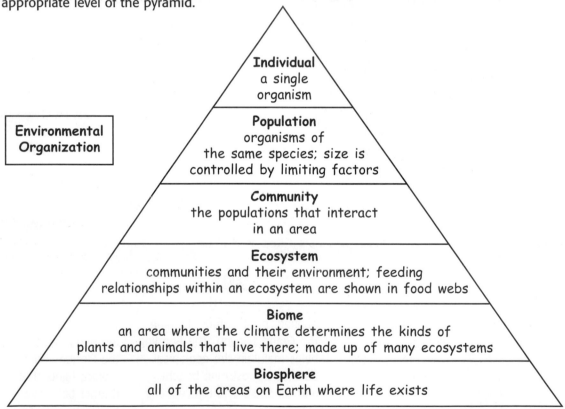

Environmental Organization

Individual
a single
organism

Population
organisms of
the same species; size is
controlled by limiting factors

Community
the populations that interact
in an area

Ecosystem
communities and their environment; feeding
relationships within an ecosystem are shown in food webs

Biome
an area where the climate determines the kinds of
plants and animals that live there; made up of many ecosystems

Biosphere
all of the areas on Earth where life exists

You Try It!

This Reading Strategy can also be used within the chapter that you are about to read. Practice making your own Pyramid Chart as directed in the Reading Strategy for Section 2. Record your work in your **Science Journal.**

Unpacking the Standards

The information below "unpacks" the standards by breaking them down into basic parts. The higher-level, academic vocabulary is highlighted and defined to help you understand the language of the standards. "What It Means" restates the standards as simply as possible.

California Standard	Academic Vocabulary	What It Means
6.5.a Students know **energy** entering ecosystems as sunlight is **transferred** by producers into **chemical** energy through photosynthesis and then from organism to organism through food webs.	**energy** (EN uhr jee) the ability to make things happen **transfer** (TRANS fuhr) to carry or cause to pass from one thing to another **chemical** (KEM i kuhl) of or having to do with the properties or actions of substances	Producers, such as plants, change energy from the sun into chemical energy through photosynthesis. Then, this chemical energy passes to and between organisms that eat other organisms.
6.5.b Students know matter is **transferred** over time from one organism to others in the food web and between organisms and the **physical** environment.	**physical** (FIZ i kuhl) able to be seen or touched	Matter moves from one living thing to another in a food web. Matter also moves between living things and their nonliving surroundings.
6.5.c Students know populations of organisms can be **categorized** by the **functions** they serve in an ecosystem.	**categorize** (KAT uh guh riez) to put into groups or classes **function** (FUHNGK shuhn) use or purpose	Living things can be identified by the role that they play, or what they do, in an ecosystem.
6.5.e Students know the number and types of organisms an ecosystem can support depends on the **resources available** and on abiotic **factors,** such as quantities of light and water, a **range** of temperatures, and soil composition.	**resource** (REE sawrs) anything that can be used to take care of a need **available** (uh VAYL uh buhl) that can be used **factor** (FAK tuhr) a condition or event that brings about a result **range** (RAYNJ) a scale or series between limits	The number and kinds of living things that can live in an ecosystem depend on the available resources and on nonliving conditions, such as the amount of light and water, the high and low temperatures, and the makeup of the soil.

16

Interactions of Living Things

The Big Idea

Organisms interact with each other and with the nonliving parts of their environment.

California Standards

Focus on Earth Sciences
6.5 Organisms in ecosystems exchange energy and nutrients among themselves and with the environment. (Sections 1, 2, and 3)

Investigation and Experimentation
6.7 Scientific progress is made by asking meaningful questions and conducting careful investigations. (Science Skills Activity)

Math
6.2.1 Number Sense

English–Language Arts
6.2.4 Reading
6.1.3 Writing

About the Photo

Giant Pacific octopuses are the largest octopuses in the world—they can grow up to 5 m (16 ft) long! Giant Pacific octopuses live in the North Pacific Ocean, including off the coast of California. They crawl along the ocean floor in search of prey. Using the suction disks on its tentacles, this giant Pacific octopus has a firm grasp on a spiny dogfish shark. The octopus will use its beak to eat the shark.

Organize

Tri-Fold

Before you read the chapter, create the FoldNote entitled "Tri-Fold." Write what you know about the interactions of living things in the column labeled "Know." Then, write what you want to know about the interactions of living things in the column labeled "Want." As you read the chapter, write what you learn about the interactions of living things in the column labeled "Learn."

Instructions for creating FoldNotes are located in the Study Skills section on p. 618 of the Appendix.

Explore Activity

🕐 15 min

Who Eats Whom?

In this activity, you will learn how organisms interact when finding (or becoming) food.

Procedure

1. On each of **five index cards,** print the name of one of the following organisms: killer whale, cod fish, krill shrimp, algae, and leopard seal.

2. On your desk, arrange the cards in a chain to show who eats whom.

3. Record the order of your cards.

4. In nature, would you expect to see more killer whales or more cod? Arrange the cards in order of the groups of organisms that have the most individuals to groups that have the fewest individuals.

Analysis

6.5.b

5. What might happen to the other organisms if algae were removed from this group? What might happen if the killer whales were removed?

6. Do any organisms in this group eat more than one kind of food? (Hint: What else might a seal, a fish, or a killer whale eat?) How could you change the order of your cards to show this information? How could you use pieces of string to show these relationships?

549

Everything Is Connected

Key Concept Organisms depend on each other and on the nonliving resources in their environment.

▶ A black bear waits patiently as a fish swims nearer. In a rush, the bear uses its paw to swipe the fish out of the water and into its mouth. The fish makes a tasty meal. Clearly, two organisms have interacted when one eats the other. But organisms interact in other ways, too. For example, a plant may depend on organisms such as a black bear to spread its seeds. Black bears eat fruits and excrete the seeds over great distances.

Studying the Web of Life

All living things are connected in the web of life. In the web of life, energy and other resources flow between organisms and their environment. Scientists who study this web specialize in ecology. **Ecology** is the study of the interactions of organisms with one another and with their environment.

The Two Parts of an Environment

An organism's environment is made up of all of the factors that affect the organism. These factors can be divided into two groups. The nonliving factors, such as water, soil, light, and temperature, make up the **abiotic** factors of the environment. The interactions between organisms in an area, such as competition, make up the **biotic** factors of the environment. Organisms depend on both of these parts to live. For example, the bear shown in **Figure 1,** depends on water to drink and catches prey, such as fish to eat.

Standards Check Do organisms depend on abiotic factors? Explain.
6.5.e

Figure 1 *The bear affects and is affected by many organisms in its environment, such as the fish and fruit that it eats.*

Organization in the Environment

At first glance, the environment may seem too complex to organize. However, the environment can be arranged into six levels, as **Figure 2** shows.

Figure 2   **The Six Levels of Environmental Organization**

Biosphere The biosphere is made up of all of the areas on Earth where organisms are found.

Biome A biome is an area where the climate typically determines the plant community, which supports an animal community.

Ecosystem An ecosystem is made up of a community of organisms and their abiotic environment.

Community A community is made up of all of the populations of organisms that live in an area and interact.

Population A population is made up of individuals that belong to the same species and live in the same area.

Individual An individual is one organism.

ecology (ee KAHL uh jee) the study of the interactions of living organisms with one another and with their environment

abiotic (AY bie AHT ik) describes the nonliving part of the environment, including water, rocks, light, and temperature

Wordwise The prefix *a-* means "not." The root *bio-* means "life." The suffix *-tic* means "pertaining to."

biotic (bie AHT ik) describes living factors in the environment

Populations

Each plant and animal is a part of a **population,** or a group of individuals of the same species that live together. For example, all of the turtles of a species that live in a salt marsh are members of a population. Individuals in a population often compete with one another for food, shelter, and mates.

Communities

A **community** is made up of all of the populations of organisms that live and interact in an area. The organisms in **Figure 3** form a salt-marsh community. The populations in a community depend on each other for many things, such as shelter and food. For example, an animal obtains energy, nutrients, and some water by eating other organisms.

Standards Check Why do animals eat other organisms? 6.5.b

Ecosystems

An **ecosystem** is made up of a community of organisms and their abiotic environment. In an ecosystem, energy and other resources flow between organisms and their physical environment. For example, the river that empties into the salt marsh carries nutrients, such as nitrogen. The cordgrass will grow more quickly because of the extra source of nutrients.

population (PAHP yoo LAY shuhn) a group of organisms of the same species that live in a specific geographical area

community (kuh MYOO nuh tee) all of the populations of species that live in the same habitat and interact with each other

ecosystem (EE koh SIS tuhm) a community of organisms and their abiotic, or nonliving, environment

Figure 3 *Examine the picture of a salt marsh.* **Which levels of environmental organization can you find in this picture?**

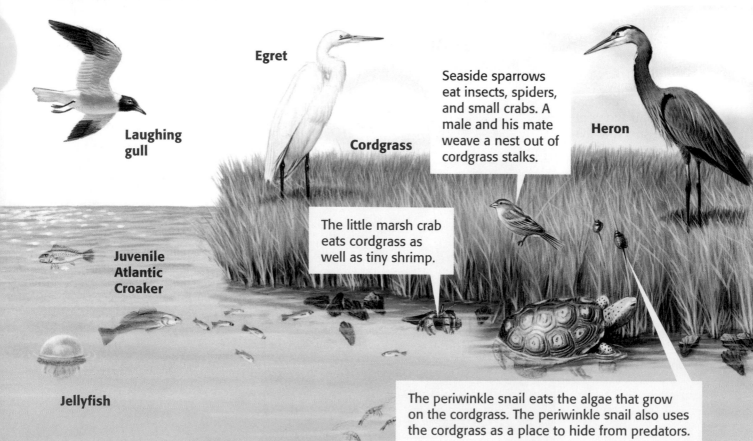

Egret

Seaside sparrows eat insects, spiders, and small crabs. A male and his mate weave a nest out of cordgrass stalks.

Heron

Cordgrass

Laughing gull

The little marsh crab eats cordgrass as well as tiny shrimp.

Juvenile Atlantic Croaker

The periwinkle snail eats the algae that grow on the cordgrass. The periwinkle snail also uses the cordgrass as a place to hide from predators.

Jellyfish

Biomes

A biome is made up of many ecosystems. A **biome** is an area where the climate typically determines the plant community, which supports an animal community. For example, a typical desert biome receives very little rainfall, is hot during the day, and is cold at night. Desert plants and animals are suited to these conditions. So, some of these desert organisms would not survive in a biome that received snow. Similar biomes are found in different parts of the world where the climate is similar. For example, the chaparral biome in California is similar to the Mediterranean scrub biome around the Mediterranean Sea.

The Biosphere

The **biosphere** is the part of Earth where life exists. It extends from the deepest parts of the ocean and Earth's crust to high in the air, where plant spores drift. Ecologists study the biosphere to learn how organisms interact with the abiotic environment—Earth's atmosphere, water, soil, and rock. The water in the abiotic environment includes fresh water, salt water, and the water that is frozen in polar icecaps and glaciers.

biome (BIE OHM) a large region characterized by a specific type of climate and certain types of plant and animal communities

biosphere (BIE oh SFIR) the part of Earth where life exists

Salt-Marsh Birds

How are salt-marsh birds adapted to living in a salt marsh? Create a brochure about salt-marsh birds and the need to protect salt-marsh habitats. Go to **go.hrw.com,** and type in the keyword HY7VR2W.

SECTION Review

6.5.b, 6.5.e

Summary

- Organisms in an ecosystem depend on other organisms and on abiotic factors for their survival.

- Energy and other resources flow between organisms and their environment.

- Biotic factors are the interactions between organisms in an area, such as competition.

- Abiotic factors include all of the nonliving things in an area, such as water and light.

Using Vocabulary

1. Write an original definition for *ecology.*

2. Use *biotic* and *abiotic* in the same sentence.

Understanding Concepts

3. **Analyzing** Use an example to explain how an abiotic factor can affect an ecosystem.

4. **Comparing** What is the difference between a community of organisms and a population of organisms?

Critical Thinking

5. **Analyzing Relationships** For what do organisms depend on cordgrass? What would happen if the cordgrass disappeared?

6. **Analyzing Ideas** Do ecosystems have borders? Explain.

Math Skills

7. **Making Conversions** The biosphere extends about 9 km above sea level and about 19 km below sea level. How thick is the biosphere in meters?

Challenge

8. **Applying Concepts** What might happen to a desert biome if the area received more rain than it normally receives over an extended period of time? Describe some of the changes that you might expect to see.

Internet Resources

For a variety of links related to this chapter, go to www.scilinks.org

Topic: Biotic and Abiotic Factors; Organization in the Environment

SciLinks code: HY70164; HY71079

Living Things Need Energy

Key Concept Energy and matter flow between organisms and their environment.

▶ Could you survive on only water and vitamins? Eating food satisfies your hunger because it provides two things you cannot live without—energy and nutrients. All organisms need energy and matter, or nutrients, to survive. For example, black-tailed prairie dogs, which live in the grasslands of North America, eat grass and seeds to get the energy they need. Like all organisms, prairie dogs require energy to carry out all life processes.

The Energy Connection

Organisms in every community can be divided into three groups based how they function in that community. These groups are producers, consumers, and decomposers. These groups also explain how organisms get the energy and nutrients they need. Examine **Figure 1** to see how energy and nutrients flow through an ecosystem.

Producers

Organisms that change the energy in sunlight into chemical energy or food are called *producers*. Producers do this through the process of *photosynthesis*. Most producers are green plants, but algae and some bacteria are also producers. Grasses are the main producers in a prairie ecosystem. Examples of producers in other ecosystems include cordgrass and algae in a salt marsh and trees in a forest.

Standards Check Why is sunlight important to producers? 6.5.a

Figure 1 *Most living things get their energy either from the sun or from eating other organisms.*

Energy Sunlight is the source of energy for almost all living things.

Producer Plants use solar energy to make food.

Primary Consumer The black-tailed prairie dog (herbivore) eats leaves and grass in the grasslands of western North America.

Secondary Consumer All of the prairie dogs in a colony watch for enemies, such as coyotes (carnivore), hawks, and badgers. Occasionally, a prairie dog is killed and eaten by a coyote.

Consumers

Not all organisms can make their own food like producers can. Some organisms must eat other organisms to obtain energy and nutrients. These organisms are called *consumers*. There are several kinds of consumers. A consumer that eats only plants is called an **herbivore,** such as a grasshopper or a bison. A consumer that eats other animals is called a **carnivore,** such as a badger or an owl. Consumers that eat both plants and animals are called **omnivores.** The grasshopper mouse is an omnivore that eats insects and grass seeds.

Scavengers are also omnivores. The turkey vulture is a scavenger in the prairie. A vulture will eat what is left after a coyote has killed and eaten part of an animal. Scavengers also eat animals and plants that have died from natural causes.

Decomposers

Organisms that get energy and nutrients by breaking down dead organisms are called *decomposers*. Bacteria, shown in **Figure 2,** and fungi are decomposers. Decomposers produce simple materials, such as water and carbon dioxide, that can be used by other organisms. Decomposers arc nature's recyclers.

Food Chains

Figure 1 shows a food chain. A **food chain** is a diagram that shows how energy and nutrients are transferred from one organism to another. Producers, such as plants, form the base of the food chain. Herbivores, such as prairie dogs, are also called *primary consumers* because they are the first consumers in the food chain. Organisms, such as coyotes, that eat primary consumers are called *secondary consumers*. Organisms that eat secondary consumers are called *tertiary consumers* (TUHR shee ER ee kuhn SOOM uhrz). A turkey vulture is a tertiary consumer because it is the third consumer in the food chain shown in **Figure 1.** But few organisms eat just one kind of food. Thus, simple food chains are rare.

herbivore (HUHR buh VAWR)
an organism that eats only plants

carnivore (KAHR nuh VAWR)
an organism that eats animals

omnivore (AHM ni VAWR)
an organism that eats both plants and animals

food chain (FOOD CHAYN) the pathway of energy transfer through various stages as a result of the feeding patterns of a series of organisms

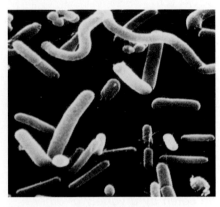

Figure 2 *All materials from dead organisms are broken down by bacteria and fungi that live in the soil.*

6.5.a Students know energy entering ecosystems as sunlight is transferred by producers into chemical energy through photosynthesis and then from organism to organism through food webs.
6.5.b Students know matter is transferred over time from one organism to others in the food web and between organisms and the physical environment.
6.5.c Students know populations of organisms can be categorized by the functions they serve in an ecosystem.
6.5.e Students know the number and types of organisms an ecosystem can support depends on the resources available and on abiotic factors, such as quantities of light and water, a range of temperatures, and soil composition.

Tertiary Consumer A turkey vulture (scavenger) may eat a dead coyote. A scavenger can pick bones completely clean.

Food Webs

The energy and nutrient connections in nature are more accurately shown by a food web than by a food chain. A **food web** is a diagram that shows the feeding relationships between organisms in an ecosystem. **Figure 3** shows a simple food web. A food web is made up of many food chains. Notice that an arrow goes from the prairie dog to the coyote and shows that the prairie dog is eaten by the coyote. The prairie dog is also eaten by the mountain lion.

Energy moves from one organism to the next in one direction in a food web. Each organism uses energy for its life processes. During these processes, some energy is lost to the environment as heat. Any energy not immediately used by an organism is stored in its cells. Only the energy stored in an organism's cells can be used by the next consumer.

food web (FOOD WEB) a diagram that shows the feeding relationships between organisms in an ecosystem

Standards Check Using the food web below, identify a secondary consumer. Explain your choice. 🐻 **6.5.b, 6.5.c**

Figure 3 *The arrows show how energy moves when one organism eats another. Most consumers eat a variety of foods and can be eaten by a variety of other consumers.*

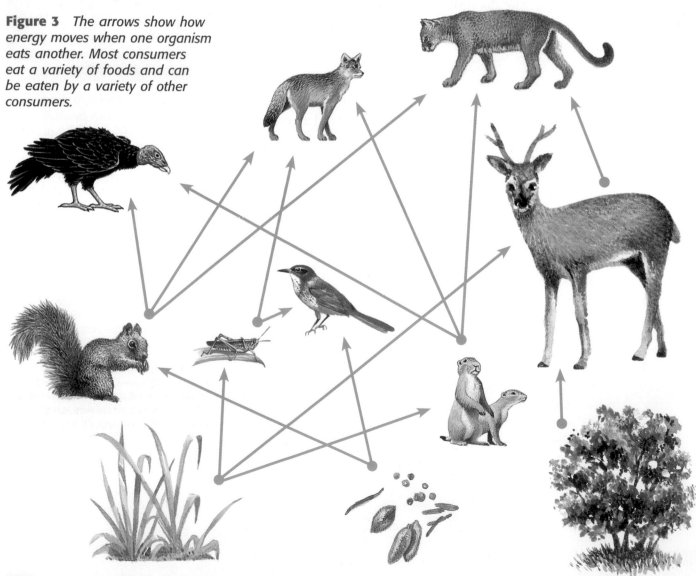

Decreasing number of organisms

Decreasing amount of energy

Figure 4 *The pyramid represents energy. As you can see, more energy is available at the base of the pyramid than at the pyramid's top.*

Energy Pyramids

Only a small part of the energy an organism obtains is transferred to the next consumer in a food chain. Thus, many more organisms have to be at the base of a food chain than at the top of a food chain. For example, in a prairie community, there must be more grass than prairie dogs and more prairie dogs than coyotes.

The amount of energy at each level of a food chain can be seen in an energy pyramid. An **energy pyramid** is a diagram that shows an ecosystem's loss of energy. Only about 10% of the energy in each level of the energy pyramid is transferred to the next level of the pyramid. An example of an energy pyramid is shown in **Figure 4.** You can see that the energy pyramid has a large base and a small top. Less energy is available at higher levels of the pyramid because most of the energy has already been used at the lower levels.

energy pyramid (EN uhr jee PIR uh mid) a triangular diagram that shows an ecosystem's loss of energy, which results as energy passes through the ecosystem's food chain

Standards Check Why are only a few animals at the top of an energy pyramid? 🐻 **6.5.b**

Wolves and the Energy Pyramid

Even a single species can be very important to the flow of energy in an environment. Gray wolves, shown in **Figure 5,** are consumers that control the populations of many other animals. Gray wolves may eat anything from a lizard to an elk. Because gray wolves are predators that are not usually preyed upon, wolves belong at the top of the energy pyramid.

Once common throughout much of the United States, gray wolves were almost wiped out as the wilderness was settled. Without wolves, some species, such as elk, were no longer controlled, and their populations began to grow. The overpopulation of elk in some areas led to overgrazing. The overgrazing left too little grass to support the elk and other herbivore populations that depended on the grass for food. Without enough food, these herbivore populations began to decline. The decline in herbivore populations was quickly followed by declines in other predator populations because there were not enough prey. Soon, almost all of the species in the area were affected by the loss of the gray wolves.

Standards Check Why did the decline of the wolf population affect the populations of other organisms in the community? 6.5.e

Figure 5 *As the wilderness was settled, the gray wolf population in the United States declined.*

Quick Lab

How Are the Organisms in a Food Chain Connected?

Try this activity to see how changes in parts of a food chain can affect the whole food chain.

6.5.b
6.5.e

▶ Try It!

1. On a desk, place **15 green beads** to represent grass, **9 brown beads** to represent elk, and **4 yellow beads** to represent wolves.

2. Roll the **numbered cube.** The number rolled represents how many elk the wolves have eaten. Remove this number of elk from the desk. Because some elk were removed, more grass can grow. Multiply the number of elk that were removed by two. This number represents how many beads of grass can be added to the desk.

3. Roll the numbered cube. The number rolled represents how much grass the elk have eaten. Multiply this number by two.

This number represents how many beads of grass should be removed from the desk. The number of wolves remains the same.

4. Roll the numbered cube. This number represents how much the grass has grown. Add this number of beads of grass to the desk.

▶ Think About It!

5. What do you think will happen to the elk and wolf populations after step 4?

6. What would happen to the balance in the ecosystem if all of the elk were eaten by the wolves?

 15 min

Balance in Ecosystems

Gray wolves were brought back to Yellowstone National Park in 1995. The reintroduced wolves soon began to breed. As they become reestablished in the park, wolves kill the old, injured, and diseased elk. This process is reducing the number of elk. The smaller elk population is letting more plants grow. So, the numbers of herbivores, such as snowshoe hares, and the carnivores that eat the hares, such as foxes, are increasing. All organisms in a food web are important for the health and balance of other organisms in the food web. However, the reintroduction of wolves is also a source of controversy. Ranchers that live near the park are worried about their livestock because wolves will eat cows and sheep if given the chance.

Energy Pyramids

In your **Science Journal,** draw an energy pyramid for a river ecosystem that has four levels—algae, insect larvae, bluegill fish, and bass. The algae get 10,000 units of energy from sunlight. If each level uses 90% of the energy it receives from the previous level, how many units of energy do the bass receive?

SECTION Review

 6.5.a, 6.5.b, 6.5.c, 6.5.e

Summary

- Producers that use photosynthesis transfer the energy in sunlight into chemical energy.
- Consumers eat producers and other organisms to obtain energy and nutrients.
- Decomposers break down all of the materials in dead organisms to obtain energy and nutrients.
- Food chains represent how energy and nutrients are transferred from one organism to another.
- Energy pyramids show how energy is lost at each level of the food chain.
- All organisms have important roles in a food web.

Using Vocabulary

❶ Use *herbivores, carnivores,* and *omnivores* in separate sentences.

Understanding Concepts

❷ **Describing** Describe how energy enters a food web through plants.

❸ **Demonstrating** Draw a food chain. Identify the producer, primary consumer, secondary consumer, and tertiary consumer.

❹ **Justifying** Explain the importance of decomposers.

❺ **Describing** Explain how producers, consumers, and decomposers are linked in a food chain.

Critical Thinking

❻ **Identifying Relationships** Explain how food chains and food webs are related.

❼ **Making Inferences** Why is it more common to find short food chains than to find long food chains?

INTERPRETING GRAPHICS Use the following graph to answer the next three questions.

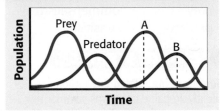

Predator and Prey Populations Over Time

❽ **Identifying Relationships** What is the relationship between the size of the predator population and the size of the prey population?

❾ **Predicting Consequences** What would happen to the prey population if the predator population was removed from this graph?

❿ **Analyzing Data** Describe what is happening at A and at B.

Types of Interactions

Key Concept Organisms depend on their relationships with each other and on the resources in their environment.

▶ Look at the kelp forest shown in **Figure 1.** How many fish do you see? How many kelp do you count? Why do you think there are more members of the seaweed population than members of the fish population? In natural communities, the sizes of populations of different organisms can vary greatly. This variation happens because everything in the environment affects every other thing.

Interactions with the Environment

Most living things produce more offspring than will survive. A female frog, for example, might lay hundreds of eggs in a small pond. In a few months, the population of frogs in that pond will be about the same as it was the year before. Why won't the pond become overrun with frogs? An organism, such as a frog, interacts with biotic and abiotic factors in its environment that can control the size of its population.

Limiting Factors

Populations cannot grow without limits, because the environment contains a limited amount of food, water, living space, and other resources. A resource that is so scarce that it limits the size of a population is called a *limiting factor*. For example, food becomes a limiting factor when a population becomes too large for the amount of food available. Any single resource can be a limiting factor to a population's size.

Standards Check How is a population of organisms affected by a limiting factor? 🐻 **6.5.e**

Figure 1 *This kelp forest is home to many species and is a good place for this sea lion to find its next meal.*

Carrying Capacity

The largest population that an environment can support is known as the **carrying capacity.** When a population grows larger than the carrying capacity, limiting factors in the environment cause individuals to die or leave. As individuals die or leave, the population size decreases.

For example, after a rainy season, producers such as plants may produce a large crop of leaves and seeds. This large amount of food may cause an herbivore, or primary consumer, population to grow. If the next year has less rainfall, there won't be enough food to support the large herbivore population. In this way, a population may become larger than the carrying capacity, but only for a small amount of time. The lack of food or other limiting factors will cause the population to decrease to a size that the environment can support.

carrying capacity (KAR ee ing kuh PAS i tee) the largest population that an environment can support at any given time

Interactions Among Organisms

Populations contain individuals of a single species that interact with one another, such as a group of rabbits of the same species feeding in the same area. Communities contain interacting populations, such as a coral reef with many species of fishes searching for food and places to live. Ecologists have described three main relationships through which species and individuals affect each other: competitive relationships, predator and prey relationships, and symbiotic relationships.

Competition

Competition happens when two or more individuals or populations try to use the same resource. Resources such as food, water, shelter, or sunlight may be in limited supply in an environment. When one individual or population uses a resource, less of the resource is available to other organisms.

Competition can happen between individuals *within* a population. The elk in Yellowstone National Park are herbivores that compete with each other for the same food plants in the park. Competition is especially high during the cold winter when many plants die. Because there aren't enough plants to eat, the size of the elk population decreases. During the warmer spring, plants grow well and support an increasing elk population.

Competition also happens *between* populations. The different plant species in **Figure 2** are competing with each other for sunlight and space.

Standards Check How is the elk population affected by winter?

🐻 6.5.e

Figure 2 *Some of the trees in this forest grow tall to reach sunlight, which reduces the amount of sunlight available to shorter plants nearby.*

Predators and Prey

Many interactions between species consist of one organism eating another to obtain energy and nutrients. The organism that is eaten is called the **prey.** The organism that eats the prey is called the **predator.** When a bird eats a worm, the worm is the prey and the bird is the predator.

Predator Adaptations

To survive, predators must be able to catch their prey. Predators have a wide variety of methods and abilities for doing so. The cheetah, for example, is able to run very quickly to catch its prey. The cheetah's speed gives the cheetah an advantage over other predators competing for the same prey.

Other predators, such as the goldenrod spider, shown in **Figure 3,** ambush their prey. The goldenrod spider blends in well with the yellow flower, so insects don't see it. All the spider has to do is wait for its next insect meal to arrive.

Prey Adaptations

Prey have their own methods and abilities to keep from being eaten. Many animals run away from predators. Prairie dogs run to their underground burrows when a predator approaches. Many small fishes, such as anchovies, swim in groups called *schools*. Antelopes and buffaloes stay in herds. All of the eyes, ears, and noses of the individuals in the group are watching, listening, and smelling for predators. This behavior increases the likelihood of spotting a potential predator.

Some prey hide from their predators by looking similar to their background. Some prey are poisonous. They may advertise their poison with bright colors to warn predators. The fire salamander, shown in **Figure 4,** sprays a poison that burns.

Figure 3 *The goldenrod spider is difficult for its insect prey to see.* **Can you see it?**

Figure 4 *Many predators have learned not to eat the fire salamander! This colorful animal will make a predator very sick.*

Camouflage

One way animals avoid being eaten is by being hard to see. A rabbit often freezes so that its natural color helps the rabbit blend into a background of shrubs or grass. Blending in with the background is called *camouflage*. Many animals mimic twigs, leaves, stones, bark, or other materials in their environment. One insect, called a walking stick, looks like a twig. Some walking sticks even sway a bit, as though a breeze were blowing.

Defensive Chemicals

The spines of a porcupine clearly signal trouble to a potential predator, but other defenses may not be as obvious. Some animals defend themselves with chemicals. The skunk and the bombardier beetle both spray predators with irritating chemicals. Bees, ants, and wasps inject a powerful acid into their attackers. The skin of both the poison arrow frog and a bird called the *hooded pitohui* contains a deadly toxin. Any predator that eats, or tries to eat, one of these animals will likely die.

Warning Coloration

Animals that have a chemical defense must be able to warn predators that they should look elsewhere for a meal. Their chemical weapons are often advertised by warning colors, as shown in **Figure 5.** Predators will avoid any animal that has the colors and patterns they associate with pain, illness, or unpleasant experiences. The most common warning colors are black, white, and bright shades of red, yellow, and orange.

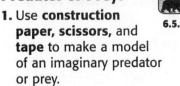

Quick Lab

Predator or Prey?

6.5.e

1. Use **construction paper, scissors,** and **tape** to make a model of an imaginary predator or prey.

2. Give the predator three characteristics that would help it catch its prey. If you choose to make a prey, give it three characteristics that would help it avoid its predator.

3. How do organisms use these kinds of adaptations?

4. What would happen if these organisms didn't have these adaptations?

⏱ 15 min

Figure 5 *The warning coloration of the yellow jacket (left) and the pitohui (above) warns predators that they are dangerous.*

Symbiosis

Some species have very close interactions with other species. **Symbiosis** is a close, long-term association between two or more species. The individuals in a symbiotic relationship can benefit from, be unaffected by, or be harmed by the relationship. Often, one species lives in or on the other species. The thousands of symbiotic relationships are often classified into three groups: mutualism, commensalism, and parasitism.

Mutualism

A symbiotic relationship in which both organisms benefit is called **mutualism.** For example, as a bee drinks the nectar from a flower, pollen is transferred from the flower to the bee. When the bee visits another flower, the pollen on the bee is transferred to the new flower. Because of these interactions, the bee finds food. And the flowers receive the pollen needed for reproduction.

Mutualism also occurs between some corals and the algae living inside those corals. In this relationship, a coral receives the extra food that the algae make by photosynthesis. In turn, these algae also receive a place to live, as **Figure 6** shows. These algae also receive some nutrients from the coral. Both organisms benefit from this relationship.

Commensalism

A symbiotic relationship in which one organism benefits and the other is unaffected is called **commensalism.** One example of commensalism is the relationship between sharks and smaller fish called *remoras.* **Figure 7** shows a shark that has a remora attached to its body. Remoras "hitch a ride" and feed on scraps of food left by sharks. The remoras benefit from this relationship, while sharks are unaffected.

symbiosis (SIM bie OH sis) a relationship in which two different organisms live in close association with each other

mutualism (MYOO choo uhl IZ uhm) a relationship between two species in which both species benefit

commensalism (kuh MEN suhl IZ uhm) a relationship between two organisms in which one organism benefits and the other is unaffected

Figure 6 *In the smaller photo above, you can see the gold-colored algae inside the coral.*

Figure 7 *The remora attached to the shark benefits from the relationship. The shark neither benefits from nor is harmed by the relationship.*

Parasitism

A symbiotic relationship in which one organism benefits while the other is harmed is called **parasitism**. The organism that benefits from this relationship is called the *parasite*. The organism that is harmed in this relationship is called the *host*. The parasite gets nourishment from its host, which weakens the host. Sometimes, a host dies and the parasite must find a new host. Parasites such as ticks and mistletoe live on the host. Parasites such as ticks often move from one host to another. Other parasites such as tapeworms live out their adult life inside the host's body.

parasitism (PAR uh SIET IZ uhm) a relationship between two species in which one species, the parasite, benefits from the other species, the host, which is harmed

Standards Check What does a parasite get from its host? 6.5.b

---

SECTION Review

 6.5.b, 6.5.e

Summary

- Limiting factors refer to the factors in the environment that keep a population from growing without limits.

- Competition happens within populations and between populations.

- A predator is an organism that kills an organism to eat all or part of that organism. The organism that is killed and eaten is called *prey*.

- Prey have features such as camouflage, chemical defenses, and warning coloration that protect them from predators.

- Mutualism, commensalism, and parasitism are the three kinds of symbiotic relationships that occur between organisms.

Using Vocabulary

1. Use *carrying capacity, mutualism, commensalism,* and *parasitism* in separate sentences.

Understanding Concepts

2. **Identifying** What are two resources for which organisms would compete?

3. **Describing** Briefly describe an example of a predator-prey relationship. Be sure to identify the predator and the prey.

Critical Thinking

4. **Identifying Relationships** Explain the probable relationship between the giant *Rafflesia* flower, which smells like rotting meat, and the carrion flies that buzz around it. (Hint: *Carrion* means "rotting flesh.")

5. **Predicting Consequences** Predict what might happen to a wolf population during spring.

6. **Applying Concepts** Explain the relationship between the carrying capacity and limiting factors.

INTERPRETING GRAPHICS

The graph below shows the growth of a population of paramecia (single-celled microorganisms) in a test tube over 18 days. Food was added to the test tube occasionally. Use the graph below to answer the next two questions.

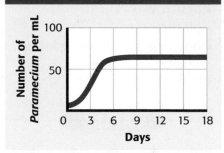

Paramecium caudatum Growth

7. **Analyzing Data** What keeps the number of paramecia at a constant level?

8. **Applying Concepts** Predict what will happen if no more food is added to the test tube.

Internet Resources

For a variety of links related to this chapter, go to www.scilinks.org

Topic: Predator/Prey
SciLinks code: HY71205

Skills Practice Lab

Too Much of a Nutrient?

Plants need nutrients, such as phosphorus and nitrogen, to grow. Compounds of phosphorus called *phosphates* are often found in detergents. Compounds of nitrogen called *nitrates* are often found in animal wastes and fertilizers. When large amounts of these nutrients enter rivers and lakes, algae and plants grow rapidly. When they die, microorganisms that decompose the dead matter use up oxygen in the water. Without oxygen, fish and other animals die. In this lab, you will observe the effect of fertilizers on organisms that live in pond water.

OBJECTIVES

Observe the effect of fertilizer on pond-water organisms.

Describe how fertilizer affects the number and type of pond-water organisms over time.

MATERIALS

- beaker, 500 mL
- distilled water, 2.25 L
- eyedropper
- liquid fertilizer
- graduated cylinder, 100 mL
- jars, 1 qt or 1 L (3)
- microscope
- microscope slides with coverslips
- pencil, wax
- plastic wrap
- pond water containing living organisms, 300 mL
- stirring rod

SAFETY

Procedure

❶ Label one jar "Control," the second jar "Fertilizer," and the third jar "Excess fertilizer."

❷ Pour 750 mL of distilled water into each jar. Add the amount of fertilizer recommended for 750 mL of water to the jar labeled "Fertilizer." Add 10 times the amount recommended for 750 mL of water to the jar labeled "Excess fertilizer." Stir the contents of each jar to dissolve the fertilizer.

❸ Obtain a sample of pond water. Stir it gently to make sure that the organisms in it are evenly distributed. Pour 100 mL of pond water into each of the three jars.

❹ Observe a drop of water from each jar under the microscope. Draw at least four of the organisms. Determine whether the organisms are producers, which are usually green, or consumers, which are usually able to move.

6.5.b Students know matter is transferred over time from one organism to others in the food web and between organisms and the physical environment.
6.5.e Students know the number and types of organisms an ecosystem can support depends on the resources available and on abiotic factors, such as quantities of light and water, a range of temperatures, and soil composition.

Investigation and Experimentation
6.7.e Recognize whether evidence is consistent with a proposed explanation.

Common Pond-Water Organisms

Volvox
(producer)

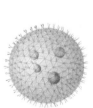
Spirogyra
(producer)

Daphnia
(consumer)

Vorticella
(consumer)

5 Describe the number of and types of organisms in the pond water.

6 Cover each jar loosely with plastic wrap. Place the jars near a sunny window but not in direct sunlight.

7 Make a prediction about how the pond organisms will grow in each of the three jars.

8 Make three tables. Title one table "Control," as shown below. Title another table "Fertilizer." Title the third table "Excess Fertilizer."

Control			
Date	Color	Odor	Other observations

DO NOT WRITE IN BOOK

9 Observe the jars when you first set them up and once every 3 days for the next 3 weeks. Note the color, the odor, and the presence of organisms. Record your observations in your tables.

10 When organisms become visible in the jars, use an eyedropper to remove a sample from each jar. Observe the sample under the microscope. How have the number of and types of organisms changed in each jar since you first looked at the pond water?

11 At the end of the 3-week period, observe a sample from each jar under the microscope. Draw at least four of the most abundant organisms, and describe how the number of and types of organisms have changed since your last observation using the microscope.

Analyze the Results

12 **Describing Events** After 3 weeks, which jar has the most abundant growth of algae?

13 **Analyzing Data** Did you observe any effects on organisms (other than algae) in the jar that had the most abundant growth of algae? Explain your answer.

Draw Conclusions

14 **Drawing Conclusions** What may have caused increased growth of algae in the jars?

15 **Evaluating Results** Did your observations match your predictions? Explain your answer.

16 **Interpreting Information** Based on these results, what can you predict about the effect resource availability in a pond?

Big Idea Question

17 **Drawing Conclusions** What does this experiment demonstrate about the relationship between organisms and the nonliving parts of their environment?

Science Skills Activity

Investigation and Experimentation

6.7.c Construct appropriate graphs from data and develop qualitative statements about the relationships between variables.

Constructing a Bar Graph

▶ Tutorial

Procedure

❶ Use the following instructions to draw the axes of your bar graph:
- Draw the axes for your graph on a sheet of graph paper.
- Title the *x*-axis with the name of the independent variable.
- Write the label for each data category on the *x*-axis. Make sure that your labels are equally spaced along the *x*-axis.
- Title the *y*-axis with the name of the dependent variable.
- Choose a scale for the *y*-axis that covers the range of values in your data set.
- Draw and label tick marks along the *y*-axis. Make sure that your tick marks are equally spaced along the *y*-axis.

❷ Complete your bar graph by doing the following:
- Draw a bar for each category in your data set. The height of each bar represents the value of the category on the *y*-axis. Make sure that your bars are equally spaced along the *y*-axis.
- Write the title of your graph at the top of your graph.

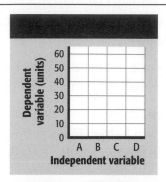

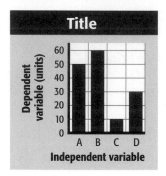

▶ You Try It!

Procedure
Use the data in **Table 1** to construct a bar graph. Then, use the bar graph to make observations about Shanthi's daily diet.

Analysis

❶ **Identify** Decide whether each of the foods in **Table 1** comes from a consumer or from a producer.

❷ **Compare** Use green to color the bars that represent food from producers. Use red to color the bars that represent consumers.

❸ **Evaluate** Which category is the largest? Does Shanthi obtain most of her nutrition directly from producers or from consumers?

❹ **Identify** Is Shanthi a primary consumer, a secondary consumer, or a tertiary consumer?

❺ **Evaluate** Would Shanthi receive more of the energy stored by producers as a primary consumer or as a secondary consumer?

Table 1	Shanthi's Average Daily Diet
Food	**Quantity (in cups)**
Rice	0.75
Vegetables	1.25
Milk	2
Chicken	0.25
Cereal	0.5
Pretzels	0.5
Fruit	1

Chapter Summary

The Big Idea

Organisms interact with each other and with the nonliving parts of their environment.

Section	Vocabulary

1 Everything Is Connected

Key Concept Organisms depend on each other and on the nonliving resources in their environment.

- Biotic factors are the effects of organisms on each other and on the environment.
- Abiotic factors are the nonliving parts of the environment.
- Ecosystems are made up of organisms, and the abiotic factors of the environment.

The bear needs fish and fruits to eat and needs water to drink.

Vocabulary

ecology p. 550
biotic p. 550
abiotic p. 550
population p. 552
community p. 552
ecosystem p. 552
biome p. 553
biosphere p. 553

2 Living Things Need Energy

Key Concept Energy and matter flow between organisms and their environment.

- Producers, consumers, and decomposers have specific functions in an ecosystem.
- Energy flows from one organism to another in food chains. Many food chains make up a food web.
- The availability of living and nonliving resources affects all organisms.

Organisms are connected in food webs.

herbivore p. 555
carnivore p. 555
omnivore p. 555
food chain p. 555
food web p. 556
energy pyramid p. 557

3 Types of Interactions

Key Concept Organisms depend on their relationships with each other and on the resources in their environment.

- Limiting factors determine the carrying capacity of an environment.
- Competition occurs when two or more organisms try to use the same resource.
- Prey have unique characteristics to avoid predation.
- Mutualism, commensalism, and parasitism are three kinds of symbiotic relationships that exist between organisms.

Plants compete with each other to obtain sunlight to make food.

carrying capacity p. 561
prey p. 562
predator p. 562
symbiosis p. 564
mutualism p. 564
commensalism p. 564
parasitism p. 565

Organize

Tri-Fold Review the FoldNote that you created at the beginning of the chapter. Add to or correct the FoldNote based on what you have learned.

Using Vocabulary

1 **Academic Vocabulary** Which of the following words is the closest in meaning to the word *transferred*?
a. changed into something else
b. passed from one thing to another
c. used to build something else
d. found everywhere

Complete each of the following sentences by choosing the correct term from the word bank.

biotic	abiotic
ecosystem	community

2 The environment includes ___ factors such as water, rocks, and light.

3 A community of organisms and their environment is called a(n) ___.

Understanding Concepts

Multiple Choice

4 A tick sucks blood from a dog. In this relationship, the tick is the ___ and the dog is the ___.
a. parasite, prey   c. parasite, host
b. predator, host   d. host, parasite

5 Nature's recyclers are
a. predators.   c. producers.
b. decomposers.   d. omnivores.

6 A beneficial association between coral and algae is an example of
a. commensalism.   c. mutualism.
b. parasitism.   d. predation.

7 The process by which energy moves through an ecosystem can be represented by
a. food chains.
b. energy pyramids.
c. food webs.
d. All of the above

8 Which of the following organisms does the base of an energy pyramid represent?
a. producers   c. herbivores
b. carnivores   d. scavengers

Short Answer

9 **Describing** Describe what happens to the energy a consumer gains when the consumer eats another organism.

10 **Describing** Explain how the food web changed when the gray wolf population declined.

11 **Comparing** How is the competition between two trees of the same species similar to the competition between two trees of different species?

12 **Evaluating** How do limiting factors affect the carrying capacity of an environment?

Writing Skills

13 **Communicating Concepts** Producers are at the bottom of every food chain or food pyramid. What are two different kinds of producers, and explain why they are necessary. What would happen to life on Earth if producers no longer existed?

Critical Thinking

14 **Concept Mapping** Use the following terms to create a concept map: *herbivores, organisms, producers, populations, ecosystems, consumers, communities, carnivores,* and *biosphere.*

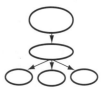

15 **Identifying Relationships** Could a balanced ecosystem contain producers and consumers but not decomposers? Why or why not?

16 **Expressing Opinions** Do you think there is a carrying capacity for humans? Explain.

17 **Applying Concepts** Why are producers at the base of food chains, food webs, and energy pyramids?

18 **Making Inferences** Producers, consumers, and decomposers play important roles in the environment. Are there any organisms that would not fall into one of these categories? Explain your answer.

INTERPRETING GRAPHICS Use the diagram below to answer the next three questions.

19 **Identifying Relationships** From the food web, identify a food chain that has a producer, a primary consumer, and a secondary consumer.

20 **Making Inferences** What will happen to the mountain lion if all of the prairie dogs become extinct? Explain.

21 **Applying Concepts** How does solar energy enter this food web?

INTERPRETING GRAPHICS Use the diagram below to answer the next three questions.

22 **Identifying Relationships** According to the energy pyramid, are there more prairie dogs than plants or more plants than prairie dogs?

23 **Making Inferences** Would an energy pyramid such as this one exist in nature?

24 **Applying Concepts** How could you change this pyramid to look like one representing a real ecosystem?

Math Skills

25 **Making Conversions** Producers are eaten by primary consumers, which are eaten by secondary consumers. Secondary consumers are eaten by tertiary consumers. What percentage of the energy stored by producers do the tertiary consumers receive?

Challenge

26 **Making Inferences** In parts of the United States, deer populations are very large. Deer wander into yards and eat garden plants. Deer also wander onto roads and can cause car accidents. Why do you think deer populations have become so large? Can you think of ways to control deer populations naturally? What do you think is happening to the vegetation in areas that have a large deer population?

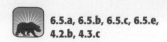
REVIEWING ACADEMIC VOCABULARY

1 Which of the following words means "able to be touched and seen"?

A physical

B feeling

C object

D visible

2 In the sentence, "Energy is transferred from one organism to another in a food chain," what does the word *transferred* mean?

A passed from one thing to another

B gathered up into a large amount

C reached out to

D communicated with

3 In the sentence, "After the experiment, they graphed the data," what does the word *data* mean?

A survey

B information

C calculations

D examples

4 Choose the appropriate form of the word *categorize* for the following sentence: "She ___ the crow as an omnivore."

A categorized

B categorize

C categorizing

D categorical

REVIEWING CONCEPTS

5 Which of the following are all examples of abiotic factors in an environment?

A water, food, and population

B trees, hills, and rivers

C water, soil, and temperature

D algae, fish, and bears

6 What is the primary source of the energy that flows through food webs on land?

A producers

B sunlight

C oxygen

D photosynthesis

7 Organisms use energy from the food they eat to fuel their life processes. Some of this energy is also

A used to make food.

B lost to the environment as heat.

C obtained through movement.

D gained through work.

8 Which of the animals shown below would be most likely to compete with a hawk for prey?

A
rabbit

C
elk

B
coyote

D
bluejay

9 What is the role of decomposers in the food chain?

A They are at the base of the food chain and provide food for primary consumers.

B They break down only bacteria, insects, fungi, and earthworms.

C They break down waste and rotting matter.

D They provide food and shelter for animals.

10 If fish in a stream begin to die because of pollution, what may happen to the ecosystem?

A The organisms in the ecosystem will all be affected in some way.

B The ecosystem will remain unchanged.

C The organisms that ate fish will reproduce faster.

D The ecosystem will continue to thrive.

11 Which of the following statements best describes the food web?

A Many individual organisms of the same species live in the same space and share resources.

B An ecosystem that is made up of a community of organisms and their environment.

C A black bear eats fruit and then spreads the fruit's seeds through its excretions.

D All life is connected by the transfer of energy and nutrients among organisms and their environment.

12 In an ecosystem located on the seashore, which organisms would most likely form the base of the energy pyramid?

A small fish

B algae

C mussels

D sea cucumbers

REVIEWING PRIOR LEARNING

13 How do bears and berries depend on each other for survival?

A Berries grow in places where bears can find them easily.

B Berries depend on bears to keep the population of berry plants down.

C Bears depend on berries as their main source of energy.

D Bears eat berries and then spread the seeds of berries by excretion.

14 Coyotes can be classified as

A producers.

B primary consumers.

C secondary consumers.

D decomposers.

15 Which organism would best fit in the empty spot in the food web shown above?

A another prairie dog

B a turkey vulture

C a fox

D a blue jay

Science in Action

Scientific Debate

How Did Dogs Become Pets?

Did humans change dogs into social and helpful creatures? Or were dogs naturally social? Did dogs start moving closer to our campfires long ago? Or did humans find dogs and bring them into our homes? The way in which dogs became our friends, companions, and helpers is still unanswered. Some scientists think that humans and training are the reasons for many of our dogs' best features. Other scientists think that dogs and humans have both changed over time to form their strong and unique bond.

Math ACTiViTY

Scientists have found fossils of dogs that are 15,000 years old. Generation time is the time between the birth of one generation and the next. If the generation time for dogs is 1.5 years, how many generations have there been in the last 15,000 years? Record your work in your **Science Journal.**

Weird Science

Can You Squirt Blood from Your Eyes?

What eats ants, has tough scaly armor, has horns, and squirts blood from its eyes? The answer is the horned lizard. Some species of horned lizards are found in California. Horned lizards have some interesting ways to defend themselves from predators, such as the coyote. For example, the colors of a horned lizard help the lizard to blend in with its environment and therefore, hide from its predators. Some horned lizards puff up so that they look larger. And the tough skin and horns of a horned lizard make the lizard hard to chew. Finally, some horned lizards squirt foul-tasting blood from their eyes to frighten away predators. These unique defensive characteristics help ensure the survival of the horned lizards.

Language Arts ACTiViTY

Imagine that you are a horned lizard. What would you eat? How would you escape from your predators? Where would you sleep? Write a short story in your **Science Journal** describing your day as a horned lizard.

Dalton Dockery

Horticulture Specialist Did you know that instead of using pesticides to get rid of insects that are eating the plants in your garden, you can use other insects? "It is a healthy way of growing vegetables without the use of chemicals and pesticides, and it reduces the harmful effects pesticides have on the environment," says Dalton Dockery, a horticulture specialist in North Carolina. Some insects, such as ladybugs and praying mantises, are natural predators of many insects that are harmful to plants. They will eat other bugs but will leave your precious plants in peace. Using bugs to drive off pests is just one aspect of natural gardening. Natural gardening takes advantage of relationships that already exist in nature and uses these interactions to our benefit. For Dockery, the best parts about being a horticultural specialist are teaching people how to preserve the environment, getting to work outside regularly, and having the opportunity to help people on a daily basis.

Social Studies ACTiViTY

Research gardening or farming techniques in other cultures. Do other cultures use any of the same aspects of natural gardening as horticultural specialists? Write a short report describing your findings in your **Science Journal.**

Internet Resources

- To learn more about careers in science, visit **www.scilinks.org** and enter the SciLinks code HY70225.

- To learn more about these Science in Action topics, visit **go.hrw.com** and type in the keyword HY7INTF.

- Check out articles related to this chapter by visiting go.hrw.com. Just type in the keyword HY7INTC.

Improving Comprehension

Graphic Organizers are important visual tools that can help you organize information and improve your reading comprehension. The Graphic Organizer below is called a *Venn diagram.* Instructions for creating other types of Graphic Organizers are located in the **Study Skills** section of the Appendix.

How to Make a Venn Diagram

❶ Draw a diagram like the one shown below. Draw one circle for each topic. Make sure that each circle partially overlaps the other circles.

❷ In each circle, write a topic that you want to compare with the topics in the other circles.

❸ In the areas of the diagram where circles overlap, write the characteristics that the topics in the overlapping circles share.

❹ In the areas of the diagram where circles do not overlap, write the characteristics that are unique to the topic of the particular circle.

When to Use a Venn Diagram

A Venn diagram is a useful tool for comparing two or three topics in science. A Venn diagram shows which characteristics the topics share and which characteristics are unique to each topic. Venn diagrams are ideal when you want to illustrate relationships in a pair or small group of topics. As you read, look for topics that have both shared and unique characteristics, and draw a Venn diagram that shows how the topics are related.

Biomes
- large areas made up of land and water ecosystems
- defined by unique plant communities that support unique animal communities
- examples: deserts, chaparrals, temperate grasslands, savannas, tundra, coniferous forests, temperate deciduous forests, and tropical rain forests

- have producers, consumers, and decomposers
- contain abiotic factors that organisms either use or have to adapt to

Ecosystems
- defined by all of their organisms and abiotic factors
- examples: land ecosystems, marine ecosystems, stream and river ecosystems, pond and lake ecosystems, and wetland ecosystems

You Try It!

This Reading Strategy can also be used within the chapter that you are about to read. Practice making your own Venn diagram as directed in the Reading Strategies for Section ❶ and Section ❹. Record your work in your **Science Journal.**

Unpacking the Standards

The information below "unpacks" the standards by breaking them down into basic parts. The higher-level, academic vocabulary is highlighted and defined to help you understand the language of the standards. "What It Means" restates the standards as simply as possible.

California Standard	Academic Vocabulary	What It Means
6.5.a Students know **energy** entering ecosystems as sunlight is **transferred** by producers into **chemical** energy through photosynthesis and then from organism to organism through food webs.	**energy** (EN uhr jee) the ability to make things happen **transfer** (TRANS fuhr) to carry or cause to pass from one thing to another **chemical** (KEM i kuhl) of or having to do with the properties or actions of substances	Producers, such as plants, change energy from the sun into chemical energy through photosynthesis. Then, this chemical energy passes to and between organisms that eat other organisms.
6.5.b Students know matter is **transferred** over time from one organism to others in the food web and between organisms and the **physical** environment.	**physical** (FIZ i kuhl) able to be seen or touched	Matter moves from one living thing to another in a food web. Matter also moves between living things and their nonliving surroundings.
6.5.c Students know populations of organisms can be **categorized** by the **functions** they serve in an ecosystem.	**categorize** (KAT uh guh RIEZ) to put into groups or classes **function** (FUHNGK shuhn) use or purpose	Living things can be identified by the role that they play, or what they do, in an ecosystem.
6.5.d Students know different kinds of organisms may play **similar** ecological **roles** in similar biomes.	**similar** (SIM uh luhr) almost the same **role** (ROHL) a part or function; purpose	Different kinds of living things may have the same function in different environments that have similar characteristics.
6.5.e Students know the number and types of organisms an ecosystem can support depends on the **resources available** and on abiotic **factors,** such as quantities of light and water, a **range** of temperatures, and soil composition.	**resource** (REE sawrs) anything that can be used to take care of a need **available** (uh VAYL uh buhl) that can be used **factor** (FAK tuhr) a condition or event that brings about a result **range** (RAYNJ) a scale or series between limits	The number and kinds of living things that can live in an ecosystem depend on the available resources and on nonliving conditions, such as the amount of light and water, the high and low temperatures, and the makeup of the soil.

Biomes and Ecosystems

The Big Idea

Biomes and ecosystems are characterized by their living and nonliving parts.

 California Standards

Focus on Earth Sciences
6.5 Organisms in ecosystems exchange energy and nutrients among themselves and with the environment. (Sections 1, 2, 3, and 4)

Investigation and Experimentation
6.7 Scientific progress is made by asking meaningful questions and conducting careful investigations. (Science Skills Activity)

Math
6.2.1 Number Sense
6.2.1 Algebra and Functions
6.1.1 Statistics, Data Analysis, and Probability

English–Language Arts
6.2.4 Reading
6.1.3 Writing

About the Photo

Where is the rest of this animal? The fringe-toed lizard can be found buried in the sands in Cadiz Dunes, California. The comblike fringes on its toes allow the lizard to dig quickly into loose sands. Buried in the sand, the lizard escapes the sweltering heat of the day and hides from its predators. So, be careful where you walk!

Organize

Three-Panel Flip Chart

Before you read this chapter, create the FoldNote entitled "Three-Panel Flip Chart." Label the flaps of the three-panel flip chart with "Land biomes," "Marine ecosystems," and "Freshwater ecosystems." As you read the chapter, write information about each topic under the appropriate flap.

Instructions for creating FoldNotes are located in the Study Skills section on p. 617 of the Appendix.

Explore Activity

⏱ 30 min

Build a Mini-Ecosystem

In this activity, you will build and observe a miniature ecosystem.

Procedure

1. Place a layer of **gravel** at the bottom of a **container,** such as a **large, wide-mouthed jar** or a **2 L soda bottle** with the top cut off. Then, add a layer of **soil.**

2. Add a **medium-sized plant** or a **few small plants** that need similar growing conditions. Choose plants that will not grow too quickly.

3. Spray **water** inside the container to moisten the soil.

4. Loosely cover the container with a **lid** or **plastic wrap.** Place the container in indirect light.

5. Describe the appearance of your ecosystem.

6.5.b
6.5.e

6. Let your mini-ecosystem grow for 6 weeks. Add more water when the soil is dry.

7. Observe your mini-ecosystem every week. Record your observations.

Analysis

8. List the nonliving and living factors that make up the ecosystem that you built.

9. Why did you need to add water? What would have happened if you had not added more water?

10. How is your mini-ecosystem similar to a real ecosystem? How is it different?

Studying the Environment

Key Concept In every environment, organisms depend on each other and on the nonliving things in the environment to survive.

What You Will Learn

- Biomes are made up of many connected ecosystems.
- Abiotic factors affect the organisms in an environment.
- All biomes have producers, consumers, and decomposers.
- Similar biomes occur in similar climates.

Why It Matters

Studying the different parts of biomes and ecosystems will help you understand how biomes and ecosystems are organized.

READING STRATEGY

Graphic Organizer In your **Science Journal,** create a Venn Diagram that compares herbivores, carnivores, and omnivores.

▶ What makes a desert different from a forest? Is it the difference in the amount of rainfall that each area receives? Or, is it because of the different kinds of organisms that live in these areas? Actually, it is both of these characteristics, along with many other characteristics, that help distinguish deserts from forests. Rainfall is a nonliving part of the environment, or an *abiotic factor.* Organisms are a living part of the environment. They rely on the abiotic factors in their environment for their survival.

How Biomes Differ from Ecosystems

Biomes are large areas made up of many connected land and water ecosystems. Therefore, biomes are typically much larger than ecosystems. An ecosystem is defined by all of its organisms and its abiotic factors. Biomes are defined by unique plant communities that support unique animal communities. The kind of plant community found in a biome is determined by the climate of the biome. *Climate* is made up of a combination of a few abiotic factors, such as the average yearly temperature and the average yearly rainfall. Some of the major land biomes on Earth are shown in **Figure 1.**

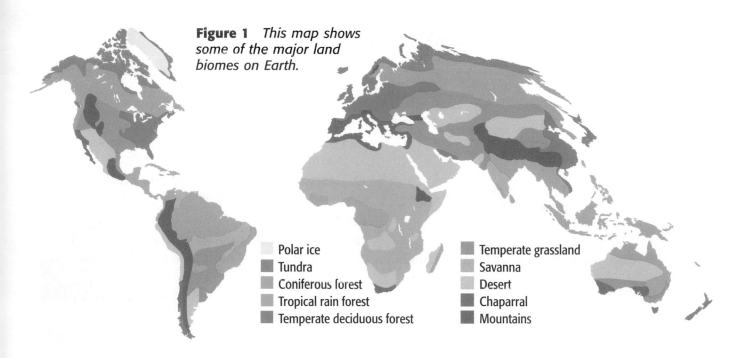

Figure 1 *This map shows some of the major land biomes on Earth.*

- Polar ice
- Tundra
- Coniferous forest
- Tropical rain forest
- Temperate deciduous forest
- Temperate grassland
- Savanna
- Desert
- Chaparral
- Mountains

Abiotic Factors of an Environment

The abiotic factors of an environment can be divided into two groups. Some abiotic factors, such as water, are resources that organisms use. Other abiotic factors, such as temperature, are conditions to which organisms must be adapted. Organisms rely on the abiotic factors in their environment in different ways. Some abiotic factors are described below.

- **Sunlight** Most producers convert the energy in sunlight into chemical energy, or food, through photosynthesis. In the oceans, there is no sunlight below 200 m. Therefore, producers that need light, such as the kelp shown in **Figure 2.** can live only in the top 200 m of the ocean. On land, fewer plants survive during seasons of lower sunlight.

- **Temperature** The cells of most organisms function best at warm temperatures. Therefore, a greater variety of organisms are found in warm environments than in environments that have extreme temperatures. Few organisms have the adaptations to survive extreme temperatures.

- **Rainfall** Generally, areas with a high amount of rainfall have rich plant growth. In turn, the plants are able to support a large number of other organisms. For example, fewer plants live in a desert than in a forest. The main reason is the difference in the amount of rainfall that each area receives.

- **Soil** Plants rely on nutrients in the soil to grow. Many plants need soil that is high in nutrients to support their growth. Nutrients in the form of fertilizers can be added to soil to increase the growth of plants.

Many other abiotic factors also affect organisms. Different abiotic factors have varying effects on different organisms.

Standards Check Is sunlight a resource? Explain. **6.5.e**

Figure 2 Producers such as kelp are limited to water depths at which they receive enough sunlight for photosynthesis.

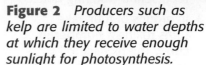

6.5.a Students know energy entering ecosystems as sunlight is transferred by producers into chemical energy through photosynthesis and then from organism to organism through food webs.
6.5.b Students know matter is transferred over time from one organism to others in the food web and between organisms and the physical environment.
6.5.c Students know populations of organisms can be categorized by the functions they serve in an ecosystem.
6.5.d Students know different kinds of organisms may play similar ecological roles in similar biomes.
6.5.e Students know the number and types of organisms an ecosystem can support depends on the resources available and on abiotic factors, such as quantities of light and water, a range of temperatures, and soil composition.

Roles of Organisms in an Environment

Different biomes and ecosystems have many kinds of organisms. However, each organism has one of three main functions, or ecological roles, in an environment. The roles are producer, consumer, or decomposer as **Figure 3** shows.

- **Producers** Producers convert energy in the environment into food. Some producers, such as plants and algae, rely on the energy in sunlight to make food. Other producers, such as some bacteria, make food from chemicals that other organisms cannot use for food-making.

- **Consumers** All animals are consumers. Consumers feed on other organisms to get the energy that they need. Three kinds of consumers are herbivores, carnivores, and omnivores. Herbivores eat only plants, and carnivores eat only animals. Omnivores eat both plants and animals.

- **Decomposers** Some bacteria and fungi are decomposers. Decomposers are consumers that obtain energy by breaking down dead organisms into simple chemicals that other organisms can use. Areas such as Antarctica are so cold that decomposition can take thousands of years.

All biomes and ecosystems have producers, consumers, and decomposers. For example, deer in South America and kangaroos in Australia are herbivores. Deer and kangaroos feed on the plants in their environment. When these organisms die, they will be decomposed by the bacteria and fungi in the environment.

Standards Check List three ecological roles of organisms in a biome or ecosystem. 🐻 **6.5.c, 6.5.d**

Figure 3 **Ecological Roles of Organisms**

Producers   **Consumer**   **Decomposer**

Similar Climates, Similar Biomes

Widely separated biomes with similar climates have similar kinds of plants and animals. You have already learned how climate varies with latitude and altitude. Temperature and rainfall also cause variations in climate. Temperature and rainfall decrease as you move from low latitudes near the equator to high latitudes at the poles. Temperature and rainfall also decrease from low altitudes near sea level to high altitudes in the mountains.

These changes in climate help explain why similar biomes are found at similar latitudes and similar altitudes. For example, much of California is at the same latitude as the area around the Mediterranean Sea. The kind of biome found in both places is called *chaparral*. Temperature and precipitation, including rainfall, of a chaparral are shown in the graph in **Figure 4.** Similarly, the same kinds of biomes are found at high altitudes all over Earth. However, regardless of climate, all biomes have organisms that play the roles of producers, consumers, and decomposers.

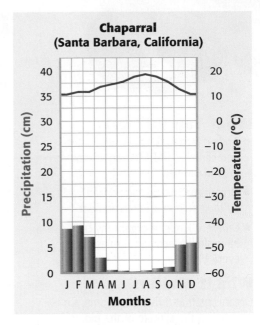

Figure 4 *This graph shows the temperature and precipitation in a chaparral biome, during a year.*

SECTION Review

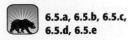
6.5.a, 6.5.b, 6.5.c, 6.5.d, 6.5.e

Summary

- Biomes are made up of many connected ecosystems.
- Some abiotic factors are resources. Other abiotic factors are conditions in the environment.
- Organisms in biomes and ecosystems can be categorized as producers, consumers, or decomposers.
- Some widely-separated biomes have similar communities of plants and animals.
- Similar biomes are found in areas that have similar climates.

Understanding Concepts

1 Applying What kind of abiotic factor are the nutrients in soil?

2 Comparing Describe the difference between a biome and an ecosystem.

3 Identifying If an organism converts energy in the environment into food, what is the ecological role of the organism?

Critical Thinking

4 Making Inferences What could you infer if two widely-separated places on Earth had similar plant communities?

5 Making Predictions At what latitudes would you expect to find a bear that hibernates during the coldest season of the year? Explain.

Math Skills

6 Making Calculations One year, a biome had the following average monthly temperatures: 12°C, 15°C, 15°C, 25°C, 30°C, 35°C, 35°C, 36°C, 28°C, 20°C, 18°C, and 16°C. What is the average annual temperature?

Challenge

7 Applying Concepts Some plants, such as the Venus' flytrap, receive a small portion of the nutrients they need by consuming insects. Would you group this organism as a producer, consumer, or decomposer? Explain.

Internet Resources

For a variety of links related to this chapter, go to www.scilinks.org
Topic: California's Environment
SciLinks code: HY7C06

Land Biomes

Key Concept The kinds of plants and animals that live in a biome are determined by the local climate.

What You Will Learn

- Abiotic factors, such as soil, water, and climate, affect the organisms in land biomes.
- Organisms can be categorized by their role in an environment.
- Different kinds of organisms can have similar ecological roles in every biome.

Why It Matters

Organisms that thrive in a biome are adapted to the climate of the biome.

Vocabulary

- desert
- chaparral
- grassland
- tundra

READING STRATEGY

Graphic Organizer In your **Science Journal,** make a Comparison Table that compares the characteristics of different land biomes.

Figure 1 *The residents of the desert biome have special adaptations to survive in a dry climate.*

▶ Why are some organisms common in some areas and not in other areas? Each biome has organisms that are adapted to the conditions in the biome, such as climate. Organisms are also adapted to using the nonliving and living resources in their biome. Therefore, there are many kinds of organisms in each biome. Each organism in a biome can be categorized as a producer, a consumer, or a decomposer.

Deserts

Very dry, and often very hot biomes are called **deserts,** such as the Mojave Desert in California. Many plants and animals are found only in deserts, and have special adaptations to live in a desert. For example, some plants have widespread roots just under the surface to take up water during a storm. Plants also often grow far apart, reducing the competition for water.

In order to survive in a desert, some animals are active only at night, when it is cooler. Some animals, such as the fringe-toed lizard, bury themselves in the loose sands. Doing so helps these animals escape the heat and avoid predators. Fringe-toed lizards are omnivores that eat insects and parts of plants. Desert tortoises are herbivores that eat flowers or leaves and store water in a large bladder under their shells. **Figure 1** shows how some plants and animals live in the desert.

Standards Check Name one adaptation that allows desert plants to survive with little water. 🐻 **6.5.e**

Cactuses store water in their stems and roots.

Some flowering plants bloom, bear seeds, and die within a few weeks after a heavy rain.

Huge ears help jack rabbits get rid of body heat.

Kangaroo rats do not need to drink. They recycle water from the foods that they eat.

Desert
- **Average Yearly Rainfall less than 25 cm (10 in.)**
- **Average Temperatures Summer: 38°C (100°F) Winter: 7°C (45°F)**

Chaparral
- Average Yearly Rainfall
  25 to 43 cm (10 to 17 in.)
- Average Temperatures
  Summer: 22°C (71.6°F)
  Winter: 17.8°C (64°F)

Figure 2 *Plants of the chaparral are adapted to recovering quickly after a natural fire.*

Chaparral

A biome that has a fairly dry climate but receives only a little more rainfall than a desert does is called a **chaparral.** In chaparral biomes, summers are warm and dry and winters are mild and wet. Chaparral can be found in California and around the Mediterranean Sea.

Chaparral is characterized by low-lying, broad-leaved evergreen shrubs and small trees that grow in dense patches, as shown in **Figure 2.** *Evergreen* plants are plants that keep their leaves all year round. Common chaparral plants include manzanita, scrub oak, and herbs. These plants have leathery leaves that help store water. During natural fires, chaparral shrubs and trees are destroyed. After a fire, the chaparral shrubs grow back more quickly than trees do. Therefore, natural fires prevent the trees from competing with the chaparral shrubs for resources such as sunlight, water, and nutrients. Natural fires are an abiotic factor that help maintain the chaparral.

Animals in the chaparral are also adapted to living in this biome. Quail, lizards, chipmunks, and mule deer are usually gray and brown, which allow them to blend into their surroundings and hide from predators. Mule deer are herbivores that eat grasses and shrubs. Quails, lizards, and chipmunks are omnivores that eat insects and parts of plants. Bobcats, gray foxes, and coyotes are carnivores that prey on many of these organisms. Coyotes also prey on bobcats and gray foxes.

Standards Check Identify the ecological role of a shrub from the chaparral and a cactus from the desert. **6.5.c, 6.5.d**

desert (DEZ uhrt) a region that has little or no plant life, long periods without rain, and extreme temperatures; usually found in hot climates

chaparral (SHAP uh RAL) a type of vegetation that includes broad-leaved evergreen shrubs and that is located in areas with hot, dry summers and mild, wet winters

6.5.c Students know populations of organisms can be categorized by the functions they serve in an ecosystem.
6.5.d Students know different kinds of organisms may play similar ecological roles in similar biomes.
6.5.e Students know the number and types of organisms an ecosystem can support depends on the resources available and on abiotic factors, such as quantities of light and water, a range of temperatures, and soil composition.

Prairie

- Average Yearly Rainfall
  25 to 75 cm (10 to 29.5 in.)
- Average Temperatures
  Summer: 30°C (86°F)
  Winter: 0°C (32°F)

Figure 3 *Bison are herbivores that once roamed North American prairies in great herds.*

Local Ecosystems

With a family member, explore the ecosystems around your home. What kinds of plants and animals live in your area? In your **Science Journal**, write a paragraph describing the plants and animals in the ecosystems near your home.

Figure 4 *In the African savanna, lions and leopards hunt zebras and wildebeests.*

Grasslands

A **grassland** is a biome in which the vegetation is mainly grasses, small flowering plants, and few trees. Grasslands are found on every continent except Antarctica. Grasslands can be divided into two main groups: temperate grasslands, such as prairies, and tropical grasslands, such as savannas.

Prairies

In temperate grasslands, such as prairies, the summers are warm, and the winters are very cold. Prairie soils are rich in nutrients because of thousands of years of decomposition. Fires, drought, and grazing prevent the growth of trees and shrubs. Prairies support small seed-eating animals, including prairie dogs and mice. Prairie dogs and mice use camouflage and burrows to hide from predators, such as the coyote. Large herbivores, such as the North American bison, shown in **Figure 3,** also live in prairies.

Savannas

A tropical grassland that has seasonal rains and scattered clumps of trees is called a *savanna*. Savannas are found in Africa, India, and South America. During the dry season, savanna grasses dry out and turn yellow. But the grasses' roots survive for many months without water. The African savanna is home to many large herbivores, such as elephants, giraffes, zebras, and wildebeests. Lions and leopards prey on these herbivores. Scavengers, such as hyenas, will eat anything that predators leave uneaten. Some of these animals are shown in **Figure 4.**

Standards Check Name an animal from the savanna that plays the same ecological role as the North American bison. 6.5.c, 6.5.d

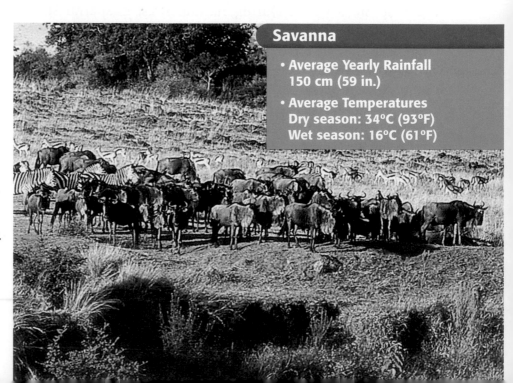

Savanna

- Average Yearly Rainfall
  150 cm (59 in.)
- Average Temperatures
  Dry season: 34°C (93°F)
  Wet season: 16°C (61°F)

Tundra
- **Average Yearly Rainfall**
  30 to 50 cm (12 to 20 in.)
- **Average Temperatures**
  Summer: 12°C (54°F)
  Winter: −26°C (−15°F)

Figure 5 *During winters in the tundra, caribou migrate to grazing grounds that have a more plentiful supply of food.*

Tundra

Imagine a place on Earth that is too cold for trees to grow. A **tundra** is a biome that has very cold temperatures and little rainfall. Tundras can be found near the North and South Poles. In a tundra, the layer of soil beneath the surface soil stays frozen year-round. This layer is called *permafrost*. Permafrost is made up of gravel and some finer materials.

During the short, cool summers, only the surface soil thaws. The surface soil is too shallow for deep-rooted plants to live. So, shallow-rooted plants, such as grasses and small shrubs, are common. Mosses and lichens (LIE kuhnz) grow beneath these plants. These plants, mosses, and lichens grow in clumps and low to the ground to resist the winds and the cold.

Animals of the tundra also have adaptations for living in this biome. Some animals, such as bears, hibernate in the winter, when food is hard to find, and the cold weather is harsh. Other animals, such as the caribou shown in **Figure 5,** migrate over large distances to find food. Many animals in the tundra also have extra layers of fat to keep them warm through the winter. During summer, the soil above the permafrost becomes muddy from melting ice and snow. Insects, such as mosquitoes, lay eggs in the mud. Birds that prey on these insects are carnivores. Other carnivores, such as wolves, prey on herbivores, including musk oxen and caribou.

grassland (GRAS LAND) a region that is dominated by grasses, that has few woody shrubs and trees, that has fertile soils, and that receives moderate amounts of seasonal rainfall

tundra (TUHN druh) a treeless plain found in the Arctic, in the Antarctic, or on the tops of mountains that is characterized by very low winter temperatures and short, cool summers

Standards Check How are the ecological roles of a lion in a savanna and a wolf in a tundra similar? 6.5.c, 6.5.d

Coniferous Forest

- **Average Yearly Rainfall**
  35 to 75 cm (14 to 29.5 in.)
- **Average Temperatures**
  Summer: 14°C (57°F)
  Winter: −10°C (14°F)

These conifer leaves are adapted to conserve water.

A coniferous forest is home to many insects and to birds that eat those insects.

Herbivores that live in the coniferous forest include deer, moose, porcupines, and squirrels.

Figure 6 *Many animals that live in a coniferous forest survive the harsh winters by hibernating or migrating to a warmer climate for the winter.*

Forests

Forest biomes receive plenty of rain, and the temperatures are not extreme. As in every biome, the kind of forest biome that develops depends on the climate of the biome. Three forest biomes are coniferous (koh NIF uhr uhs) forests, temperate deciduous (dee SIJ oo uhs) forests, and tropical rain forests.

Coniferous Forests

Most of the trees in a coniferous forest are called *conifers.* Conifers produce seeds in cones. Conifers also have special needle-shaped leaves covered in a thick, waxy coating. These characteristics prevent water loss and protect the needles from cold damage. Most conifers are evergreens because they keep many of their leaves year-round. Because decomposition is slow, the ground beneath large conifers is often covered by a thick layer of needles. Also, very little light reaches the ground, so few large plants grow beneath conifers.

Figure 6 shows a coniferous forest and some of the animals that live there. Squirrels and insects live in coniferous forests. Birds, such as finches, chickadees, and jays, are also common in these forests. Like squirrels, these birds are omnivores because they eat plants, seeds, and insects. Herbivores, such as porcupines, elk, and moose, also live in coniferous forests.

Temperate Deciduous Forests

Have you seen leaves change color in the fall? Have you seen trees lose all of their leaves? If so, you have seen deciduous trees, such as oaks and maples. The word *deciduous* comes from a Latin word that means "to fall off." Some deciduous trees shed their leaves to save water during the winter or during the dry season. Other deciduous trees shed their leaves because the leaves are damaged by the cold. Leaves and other materials decompose on the forest floor and keep the soil fertile. Fertile soils and the sunlight that reaches the forest floor allow for the growth of small trees and shrubs.

Animals use different layers of the forest. For example, black bears and rabbits live on the forest floor. Black bears are omnivores that eat nuts, berries, and animals, such as rabbits. Rabbits are herbivores that feed on plants. Squirrels feed on nuts. Squirrels move between the forest floor and the tree tops or *forest canopy*. Birds, such as woodpeckers, nest in the canopy. Woodpeckers that feed on only insects are carnivores. **Figure 7** shows some of the animals that live in this biome.

Standards Check Why can more plants grow on the floors of deciduous forests than on the floors of coniferous forests? 6.5.e

Hibernation and Weight

Black bears enter a light hibernation during the coldest parts of the year. While in hibernation, black bears have lower body temperatures and heart rates. They are also inactive and must live off their store of fat. A black bear weighs 92 kgs before hibernation. After hibernation, the bear is 30% lighter. Calculate the bear's new weight. Record your work in your **Science Journal.**

Figure 7 *In a temperate deciduous forest, mammals, birds, and reptiles thrive on the many leaves, seeds, nuts, and insects.*

In forests, plant growth happens in layers. The leafy tops of the trees reach high above the forest floor, where the leaves can get sunlight.

Woody shrubs catch the light that filters through the trees.

Ferns and mosses are scattered across the forest floor. Flowering plants often bloom in early spring, before the trees grow new leaves.

Temperate Deciduous Forest

• Average Yearly Rainfall
75 to 125 cm (29.5 to 49 in.)

• Average Temperatures
Summer: 28°C (82°F)
Winter: 6°C (43°F)

589

Tropical Rain Forests

Tropical rain forest biomes are the most diverse places on Earth. This means that tropical rain forest biomes have more kinds of plants and animals than any other biome does. Tropical rain forests have warm temperatures and receive a high amount of rainfall, which supports a high diversity of plants. In turn, the plants support a high diversity of animals. Many animals live on the forest floor, but most animals live in the canopy. Birds, such as the toucan shown in **Figure 8,** are omnivores that eat fruits, reptiles, and other birds. Carnivores, such as harpy eagles, eat other animals, such as howler monkeys. Howler monkeys are primarily herbivores that eat fruits, nuts, and leaves. However, howler monkeys may also eat the maggots found in fruits.

You may think that because of its diversity, the rain forest has nutrient-rich soil. However, most of the nutrients in the tropical rain forest are in the plants. The soil is actually very nutrient poor and thin. Because the soil is so thin, many trees grow above-ground roots for extra support.

Standards Check Identify a consumer found in a tropical rain forest.
🐻 **6.5.c, 6.5.d**

Figure 8 *Tropical rain forests have a greater diversity of organisms than any other biome does.*

Trees form a continuous green roof, or canopy, that may extend 60 m above the forest floor.

Woody vines climb the tree trunks to reach sunlight.

Little light reaches the ground. Low-growing plants in the rain forest don't need a lot of light.

Tropical Rain Forest

• **Average Yearly Rainfall** up to 400 cm (157.5 in.)

• **Average Temperatures** Daytime: 34°C (93°F) Nighttime: 20°C (68°F)

Summary

- A biome is characterized by a unique plant community. The plants, in turn, support unique animal communities.

- Plants and animals in a biome are adapted to the climate of the biome.

- Each organism in a biome can be categorized into the ecological role of a producer, a consumer, or a decomposer.

- Deserts are very dry and often very hot. Deserts support plants and animals that use little water.

- Chaparral biomes are fairly dry biomes that support dense patches of shrubs and trees. Animals in the chaparral blend into their surroundings to avoid predators.

- Tundras are cold areas that have permafrost and receive very little rainfall. Tundras support low-growing plants and few animals.

- Grasslands are areas where grasses are the main plants. Prairies have hot summers and cold winters. Savannas have wet and dry seasons.

- Three forest biomes are temperate deciduous forests, coniferous forests, and tropical rain forests.

Using Vocabulary

1 Use *chaparral* and *tundra* in separate sentences.

2 Write an original definition for *grasslands* and *desert*.

Understanding Concepts

3 **Describing** What are the major land biomes discussed in this section? What characteristics do all biomes share?

4 **Identifying** How are organisms categorized in land biomes? Give an example of each category.

5 **Applying** What is the ecological role of a leopard in the savanna and of a harpy eagle in the rain forest?

INTERPRETING GRAPHICS Use the bar graph below to answer the next two questions.

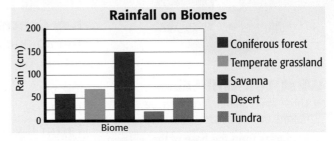

Rainfall on Biomes

6 **Identifying** Which biomes receive 50 cm or more of rain each year?

7 **Identifying** Which biome receives the smallest amount of rain? Which receives the largest amount of rain?

Critical Thinking

8 **Making Inferences** While excavating an area in the desert, a scientist discovers the fossils of very large trees and ferns. What might the scientist conclude about biomes in this area?

9 **Analyzing Ideas** Tundra receives very little rainfall. Could a tundra accurately be called a frozen desert? Explain your answer.

10 **Identifying Relationships** You are looking after a friend's plant. The plant needs a warm environment, lots of water, and very little sunlight. To which biome do you think the plant would be best adapted? Explain your answer.

Challenge

11 **Making Inferences** You are studying an area in which the temperatures are usually moderate. However, extreme temperatures occur on one or two days of the year. Which organisms would survive better in this area: organisms that are adapted to moderate temperatures or those that can tolerate extreme temperatures? Explain.

Internet Resources

For a variety of links related to this chapter, go to www.scilinks.org

Topic: Forests; Wildfires in California
SciLinks code: HY70609; HY7C12

Marine Ecosystems

Key Concept Organisms in marine ecosystems depend on the abiotic factors and biotic factors in their environment.

READING STRATEGY

Outlining In your **Science Journal,** create an outline of the section. Use the headings from the section in your outline.

▶ What covers almost three-fourths of Earth's surface? What holds the largest animals and some of the smallest organisms on Earth? If your answer to both questions is *oceans,* you are correct! Earth's oceans contain many kinds of ecosystems. Scientists call ecosystems in the ocean *marine ecosystems.*

Depth and Sunlight

Marine ecosystems are shaped by abiotic factors. Two of these factors are water depth and the amount of sunlight that passes through water. The average depth of the oceans is 4,000 m, but sunlight does not reach deeper than 200 m. Therefore, producers that perform photosynthesis, such as algae and phytoplankton, can survive only above 200 m. **Phytoplankton** are tiny producers that float near the surface of the ocean. Algae and phytoplankton form the base of most of the ocean's food chains. Tiny producers and large consumers can be found near the surface of the oceans, as shown in **Figure 1.**

Standards Check Why are phytoplankton important to marine ecosystems? 🐻 **6.5.a, 6.5.c**

phytoplankton
(FIET oh PLANGK tuhn) the microscopic, photosynthetic organisms that float near the surface of marine or fresh water
Wordwise The prefix *phyto-* means "plant."

Figure 1 *Marine ecosystems support a broad diversity of life. Large humpback whales and tiny phytoplankton live in the oceans.*

Temperature

A third abiotic factor in marine ecosystems is the temperature of the water. Ocean water becomes colder as it becomes deeper. However, the temperature change is not gradual, as **Figure 2** shows. Because the water in the surface zone is heated by the sun, it is much warmer than the rest of the ocean. Temperatures in the surface zone vary with latitude. Areas of the ocean along the equator are warmer than areas closer to the poles. Surface-zone temperatures also vary with season.

Water temperature affects the animals that live in marine ecosystems. For example, fishes that live near the poles have a special chemical in their blood to prevent them from freezing. In contrast, animals that live in coral reefs need warm water to live. Most marine organisms live in the warm waters of the surface zone. Some animals, such as whales, migrate from cold areas near the poles to warm areas near the equator to reproduce. Water temperature also affects whether some animals, such as barnacles, can eat. If the water is too hot or too cold, these animals may not be able to eat. A sudden change in temperature may cause these animals to die.

Standards Check Give an example of how temperature affects marine animals. 🐻 **6.5.e**

6.5.a Students know energy entering ecosystems as sunlight is transferred by producers into chemical energy through photosynthesis and then from organism to organism through food webs.
6.5.c Students know populations of organisms can be categorized by the functions they serve in an ecosystem.
6.5.e Students know the number and types of organisms an ecosystem can support depends on the resources available and on abiotic factors, such as quantities of light and water, a range of temperatures, and soil composition.

Figure 2 Ocean Temperature Zones

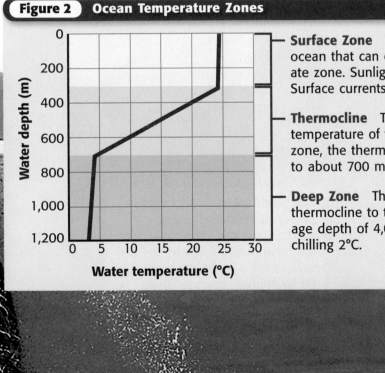

Surface Zone The surface zone is the warm, top layer of the ocean that can extend to 300 m below sea level in a temperate zone. Sunlight heats the top 100 m of the surface zone. Surface currents mix the warm water with cooler water below.

Thermocline The thermocline is a layer of water where the temperature of the sea water changes rapidly. In a temperate zone, the thermocline can extend from 300 m below sea level to about 700 m below sea level.

Deep Zone This bottom layer extends from the base of the thermocline to the ocean floor. The ocean floor is at an average depth of 4,000 m, where the temperature averages a chilling 2°C.

Major Zones in the Ocean

The ocean can be divided into zones based on distance from the shore, water depth, amount of sunlight in the zone, and water temperature. Organisms are adapted to the ocean zones, as shown in **Figure 3**.

The Intertidal Zone

The intertidal zone is the zone where the ocean meets the shore. This zone is exposed to air for part of the day and also to waves. Organisms of this zone are adapted to survive exposure to air and to keep from being washed away by waves.

The Neritic Zone

The neritic zone (nee RIT ik ZOHN), is farther from shore. In this zone, the water becomes deeper as the ocean floor starts to slope downward. The water is warmer than deeper ocean waters and receives a lot of sunlight. Therefore, corals and producers thrive in this zone. Consumers in this zone include sea urchins, some fishes, and sea turtles that eat algae.

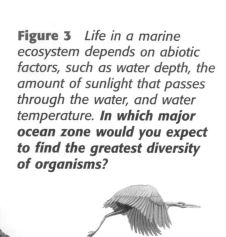

Figure 3 *Life in a marine ecosystem depends on abiotic factors, such as water depth, the amount of sunlight that passes through the water, and water temperature.* **In which major ocean zone would you expect to find the greatest diversity of organisms?**

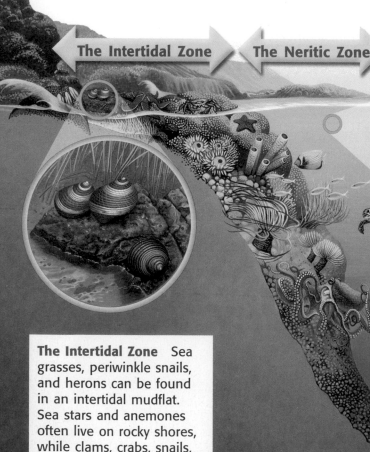

The Intertidal Zone | **The Neritic Zone**

The Intertidal Zone Sea grasses, periwinkle snails, and herons can be found in an intertidal mudflat. Sea stars and anemones often live on rocky shores, while clams, crabs, snails, and conchs are common on sandy beaches.

The Neritic Zone Although phytoplankton are the major producers in this zone, seaweeds are common, too. Sea turtles and dolphins live in the neritic zone. Other animals, such as corals, sponges, and colorful fishes, contribute to this vivid seascape.

The Oceanic Zone

In the oceanic zone, the sea floor drops sharply. This zone extends from the surface to the deep waters of the open ocean. Phytoplankton live near the surface, where there is sunlight. Consumers such as fishes, whales, and sharks live in this zone. Some of these animals live deep in the oceanic zone, where the sunlight does not reach. These animals feed on each other and on material that sinks from the surface waters.

Standards Check What do animals deep in the oceanic zone rely on for food? 6.5.e

The Abyssal Zone

The abyssal zone is the ocean floor. The abyssal zone does not get any sunlight. This zone is also very cold. Fishes, worms, and crabs have special adaptations for living in this zone. Many of these consumers feed on material that sinks from above. Some organisms, such as the angler fish, eat smaller fishes. Other organisms, such as bacteria, are decomposers and help break down dead organisms.

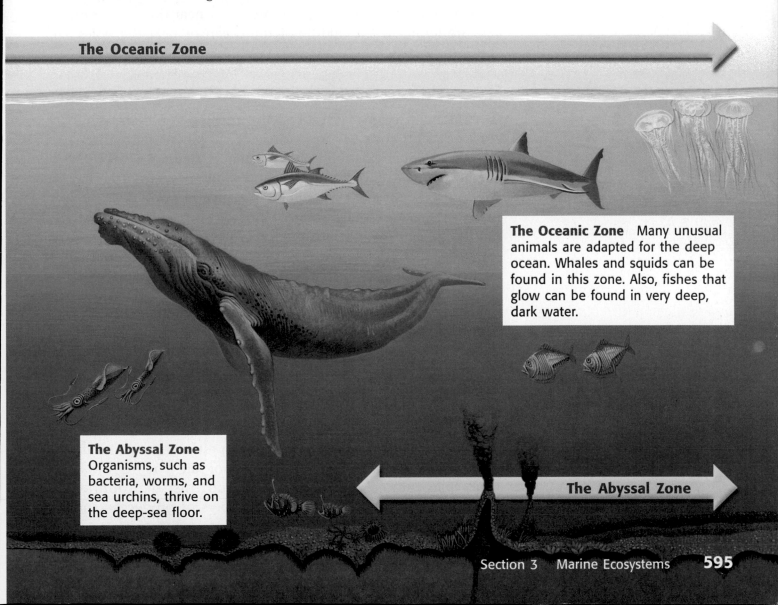

The Oceanic Zone

The Oceanic Zone Many unusual animals are adapted for the deep ocean. Whales and squids can be found in this zone. Also, fishes that glow can be found in very deep, dark water.

The Abyssal Zone Organisms, such as bacteria, worms, and sea urchins, thrive on the deep-sea floor.

The Abyssal Zone

Figure 4 *Organisms such as sea anemones and sea stars attach themselves to rocks and reefs. These organisms must be able to survive both wet and dry conditions.*

Kinds of Marine Ecosystems

Life on Earth depends on the ocean. Through evaporation, the ocean provides most of the water that makes up Earth's precipitation. Ocean temperatures and currents affect world climates and wind patterns. Humans and many animals depend on the ocean for food and water.

There are many ecosystems in the different zones of the ocean. Some marine ecosystems are on or near the shore. Others are found in the middle of the ocean or near the poles.

Standards Check How do the oceans affect life on Earth? 6.5.e

Intertidal Ecosystems

Different intertidal ecosystems include mudflats, sandy beaches, and rocky shores. Intertidal organisms are able to live both underwater and out of water as **Figure 4** shows. The organisms that live in mudflats and sandy beaches often burrow into the ground. Consumers that live in these areas such as worms, clams, and crabs are eaten by shorebirds. On rocky shores, organisms have adaptations to keep from being swept away by crashing waves. For example, seaweeds use rootlike structures called *holdfasts* to attach themselves to rocks. Other organisms, such as barnacles, attach themselves to rocks with a special cement. Sea stars feed on these organisms.

Estuaries

estuary (ES tyoo er ee) an area where fresh water mixes with salt water from the ocean

An area where salt water from the ocean flows into the mouth of a stream or river is called an **estuary**. In estuaries, the salt water from the ocean and the fresh water from rivers and are always mixing. Therefore, the amount of salt in the water is always changing. Organisms that live in estuaries must be able to survive the changing concentrations of salt. The fresh water that spills into an estuary is rich in nutrients. High nutrient levels in the water support large numbers of producers, such as algae. The algae, in turn, support many consumers.

Coral Reefs

Coral reefs are named for *corals,* the animals that form these reefs. Most corals are made up of many individuals living in a group or colony. Living in the tissues of many of these corals are algae. Both the coral and the algae receive benefits from the mutualistic relationship that they have.

Most coral reefs are found in warm, shallow areas of the neritic zone. The structure of a coral reef is mainly based on the skeletons of *stony corals.* The skeleton of a stony coral is made of calcium carbonate. When stony corals die, their hard skeletons remain. New corals grow on these remains. Over time, layers of skeletons build up and form a reef. This reef provides a home for many marine animals and algae as **Figure 5** shows. These organisms include fishes, sponges, sea stars, and sea urchins.

Figure 5 *A coral reef is one of the most biologically diverse ecosystems on Earth.*

Kelp Forests

Kelp forests are found in cold, shallow areas of the neritic zone. Kelp are large brown algae that grow well in nutrient-rich areas, such as areas along the coast of California. Kelp are attached to the ocean floor by holdfasts. Some kelp can grow up to 60 cm per day and can be more than 33 m long. Their tops can be seen floating on the surface of the ocean. Many organisms, such as sea otters, fishes, crabs, and sea urchins, are found in kelp forests. Sea urchins are primary consumers that eat the algae growing on rocks. Sea otters are secondary consumers that eat many organisms, including sea urchins. Sometimes, sea otters wrap themselves in kelp to stay afloat while they take a nap.

Standards Check Explain why sea otters are called *secondary consumers.* 6.5.c

Figure 6 *These vent worms use the food made by the large populations of bacteria that live in their bodies.*

Deep-Sea Hydrothermal Vents

Deep-sea hydrothermal vents are found in the abyssal zone. These vents release water with temperatures as hot as 360°C and toxic chemicals. **Figure 6** shows some of the different kinds of organisms, such as worms and crabs, that live near these vents. Vent worms are unusual because bacteria live in their bodies. These bacteria make their own food from the chemicals released from the vents. The extra food that the bacteria make is transferred to the worm. These bacteria are considered to be producers because they can make their own food. This mutualistic relationship between the bacteria and the vent worms is similar to the relationship between some algae and corals.

The Sargasso Sea

An ecosystem called the *Sargasso Sea* (sahr GAS oh SEE) is found only in the middle of the Atlantic Ocean. Floating rafts of algae called *sargassums* (sahr GAS uhmz) make up the base of this ecosystem. Sargassums float because parts of these algae are filled with air. Many animals live in this ecosystem. Most of these animals are omnivores and can eat many kinds of organisms throughout the year. Some of these animals, such as the sargasso fish seen in **Figure 7,** are the same color as sargassums. Its color helps the sargasso fish hide from its predators.

Polar Ice

The Arctic Ocean and the ocean around Antarctica make up another kind of marine ecosystem. These icy waters are rich in nutrients and support large numbers of phytoplankton. In turn, these plankton support other organisms, such as fishes and krill. Krill are tiny shrimplike organisms that some whales rely on for food. Seals feed on fishes that eat krill and are, in turn, eaten by polar bears.

Standards Check Name one abiotic factor that helps support large numbers of phytoplankton in the Arctic Ocean. 6.5.e

Figure 7 *This sargasso fish is adapted to living in the algae. Its color and shape help the fish hide from predators.*

Quick Lab

6.5.c

How to Categorize Organisms

Organisms can be categorized by the ecological role they serve in an ecosystem. Try this activity to identify the roles of some organisms.

▶ Try It!

1. Divide a **large, blank piece of paper** into three horizontal rows. Label the bottom row "Producer." Label the middle row "Primary consumer." Label the top row "Secondary consumer."

2. Obtain a stack of **flashcards** from your teacher. Categorize the flashcards into two groups: producers that make their own food and consumers that eat other organisms to obtain the energy they need.

3. Then, place all of the producers in the bottom row.

4. Consumers that eat producers are the primary consumers. Place the primary consumers in the second row, directly above the producers that they consume.

5. Secondary consumers prey on primary consumers. Place the secondary consumers in the top row, directly above their prey.

▶ Think About It!

6. Do you seen any patterns among producers? Do you seen any patterns among consumers?

7. What is transferred between the organisms as one organism eats another?

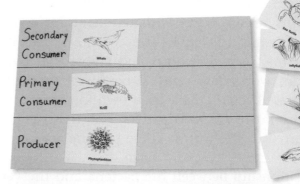

 15 min

Summary

- Abiotic factors that affect marine ecosystems are water temperature, water depth, and the amount of light that passes through the water.

- Producers convert solar energy or chemicals from the environment into food, or a form of chemical energy that can be used by organisms.

- Phytoplankton and algae form the base of most of the ocean's food chains. Bacteria that make food from only the chemicals in their environment also form the base of some food chains in the ocean.

- Four ocean zones are the intertidal zone, the neritic zone, the oceanic zone, and the abyssal zone.

- Intertidal ecosystems, coral reefs, estuaries, kelp forests, deep-sea vents, the Sargasso Sea, and polar ice are some marine ecosystems. These ecosystems have unique abiotic factors that support unique communities of organisms with different ecological roles.

Understanding Concepts

1 **Identifying** What are three abiotic factors that affect marine ecosystems?

2 **Comparing** Describe four major ocean zones. How do they differ from each other?

3 **Describing** Describe a marine ecosystem. Make sure to include the organisms that live there, what they consume, and their ecological role in the ecosystem.

Critical Thinking

4 **Evaluating Hypotheses** Are bacteria that live in deep sea vent worms, and phytoplankton that live in the ocean, producers? Explain.

5 **Identifying Relationships** Many fishes and other organisms that live in the deep ocean produce light. What are two ways in which this light may be useful?

6 **Applying Concepts** Imagine that you are studying animals that live in intertidal zones. You just discovered a new animal. Describe the animal and the adaptations the animal has for living in the intertidal zone.

INTERPRETING GRAPHICS Use the line graph below to answer the next two questions.

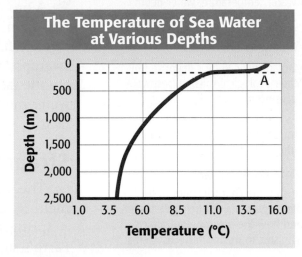

The Temperature of Sea Water at Various Depths

7 **Applying Concepts** In which ocean zone does the dotted line occur? What does it represent?

8 **Analyzing Relationships** According to this graph, at what depth would a fish need a chemical to prevent its blood from freezing?

Math Skills

9 **Making Calculations** The ocean covers about 71% of Earth's surface. If the total surface area of Earth is about 510 million square kilometers, how many square kilometers are covered by the ocean?

Challenge

10 **Making Inferences** Animals in the Sargasso Sea hide from predators by blending in with the sargassum. Other than color, how can animals blend in with sargassum?

Internet Resources

For a variety of links related to this chapter, go to www.scilinks.org

Topic: Marine Ecosystems; California's Coasts

SciLinks code: HY70911; HY7C07

Freshwater Ecosystems

Key Concept Organisms in freshwater ecosystems depend on the abiotic and biotic factors in their environment.

What You Will Learn

● Water temperature, water depth, and nutrients are some abiotic factors that affect organisms in freshwater ecosystems.

● Organisms can be categorized by their ecological roles in freshwater ecosystems.

● As a pond or lake becomes a forest, it supports different kinds of organisms.

Why It Matters

Studying the characteristics of fresh water organisms will help you understand how the environment affects organisms in freshwater ecosystems.

Vocabulary

• littoral zone   • wetland
• open-water zone   • marsh
• deep-water zone   • swamp

READING STRATEGY

Graphic Organizer In your **Science Journal,** create a Venn Diagram that compares various characteristics of wetland ecosystems.

▶ A brook bubbles over rocks. A mighty river thunders through a canyon. A calm swamp echoes with the sounds of frogs and birds. What do these places have in common? Brooks, rivers, and swamps are examples of freshwater ecosystems. An important abiotic factor that affects freshwater ecosystems is how quickly water moves. Freshwater ecosystems are also affected by abiotic factors, such as water temperature, water depth, and nutrients.

Stream and River Ecosystems

The water in brooks, streams, and rivers may flow from melting ice or snow. Or the water may come from a spring. A spring is a place where water flows from underground to Earth's surface. Each stream of water that joins a larger stream is called a *tributary* (TRIB yoo TER ee). As more tributaries join a stream, the stream contains more water. The stream becomes stronger and wider. A very strong, wide stream is called a *river*. **Figure 1** shows how a river develops.

Stream and river ecosystems are full of life. Plants typically line the edges of streams and rivers. Fishes live in the open waters. Clams and snails live in the mud at the bottom of a stream or river.

Organisms that live in fast-moving water have adaptations to keep from being washed away. Some producers, such as algae and moss, are attached to rocks. Consumers such as tadpoles use suction disks to hold themselves to rocks. Other consumers, such as insects, live under rocks.

Figure 1 *Rivers become larger as more tributaries flow into them.*

6.5.c Students know populations of organisms can be categorized by the functions they serve in an ecosystem.
6.5.e Students know the number and types of organisms an ecosystem can support depends on the resources available and on abiotic factors, such as quantities of light and water, a range of temperatures, and soil composition.

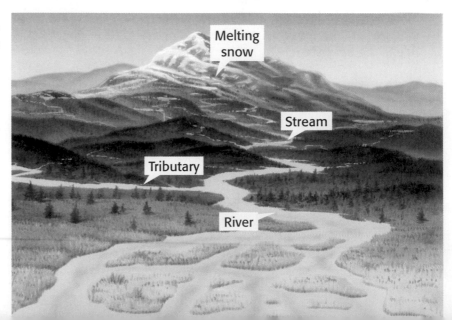

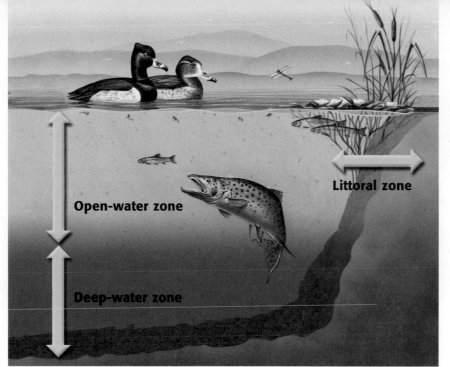

Open-water zone

Littoral zone

Deep-water zone

Figure 2 *Ponds and lakes can be divided into three zones. Each zone has different organisms and abiotic factors.*

Pond and Lake Ecosystems

Ponds and lakes have different ecosystems than streams and rivers do. **Figure 2** shows the zones of a typical lake.

Life near Shore

The area of water closest to the edge of a lake or pond is called the **littoral zone.** Sunlight reaches the bottom of the littoral zone. This sunlight allows producers, such as algae, to grow in this zone. Plants such as cattails and rushes, grow near the shore. Floating plants, such as water lilies, grow farther from the shore. The plants and algae of the littoral zone are eaten by many animals. These plants are also home to consumers, such as snails and insects. Consumers that live in the mud include clams and worms. Consumers such as fishes and snakes also live in this zone.

Life Away from Shore

The area of a lake or pond that extends from the littoral zone across the top of the water is called the **open-water zone.** The open-water zone is as deep as sunlight can reach. So, producers such as photosynthetic plankton grow well here. This zone is also home to bass, lake trout, and other consumers. Beneath the open-water zone is the **deep-water zone,** where no sunlight reaches. So, photosynthetic organisms cannot grow in this zone. Scavengers such as catfish and crabs live here and feed on dead organisms that sink from above. Decomposers, such as fungi and bacteria, also help break down dead organisms.

Standards Check Name a producer and a consumer that typically live in lake ecosystems. 🐻 6.5.c

littoral zone (LIT uh ruhl ZOHN) the shallow zone of a lake or pond where light reaches the bottom and nurtures plants

open-water zone (OH puhn WAWT uhr ZOHN) the zone of a pond or lake that extends from the littoral zone and that is only as deep as light can reach

deep-water zone (DEEP WAWT uhr ZOHN) the zone of a lake or pond below the open-water zone, where no light reaches

Wetland Ecosystems

An area of land that is sometimes underwater or whose soil contains a great deal of moisture is called a **wetland.** Wetlands support many kinds of plants and animals. Wetlands also play an important role in flood control. During heavy rains or spring snowmelts, wetlands soak up large amounts of water. The water in wetlands also moves deeper into the ground. So, wetlands help replenish underground water supplies.

Marshes

A treeless wetland ecosystem where producers such as grasses grow is called a **marsh.** A freshwater marsh is shown in **Figure 3.** Freshwater marshes are often found in shallow areas along the shores of lakes, ponds, rivers, and streams. The plants in a marsh vary depending on the depth of the water and the location of the marsh. Grasses, reeds, bulrushes, and wild rice are common marsh plants. Consumers, such as muskrats, turtles, frogs, and birds, also live in marshes.

Swamps

A wetland ecosystem in which producers such as trees and vines grow is called a **swamp.** Swamps, like the one shown in **Figure 4,** are found in low-lying areas and beside slow-moving rivers. Most swamps are flooded for part of the year, depending on rainfall. Willows, baldcypresses, and oaks are common swamp trees. Vines, such as poison ivy, grow up tree trunks. Plants, such as orchids, may hang from tree branches. Water lilies and other plants grow in standing water. Plants that grow in standing water are adapted to growing in waters with low oxygen levels. Many consumers, such as fishes, snakes, and birds, also live in swamps.

Figure 3 *This painted turtle suns itself on a log in a freshwater marsh.*

wetland (WET LAND) an area of land that is periodically underwater or whose soil contains a great deal of moisture

marsh (MAHRSH) a treeless wetland ecosystem where plants such as grasses grow

swamp (SWAHMP) a wetland ecosystem in which shrubs and trees grow

Figure 4 *The trunks of these trees are adapted to give the trees more support in the wet, soft soil of a swamp.*

How Ecosystems Can Change

Did you know that a lake or pond can disappear? Water entering a standing body of water usually carries nutrients and sediment. These materials settle to the bottom of the pond or lake. Dead leaves from overhanging trees and decaying plant and animal life also settle to the bottom. Then, bacteria decompose this material. This process uses oxygen, an abiotic factor. Decreasing levels of oxygen can affect the kinds of animals that can survive in the pond or lake. For example, many fishes would not be able to survive with less oxygen in the water.

Over time, the pond or lake is filled with sediment. New kinds of plants grow in the new soil. Shallow areas fill in first. So, plants slowly grow closer and closer to the center of the pond or lake. What is left of the lake or pond becomes a wetland. As the soils dry out and the oxygen levels increase, forest plants can grow. Forest plants will, in turn, support forest animals. In this way, a pond or lake can become a forest.

Standards Check How might the decomposition of dead plant and animal life in a pond affect the fish that live there? 6.5.e

INTERNET ACTIVITY

Earth Biome Brochure

How do you choose where you would like to live? Create a brochure to help plants, animals, and people find the best place to live. Go to **go.hrw.com,** and type in the keyword HY7ECOW.

SECTION Review

6.5.c, 6.5.e

Summary

- Each kind of freshwater ecosystem supports different communities of organisms because each ecosystem has different abiotic factors.

- Organisms can be categorized as producers, consumers, and decomposers in freshwater ecosystems.

- Changes in abiotic factors, such as an increase in sediment and a decrease in oxygen, can cause lake organisms to die. Eventually, further changes can lead to the development of a forest.

Understanding Concepts

1. **Identifying** What are two producers and two consumers found in swamp ecosystems?

2. **Describing** Describe what happens as a lake becomes a forest.

3. **Analyzing** Why can't photosynthetic organisms grow in the deep-water zone of a lake?

Critical Thinking

4. **Making Inferences** A river is slowly drying up. What do you think will happen to the plants that grow on the edge of the river and the algae that grow on the rocks in the river? Explain.

5. **Applying Concepts** Imagine a steep, rocky stream. What kinds of adaptations might animals living in this stream have? What might happen to animals without these adaptations? Explain.

Math Skills

6. **Making Calculations** Sunlight can penetrate a certain lake to a depth of 15 m. The lake is 5.5 times as deep as the depth to which light can penetrate. In meters, how deep is the lake?

Challenge

7. **Making Inferences** Fungi and bacteria decompose material in many freshwater ecosystems. Would you expect to find any freshwater ecosystems that did not have decomposers? Explain.

Internet Resources

For a variety of links related to this chapter, go to www.scilinks.org
Topic: Freshwater Ecosystems; California's Freshwater
SciLinks code: HY70621; HY7C05

Inquiry Lab

Discovering Mini-Ecosystems

In your study of ecosystems, you learned that a biome is a very large region that is made up of many connected ecosystems. For example, a coniferous forest biome may include a river ecosystem, a wetland ecosystem, and a lake ecosystem. Each of those ecosystems may include several other smaller, related ecosystems. Even cities have mini-ecosystems! You may find a mini-ecosystem on a patch of sidewalk, in a puddle of rainwater, under a leaky faucet, in a shady area, or under a rock. In this activity, you will design a method for comparing two different mini-ecosystems found near your school.

OBJECTIVES

Observe two different mini-ecosystems.

Identify the different abiotic factors that characterize each mini-ecosystem.

Describe how organisms are adapted to the abiotic factors in each ecosystem.

MATERIALS

- items to be determined by the students and approved by the teacher

SAFETY

Ask a Question

1 Examine the grounds around your school, and select two different areas you wish to investigate. Write a question that you want to answer about your mini-ecosystems. For example, you may want to know what kinds of organisms live in each area or how many organisms there are in each area. Be sure to get your teacher's approval before you begin.

Form a Hypothesis

2 Now, turn your question into a hypothesis that you can test. For example, if you wanted to know how many different organisms were in each mini-ecosystem, you might form this hypothesis: "There are more different kinds of organisms in one mini-ecosystem than in the other."

6.5.b Students know matter is transferred over time from one organism to others in the food web and between organisms and the physical environment.

6.5.e Students know the number and types of organisms an ecosystem can support depends on the resources available and on abiotic factors, such as quantities of light and water, a range of temperatures, and soil composition.

Investigation and Experimentation
6.7.a Develop a hypothesis.
6.7.b Select and use appropriate tools and technology (including calculators, computers, balances, spring scales, microscopes, and binoculars) to perform tests, collect data, and display data.

Mini-Ecosystem A					
Date	Time	Temperature (°C)	Other abiotic factors	Animals and their adaptations	Plants and their adaptations
			DO NOT WRITE IN BOOK		

Test the Hypothesis

3 For each mini-ecosystem, make a data table to record your observations. An example of a data table is shown above. Recording abiotic factors in each mini-ecosystem may help explain your results. Each data table should be large enough for you to record three sets of observations.

4 Observe your mini-ecosystem for 15 min. Make sure to enter your observations accurately and thoroughly in your data table.

5 Wait 24 h, and then observe your mini-ecosystems again at the same time of day that you observed them the day before. Record your observations.

6 Wait 1 week, and then observe your mini-ecosystems again at the same time of day. Record your observations.

Analyze the Results

7 **Interpreting Information**   What are two differences between the mini-ecosystems? Identify the factors that set each mini-ecosystem apart from its surrounding area.

8 **Analyzing Results**   How do the populations of your mini-ecosystems compare? Which mini-ecosystem has more organisms? Does one mini-ecosystem have more different kinds of organisms than the other?

9 **Interpreting Information**   If you observed your mini-ecosystem more than once a day, did you notice any differences in your observations at different times of day? What reasons can you think of for these differences?

10 **Identifying Patterns**   Did you identify any abiotic factors that supported a kind of organism that was in one mini-ecosystem but not in the other?

11 **Identifying Patterns**   Identify some of the adaptations that the organisms living in your two mini-ecosystems have. Describe how the adaptations help the organisms survive in their environment.

Draw Conclusions

12 **Applying Conclusions**   Was your hypothesis correct? If your hypothesis was correct, how could this information be helpful if the school needed to build a new library in one of the two areas that you studied?

13 **Applying Conclusions**   Write a report that describes and compares your mini-ecosystems with those of your classmates.

Big Idea Question

14 **Identifying Patterns**   How did the abiotic factors in each mini-ecosystem support different kinds of organisms?

Science Skills Activity

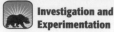

Investigation and Experimentation
6.7.e Recognize whether evidence is consistent with a proposed explanation.

Organizing and Analyzing Evidence

▶ Tutorial

After scientists make observations and collect data, they develop explanations based on all the evidence. In order to develop explanations, scientists must organize and analyze the evidence. Use the following instructions to organize observations and data from notes recorded at a field site.

Procedure

1 Read the field notes once to understand the main subject of the notes. Read the field notes a second time to identify different categories of information that are provided in the notes.

2 Create a table to organize the information. For example, if you identify four categories of information, create a table with four columns. A sample table is shown at right.

3 Label each column, and record information from the notes into the appropriate column.

Month:			
Temp. (°C)	Rainfall (cm)	Animals	Birds

4 As you record information into the table, cross out the corresponding information in the notes so that you can see your progress.

5 Once all of the notes have been organized, you can begin analyzing the evidence in the table to identify patterns.

▶ You Try It!

Procedure

The passage at right was taken from a scientist's field notes. Create a table to organize the scientist's observations and data. Then, analyze all of the evidence to determine which land biome the notes describe.

Analysis

1 **Identifying Patterns** What kind of biome is likely to have this combination of abiotic and biotic factors? Explain your reasoning.

2 **Evaluating Evidence** In which parts of the world would you find this kind of biome? Explain.

3 **Making Inferences** What would happen if the biome received decreasing amounts of rain?

4 **Evaluating Processes** What other ways could you represent the information in the notes from the field site?

Month: July

It has been quite hot again today. Temperatures have been about 32°C during the day and 20°C at night for the last month. It has also rained a lot every afternoon. Very little sunlight reaches us through the trees, so we have to be careful when we walk around. Every day, we continue to find new species of brightly colored animals, birds, insects, and plants. Many plants are actually growing in the tree branches and have roots growing downward. What an amazing place this is!

Chapter Summary

The Big Idea Biomes and ecosystems are characterized by their living and nonliving parts.

Section

Vocabulary

❶ Studying the Environment

Key Concept In every environment, organisms depend on each other and on the nonliving things in the environment to survive.

- Biomes are made up of many connected ecosystems.
- Abiotic factors affect the organisms in an environment.
- All biomes have producers, consumers, and decomposers.
- Similar biomes occur in similar climates.

❷ Land Biomes

Key Concept The kinds of plants and animals that live in a biome are determined by the local climate.

- Abiotic factors, such as soil, water, and climate, affect the organisms in land biomes.
- Organisms can be categorized by their role in an environment.
- Different kinds of organisms can have similar ecological roles in every biome.

desert p. 584
chaparral p. 585
grassland p. 586
tundra p. 587

❸ Marine Ecosystems

Key Concept Organisms in marine ecosystems depend on the abiotic factors and biotic factors in their environment.

- Three main abiotic factors shape marine ecosystems.
- Producers form the base of the ocean's food chains.
- There are four major ocean zones.
- Different marine ecosystems support different communities of organisms.

phytoplankton p. 592
estuary p. 596

❹ Freshwater Ecosystems

Key Concept Organisms in freshwater ecosystems depend on the abiotic and biotic factors in their environment.

- Water temperature, water depth, and nutrients are some abiotic factors that affect organisms in freshwater ecosystems.
- Organisms can be categorized by their ecological roles in freshwater ecosystems.
- As a pond or lake becomes a forest, it supports different kinds of organisms.

littoral zone p. 601
open-water zone p. 601
deep-water zone p. 601
wetland p. 602
marsh p. 602
swamp p. 602

Chapter Review

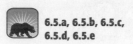

6.5.a, 6.5.b, 6.5.c,
6.5.d, 6.5.e

Organize

Three-Panel Flip Chart   Review the FoldNote that you created at the beginning of the chapter. Add to or correct the FoldNote based on what you have learned.

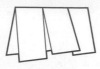

Using Vocabulary

1 **Academic Vocabulary**   In the sentence "Organisms can be categorized according to their roles in an ecosystem," what does the word *categorized* mean?
  a. grouped   **c.** collected
  b. separated   **d.** derived

For each pair of terms, explain how the meanings of the terms differ.

2 *savanna* and *biome*

3 *open-water zone* and *deep-water zone*

Understanding Concepts

Multiple Choice

4 Which of the following organisms has the same ecological role as lions in the savanna?
  a. algae in the ocean
  b. coyotes in the chaparral
  c. grasshoppers in the prairie
  d. none of the above

5 In which major ocean zone are algae and animals exposed to air for part of the day?
  a. intertidal zone
  b. neritic zone
  c. oceanic zone
  d. benthic zone

6 An abiotic factor in marine ecosystems is
  a. the temperature of the water.
  b. the depth of the water.
  c. the amount of sunlight that passes through the water.
  d. All of the above

7 Which of the following statements about organisms and their ecosystems is true?
  a. Organisms are adapted to the ecosystems in which they live.
  b. The abiotic factors in an environment are determined only by the local organisms.
  c. Similar organisms play different roles in different ecosystems.
  d. All organisms will thrive in any ecosystem.

Short Answer

8 **Identifying**   In which category do organisms that break down dead organisms belong? Where can you find these organisms?

9 **Comparing**   How do producers differ from consumers?

10 **Describing**   Explain how a small lake can eventually become a forest.

11 **Describing**   Describe three zones in the ocean.

12 **Listing**   What are three abiotic factors in land biomes? three abiotic factors in marine ecosystems? an abiotic factor in freshwater ecosystems?

13 **Describing**   How do rivers form?

Writing Skills

14 **Communicating Concepts**   A scientist has a new hypothesis. The scientist thinks that savannas and deserts are part of one biome rather than two separate biomes. Using what you've learned, decide if the scientist's hypothesis is correct. Write your answer in a short essay that explains your opinion.

Critical Thinking

15 **Concept Mapping**   Use the following terms to create a concept map: *plants and animals, tropical rain forest, tundra, biomes, permafrost, canopy, desert,* and *climate.*

16 Making Inferences Phytoplankton use photosynthesis to make chemical energy. They need sunlight for photosynthesis. Which of the four major ocean zones can support phytoplankton growth? Explain.

17 Applying Concepts Imagine that you are a scientist. You are studying an area that gets about 100 cm of rain each year. The average summer temperatures are near 30°C. What biome are you in? What plants and animals are likely to live in this area? If you stayed in this area for the winter, what kinds of preparations might you need to make?

18 Making Inferences A cactus is adapted to living in areas with very little water. Joe wants to plant his cactus in a thick, nutrient-rich soil that holds a lot of water. What will happen to the cactus? Explain your answer.

19 Making Inferences In which category do plants belong? Explain why they are categorized in this group.

20 Making Inferences What information would you have to collect in order to assign an ecological role to a newly discovered organism?

INTERPRETING GRAPHICS Use the image below to answer the next three questions.

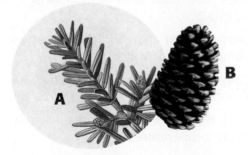

21 Identifying Relationships How does the shape of the leaf in A help the plant survive the abiotic factors in its environment?

22 Making Inferences What kinds of plants have the structures shown in A and B?

23 Applying Concepts Would you expect to find the plants represented in A and B in a desert? Explain why or why not.

INTERPRETING GRAPHICS Use the graph below to answer the next three questions.

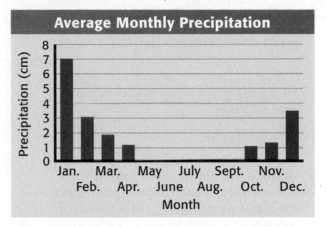

24 Analyzing Data How many centimeters of rain fell in the region during the year?

25 Analyzing Data Which are the five driest months of the year?

26 Making Inferences Name one adaptation that plants in this biome might have.

Math Skills

27 Making Calculations Some desert reptiles hunt for food only at sunrise and sunset. A lizard may need to be in the sun for 20 min after a cold night before it can be active. In a desert where the sun rises between 5:00 A.M. and 6:00 A.M. and sets between 7:30 P.M. and 8:15 P.M., how many hours of the day can the lizard use to hunt?

Challenge

28 Identifying Patterns Algae on coral-reef ecosystems convert solar energy into chemical energy. Fishes eat algae to obtain energy, and larger fish eat the smaller fish. In deep-sea vent ecosystems, some bacteria make their own food from the chemicals released by the vents. Other organisms, such as crabs and shrimp, may consume these bacteria to obtain energy. Fishes then eat these crabs and shrimp. Identify which organisms have the same ecological roles in these two ecosystems.

REVIEWING ACADEMIC VOCABULARY

1 In the sentence "Bacteria have an important function in the ecosystem," what does the word *function* mean?

A purpose

B property

C location

D organization

2 Choose the appropriate form of *categorize* for the following sentence: "Organisms can be ___ in a variety of ways."

A category

B categories

C categorize

D categorized

3 Which of the following words means "the surrounding conditions acting on an organism"?

A biome

B environment

C factors

D location

4 In the sentence "Plants play a key role in Earth's biomes," what does the word *role* mean?

A a part performed in a process

B a method of completing a task

C a specific location in an area

D a difficult goal to be reached

5 Which of the following words means "a set of values between two limits"?

A range

B variety

C diversity

D difference

REVIEWING CONCEPTS

6 Which of the following is an important abiotic factor in a river?

A the diversity of life in the river

B the speed at which the water flows

C the predators living near the river

D the direction in which the river flows

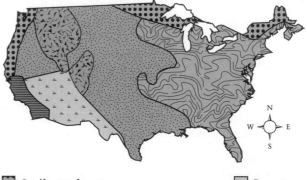

::: Coniferous forest   ▫ Desert

▨ Temperate deciduous forest   ▤ Chaparral

▦ Temperate grassland   ▧ Mountains

7 The map above shows some of the biomes of the United States. How are trees in the eastern part of the United States adapted to their environment?

A They grow taller than trees in most forests.

B They grow far apart, which reduces the competition for water.

C They shed leaves during the long winter months, which helps reduce water loss.

D Their thick bark helps them survive in arctic temperatures.

8 Which of the following is a producer that can live in the open-water zone of a lake?

A cattails

B lake trout

C photosynthetic plankton

D fungi

9 Which of the following types of life is most likely to be found in the ocean's abyssal zone?

  A sea grass that converts sunlight into chemical energy

  B phytoplankton

  C a sea turtle that needs air to breathe

  D a sea urchin that does not need sunlight

10 Which type of animal is most likely to live in a tundra?

  A a rodent that needs warm, dry weather in order to survive

  B a bird that can live in rainy, hot weather

  C a mammal adapted to cold, dry weather

  D an insect that lives in trees

11 What do scavengers in the savanna do?

  A They eat shrubs and other small plants.

  B They eat grasses and seeds.

  C They eat rodents and lizards.

  D They eat waste and dead animals.

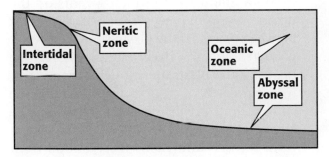

12 The diagram above shows zones in the ocean. Which part of the ocean does not get any sunlight and is also very cold?

  A the intertidal zone

  B the neritic zone

  C the oceanic zone

  D the abyssal zone

REVIEWING PRIOR LEARNING

13 Why are sea otters called *secondary consumers*?

  A They eat the remains of dead animals.

  B They eat animals that consume algae.

  C They convert sunlight into chemical energy.

  D They are eaten by other animals.

14 Which of the following is a biotic part of a rain forest biome?

  A soil

  B rainfall

  C humidity

  D fungi

15 Which of the following pairs of organisms are producers in their ecosystems?

  A cactuses and vultures

  B turtles and lions

  C lichens and bacteria

  D trees and algae

16 What benefit do the skeletons of corals provide to a marine ecosystem?

  A Skeletons of corals provide food for fish.

  B Skeletons of corals provide homes for organisms.

  C Skeletons of corals decompose to provide soil for sea grasses.

  D Skeletons of corals regenerate into new corals.

Standards Assessment

Science in Action

Scientific Debate

Studying Mars at Mono Lake

For more than a million years, salts and minerals have been collecting in Mono Lake, California. As water evaporates, these salts crystallize into formations called *tufa towers*. Microbes and other organisms have been fossilized in these towers. Birds and brine shrimp are also a part of the fragile and unique ecosystem of Mono Lake. But did you know that scientists are studying Mono Lake to learn more about the planet Mars? Scientists think that areas on Mars that were once similar to Mono Lake are promising places to search for fossils. Fossils can provide evidence that there was once life on Mars.

Language Arts ACTiViTY

Developers often clear natural habitats to build areas for people to live and work. Research how natural habitats are protected on your own. Then, in your **Science Journal,** write an essay discussing the pros and cons of protecting natural habitats such as Mono Lake.

Scientific Discoveries

Ocean Vents

Imagine the deepest parts of the ocean. There is no light at all, and it is very cold. Some of the animals that live here have found a unique place to live—vents on the ocean floor. Water seeps into the Earth's crust between plates on the ocean floor. The water is heated and absorbs chemicals. When the heated water blasts up through ocean vents, it is hundreds of degrees warmer than the surrounding ocean water! Bacteria use the chemicals from the ocean vents to live. In turn, mussels and clams receive food from the bacteria. Without ocean vents, these organisms would not survive as well.

Math ACTiViTY

The temperature of the water released by an ocean vent is 360°C. The average water temperature at the sea floor is 2°C. By what percentage will the temperature of the water from the vent decrease as it mixes with cold ocean water at the sea floor? Record your work in your **Science Journal.**

Alfonso Alonso-Mejía

Ecologist During the winter, ecologist Alfonso Alonso-Mejía visits sites in central Mexico where millions of monarch butterflies spend the winter. Unfortunately, the monarchs' winter habitat is threatened by human activity. Only nine of the monarchs' wintering sites remain. Five of the sites are set aside as sanctuaries for monarchs, but these sites are threatened by people who cut down fir trees for firewood or for commercial purposes.

Alonso-Mejía discovered that monarchs depend on understory vegetation, bushlike plants that grow beneath fir trees, to survive. When the temperature is low, monarchs can climb understory vegetation until they are at least 10 cm above the ground. This tiny difference in elevation can ensure that monarchs are warm enough to survive. Because of Alonso-Mejía's discovery, Mexican conservationists are working to protect understory vegetation and monarchs.

Social Studies ACTIVITY

Use your school library or the Internet to research the routes that monarchs use to migrate to Mexico. Draw a map illustrating your findings. Record your work in your **Science Journal.**

Internet Resources

- To learn more about careers in science, visit **www.scilinks.org** and enter the SciLinks code HY70225.

- To learn more about these Science in Action topics, visit **go.hrw.com** and type in the keyword HY7ECOF.

- Check out articles related to this chapter by visiting **go.hrw.com.** Just type in the keyword HY7ECOC.

Appendix

Contents

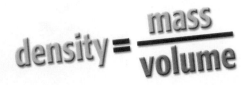

Study Skills: Making and Using FoldNotes

Have you ever tried to study for a test or quiz but didn't know where to start? Or have you read a chapter and found that you can remember only a few ideas? Well, FoldNotes are a fun and exciting way to help you learn and remember the ideas you encounter as you learn science!

FoldNotes are tools that you can use to organize concepts. One FoldNote focuses on a few main concepts. FoldNotes help you learn and remember how the concepts fit together. FoldNotes can help you see the "big picture." Below, you will find instructions for building 10 different FoldNotes.

Pyramid

A pyramid provides a unique way for taking notes. The three sides of the pyramid can summarize information into three categories. Use the pyramid as a tool for studying information in a chapter.

1. Place a **sheet of paper** in front of you. Fold the lower left-hand corner of the paper diagonally to the opposite edge of the paper.

2. Cut off the tab of paper created by the fold (at the top).

3. Open the paper so that it is a square. Fold the lower right-hand corner of the paper diagonally to the opposite corner to form a triangle.

4. Open the paper. The creases of the two folds will have created an X.

5. Using **scissors,** cut along one of the creases. Start from any corner, and stop at the center point to create two flaps. Use **tape** or **glue** to attach one of the flaps on top of the other flap.

Double-Door Fold

A double-door fold is useful when you want to compare the characteristics of two topics. The double-door fold can organize characteristics of the two topics side by side under the flaps. Similarities and differences between the two topics can then be easily identified.

1. Fold a **sheet of paper** in half from the top to the bottom. Then, unfold the paper.

2. Fold the top and bottom edges of the paper to the center crease.

Booklet

A booklet is a useful tool for taking notes as you read a chapter. Each page of the booklet can contain a main topic from the chapter. Write details of each main topic on the appropriate page to create an outline of the chapter.

1. Fold a **sheet of paper** in half from left to right. Then, unfold the paper.

2. Fold the sheet of paper in half again from the top to the bottom. Then, unfold the paper.

3. Refold the sheet of paper in half from left to right.

4. Fold the top and bottom edges to the center crease.

5. Completely unfold the paper.

6. Refold the paper from top to bottom.

7. Using **scissors,** cut a slit along the center crease of the sheet from the folded edge to the creases made in step 4. Do not cut the entire sheet in half.

8. Fold the sheet of paper in half from left to right. While holding the bottom and top edges of the paper, push the bottom and top edges together so that the center collapses at the center slit. Fold the four flaps to form a four-page book.

Layered Book

A layered book is a useful tool for taking notes as you read a chapter. The four flaps of the layered book can summarize information into four categories. Write details of each category on the appropriate flap to create a summary of the chapter.

1. Lay one **sheet of paper** on top of **another sheet.** Slide the top sheet up so that 2 cm of the bottom sheet is showing.

2. Holding the two sheets together, fold down the top of the two sheets so that you see four 2 cm tabs along the bottom.

3. Using a stapler, staple the top of the FoldNote.

Key-Term Fold

A key-term fold is a useful for studying definitions of key terms in a chapter. Each tab can contain a key term on one side and its definition on the other. Use the key-term fold to quiz yourself on the definitions of the key terms in a chapter.

1. Fold a **sheet of lined notebook paper** in half from left to right.

2. Using **scissors,** cut along every third line from the right edge of the paper to the center fold to make tabs.

Four-Corner Fold

A four-corner fold is useful when you want to compare the characteristics of four topics. The four-corner fold can organize the characteristics of the four topics side by side under the flaps. Similarities and differences between the four topics can then be easily identified.

1. Fold a **sheet of paper** in half from left to right. Then, unfold the paper.

2. Fold each side of the paper to the crease in the center of the paper.

3. Fold the paper in half from the top to the bottom. Then, unfold the paper.

4. Using **scissors,** cut the top flap creases made in step 3 to form four flaps.

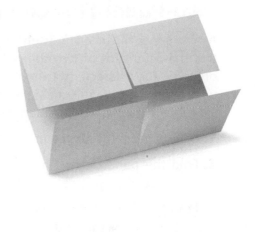

Three-Panel Flip Chart

A three-panel flip chart is useful when you want to compare the characteristics of three topics. The three-panel flip chart can organize the characteristics of the three topics side by side under the flaps. Similarities and differences between the three topics can then be easily identified.

1. Fold a **piece of paper** in half from the top to the bottom.

2. Fold the paper in thirds from side to side. Then, unfold the paper so that you can see the three sections.

3. From the top of the paper, cut along each of the vertical fold lines to the fold in the middle of the paper. You will now have three flaps.

Table Fold

A table fold is a useful tool for comparing the characteristics of two or three topics. In a table fold, all topics are described in terms of the same characteristics so that you can easily make a thorough comparison.

1. Fold a **piece of paper** in half from the top to the bottom. Then, fold the paper in half again.

2. Fold the paper in thirds from side to side.

3. Unfold the paper completely. Carefully trace the fold lines by using a pen or pencil.

Two-Panel Flip Chart

A two-panel flip chart is useful when you want to compare the characteristics of two topics. The two-panel flip chart can organize the characteristics of the two topics side by side under the flaps. Similarities and differences between the two topics can then be easily identified.

1. Fold a **piece of paper** in half from the top to the bottom.

2. Fold the paper in half from side to side. Then, unfold the paper so that you can see the two sections.

3. From the top of the paper, cut along the vertical fold line to the fold in the middle of the paper. You will now have two flaps.

Tri-Fold

A tri-fold is a useful tool that helps you track your progress. By organizing the chapter topic into what you know, what you want to know, and what you learn, you can see how much you have learned after reading a chapter.

1. Fold a piece a paper in thirds from the top to the bottom.

2. Unfold the paper so that you can see the three sections. Then, turn the paper sideways so that the three sections form vertical columns.

3. Trace the fold lines by using a **pen** or **pencil.** Label the columns "Know," "Want," and "Learn."

Study Skills: Making and Using Graphic Organizers

Have you ever wished that you could "draw out" the many concepts you learn in your science class? Sometimes, being able to see how concepts are related really helps you remember what you've learned. Graphic Organizers do just that! They give you a way to draw or map out concepts.

All you need to make a Graphic Organizer is a piece of paper and a pencil. Below you will find instructions for nine different Graphic Organizers designed to help you organize the concepts you'll learn in this book.

Concept Map

How to Make a Concept Map

1. Identify main ideas from the text, and write the ideas as short phrases or single words.

2. Select a main concept. Place this concept at the top or center of a piece of paper.

3. Place other ideas under or around the main concept based on their relationship to the main concept. Draw a circle around each idea.

4. Draw lines between the concepts, and add linking words to connect the ideas.

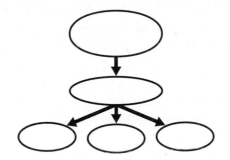

When to Use a Concept Map

Concept maps are useful when you are trying to identify how several ideas are connected to a main concept. Concept maps may be based on vocabulary terms or on main topics from the text. As you read about science, look for terms that can be organized in a concept map.

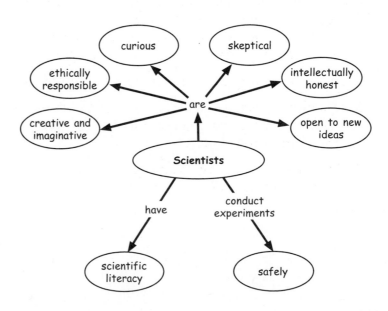

Cause-and-Effect Map

How to Make a Cause-and-Effect Map

1. Draw a box, and write a cause in the box. You can have as many cause boxes as you want. The diagram shown here is one example of a cause-and-effect map.

2. Draw another box to the right of the cause box to represent an effect. You can have as many effect boxes as you want. Draw arrows from each cause box to the appropriate effect boxes.

3. In the cause boxes, explain the process that makes up the cause. In the effect boxes, write a description of the effect or details about the effect.

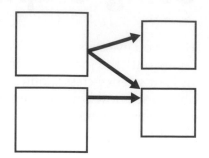

When to Use a Cause-and-Effect Map

A cause-and-effect map is a useful tool for illustrating a specific type of scientific process. Use a cause-and-effect map when you want to describe how, when, or why one event causes another event. As you read, look for events that are either causes or results of other events, and draw a cause-and-effect map that shows the relationships between the events.

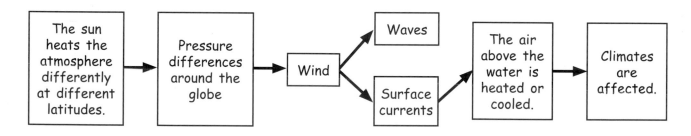

Spider Map

How to Make a Spider Map

1. Draw a diagram like the one shown here. In the circle, write the main topic.

2. From the circle, draw legs to represent the main ideas or characteristics of the topic. Draw as many legs as you want to draw. Write an idea or characteristic along each leg.

3. From each leg, draw horizontal lines. As you read the chapter, write details about each idea on the idea's horizontal lines. To add more details, make the legs longer and add more horizontal lines.

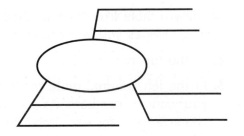

When to Use a Spider Map

A spider map is an effective tool for classifying the details of a specific topic in science. A spider map divides a topic into ideas and details. As you read about a topic, look for the main ideas or characteristics of the topic. Within each idea, look for details. Use a spider map to organize the ideas and details of each topic.

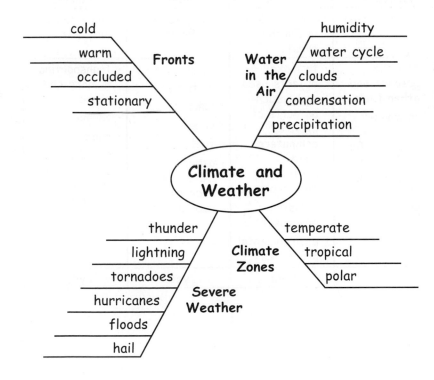

Appendix

Comparison Table

How to Make a Comparison Table

1. Draw a table like the one shown here. Draw as many columns and rows as you want to draw.

2. In the top row, write the topics that you want to compare.

3. In the left column, write the general characteristics that you want to compare. As you read the chapter, fill in the characteristics for each topic in the appropriate boxes.

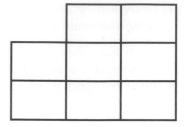

When to Use a Comparison Table

A comparison table is useful when you want to compare the characteristics of two or more topics in science. Organizing information in a table helps you compare several topics at one time. In a table, all topics are described in terms of the same list of characteristics, which helps you make a thorough comparison. As you read, look for topics whose characteristics you may want to compare in a table.

	Oxygen	Petroleum	Minerals	Plants	Animals
Where they are found	• the atmosphere	• Earth's crust	• various places in Earth's crust	• many places on Earth	• many places on Earth
Examples of what they are used for	• life processes • rocket fuel	• to make gasoline and other fuels • to manufacture polymers for products such as plastics, clothing, and plumbing supplies	• to make objects used daily, such as parts of bicycles, computers, food containers, and airplanes • industrial processes • environmental processes	• food • clothing • lumber • paper • fuel • other materials, such as rubber	• transporting humans and cargo • farming • food • fertilizer and fuel (in the case of animal wastes)
Renewable?	yes	no	some	yes	yes

Appendix

Venn Diagram

How to Make a Venn Diagram

1. Draw a diagram like the one shown here. Draw one circle for each topic. Make sure that each circle partially overlaps the other circles.

2. In each circle, write a topic that you want to compare with the topics in the other circles.

3. In the areas of the diagram where circles overlap, write the characteristics that the topics in the overlapping circles share.

4. In the areas of the diagram where circles do not overlap, write the characteristics that are unique to the topic of the particular circle.

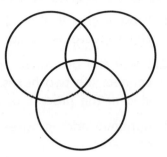

When to Use a Venn Diagram

A Venn diagram is a useful tool for comparing two or three topics in science. A Venn diagram shows which characteristics the topics share and which characteristics are unique to each topic. Venn diagrams are ideal when you want to illustrate relationships in a pair or small group of topics. As you read, look for topics that have both shared and unique characteristics, and draw a Venn diagram that shows how the topics are related.

Biomes
- large areas made up of land and water ecosystems
- defined by unique plant communities that support unique animal communities
- examples: deserts, chaparrals, temperate grasslands, savannas, tundra, coniferous forests, temperate deciduous forests, and tropical rain forests

- have producers, consumers, and decomposers
- contain abiotic factors that organisms either use or have to adapt to

Ecosystems
- defined by all of their organisms and abiotic factors
- examples: land ecosystems, marine ecosystems, stream and river ecosystems, pond and lake ecosystems, and wetland ecosystems

Appendix

Process Chart

How to Make a Process Chart

1. Draw a box. In the box, write the first step of a process, chain of events, or cycle.

2. Under the box, draw another box, and draw an arrow to connect the two boxes. In the second box, write the next step of the process or the next event in the timeline.

3. Continue adding boxes until each step of the process, chain of events, or cycle is written in a box. For cycles only, draw an arrow to connect the last box and the first box.

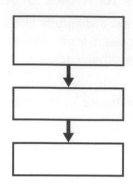

When to Use a Process Chart

Science is full of processes. A process chart shows the steps that a process takes to get from one point to another point. Timelines, chains of events, and cycles are examples of the kinds of information that can be organized well in a process chart. As you read, look for information that is described in steps or in a sequence, and draw a process chart that shows the progression of the steps or sequence.

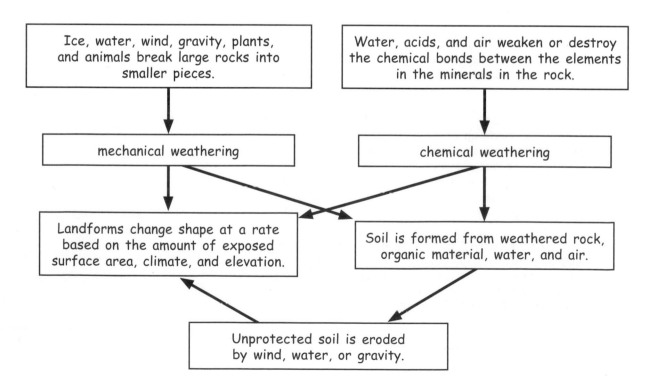

Idea Wheel

How to Make an Idea Wheel

1. Draw a circle. Draw a larger circle around the first circle. Divide the ring between the circles into sections by drawing lines from one circle to the other across the ring. Divide the ring into as many sections as you want.

2. Write a main idea or topic in the smaller circle. Label each section in the ring with a category or characteristic of the main idea.

3. In each section of the ring, include details that are unique to the topic.

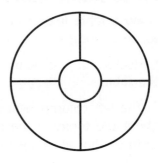

When to Use an Idea Wheel

An idea wheel is an effective type of visual organization in which ideas in science can be divided into categories or parts. It is also a useful way to illustrate characteristics of a main idea or topic. As you read, look for topics that are divided into ideas or categories that can be organized around an idea wheel.

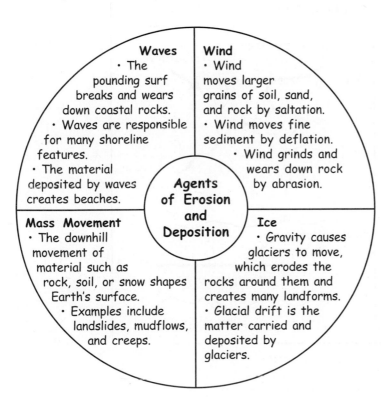

Combination Notes

How to Make Combination Notes

1. Draw a table like the one shown here. Draw the columns to be as long as you want them to be.

2. Write the topic of your notes in the section at the top of the table.

3. In the left column, write important phrases or sentences about the topic. In the right column, draw diagrams or pictures that illustrate the information in the left column.

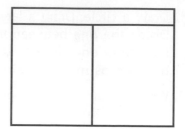

When to Use Combination Notes

Combination notes let you express scientific information in words and pictures at the same time. Use combination notes to express information that a picture could help explain. The picture could be a diagram, a sketch, or another useful visual representation of the written information in your notes.

Rivers and Groundwater	
Rivers • A **river system** is a network of streams and rivers that drain an area of its runoff. • A stream that flows into a lake or into a larger stream is called a **tributary**. **Groundwater** • **Groundwater** is the water in rocks below Earth's surface. • The rock layer that stores the groundwater and allows it to flow is called an **aquifer**. • The upper surface of the underground water is called the **water table**.	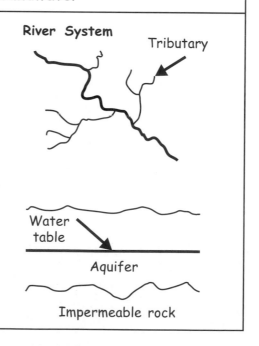

Pyramid Chart

How to Make a Pyramid Chart

1. Draw a triangle that is divided into sections like the one shown here. Draw as many sections as you need to draw.

2. Draw a box to the left of the triangle, as shown in the example. Write the topic of your pyramid chart in the box.

3. In each section of your triangle, write information about the topic in the appropriate level of the pyramid.

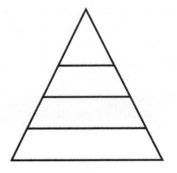

When to Use a Pyramid Chart

A pyramid chart is used to organize information in a hierarchy of importance, detail, or magnitude. As the shape of the pyramid suggests, the pyramid's bottom level contains information that is largest in terms of magnitude and broadest, or least specific, in terms of detail. As you read about science, look for information that you can organize into a hierarchy.

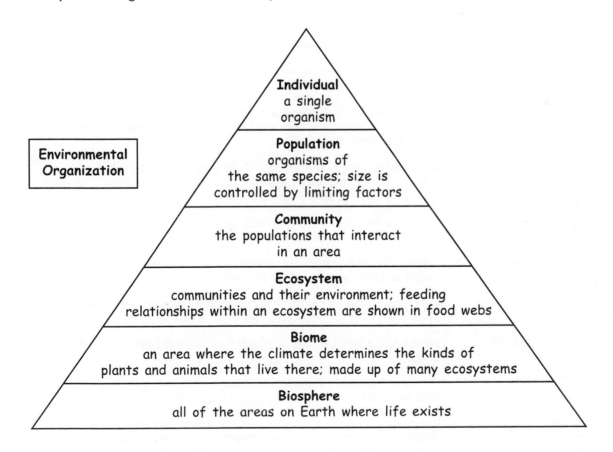

Environmental Organization

Individual
a single organism

Population
organisms of the same species; size is controlled by limiting factors

Community
the populations that interact in an area

Ecosystem
communities and their environment; feeding relationships within an ecosystem are shown in food webs

Biome
an area where the climate determines the kinds of plants and animals that live there; made up of many ecosystems

Biosphere
all of the areas on Earth where life exists

Understanding Word Parts

Many scientific words are made up of parts based on Greek and Latin languages. Understanding the meaning of the parts will help you understand the meaning of the scientific words. The table below provides a definition and an example of prefixes, roots, and suffixes that you will see in this textbook.

Prefix	Definition	Example
anti-	against	anticyclone: the rotation of air around a high-pressure center in the direction against, or opposite to, Earth's rotation
com-	together	composite volcano: a volcano made up of layers of lava and pyroclastic material deposited together in alternating layers
counter-	opposite; contrary to	counterclockwise: in a direction opposite to that in which the hands of a clock move
epi-	upon	epicenter: the point on Earth's surface directly above an earthquake's starting point, or focus
im-	against; not	impermeable: describes something that does not allow water to pass through
in-	in; into	infiltration: the ability of water to move in soil
infra-	below; beneath	infrared: describes invisible rays just beyond, or below, the red end of the visible spectrum
inter-	between; among	intertidal zone: an area along ocean shorelines that lies between low and high water lines
meta-	after; changed	metamorphism: the process in which one type of rock changes into metamorphic rock because of chemical processes or changes in temperature and pressure
non-	not	nonpoint-source pollution: pollution that comes from many sources rather than from a single, specific site; pollution that does not come from a single source
per-	through	permeability: the ability of a rock or sediment to let fluids pass through its open spaces, or pores
sub-	aside; away; under	subduction: the process by which one lithospheric plate moves under another as a result of tectonic forces
super-	above; over	superposition: a principle that states that younger rocks lie above older rocks if the layers have not been disturbed
sym-	with; together	symbiosis: a relationship in which two different organisms live together
ultra-	beyond; exceedingly	ultraviolet: a band of electromagnetic radiation that has wavelengths that are shorter than the wavelengths of violet light; beyond violet
un-	not; the lack of	unconformity: a break in the geologic record created when rock layers are eroded or when sediment is not deposited for a long period of time; a gap in the rock record that does not show a continuous record of geologic time

Word root	Definition	Example
batho	depth	batholith: a large body of igneous rock that forms when magma solidifies deep beneath Earth's surface
eco	environment	ecosystem: a community of organisms and their abiotic, or nonliving, environment; a system consisting of organisms and their nonliving environment
geo	earth	geology: the scientific study of the origin, history, and structure of Earth and the processes that shape Earth
hydro	water	hydroelectric energy: electrical energy produced by the flow of water
lith	stone	lithosphere: the solid, outer layer of Earth that consists of crustal rock and the rigid upper part of the mantle
micro	small	microclimate: the climate of a small area
paleo	old	paleontology: the scientific study of fossils
pyr	fire	pyroclastic material: fragments of rock that form during a volcanic eruption
sed	to sit; to settle	sediment: fragments of organic or inorganic material that are transported and deposited by wind, water, or ice and that settle, or accumulate, in layers on Earth's surface
sphere	ball; globe	atmosphere: a mixture of gases that surrounds a planet or moon
terra	earth; land	terrane: a piece of Earth's lithosphere that has a unique geologic history and that may be part of a larger piece of lithosphere, such as a continent
thermo	heat	thermosphere: the uppermost layer of the atmosphere, in which temperature increases as altitude increases

Suffix	Definition	Example
-fer	to carry	aquifer: a body of rock or sediment that stores groundwater and allows the flow of groundwater; rock that carries water
-gram	thing written	seismogram: a tracing of earthquake motion that is recorded by a seismograph; a written record of earthquake motion
-ion	act of	erosion: the action of wind, water, ice, or gravity that transports soil and sediment from one location to another
-ism	a belief in	uniformitarianism: a principle that geologic processes that occurred in the past can be explained by current geologic processes; the belief that past geologic processes can be explained by geologic processes that are happening right now
-logy	the science of	paleontology: the scientific study of fossils
-meter	to measure	thermometer: an instrument that measures and indicates temperature

Common Words with Multiple Meanings

Scientific words may have common meanings that you already know. Understanding the difference between common meanings and scientific meanings will help you develop a scientific vocabulary. The table below provides common and scientific meanings for words that you will see in this textbook.

Word	Common meaning	Scientific meaning
atmosphere	a general mood or social environment	a mixture of gases that surrounds a planet or moon
channel	a band of frequencies of sufficient width for a single radio or television communication	the path that a stream follows
cloud	to darken or obscure	a collection of small water droplets or ice crystals suspended in the air, which forms when the air is cooled and condensation occurs
community	all of the people living in a particular area	all of the populations of species that live in the same habitat and interact with each other
consumer	a person who buys goods or services for personal needs	an organism that eats other organisms or organic matter
core	the hard central part of fruit that contains the seeds	the central part of Earth below the mantle
creep	to move slowly	the slow downhill movement of weathered rock material
crust	the hard, crisp outer part of bread	the thin and solid outermost layer of Earth above the mantle
current	at the present time	a horizontal movement of water in a well-defined pattern, such as a river or stream; the movement of air in a certain direction
date	an engagement to go out socially	to measure the age of an event or object
divide	to separate into parts	the boundary between drainage areas that have streams that flow in opposite directions
element	a distinct group within a larger group or community	a substance that cannot be separated or broken down into simpler substances by chemical means
fault	responsibility for a mistake	a break in a body of rock along which one block slides relative to another

Word	Common meaning	Scientific meaning
focus	a center of activity or attention	the location within Earth along a fault at which the first motion of an earthquake occurs
fold	to bend or press	a form of ductile strain in which rock layers bend, usually as a result of compression
front	the part of something that faces forward	the boundary between air masses of different densities and usually different temperatures
gas	short for *gasoline*; a liquid fuel used by vehicles, such as cars and buses	a form of matter that does not have a definite volume or shape
kettle	a metal container for boiling or cooking things	a bowl-shaped depression in a glacial drift deposit
law	a rule of conduct established by the government	a descriptive statement or equation that reliably predicts events under certain conditions
legend	a romanticized story or myth	a list of map symbols and their meanings
mass	a quantity of matter that has an unspecified shape	a measure of the amount of matter in an object
matter	a subject of concern or topic of discussion	anything that has mass and takes up space
period	a punctuation mark used to indicate the end of a sentence	a unit of geologic time that is longer than an epoch but shorter than an era
plate	a shallow dish from which food is eaten	a large piece of the lithosphere (tectonic plate)
relief	any aid given in times of need	the difference between the highest and lowest elevations in a given area; the variations in elevation of a land surface
scale	a machine used to measure weight	the relationship between the measurements on a model, map, or diagram and the actual measurement or distance
tension	mental or nervous strain	stress that occurs when forces act to stretch an object
theory	an assumption based on limited knowledge	a system of ideas that explains many related observations and is supported by a large body of evidence acquired through scientific investigation
vent	to give expression to feelings	an opening at the surface of Earth through which volcanic material passes
volume	a measure of how loud a sound is	a measure of the size of a body or region in three-dimensional space
weather	to pass through safely or to survive	the short-term state of the atmosphere, including temperature, humidity, precipitation, wind, and visibility
wind	to cause to be out of breath	the movement of air caused by differences in air pressure

Appendix

Math Refresher

Science requires an understanding of many math concepts. The following pages will help you review some important math skills.

Averages

An **average**, or **mean**, simplifies a set of numbers into a single number that *approximates* the value of the set.

> **Example:** Find the average of the following set of numbers: 5, 4, 7, and 8.

Step 1: Find the sum.
$$5 + 4 + 7 + 8 = 24$$

Step 2: Divide the sum by the number of numbers in your set. Because there are four numbers in this example, divide the sum by 4.
$$\frac{24}{4} = 6$$

The average, or mean, is **6.**

Ratios

A **ratio** is a comparison between numbers, and it is usually written as a fraction.

> **Example:** Find the ratio of thermometers to students if you have 36 thermometers and 48 students in your class.

Step 1: Make the ratio.
$$\frac{36 \text{ thermometers}}{48 \text{ students}}$$

Step 2: Reduce the fraction to its simplest form.
$$\frac{36}{48} = \frac{36 \div 12}{48 \div 12} = \frac{3}{4}$$

The ratio of thermometers to students is **3 to 4,** or $\frac{3}{4}$. The ratio may also be written in the form 3:4.

Proportions

A **proportion** is an equation that states that two ratios are equal.
$$\frac{3}{1} = \frac{12}{4}$$

To solve a proportion, first multiply across the equal sign. This is called *cross-multiplication*. If you know three of the quantities in a proportion, you can use cross-multiplication to find the fourth.

> **Example:** Imagine that you are making a scale model of the solar system for your science project. The diameter of Jupiter is 11.2 times the diameter of Earth. If you are using a plastic-foam ball that has a diameter of 2 cm to represent Earth, what must the diameter of the ball representing Jupiter be? $\frac{11.2}{1} = \frac{x}{2 \text{ cm}}$

Step 1: Cross-multiply.
$$\frac{11.2}{1} \diagdown\hspace{-1em}\diagup \frac{x}{2}$$
$$11.2 \times 2 = x \times 1$$

Step 2: Multiply.
$$22.4 = x \times 1$$

Step 3: Isolate the variable by dividing both sides by 1.
$$x = \frac{22.4}{1}$$
$$x = 22.4 \text{ cm}$$

You will need to use a ball that has a diameter of **22.4** cm to represent Jupiter.

Percentages

A **percentage** is a ratio of a given number to 100.

> **Example:** What is 85% of 40?

Step 1: Rewrite the percentage by moving the decimal point two places to the left.

$$0.\underset{\smile}{8}5$$

Step 2: Multiply the decimal by the number that you are calculating the percentage of.

$$0.85 \times 40 = 34$$

85% of 40 is **34.**

Decimals

To **add** or **subtract decimals,** line up the digits vertically so that the decimal points line up. Then, add or subtract the columns from right to left. Carry or borrow numbers as necessary.

> **Example:** Add the following numbers: 3.1415 and 2.96.

Step 1: Line up the digits vertically so that the decimal points line up.

$$\begin{array}{r} 3.1415 \\ + 2.96 \\ \hline \end{array}$$

Step 2: Add the columns from right to left, and carry when necessary.

$$\begin{array}{r} {}^{1}\,{}^{1} \\ 3.1415 \\ + 2.96 \\ \hline 6.1015 \end{array}$$

The sum is **6.1015.**

Fractions

Numbers tell you how many; **fractions** tell you *how much of a whole*.

> **Example:** Your class has 24 plants. Your teacher instructs you to put 5 plants in a shady spot. What fraction of the plants in your class will you put in a shady spot?

Step 1: In the denominator, write the total number of parts in the whole.

$$\frac{?}{24}$$

Step 2: In the numerator, write the number of parts of the whole that are being considered.

$$\frac{5}{24}$$

So, $\frac{5}{24}$ of the plants will be in the shade.

Reducing Fractions

It is usually best to express a fraction in its simplest form. Expressing a fraction in its simplest form is called *reducing* a fraction.

> **Example:** Reduce the fraction $\frac{30}{45}$ to its simplest form.

Step 1: Find the largest whole number that will divide evenly into both the numerator and denominator. This number is called the *greatest common factor* (GCF).

Factors of the numerator 30:
1, 2, 3, 5, 6, 10, **15,** 30

Factors of the denominator 45:
1, 3, 5, 9, **15,** 45

Step 2: Divide both the numerator and the denominator by the GCF, which in this case is 15.

$$\frac{30}{45} = \frac{30 \div 15}{45 \div 15} = \frac{2}{3}$$

Thus, $\frac{30}{45}$ reduced to its simplest form is $\frac{2}{3}$.

Adding and Subtracting Fractions

To **add** or **subtract fractions** that have the **same denominator,** simply add or subtract the numerators.

Examples:

$$\frac{3}{5} + \frac{1}{5} = ? \quad \text{and} \quad \frac{3}{4} - \frac{1}{4} = ?$$

Step 1: Add or subtract the numerators.

$$\frac{3}{5} + \frac{1}{5} = \frac{4}{} \quad \text{and} \quad \frac{3}{4} - \frac{1}{4} = \frac{2}{}$$

Step 2: Write the sum or difference over the denominator.

$$\frac{3}{5} + \frac{1}{5} = \frac{4}{5} \quad \text{and} \quad \frac{3}{4} - \frac{1}{4} = \frac{2}{4}$$

Step 3: If necessary, reduce the fraction to its simplest form.

$$\frac{4}{5} \text{ cannot be reduced, and } \frac{2}{4} = \frac{1}{2}.$$

To **add** or **subtract fractions** that have **different denominators,** first find the least common denominator (LCD).

Examples:

$$\frac{1}{2} + \frac{1}{6} = ? \quad \text{and} \quad \frac{3}{4} - \frac{2}{3} = ?$$

Step 1: Write the equivalent fractions that have a common denominator.

$$\frac{3}{6} + \frac{1}{6} = ? \quad \text{and} \quad \frac{9}{12} - \frac{8}{12} = ?$$

Step 2: Add or subtract the fractions.

$$\frac{3}{6} + \frac{1}{6} = \frac{4}{6} \quad \text{and} \quad \frac{9}{12} - \frac{8}{12} = \frac{1}{12}$$

Step 3: If necessary, reduce the fraction to its simplest form.

The fraction $\frac{4}{6} = \frac{2}{3}$, and $\frac{1}{12}$ cannot be reduced.

Multiplying Fractions

To **multiply fractions,** multiply the numerators and the denominators together, and then reduce the fraction to its simplest form.

Example:

$$\frac{5}{9} \times \frac{7}{10} = ?$$

Step 1: Multiply the numerators and denominators.

$$\frac{5}{9} \times \frac{7}{10} = \frac{5 \times 7}{9 \times 10} = \frac{35}{90}$$

Step 2: Reduce the fraction.

$$\frac{35}{90} = \frac{35 \div 5}{90 \div 5} = \frac{7}{18}$$

Dividing Fractions

To **divide fractions,** first rewrite the divisor (the number you divide by) upside down. This number is called the *reciprocal* of the divisor. Then multiply and reduce if necessary.

Example:

$$\frac{5}{8} \div \frac{3}{2} = ?$$

Step 1: Rewrite the divisor as its reciprocal.

$$\frac{3}{2} \rightarrow \frac{2}{3}$$

Step 2: Multiply the fractions.

$$\frac{5}{8} \times \frac{2}{3} = \frac{5 \times 2}{8 \times 3} = \frac{10}{24}$$

Step 3: Reduce the fraction.

$$\frac{10}{24} = \frac{10 \div 2}{24 \div 2} = \frac{5}{12}$$

Appendix

Scientific Notation

Scientific notation is a short way of representing very large and very small numbers without writing all of the place-holding zeros.

Example: Write 653,000,000 in scientific notation.

Step 1: Write the number without the place-holding zeros.

653

Step 2: Place the decimal point after the first digit.

6.53

Step 3: Find the exponent by counting the number of places that you moved the decimal point.

6.53000000

The decimal point was moved eight places to the left. Therefore, the exponent of 10 is positive 8. If you had moved the decimal point to the right, the exponent would be negative.

Step 4: Write the number in scientific notation.

$$6.53 \times 10^8$$

Finding Area

Area is the number of square units needed to cover the surface of an object.

Formulas:

area of a square = side × side

area of a rectangle = length × width

area of a triangle = $\frac{1}{2}$ × base × height

Examples: Find the areas.

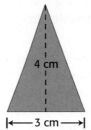

Triangle

area = $\frac{1}{2}$ × base × height

area = $\frac{1}{2}$ × 3 cm × 4 cm

area = **6 cm²**

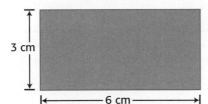

Rectangle

area = length × width

area = 6 cm × 3 cm

area = **18 cm²**

Square

area = side × side

area = 3 cm × 3 cm

area = **9 cm²**

Finding Volume

Volume is the amount of space that something occupies.

Formulas:

volume of a cube = side × side × side

volume of a prism = area of base × height

Examples: Find the volume of the solids.

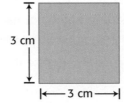

Cube

volume = side × side × side

volume = 4 cm × 4 cm × 4 cm

volume = **64 cm³**

Prism

volume = area of base × height

volume = (area of triangle) × height

volume = ($\frac{1}{2}$ × 3 cm × 4 cm) × 5 cm

volume = 6 cm² × 5 cm

volume = **30 cm³**

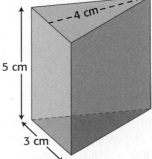

Making Graphs

Line Graphs

Line graphs are most often used to demonstrate continuous change. For example, Mr. Smith's students analyzed the population records for their hometown, Appleton, between 1900 and 2000. Examine the data at right.

Because the year and the population change, they are the *variables*. The population is determined by, or dependent on, the year. Therefore, the population is called the **dependent variable,** and the year is called the **independent variable.** Each set of data is called a **data pair.** To prepare a line graph, you must first organize data pairs into a table like the one at right.

Population of Appleton, 1900–2000	
Year	Population
1900	1,800
1920	2,500
1940	3,200
1960	3,900
1980	4,600
2000	5,300

How to Make a Line Graph

1. Place the independent variable along the horizontal (x) axis. Place the dependent variable along the vertical (y) axis.

2. Label the x-axis "Year" and the y-axis "Population." Look at your largest and smallest values for the population. For the y-axis, determine a scale that will provide enough space to show these values. You must use the same scale for the entire length of the axis. Next, find an appropriate scale for the x-axis.

3. Choose reasonable starting points for each axis.

4. Plot the data pairs as accurately as possible.

5. Choose a title that accurately represents the data.

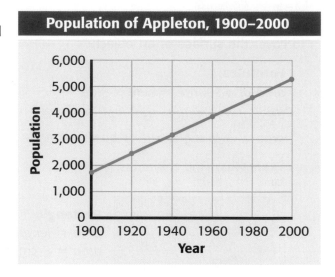

Population of Appleton, 1900–2000

How to Determine Slope

Slope is the ratio of the change in the y-value to the change in the x-value, or "rise over run."

1. Choose two points on the line graph. For example, the population of Appleton in 2000 was 5,300 people. Therefore, you can define point *a* as (2000, 5,300). In 1900, the population was 1,800 people. You can define point *b* as (1900, 1,800).

2. Find the change in the y-value. (y at point *a*) − (y at point *b*) = 5,300 people − 1,800 people = 3,500 people

3. Find the change in the x-value. (x at point *a*) − (x at point *b*) = 2000 − 1900 = 100 years

4. Calculate the slope of the graph by dividing the change in y by the change in x.

$$slope = \frac{change\ in\ y}{change\ in\ x}$$

$$slope = \frac{3,500\ people}{100\ years}$$

$$slope = 35\ people\ per\ year$$

In this example, the population in Appleton increased by a fixed amount each year. The graph of these data is a straight line. Therefore, the relationship is **linear.** When the graph of a set of data is not a straight line, the relationship is **nonlinear.**

Using Algebra to Determine Slope

The equation in step **4** may also be arranged to be

$$y = kx$$

where y represents the change in the y-value, k represents the slope, and x represents the change in the x-value.

$$slope = \frac{change\ in\ y}{change\ in\ x}$$

$$k = \frac{y}{x}$$

$$k \times x = \frac{y \times x}{x}$$

$$kx = y$$

Bar Graphs

Bar graphs are useful for comparing data values. For example, if you want to compare the amounts of several types of municipal solid waste, you might use a bar graph. The table at right contains the data used to make the bar graph below.

How to Make a Bar Graph

1 Use an appropriate scale and a reasonable starting point for each axis.

2 Label the axes, and plot the data.

3 Choose a title that accurately represents the data.

United States Municipal Solid Waste	
Material	**Percentage of total waste**
Paper	38.1
Yard waste	12.1
Food waste	10.9
Plastics	10.5
Metals	7.8
Rubber, leather, and textiles	6.6
Glass	5.5
Wood	5.3
Other	3.2

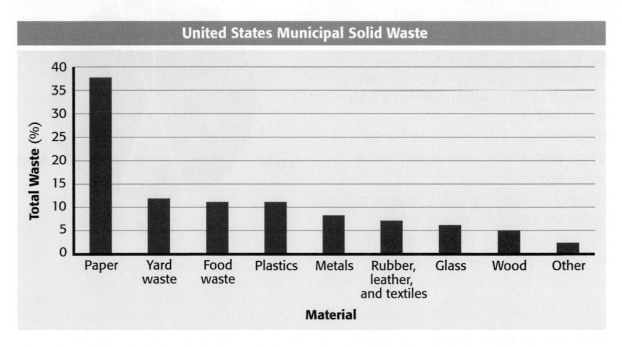

Appendix

Pie Graph

A pie graph shows how each group of data relates to all of the data. Each part of the circle forming the graph represents a category of the data. The entire circle represents all of the data. For example, a biologist studying a hardwood forest found that there were five types of trees. The data table at right summarizes the biologist's findings.

Hardwood Trees	
Type of tree	**Number found**
Oak	600
Maple	750
Beech	300
Birch	1,200
Hickory	150
Total	3,000

How to Make a Pie Graph

1 To make a pie graph of these data, first find what percentage all of the trees of each type of tree represents. Divide the number of trees of each type by the total number of trees, and multiply by 100.

$$\frac{600 \text{ oak}}{3,000 \text{ trees}} \times 100 = 20\%$$

$$\frac{750 \text{ maple}}{3,000 \text{ trees}} \times 100 = 25\%$$

$$\frac{300 \text{ beech}}{3,000 \text{ trees}} \times 100 = 10\%$$

$$\frac{1,200 \text{ birch}}{3,000 \text{ trees}} \times 100 = 40\%$$

$$\frac{150 \text{ hickory}}{3,000 \text{ trees}} \times 100 = 5\%$$

2 Now, determine the size of the wedges that make up the pie graph. Multiply each percentage by 360°. Remember that a circle contains 360°.

20% × 360° = 72°   25% × 360° = 90°

10% × 360° = 36°   40% × 360° = 144°

 5% × 360° = 18°

3 Check that the sum of the percentages is 100 and that the sum of the degrees is 360.

20% + 25% + 10% + 40% + 5% = 100%

72° + 90° + 36° + 144° + 18° = 360°

4 Use a compass to draw a circle and mark the center of the circle.

5 Then, use a protractor to draw angles of 72°, 90°, 36°, 144°, and 18° in the circle.

6 Finally, label each part of the graph, and choose an appropriate title.

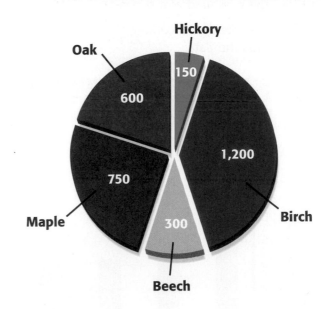

A Community of Hardwood Trees

Physical Science Refresher

Atoms and Elements

Every object in the universe is made up of particles of some kind of matter. **Matter** is anything that takes up space and has mass. All matter is made up of elements. An **element** is a substance that cannot be separated into simpler components by ordinary chemical means. The reason is that each element consists of only one kind of atom. An **atom** is the smallest unit of an element that maintains the properties of that element.

Atomic Structure

Atoms are made up of small particles called **subatomic particles.** The three major types of subatomic particles are **electrons, protons,** and **neutrons.** Electrons have a negative electric charge, protons have a positive electric charge, and neutrons have no electric charge. The protons and neutrons are packed close to one another to form the **nucleus.** The protons give the nucleus a positive charge. Electrons are most likely to be found in regions around the nucleus called **electron clouds.** The negatively charged electrons are attracted to the positively charged nucleus. An atom may have several energy levels in which electrons are located.

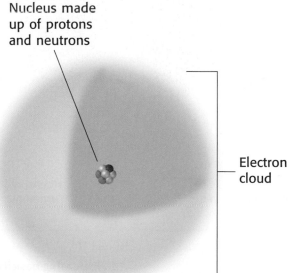

Nucleus made up of protons and neutrons

Electron cloud

Atomic Number

To help in the identification of elements, scientists have assigned an **atomic number** to each kind of atom. The atomic number is the number of protons in the atom. Atoms that have the same number of protons are the same kind of element. In an uncharged, or electrically neutral, atom, the numbers of protons and electrons are equal. Therefore, the atomic number equals the number of electrons in an uncharged atom. The number of neutrons, however, can vary for a given element. Atoms of the same element that have different numbers of neutrons are called **isotopes.**

Periodic Table of the Elements

In the periodic table, the elements are arranged from left to right in order of increasing atomic number. Each element in the table is in a separate box. An uncharged atom of each element has one more electron and one more proton than does an uncharged atom of the element to its left. Each horizontal row of the table is called a **period.** Changes in chemical properties of elements across a period correspond to changes in the electron arrangements of the atoms of the elements. Each vertical column of the table, known as a **group,** lists elements that have similar properties. The elements in a group have similar chemical properties because their atoms have the same number of electrons in their outer energy level. For example, the elements helium, neon, argon, krypton, xenon, and radon have similar properties and are known as the *noble gases*.

Molecules and Compounds

When two or more elements are joined chemically, the resulting substance is called a **compound.** A compound is a new substance whose properties differ from the properties of the elements that compose the compound. For example, water, H_2O, is a compound formed when hydrogen, H, and oxygen, O, combine. The smallest complete unit of a compound that has the properties of that compound is called a **molecule.** A chemical formula indicates the elements in a compound. It also indicates the relative number of atoms of each element present. The chemical formula for water is H_2O, which indicates that each water molecule consists of two atoms of hydrogen and one atom of oxygen. The subscript number after the symbol for an element indicates how many atoms of that element are in a single molecule of the compound.

Acids, Bases, and pH

An **ion** is an atom or group of atoms that has an electric charge because it has lost or gained one or more electrons. When an acid, such as hydrochloric acid, HCl, is mixed with water, it separates into ions. An **acid** is a compound that produces hydrogen ions, H^+, in water. The hydrogen ions then combine with water molecules to form hydronium ions, H_3O^+. A **base,** on the other hand, is a substance that produces hydroxide ions, OH^-, in water.

To determine whether a solution is acidic or basic, scientists use pH. The **pH** is a measure of the hydronium ion concentration in a solution. The pH scale ranges from 0 to 14. The middle point, pH = 7, is neutral—neither acidic nor basic. Acids have a pH less than 7; bases have a pH greater than 7. The lower the number is, the more acidic the solution. The higher the number is, the more basic the solution.

Chemical Equations

A chemical reaction occurs when a chemical change takes place. (In a chemical change, new substances that have new properties form.) A chemical equation is a useful way of describing a chemical reaction by means of chemical formulas. The equation indicates what substances react and what the products are. For example, when carbon and oxygen combine, they can form carbon dioxide. The equation for the reaction is as follows: $C + O_2 \rightarrow CO_2$.

pH Measurements of Some Comon Substances

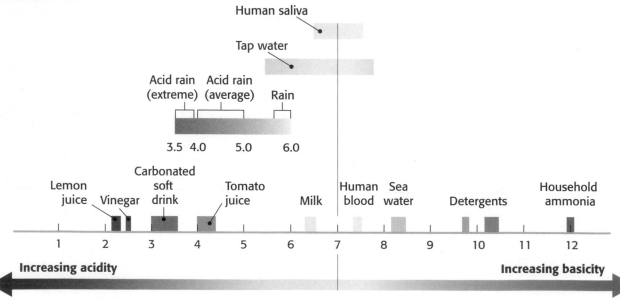

Physical Science Laws and Principles

Newton's Laws of Motion

Newton's first law of motion states that an object at rest remains at rest and an object in motion remains in motion at constant speed and in a straight line unless acted on by an unbalanced force.

The first part of the law explains why a football will remain on a tee until it is kicked off or until a gust of wind blows it off.

The second part of the law explains why a bike rider will continue moving forward after the bike comes to an abrupt stop. Gravity and the friction of the sidewalk will eventually stop the rider.

Newton's second law of motion states that the acceleration of an object depends on the mass of the object and the amount of force applied.

The first part of the law explains why the acceleration of a 4 kg bowling ball will be greater than the acceleration of a 6 kg bowling ball if the same force is applied to both balls.

The second part of the law explains why the acceleration of a bowling ball will be larger if a larger force is applied to the bowling ball.

The relationship of acceleration (a) to mass (m) and force (F) can be expressed mathematically by the following equation:

$$acceleration = \frac{force}{mass}, \text{ or } a = \frac{F}{m}$$

This equation is often rearranged to the form

$$force = mass \times acceleration, \text{ or } F = m \times a$$

Newton's third law of motion states that whenever one object exerts a force on a second object, the second object exerts an equal and opposite force on the first.

This law explains that a runner is able to move forward because of the equal and opposite force that the ground exerts on the runner's foot after each step.

Law of Conservation of Mass

Mass cannot be created or destroyed during ordinary chemical or physical changes.

The total mass in a closed system is always the same no matter how many physical changes or chemical reactions occur.

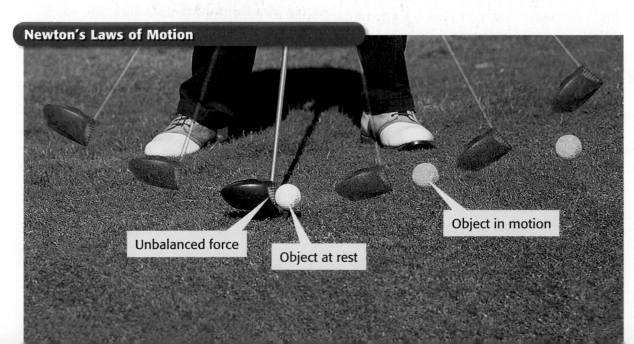

Newton's Laws of Motion

Unbalanced force

Object at rest

Object in motion

Law of Universal Gravitation

All objects in the universe attract each other by a force called *gravity*. The size of the force depends on the masses of the objects and the distance between the objects.

The first part of the law explains why lifting a bowling ball is much harder than lifting a marble. Because the bowling ball has a much larger mass than the marble does, the amount of gravity between Earth and the bowling ball is greater than the amount of gravity between Earth and the marble.

The second part of the law explains why a satellite can remain in orbit around Earth. The satellite is carefully placed at a distance great enough to prevent Earth's gravity from immediately pulling the satellite down but small enough to prevent the satellite from completely escaping Earth's gravity and wandering off into space.

Law of Conservation of Energy

Energy can be neither created nor destroyed.

The total amount of energy in a closed system is always the same. Energy can be changed from one form to another, but all of the different forms of energy in a system always add up to the same total amount of energy no matter how many energy conversions occur.

Charles's Law

Charles's law states that for a fixed amount of gas at a constant pressure, the volume of the gas increases as the temperature of the gas increases. Likewise, the volume of the gas decreases as the temperature of the gas decreases.

If a basketball that was inflated indoors is left outside on a cold winter day, the air particles inside the ball will move more slowly. They will hit the sides of the basketball less often and with less force. The ball will get smaller as the volume of the air decreases.

Boyle's Law

Boyle's law states that for a fixed amount of gas at a constant temperature, the volume of a gas increases as the pressure of the gas decreases. Likewise, the volume of a gas decreases as its pressure increases.

If an inflated balloon is pulled down to the bottom of a swimming pool, the pressure of the water on the balloon increases. The pressure of the air particles inside the balloon must increase to match that of the water outside, so the volume of the air inside the balloon decreases.

Pascal's Principle

Pascal's principle states that a change in pressure at any point in an enclosed fluid will be transmitted equally to all parts of that fluid.

When a mechanic uses a hydraulic jack to raise an automobile off the ground, he or she increases the pressure on the fluid in the jack by pushing on the jack handle. The pressure is transmitted equally to all parts of the fluid-filled jacking system. As fluid presses the jack plate against the frame of the car, the car is lifted off the ground.

Archimedes' Principle

Archimedes' principle states that the buoyant force on an object in a fluid is equal to the weight of the volume of fluid that the object displaces.

A person floating in a swimming pool displaces 20 L of water. The weight of that volume of water is about 200 N. Therefore, the buoyant force on the person is 200 N.

Bernoulli's Principle

Bernoulli's principle states that as the speed of a moving fluid increases, the fluid's pressure decreases.

The lift on an airplane wing can be explained in part by using Bernoulli's principle. Because of the shape of the wing, the air moving over the top of the wing is moving faster than the air below the wing. This faster-moving air above the wing exerts less pressure than the slower-moving air below it does. The resulting increased pressure below exerts an upward force and pushes the wing up.

Law of Reflection

The **law of reflection** states that the angle of incidence is equal to the angle of reflection. This law explains why light reflects off a surface at the same angle that the light strikes the surface.

Law of Reflection

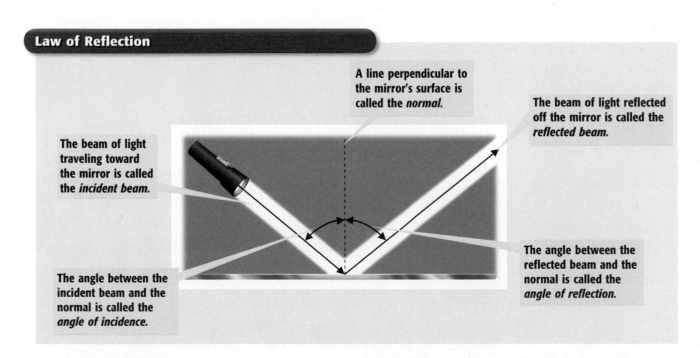

The beam of light traveling toward the mirror is called the *incident beam.*

A line perpendicular to the mirror's surface is called the *normal.*

The beam of light reflected off the mirror is called the *reflected beam.*

The angle between the incident beam and the normal is called the *angle of incidence.*

The angle between the reflected beam and the normal is called the *angle of reflection.*

Useful Equations

Average Speed

The rate at which an object moves is its *speed*. Speed depends on the distance traveled and the time taken to travel that distance. **Average speed** is calculated using the following equation:

$$average\ speed = \frac{total\ distance}{total\ time}$$

> **Example:** A bicycle messenger traveled a distance of 136 km in 8 h. What was the messenger's average speed?
>
> $$\frac{136\ km}{8\ h} = 17\ km/h$$
>
> The messenger's average speed was **17 km/h.**

Velocity

The speed of an object in a particular direction is **velocity.** Speed and velocity are not the same even though they are calculated by using the same equation. Velocity must include a direction, so velocity is described as speed in a certain direction. For example, the speed of a plane that is traveling south at 600 km/h is 600 km/h. The velocity of a plane that is traveling south at 600 km/h is 600 km/h south.

Velocity can also be thought of as the rate of change of an object's position. An object's velocity remains constant only if its speed and direction don't change. Therefore, constant velocity occurs only along a straight line.

Average Acceleration

The rate at which velocity changes is called *acceleration*. **Average acceleration** can be calculated by using the following equation:

$$\frac{average}{acceleration} = \frac{final\ velocity - starting\ velocity}{time\ it\ takes\ to\ change\ velocity}$$

> **Example:** Calculate the average acceleration of an Olympic sprinter who reached a velocity of 20 m/s south at the finish line of a 100 m dash. The race was in a straight line and lasted 10 s.
>
> $$\frac{20\ m/s - 0\ m/s}{10\ s} = 2\ m/s/s$$
>
> The sprinter's average acceleration was **2 m/s/s south.**

The winner of this race is the athlete who has the greatest average speed.

Net Force

Forces in the Same Direction

When forces are in the same direction, add the forces together to determine the net force.

> **Example:** Calculate the net force on a stalled car that is being pushed by two people. One person is pushing with a force of 13 N northwest, and the other person is pushing with a force of 8 N in the same direction.
>
> $$13\ N + 8\ N = 21\ N$$
>
> The net force is **21 N northwest.**

Forces in Opposite Directions

When forces are in opposite directions, subtract the smaller force from the larger force to determine the net force. The net force will be in the direction of the larger force.

> **Example:** Calculate the net force on a rope that is being pulled on each end. One person is pulling on one end of the rope with a force of 12 N south. Another person is pulling on the opposite end of the rope with a force of 7 N north.
>
> $$12\ N - 7\ N = 5\ N$$
>
> The net force is **5 N south.**

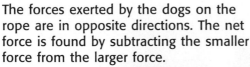

The forces exerted by the dogs on the rope are in opposite directions. The net force is found by subtracting the smaller force from the larger force.

Pressure

Pressure is the force exerted over a given area. The SI unit for pressure is the pascal (Pa).

$$pressure = \frac{force}{area}$$

> **Example:** Calculate the pressure of the air in a soccer ball if the air exerts a force of 25,000 N over an area of 0.15 m².
>
> $$pressure = \frac{25{,}000\ N}{1\ m^2} = \frac{167{,}000\ N}{m^2} = 167{,}000\ Pa$$
>
> The pressure of the air inside the soccer ball is **167,000 Pa.**

Density

The mass per unit volume of a substance is **density.** Thus, a material's density is the amount of matter it contains in a given space. To find density, you must measure both mass and volume. Density is calculated by using the following equation:

$$density = \frac{mass}{volume}$$

> **Example:** Calculate the density of a sponge that has a mass of 10 g and a volume of 40 cm³.
>
> $$\frac{10\ g}{40\ cm^3} = \frac{0.25\ g}{cm^3}$$
>
> The density of the sponge is $\frac{0.25\ g}{cm^3}$.

Appendix

Concentration

A measure of the amount of one substance that is dissolved in another substance is **concentration.** The substance that is dissolved is the solute. The substance that dissolves another substance is the solvent. Concentration is calculated by using the following equation:

$$concentration = \frac{mass\ of\ solute}{volume\ of\ solvent}$$

Example: Calculate the concentration of a solution in which 10 g of sugar is dissolved in 125 mL of water.

$$\frac{10\ g\ of\ sugar}{125\ mL\ of\ water} = \frac{0.08\ g}{mL}$$

The concentration of this solution is $\frac{0.08\ g}{mL}$.

These solutions were made by using the same volume of water. But less solute was dissolved in the beaker on the left. So, the concentration of the solution on the left is lower than the concentration of the solution on the right.

Work

Work is done by exerting a force through a distance. Work is expressed in joules (J), which are equivalent to newton-meters (N•m).

$$work = force \times distance$$

Example: Calculate the amount of work done by a man who lifts a 100 N toddler 1.5 m off the floor.

$$work = 100\ N \times 1.5\ m = 150\ N•m = 150\ J$$

The man did **150 J** of work.

Power

Power is the rate at which work is done. Power is expressed in watts (W), which are equivalent to joules per second (J/s).

$$power = \frac{work}{time}$$

Example: Calculate the power of a weightlifter who raises a 300 N barbell 2.1 m off the floor in 1.25 s.

$$work = 300\ N \times 2.1\ m = 630\ N•m = 630\ J$$

$$power = \frac{30\ J}{1.25\ s} = \frac{504\ J}{s} = 504\ W$$

The weightlifter's power is **504 W.**

Appendix

Heat

Heat is the energy transferred between objects that are at different temperatures. Heat is expressed in joules (J). In general, if you know an object's mass, change in temperature, and specific heat, you can calculate heat. Specific heat is the amount of energy needed to change the temperature of 1 kg of a substance by 1°C. Specific heat is expressed in joules per kilogram-degree Celsius (J/kg•°C).

heat = specific heat × mass × *change in temperature*

Example: Calculate the heat transferred to a mass of 0.2 kg of water to change the temperature of the water from 25°C to 80°C. The specific heat of water is 4,184 J/kg•°C.

heat = 4,184 J/kg•°C × 0.2 kg × (80°C − 25°C) = 46,024 J

The heat transferred is **46,024 J.**

Work and Heat

James Joule, an English scientist, performed experiments to explore the relationship between **work** and **heat.** He found that a given amount of work always generated the same amount of heat. By applying the law of conservation of energy, we know that the amount of heat generated can never be larger than the work done.

Example: What is the maximum amount of heat that can be generated from the work done if a force of 75 N is exerted over a distance of 5 m?

work = 75 N × 5 m = 375 N•m = 375 J

The maximum amount of heat that can be generated is **375 J.**

Example: A force of 299 N is exerted through a distance of 210 m. The resulting work is converted into heat and absorbed by 2.0 kg of water. What is the maximum change in temperature if the specific heat of water is 4,184 J/kg•°C?

work = 299 N × 210 m = 62,790 N•m = 62,790 J

$$\text{change in temperature} = \frac{\text{heat}}{\text{mass} \times \text{specific heat}}$$

$$\text{change in temperature} = \frac{62{,}790 \text{ J}}{2.0 \text{ kg} \times 4{,}184 \text{ J/kg•°C}} = 7.5°C$$

The maximum change in temperature is **7.5°C.**

As the air in this balloon absorbs heat, the temperature of the air rises.

Appendix

Scientific Methods

The ways in which scientists answer questions and solve problems are called **scientific methods.** The same steps are often used by scientists as they look for answers. However, there is more than one way to use these steps. Scientists may use all of the steps or just some of the steps during an investigation. They may even repeat some of the steps. The goal of using scientific methods is to come up with reliable answers and solutions.

Six Steps of Scientific Methods

 Good questions come from careful **observations.** You make observations by using your senses to gather information. Sometimes, you may use instruments, such as microscopes and telescopes, to extend the range of your senses. As you observe the natural world, you will discover that you have many more questions than answers. These questions drive investigations.

Questions beginning with *what, why, how,* and *when* are important in focusing an investigation. Here is an example of a question that could lead to an investigation.

Question: How does acid rain affect plant growth?

 After you ask a question, you need to form a **hypothesis.** A hypothesis is a clear statement of what you expect the answer to your question to be. Your hypothesis will represent your best "educated guess" based on what you have observed and what you already know. A good hypothesis is testable. Otherwise, the investigation can go no further. Here is a hypothesis based on the question "How does acid rain affect plant growth?"

Hypothesis: Acid rain slows plant growth.

The hypothesis can lead to predictions. A prediction is what you think the outcome of your experiment or data collection will be. Predictions are usually stated in an if-then format. Here is a sample prediction for the hypothesis that acid rain slows plant growth.

Prediction: If a plant is watered with only acid rain (which has a pH of 4), then the plant will grow at half its normal rate.

3 Test the Hypothesis

After you have formed a hypothesis and made a prediction, your hypothesis should be tested. One way to test a hypothesis is with a controlled experiment. A **controlled experiment** tests only one factor at a time. In an experiment to test the effect of acid rain on plant growth, the **control group** would be watered with normal rainwater. The **experimental group** would be watered with acid rain. All of the plants should receive the same amount of sunlight and water each day. The air temperature should be the same for all groups. However, the acidity of the water will be a variable. In fact, any factor that differs from one group to another is a **variable.** If your hypothesis is correct, then the acidity of the water and plant growth are *dependant variables.* The amount that a plant grows is dependent on the acidity of the water. However, the amount of water and the amount of sunlight received by each plant are *independent variables.* Either of these factors could change without affecting the other factor.

Sometimes, the nature of an investigation makes a controlled experiment impossible. For example, Earth's core is surrounded by thousands of meters of rock. Under such circumstances, a hypothesis may be tested by making detailed observations.

4 Analyze the Results

After you have completed your experiments, made your observations, and collected your data, you must analyze all of the information that you have gathered. Tables and graphs are often used in this step to organize the data.

5 Draw Conclusions

After analyzing your data, you can determine if your results support your hypothesis. If your hypothesis is supported, you (or others) might want to repeat the observations or experiments to verify your results. If your hypothesis is not supported by the data, you may have to check your procedure for errors. You may even have to reject your hypothesis and make a new one. If you cannot draw a conclusion from your results, you may have to try the investigation again or carry out further observations or experiments.

6 Communicate Results

After any scientific investigation, you should report your results. By preparing a written or oral report, you let others know what you have learned. They may repeat your investigation to see if they get the same results. Your report may even lead to another question and then to another investigation.

Scientific Methods in Action

Scientific methods contain loops in which several steps may be repeated over and over again. In some cases, certain steps are unnecessary. Thus, there is not a "straight line" of steps. For example, sometimes scientists find that testing one hypothesis raises new questions and new hypotheses to be tested. And sometimes, testing the hypothesis leads directly to a conclusion. Furthermore, the steps in scientific methods are not always used in the same order. Follow the steps in the diagram, and see how many different directions scientific methods can take you.

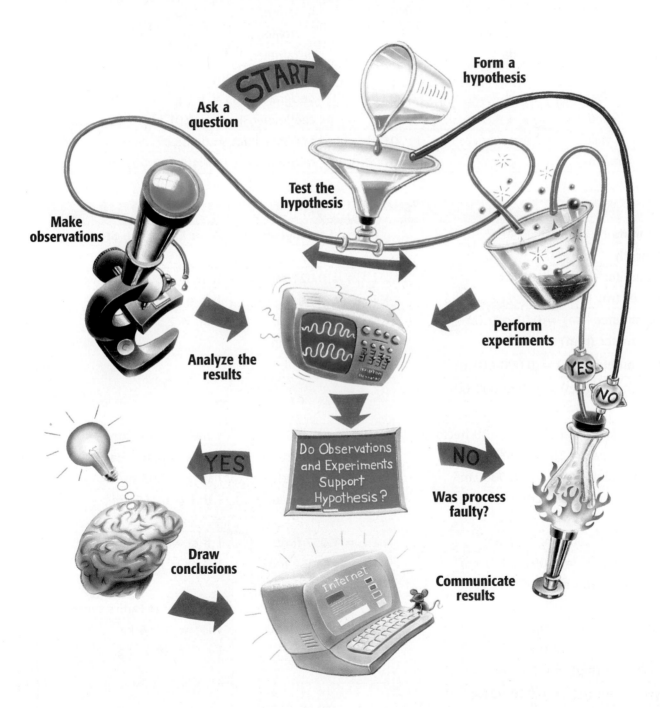

START

Ask a question

Form a hypothesis

Test the hypothesis

Make observations

Perform experiments

Analyze the results

YES

NO

Do Observations and Experiments Support Hypothesis?

YES

NO

Was process faulty?

Draw conclusions

Communicate results

Internet

SI Measurement

The International System of Units, or SI, is the standard system of measurement used by many scientists. Using the same standards of measurement makes it easier for scientists to communicate with one another.

SI works by combining prefixes and base units. Each base unit can be used with different prefixes to define smaller and larger quantities. The table below lists common SI prefixes.

SI Prefixes			
Prefix	**Symbol**	**Factor**	**Example**
kilo-	k	1,000	kilogram, 1 kg = 1,000 g
hecto-	h	100	hectoliter, 1 hL = 100 L
deka-	da	10	dekameter, 1 dam = 10 m
		1	meter, liter, gram
deci-	d	0.1	decigram, 1 dg = 0.1 g
centi-	c	0.01	centimeter, 1 cm = 0.01 m
milli-	m	0.001	milliliter, 1 mL = 0.001 L
micro-	μ	0.000 001	micrometer, 1 μm = 0.000 001 m

SI Conversion Table		
SI units	**From SI to English**	**From English to SI**
Length		
kilometer (km) = 1,000 m	1 km = 0.621 mi	1 mi = 1.609 km
meter (m) = 100 cm	1 m = 3.281 ft	1 ft = 0.305 m
centimeter (cm) = 0.01 m	1 cm = 0.394 in.	1 in. = 2.540 cm
millimeter (mm) = 0.001 m	1 mm = 0.039 in.	
micrometer (μm) = 0.000 001 m		
nanometer (nm) = 0.000 000 001 m		
Area		
square kilometer (km^2) = 100 hectares	1 km^2 = 0.386 mi^2	1 mi^2 = 2.590 km^2
hectare (ha) = 10,000 m^2	1 ha = 2.471 acres	1 acre = 0.405 ha
square meter (m^2) = 10,000 cm^2	1 m^2 = 10.764 ft^2	1 ft^2 = 0.093 m^2
square centimeter (cm^2) = 100 mm^2	1 cm^2 = 0.155 $in.^2$	1 $in.^2$ = 6.452 cm^2
Volume		
liter (L) = 1,000 mL = 1 dm^3	1 L = 1.057 fl qt	1 fl qt = 0.946 L
milliliter (mL) = 0.001 L = 1 cm^3	1 mL = 0.034 fl oz	1 fl oz = 29.574 mL
microliter (μL) = 0.000 001 L		
Mass		*Equivalent weight at Earth's surface
kilogram (kg) = 1,000 g	1 kg = 2.205 lb*	1 lb* = 0.454 kg
gram (g) = 1,000 mg	1 g = 0.035 oz*	1 oz* = 28.350 g
milligram (mg) = 0.001 g		
microgram (μg) = 0.000 001 g		

Measuring Skills

Using a Graduated Cylinder

When using a graduated cylinder to measure volume, keep the following procedures in mind:

1. Place the cylinder on a flat, level surface before measuring liquid.

2. Move your head so that your eye is level with the surface of the liquid.

3. Read the mark closest to the liquid level. On glass graduated cylinders, read the mark closest to the center of the curve in the liquid's surface.

Using a Meterstick or Metric Ruler

When using a meterstick or metric ruler to measure length, keep the following procedures in mind:

1. Place the ruler firmly against the object that you are measuring.

2. Align one edge of the object exactly with the 0 end of the ruler.

3. Look at the other edge of the object to see which of the marks on the ruler is closest to that edge. (Note: Each small slash between the centimeters represents a millimeter, which is one-tenth of a centimeter.)

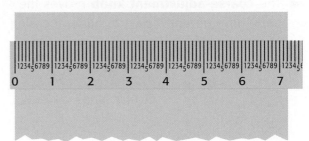

Using a Triple-Beam Balance

When using a triple-beam balance to measure mass, keep the following procedures in mind:

1. Make sure the balance is on a level surface.

2. Place all of the countermasses at 0. Adjust the balancing knob until the pointer rests at 0.

3. Place the object to be measured on the pan. **Caution:** Do not place hot objects or chemicals directly on the balance pan.

4. Move the largest countermass along the beam to the right until it is at the last notch that does not tip the balance. Follow the same procedure with the next-largest countermass. Then, move the smallest countermass until the pointer rests at 0.

5. Add the readings from the three beams together to determine the mass of the object.

6. When determining the mass of crystals or powders, first find the mass of a piece of filter paper. Then, add the crystals or powder to the paper, and remeasure. The actual mass of the crystals or powder is the total mass minus the mass of the paper. When finding the mass of liquids, first find the mass of the empty container. Then, find the combined mass of the liquid and container. The mass of the liquid is the total mass minus the mass of the container.

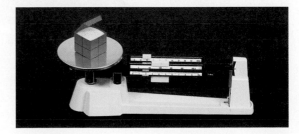

Using the Microscope

Parts of the Compound Light Microscope

- The **ocular lens** magnifies the image 10×.
- The **low-power objective** magnifies the image 10×.
- The **high-power objective** magnifies the image either 40× or 43×.
- The **revolving nosepiece** holds the objectives and can be turned to change from one magnification to the other.
- The **body tube** maintains the correct distance between the ocular lens and objectives.
- The **coarse-adjustment knob** moves the body tube up and down to allow focusing of the image.

- The **fine-adjustment knob** moves the body tube slightly to bring the image into sharper focus. It is usually located in the center of the coarse-adjustment knob.
- The **stage** supports a slide.
- **Stage clips** hold the slide in place for viewing.
- The **diaphragm** controls the amount of light coming through the stage.
- The light source provides a **light** for viewing the slide.
- The **arm** supports the body tube.
- The **base** supports the microscope.

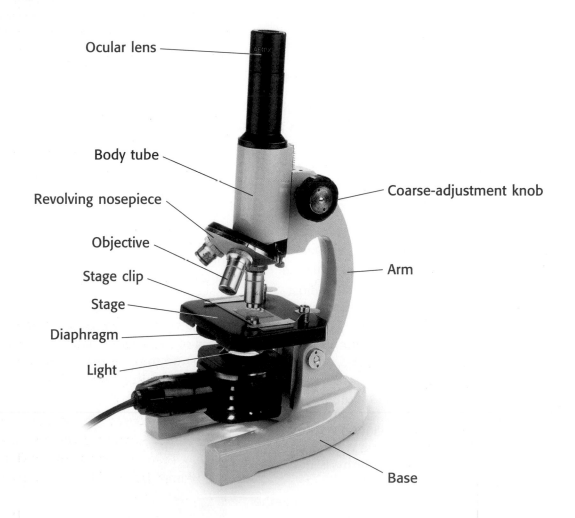

Ocular lens

Body tube

Revolving nosepiece

Objective

Stage clip

Stage

Diaphragm

Light

Coarse-adjustment knob

Arm

Base

Appendix

Proper Use of the Compound Light Microscope

1 Use both hands to carry the microscope to your lab table. Place one hand beneath the base, and use the other hand to hold the arm of the microscope. Hold the microscope close to your body while carrying it to your lab table.

2 Place the microscope on the lab table at least 5 cm from the edge of the table.

3 Check to see what type of light source is used by your microscope. If the microscope has a lamp, plug it in and make sure that the cord is out of the way. If the microscope has a mirror, adjust the mirror to reflect light through the hole in the stage.
Caution: If your microscope has a mirror, do not use direct sunlight as a light source. Direct sunlight can damage your eyes.

4 Always begin work with the low-power objective in line with the body tube. Adjust the revolving nosepiece.

5 Place a prepared slide over the hole in the stage. Secure the slide with the stage clips.

6 Look through the ocular lens. Move the diaphragm to adjust the amount of light coming through the stage.

7 Look at the stage from eye level. Slowly turn the coarse adjustment to lower the objective until the objective almost touches the slide. Do not allow the objective to touch the slide.

8 Look through the ocular lens. Turn the coarse adjustment to raise the low-power objective until the image is in focus. Always focus by raising the objective away from the slide. Never focus the objective downward. Use the fine adjustment to sharpen the focus. Keep both eyes open while viewing a slide.

9 Make sure that the image is exactly in the center of your field of vision. Then, switch to the high-power objective. Focus the image by using only the fine adjustment. Never use the coarse adjustment at high power.

10 When you are finished using the microscope, remove the slide. Clean the ocular lens and objectives with lens paper. Return the microscope to its storage area. Remember to use both hands when carrying the microscope.

Making a Wet Mount

1 Use lens paper to clean a glass slide and a coverslip.

2 Place the specimen that you wish to observe in the center of the slide.

3 Using a medicine dropper, place one drop of water on the specimen.

4 Hold the coverslip at the edge of the water and at a 45° angle to the slide. Make sure that the water runs along the edge of the coverslip.

5 Lower the coverslip slowly to avoid trapping air bubbles.

6 Water might evaporate from the slide as you work. Add more water to keep the specimen fresh. Place the tip of the medicine dropper next to the edge of the coverslip. Add a drop of water. (You can also use this method to add stain or solutions to a wet mount.) Remove excess water from the slide by using the corner of a paper towel as a blotter. Do not lift the coverslip to add or remove water.

Periodic Table of the Elements

Each square on the table includes an element's name, chemical symbol, atomic number, and atomic mass.

The color of the chemical symbol indicates the physical state at room temperature. Carbon is a solid.

6	Atomic number
C	Chemical symbol
Carbon	Element name
12.0	Atomic mass

The background color indicates the type of element. Carbon is a nonmetal.

Period 1

| 1 |
| **H** |
| Hydrogen |
| 1.0 |

Background

Metals	
Metalloids	
Nonmetals	

Chemical symbol

Solid	
Liquid	
Gas	

	Group 1	Group 2
Period 2	3 **Li** Lithium 6.9	4 **Be** Beryllium 9.0
Period 3	11 **Na** Sodium 23.0	12 **Mg** Magnesium 24.3

	Group 1	Group 2	Group 3	Group 4	Group 5	Group 6	Group 7	Group 8	Group 9
Period 4	19 **K** Potassium 39.1	20 **Ca** Calcium 40.1	21 **Sc** Scandium 45.0	22 **Ti** Titanium 47.9	23 **V** Vanadium 50.9	24 **Cr** Chromium 52.0	25 **Mn** Manganese 54.9	26 **Fe** Iron 55.8	27 **Co** Cobalt 58.9
Period 5	37 **Rb** Rubidium 85.5	38 **Sr** Strontium 87.6	39 **Y** Yttrium 88.9	40 **Zr** Zirconium 91.2	41 **Nb** Niobium 92.9	42 **Mo** Molybdenum 95.9	43 **Tc** Technetium (98)	44 **Ru** Ruthenium 101.1	45 **Rh** Rhodium 102.9
Period 6	55 **Cs** Cesium 132.9	56 **Ba** Barium 137.3	57 **La** Lanthanum 138.9	72 **Hf** Hafnium 178.5	73 **Ta** Tantalum 180.9	74 **W** Tungsten 183.8	75 **Re** Rhenium 186.2	76 **Os** Osmium 190.2	77 **Ir** Iridium 192.2
Period 7	87 **Fr** Francium (223)	88 **Ra** Radium (226)	89 **Ac** Actinium (227)	104 **Rf** Rutherfordium (261)	105 **Db** Dubnium (262)	106 **Sg** Seaborgium (266)	107 **Bh** Bohrium (264)	108 **Hs** Hassium (277)	109 **Mt** Meitnerium (268)

A row of elements is called a *period*.

A column of elements is called a *group* or *family*.

Values in parentheses are the mass numbers of those radioactive elements' most stable or most common isotopes.

These elements are placed below the table to allow the table to be narrower.

Lanthanides	58 **Ce** Cerium 140.1	59 **Pr** Praseodymium 140.9	60 **Nd** Neodymium 144.2	61 **Pm** Promethium (145)	62 **Sm** Samarium 150.4
Actinides	90 **Th** Thorium 232.0	91 **Pa** Protactinium 231.0	92 **U** Uranium 238.0	93 **Np** Neptunium (237)	94 **Pu** Plutonium (244)

Topic: **Periodic Table**
Go To: **go.hrw.com**
Keyword: **HN0 PERIODIC**
Visit the HRW Web site for updates on the periodic table.

Group 18

						Group 18
						2 **He** Helium 4.0

This zigzag line reminds you where the metals, nonmetals, and metalloids are.

Group 13	Group 14	Group 15	Group 16	Group 17	
5 **B** Boron 10.8	6 **C** Carbon 12.0	7 **N** Nitrogen 14.0	8 **O** Oxygen 16.0	9 **F** Fluorine 19.0	10 **Ne** Neon 20.2
13 **Al** Aluminum 27.0	14 **Si** Silicon 28.1	15 **P** Phosphorus 31.0	16 **S** Sulfur 32.1	17 **Cl** Chlorine 35.5	18 **Ar** Argon 39.9

Group 10	Group 11	Group 12						
28 **Ni** Nickel 58.7	29 **Cu** Copper 63.5	30 **Zn** Zinc 65.4	31 **Ga** Gallium 69.7	32 **Ge** Germanium 72.6	33 **As** Arsenic 74.9	34 **Se** Selenium 79.0	35 **Br** Bromine 79.9	36 **Kr** Krypton 83.8
46 **Pd** Palladium 106.4	47 **Ag** Silver 107.9	48 **Cd** Cadmium 112.4	49 **In** Indium 114.8	50 **Sn** Tin 118.7	51 **Sb** Antimony 121.8	52 **Te** Tellurium 127.6	53 **I** Iodine 126.9	54 **Xe** Xenon 131.3
78 **Pt** Platinum 195.1	79 **Au** Gold 197.0	80 **Hg** Mercury 200.6	81 **Tl** Thallium 204.4	82 **Pb** Lead 207.2	83 **Bi** Bismuth 209.0	84 **Po** Polonium (209)	85 **At** Astatine (210)	86 **Rn** Radon (222)
110 **Ds** Darmstadtium (281)	111 **Uuu** Unununium (272)	112 **Uub** Ununbium (285)	113 **Uut** Ununtrium (284)	114 **Uuq** Ununquadium (289)	115 **Uup** Ununpentium (288)			

The discovery of elements 113, 114, and 115 has been reported but not confirmed.

The names and three-letter symbols of elements are temporary. They are based on the atomic numbers of the elements. Official names and symbols will be approved by an international committee of scientists.

63 **Eu** Europium 152.0	64 **Gd** Gadolinium 157.2	65 **Tb** Terbium 158.9	66 **Dy** Dysprosium 162.5	67 **Ho** Holmium 164.9	68 **Er** Erbium 167.3	69 **Tm** Thulium 168.9	70 **Yb** Ytterbium 173.0	71 **Lu** Lutetium 175.0
95 **Am** Americium (243)	96 **Cm** Curium (247)	97 **Bk** Berkelium (247)	98 **Cf** Californium (251)	99 **Es** Einsteinium (252)	100 **Fm** Fermium (257)	101 **Md** Mendelevium (258)	102 **No** Nobelium (259)	103 **Lr** Lawrencium (262)

Appendix

Properties of Common Minerals

Silicate Minerals

Mineral	Color	Luster	Streak	Hardness
Beryl	deep green, pink, white, bluish green, or yellow	vitreous	white	7.5–8
Chlorite	green	vitreous to pearly	pale green	2–2.5
Garnet	green, red, brown, black	vitreous	white	6.5–7.5
Hornblende	dark green, brown, or black	vitreous	none	5–6
Muscovite	colorless, silvery white, or brown	vitreous or pearly	white	2–2.5
Olivine	olive green, yellow	vitreous	white or none	6.5–7
Orthoclase	colorless, white, pink, or other colors	vitreous	white or none	6
Plagioclase	colorless, white, yellow, pink, green	vitreous	white	6
Quartz	colorless or white; any color when not pure	vitreous or waxy	white or none	7

Native Elements

Mineral	Color	Luster	Streak	Hardness
Copper	copper-red	metallic	copper-red	2.5–3
Diamond	pale yellow or colorless	adamantine	none	10
Graphite	black to gray	submetallic	black	1–2

Carbonates

Mineral	Color	Luster	Streak	Hardness
Aragonite	colorless, white, or pale yellow	vitreous	white	3.5–4
Calcite	colorless or white to tan	vitreous	white	3

Halides

Mineral	Color	Luster	Streak	Hardness
Fluorite	light green, yellow, purple, bluish green, or other colors	vitreous	none	4
Halite	white	vitreous	white	2.0–2.5

Oxides

Mineral	Color	Luster	Streak	Hardness
Hematite	reddish brown to black	metallic to earthy	dark red to red-brown	5.6–6.5
Magnetite	iron-black	metallic	black	5.5–6.5

Sulfates

Mineral	Color	Luster	Streak	Hardness
Anhydrite	colorless, bluish, or violet	vitreous to pearly	white	3–3.5
Gypsum	white, pink, gray, or colorless	vitreous, pearly, or silky	white	2.0

Sulfides

Mineral	Color	Luster	Streak	Hardness
Galena	lead-gray	metallic	lead-gray to black	2.5–2.8
Pyrite	brassy yellow	metallic	greenish, brownish, or black	6–6.5

Nonsilicate Minerals

Appendix

Density (g/cm³)	Cleavage, Fracture, Special Properties	Common Uses
2.6–2.8	1 cleavage direction; irregular fracture; some varieties fluoresce in ultraviolet light	gemstones, ore of the metal beryllium
2.6–3.3	1 cleavage direction; irregular fracture	
4.2	no cleavage; conchoidal to splintery fracture	gemstones, abrasives
3.0–3.4	2 cleavage directions; hackly to splintery fracture	
2.7–3	1 cleavage direction; irregular fracture	electrical insulation, wallpaper,
3.2–3.3	no cleavage; conchoidal fracture	gemstones, casting
2.6	2 cleavage directions; irregular fracture	porcelain
2.6–2.7	2 cleavage directions; irregular fracture	ceramics
2.6	no cleavage; conchoidal fracture	gemstones, concrete, glass, porcelain, sandpaper, lenses
8.9	no cleavage; hackly fracture	wiring, brass, bronze, coins
3.5	4 cleavage directions; irregular to conchoidal fracture	gemstones, drilling
2.3	1 cleavage direction; irregular fracture	pencils, paints, lubricants, batteries
2.95	2 cleavage directions; irregular fracture; reacts with hydrochloric acid	no important industrial uses
2.7	3 cleavage directions; irregular fracture; reacts with weak acid; double refraction	cements, soil conditioner, whitewash, construction materials
3.0–3.3	4 cleavage directions; irregular fracture; some varieties fluoresce	hydrofluoric acid, steel, glass, fiberglass, pottery, enamel
2.1–2.2	3 cleavage directions; splintery to conchoidal fracture; salty taste	tanning hides, salting icy roads, food preservation
5.2–5.3	no cleavage; splintery fracture; magnetic when heated	iron ore for steel, pigments
5.2	no cleavage; splintery fracture; magnetic	iron ore
3.0	3 cleavage directions; conchoidal to splintery fracture	soil conditioner, sulfuric acid
2.3	3 cleavage directions; conchoidal to splintery fracture	plaster of Paris, wallboard, soil conditioner
7.4–7.6	3 cleavage directions; irregular fracture	batteries, paints
5	no cleavage; conchoidal to splintery fracture	sulfuric acid

Appendix

Temperature Scales

Temperature can be expressed by using three scales: the Fahrenheit, Celsius, and Kelvin scales. The SI unit for temperature is the kelvin (K). Although 0 K is much colder than 0°C, a change of 1 K is equal to a change of 1°C.

Three Temperature Scales

	Fahrenheit	Celsius	Kelvin
Water boils	212°	100°	373
Body temperature	98.6°	37°	310
Room temperature	68°	20°	293
Water freezes	32°	0°	273

Temperature Conversion Table

Conversion	Equation	Example
degrees Celsius to degrees Fahrenheit °C → °F	$°F = \left(\dfrac{9}{5} \times °C\right) + 32$	Convert 45°C to °F. $°F = \left(\dfrac{9}{5} \times 45°C\right) + 32 = 113°F$
degrees Fahrenheit to degrees Celsius °F → °C	$°C = \dfrac{5}{9} \times (°F - 32)$	Convert 68°F to °C. $°C = \dfrac{5}{9} \times (68°F - 32) = 20°C$
degrees Celsius to kelvins °C → K	$K = °C + 273$	Convert 45°C to K. $K = 45°C + 273 = 318\ K$
kelvins to degrees Celsius K → °C	$°C = K - 273$	Convert 32 K to °C. $°C = 32K - 273 = -241°C$

English and Spanish Glossary

with Academic Vocabulary

A

abiotic (AY bie AHT ik) describes the nonliving part of the environment, including water, rocks, light, and temperature (550)

abiótico término que describe la parte sin vida del ambiente, incluyendo el agua, las rocas, la luz y la temperatura (550)

abrasion (uh BRAY zhuhn) the grinding and wearing away of rock surfaces through the mechanical action of other rock or sand particles (299, 341)

abrasión proceso por el cual las superficies de las rocas se muelen o desgastan por medio de la acción mecánica de otras rocas y partículas de arena (299, 341)

abyssal plain (uh BIS uhl PLAYN) a large, flat, almost level area of the deep-ocean basin (409)

llanura abisal un área amplia, llana y casi plana de la cuenca oceánica profunda (409)

accreted terrane (uh KREET uhd ter RAYN) a piece of lithosphere that becomes part of a larger landmass when tectonic plates collide at a convergent boundary (213)

terreno acrecentado un pedazo de litosfera que se vuelve parte de una masa de tierra mayor cuando las placas tectónicas chocan en un límite convergente (213)

acid precipitation (AS id pree SIP uh TAY shuhn) rain, sleet, or snow that contains a high concentration of acids (164, 301, 487)

precipitación ácida lluvia, aguanieve o nieve que contiene una alta concentración de ácidos (164, 301, 487)

air mass (ER MAS) a large body of air throughout which temperature and moisture content are similar (512)

masa de aire un gran volumen de aire, cuya temperatura y cuyo contenido de humedad son similares en toda su extensión (512)

air pollution (ER puh LOO shuhn) the contamination of the atmosphere by the introduction of pollutants from human and natural sources (484)

contaminación del aire la contaminación de la atmósfera debido a la introducción de contaminantes provenientes de fuentes humanas y naturales (484)

air pressure (ER PRESH uhr) the measure of the force with which air molecules push on a surface (471)

presión del aire la medida de la fuerza con la que las moléculas del aire empujan contra una superficie (471)

alluvial fan (uh LOO vee uhl FAN) a fan-shaped mass of material deposited by a stream when the slope of the land decreases sharply (375)

abanico aluvial masa en forma de abanico de materiales depositados por un arroyo cuando la pendiente del terreno disminuye bruscamente (375)

*appropriate (uh PROH pree it) correct for the use; proper (41)

apropiado correcto para un determinado uso; adecuado (41)

aquifer (AK wuh fuhr) a body of rock or sediment that stores groundwater and allows the flow of groundwater (378)

acuífero un cuerpo rocoso o sedimento que almacena agua subterránea y permite que fluya (378)

area (ER ee uh) a measure of the size of a surface or a region (47)

área una medida del tamaño de una superficie o región (47)

Glossary

*Academic Vocabulary

asthenosphere (as THEN uh SFIR) the soft layer of the mantle on which the tectonic plates move (191)

astenosfera la capa blanda del manto sobre la que se mueven las placas tectónicas (191)

atmosphere (AT muhs FIR) a mixture of gases that surrounds a planet or moon (470)

atmósfera una mezcla de gases que rodea un planeta o una luna (470)

* **available** (uh VAYL uh buhl) that can be used (295, 547, 577)

disponible que se puede usar (295, 547, 577)

B

batholith (BATH oh LITH) a large mass of igneous rock in Earth's crust that, if exposed at the surface, covers an area of at least 100 km² (212)

batolito una masa grande de rocas ígneas en la corteza terrestre que, expuesta en la superficie, cubre un área de al menos 100 km² (212)

beach (BEECH) an area of the shoreline that is made up of deposited sediment (336)

playa un área de la costa que está formada por sedimento depositado (336)

bedrock (BED RAHK) the layer of rock beneath soil (308)

lecho de roca la capa de rocas que está debajo del suelo (308)

biomass (BIE oh MAS) plant material, manure, or any other organic matter that is used as an energy source (171)

biomasa materia vegetal, estiércol o cualquier otra materia orgánica que se usa como fuente de energía (171)

biome (BIE OHM) a large region characterized by a specific type of climate and certain types of plant and animal communities (553)

bioma una región extensa caracterizada por un tipo de clima específico y ciertos tipos de comunidades de plantas y animales (553)

biosphere (BIE oh SFIR) the part of Earth where life exists; includes all of the living organisms on Earth (553)

biosfera la parte de la Tierra donde existe la vida; comprende todos los seres vivos de la Tierra (553)

biotic (bie AHT ik) describes living factors in the environment (550)

biótico término que describe los factores vivientes del ambiente (550)

C

carbon cycle (KAHR buhn SIE kuhl) the movement of carbon from the nonliving environment into living things and back (109)

ciclo del carbono el movimiento del carbono del ambiente sin vida a los seres vivos y de los seres vivos al ambiente (109)

carnivore (KAHR nuh VAWR) an organism that eats animals (555)

carnívoro un organismo que se alimenta de animales (555)

carrying capacity (KAR ee ing kuh PAS i tee) the largest population that an environment can support at any given time (561)

capacidad de carga la población más grande que un ambiente puede sostener en cualquier momento (561)

* **categorize** (KAT uh guh RIEZ) to put into groups or classes (547, 577)

clasificar ordenar por grupos o clases (547, 577)

channel (CHAN uhl) the path that a stream follows (369)

canal el camino que sigue un arroyo (369)

chaparral (SHAP uh RAL) a type of vegetation that includes broad-leaved evergreen shrubs and that is located in areas with hot, dry summers and mild, wet winters (585)

chaparral un tipo de vegetación que incluye arbustos de hoja perenne y ancha, y que se ubica en áreas donde los veranos son calientes y secos y los inviernos son templados y húmedos (585)

*Academic Vocabulary

chemical (KEM i kuhl) of or having to do with the properties or actions of substances (547, 577)

químico perteneciente o relativo a las propiedades o acciones de las sustancias (547, 577)

chemical energy (KEM i kuhl EN uhr jee) the energy released when a chemical compound reacts to produce new compounds (168)

energía química la energía que se libera cuando un compuesto químico reacciona para producir nuevos compuestos (168)

chemical weathering (KEM i kuhl WETH uhr ing) the process by which rocks break down as a result of chemical reactions (301)

desgaste químico el proceso por medio del cual las rocas se fragmentan como resultado de reacciones químicas (301)

climate (KLIE muht) the average weather conditions in an area over a long period of time (520)

clima las condiciones promedio del tiempo en un área durante un largo período de tiempo (520)

cloud (KLOWD) a collection of small water droplets or ice crystals suspended in the air, which forms when the air is cooled and condensation occurs (510)

nube un conjunto de pequeñas gotitas de agua o cristales de hielo suspendidos en el aire, que se forma cuando el aire se enfría y ocurre condensación (510)

coal (KOHL) a fossil fuel that forms underground from partially decomposed plant material (160)

carbón un combustible fósil que se forma en el subsuelo a partir de materiales vegetales parcialmente descompuestos (160)

commensalism (kuh MEN suhl iz uhm) a relationship between two organisms in which one organism benefits and the other is unaffected (564)

comensalismo una relación entre dos organismos en la que uno se beneficia y el otro no es afectado (564)

*   **communicate** (kuh MYOO ni KAYT) to make known; to tell (5)

    comunicar hacer saber; decir (5)

community (kuh MYOO nuh tee) all of the populations of species that live in the same habitat and interact with each other (552)

comunidad todas las poblaciones de especies que viven en el mismo hábitat e interactúan entre sí (552)

*   **computer** (kuhm PYOOT uhr) an electronic device that stores, retrieves, and calculates data (41)

    computadora un dispositivo electrónico que almacena, recupera y calcula datos (41)

condensation (KAHN duhn SAY shuhn) the change of state from a gas to a liquid (509)

condensación el cambio de estado de gas a líquido (509)

conduction (kuhn DUHK shuhn) the transfer of energy as heat through a material (94, 476)

conducción la transferencia de energía en forma de calor a través de un material (94, 476)

*   **consequence** (KAHN si KWENS) the effect, or result, of an action or process (155)

    consecuencia el efecto, o resultado, de una acción o un proceso (155)

conservation (KAHN suhr VAY shuhn) the preservation and wise use of natural resources (382)

conservación la preservación y el uso inteligente de los recursos naturales (382)

*   **consistent** (kuhn SIS tuhnt) in agreement (5, 41)

    conforme de acuerdo (5, 41)

*   **construct** (kuhn STRUHKT) to build; to make from parts (41)

    construir armar; hacer con partes (41)

*   **construction** (kuhn STRUHK shuhn) the type of buildings in an area; the way something is built (229)

    construcción el tipo de edificios que hay en un área; la forma en que algo está construido (229)

consume (kuhn SOOM) to use up (155)

   consumir agotar (155)

continental drift (KAHN tuh NENT uhl DRIFT) the hypothesis that a single large landmass broke up into smaller landmasses to form the continents, which then drifted to their present locations; the movement of continents (193)

   deriva continental la hipótesis de que una sola masa de tierra se dividió en masas de tierra más pequeñas para formar los continentes, los cuales se fueron a la deriva hasta terminar en sus ubicaciones actuales; el movimiento de los continentes (193)

controlled experiment (kuhn TROHLD ek SPER uh muhnt) an experiment that tests only one factor at a time by using a comparison of a control group with an experimental group (19)

   experimento controlado un experimento que prueba sólo un factor a la vez, comparando un grupo de control con un grupo experimental (19)

convection (kuhn VEK shuhn) the movement of matter due to differences in density; the transfer of energy due to the movement of matter (86, 94, 477)

   convección el movimiento de la materia debido a diferencias en la densidad; la transferencia de energía debido al movimiento de la materia (86, 94, 477)

convection current (kuhn VEK shuhn KUHR uhnt) any movement of matter that results from differences in density; may be vertical, circular, or cyclical (87, 441, 477)

   corriente de convección cualquier movimiento de la materia que se produce como resultado de diferencias en la densidad; puede ser vertical, circular o cíclico (87, 441, 477)

*conversion (kuhn VUHR zhuhn) a change from one form or state to another (155)

   transformación cambio de una forma o estado a otra forma o estado (155)

*convert (kuhn VUHRT) to change from one form to another (155)

   transformarse cambiar de una forma a otra (155)

core (KAWR) the central part of Earth below the mantle (85, 190)

   núcleo la parte central de la Tierra, debajo del manto (85, 190)

Coriolis effect (KAWR ee OH lis e FEKT) the curving of the path of a moving object from an otherwise straight path due to Earth's rotation (438, 481)

   efecto de Coriolis la desviación de la trayectoria recta que experimentan los objetos en movimiento debido a la rotación de la Tierra (438, 481)

creep (KREEP) the slow downhill movement of weathered rock material (350)

   arrastre el movimiento lento y descendente de materiales rocosos desgastados (350)

crust (KRUHST) the thin and solid outermost layer of Earth above the mantle (85, 190)

   corteza la capa externa, delgada y sólida de la Tierra, que se encuentra sobre el manto (85, 190)

*cycle (SIE kuhl) a repeating series of changes (81, 363, 433, 467, 503)

   ciclo una serie de cambios que se repiten (81, 363, 433, 467, 503)

cyclone (SIE KLOHN) an area in the atmosphere that has lower pressure than the surrounding areas and has winds that spiral toward the center (514)

   ciclón un área de la atmósfera que tiene una presión menor que la de las áreas circundantes y que tiene vientos que giran en espiral hacia el centro (514)

D

data (DAYT uh) any pieces of information acquired through observation or experimentation (19)

   datos cualquier parte de la información que se adquiere por medio de la observación o experimentación (19)

*data (DAYT uh) facts or figures; information (41)

   datos hechos o números; información (41)

*Academic Vocabulary

deep current (DEEP KUHR uhnt) a streamlike movement of ocean water far below the surface (439)

corriente profunda un movimiento del agua del océano que es similar a una corriente y ocurre debajo de la superficie (439)

deep-water zone (DEEP WAWT uhr ZOHN) the zone of a lake or pond below the open-water zone, where no light reaches (601)

zona de aguas profundas la zona de un lago o laguna debajo de la zona de aguas abiertas, a donde no llega la luz (601)

deflation (dee FLAY shuhn) a form of wind erosion in which fine, dry soil particles are blown away (341)

deflación una forma de erosión del viento en la que se mueven partículas de suelo finas y secas (341)

delta (DEL tuh) a fan-shaped mass of material deposited at the mouth of a stream (375)

delta un depósito de materiales que tiene forma de abanico y que se deposita en la desembocadura de un río (375)

deposition (DEP uh ZISH uhn) the process in which material is laid down (374)

deposición el proceso por medio del cual un material se deposita (374)

* **derive** (di RIEV) to figure out by reasoning (187, 229, 397)

deducir entender mediante el razonamiento (187, 229, 397)

desalination (DEE SAL uh NAY shuhn) a process of removing salt from ocean water (413)

desalación (o desalinización) un proceso de remoción de sal del agua del océano (413)

desert (DEZ uhrt) a region that has little or no plant life, long periods without rain, and extreme temperatures; usually found in hot climates (584)

desierto una región con poca vegetación o sin vegetación, largos períodos sin lluvia y temperaturas extremas; generalmente se ubica en climas calientes (584)

dew point (DOO POYNT) at constant pressure and water vapor content, the temperature at which the rate of condensation equals the rate of evaporation (507)

punto de rocío a presión y contenido de vapor de agua constantes, la temperatura a la que la tasa de condensación es igual a la tasa de evaporación (507)

differential weathering (DIF uhr EN shuhl WETH uhr ing) the process by which softer, less weather resistant rocks wear away at a faster rate than harder, more weather resistant rocks do (304)

desgaste diferencial el proceso por medio cual las rocas más blandas y menos resistentes al clima se desgastan a una tasa más rápida que las rocas más duras y resistentes al clima (304)

* **display** (di SPLAY) to show (41)

presentar mostrar (41)

* **distribute** (di STRIB yoot) to spread out over an area (397, 433, 467, 503)

distribuir extender sobre un área (397, 433, 467, 503)

* **distribution** (DIS tri BYOO shuhn) the relative arrangement of objects or organisms in time or space (187, 229, 397)

distribución disposición relativa de objetos u organismos en el tiempo o el espacio (187, 229, 397)

divide (duh VIED) the boundary between drainage areas that have streams that flow in opposite directions (368)

división el límite entre áreas de drenaje que tienen corrientes que fluyen en direcciones opuestas (368)

* **dominant** (DAHM uh nuhnt) having the greatest effect (329, 363)

dominante que tiene el mayor efecto (329, 363)

Glossary

dune (DOON) a mound of wind-deposited sand that moves as a result of the action of wind (342)

duna un montículo de arena depositada por el viento que se mueve como resultado de la acción de éste (342)

* **dynamic** (die NAM ik) active; tending toward change (295, 329, 363)

dinámico activo; que tiende al cambio (295, 329, 363)

E

earthquake (UHRTH KWAYK) a movement or trembling of the ground that is caused by a sudden release of energy when rocks along a fault move (232)

terremoto un movimiento o temblor del suelo causado por una liberación súbita de energía que se produce cuando las rocas ubicadas a lo largo de una falla se mueven (232)

ecology (ee KAHL uh jee) the study of the interactions of living organisms with one another and with their environment (550)

ecología el estudio de las interacciones de los seres vivos entre sí mismos y entre sí mismos y su ambiente (550)

ecosystem (EE koh SIS tuhm) a community of organisms and their abiotic, or nonliving, environment (552)

ecosistema una comunidad de organismos y su ambiente abiótico o no vivo (552)

elastic rebound (ee LAS tik REE BOWND) the sudden return of elastically deformed rock to its undeformed shape (235)

rebote elástico ocurre cuando una roca deformada elásticamente vuelve súbitamente a su forma no deformada (235)

electromagnetic spectrum (ee LEK troh mag NET ik SPEK truhm) all of the frequencies or wavelengths of electromagnetic radiation (99, 475)

espectro electromagnético todas las frecuencias o longitudes de onda de la radiación electromagnética (99, 475)

elevation (EL uh VAY shuhn) the height of an object above sea level (64, 524)

elevación la altura de un objeto sobre el nivel del mar (64, 524)

El Niño (el NEEN yoh) a change in the water temperature in the Pacific Ocean that produces a warm current (445)

El Niño un cambio en la temperatura del agua superficial del océano Pacífico que produce una corriente caliente (445)

* **energy** (EN uhr jee) the ability to make things happen (81, 125, 155, 295, 329, 363, 433, 467, 503, 547, 577)

energía la capacidad de hacer que las cosas ocurran (81, 125, 155, 295, 329, 363, 433, 467, 503, 547, 577)

energy pyramid (EN uhr jee PIR uh mid) a triangular diagram that shows an ecosystem's loss of energy, which results as energy passes through the ecosystem's food chain (557)

pirámide de energía un diagrama triangular que muestra la pérdida de energía en un ecosistema, producida a medida que la energía pasa a través de la cadena alimenticia del ecosistema (557)

energy resource (EN uhr jee REE SAWRS) a natural resource that humans use to generate energy (158)

recurso energético un recurso natural que utilizan los humanos para generar energía (158)

epicenter (EP i SENT uhr) the point on Earth's surface directly above an earthquake's starting point, or focus (238)

epicentro el punto de la superficie de la Tierra que queda justo arriba del punto de inicio, o foco, de un terremoto (238)

equator (ee KWAYT uhr) the imaginary circle halfway between the poles that divides the Earth into the Northern and Southern Hemispheres (57)

ecuador el círculo imaginario que se encuentra a la mitad entre los polos y divide a la Tierra en los hemisferios norte y sur (57)

*Academic Vocabulary

Glossary

*erode (ee ROHD) to wear away (295, 363)

erosionar desgastar (295, 363)

erosion (ee ROH zhuhn) the process by which wind, water, ice, or gravity transports soil and sediment from one location to another (315, 366)

erosión el proceso por medio del cual el viento, el agua, el hielo o la gravedad transporta tierra y sedimentos de un lugar a otro (315, 366)

estuary (ES tyoo er ee) an area where fresh water mixes with salt water from the ocean (596)

estuario un área donde el agua dulce de los ríos se mezcla con el agua salada del océano (596)

*evidence (EV uh duhns) information showing whether an idea or belief is true or valid (5, 41, 187, 229, 397)

prueba información que demuestra si una idea o creencia es verdadera o válida (5, 41, 187, 229, 397)

exfoliation (eks FOH lee AY shuhn) the process by which sheets of rock peel away from a large body of rock because pressure is removed (299)

exfoliación el proceso mediante el cual capas de roca se separan de un cuerpo rocoso grande al dejar de aplicarse presión (299)

F

*factor (FAK tuhr) a condition or event that brings about a result (155, 295, 547, 577)

factor una condición o un suceso que produce un resultado (155, 295, 547, 577)

fault (FAWLT) a break in a body of rock along which one block slides relative to another (206)

falla una grieta en un cuerpo rocoso a lo largo de la cual un bloque se desliza respecto a otro (206)

*feature (FEE chuhr) the shape or form of a thing; characteristic (187)

característica la forma particular de una cosa (187)

felsic (FEL sik) describes magma or igneous rock that is rich in feldspars and silica and that is generally light in color (274)

félsico término que describe un tipo de magma o roca ígnea que es rica en feldespatos y sílice y generalmente tiene un color claro (274)

first aid (FUHRST AYD) emergency medical care for someone who has been hurt or who is sick (29)

primeros auxilios atención médica de emergencia para una persona que se lastimó o está enferma (29)

floodplain (FLUHD PLAYN) an area along a river that forms from sediments deposited when the river overflows its banks (376)

llanura de inundación un área a lo largo de un río formada por sedimentos que se depositan cuando el río se desborda (376)

focus (FOH kuhs) the location within Earth along a fault at which the first motion of an earthquake occurs (238)

foco el lugar dentro de la Tierra a lo largo de una falla donde ocurre el primer movimiento de un terremoto (238)

folding (FOHLD ing) the bending of rock layers due to stress (205)

plegamiento fenómeno que ocurre cuando las capas de roca se doblan debido a la compresión (205)

food chain (FOOD CHAYN) the pathway of energy transfer through various stages as a result of the feeding patterns of a series of organisms (555)

cadena alimenticia la vía de transferencia de energía través de varias etapas, que ocurre como resultado de los patrones de alimentación de una serie de organismos (555)

food web (FOOD WEB) a diagram that shows the feeding relationships between organisms in an ecosystem (556)

red alimenticia un diagrama que muestra las relaciones de alimentación entre los organismos de un ecosistema (556)

Glossary

fossil fuel (FAHS uhl FYOO uhl) a nonrenewable energy resource formed from the remains of organisms that lived long ago; examples include oil, coal, and natural gas (158)

combustible fósil un recurso energético no renovable formado a partir de los restos de organismos que vivieron hace mucho tiempo; algunos ejemplos incluyen el petróleo, el carbón y el gas natural (158)

front (FRUHNT) the boundary between air masses of different densities and usually different temperatures (512)

frente el límite entre masas de aire de diferentes densidades y, normalmente, diferentes temperaturas (512)

*function (FUHNGK shuhn) use or purpose (547, 577)

función uso o propósito (547, 577)

G

gasohol (GAS uh HAWL) a mixture of gasoline and alcohol that is used as a fuel (171)

gasohol una mezcla de gasolina y alcohol que se usa como combustible (171)

geologic map (JEE uh LAHJ ik MAP) a map that records geologic information, such as rock units, structural features, mineral deposits, and fossil localities (68)

mapa geológico mapa que registra la información geológica, como las unidades rocosas, las características estructurales, los depósitos minerales y la ubicación de los fósiles (68)

geothermal energy (JEE oh THUHR muhl EN uhr jee) the energy produced by heat within Earth (172)

energía geotérmica la energía producida por el calor del interior de la Tierra (172)

glacial drift (GLAY shuhl DRIFT) the rock material carried and deposited by glaciers (346)

deriva glacial el material rocoso que es transportado y depositado por los glaciares (346)

glacier (GLAY shuhr) a large mass of moving ice (344)

glaciar una masa grande de hielo en movimiento (344)

global warming (GLOH buhl WAWRM ing) a gradual increase in average global temperature (531)

calentamiento global un aumento gradual de la temperatura global promedio (531)

grassland (GRAS LAND) a region that is dominated by grasses, that has few woody shrubs and trees, that has fertile soils, and that receives moderate amounts of seasonal rainfall (586)

pradera una región en la que predomina la hierba, tiene algunos arbustos leñosos y árboles y suelos fértiles, y recibe cantidades moderadas de precipitaciones estacionales (586)

greenhouse effect (GREEN HOWS e FEKT) the warming of the surface and lower atmosphere of Earth that occurs when water vapor, carbon dioxide, and other gases absorb and reradiate thermal energy (478, 532)

efecto invernadero el calentamiento de la superficie y de la parte más baja de la atmósfera, el cual se produce cuando el vapor de agua, el dióxido de carbono y otros gases absorben y vuelven a irradiar la energía térmica (478, 532)

H

heat (HEET) the energy transferred between objects that are at different temperatures (92)

calor la transferencia de energía entre objetos que están a temperaturas diferentes (92)

heat flow (HEET FLOH) another term for *heat transfer,* the transfer of energy from a warmer object to a cooler object (98)

flujo de calor otro término para la transferencia de calor, transferencia de energía de un objeto más caliente a un objeto más frío (98)

herbivore (HUHR buh VAWR) an organism that eats only plants (555)

herbívoro un organismo que sólo come plantas (555)

*Academic Vocabulary

Glossary

humidity (hyoo MID uh tee) the amount of water vapor in the air (507)

humedad la cantidad de vapor de agua que hay en el aire (507)

humus (HYOO muhs) dark, organic material formed in soil from the decayed remains of plants and animals (310)

humus material orgánico obscuro que se forma en la tierra a partir de restos de plantas y animales en descomposición (310)

hydroelectric energy (HIE DROH ee LEK trik EN uhr gee) electrical energy produced by the flow of water (170)

energía hidroeléctrica energía eléctrica producida por el flujo del agua (170)

hypothesis (hie PAHTH uh sis) a testable idea or explanation that leads to scientific investigation (18)

hipótesis una idea o explicación que conlleva a la investigación científica y que se puede probar (18)

I

ice age (IES AYJ) a long period of climatic cooling during which the continents are glaciated repeatedly (528)

edad de hielo un largo período de enfriamiento del clima, durante el cual los continentes se ven repetidamente sometidos a la glaciación (528)

*__identify__ (ie DEN tuh FIE) to point out or pick out (5)

identificar señalar o elegir (5)

intensity (in TEN suh tee) in Earth science, the amount of damage caused by an earthquake (241)

intensidad en las ciencias de la Tierra, la cantidad de daño causado por un terremoto (241)

*__interpret__ (in TUHR pruht) to tell or explain the meaning of (5, 41)

interpretar decir o explicar el significado de algo (5, 41)

*__investigation__ (in VES tuh GAY shuhn) a detailed search for answers (5)

investigación búsqueda cuidadosa de respuestas (5)

*__involve__ (in VAHLV) to be a part of (155)

implicar formar parte de (155)

*__involve__ (in VAHLV) to have as a part of (397, 433, 467)

consistir tener como parte (397, 433, 467)

L

lahar (LAH HAHR) a mudflow that forms when volcanic ash and debris mix with water during a volcanic eruption (279)

lahar un flujo de lodo que se forma cuando la ceniza y otros detritos volcánicos se mezclan con agua durante una erupción volcánica (279)

landslide (LAND SLIED) the sudden movement of rock and soil down a slope (349)

derrumbamiento el movimiento súbito hacia abajo de rocas y suelo por una pendiente (349)

La Niña (lah NEEN yuh) a change in the Eastern Pacific Ocean in which the surface water temperature becomes unusually cool (445)

La Niña un cambio en el océano Pacífico oriental por el cual el agua superficial se vuelve más fría que de costumbre (445)

latitude (LAT uh TOOD) the distance north or south from the equator; expressed in degrees (57, 521)

latitud la distancia hacia el norte o hacia el sur del ecuador; se expresa en grados (57, 521)

lava (LAH vuh) magma that flows onto Earth's surface; the rock that forms when lava cools and solidifies (270)

lava magma que fluye a la superficie terrestre; la roca que se forma cuando la lava se enfría y se solidifica (270)

Glossary

law (LAW) a descriptive statement or equation that reliably predicts events under certain conditions (53)

ley una ecuación o afirmación descriptiva que predice sucesos de manera confiable en determinadas condiciones (53)

***layer** (LAY uhr) a separate or distinct portion of matter that has thickness (81, 187)

capa una parte separada o diferenciada de materia que tiene espesor (81, 187)

lightning (LIET ning) an electric discharge that takes place between two oppositely charged surfaces, such as between a cloud and the ground, between two clouds, or between two parts of the same cloud (515)

relámpago una descarga eléctrica que ocurre entre dos superficies que tienen carga opuesta, como por ejemplo, entre una nube y el suelo, entre dos nubes o entres dos partes de la misma nube (515)

lithosphere (LITH oh sFIR) the solid, outer layer of Earth that consists of the crust and the rigid upper part of the mantle (191)

litosfera la capa externa y sólida de la Tierra que está formada por la corteza y la parte superior y rígida del manto (191)

littoral zone (LIT uh ruhl ZOHN) the shallow zone of a lake or pond where light reaches the bottom and nurtures plants (601)

zona litoral la zona poco profunda de un lago o una laguna donde la luz llega al fondo y nutre a las plantas (601)

***location** (loh KAY shuhn) a place or position (187, 229, 263, 397)

ubicación lugar o posición (187, 229, 263, 397)

load (LOHD) the materials carried by a stream (370)

carga los materiales que lleva un arroyo (370)

longitude (LAHN juh TOOD) the distance east or west from the prime meridian; expressed in degrees (58)

longitud la distancia angular hacia el este o hacia el oeste del primer meridiano; se expresa en grados (58)

longshore current (LAWNG SHAWR KUHR uhnt) a water current that travels near and parallel to the shoreline (337)

corriente de ribera una corriente de agua que se desplaza cerca de la costa y paralela a ella (337)

M

mafic (MAF ik) describes magma or igneous rock that is rich in magnesium and iron and that is generally dark in color (270)

máfico término que describe un tipo de magma o roca ígnea que es rica en magnesio y hierro y generalmente tiene un color oscuro (270)

magma (MAG muh) liquid rock produced under Earth's surface; igneous rocks are made of magma (266)

magma roca líquida producida debajo de la superficie terrestre; las rocas ígneas están hechas de magma (266)

magnitude (MAG nuh TOOD) a measure of the strength of an earthquake (240)

magnitud una medida de la intensidad de un terremoto (240)

***major** (MAY juhr) of great importance or large scale (81, 187, 229, 263, 363, 397, 433, 467, 503)

principal de gran importancia o gran escala (81, 187, 229, 263, 363, 397, 433, 467, 503)

***manipulate** (muh NIP yoo LAYT) to affect or control (5)

manipular afectar o controlar (5)

mantle (MAN tuhl) the layer of rock between Earth's crust and core (85, 190)

manto la capa de roca que se encuentra entre la corteza terrestre y el núcleo (85, 190)

map (MAP) a representation of the features of a physical body such as Earth (56)

mapa una representación de las características de un cuerpo físico, tal como la Tierra (56)

Glossary

marsh (MAHRSH) a treeless wetland ecosystem where plants such as grasses grow (602)

pantano un ecosistema pantanoso sin árboles, donde crecen plantas tales como el pasto (602)

mass (MAS) a measure of the amount of matter in an object (47)

masa una medida de la cantidad de materia que tiene un objeto (47)

mass movement (MAS MOOV muhnt) the movement of a large mass of sediment or a section of land down a slope (348)

movimiento masivo el movimiento hacia abajo por una pendiente de una gran masa de sedimento o una sección de terreno (348)

material resource (muh TIR ee uhl REE SAWRS) a natural resource that humans use to make objects or to consume as food and drink (138)

recurso material un recurso natural que utilizan los seres humanos para fabricar objetos o para consumir como alimento o bebida (138)

mechanical weathering (muh KAN i kuhl WETH uhr ing) the process by which rocks break down into smaller pieces by physical means (298)

desgaste mecánico el proceso por medio del cual las rocas se rompen en pedazos más pequeños mediante medios físicos (298)

mesosphere (MES oh SFIR) the layer of the atmosphere between the stratosphere and the thermosphere and in which temperature decreases as altitude increases (473)

mesosfera la capa de la atmósfera que se encuentra entre la estratosfera y la termosfera, en la cual la temperatura disminuye al aumentar la altitud (473)

meter (MEET uhr) the basic unit of length in the SI (symbol, m) (47)

metro la unidad fundamental de longitud en el sistema internacional de unidades (símbolo: m) (47)

mid-ocean ridge (MID OH shuhn RIJ) a long, undersea mountain chain that forms along the floor of the major oceans (410)

dorsal oceánica una larga cadena submarina de montañas que se forma en el suelo de los principales océanos (410)

mineral (MIN uhr uhl) a natural, usually inorganic solid that has a characteristic chemical composition and an orderly internal structure (132)

mineral un sólido natural, normalmente inorgánico, que tiene una composición química característica y una estructura interna ordenada (132)

model (MAHD'l) a pattern, plan, representation, or description designed to show the structure or workings of an object, system, or concept (51)

modelo un diseño, plan, representación o descripción cuyo objetivo es mostrar la estructura o funcionamiento de un objeto, sistema o concepto (51)

mudflow (MUHD FLOH) the flow of a mass of mud or rock and soil mixed with a large amount of water (350)

flujo de lodo el flujo de una masa de lodo o roca y suelo mezclados con una gran cantidad de agua (350)

mutualism (MYOO choo uhl IZ uhm) a relationship between two species in which both species benefit (564)

mutualismo una relación entre dos especies en la que ambas se benefician (564)

N

natural gas (NACH uhr uhl GAS) a mixture of gaseous hydrocarbons located under the surface of Earth, often near petroleum deposits; used as a fuel (159)

gas natural una mezcla de hidrocarburos gaseosos que se encuentran debajo de la superficie de la Tierra, normalmente cerca de los depósitos de petróleo, y los cuales se usan como combustible (159)

Glossary

natural resource (NACH uhr uhl REE SAWRS) any natural material that is used by humans, such as water, petroleum, minerals, forests, and animals (128)

recurso natural cualquier material natural que es utilizado por los seres humanos, como agua, petróleo, minerales, bosques y animales (128)

neap tide (NEEP TIED) a tide of minimum range that occurs during the first and third quarters of the moon (454)

marea muerta una marea que tiene un rango mínimo, la cual ocurre durante el primer y el tercer cuartos de la Luna (454)

nitrogen cycle (NIE truh juhn SIE kuhl) the process in which nitrogen circulates among the air, soil, water, plants, and animals in an ecosystem (110)

ciclo del nitrógeno el proceso por medio del cual el nitrógeno circula en el aire, el suelo, el agua, las plantas y los animales de un ecosistema (110)

nonpoint-source pollution (NAHN POYNT SAWRS puh LOO shuhn) pollution that comes from many sources rather than from a single, specific site (416)

contaminación no puntual contaminación que proviene de muchas fuentes, en lugar de provenir de un solo sitio específico (416)

nonrenewable resource (NAHN ri NOO uh buhl REE SAWRS) a resource that forms at a rate that is much slower than the rate at which the resource is consumed (129)

recurso no renovable un recurso que se forma a una tasa que es mucho más lenta que la tasa a la que se consume (129)

nuclear energy (NOO klee uhr EN uhr jee) the energy released by a fission or fusion reaction; the binding energy of the atomic nucleus (166)

energía nuclear la energía liberada por una reacción de fisión o fusión; la energía de enlace del núcleo atómico (166)

O

ocean trench (OH shuhn TRENCH) a long, narrow, and steep depression on the ocean floor that forms when one tectonic plate subducts beneath another plate; trenches run parallel to volcanic island chains or to the coastlines of continents; also called a *trench* or a *deep-ocean trench* (411)

fosa oceánica una depresión larga, angosta y empinada que se encuentra en el fondo del océano y se forma cuando una placa tectónica se subduce bajo otra; las fosas submarinas corren en forma paralela a cadenas de islas volcánicas o a las costas continentales; también denominada *fosa* o *fosa oceánica profunda* (411)

omnivore (AHM ni VAWR) an organism that eats both plants and animals (555)

omnívoro un organismo que come tanto plantas como animales (555)

open-water zone (OH puhn WAWT uhr ZOHN) the zone of a pond or lake that extends from the littoral zone and that is only as deep as light can reach (601)

zona de aguas superiores la zona de un lago o una laguna que se extiende desde la zona litoral y cuya profundidad sólo alcanza hasta donde penetra la luz (601)

ore (AWR) a natural material whose concentration of economically valuable minerals is high enough for the material to be mined profitably (134)

mena un material natural cuya concentración de minerales con valor económico es suficientemente alta como para que el material pueda ser explotado de manera rentable (134)

P

parasitism (PAR uh SIET IZ uhm) a relationship between two species in which one species, the parasite, benefits from the other species, the host, which is harmed (565)

parasitismo una relación entre dos especies en la que una, el parásito, se beneficia de la otra, el huésped, que resulta perjudicada (565)

*Academic Vocabulary

parent rock (PER uhnt RAHK) a rock formation that is the source of soil (308)

roca precursora una formación rocosa que es la fuente a partir de la cual se origina el suelo (308)

petroleum (puh TROH lee uhm) a liquid mixture of complex hydrocarbon compounds; used widely as a fuel source (139, 159)

petróleo una mezcla líquida de compuestos hidrocarburos complejos; se usa ampliamente como una fuente de combustible (139, 159)

*phenomenon (fuh NAHM uh NUHN) any fact or event that can be sensed or described scientifically (plural, *phenomena*) (5, 81, 363, 433, 467, 503)

fenómeno cualquier hecho o suceso que se puede percibir o describir por medios científicos (5, 81, 363, 433, 467, 503)

*physical (FIZ i kuhl) able to be seen or touched (547, 577)

físico que se puede ver o tocar (547, 577)

phytoplankton (FIET oh PLANGK tuhn) the microscopic, photosynthetic organisms that float near the surface of marine or fresh water (592)

fitoplancton los organismos microscópicos fotosintéticos que flotan cerca de la superficie del agua dulce o marina (592)

plate tectonics (PLAYT tek TAHN iks) the theory that explains how large pieces of Earth's outermost layer, called *tectonic plates,* move and change shape (198)

tectónica de placas la teoría que explica cómo se mueven y cambian de forma las placas tectónicas, que son grandes porciones de la capa más externa de la Tierra (198)

point-source pollution (POYNT SAWRS puh LOO shuhn) pollution that comes from a specific site (417)

contaminación puntual contaminación que proviene de un lugar específico (417)

population (PAHP yoo LAY shuhn) a group of organisms of the same species that live in a specific geographical area (552)

población un grupo de organismos de la misma especie que viven en un área geográfica específica (552)

precipitation (pree SIP uh TAY shuhn) any form of water that falls to Earth's surface from the clouds (511)

precipitación cualquier forma de agua que cae de las nubes a la superficie de la Tierra (511)

predator (PRED uh tuhr) an organism that kills and eats all or part of another organism (562)

depredador un organismo que mata y se alimenta de otro organismo o de parte de él (562)

prey (PRAY) an organism that is killed and eaten by another organism (562)

presa un organismo al que otro organismo mata para alimentarse de él (562)

*primarily (prie MER uh lee) mainly (81, 187)

fundamentalmente principalmente (81, 187)

prime meridian (PRIEM muh RID ee uhn) the meridian, or line of longitude, that is designated as 0° longitude (58)

meridiano de Greenwich el meridiano, o línea de longitud, que se designa como longitud 0° (58)

*process (PRAH SES) a set of steps, events, or changes (155, 295, 329, 363)

proceso una serie de pasos, sucesos o cambios (155, 295, 329, 363)

Q

*qualitative (KWAWL i TAYT iv) descriptive information that is not expressed as a number and is based on comparisons between traits (41)

cualitativo información descriptiva que no se expresa con números y se basa en comparaciones entre distintos rasgos (41)

R

radiation (RAY dee AY shuhn) the transfer of energy as electromagnetic waves (95, 474)

radiación la transferencia de energía en forma de ondas electromagnéticas (95, 474)

*range (RAYNJ) a scale or series between limits (295, 547, 577)

rango escala o serie entre dos límites (295, 547, 577)

recycling (ree SIE kling) the process of recovering valuable or useful materials from waste or scrap (131)

reciclar el proceso de recuperar materiales valiosos o útiles de los desechos o de la basura (131)

*region (REE juhn) an area (229)

región área (229)

relative humidity (REL uh tiv hyoo MID uh tee) the ratio of the amount of water vapor in the air to the amount of water vapor needed to reach saturation at a given temperature (507)

humedad relativa la proporción de la cantidad de vapor de agua que hay en el aire respecto a la cantidad de vapor de agua que se necesita para alcanzar la saturación a una temperatura dada (507)

*release (ri LEES) to set free; to let go (155)

liberar poner en libertad; soltar (155)

relief (ri LEEF) the variations in elevation of a land surface (65)

relieve la diferencia entre las elevaciones más altas y las más bajas en un área dada; las variaciones en elevación de una superficie de terreno (65)

remote sensing (re MOHT SENS ing) the process of gathering and analyzing information about an object without physically being in touch with the object (60)

teledetección el proceso de recopilar y analizar información acerca de un objeto sin estar en contacto físico con el objeto (60)

renewable resource (ri NOO uh buhl REE SAWRS) a natural resource that can be replaced at the same rate at which the resource is consumed (129)

recurso renovable un recurso natural que puede reemplazarse a la misma tasa a la que se consume (129)

*resource (REE SAWRS) anything that can be used to take care of a need (125, 155, 295, 363, 547, 577)

recurso cualquier cosa que se puede usar para satisfacer una necesidad (125, 155, 295, 363, 547, 577)

*response (ri SPAHNS) an action brought on by another action; a reaction (187)

respuesta una acción provocada por otra acción; una reacción (187)

rock cycle (RAHK SIE kuhl) the series of processes in which rock forms, changes from one type to another, is destroyed, and forms again by geologic processes (105)

ciclo de las rocas la serie de procesos por medio de los cuales una roca se forma, cambia de un tipo a otro, se destruye y se forma nuevamente por procesos geológicos (105)

rock fall (RAHK FAHL) the rapid mass movement of rock down a steep slope or cliff (349)

desprendimiento de rocas el movimiento rápido y masivo de rocas por una pendiente empinada o un precipicio (349)

*role (ROHL) a part or function; purpose (577)

papel parte o función; propósito (577)

S

salinity (suh LIN uh tee) a measure of the amount of dissolved salts in a given amount of liquid (401)

salinidad una medida de la cantidad de sales disueltas en una cantidad determinada de líquido (401)

*Academic Vocabulary

674   English and Spanish Glossary

Glossary

saltation (sal TAY shuhn) the movement of sand or other sediments by short jumps and bounces that is caused by wind or water (340)

saltación el movimiento de la arena u otros sedimentos por medio de saltos pequeños y rebotes debido al viento o al agua (340)

scientific literacy (SIE uhn TIF ik LIT uhr uh see) the understanding of the methods of scientific inquiry, the scope of scientific knowledge, and the role of science in society (12)

cultura científica el entendimiento de los métodos de investigación científica, el campo del conocimiento científico y el papel de las ciencias en la sociedad (12)

scientific methods (SIE uhn TIF ik METH uhds) a series of steps followed to solve problems (17)

métodos científicos una serie de pasos que se siguen para solucionar problemas (17)

sea-floor spreading (SEE FLAWR SPRED ing) the process by which new oceanic lithosphere forms as magma rises to Earth's surface and solidifies at a mid-ocean ridge (196)

expansión del suelo marino el proceso por medio del cual se forma nueva litosfera oceánica (suelo marino) a medida que el magma se eleva a la superficie de la Tierra y se solidifica en una dorsal oceánica (196)

seismic gap (SIEZ mik GAP) an area along a fault where relatively few earthquakes have occurred recently but where strong earthquakes have occurred in the past (245)

brecha sísmica un área a lo largo de una falla donde han ocurrido relativamente pocos terremotos recientemente, pero donde se han producido terremotos fuertes en el pasado (245)

seismic wave (SIEZ mik WAYV) a wave of energy that travels through the Earth and away from an earthquake in all directions (235)

onda sísmica una onda de energía que viaja a través de la Tierra y se aleja de un terremoto en todas direcciones (235)

*select (suh LEKT) to choose; to pick out (41)

seleccionar elegir; escoger (41)

*sequence (SEE kwuhns) the order in which things come or events happen (5)

secuencia orden en que vienen las cosas u ocurren los sucesos (5)

shoreline (SHAWR LIEN) the boundary between land and a body of water (332)

orilla el límite entre la tierra y una masa de agua (332)

*similar (SIM uh luhr) almost the same (577)

similar casi igual (577)

skepticism (SKEP ti SIZ uhm) a habit of mind in which a person questions the validity of accepted ideas (9)

escepticismo un hábito de la mente que hace que la persona cuestione la validez de las ideas aceptadas (9)

soil (SOYL) a loose mixture of rock fragments, organic material, water, and air that can support the growth of vegetation (308)

suelo una mezcla suelta de fragmentos de roca, material orgánico, agua y aire en la que puede crecer vegetación (308)

soil conservation (SOYL KAHN suhr VAY shuhn) a method to maintain the fertility of the soil by protecting the soil from erosion and nutrient loss (314)

conservación del suelo un método para mantener la fertilidad del suelo protegiéndolo de la erosión y la pérdida de nutrientes (314)

solar energy (SOH luhr EN uhr jee) the energy received by Earth from the sun in the form of radiation (169)

energía solar la energía que la Tierra recibe del Sol en forma de radiación (169)

*source (SAWRS) the thing from which something else comes (81, 155, 363, 433, 467, 503)

fuente el lugar de donde viene una cosa (81, 155, 363, 433, 467, 503)

Glossary

spring tide (SPRING TIED) a tide of increased range that occurs two times a month, at the new and full moons (454)

marea viva una marea de mayor rango que ocurre dos veces al mes, durante la luna nueva y la luna llena (454)

stratified drift (STRAT uh FIED DRIFT) a glacial deposit that has been sorted and layered by the action of streams or meltwater (347)

deriva estratificada un depósito glacial que ha formado capas debido a la acción de los arroyos o de las aguas de ablación (347)

stratosphere (STRAT uh SFIR) the layer of the atmosphere that is above the troposphere and in which temperature increases as altitude increases (472)

estratosfera la capa de la atmósfera que se encuentra encima de la troposfera y en la que la temperatura aumenta al aumentar la altitud (472)

surface current (SUHR fis KUHR uhnt) a horizontal movement of ocean water that is caused by wind and that occurs at or near the ocean's surface (436, 525)

corriente superficial un movimiento horizontal del agua del océano que es producido por el viento y que ocurre en la superficie del océano o cerca de ella (436, 525)

swamp (SWAHMP) a wetland ecosystem in which shrubs and trees grow (602)

ciénaga un ecosistema de pantano en el que crecen arbustos y árboles (602)

symbiosis (SIM bie OH sis) a relationship in which two different organisms live in close association with each other (564)

simbiosis una relación en la que dos organismos diferentes viven estrechamente asociados uno con el otro (564)

T

*technology (tek NAHL uh jee) tools, including electronic products (41)

tecnología herramientas; incluye los productos electrónicos (41)

tectonic plate (tek TAHN ik PLAYT) a block of lithosphere that consists of the crust and the rigid, outermost part of the mantle (198)

placa tectónica un bloque de litosfera formado por la corteza y la parte rígida y más externa del manto (198)

temperature (TEM puhr uh chuhr) a measure of how hot (or cold) something is; specifically, a measure of the average kinetic energy of the particles in an object (48, 90)

temperatura una medida de qué tan caliente (o frío) está algo; específicamente, una medida de la energía cinética promedio de las partículas de un objeto (48, 90)

theory (THEE uh ree) a system of ideas that explains many related observations and is supported by a large body of evidence acquired through scientific investigation (53)

teoría un sistema de ideas que explica muchas observaciones relacionadas y que está respaldado por una gran cantidad de pruebas obtenidas mediante la investigación científica (53)

thermal energy (THUHR muhl EN uhr jee) the kinetic energy of a substance's atoms (93)

energía térmica la energía cinética de los átomos de una sustancia (93)

thermocline (THUHR moh KLIEN) a layer in a body of water in which water temperature drops with increased depth faster than it does in other layers (403)

termoclina una capa en una masa de agua en la que, al aumentar la profundidad, la temperatura del agua disminuye más rápido de lo que lo hace en otras capas (403)

thermosphere (THUHR moh SFIR) the uppermost layer of the atmosphere, in which temperature increases as altitude increases (473)

termosfera la capa más alta de la atmósfera, en la cual la temperatura aumenta a medida que la altitud aumenta (473)

thunder (THUHN duhr) the sound caused by the rapid expansion of air along an electrical strike (515)

trueno el sonido producido por la expansión rápida del aire a lo largo de una descarga eléctrica (515)

*Academic Vocabulary

Glossary

tide (TIED) the periodic rise and fall of the water level in the oceans and other large bodies of water (452)

marea el ascenso y descenso periódico del nivel del agua en los océanos y otras masas grandes de agua (452)

till (TIL) unsorted rock material that is deposited directly by a melting glacier (346)

arcilla glaciárica material rocoso desordenado que deposita directamente un glaciar que se está derritiendo (346)

topographic map (TAHP uh GRAF ik MAP) a map that shows the surface features of Earth (64)

mapa topográfico un mapa que muestra las características superficiales de la Tierra (64)

tornado (tawr NAY doh) a destructive, rotating column of air that has very high wind speeds and that may be visible as a funnel-shaped cloud (516)

tornado una columna destructiva de aire en rotación cuyos vientos se mueven a velocidades muy altas y que puede verse como una nube con forma de embudo (516)

***transfer** (TRANS fuhr) (v.) to carry or cause to pass from one thing to another (81, 467, 547, 577)

transferir transportar algo o hacer que pase de una cosa a otra (81, 467, 547, 577)

***transport** (trans PAWRT) to carry from one place to another (295, 363)

transportar llevar de un lugar a otro (295, 363)

tributary (TRIB yoo TER ee) a stream that flows into a lake or into a larger stream (368)

afluente un arroyo que fluye a un lago o a otro arroyo más grande (368)

troposphere (TROH poh SFIR) the lowest layer of the atmosphere, in which temperature decreases at a constant rate as altitude increases (472)

troposfera la capa inferior de la atmósfera, en la que la temperatura disminuye a una tasa constante a medida que la altitud aumenta (472)

tsunami (tsoo NAH mee) a giant ocean wave that forms after a volcanic eruption, submarine earthquake, or landslide (249)

tsunami una ola gigante del océano que se forma después de una erupción volcánica, terremoto submarino o desprendimiento de tierras (249)

tundra (TUHN druh) a treeless plain found in the Arctic, in the Antarctic, or on the tops of mountains that is characterized by very low winter temperatures and short, cool summers (587)

tundra una llanura sin árboles situada en la región ártica o antártica o en la cumbre de las montañas; se caracteriza por temperaturas muy bajas en el invierno y veranos cortos y frescos (587)

U

undertow (UHN duhr TOH) a subsurface current that is near shore and that pulls objects out to sea (337)

resaca un corriente subsuperficial que está cerca de la orilla y que arrastra los objetos hacia el mar (337)

upwelling (UHP WEL ing) the movement of deep, cold, and nutrient-rich water to the surface (447)

surgencia el movimiento de las aguas profundas, frías y ricas en nutrientes hacia la superficie (447)

***utility** (yoo TIL uh tee) usefulness (155)

utilidad que se puede usar (155)

V

***variable** (VER ee uh buhl) a factor that changes in an experiment in order to test a hypothesis (41)

variable factor que se cambia en un experimento para poner a prueba una hipótesis (41)

***vary** (VER ee) to differ; to have more than one possible state (229)

variar ser distinto; tener más de un estado posible (229)

Glossary

*visible (VIZ uh buhl) that can be seen (81, 467, 503)

visible que se puede ver (81, 467, 503)

volcano (vahl KAY noh) a vent or fissure in Earth's surface through which magma and gases are expelled (266)

volcán una chimenea o fisura en la superficie de la Tierra a través de la cual se expulsan magma y gases (266)

volume (VAHL yoom) a measure of the size of a body or region in three-dimensional space (48)

volumen una medida del tamaño de un cuerpo o región en un espacio de tres dimensiones (48)

W

water cycle (WAWT uhr SIE kuhl) the continuous movement of water between the atmosphere, the land, and the oceans (108, 367)

ciclo del agua el movimiento continuo del agua entre la atmósfera, la tierra y los océanos (108, 367)

water pollution (WAWT uhr puh LOO shuhn) waste matter or other material that is introduced into water and that is harmful to organisms that live in, drink, or are exposed to the water (380)

contaminación del agua material de desecho u otro material que se introduce en el agua y que daña a los organismos que viven en el agua, la beben o están expuestos a ella (380)

watershed (WAWT uhr SHED) the area of land that is drained by a river system (368)

cuenca hidrográfica el área del terreno que es drenada por un sistema de ríos (368)

water table (WAWT uhr TAY buhl) the upper surface of underground water (378)

capa freática el nivel más alto del agua subterránea (378)

wave (WAYV) a periodic disturbance in a solid, liquid, or gas as energy is transmitted through a medium (448)

onda una perturbación periódica en un sólido, líquido o gas que se transmite a través de un medio en forma de energía (448)

weather (WETH uhr) the short-term state of the atmosphere, including temperature, humidity, precipitation, wind, and visibility (506)

tiempo el estado de la atmósfera a corto plazo que incluye la temperatura, la humedad, la precipitación, el viento y la visibilidad (506)

weathering (WETH uhr ing) the natural process by which atmospheric and environmental agents, such as wind, rain, and temperature changes, disintegrate and decompose rocks (298)

weathering el proceso natural por medio del cual los agentes atmosféricos o ambientales, como el viento, la lluvia y los cambios de temperatura, desintegran y descomponen las rocas (298)

wetland (WET LAND) an area of land that is periodically underwater or whose soil contains a great deal of moisture (602)

pantano un área de tierra que está periódicamente bajo el agua o cuyo suelo contiene una gran cantidad de humedad (602)

wind (WIND) the movement of air caused by differences in air pressure (480)

viento el movimiento de aire producido por diferencias en la presión barométrica (480)

wind power (WIND POW uhr) the use of a windmill to drive an electric generator (168)

potencia eólica el uso de un molino de viento para hacer funcionar un generador eléctrico (168)

---

*Academic Vocabulary

Index

Boldface page numbers refer to illustrative material, such as figures, tables, margin elements, photographs, and illustrations.

A

Index

Index

Index

Index

Index

Index

Index

Index

Index

X

Y

Index

Acknowledgments

continued from p. ii

Senior Advisors

Susana E. Deustua, Ph.D.
Director of Educational Activities
American Astronomical Society
Washington, D.C.

Frances Marie Gipson, MA
*Director of the UCLA and District 3
    LAUSD Partnership*
Department of Secondary Literacy
University of California, Los Angeles; Center X
Los Angeles, California

Ron Hage
Science Partner
University of California, Los Angeles;
    Los Angeles Unified School District
Los Angeles, California

James E. Marshall, Ph.D.
Professor of Science Education
Department of Curriculum and Instruction
California State University, Fresno
Fresno, California

Richard D. McCallum, Ph.D.
Research Specialist
Graduate School of Education
University of California, Berkeley
Berkeley, California

Advisors

Kristin L. Baker
Science Teacher
Starr King School
Carmichael, California

Laura L. Bauer
Department Chair
Toby Johnson Middle School
Elk Grove, California

Jack Bettencourt
Science Department Chair
Joseph Kerr Middle School
Elk Grove, California

Rebecca Buschang
Science Partner
University of California, Los Angeles;
    Los Angeles Unified School District
Los Angeles, California

Eddyce Pope Moore
Science Teacher
Daniel Webster Middle School
Los Angeles, California

Kim O'Donnell
Science Teacher
Earle E. Williams Middle School
Tracy, California

Theresa Pearse
Science Teacher
Fremont Middle School
Stockton, California

Manuel Sanchez
Science Department Chair
Greer Middle School
Galt, California

Chuck Schindler
Secondary Math and Science Coordinator
San Bernardino City Unified School District
San Bernardino, California

William W. Tarr Jr., Ed.D.
Coordinator, Secondary Periodic Assessments
Los Angeles Unified School District
Los Angeles, California

Hong Tran
Science Teacher
Westlake Middle School
Oakland, California

Academic Reviewers

David Ackerly, Ph.D.
Associate Professor
Department of Integrative Biology
University of California, Berkeley
Berkeley, California

Paul D. Asimow, Ph.D.
*Associate Professor of Geology and
    Geochemistry*
Division of Geological and Planetary Sciences
California Institute of Technology
Pasadena, California

Magali I. Billen, Ph.D.
Assistant Professor
Department of Geology
University of California, Davis
Davis, California

Howard B. Bluestein, Ph.D.
George Lynn Cross Research Professor
School of Meteorology
The University of Oklahoma
Norman, Oklahoma

Emily E. Brodsky, Ph.D.
Assistant Professor of Geophysics
Department of Earth and Space Sciences
University of California, Los Angeles
Los Angeles, California

Eileen Cashman, Ph.D.
Associate Professor
Department of Environmental
    Resources Engineering
Humboldt State University
Arcata, California

Katherine Kelly Ellins, Ph.D.
Program Manager
Institute for Geophysics; Jackson
    School of Geosciences
The University of Texas at Austin
Austin, Texas

Jay Famiglietti, Ph.D.
Professor of Earth System Science
Department of Earth System Science
University of California, Irvine
Irvine, California

Daniel M. Fernandez, Ph.D.
Associate Professor
Division of Science and Environmental Policy
California State University, Monterey Bay
Seaside, California

Dennis Fitzsimons, Ph.D.
Associate Professor of Geography
Department of Geography
Humboldt State University
Arcata, California

Robert Fovell, Ph.D.
Associate Professor
Department of Atmospheric and Oceanic
    Sciences
University of California, Los Angeles
Los Angeles, California

Catherine Gautier, D. Es Sc.
Professor of Geography
Geography Department
University of California, Santa Barbara
Santa Barbara, California

Sarah Gille, Ph.D.
Associate Professor of Oceanography
Scripps Institution of Oceanography;
    Department of Mechanical and
    Aerospace Engineering
University of California, San Diego
La Jolla, California

David D. Gillette, Ph.D.
Colbert Curator of Paleontology
Museum of Northern Arizona
Flagstaff, Arizona

Brian Hausback, Ph.D.
Professor
Geology Department
California State University, Sacramento
Sacramento, California

Mitchell M. Johns, Ph.D.
Associate Professor of Soil Science
College of Agriculture
California State University, Chico
Chico, California

Lloyd Kitazono, Ph.D.
Professor
California Maritime Academy
Vallejo, California

W. Richard Laton, Ph.D., PG, CPG
Assistant Professor of Hydrogeology
Department of Geological Sciences
California State University, Fullerton
Fullerton, California

John P. Monteverdi, Ph.D.
Professor of Meteorology
Department of Geosciences
San Francisco State University
San Francisco, California

Laura Rademacher, Ph.D.
Assistant Professor
Department of Geosciences
University of the Pacific
Stockton, California

Eric M. Riggs, Ph.D.
*Associate Professor of Geology and
   Geoscience Education*
Department of Geological Sciences
San Diego State University
San Diego, California

Kenneth Rubin, Ph.D.
Associate Professor of Geology
Department of Geology and Geophysics
University of Hawaii at Manoa
Honolulu, Hawaii

Brandon E. Schwab, Ph.D.
Assistant Professor
Department of Geology
Humboldt State University
Arcata, California

Susan Y. Schwartz, Ph.D.
Professor of Earth Sciences
Earth Sciences Department
University of California, Santa Cruz
Santa Cruz, California

Randal J. Southard, Ph.D.
Professor of Soils and Soil Scientist
Department of Land, Air and
   Water Resources
University of California, Davis
Davis, California

John J. Stachowicz, Ph.D.
Associate Professor of Evolution and Ecology
Section of Evolution and Ecology
University of California, Davis
Davis, California

Joann M. Stock, Ph.D.
Professor of Geology and Geophysics
Division of Geological and Planetary Sciences
California Institute of Technology
Pasadena, California

Slawek Tulaczyk, Ph.D.
Associate Professor of Earth Science
Earth Sciences Department
University of California, Santa Cruz
Santa Cruz, California

Suzanne P. Wechsler, Ph.D.
Assistant Professor
Department of Geography
California State University, Long Beach
Long Beach, California

Elizabeth Wenk, Ph.D.
Visiting Scholar
University Herbarium
University of California, Berkeley
Berkeley, California

Adam D. Woods, Ph.D.
Assistant Professor of Geology
Department of Geological Sciences
California State University, Fullerton
Fullerton, California

Charlie Zender, Ph.D.
Associate Professor of Earth System Science
Department of Earth System Science
University of California, Irvine
Irvine, California

Teacher Reviewers

Marilyn K. Bachman
Science Teacher
Montecito Union School
Santa Barbara, California

Karen Benitez
Science Teacher
George V. LeyVa Middle School
San Jose, California

Sara Brownell
Science Teacher
Sutter Middle School
Folsom, California

Dana Carrigan
Vice Principal
Cordova High School
Rancho Cordova, California

Ann Marie Cica
Science Teacher
Bret Harte Middle School
San Jose, California

Michelle B. Emelle
Science Teacher
Audubon Middle School
Los Angeles, California

Lisa A. Ernst
Earth Science Teacher
Alice Fong Yu K-8
San Francisco, California

Christine Erskine, MA
Science Teacher
Brier School
Fremont, California

Catherine D. Haynes
Science Teacher
El Segundo Middle School
El Segundo, California

Joseph A. Himden
Science Teacher
John F. Kennedy Academy
Dinuba, California

Kimberly Klein
Science Teacher
Kennedy Middle School
Barstow, California

Carol Lindstrom
Science Teacher and Curriculum Specialist
Herman Intermediate School
San Jose, California

Katrina Minck
Science Teacher
Manhattan Beach Middle School
Redondo Beach, California

Susan Nora Papson, M.S.
Earth Science Teacher
Graham Middle School
Mountain View, California

Zamaria Rocio
Science Teacher and Department Chair
Horace Mann Middle School
San Diego, California

Stephanie Wasserman
Science Teacher
Daniel Webster Middle School
Los Angeles, California

Lisé Whitfield
Science Teacher
Latino College Preparatory Academy
San Jose, California

Lab Development

Kenneth E. Creese
Science Teacher
White Mountain Junior High School
Rock Springs, Wyoming

Linda A. Culp
Department Chair and Science Teacher
Thorndale High School
Thorndale, Texas

Michael A. DiSpezio
Professional Development Specialist
JASON Project
Cape Cod, Massachusetts

Bruce M. Jones
Department Chair and Science Teacher
The Blake School
Minneapolis, Minnesota

Shannon Miller
Science and Math Teacher
Llano Junior High School
Llano, Texas

Robert Stephen Ricks
Special Services Teacher
Department of Classroom Improvement
Alabama State Department of Education
Montgomery, Alabama

James J. Secosky
Science Teacher
Bloomfield Central School
Bloomfield, New York

Lab Testing

Marilyn K. Bachman
Science Teacher
Montecito Union School
Santa Barbara, California

Lars Blomberg
Science Teacher
Black Diamond Middle School
Antioch, California

Brian Conrad
Science Teacher
George LeyVa Middle School
San Jose, California

Rhonda Dupar
Science Teacher
La Colina Junior High School
Santa Barbara, California

Lisa A. Ernst
Earth Science Teacher
Alice Fong Yu K-8
San Francisco, California

Christine Erskine, MA
Science Teacher
Brier School
Fremont, California

Dan Judnick
Department Chair and Science Teacher
Bernal Intermediate School
San Jose, California

Carol Lindstrom
Science Teacher and Curriculum Specialist
Herman Intermediate School
San Jose, California

Frank D. Lucio
Science Teacher
Olive Peirce Middle School
Ramona, California

Susan Nora Papson, M.S.
Earth Science Teacher
Graham Middle School
Mountain View, California

Anne Stephens, MA
Science Teacher
Marsh Junior High School
Co-Director, Hands-on Science Lab
College of Natural Sciences
California State University, Chico
Chico, California

Feature Development

Katy Z. Allen
Hatim Belyamani
John A. Benner
David Bradford
Jennifer Childers
Mickey Coakley
Susan Feldkamp
Jane Gardner
Erik Hahn
Christopher Hess
Abby Jones
Deena Kalai
Charlotte W. Luongo, MSc
Michael May
Persis Mehta, Ph.D.
Eileen Nehme, MPH
Catherine Podeszwa
Dennis Rathnaw
Daniel B. Sharp
John M. Stokes
April Smith West
Molly F. Wetterschneider

Staff Credits

The people who contributed to **Holt California Earth Science** are listed below. They represent editorial, design, production, emedia, and permissions.

Chris Allison, Wesley M. Bain, Juan Baquera, Angela Beckmann, Ed Blake, Marc Burgamy, Rebecca Calhoun, Kimberly Cammerata, Soojinn Choi, Julie Dervin, Michelle Dike, Lydia Doty, Jen Driscoll, Diana Goetting, Angela Hemmeter, Tim Hovde, Wilonda Ieans, Elizabeth Ihry, Jevara Jackson, Simon Key, Jane A. Kirschman, Cathy Kuhles, Denise Mahoney, Michael Mazza, Kristen McCardel, Richard Metzger, Christina Murray, Micah Newman, Janice Noske, Dustin Ognowski, Joeleen Ornt, Laura Prescott, Bill Rader, Jim Ratcliffe, Peter Reid, Michael Rinella, Kelly Rizk, Jeff Robinson, Audrey Rozsypal, Beth Sample, Kay Selke, Chris Smith, Dawn Marie Spinozza, Sherry Sprague, Jeff Streber, Roshan Strong, Jeannie Taylor, Bob Tucek, Tam Voynick, Clay Walton, Kira J. Watkins, Ken Whiteside, Holly Whittaker, David Wisnieski, Monica Yudron

Credits

Abbreviations used: (t) top, (c) center, (b) bottom, (l) left, (r) right, (bkgd) background

PHOTOGRAPHY

Front Cover Larry Ulrich

Table of Contents iv, Paul Fraughton/HRW; v (tl), Peter Van Steen/HRW; v (bl), AP Photo/Joe Giblin; vi (bl), Alberto Incrocci/Getty Images/The Image Bank; vi (br), Corbis; vii (b), Bob Rowan; Progressive Image/CORBIS; vii (c), Junko Kimura/Getty Images; viii, Jose Fuste Raga/CORBIS; ix, Royalty-Free/Corbis; x (cl), Digital Image copyright © 2005 EyeWire; x (cr), David Cumming; Eye Ubiquitous/CORBIS; x (b),Tom Bean/CORBIS; xi (tl), R.L. Schuster, U.S. Geological Survey; xi (b), Yann Arthus-Bertrand/CORBIS; xii, John A. Rizzo/PhotoDisc/Getty Images; xiii, Peter Van Steen/HRW; xiv, William James Warren/CORBIS; xv, Leroy Simon/Visuals Unlimited; xvi, David Fleetham/Visuals Unlimited

Safety First! xxx, Sam Dudgeon/HRW; xxxi (t), John Langford/HRW; xxxi (b), xxxii (br) & xxxii (t), Sam Dudgeon/HRW; xxxii (bl), Stephanie Morris/HRW; xxxiii (tl), Sam Dudgeon/HRW; xxxiii (tr), Jana Birchum/HRW; xxxiii (b), Sam Dudgeon/HRW

Unit One 2 (tl); Ed Reschke/Peter Arnold, Inc.; 2 (c), Francois Gohier; 2 (b), Smithsonian Air and Space Museum; 2 (tl), T.A. Wiewandt/DRK Photo; 3 (tl), Uwe Fink/University of Arizona, Department of Planetary Sciences, Lunar & Planetary Laboratory; 3 (tr), Hulton Archive/Getty Images; 3 (stone) Adam Woolfitt/British Museum/Woodfin Camp & Assocites, Inc.; 3 (c), K. Segerstrom/USGS; 3 (bl), NASA; 3 (br), Iziko Museums of Cape Town

Chapter One 6-7, Louie Psihoyos/psihoyos.com; 7 (br), Sam Dudgeon/HRW; 8, K & K Ammann/Bruce Coleman Inc.; 9 (b), John Morrison/Morrison Photography; 9 (r), Erich Hartmann/Magnum Photos; 9 (t), Roy Toft/National Geographic/Getty Images; 10, Sam Dudgeon/HRW; 11 (l), NASA-MSFC; 11 (cr), Bobby Yip/Reuters/CORBIS; 11 (br), The Scotsman/CORBIS SYGMA; 12, Sam Dudgeon/HRW; 13 (r), Ramiro Molina/Nomitex/NewsCom; 13 (l), Goddard Space Flight Center Scientific Visualization Studio/NASA; 14, 004 Stefanie Felix, All Rights Reserved; 15, HRW; 18, Courtesy of Dr. David Gillette; 21, PhotoDisc/Getty Images; 22, Paul Fraughton/HRW; 24, Michael Newman/PhotoEdit; 25, 27 & 28, Victoria Smith/HRW; 30, Andy Christiansen/HRW; 31, Mikael Karlsson/Alamy; 33 (t), K & K Ammann/Bruce Coleman Inc.; 33 (b), Victoria Smith/HRW; 38 (l), The Stuart News, Carl Rivenbark/AP/Wide World Photos; 38 (r), Palomar Observatory/California Institute of Technology; 39, Wes Skiles/Karst Productions, Inc.

Chapter Two 42-3, NASA/Corbis; 43 (br), John Morrison/Morrison Photography; 44, Peter Van Steen/HRW; 45 (cr), Sam Dudgeon/HRW; 45 (tr, tc, bc, bl & tl) & 46 (bc), Victoria Smith/HRW; 46 (cl), Sam Dudgeon/HRW; 47 (t), Peter Van Steen/HRW; 47 (b), Sam Dudgeon/HRW; 48, Peter Van Steen/HRW; 50, Andy Christiansen/HRW; 52, Peter Essick/Aurora; 53, Dr. Juerg Alean/Photo Researchers, Inc.; 56, Guy Grenier/Masterfile; 57 (tr), Tom Pantages Photography; 59, Rand McNally; 60, Space Imaging; 61 (b), Getty/NewsCom; 63, Rand McNally; 65, United States Geological Survey; 66, John Morrison/Morrison Photography; 67 & 68, United States Geological Survey; 70, John Morrison/Morrison Photography; 71, Sam Dudgeon/HRW; 72, United States Geological Survey; 73 (t), Sam Dudgeon/HRW; 73 (tc), Andy Christiansen/HRW; 74 & 75, United States Geological Survey; 78 (r), JPL/NASA; 79 (l), Victoria Smith/HRW; 80 (r), Bettman/CORBIS; 80 (bl), Layne Kennedy/CORBIS

Chapter Three 82-83, Darlyne A. Murawski/Peter Arnold, Inc.; 83 (br), John Morrison/Morrison Photography; 84, Getty Images; 86 (b), Howard Sokol/Index Stock Imagery; 86 (t), Tom Bean/Photographer's Choice/Getty Images; 87, Tom Van Sant, Geosphere/Photo Researchers, Inc.; 91, AP Photo/Joe Giblin; 92, Sam Dudgeon/HRW; 93 & 94, John Langford/HRW; 95 (b), John Morrison/Morrison Photography; 95 (tr), John Langford/HRW; 96 (b), Sam Dudgeon/HRW; 99 (tl), NRAO/AUI/NSF; 99 (tc), NASA/JIAS/SPL/Photo Researchers, Inc.; 99 (cr), SOHO/EAS/NASA; 99 (cl), NOAN SPL/Photo Researchers, Inc.; 99 (tr), NASA/JIAS/SPL/Photo Researchers, Inc.; 102, John Morrison/Morrison Photography; 105 (r), Sam Dudgeon/HRW; 105 (t), Joyce Photographics/Photo Researchers, Inc.; 105 (tl), Getty Images; 105 (bl), Pat Lanza/Bruce Coleman Inc.; 105 (b), James Watt/Animals Animals/Earth Scenes; 106 (l), Dorling Kindersley; 106 (b & r), Sam Dudgeon/HRW; 107 (r & l), Breck P. Kent; 107 (br), Andy Christiansen/HRW; 107 (bl), Victoria Smith/HRW; 113, Sam Dudgeon/HRW; 115 (t), Tom Van Sant, Geosphere/Photo Researchers, Inc.; 115 (br), Sam Dudgeon/HRW; 115 (b), Joyce Photographics/Photo Researchers, Inc.; 115 (bl), Getty Images; 115 (l), Pat Lanza/Bruce Coleman, Inc.; 115 (b), James Watt/Animals Animals/Earth Scenes; 120 (l), Dan Winters Photography; 120 (r), Bart Harris/Alamy; 121 (l), Solar Survival Architecture; 121 (r), Singeli Agnew/Taos News

Unit Two 122 (tl), Science Photo Library/Photo Researchers, Inc; 122 (c) Francois Gohier; 122 (bl), UPI/ Bettmann/CORBIS; 122 (br), Thomas Laird/Peter Arnold, Inc; 123 (tl), Science VU/Visuals Unlimited; 123 (tr), SuperStock; 123 (cl), AP/Wide World Photos; 123 (cr), NASA/Image State; 123 (br), File/AP/Wide World Photos

Chapter Four 126, Novovitch/Liaison/Getty Images; 127 (br), John Morrison/Morrison Photography; 127, Roger Ressmeyer/CORBIS; 128 (l), Russell Illiq/Photodisc/gettyimages; 128 (c), Andy Christiansen/HRW; 128 (r), Mark Lewis/Getty Images/Stone; 129 (br), John Morrison/Morrison Photography; 129 (tl), James Randklev/Getty Images/Stone; 129 (tr), Myrleen Fergusson Cate/PhotoEdit; 130, Victoria Smith/HRW; 131, HRW; 132 (c), Victoria Smith/HRW; 132 (l), Breck P. Kent; 133 (cl), Sam Dudgeon/HRW; 133 (cr), Visuals Unlimited/Ken Lucas; 133 (r), Sam Dudgeon/HRW; 134 (bl), Lester Lefkowitz/CORBIS; 134 (r), Wernher Krutein, 135 (br), John Morrison/Morrison Photography; 135 (tr), Stewart Cohen/Index Stock Photography, Inc.; 136, Digital Image copyright © 2005 PhotoDisc; 137, Point-of-View/Alamy; 138, CORBIS; 139 (tl), Photo Disc/Getty Images; 139 (tc), Still Pictures/Peter Arnold, Inc.; 139 (tr), Sam Dudgeon/HRW; 139 (br), Chuck Savage/CORBIS; 140 (tl), GRANT HEILMAN/Heilmanphoto; 140 (tr), B. Peebles/Stock Photos/zefa/Corbis; 140 (t), ANDREW LAMBERT PHOTOGRAPHY/PHOTO RESEARCHERS, INC.; 140 (b), The Image Bank/Getty Images; 140 (cr), Danny Lehman/CORBIS; 140 (cl), E. R. Degginger/Photo Researchers, Inc.; 140 (br), ANDREW LAMBERT PHOTOGRAPHY/PHOTO RESEARCHERS, INC.; 140 (c), Fritz Polking/Visuals Unlimited; 141 (br), John Morrison/Morrison Photography; 141 (l), Holt Studios International Ltd/Alamy; 141 (inset), altrendo images/Getty Images; 143, Jose Fuste Raga/CORBIS; 144, Victoria Smith/HRW; 146, California Geological Survey; 147 (b), Holt Studios International Ltd/Alamy; 147 (t), Andy Christiansen/HRW; 147 (c), Wernher Krutein; 152 (l), Ken Lucas/Visuals Unlimited; 152 (r), ESCH THIERRY/Paris MATCH/Gamma; 153 (r), Will & Dennie McIntyre/McIntyre Photography; 153 (l), Mark Schneider/Visuals Unlimited

Chapter Five 156-7, ML Sinibaldi/CORBIS; 157 (br), John Morrison/Morrison Photography; 158, Data courtesy Marc Imhoff of NASA GSFC and Christopher Elvidge of NOAA NGDC. Image by Craig Mayhew and Robert Simmon, NASA GSFC; 159, Mark Green/Getty Images/Taxi; 160 (t), Craig Learoyd; 160 (b), John Morrison/Morrison Photography; 162, Barry Runk/Stan/Grant Heilman Photography, Inc.; 163, Alberto Incrocci/Getty Images/The Image Bank; 164 (tr), 1994 NYC Parks Photo Archive/Fundamental Photographs; 164 (tl), 1994 Kristen Brochmann/Fundamental Photographs; 164 (b), Martin Harvey; 167 (t), Reuters/CORBIS; 168, Bob Rowan; Progressive Image/CORBIS; 169, John Morrison/Morrison Photography; 170, Mark Gibson; 171, G.R. Roberts Photo Library; 174 & 175, Victoria Smith/HRW; 182 (r), Junko Kimura/Getty Images; 182 (l), Corbis; 183 (t), Courtesy of Los Alamos National Laboratories; 183 (b), Corbis Images

Unit Three 184 (tl), Charles Scribner's Sons NY, 1906; 184 (bl), USGS/NASA/Science Source/Photo Researchers, Inc.; 185 (tr), Bettmann/CORBIS; 185 (c), Lambert/Hulton Archive/Getty Images; 185 (cr), Steve Winter/National Geographic Society; 185 (cl), Randy Duchaine/Corbis Stock Market; 185 (b), Robotics Institute Carnegie Mellon University; 292 (bl), Detail of The Age of Reptiles, a mural by Rudolph F. Zallinger. ©1996, 1975, 1985, 1989, Peabody Museum of Natural History, Yale University, New Haven, Connecticut, USA

Chapter Six 188-9, James Balog/Getty Images/Stone; 189 (br), John Morrison/Morrison Photography; 193, Ken Lucas/Visuals Unlimited; 195, John Morrison/Morrison Photography; 204, Peter Van Steen/HRW; 207, John Morrison/Morrison Photography; 208 (b), Michele & Tom Grimm Photography; 208 (t), Jay Dickman/CORBIS; 209, Royalty-Free/Corbis; 212, Jose Fuste Raga/CORBIS; 213 (b), John Morrison/Morrison Photography; 214 (c), Ken Lucas/Visuals Unlimited; 215, Tom Bean/CORBIS; 219, Victoria Smith/HRW; 221, Ken Lucas/Visuals Unlimited; 226 (c), Painting © Fran Seigel; 226 (tr), Photo by S. Thorarinsson/Solar-Filma/Sun Film-15/3/ Courtesy of Edward T. Baker, Pacific Marine Environmental Laboratory, NOAA; 226 (l), Gary Glatzmaier; 227 (r), Bettmann/CORBIS

Chapter Seven 230-31, Roger Ressmeyer/CORBIS; 231 (br), John Morrison/Morrison Photography; 235 (tr), Roger Ressmeyer/CORBIS; 236, HRW; 239, Earth Images/Getty Images/Stone; 241, Bettmann/CORBIS; 243 (tr), Royalty-Free/Corbis; 246 (l), John Morrison/Morrison Photography; 248, David Parker/Photo Researchers, Inc.; 250 (tl), AP Photo/Greg Baker; 250 (br), John Morrison/Morrison Photography; 257 (tr), Earth Images/Getty Images/Stone; 260 (r), Courtesy Stephen H. Hickman, USGS; 260 (l), Bettmann/CORBIS; 261 (cr), Todd Bigelow/HRW; 261 (b), Corbis Images